History of Creativity

in the Arts, Science, & Technology

PRE-1500

SECOND EDITION

BRENT STRONG ■ MARK DAVIS
BRIGHAM YOUNG UNIVERSITY

Kendall Hunt
publishing company

ISBN 978-0-7575-8620-0

Printed in the United States of America
10 9 8 7 6 5 4 3 2 1

Contents

Chapter 15 ■ Byzantium: Creativity Holding On 357

Chapter 16 ■ Islam: Creativity in the Desert 375

Chapter 17 ■ Early Medieval Europe: Creativity Dimmed 387

Chapter 18 ■ Nations, Crusades, and Mongols: Creativity Rekindled 415

Chapter 19 ■ Church and University: Creative Thinking 439

Chapter 20 ■ Middle Ages Architecture: High Creativity 459

Preface

From the Dawn of History to 1500 a.d.

This is the first volume of a highly unique textbook for Civilization and World History courses and an exciting history book for the general-interest reader. By looking through the lens of creativity, we can see historical trends, differences between cultures, influences of technical advances on the direction of societies, and other elements of civilization with fresh perspectives. Periods of great creative output, like the Golden Age of Greece, are understood with new insights. Interesting comparisons can be made between the nature of creativity in various societies as, for instance, Greece and Rome. The causes of low creativity in periods such as the early Middle Ages are examined, especially in light of the later environment that sparked new bursts of creativity.

Sometimes the creative step seems trivial, but the consequences are immense. For example, the mere addition of vowels to the Greek alphabet does not seem to be much of an improvement over the existing Semitic alphabets of Mesopotamia. However, because the new Greek alphabet could then mimic speech, it empowered Greek speakers and therefore contributed to the broadening of political power that was the basis of democracy. Moreover, the less ambiguous nature of the Greek alphabet allowed philosophy to flourish. The improved clarity also permitted science and history to emerge. The beauty of the written word contributed to the rise of Greek drama and literature. We see, therefore, that the small creative step was critical to the development of Greek culture which became an important foundation for all of western civilization.

Because creativity is so valuable in describing innovations and progress, it is a wonderful vehicle to integrate our learning about the arts, technology, science, politics, economics, and most other facets of civilization. This integration is emphasized throughout the book, both within a particular era and across the centuries.

This book is the result of a collaboration of two disciplines–history and engineering/science, each represented by one of the authors. We want to tell you how it came about so that you can see our objectives and the rather unusual linkage of history and creativity in the light of our thinking. Our story, which began several years ago, will be told by Dr. Strong:

> *I felt that the College of Engineering and Technology at Brigham Young University, of which I am a member, should be more involved in the wider campus community. Most of the faculty in my college were focused in their own narrow fields and rarely interacted with students outside our college. I thought that situation was sad because, in my opinion, engineering and technology faculty have some insights into the world that are important for students in general, regardless of major. I felt that a general education class was the most appropriate route to interact with a wider collection of students. To this end, the Civilization general education requirement*

at Brigham Young University seemed to invite my participation. This two-semester sequence was structured so that any department could teach the course within a set of minimum expectations and criteria, and with approval of the Faculty General Education Council. It was currently being taught by departments as diverse as History, Humanities, Philosophy, English, Music, and Art. Each department gave the course its own flavor. Some taught the course with intensive readings and with only enough history to provide the setting; others were just the opposite.

Since one of my goals was to reach students in a wide variety of disciplines, I searched for an overall theme that would appeal to students of all majors. I felt that the theme had to be something that was common to engineering and technology, to humanities, and to history. Ideally, it would also be something that fit my personal background. I reasoned that there are many similarities between technology and the arts. I have been told that the word "techne," from which we get "technology," meant both art and craft in the ancient Greek. I also noted that other words seem to cross over between science and the humanities, such as Plato's Forms which are remembered in the word we use for mathematical models—formulas. Also, the word "scientist" was invented in the seventeenth century as an analogy to the word "artist."

I eventually concluded that creativity was a common and critical thread for all of the fields I sought to include. In fact, creativity is probably required for all types of people who make significant contributions to our civilization. The examination of creative people and creative periods seemed to be a way to link science, technology, and the arts throughout history. It also seemed to be a fun and interesting way to bring diverse groups together in discussions, so that they could learn from each other. Furthermore, it was consistent with my own background. I received my doctorate in a rather theoretical branch of chemistry but I had always loved diversity and graduated with a Bachelor of Arts rather than the traditional Bachelor of Science. I worked in the chemical industry and found great fulfillment in both plastics research and manufacturing of new plastic products. The concreteness of these jobs seemed to complete the theoretical aspects of chemistry for me. In all of them, I found that creativity and problem solving were critical to success. When I changed companies and became a businessman, I found a whole new world, very different but equally exciting. Then, after several more years, I left to enter academia. Initially I was thrust again into research. There, again, I found creativity an invaluable skill for success. I agree with Robert Woodward (a Nobel laureate), who said:

There are two basic tools of synthetic activities: the science of chemistry with its laws and principles, and the body of experimental, manipulative techniques. Beyond that, chemical synthesis is entirely a creative activity, in which art, design, imagination, and inspiration play a predominant role.[1]

The art, design, imagination, and inspiration associated with my work led me to a study of the nature of creativity. I began to observe that some aspects of creativity are similar in many fields. Creativity in engineering design is not too different from creativity in painting. Creativity in manufacturing engineering has many elements that are similar to creativity in dance. Music creativity is like business entrepreneurship. I then grew to believe that creativity was integral with history and could give insights to historical periods that were both unique and useful. Hence, the History of Creativity in the Arts, Science, and Technology was born.

When Brent Strong began to work toward actually teaching the class, he joined forces with Mark Davis, an historian, who agreed to bring the traditional perspective to the class when appropriate. We have continued to enjoy each other's perspectives and have mutually grown. We have, in the process, learned a great deal, especially about creativity and history.

One of the advantages of this text is the supplemental readings. These give the readers an opportunity to sample primary documents and, thereby, sense directly the creativity of several important writings.

The students in the classes we have taught report that their personal creativity capabilities have been enhanced by the focus of the course on the nature of creativity throughout history. This improved student capability adds to the value of the class over more traditional civilization and history courses and, we believe, furthers the purpose of education.

Notes

1. Robert Woodward, Quoted in *Creative People at Work,* Doris B. Wallace and Howard E. Gruber (Oxford: Oxford University Press, 1989) 232–233.

Preface to the Second Edition

To enrich the experience of history gained from reading this text, a supplement containing selections from important primary writings throughout history has been developed. Normally these supplemental readings are assigned to be read along with the text. In this 2nd Edition, that supplement has been integrated into this book (Pre-1500) at the end of the appropriate chapters and into the text for the second semester class (1500-Present).

Prologue

> The psychological conditions which make a society or an epoch creative and consistently original have been little studied, but it seems likely that social conditions analogous to those seen in individual creativity are important. Freedom of expression and movement, lack of fear of dissent and contradiction, a willingness to break with custom, a spirit of play as well as of dedication to work, purpose on a grand scale; these are some of the attributes which a creative social entity, whether vast or tiny, can be expected to have.
>
> —Frank Barron (Institute of Personality Assessment and Research, University of California, Berkeley)

Creativity and History

What Is Creativity?

If we are going to study the history of creativity, we should understand the basic definition and elements of creativity, so that we can recognize it when we encounter it in an historical setting. Many definitions of creativity have been proposed by experts in the field, but we find the following definition to be both intuitive and logical. **Creativity is a way of thinking and doing (innovation) that brings unexpected, original, and valuable ideas to fruition.** Notice that the definition requires that both thinking and doing are part of creativity, and that originality plays an important part. Also, fruition or accomplishment is involved. These critical elements of creativity can be summarized from the important study of creativity adapted from Wallace and Gruber[1] as follows:

Elements of Creativity

- Value
- Intention
- Novel
- Excellent

Note: These can be remembered using the mnemonic VINE.

They proposed that all creativity must have uniqueness or novelty but that this element alone does not guarantee creativity, nor does it explain the extent of the creativity. For example, if a person does something that is unique to them—say, visit New York City for the first time—we would not consider that to be creative, since millions have done it previously. This problem of uniqueness is more difficult when the act of the person is something like making a painting. Let's assume two cases. First case: The painting is a copy of a painting done originally by Picasso. Most people, including us, would not consider this to be a creative act since the copy was not original, even though the person painting the copy would see their own work as creative because they had never attempted such a thing before. Second case: The painting is not a copy but is an original. The artist would surely claim uniqueness and we would agree. However, the work may be quite amateurish and may not contain any elements of good painting, such as aesthetic value, and we would dismiss it and say it is not really creative. **Therefore, for something to be creative it must be novel, but it must also be good or valuable.**

In making this limitation on creativity we have invoked another element in Wallace and Gruber's criteria: value. We generally believe that creativity is exhibited in those things that have value for us. Along this line, the story is told of a man who approached Picasso and saw a cubist-style painting that Picasso had for sale. The man laughed at the price Picasso was asking and said, "My own daughter could produce a painting just as good as this." Picasso then responded, "Congratulations sir, your daughter is a genius." Douglas Hofstadter tried to address this same issue of value in his book *Gödel, Escher, Bach,* and commented, "Perhaps what differentiates highly creative ideas from ordinary ones is some combined sense of beauty, simplicity, and harmony."[2] The laws of patentability for technical inventions also seem to place importance on value. For something to be patented it must be unique (not part of the public domain), valued or useful, and reduced to practice.

The problem of value is a difficult one. We don't really consider things that are unique only to an individual as creative, yet to the individual they are. This problem has been addressed by talking about two kinds of creativity—little "c" creativity and big "C" creativity. Those acts that are creative only to the person performing them are called little "c." Those that have value in the world (usually defined as those who are experts in the domain in which the creative act would belong) are big "C" creativity. Sometimes the experts are wrong. For instance, the world little appreciated the work of J.S. Bach or of Vincent Van Gogh before they died. Those works were then not considered big "C" creative, but today, many years later, they most certainly are. In spite of these problems, the concept of value still seems to be worthwhile as a criterion for creativity, as it separates those acts that have value to the world and can make a difference. In our study of historical creativity, we have the advantage of perspective, and can therefore more easily assign value as being some creative act that changed the course of history. **We will, therefore, exclusively look at big "C" creativity.**

Another element of creativity—intent—is likewise difficult. The issue concerns the nature of luck or serendipity (finding values of things not sought for). Most people would not consider a lucky event, such as hitting the right number on a roulette table, to be creative. But what about events such as the discovery of penicillin by Alexander Fleming, who was working in his laboratory and found a contaminated Petri dish in which the bacteria had been mysteriously killed by a mold that may have fallen into the Petri dish during Fleming's lunch? Another case was Louis Pasteur's discovery of the principle of inoculation, which came to him because of a mistake in the way chickens were being treated with live serum. Perhaps Pasteur's own comment is the best answer to whether such events are creative. He said, "Chance favors the prepared mind." In other words, the intent had been present from the beginning of the investigation and the chance occurrence was recognized because the investigator was prepared to see it. Benjamin Franklin expressed a similar sentiment: "Diligence is the mother of good luck"; similarly, Robert Woodward, the Nobel Prize laureate in chemistry said, "It takes a lot of work to get to the point where one can be lucky." **We will, therefore, consider creative only those events or products that were intended by their creator.**

The last of the elements of creativity is excellence. We appreciate the creative excellence of a musical performance that moves our spirits, even though the music was written many years ago and is therefore not unique at that moment. While it is true that the interpretation was unique, we also comment on the magnificence of the skill of the performer. This level of skill is appreciated when it goes beyond what is common. Mozart's playing as a child prodigy is this type of creativity. Usually a high level of skill is achieved only with much hard work over a long period of time. Several experts on creativity have noticed that creative works usually occur only after the person has been working in the field for about ten years. This applies even to Mozart, whose early compositions are rarely played today (not highly valued) because they are not as good as those that were written after he had been composing for ten years (which still meant he was in his teens). This long-term diligence to the field is called continuance. **When this diligence results in excellence, it is an element of creativity.**

Creativity and the History of Civilization

The concepts of creativity which we have discussed do not directly address the environment in which the creativity is done. That environment might be personal—related to the personality or family situation of the individual—or it might be social—related to the society in which the individual lives. These factors will be important in our examination of history because they will help us better understand the creative process. However, we might also consider applying the elements of creativity and the factors of the environment to entire societies. We might ask the question, "Do the creative acts of individuals relate to the creativity of a society?" Frank Barron's quotation at the beginning of this Prologue indicates that personal creativity can likely be applied to civilizations. We believe he is correct. These social conditions will be a major focus of this book. We will also look at the relationship between creativity and change. We know that great leaders are often associated with change, and that managing these changes usually needs unique thinking and clever implementation, which are, of course, elements of creativity. Since leadership is a critical element in history, we can link change, history, leadership, and creativity. This is a different perspective on history from that normally taken by historians, but perhaps one that is appealing to the reader (and to us).

Purposes

Teaching a survey course like the history of civilization (and all civilization classes are of this type), is like walking down a hallway in a long building. We might occasionally stop and open a door to look inside and then move on. We rarely take enough time to go into the room. Each room in a civilization class is a different period or topic. We might look through the door and see one or two paintings or hear some music or meet a person, but not much more. After the brief overview of the house, we need to go back to some of the rooms and enter them so that we can get some deeper understanding. Our hope is that this survey of history through the paradigm of creativity will entice the reader to choose a few rooms to enter and learn in depth. We also hope to give a unique perspective on civilization so that people can learn new concepts and, perhaps, help solve some of the very complex problems in the world that have resisted solution because people have looked at them too narrowly.

As with all studies of civilization, one purpose is to become well educated in the sense that the basic principles of civilization and societies are understood, the great people are known and their works valued, and different cultures are appreciated. Achieving this status with the history of our civilization will be a basis for discussion with other people, self-confidence, development of skills, and background for observation and analysis of the world, and will provide a basis for thinking. We are reminded that education is what remains after you have forgotten what you've learned. Indeed, **the most important thing you learn in school is how to learn.**

The study of historical creativity is not without some other potential benefits. We hope that readers will understand both history and creativity better. Perhaps the new approach will help those who might not like history see it with new understanding and interest. To assist in this quest, the focus of this book will be on the people and events of history, with very little concentration on the dates and hard facts. We feel that these can be looked up in references if they are needed. Nevertheless, a timeline is provided, so that readers can keep straight the timing of the various epochs and events discussed.

We also hope that students will improve their own creativity. Edward De Bono, a world expert in creativity, was asked whether creativity resulted from skill, talent, or personality. He said that it came from all three, but he would focus only on the skill, because that can be learned and, therefore, people will gain the confidence to improve their creativity.[3] We, too, will try to improve the understanding of creativity so that the skills and situational effects can be learned and controlled and, thereby, readers might improve their personal creativity. This may take some changes in personal habits and also some changes in environment. With effort, both of these can be accomplished.

In order to understand creativity and history, we should be prepared to ask some new questions concerning each of the civilizations and historical characters we encounter. Some of those questions might be the following:

- What are the effects of war (or peace) on creativity? (We can consider, too, whether personal security or living in a chaotic environment increases personal creativity.)
- Does isolation of a society improve its creativity? (Similarly, are creative people better when they are isolated, or does participation with a group improve creativity?)
- What does uniqueness really mean with respect to a creative development? Could the development be based on previous concepts and works done by others? (Has any individual ever created something that was not, at least in principle, based on the knowledge gained from the accomplishment of others?)
- What factors can extinguish creativity? Do these factors apply to societies in general, or should we examine how societal norms affect individuals? (What spurs an individual to be more creative or, conversely, prevents someone from pursuing creative activities?)
- Does the availability of time for creative work make a major difference to a society? That is, must a society provide leisure time for its creative individuals, or do people continue in creativity even though they are pressed to just meet personal needs?
- Is creativity a function of the environment? What can a society do to promote creativity?

Finally, we hope that this book will be an example for others to cross from one academic discipline to another. We think that people will be enriched when they make the effort to enter the foreign territory of other fields. It is true that we might make mistakes by this crossover action, as we may have made in this book. Please forgive us. But, remember what Albert Einstein said: "Anyone who has never made a mistake has never tried anything new." When we enter into another field, we will gain a greater appreciation of the thinking, methods, and understandings usually practiced in those other fields. Remember that the term "narrow-mindedness" implies less than the entire scope of thinking. It is constrictive and divisive. As we gain knowledge in other fields, we will likely enrich work in our own field because of our increased ability to think laterally. But, we may also work diligently and thus make unique and valued contributions in the new field. That would, of course, result in a new creative work.

Notes

1. Doris B. Wallace and Howard E. Gruber, *Creative People at Work* (Oxford: Oxford University Press, 1989), 28–29 (extracted).
2. Douglas R. Hofstadter, *Gödel, Escher, Bach: An Eternal Golden Braid* (New York: Vintage, 1989), 673.
3. Edward De Bono, *Six Thinking Hats* (Back Bay Books, 1999), 138.

Suggested Readings

Adams, James L., *Conceptual Blockbusting,* Addison-Wesley, 1986.

Csikszentmihalyi, Mihaly, *Creativity,* HarperPerennial, 1997.

De Bono, Edward, *The Mechanism of Mind,* Penguin, 1969.

De Bono, Edward, *Lateral Thinking,* Harper and Row, 1970.

De Bono, Edward, *Six Thinking Hats,* Back Bay Books, 1999.

Gardner, Howard, *Creating Minds,* BasicBooks, 1993.

Gardner, Howard, *Extraordinary Minds,* BasicBooks, 1994.

Ghiselin, Brewster, *The Creative Process,* University of California Press, 1952.

Goleman, Daniel, Paul Kaufman, and Michael Ray, *The Creative Spirit,* Plume, 1993.

Hofstadter, Douglas R., *Gödel, Escher, Bach,* Vintage, 1989.

Koestler, Arthur, *The Act of Creation,* Penguin, 1964.

Robert, Royston M., *Serendipity,* John Wiley & Sons, Inc., 1989.

Simonton, Dean Keith, *Genius, Creativity and Leadership,* Harvard University Press, 1984.

Simonton, Dean Keith, *Origins of Genius,* Oxford University Press, 1999.

Sternberg, Robert J. (ed.), *Handbook of Creativity,* Cambridge University Press, 1999.

Thorpe, Scott, *How to Think Like Einstein,* Barnes & Noble, 2000.

Wallace, Doris B. and Howard E. Gruber, *Creative People at Work,* Oxford University Press, 1989.

Weiner, Robert Paul, *Creativity and Beyond,* State University of New York Press, 2000.

Civilization

Creativity Begins to Flow

> At certain epochs man has felt conscious of something about himself—body and spirit—which was outside the day-to-day struggle for existence and the night-to-night struggle with fear; and he has felt the need to develop these qualities of thought and feeling so that they might approach as nearly as possible to an ideal of perfection—reason, justice, physical beauty, all of them in equilibrium. He has managed to satisfy this need in various ways—through myths, through dance and song, through systems of philosophy and through the order that he has imposed upon the visible world.
>
> —*Kenneth Clark,* Civilisation *(BBC television series)*

The Earliest Beginnings of Civilization

As best we can determine from the historical record, sometime between the years 4000 and 3500 B.C. humankind advanced sufficiently so that civilization began. As Kenneth Clark has indicated in the above quotation, the founding of civilization required that people move outside their rudimentary life of all-consuming drudgery and into a new mindset. This mindset lifted their spirits and expanded their visions. They began to be concerned about reason, justice, beauty, and a wealth of other concepts that invigorated their minds as never before. They also developed a desire to rise above mere survival and improve the environment around them. The conception of these liberating ideas and the implementation of them into reality were made possible by personal and collective creativity. Some societies exhibited great creativity and progress while others were lethargic and constrictive. Some of these civilizations were more or less isolated; others clearly interacted, sometimes borrowing from their neighboring societies and, in other instances, building upon previous civilizations. This book examines the creative nature of these civilizations and the environments that fostered or impeded that creativity. In some cases key individuals played a critical role in the creativity of the age or otherwise exhibited great personal creativity. These individuals will also be examined. Creativity has not just been a factor that occasionally accompanies the progress of humankind but is the generator that powers changes in human life and has led to the continuing development and enrichment of civilization.

With the beginnings of civilization we also come to the beginnings of history. Of course, that is not exactly true, as every small and boring detail from every human's life is actually history. However, just as people left their totally mundane existence and entered a higher realm, their historical record similarly rose to become more than just a sterile record of daily routines but, rather, to document the changes and progress that was occurring in their lives. We see, therefore, the interconnection of history, civilization, change, and creativity. In essence, the most meaningful history is the record of changes, of new ideas, and of innovations. The history of civilization is, therefore, the History of Creativity.

That is not to say that pre-civilized people totally lacked creativity. On the contrary, pre-civilized people (pre-historical people) and cultures made the necessary creative steps that led to eventual civilization. Pre-civilized people made important discoveries, such as the use of tools and the domestication and storage of grains, and without these creative flourishes civilization would not have been possible. Furthermore, pre-civilized cultures were also responsible for some artistic creativity, such as the beautiful cave art at Lascaux, France. But these efforts were, in general, isolated and probably serendipitous. We see little evidence of intentional and systematic development of creative works in pre-historic societies.

Creativity and change occurred much more slowly among pre-civilized peoples than among the later civilized cultures because, at least in part, pre-civilized people tended to spend so much of their time and energy on mere survival. The founding of civilization was probably not even noticed or realized by those early men and women who caused these important changes to occur. Slowly, over years, decades, and even centuries, people accumulated their experiences with life—especially in technology, science, and the arts—to bring together the critical elements that would allow them to leave behind their scattered, nomadic way of life and enter into a new way of living that has become known as civilization.

We must be careful using the word "civilized." While it is true that civilization began with the onset of history and effective creativity, we should not imply that "civilized" peoples left behind all their barbarous practices and were always more refined than pre-civilized peoples. For example, even one thousand years after their "civilization," it was legal in Canaanite towns for a man to kill his wife during "the fifty," or the fifty hottest days of summer, as it was felt that under such conditions no man could be held responsible for his actions toward a nagging woman. Furthermore, the practice of human sacrifice, especially of children, was much more prevalent among "civilized" peoples than among "pre-civilized" ones. In spite of the occasional non-civilized behaviors of civilized people, the emergence of civilization did bring about cultural improvement. That improvement was most readily apparent in, and was accelerated by, the movement of people into stationary, cooperative societies.

The Rise of Cities

The enhancement of creativity through the development of cities is undoubtedly related to the synergy that occurs when people of different talents and abilities work together cooperatively. Those city-based societies were more complex and more highly structured than the earlier hunter-gatherer societies. Examples of the complexities of urban society included specialization of labor, cooperative ventures in business, expansion and organization of trade, sophisticated government, elaborate entertainments, and military protection. In that complexity humankind found benefits that have proven, overall, to be so desirable that urban societies have dominated human progress ever since the original establishment of cities at the dawn of history.

It is instructive to note that the root of the word "civilization" means "city dweller," thus suggesting that even with the coining of the word, the linkage of civilization with city was appreciated. In addition, the root of an ancient Shang Dynasty Chinese character for city, yi, has at its core the twin concepts of submission to authority and an enclosure providing protection from danger. While it is true that living in association with other people requires that each individual give up some personal freedom of action to the authority that administers the city, the protection afforded by group living and the enhanced opportunities that come from collective efforts have proven to be so desirable that people have been willing to sacrifice some personal freedoms to achieve these collective benefits.

Some people may criticize city life and yearn for the simplicity of life as a "noble savage," especially those who view modern society as corrupt and damaging. These people often believe that pre-civilized people lived in harmony with nature and with their fellow humans. However, the contrary seems to be the actual case. Cities became popular, in part, because of the protection they afforded from the constant warfare of most tribal societies. Lawrence Keeley, in his book *War Before Civilization,* which reported on his study of many pre-historic civilizations, found that war in the pre-historic past was just as frequent and at least as brutal as war in modern times. Furthermore, because pre-historic populations were tribal and relatively small, war was more personal in those times and, therefore, more frightening. Keeley said, "The antidote to war is an effective political organization with legislative, judicial, and police powers, whether its scale comprises a family band, a village, a tribe, a chiefdom, a city-state, a nation, or the whole earth. Obviously, the larger the scale and the longer the life span of any such political organization, the more general and enduring is the extent of peace."[1] People sought protection and found it, at least to some degree, in cities.

The essential elements that came together to allow a more complex and beneficial society (what we have termed civilization and urban dwelling) include the following:

- **Food in abundance** (without requiring that everyone be involved in farming, and including a distribution system linking the urban and agricultural sectors);
- **Labor specialization** (including trade, manufacturing, and other creative endeavors);
- **Order and organization of society** (usually based in government, religion, or a combination of the two); and
- **Writing system.**

NOTE: These can be remembered using the mnemonic FLOW.

The first of these elements, producing sufficient food, was based on what may have been the greatest creative achievement of pre-history–the domestication of grains. This was the development on which all the other essential features of urban society depended. Agriculture allowed both a localization of and an increase in population. Agriculture also provided an incentive for technological development in agronomy, tools, and materials.

The domestication of grains required a high degree of creativity but also, perhaps, a type of creativity not normally appreciated. That creativity involved the recognition of an opportunity that may not have been specifically a problem demanding the attention of the people. There is little evidence that people were starving and that grain was domesticated in response to their hunger. Rather, it seems logical to assume that someone recognized the possibility of growing more food if certain changes could be made in some plants and in the methods used to grow and harvest them. To that perceptive person there then seemed to be some benefit from the domestication of the grain, perhaps a social benefit because that person, or persons, didn't like the nomadic life and felt that domestication would be a way to settle down comfortably. To enable domestication, the seeds of the wild grasses (the logical precursor plants to domesticated grains) needed to be relatively large (at least ten times heavier than the median size for wild grass species), to be retained by the plant until harvest (as opposed to being scattered by the wind or dropping on the ground), to be of appropriate nutritional value, to be storable for long periods, to be easily processed into a convenient raw form (such as flour that is not too oily and won't quickly spoil), and to be useful for making bread or some other easily consumable product. Jared Diamond, in his book *Guns, Germs and Steel,* reports that only 56 types of wild seeds were appropriate for possible domestication for commercial purposes. Of these, Eurasia had 32 types, with the next continent in number of seeds having only 11. Hence, the probability of domesticating grains was much higher in Eurasia than in other continents. Moreover, the climate of the Mediterranean zone of Eurasia (the Fertile Crescent) was especially favorable for growing the seeds.[2] This probably contributed to the development of civilization first in Mediterranean Eurasia, specifically in Mesopotamia. But, we will see other reasons why this location was the birthplace of civilization.

With sufficient food, the members of society were able to specialize their labor according to their abilities and desires. Not everyone needed to be a farmer because those who *were* farmers could produce more food than they needed for their own family. They sold the excess. The marketplace therefore became a reality and the essential supportive functions such as distribution, finance, bookkeeping, and marketing inevitably followed. The needs of living in a city required that manufacturing be developed to provide shelter and other basic commodities. Artisans sprang up to make these and other goods, some of which required great skill and specialization. Some goods were artistic, that is, not specifically tied to survival, but desired nonetheless. The net result was that the variety of goods increased and people were, in general, able to work more effectively because they could work in areas they enjoyed. This change in the way people worked is called the **division of labor.**

The benefits of the division of labor were classically outlined by Adam Smith in his book *The Wealth of Nations,* written in 1776, but are still accurate in describing how specialization of labor would have been effective even in the ancient world. He used the making of pins to illustrate how efficiencies were vastly improved when jobs were specialized, versus when one person did all of the tasks. In the ancient world the specialization might have been where one person made flour, another made the flour sacks, another made the machinery to grind the flour, and yet another baked the bread. Here is Adam Smith's analysis.

> *The greatest improvement in the productive powers of labour, and the greatest part of the skill, dexterity, and judgment with which it is anywhere directed, or applied, seem to have been the effects of the division of labour. To take an example, therefore, from a very trifling manufacture; but one in which the division of labour has been very often taken notice of, the trade of the pin-maker; a workman not educated to this business (which the division of labor has rendered a distinct trade), nor acquainted with the use of the machinery employed in it (to the invention of which the same division of labour has probably given occasion), could scarce, perhaps, with his utmost industry, make one pin in a day, and certainly could not make twenty. But in the way in which this business is now carried on, not only the whole work is a peculiar trade, but it is divided into a number of branches, of which the greater part are likewise peculiar trades. One man draws out the wire, another straights it, a third cuts it, a fourth points it, a fifth grinds it at the top for receiving the head; to make the head requires three distinct operations; to put it on is a peculiar business, to whiten the pins is another; it is even a trade by itself to put them into the paper; and the important business of making a pin is, in this manner, divided into about eighteen distinct operations. I have seen a small manufactory of this kind where ten men only were employed, and where some of them consequently performed two or three distinct operations. Those ten persons, therefore, could make among them upwards of forty-eight thousand eight hundred pins in a day. Each person . . . might be considered as making four thousand eight hundred pins in a day. But if they had all wrought separately and independently, and without any of them hav-*

ing been educated to this peculiar business, they could certainly not each of them have made twenty, perhaps not one pin in a day.[3]

The specialization of labor is obviously a critical part of the development of manufactured goods. Cities facilitated such specialization of labor and were, therefore, a critical element in the development of manufactured goods and the growth of civilization.

Think about the incredible need for creativity as people began to gather into cities. This gathering required solving problems such as water supply, sewers, roads, home construction, perimeter walls, and a myriad of other small problems that occur just because of high population density. Moreover, imagine the creativity required when people began to work in new jobs (such as millers, bakers, shoemakers, butchers, etc.) and, for the first time, felt the pressure of competition. Some people chose occupations that were artistic, and these clearly depended on both skill and creativity to succeed. It is no wonder that civilization, that is, moving into cities, both required and fostered creativity.

The resulting complexity in society, where many people had different roles, required that order and organization be developed, inevitably leading to a hierarchy within the society. Most of the ancient societies ranked nobility and military officers at the top, followed by religious officials, landowners, and bureaucrats. The religious officials, landowners, and bureaucrats became the most influential advisors to the royalty, with the relative importance of each depending on the nature and culture of the particular society. We will see examples where each of the groups takes the dominant advisory role even in the earliest societies. Because of their specialized skills, artisans and merchants were ranked slightly higher than farm workers. Slaves were at the bottom of the society.

The entire system required a method of communication, both oral and written, so that, for example, business transactions could be recorded and knowledge passed reliably from one generation to another. Writing was critical to this communication, and was the lubricant that made everything else work.

Three general types of writing systems were developed in the ancient world; those same types persist today. While languages typically use some of each of the three types, most ancient and modern languages are dominated by one of the types of systems, so we can conveniently generalize to gain insights into language development and use by examining the three types separately.

- **Logograms**—writing systems in which a symbol represents an idea or a whole word. Examples include Egyptian hieroglyphics and Chinese characters, as well as some modern characters such as +, %, and $.
- **Syllabaries**—writing systems in which a symbol represents a syllable. Examples include shorthand, Korean script, and languages for the blind.
- **Alphabets**—writing systems in which a symbol represents a sound. Examples include the Roman, Greek, and Cyrillic alphabets.

Figure 1.1 depicts examples of the three types of writing systems. The Chinese script is modern. The Korean script is old. The example of the Roman alphabet is from medieval times.

Even when all four of the critical elements—food production, specialization of labor, social order, and writing—were present for civilization, some locations seemed to be especially beneficial for starting civilized, urban societies. We will now examine those locations.

Ancient River Societies

The earliest areas in which all of the critical elements for civilization were brought together and which therefore experienced an explosion of creativity were the river valley civilizations of Mesopotamia, Egypt, India, and China. It is not by chance that the river valleys were the cradles of civilization. The rivers provided a nutrient-rich silt that refurbished the land, water for irrigation during dry periods, supplementary food supplies such as small animals and birds, transportation for supplies and products, and communication pathways.

Logograms (Chinese)

Syllabanes (old Korean)

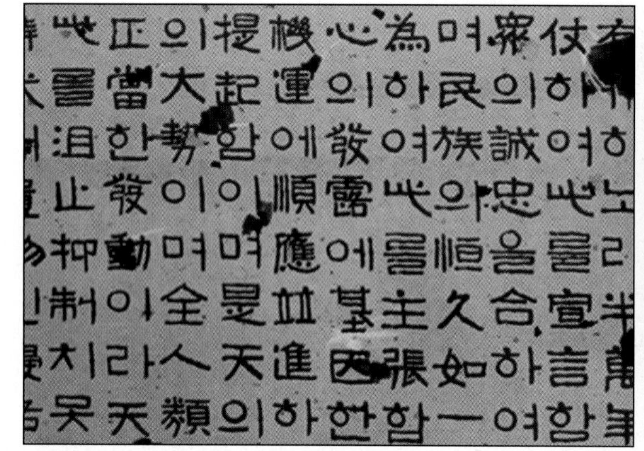

Alphabets (Medieval Roman)

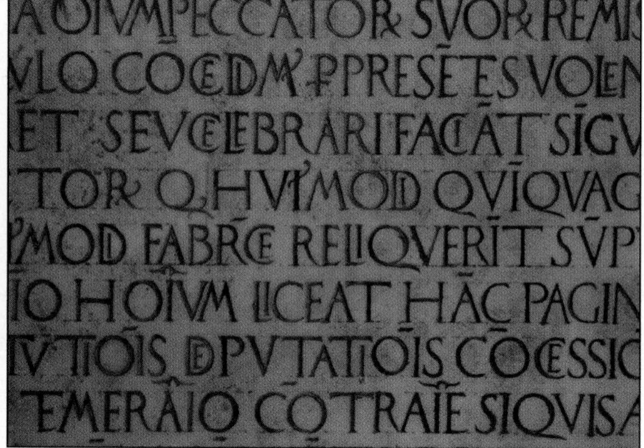

Figure 1.1 ■ Three writing systems: **A)** Logograms (Chinese), **B)** Syllabanes (old Korean), **C)** Alphabets (Medieval Roman). *A) © 2010 by betamax. Used under license of Shutterstock, Inc. B) © 2010 by megumi ito. Used under license from Shutterstock, Inc. C) © 2010 by alehnia. Used under license of Shutterstock, Inc.*

In addition, all of these societies had pleasant climates with long growing seasons.

These four early river civilizations were similar in many ways, but were also unique in how they developed and in what they contributed to the advancement of mankind. We begin our examinations of civilization and creativity by looking at, in turn, each of these river societies, from their beginnings to the end of their major influence on the ancient world. We will discuss the historical events but will also continuously note the creative developments that accompanied the political, military, social, artistic, and technological occurrences in each of the societies. We will also occasionally pause to ask why a particular individual or society was creative in a particular way and at a particular time.

Reliable historical data about these ancient societies is sometimes difficult to obtain. Some data is archeological in origin and some is from literature. We have, in general, consulted a wide variety of sources for the information we have used. When those sources differ or even conflict, we have chosen the version that we believe fits most closely with the facts as we perceive them.

Two of these societies—Mesopotamia and Egypt—are coincident with the people described in the Bible; in fact, the river societies often interacted with the Biblical societies. Some authors choose to ignore the Biblical connections. We take the opposite view. Not only do we consider the Bible to be a valid historical document (as well as a religious text), but we have found that the events of the ancient world can be made more interesting and relevant when tied to the Biblical stories familiar to most people of Christian-Judaic-Islamic origins.

Timeline—Important Dates

Date	Event
4000–3500 B.C.	*Domestication of grains*
4000–3500 B.C.	*Establishment of cities in selected river valleys*
About 3500 B.C.	*Division of labor in cities*
About 3500 B.C.	*Establishment of a hierarchy within the cities*
About 3500 B.C.	*Creation of effective writing systems*

Notes

1. Lawrence H. Keeley, *War Before Civilization* (Oxford: Oxford University Press, 1996), 181.
2. Jared Diamond, *Guns, Germs, and Steel* (New York: Norton, 1999), 139–142.
3. Adam Smith, *The Wealth of Nations* (1776; New York: Penguin, 1986), 109–110.

Suggested Readings

Derry, T. K. and Trevor I. Williams, *A Short History of Technology,* Oxford University Press, 1960.

Diamond, Jared, *Guns, Germs, and Steel,* Norton, 1999.

Keegan, John, *A History of Warfare,* Vintage, 1993.

Keeley, Lawrence H., *War Before Civilization,* Oxford University Press, 1996.

Kirby, Richard Shelton, Sidney Withington, Arthur Burr Darling, and Frederick Gridley Kilgour, *Engineering in History,* Dover, 1990.

Roberts, J. M., *A Short History of the World,* Element, 1996.

Smith, Adam, *The Wealth of Nations,* Penguin, 1989.

Mesopotamia
Seeds of Creativity

> If a man has accused another of laying a death spell upon him, but has not proved it, the accused shall go to the sacred river, he shall plunge in the sacred river, and if the sacred river shall conquer him, he that accused him shall take possession of his house. If the sacred river shall show his innocence and he is saved, his accuser shall be put to death. He that plunged in the sacred river shall appropriate the house of him that accused him.
>
> —Code of Hammurabi

The Rivers and the Land

As far as we can tell, the domestication of grains occurred first in the valleys of the Tigris and Euphrates rivers (modern-day Iraq) between about 4000 and 3500 B.C. and, as we have already seen, that creative development was the key to the beginning of civilization. The fertile area between the Tigris and Euphrates rivers where the first cities were founded has been named Mesopotamia, which means "between the rivers." The civilizations of Mesopotamia spread outside the river valleys to the area along the Mediterranean coast in what became known as Syria, Lebanon, Israel, and Palestine. (Some authorities expand the area to include Egypt.) This larger region is frequently called the Fertile Crescent, a name that reflects the crescent shape of this region. A map of Mesopotamia and the Fertile Crescent is given in Figure 2.1.

As can be seen from the quotation given at the beginning of this chapter, the river was not just a source of water for agriculture, but was integral in daily life and was sacred, sometimes even determining whether a person lived or died. The Code of Hammurabi, from which the quotation was taken, was the first, written, legal code; it helped to define the Mesopotamian society. But, before we look at the society, we will examine the land and the rivers.

Even though the Tigris and Euphrates Rivers were very important in enabling the Mesopotamian civilization to begin, some basic problems were encountered that had to be overcome for the civilization to flourish over the long term. The creative ways in which these problems were solved

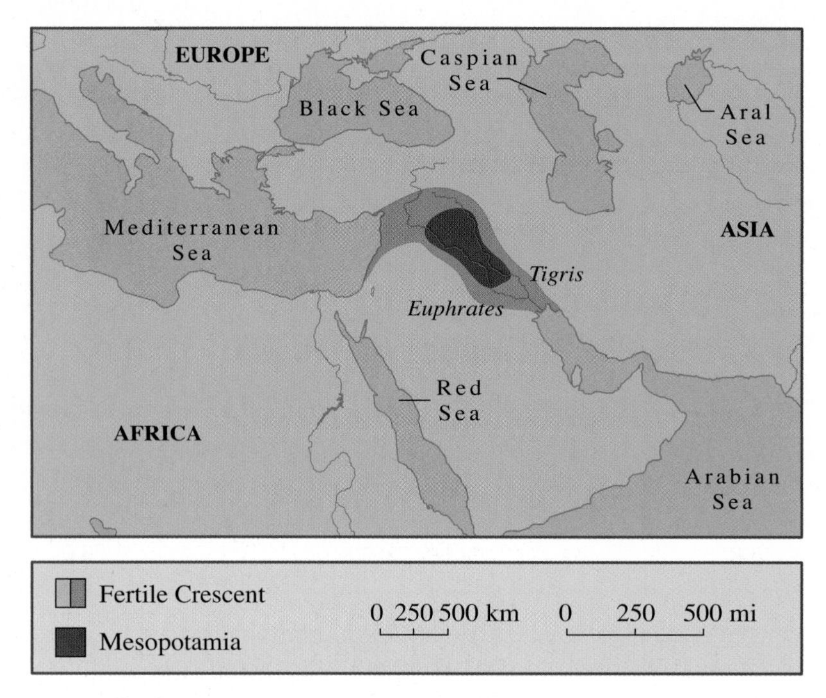

Figure 2.1 ■ Mesopotamia and the Fertile Crescent.

attest to the vigor and determination of the Mesopotamian people.

The Tigris and Euphrates Rivers are heavily laden with beneficial silt, but the timing of the annual flooding of these rivers, which would spread that silt over the countryside, does not coincide with the growing season of grains and other important crops, thus making the floods as detrimental as they are helpful. The first solution to this problem of flood timing was to control the flooding through a series of dams and catch basins, which were connected to canals so that irrigation could be used to supply water during the dry season when rains were minimal. Although this irrigation system seemed to solve the water problem, over time salts built up in the poorly drained soils and crop yields began to diminish. To solve this problem, other solutions were required.

One solution was simply to move to new land and reconstruct the civilization. This occasionally happened, but was, of course, too costly to continue. Another solution was to flush the soil with large amounts of water so that the salts would be driven so deep into the soil that they were below the root zones of the plants. However, the poor drainage of the soil complicated this option. A more innovative solution was created when the people constructed the irrigation system so that flushing occurred by moving the water from the higher-elevation Euphrates River to the lower Tigris River. In this way the land was rejuvenated by the rich silt in the river but the salts were swept across the land into the Tigris and then out to sea. This type of irrigation system proved to work very well, so long as it was maintained. With this innovation, Mesopotamia was fertile and productive over the long term and, therefore, able to sustain the various societies that controlled it. We see, therefore, that from the outset, agriculture in the very first area of its domestication required considerable creativity to sustain it. This reliance on sustained creativity will be seen throughout history, and will be a hallmark of thriving and changing societies.

Mesopotamia was a land of constant change, challenge, and upheaval because of the many conquests of the area by invading empires. Each conquest brought new lifestyles and the need to change, but it also brought creative ideas. We will discuss the creative ideas of each Mesopotamian empire and also consider the reasons that each empire was supplanted by another. In general, the empires were in a state of decay when the conquerors entered, but then, we may only be aware of the successful conquests and a society that is not decayed might have the vitality to resist invasions which, because they were not successful, are lost to the historical record. We seem to be able to note that, in general, the repeated infusion of new conquering people gives renewed creative vigor and, without the invasions, Mesopotamia would have decayed into a state of uncreative lethargy rather than the vigorous and progressive place that actually resulted. We will also briefly explore the origin of each conquering people and hope to determine their creative state at the time of their conquest.

Sumerians

The first group to control Mesopotamia were the Sumerians, who governed the area, chiefly in the southern end of Mesopotamia, from 3500 B.C. to 2350 B.C. Written history does not give us much information about the specific origin of the Sumerians, and their language, which is unrelated to any other, gives us no clues about origins. Their lives seem to have been very strongly influenced by their religion, a polytheistic faith that had gods associated with nearly everything in their environment. (Archeologists have found statuettes from Sumerian temples that seem to confirm this polytheism.) Success in life was believed to depend on keeping the gods happy through devotions and sacrifices, as was typical of most polytheistic pagan religions. Whenever a disaster struck, the people tended to blame it on a dissatisfied god. Therefore, the duty of every family included making the appropriate sacrifices so that the gods would not be angry. Priests, who assisted in these sacrifices, were powerful, but acted under the direction of the king, who was both the ruler and the military leader. The need for military leadership in this land of relatively open boundaries and constant threat from outside groups kept the kings in charge.

The cities of the Sumerians were quite large and often enclosed within large, rectangular walls. Within the cities the main streets were wide, perhaps for victory parades or religious processions, and seemed to culminate at large pyramid-like religious edifices called **ziggurats.** The ziggurats served as temples, tombs, and government sites. The ziggurats were built of dried mud bricks with gates of solid brass, and were decorated with dozens of brightly colored lions. A long staircase led to the top, where a shrine to a chief god was located. The shrine contained a bed and golden table, supposedly so that the god could sleep and eat there.

One of the ziggurats is traditionally associated with the tower of Babel. This association is especially interesting because the Sumerian language is not related to any other, thus suggesting that Sumerian might have been the language that pre-dated the confusion of tongues. Ziggurats were also constructed by many of the societies that succeeded the Sumerians, so this part of their culture was retained and became typical of the Mesopotamian region. Figure 2.2 shows the ruins of a ziggurat.

Some buildings in the cities were quite large, probably for royalty, while the majority of houses

Figure 2.2 ■ Ziggurat ruins. *Image © Dean Conger/ Corbis.*

were small and crowded closely together. Artisans who practiced the same trade, such as shoemakers or weavers, had shops located in the same general area and often along the same street. Although we don't know the origin of the wheel, the Sumerians were the first to develop wheeled vehicles for practical applications. These vehicles not only assisted in general transportation and war, but also promoted widespread trade. Some evidence in the cities indicates that trade may have been with cultures as far away as Egypt and India.

Cuneiform (which means wedge writing), as the Sumerian written language came to be called, was developed as a means of keeping track of inventories, credits, debits, and other business transactions. Cuneiform began simply as **pictograms** (where wheat was a picture of wheat, but one person's picture of wheat might not look like another's picture of wheat). Later these pictograms developed into **ideograms** (where wheat was a stylized picture of wheat, but everyone drew the same picture when they meant wheat). As time passed the use of ideograms expanded to include phonetically related symbols.

Cuneiform was written on soft clay tablets, using a sharpened reed or stick, which made a wedge-shaped indentation; the tablets were then baked to harden and preserve them. There were about 1,200 characters in cuneiform, and the ability to be able to read and write cuneiform was the key to success and advancement in Sumerian Mesopotamia. Cuneiform had the advantage that it could be adapted to many different languages, much like the Roman alphabet is used by many languages. Therefore, as the various empires came and went in Mesopotamia, many of the empires adopted cuneiform as their writing method. Hundreds of cuneiform clay tablets survive, and over 90 percent of them are records of commercial transactions. One such tablet is shown in Figure 2.3.

The Sumerians controlled Mesopotamia until around 2350 B.C., when a Semitic people (descended from the Biblical Shem and speaking a Semitic language similar to Arabic or Hebrew) conquered them. By this time a series of internal battles had greatly weakened the Sumerian empire, thus making it ripe for conquest.

Figure 2.3 ■ Cuneiform tablet. *Image © Christie's Images/Corbis.*

Akkadians/Early Babylonians

The Semitic conquerors chose the city of Akkad as their headquarters, and this period is called the Akkadian or Semitic Period. Later the capital was moved from Akkad to Babylonia, and so these same Semitic people are also called the Babylonians. (Since a much later empire was also centered in Babylonia, this first period in which Babylon was a capital is called the Akkadian or Early Babylonian Period.) The Akkadian/Early Babylonian Period lasted until about 1650 B.C.

Sargon I, the first Akkadian king, was powerful, and expanded the empire from the southern Tigris and Euphrates valley northward through Syria to the Taurus Mountains, which form the southern boundary of present-day Turkey. He was able to do this by creating the first standing army, thus keeping his men constantly trained and ready to fight. Then, in order to pay for the immense cost of keeping a standing army (after all, these are men who did not produce anything), he continually sent them to conquer new territories so that they could be paid from the spoils of war. This was a creative innovation; standing armies changed the nature of warfare. He was also creative in controlling and administering the vast territory over which he ruled. He established royal servants, who supervised vast estates throughout the territory. These royal servants generally administered well, thus fostering economic vigor through trade and intelligent division of labor.

As we shall see repeated many times throughout history, periods of military expansion are often (although not always) also periods of creativity. The generally positive linkage between warfare and creativity may occur because the needs of the active military might demand creative improvements in weaponry and tactics, much like during the expansion of the Roman Empire and the arms race between the United States and the Soviet Union from the 1950s to the 1980s. The creativity-war linkage might also occur because of the beneficial interactions between peoples who might otherwise have been isolated. This latter situation was one of the benefits to Europe following the Crusades; more of that will be discussed later in this book.

Figure 2.4 ■ Stele pillar depicting King Hammurabi and containing his code. *© 2010 by John Said. Used under license of Shutterstock, Inc.*

One of the world's oldest known literary documents is the Akkadian poem entitled *The Epic of Gilgamesh,* which was written about the year 2000 B.C. This epic tells the legendary story of Gilgamesh, a Sumerian ruler, as he traveled the earth seeking adventure and eternal life. It says something about Sumerian culture that even the hero Gilgamesh ultimately failed in his quest to become immortal, and returned home to die. An interesting saga within the *Epic of Gilgamesh* is a story of a great flood that is surprisingly similar to the story found in Genesis.

The cultural pinnacle of the first Babylonian Period came during the rule of their great King **Hammurabi,** about 1750 B.C. Hammurabi was brilliant and well-rounded. He personally supervised innovations in navigation, agriculture, tax collection, and temple erection. He can be favorably compared with other multi-faceted leaders like Pericles of Athens (fifth century B.C.) and Frederick the Great of Prussia (eighteenth century A.D.). These creative leaders seemed to lay a foundation for greatness that survived many years. Perhaps the most important of his innovations was, however, history's first known set of laws: the Code of Hammurabi. The Code of Hammurabi was written on a basalt rock stele (pillar) and is now in the Louvre. (See Figure 2.4.) The stele has a depiction of Hammurabi and, below the picture, the text of the code, written in cuneiform characters. The language is Akkadian.

The development of a written law code that, in theory at least, even Hammurabi himself was subject to, was unique and creative. The reasoning behind it, however, may have been even more so. Hammurabi was familiar with the history of his own people and the Sumerians before them in controlling Mesopotamia, and realized that there were key difficulties in governing an empire such as his. Through military conquest Hammurabi's empire was large and far-flung and its inhabitants were quite ethnically diverse. By writing down a basic law, rather than ruling by just whim and decree as previous kings had done, he could ensure some measure of uniformity throughout his land, and create a feeling of inclusion amongst his various subjects. This reduced the resentment of subjugated peoples and the possibility of revolt.

The Code of Hammurabi has many characteristics that are similar to the Mosaic Law found in the Bible. For example, both outline many crimes that are punishable by death. Although most of these capital crimes are similar (such as murder and adultery), some are unique to the Hammurabi Code, such as aiding a fleeing slave or stealing from the temple. Both codes are also retributive; that is, they require an eye for an eye. However, both codes also allow compensation with money for some crimes. One major difference between the Mosaic Law and the Hammurabi Code is that the Mosaic Law was given to Moses by God, whereas the Hammurabi Code was not divinely inspired but, rather, a collection of current Babylonian practices plus concepts initiated by Hammurabi. Another difference is that the Mosaic Law applies equally to everyone, regardless of social position, whereas the Code of Hammurabi is more lenient for higher ranking individuals in some crimes.

Hammurabi's Code was set up so that the punishment would fit the crime, sometimes with an especially poetic justice. For example, burglars who dug through walls were killed and then buried in the wall; tavern owners who watered down their drinks were drowned; physicians whose patients died could lose a hand. (A physician's text from this era encourages physicians to avoid treating dying patients.) Hammurabi's Code also established a procedure where the accused was given a trial; and a provision where the accuser was punished if the accusation couldn't be proved.

Hammurabi also made other changes to make Babylonian life better that helped him to govern more effectively. A governmental bureaucracy was created to oversee the more remote parts of his empire, much like the administrators of Sargon I, but Hammurabi's administrators were paid directly by the government rather than from lands they administered within the territories. This gave Hammurabi more direct control. He established certain cities as trade cities, to help encourage trade and production. Finally, rather than send his army on a continual series of wars to pay for their upkeep, he spread the army throughout already conquered areas and had the local peoples' taxes pay for them. This practice allowed him to avoid continuous, costly military entanglements, and was a good way to keep an eye on conquered peoples.

The Babylonians developed a truly creative and remarkable number system. It was based on the number 60 (and was therefore called sexigesimal). Just as our system uses decimal place holders (units, tens, hundreds, etc.), the Babylonian system used place holders based on 60. Therefore, where we have units, they also had units. But, where our second position is for tens, their second position was for 60. Their third position was for 3600, and so on. We are not quite sure why the Babylonians chose 60 as the basis of their number system, but it seems to have been related to the high number of factors for 60. (It can be divided evenly by 1, 2, 3, 4, 5, 6, 10, 12, 15, 20, and 30). This gave 60 a type of numerical compatibility that the Babylonians believed was special. Another number important to them was 360, perhaps for the same reason. Perhaps the Babylonians also gave 360 special importance because it approximated the number of days in the year.

Early Babylonian dominance was not to last forever in Mesopotamia. The kings who succeeded Hammurabi suffered from many border wars with the various tribes surrounding the empire, and also from dissent within the empire from tribes not fully pacified. Hence, as with the Sumerian, the Akkadian/Early Babylonian Empire fell into decline.

Hittites

Around 1650 B.C. a new power, the Hittites, rose north of the Akkadian empire and swept in to dominate the region. The Hittites were from Anatolia (present-day Turkey) and spoke an Indo-European language. They were tribal and fierce, but their greatest asset was knowledge of how to smelt and form iron. They ushered in the Iron Age, but, just like an inventor who cannot get a patent, they were careful about their secrets.

At some point, Hittite smiths had learned the technique of heating iron to the high temperature needed for shaping it into useful forms and then cooling it properly to obtain a hard structure. Iron was much harder and sturdier than bronze, the predominant metal of the Akkadians, and was therefore better for use in both warfare and farming. Thus, the warlike Hittites would use their superior weaponry (including much improved iron-wheeled chariots, battering rams, and improved infantry weapons) to take over Mesopotamia and its other peoples, and then introduce iron for farming tools (plowshares, axes, etc.) to the newly conquered peoples, which in turn raised the level of agricultural productivity.

The importance of a high-technology material has been commonly recognized by historians. One system of naming major epochs is to call them after the most advanced material of the age. The Stone Age featured stone (actually ceramic) technology for items like pots and dishes, which enabled trade in commodities like wine and oil, as well as providing civilization with important implements like dishes, cups, boxes, and writing materials. The Bronze Age followed the stone age. Undoubtedly bronze was discovered rather than specifically developed. Copper, which is the major component in bronze, can be smelted quite easily from ore. If, by chance, this was done in the presence of tin, bronze would be made. The superior hardness of bronze over pure copper would then lead some creative and observant person to investigate how the new, improved material came about. Other alloys of copper, such as brass (copper and zinc), would undoubtedly be either discovered or developed once the concept of alloying with copper became known.

However, a new technology was required for the development of iron; that technology seemed to be developed first by the Hittites. Although iron ore is abundant and easily accessible, it does not smelt easily because of the much higher temperature that is required compared to the conditions for smelting copper. In fact, the temperature required for iron is higher than the temperature of a fire from burning most ordinary woods. Someone eventually discovered that, by burning the wood to charcoal and then burning the charcoal while blowing air onto it, the higher temperatures for smelting iron could be obtained. The inclusion of carbon to give iron its hardness would have been almost automatic with charcoal as the fuel in the fire. The working of iron also required higher temperatures than for copper alloys, but, presumably, once the smelting temperatures were obtained, the working temperatures would also be easily achieved. Therefore, with some diligence and insight, the Hittites developed iron technology and the world entered the Iron Age. They carefully guarded their secrets and used these new materials to conquer all of Mesopotamia but, once someone has made a discovery and that discovery becomes widely used, others seem to be able to figure out or, perhaps, steal the secret. This has been the pattern from the Iron Age to the Nuclear Age. This pattern reveals both similarities and differences in creativity between the originator of an idea and a copier. Creativity is obvious in the originator and, occasionally, creativity might also be shown in the work of the copier to uncover the secret, but the creativity of the originator is generally more esteemed.

Phoenicians/Philistines/Sea Peoples

The secret of making iron would remain almost exclusively in Hittite control until they lost their empire to the Phoenicians, who were also called the Philistines. The Phoenicians may have been the Sea Peoples mentioned in ancient texts, or may have simply united with the Sea Peoples during some part of their history. Either way, the Phoenicians rose to power about 1200 B.C. The Philistines continued to dominate the coastal area (then called Canaan) because of their knowledge of iron-working as attested in the Bible throughout the Biblical period of the Judges and well into the reigns of Saul, David and Solomon.

> And the children of Israel cried unto the Lord: for he [Jabin, King of Canaan] had nine hundred chariots of iron; and twenty years he mightily oppressed the children of Israel.
>
> —Judges 4:3

> Now there was no smith found throughout all the land of Israel: for the Philistines said, Lest the Hebrews make them swords or spears: But all the Israelites went down to the Philistines, to sharpen every man his share, and his coulter, and his axe, and his mattock. Yet they had a file for the mattocks, and for the coulters, and for the forks, and for the axes, and to sharpen the goads. So it came in the day of the battle, that there was neither sword nor spear found in the hand of any of the people that were with Saul and Jonathan: but with Saul and with Jonathan his son was there found.
>
> —1 Samuel 13:19–22

The Phoenicians were traders, and seemed to have understood the importance of controlling ports throughout their trading area. We see this in the many colonies the Phoenicians established around the Mediterranean Sea and even into the Atlantic Ocean. Some of these colonies became very important trade centers in their own region and one, Carthage, dominated trade in the western Mediterranean until the second century B.C., when they were defeated by the Romans in the Punic Wars.

This vast trading area required good administration and communications. An innovation in communications is one of the contributions of the Phoenicians: the alphabet. This alphabet was substantially different from the cuneiform method of writing, since cuneiform was a combination of pictographic and syllabic but the alphabet was based on sounds. However, because the Phoenicians spoke a Semitic language that is dominated by the consonant sounds, the vowels were not written; consequently, the written texts were inherently confusing, and remained mostly business-related. The lack of written vowels has caused some interesting problems in translation, since the linkage between the written letters and the word they represent is often difficult. For instance (using English words to illustrate), *"mn"* could stand for man, moon, mean, mine, and many other words. Nevertheless, the Phoenician alphabet was the precursor to the Greek and Roman alphabets, which have continued to the present time.

Since the Phoenicians were traders, they needed goods to trade—and the more expensive the goods, the more money they could make for each voyage. With tremendous creativity, the Phoenicians invented one of the most luxurious of all ancient materials: the dye for royal purple. This dye was obtained by crushing and then extracting the color from a small shellfish found off the coast of Phoenicia and its colonies in Africa. The dye is named Tyrian purple for the city in Phoenicia, Tyre, that was the center of the industry.

The Phoenicians are given credit for the invention of glass, which also became a highly prized trading commodity. They also developed great skill in shipbuilding and building construction. That latter skill was demonstrated when King Solomon of the Jews asked the Phoenicians to assist in the construction of the great temple. Solomon used Phoenician cedars (called today the Cedars of Lebanon) for the temple. Among other items traded by the Phoenicians were embroideries, linen, metalwork, ivory, ebony, silk, amber, spices, incense, and precious metals. Clearly they were importing some of the goods to be resold elsewhere. This is, of course, the heart of a trading economy.

Israelites

The Israelites rose to their most powerful position during the time when the Phoenicians controlled the coastal regions of Mesopotamia. Under Saul, David, and Solomon, the Israelites expanded their kingdom to include most of the territory south of present-day Syria and north of the Negev desert, with the exception of some of the coastal areas that were still under the Phoenicians (called Philistines in the Bible), although the Phoenicians paid tribute to the Israelite kings during the time of the strongest kings.

Except for the brief period when Saul, David, and Solomon were kings, the land of the Hebrews was usually under the domination of one of the greater Mesopotamian empires. However, because several major overland trade routes passed through Hebrew territory, the major empires fought over control of the territory, giving, perhaps, importance to the area that would not otherwise have occurred.

Assyrians

Another conquering group were the Assyrians, an extremely warlike and vicious people who came from within the territory of the old Babylonian Empire. They lived inland, somewhat further north along the Tigris River than Babylon. Although this people had been in that area for many years as a minor power, they rose to eminence somewhere around 900 B.C. The Assyrian capital was Ninevah, which, at the time of Jonah in the Bible, was a wicked and frightening place. The Assyrians would sweep down on a weaker civilization, conquer them, and then adopt the aspects of the conquered culture that were appealing to them. The Assyrians would often carry off the people they conquered and bring in new people to occupy the vacated territory, thus ensuring that the Assyrians could control the territory as they wished. This is what happened in 721 B.C. when the Assyrians conquered the northern ten tribes of Israel and resettled the territory with people from across the Jordan River. These new settlers became known as the Samaritans. Since the Bible has no further record of the tribes that were carried away by the Assyrians, the ten tribes of the northern kingdom of Israel are known as the Lost Ten Tribes.

Later Babylonians, Medes, and Persians

After the Assyrians had lost their control (around 700 B.C.), Mesopotamia fell into the hands of a new Babylonian regime that ruled for a brief period. This regime, sometimes called the Chaldean Empire, was, in turn, conquered by the Medes, who then effectively merged with a group from the east called the Persians. (The Medes and Persians were from the area of present-day Iran, with the Medes originating in the western part of that territory and the Persians coming from the eastern part.) All of these civilizations will be discussed together because they tended to run together culturally; the time frame from one to the next was relatively short, although, when finally established, the Persian Empire was the largest the world had yet known, and lasted several hundred years.

The kings of this period, such as Nebuchadnezzar, Cyrus the Great, Xerxes, and Darius, were extremely powerful. They built a huge empire and developed strong bureaucratic control to supervise it. They also instituted king-worship, as discussed in the stories of Daniel in the Lion's Den and of Shadrach, Meshach, and Abed-Nego in the Bible. Under the rule of these kings, we see great creativity in government and in city planning and art, as evidenced by the Hanging Gardens of Babylon, one of the Seven Wonders of the Ancient World. The hanging gardens consisted of a series of terraces rising above the river, with beautiful flowers and shrubs growing on each of the levels. The entire complex was watered by a sophisticated irrigation system similar to some of the drip-irrigation systems employed today. The city of Babylon became a symbol for the magnificence of these empires. The walls of the city were decorated with animals made from colored tiles, as shown in Figure 2.5. The walls, gardens, palaces, and other parts of the city creatively communicated the glory of the empires, often intimidating both citizens and foreigners.

During the later part of the Persian period we also begin to see the rise of ethical monotheism, a trend that would eventually embrace most of Western civilization and culture in the form of Christianity. (Ethical monotheism had already existed in Canaan/Israel from the days of Abraham, some 1500 years previous to the Persian dynasty, but was confined to the Hebrew people because this religion was associated with them as a chosen people.) The most important of these new monotheistic religions was Zoroastrianism, which arose in Persia in the seventh century B.C. This

Figure 2.5 ■ Lion and horse depicted on Babylonian walls. *© 2010 by John Said. Used under license of Shutterstock, Inc.*

religion was founded by **Zarathustra,** a prophet who used fire as an element of worship. The three wise men of the New Testament story of Christ's birth were likely Zoroastrians. This religion was expelled from Persian about 700 A.D. and fled to India, where they now have small groups of adherents in the areas of Bombay and Calcutta. In India they are known as the Parsi.

The Persians were adept at celestial measurements and predictions, and developed the **zodiac,** a method of measuring the movement of the earth through the year by noting its position with respect to twelve constellations, each located in a different part of the sky. The predictive nature of astrology, using the zodiac, is based on the reasonable observation that many events on earth, such as the seasons and the tides, depend upon celestial bodies. These obvious dependencies were extended to the planets and other celestial phenomena to give the complex predictions now associated with astrology. In the ancient world, there was no difference between astrology and astronomy.

The strong emphasis of the Babylonians, Medes, and Persians on astronomy (astrology), and the powerful number system they used, based on 60 and 360, have given us a legacy today. We still use 60 minutes in the hour and 60 seconds in the minute. A circle has 360 degrees and angles are divided into minutes and seconds, just like time. All of these are from the ancient Babylonians, Medes, and Persians.

From roughly 3500 to 333 B.C., Mesopotamia existed as the center of one empire or another. Each of these empires was overthrown by another group, usually because the ruling empire had fallen into decline, thus providing an opportunity for the new regime. In almost every instance, the new regimes brought a new burst of creativity, and the civilization of the entire region sprinted ahead.

In 333 B.C. the Greek general Alexander the Great marched with his armies and conquered Mesopotamia. This conquest was somewhat different from the others. The Persian Empire was still very powerful and very much in control of their territories. However, as we shall see later when we discuss Alexander, the rash and proud young Macedonian king was able to defeat the greatest empire in the world at that time. He used great creativity in tactics, and a determination that was destined to succeed. After Alexander's death, his generals divided the empire, and Mesopotamia came under the control of Seleucus. His descendants ruled the area until the time of the Romans, around 50 B.C. (Later, from time to time, small parts of the territory were controlled by other groups, such as the Maccabees, Jewish patriots who were able to form an independent territory about 170 B.C.)

We will discuss the events of Mesopotamia again when we examine the conquests of Alexander and of the Romans. Then, later, we will see conflicts in Mesopotamia between the Christian

Byzantine Empire and the rising Muslim tribes sweeping into the area from Arabia. Mesopotamia became, for many years, the center of the Islamic Empire, with various headquarters either in the area or in surrounding territories. It remained an important part of the Ottoman Empire until the end of World War I. Then, after World War II it again took on great political and religious importance, continuing until today.

Timeline—Important Dates

Date	Event
4000–3000 B.C.	*Initiation of the society*
3500–2350 B.C.	*Sumerians control Mesopotamia*
2350–1650 B.C.	*Akkadians (early Babylonians) control Mesopotamia*
1750 B.C.	*Rule of Hammurabi*
1650 B.C.	*Conquest by the Hittites*
1200 B.C.	*Conquest (coastal) by the Phoenicians/Sea People*
1100–1000 B.C.	*Height of Hebrew power (Saul, David, Solomon)*
900 B.C.	*Conquest by the Assyrians*
721 B.C.	*Loss of the northern kingdom of Israel (10 tribes)*
700 B.C.	*Rise of the Later Babylonian (Chaldean) empire*
600 B.C.	*Rise of the Medes*
500 B.C.	*Rise of the Persians*
333 B.C.	*Conquest of the Persians by Alexander the Great*
50 B.C.	*Conquest of Mesopotamian area by the Romans*

Suggested Readings

Abbott, Walter M., SJ, Rabbi Arthur Gilbert, Rolfe Lanier Hunt, and J. Carter Swaim, *The Bible Reader,* Bruce Publishing Company, 1969.

Boorstin, Daniel J., *The Discoverers,* Vintage Books, 1985.

Cahill, Thomas, *The Gifts of the Jews,* Nan A. Talese/ Anchor Books, 1998.

Gabel, John B., Charles B. Wheeler, and Anthony D. York, *The Bible as Literature,* 3rd ed., Oxford University Press, 1996.

Gordon, Cyrus H. and Gary A. Rendsburg, *The Bible and the Ancient Near East,* Norton, 1997.

Keller, Werner, *The Bible as History,* William Neil (tr.), Bantam Books, 1980.

Michener, James, *The Source,* Ballantine Books, 1965.

Potok, Chaim, *Wanderings,* Fawcett, 1978.

Pritchard, J. B. (ed.), *The Ancient Near East,* Princeton University Press, 1958.

Article 1
Code of Hammurabi

Introduction

Hammurabi was the king of the kingdom of Babylon in the 18th Century BC. This establishes the Code of Hammurabi as the first known set of laws to be written (pre-dating Moses by about four centuries). The code was found inscribed on a stone in the Mesopotamian area at the beginning of the 20th Century AD. The code was written in cuneiform, the ancient language of Mesopotamia that is characterized by wedge-shaped letters, usually inscribed into clay tablets which were then hardened.

Although the code states that Hammurabi was called by the gods to cause justice to prevail in the land and to destroy the wicked and evil, no religious statements are contained in the code and the code was not, itself, considered to have come from the gods. Rather, the code is a compilation of the practices and wisdom of the Mesopotamian people and focuses on criminal law. It outlines the punishments that would be given for various crimes. The punishments are, in general, based on retaliation such as "an eye for an eye" similar in many ways to the Hebraic code outlined in the Bible. But unique to the Hammurabi law code is the changing severity of the punishment based on social status. A nobleman would receive a light punishment for the same crime that would bring capital punishment to a guilty slave. Nevertheless, the law is applied to all classes of people. The readings are some of the most important sections of the code and should be compared to other ancient legal codes (such as the Biblical laws) and to modern laws.

Code

1. If a man has accused another of laying a death spell upon him, but has not proved it, he shall be put to death.
2. If a man has accused another of laying a spell upon him, but has not proved it, the accused shall go to the sacred river, he shall plunge in the sacred river, and if the sacred river shall conquer him, he that accused him shall take possession of his house. If the sacred river shall show his innocence and he is saved, his accuser shall be put to death. He that plunged in the sacred river shall appropriate the house of him that accused him.
3. If a man has borne false witness in a trial, or has not established the statement that he has made, if that case be a capital trial, that man shall be put to death.
4. If he has borne false witness in a civil law case, he shall pay the damages in that suit.
5. If a judge has given a verdict, rendered a decision, granted a written judgment, and afterward has altered his judgment, that judge shall be prosecuted for altering the judgment he gave and shall pay twelvefold the penalty laid down in that judgment. Further, he shall be publicly expelled from

his judgment-seat and shall not return nor take his seat with the judge at a trial.

6. If a man has stolen goods from a temple, or house, he shall be put to death; and he that has received the stolen property from him shall be put to death.

* * *

14. If a man has stolen a child, he shall be put to death.
15. If a man has induced either a male or female slave from the house of a patrician, or plebeian, to leave the city, he shall be put to death.
16. If a man has harbored in his house a male or female slave from patrician's or plebeian's house, and has not caused the fugitive to leave on the demand of the officer over the slaves condemned to public forced labor, that householder shall be put to death.

* * *

22. If a man has committed highway robbery and has been caught that man shall be put to death.
23. If the highwayman has not been caught, the man that has been robbed shall state on oath what he has lost and the city or district governor in whose territory or district the robbery took place shall restore to him what he has lost.

* * *

25. If a fire has broken out in a man's house and one who has come to put it out has coveted the property of the householder and appropriated any of it, that man shall be cast into the self-same fire.
108. If the mistress of a beer-shop has not received corn as the price of beer or has demanded silver on an excessive scale, and has made the measure of beer less than the measure of corn, that beer-seller shall be prosecuted and drowned.

* * *

128. If a man has taken a wife and has not executed a marriage-contract, that woman is not a wife.
129. If a man's wife be caught lying with another, they shall be strangled and cast into the water. If the wife's husband would save his wife, the king can save his servant.
130. If a man has ravished another's betrothed wife, who is a virgin, while still living in her father's house, and has been caught in the act, that man shall be put to death; the woman shall go free.
131. If a man's wife has been accused by her husband, and has not been caught lying with another, she shall swear her innocence, and return to her house.
132. If a man's wife has the finger pointed at her on account of another, but has not been caught lying with him, for her husband's sake she shall plunge into the sacred river.

* * *

142. If a woman has hated her husband and has said, "You shall not possess me," her past shall be inquired into, as to what she lacks. If she has been discreet, and has no vice, and her husband has gone out, and has greatly belittled her, that woman has no blame, she shall take her marriage-portion and go off to her father's house.
143. If she has not been discreet, has gone out, ruined her house, belittled her husband, she shall be drowned.

* * *

152. From the time that that woman entered into the man's house they together shall be liable for all debts subsequently incurred.

153. If a man's wife, for the sake of another, has caused her husband to be killed, that woman shall be impaled.
159. If a man, who has presented a gift to the house of his prospective father-in-law and has given the brideprice, has afterward looked upon another woman and has said to his father-in-law, "I will not marry your daughter"; the father of the girl shall keep whatever he has brought as a present.
160. If a man has presented a gift to the house of his prospective father-in-law, and has given the brideprice, but the father of the girl has said, "I will not give you my daughter," the father shall return double all that was presented him.

* * *

195. If a son has struck his father, his hands shall be cut off.
196. If a man has knocked out the eye of a patrician, his eye shall be knocked out.
197. If he has broken the limb of a patrician, his limb shall be broken.
198. If he has knocked out the eye of a plebeian or has broken the limb of a plebeian, he shall pay one mina of silver.
199. If he has knocked out the eye of a patrician's servant, or broken the limb of a patrician's servant, he shall pay half his value.
200. If a partician has knocked out the tooth of a man that is his equal, his tooth shall be knocked out.
201. If he has knocked out the tooth of a plebeian, he shall pay one-third of a mina of silver.
202. If a man has smitten the privates of a man, higher in rank than he, he shall be scourged with sixty blows of an ox-hide scourge, in the assembly.

* * *

209. If a man has struck a free woman with child, and has caused her to miscarry, he shall pay ten shekels for her miscarriage.
210. If that woman die, his daughter shall be killed.

* * *

218. If a surgeon has operated with the bronze lancet on a patrician for a serious injury, and has caused his death, or has removed a cataract for a patrician, with the bronze lancet, and has made him lose his eye, his hands shall be cut off.

* * *

229. If a builder has built a house for a man, and has not made his work sound, and the house he built has fallen, and caused the death of its owner, that builder shall be put to death.
230. If it is the owner's son that is killed, the builder's son shall be put to death.
231. If it is the slave of the owner that is killed, the builder shall give slave for slave to the owner of the house.

Article 2
The Bible: Exodus and I Samuel

Introduction

Although small on a global scale, the Hebrew nation has influenced western civilization as few other nations have. From its origin, around 1800 BC, in a small family of nomads, the house of Israel (named after one of its early patriarchs) managed to preserve its identity in the face of internal squabbles, drought, four hundred years of Egyptian slavery, and repeated conquest by larger neighbors like Egypt, Syria, Babylon, and Rome. Ultimately, the unique identity and message of this nation became a contributing factor of great significance to the entire western world. The Hebrews passed their message on to the world in the form of the Bible. This book, to them, represented the word of God and, therefore, had a far greater meaning and permanency than did the words of even the greatest thinkers of humanity. Many other cultures, among them the Christians and the Muslims, also accept the Bible as the word of God, hence giving its teachings special significance even in modern culture.

Perhaps no men figured more prominently in the ancient Hebrew culture than did Moses and David. Accompanied by events and manifestations that have gained almost archetypal fame, Moses led the Israelites out of Egyptian enslavement around 1300 BC. This story is told in Exodus, the second book in the Bible. Before the wandering nation had yet established a permanent home, Moses presented them with Ten Commandments accompanied by a set of laws. These represented the will of God in the way the people were to conduct themselves both with respect to God and each other. The laws which governed the details of criminal law are referred to as retributive, that is, they exact a punishment that is designed to fit the crime. These commandments and laws established a system by which the nation would be governed and laid a foundation upon which modern Judaism and Christianity would later build. The Ten Commandments and some of the most important other laws are contained in the excerpted readings.

Two and a half centuries later, a Hebrew shepherd named David rose from humble beginnings to become king over a united Kingdom of Israel at the height of its power and glory. As discussed in the book of 1 Samuel, David volunteered to fight Goliath, a Philistine enemy who was gigantic in size. David's story became a legendary rallying cry for his small, yet determined people, much like the epic poems of Homer did for the Greeks. Even the concept of battle between two champions is similar between the accounts of David and Achilles, a hero of the Trojan War. The readings contain this famous story of David and Goliath that has been an inspiration to so many artists and writers throughout western history.

Today Moses and David not only hold places of epic significance among Jews, but their writings and legacy have left an ineradicable mark on western civilization as a whole.

Exodus

Chapter 20

AND God spake all these words, saying,

2 I *am* the LORD thy God, which have brought thee out of the land of Egypt, out of the house of bondage.

3 Thou shalt have no other gods before me.

4 Thou shalt not make unto thee any graven image, or any likeness *of any thing* that **is** in heaven above, or that *is* in the earth beneath, or that *is* in the water under the earth:

5 Thou shalt not bow down thyself to them, nor serve them: for I the LORD thy God *am* a jealous God, visiting the iniquity of the fathers upon the children unto the third and fourth *generation* of them that hate me;

6 And shewing mercy unto thousands of them that love me, and keep my commandments.

7 Thou shalt not take the name of the LORD thy God in vain; for the LORD will not hold him guiltless that taketh his name in vain.

8 Remember the sabbath day, to keep it holy.

9 Six days shalt thou labour, and do all thy work:

10 But the seventh day **is** the sabbath of the LORD thy God: *in it* thou shalt not do any work, thou, nor thy son, nor thy daughter, thy manservant, nor thy maidservant, nor thy cattle, nor thy stranger that *is* within thy gates:

11 For *in* six days the LORD made heaven and earth, the sea, and all that in them *is,* and rested the seventh day: wherefore the LORD blessed the sabbath day, and hallowed it.

12 ¶ Honour thy father and thy mother: that thy days may be long upon the land which the LORD thy God giveth thee.

13 Thou shalt not kill.

14 Thou shalt not commit adultery.

15 Thou shalt not steal.

16 Thou shalt not bear false witness against thy neighbour.

17 Thou shalt not covet thy neighbour's house, thou shalt not covet thy neighbour's wife, nor his manservant, nor his maidservant, nor his ox, nor his ass, nor any thing that *is* thy neighbour's.

Chapter 21

12 ¶ He that smiteth a man, so that he die, shall be surely put to death.

13 And if a man lie not in wait, but God deliver *him* into his hand; then I will appoint thee a place whither he shall flee.

14 But if a man come presumptuously upon his neighbour, to slay him with guile; thou shalt take him from mine altar, that he may die.

15 ¶ And he that smiteth his father, or his mother, shall be surely put to death.

16 ¶ And he that stealeth a man, and selleth him, or if he be found in his hand, he shall surely be put to death.

17 ¶ And he that curseth his father, or his mother, shall surely be put to death.

18 ¶ And if men strive together, and one smite another with a stone, or with *his* fist, and he die not, but keepeth *his* bed:

19 If he rise again, and walk abroad upon his staff, then shall he that smote *him* be quit: only he shall pay *for* the loss of his time, and shall cause *him* to be thoroughly healed.

20 ¶ And if a man smite his servant, or his maid, with a rod, and he die under his hand; he shall be surely punished.

21 Notwithstanding, if he continue a day or two, he shall not be punished: for he *is* his money.

22 ¶ If men strive, and hurt a woman with child, so that her fruit depart *from her,* and yet no mischief follow: he shall be surely punished, according as the woman's husband will lay upon him; and he shall pay as the judges *determine.*

23 And if *any* mischief follow, then thou shalt give life for life,

24 Eye for eye, tooth for tooth, hand for hand, foot for foot,

25 Burning for burning, wound for wound, stripe for stripe.

26 ¶ And if a man smite the eye of his servant, or the eye of his maid, that it perish; he shall let him go free for his eye's sake.

27 And if he smite out his manservant's tooth, or his maidservant's tooth; he shall let him go free for his tooth's sake.

28 ¶ If an ox gore a man or a woman, that they die: then the ox shall be surely stoned, and his flesh shall not be eaten; but the owner of the ox *shall be* quit.

29 But if the ox were wont to push with his horn in time past, and it hath been testified to his owner, and he hath not kept him in, but that he hath killed a man or a woman; the ox shall be

stoned, and his owner also shall be put to death.

32 If the ox shall push a manservant or a maidservant; he shall give unto their master thirty shekels of silver, and the ox shall be stoned.

Chapter 22

9 For all manner of trespass, *whether it be* for ox, for ass, for sheep, for raiment, *or* for any manner of lost thing, which *another* challengeth to be his, the cause of both parties shall come before the judges; *and* whom the judges shall condemn, he shall pay double unto his neighbour.

20 ¶ He that sacrificeth unto *any* god, save unto the LORD only, he shall be utterly destroyed.

21 ¶ Thou shalt neither vex a stranger, nor oppress him: for ye were strangers in the land of Egypt.

22 ¶ Ye shall not afflict any widow, or fatherless child.

23 If thou afflict them in any wise, and they cry at all unto me, I will surely hear their cry;

24 And my wrath shall wax hot, and I will kill you with the sword; and your wives shall be widows, and your children fatherless.

Chapter 23

1 THOU shalt not raise a false report: put not thine hand with the wicked to be an unrighteous witness.

2 ¶ Thou shalt not follow a multitude to do evil; neither shalt thou speak in a cause to decline after many to wrest *judgment:*

3 ¶ Neither shalt thou countenance a poor man in his cause.

4 ¶ If thou meet thine enemy's ox or his ass going astray, thou shalt surely bring it back to him again.

5 If thou see the ass of him that hateth thee lying under his burden, and wouldest forbear to help him, thou shalt surely help with him.

I Samuel

Chapter 17

1 Now the Philistines gathered together their armies to battle, and were gathered together at Shochoh, which *belongeth* to Judah, and pitched between Shochoh and Azekah, in Ephes-dammim.

2 And Saul and the men of Israel were gathered together, and pitched by the valley of Elah, and set the battle in array against the Philistines.

3 And the Philistines stood on a mountain on the one side, and Israel stood on a mountain on the other side: and *there was* a valley between them.

4 ¶ And there went out a champion out of the camp of the Philistines, named Goliath, of Gath, those height *was* six cubits and a span.

5 And *he had* an helmet of brass upon his head, and he *was* armed with a coat of mail; and the weight of the coat *was* five thousand shekels of brass.

6 And *he had* greaves of brass upon his legs; and a target of brass between his shoulders.

7 And the staff of his spear *was* like a weaver's beam; and his spear's head *weighed* six hundred shekels of iron: and one bearing a shield went before him.

8 And he stood and cried unto the armies of Israel, and said unto them, Why are ye come out to set *your* battle in array? *am* not I a Philistine, and ye servants to Saul? choose you a man for you, and let him come down to me.

9 If he be able to fight with me, and to kill me, then will we be your servants: but if I prevail against him, and kill him, then shall ye be our servants, and serve us.

10 And the Philistine said, I defy the armies of Israel this day; give me a man, that we may fight together.

11 When Saul and all Israel heard those words of the Philistine, they were dismayed, and greatly afraid.

12 ¶ Now David *was* the son of that Ephrathite of Beth-lehem-judah, whose name *was* Jesse; and he had eight sons: and the man went among men *for* an old man in the days of Saul.

13 And the three eldest sons of Jesse went *and* followed Saul to the battle: and the names of his three sons that went to the battle *were* Eliab the firstborn, and next unto him Abinadab, and the third Shammah.

14 And David *was* the youngest: and the three eldest followed Saul.

15 But David went and returned from Saul to feed his father's sheep at Beth-lehem.

16 And the Philistine drew near morning and evening, and presented himself forty days.

17 And Jesse said unto David his son. Take now for thy brethren an ephah of this parched *corn,* and these ten loaves, and run to the camp to thy brethren;

18 And carry these ten cheeses unto the captain of *their* thousand, and look how thy brethren fare, and take their pledge.

19 Now Saul, and they, and all the men of Israel, *were* in the valley of Elah, fighting with the Philistines.

20 ¶ And David rose up early in the morning, and left the sheep with a keeper, and took, and went, as Jesse had commanded him; and he came to the trench, as the host was going forth to the fight, and shouted for the battle.

21 For Israel and the Philistines had put the battle in array, army against army.

22 And David left his carriage in the hand of the keeper of the carriage, and ran into the army, and came and saluted his brethren.

23 And as he talked with them, behold, there came up the champion, the Philistine of Gath, Goliath by name, out of the armies of the Philistines, and spake according to the same words: and David heard *them.*

24 And all the men of Israel, when they saw the man, fled from him, and were sore afraid.

25 And the men of Israel said, Have ye seen this man that is come up? surely to defy Israel is he come up: and it shall be, *that* the man who killeth him, the king will enrich him with great riches, and will give him his daughter, and make his father's house free in Israel.

26 And David spake to the men that stood by him, saying, What shall be done to the man that killeth this Philistine, and taketh away the reproach from Israel? for who *is* this uncircumcised Philistine, that he should defy the armies of the living God?

27 And the people answered him after this manner, saying, So shall it be done to the man that killeth him.

28 ¶ And Eliab his eldest brother heard when he spake unto the men; and Eliab's anger was kindled, against David, and he said, Why camest thou down hither? and with whom hast thou left those few sheep in the wilderness? I know thy pride, and the naughtiness of thine heart; for thou art come down that thou mightest see the battle.

29 And David said, What have I now done? *Is there* not a cause?

30 ¶ And he turned from him toward another, and spake after the same manner: and the people answered him again after the former manner.

31 And when the words were heard which David spake, they rehearsed *them* before Saul: and he sent for him.

32 ¶ And David said to Saul, Let no man's heart fail because of him; thy servant will go and fight with this Philistine.

33 And Saul said to David, Thou art not able to go against this Philistine to fight with him: for thou art *but* a youth, and he a man of war from his youth.

34 And David said unto Saul, Thy servant kept his father's sheep, and there came a lion, and a bear, and took a lamb out of the flock:

35 And I went out after him, and smote him, and delivered *it* out of his mouth: and when he arose against me, I caught *him* by his beard, and smote him, and slew him.

36 Thy servant slew both the lion and the bear: and this uncircumcised Philistine shall be as one of them, seeing he hath defied the armies of the living God.

37 David said moreover, The LORD that delivered me out of the paw of the lion, and out of the paw of the bear, he will deliver me out of the hand of this Philistine. And Saul said unto David, Go, and the LORD be with thee.

38 ¶ And Saul armed David with his armour, and he put an helmet of brass upon his head; also he armed him with a coat of mail.

39 And David girded his sword upon his armour, and he assayed to go; for he had not proved *it.* And David said unto Saul, I cannot go with these; for I have not proved *them.* And David put them off him.

40 And he took his staff in his hand, and chose him five smooth stones out of the brook, and put them in a stepherd's bag which he had, even in a scrip; and his sling *was* in his hand: and he drew near to the Philistine.

41 And the Philistine came on and drew near unto David; and the man that bare the shield *went* before him.

42 And when the Philistine looked about, and saw David, he disdained him: for he was *but* a youth, and ruddy, and of a fair countenance.

43 And the Philistine said unto David, *Am* I a dog, that thou comest to me with staves? And the Philistine cursed David by his gods.

44 And the Philistine said to David; Come to me, and I will give thy flesh unto the fowls of the air, and to the beasts of the field.

45 Then said David to the Philistine, Thou comest to me with a sword, and with a spear, and with a shield: but I come to thee in the time of the LORD of hosts, the God of the armies of Israel, whom thou hast defied.

46 This day will the LORD deliver thee into mine hand; and I will smite thee, and take thine head from thee and I will give the carcases of the host of the Philistines this day into to the fowls of the air, and to the wild beasts of the earth; that all the with may know that there is a God in Israel.

47 And all this assembly shall know that the LORD saveth not with sword and spear: for the battle *is* the LORD's, and he will give you into our hands.

48 And it came to pass, when the Philistine arose, and came and drew nigh to meet David, that David hasted, and ran toward the army to meet the Philistine.

49 And David put his hand in his bag, and took thence a stone, and slang *it,* and smote the Philistine in his forehead, that the stone sunk into his forehead; and he fell upon his face to the earth.

50 So David prevailed over the Philistine with a sling and with a stone, and smote the Philistine, and slew him; but *there was* no sword in the hand of David.

51 Therefore David ran, and stood upon the Philistine, and took his sword, and drew it out of the sheath thereof, and slew him, and cut off his head therewith. And when the Philistines saw their champion was dead, they fled.

52 And the men of Israel and of Judah arose, and shouted, and pursued the Philistines, until thou come to the valley, and to the gates of Ekron. And the wounded of the Philistines fell down by the way to Shaaraim, even unto Gath, and unto Ekron.

53 And the children of Israel returned from chasing after the Philistines, and they spoiled their tents.

54 And David took the head of the Philistine, and brought it to Jerusalem; but he put his armour in his tent.

55 ¶ And when Saul saw David go forth against the Philistine, he said unto Abner, the captain of the host, Abner, whose son *is* this youth? And Abner said, As thy soul liveth, O king, I cannot tell.

56 And the king said, Enquire thou whose son the stripling *is.*

57 And as David returned from the slaughter of the Philistine, Abner took him, and brought him before Saul with the head of the Philistine in his hand.

58 And Saul said to him, Whose son *art* thou, *thou* young man? And David answered, I *am* the son of thy servant Jesse the Beth-lehemite.

Egypt
Creativity for Eternity

> O my heart of my being! Do not rise up against me as witness, Do not oppose me in the tribunal, Do not rebel against me before the guardian of the scales!
>
> —The Papyrus of Ani *translated by E. A. Wallis Budge*

Geography and Stability

Almost as old and probably just as important to the ancient world as Mesopotamia was the civilization established along the banks of the Nile River in Egypt. This civilization differed markedly from Mesopotamia in many ways, even though the two existed at the same time and, to some extent, interacted. Whereas the Mesopotamian civilization was a series of kingdoms and empires, repeatedly invaded and conquered, Egypt existed as an independent or semi-independent state for over 2,500 years, from the beginning of recorded history (about 3500 B.C.) to the eventual dissolution of the Egyptian ruling dynasties around 1000 B.C. and, even then, continued as an important state under foreign rulers until the end of the Roman Empire.

Whereas the creativity of Mesopotamia was infused from foreign conquerors, the creativity of Egypt (and it was very impressive indeed) came from religious forces. The most important of those forces was the Egyptian belief in the afterworld, the final judgment of the spirit, and an after life. This final judgment is shown in Figure 3.1 and described in prayer in the quotation at the beginning of this chapter. The dead person is brought to the scales of judgment and the person's heart is weighed against a sacred feather. If the heart is heavier than the feather, the person's life was burdened with guilt and evil. If the heart is light, then the person can pass the gods and enter into an eternal afterlife. We will explore those creativity-inspiring forces and others as we discuss the history of this second of the great ancient river societies.

Egypt's geography was both its greatest blessing and its ultimate downfall. The Nile River and its delta seemed to be the perfect place for a civilization to spring up. Egypt received almost no rainfall, but the annual flooding of the Nile River and the simple irrigation that could be used later allowed enough crops to be raised along its banks that Egypt could support and feed a very large

Figure 3.1 ■ *The Last Judgment of the Egyptians.* Image © Gianni Dagli Orti/Corbis.

population without resorting to interactions with the outside world. One of the gifts of the Nile River was that its flooding was very predictable. The Nile not only flooded annually, but it did so at nearly the exact same time of year, almost down to the day, and with nearly the same volume. This was quite advantageous for farming because it allowed the Egyptians to plan ahead and not plant too early or too late to take advantage of the river's flooding. The relative constancy of the volume of water also was useful because the leaders knew approximately how much land would be useful for planting.

Furthermore, the flooding was gentle, so that large areas were inundated but soil was not swept away. After the water drained, it left a new layer of soil from the silt that the river had carried with it. The new soil was always rich in nutrients and minerals, and this had two positive effects on Egyptian agriculture. First, Egyptian crops were plentiful and healthy, and second, even more importantly, the soil was renewed every year and never ran low on nutrients. This meant that the Egyptians could plant over and over again in the same place for 3,000 years without depleting or damaging the soil. Salt buildup was not a problem, because the inundation washed the salts downward into the easily drained soil.

Another important consideration of Egyptian geography was the relative isolation and safety from attack, afforded by the nearly impassible deserts on the south and west and by the Mediterranean Sea on the north and the Red Sea on the east, which, in the days of primitive sailing, were effective barriers to conquest. The only reasonable route for a potential invader was from the northeast over the Isthmus of Suez (the narrow land bridge between the Mediterranean Sea and the Red Sea), and this gap proved to be fairly easy for the Egyptians to defend. Even in the late period of Egyptian history when Egypt became dominated by outside rulers, its geography still kept it so isolated that Egypt kept intact its own laws, culture, and religion. A map of Egypt is given in Figure 3.2.

Hence, unlike Mesopotamia, the history of Egypt is not dominated by invasions. Rather, it is a series of long dynasties of consecutive ruling houses, interrupted only occasionally and briefly by invaders. Even when those invaders came, the strong cultural heritage of the Egyptians seemed to overwhelm the invading culture, thus resulting in a return to nearly the same cultural pattern as before. Little change occurred from dynasty to dynasty.

Initially, however, Egyptian life was full of change. The beginning settlers needed to establish a civilization, and that required much innovation and dynamic creativity. Multiple tribes lived within the territory, and these all needed to be subdued if a strong, united empire was to be formed within those safe boundaries. And, as we shall see, the religion of the Egyptians required special temples and burial places, which demanded strong

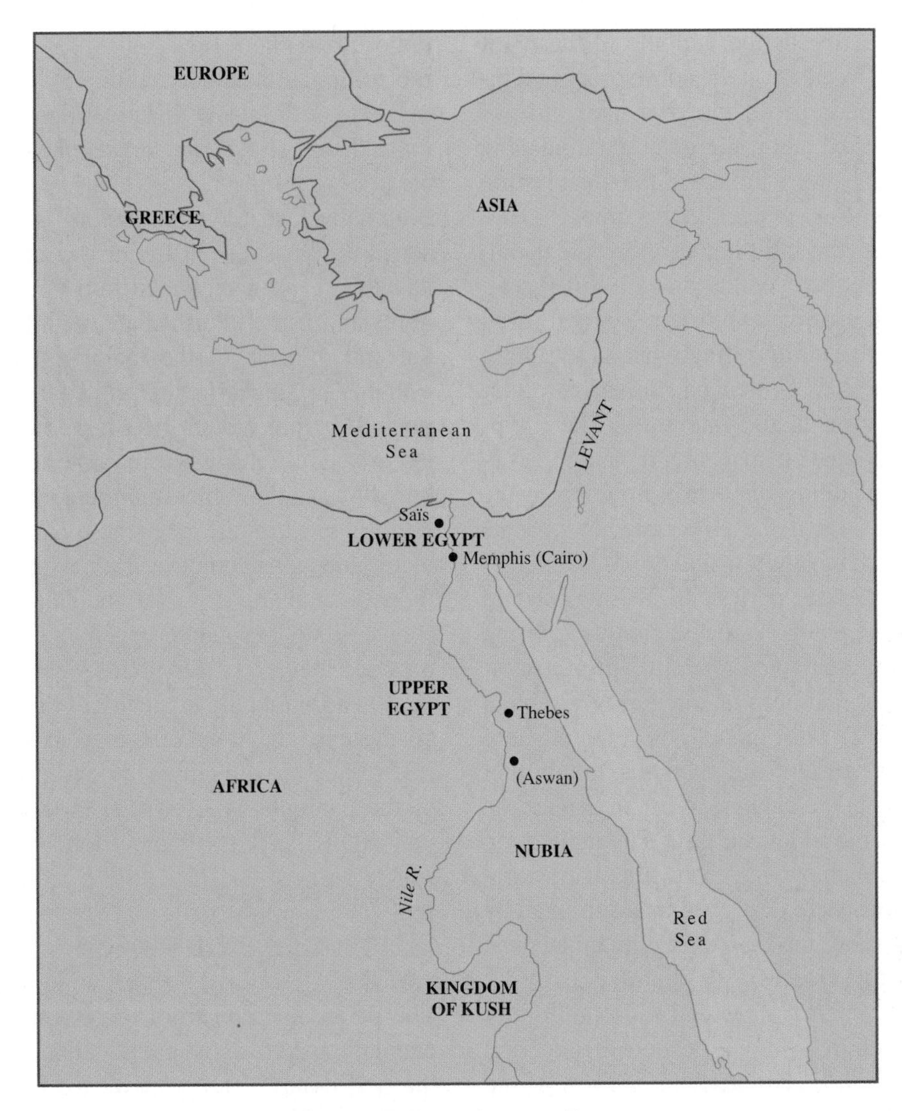

Figure 3.2 ■ *Ancient Egypt.*

creative effort. This dynamic period was the time when great creativity was obvious.

If the Nile River itself created an environment suitable for a large and stable civilization to develop, then its bountiful generosity produced the effect of serving as another spur to Egypt's early creativity. The relative ease of Egyptian agriculture meant that there was a surplus of labor. The pharaohs, knowing the danger inherent in too many people with nothing to do, kept the masses busy by putting them to work on elaborate and enormous construction projects, such as the Great Pyramids, the Sphinx, and later the temples of Luxor and Thebes. We will talk more about these great building projects later. Contrary to popular belief, slaves did not do most of the work.

It is a tribute to the power of the social order of Egypt that the simple command of a pharaoh was enough to put thousands to work willingly on projects that would be creative and challenging even with modern construction equipment and techniques, and must have seemed next to impossible in an age that had not even discovered metal tools. However, the pharaoh was a demigod, part human and part deity, and, as an important link between the worlds of life and death, he enjoyed the implicit trust of the Egyptian people. For the masses to have questioned a pharaoh's commands, even in a matter as daunting as the building of the pyramids, would be to question the entire order and hierarchy of Egyptian life. Thus, over the course of several centuries of labor, the great pyramids and temples and tombs were built, and remain a lasting creative legacy of Egypt even to this time.

However, in the building of these great edifices we also see the eventual downfall of Egypt. After the initial creative explosion, Egypt refused to change, for fear of upsetting what had brought them to greatness as evidenced in their carefully preserved monuments and mummies. The Egyptians were afraid that an upset might change all aspects of life, including the yearly flooding of the life-giving Nile, for if the Nile failed to give its yearly gift, much of Egypt would die. If it failed to do so for an extended period, all of Egypt would be lost. Even the pharaohs lost the ability to bring about change in their own kingdom. The preservation of the status quo became integral to Egyptian religion. Priests, who gained more and more power at the expense of the pharaohs, taught that change would put the balance of life in danger. As the centuries came and went, Egyptian civilization and culture were able to survive while many early peer civilizations were destroyed or assimilated by other cultures—but the cost of Egyptian survival was the loss of its creativity.

As Egypt became more and more culturally stagnant, it withdrew into a cocoon of isolation until it had very little contact with the rest of the world. After 3,000 years its art, religion, and culture were nearly identical to what they had been at the dawn of Egyptian civilization. Even when the Persians made Egypt a vassal state in the sixth century B.C., Egypt's geographic and cultural isolation was so effective that Egypt was practically untouched by Persian culture.

The Egyptians were vulnerable to the military forces and culture of Alexander the Great. He conquered Egypt quickly, almost as a sideshow to his main focus of devouring the Persian heartland, but even Alexander was caught by the timeless forces of Egypt. He journeyed to a sacred desert shrine where, obligingly, the priests declared him to be a pharaoh-like demigod. Then, with that mandate for immortality, Alexander felt qualified to establish himself as an emperor in the Persian sense (as opposed to the Greek sense). But we will talk more about Alexander and his legacy later.

Now, let's look at this great Egyptian culture in more detail, so that we can see the causes of their creativity and the reasons that creative force was eventually lost. Egyptian history is divided into a series of dynasties (31 by most counts). These dynasties are further divided into three major kingdoms and some intermediate periods which cause the end of each of the major kingdom periods. There is also an early time, called the **pre-dynastic period,** before written history and before the first dynasty. We will give some dates for the various kingdoms and for other important events associated with Egypt. In most cases these dates are approximate, and considerable variation is found among modern scholars. However, the dates do serve as a way to relate Egyptian events to one another and to outside events. The Egyptians were very proud of their history and the longevity of their governmental system, and thus kept reasonable lists of the rulers. Hence, with only a few exceptions, the order of the pharaohs is known, even though the dates may not be known with precision.

Pre-Dynastic Period

The period of time from the initial settlement of people in the Nile River valley (about 3500 B.C.) to the first dynasty (about 3100 B.C.) was a time of tribal, nomadic wandering with only loose associations. The Egyptian territory was roughly divided into two main sections—upper and lower Egypt. Upper Egypt was that portion upriver, that is, central and southern Egypt. Lower Egypt was the area north of Central Egypt toward the Mediterranean. Even in this early period, some boats had been built to allow travel along the Nile. These simple boats were often made of reeds and might have had a sail that helped propel the boats upriver. Since the boats could not easily pass the cataract, that served as a logical dividing point between the two Egypts.

The Egyptian people had not yet developed the prerequisite elements needed for a stationary civilization to begin. Even though there may have been agriculture and sufficient food, there were no cities and little division of labor. There was no writing and so we know little about pre-dynastic Egypt except for the small amount told to us by the writings of the later periods, when Egypt became a full-fledged civilization.

Old Kingdom

Eventually one of the tribal rulers, known as Narmur or Menes (as named by the Greeks), gained sufficient strength to subdue the other tribes and unite the kingdoms of upper and lower Egypt. **Narmur** created a crown that combined the crowns for upper and lower Egypt to commemorate this unification, and that crown became the model for the crowns of all subsequent pharaohs. Menes built the city of Memphis (not far from modern-day Cairo in lower Egypt) and made it the capital of the combined kingdom. He was immensely powerful as a king and military ruler, and the people worshiped him as a man-god and as the intermediary between humans and the many gods that made up the Egyptian deities.

Papyrus, surely a creative invention, was first made during the time of Narmur. Early ideograms (writing with pictures) were written on papyrus sheets to honor him and his works. This ideogram writing eventually led to the development of **hieroglyphs,** another major creative invention that was used for over 2,000 years. We should note that hieroglyphs means "sacred writings." The name may come from two sources. First, most of the writing concerned pharaohs (who are man-gods) or were religious texts about the other gods. Second, the writing was done by the priests.

Later in the Old Kingdom we see the erection of pyramids as burial places for the pharaohs. Initially, these pyramids were built as layered or stepped structures. Successive Old Kingdom pharaohs built larger and higher pyramids (supposedly to gain more glory for themselves) with smooth sides, but eventually a problem was encountered. The angles of the sides of these old pyramids were so steep that when the pyramids reached a certain height, they collapsed. The next pyramids were, therefore, bent with two angles of incline. In these, the lower part of the pyramid used a gradual angle and the top used a steeper angle. Eventually the engineers were able to find an angle that gave a rapid rise in the structure but would not collapse. With these discoveries, the engineers were able to build the great pyramids of Giza (an area not too far from Memphis). Both a stepped pyramid and the great pyramids are shown in Figure 3.3.

Visitors to the great pyramids are impressed by their size but are even more impressed by going inside the pyramids and seeing quite large chambers whose ceilings had to be built to withstand the incredible weight of the stones of the pyramid above the chambers. We are not sure how the Egyptians constructed the pyramids, but some theorize that mud ramps were used to transport the huge blocks up the sides and into the center of the structure. Similar mud ramps were certainly used to build high walls and other structures, as

Figure 3.3 ■ **A)** *Stepped pyramid.* Image © 2006 Jupiter Images Corporation. **B)** *Great pyramids of Giza.* *Image © 2006 Jupiter Images Corporation.*

some of those mud ramps on other structures were not removed and can still be seen today. However they were built, the pyramids are truly creative engineering endeavors.

The pyramids were also creative public works projects. Many historians now believe that the labor to build the pyramids was not slaves but, rather, Egyptian people who were between wars and needed to be kept busy. That concept (make-work projects) in itself was creative, and gave an indication of the concept of stability within the relationship of people and government that was so characteristic of Egypt.

The pyramids also reflect the commitment of the pharaoh to religion (which was developed in detail during the Old Kingdom) and, especially, the belief in life after death. The Egyptians believed that continuation of life after this one depended on three things:

- having one's name preserved in writing (usually as part of the hieroglyphics on a temple or tomb),
- being buried on Egyptian soil (hence the absence of occupation of foreign territories by the Egyptians who always wanted to be buried on Egyptian soil), and
- being properly prepared for the next life (which is reflected in emphasis on embalming and other rituals associated with death).

The Egyptian people must surely have thought that if the afterlife were not real, no one would go to the expense and effort to build a great pyramid. Therefore, the very existence of the pyramids was a testament to the belief of the Egyptians in an afterlife and their commitment to religion.

Like the Mesopotamians, the Egyptians were careful observers of the heavens and of earthly events which marked the passage of time. The Egyptians developed an accurate calendar of 12 months of 30 days, each subdivided into three 10-day periods, thus giving a regular year of 360 days. The solar year was matched by adding 5 days as holidays at the end of each year.

The Egyptians also developed a number system but, unlike the Mesopotamians, the Egyptian system was based on 10. They used an accumulative system from 0 to 9 (somewhat like the way dots accumulate on a pair of dice) but then used a new symbol to designate a 10. Designation symbols were also given for 100, 1000, and so on. This system proved to be very useful, and spurred Egyptian excellence in mathematics and technical record-keeping.

Art in the Old Kingdom set a standard that was used for the remainder of the Egyptian period. The art was representational rather than realistic. Important characters were made larger than non-important ones. The poses of the figures were standardized in both statues and in drawings. In statues, the most common pose was forward-facing, with the body also fully to the front, the arms at the side and one foot slightly forward. The faces were generic, that is, not meant to represent a particular person. In drawings, the most common pose was with the body facing the front but with the face turned to profile. The feet were also turned to the side. In drawings, the body position and the arms were positioned to represent the task that was being done at the time. The drawings are shown in Figure 3.1 and the sculpture is in Figure 3.4.

The Old Kingdom was the Golden Age for Egypt. Its pyramids, hieroglyphs, buildings, art, and even religion were constant reminders of the glory and creativity that characterized this period. Reaching that same level of creativity was a goal for all subsequent periods, but the standard of the Old Kingdom was never reached again. We might ask, "What was the reason for the creativity during the Old Kingdom?" Some reasons might be the energy associated with forming a country and the innovation that often comes from conquering areas, both in learning what the new area has developed and from the needs of war to enable the conquest. The conquests also provided the wealth and other resources that were needed to create these works. In this regard, the creativity of the Old Kingdom is like the creativity of Mesopotamia—dependent on conquest.

Much credit must also be given to the pharaohs of the Old Kingdom, who drove the society to create even during the periods when conquest was not important. The pharaohs understood that the people

Figure 3.4 ■ *Typical Egyptian sculpture. Image from Corel.*

could be motivated to creativity by the concepts of Egyptian greatness, religion, and glory. This motivation for creativity from the pharaohs and from a unique culture had to be coupled with the means of bringing it about, but history shows that strong leaders, who know how to motivate their people, are capable of great accomplishments.

The Old Kingdom ended when the leaders became weak and internal chaos took over. This period of weakness is called the First Intermediate Period; it lasted from about 2200 B.C. to 2000 B.C. Little of creative value occurred during this brief period.

Middle Kingdom

The Middle Kingdom, which only lasted from 2000 B.C. to 1800 B.C., was not a period of great creativity. The dynasties during this period attempted to recapture the glory of the past but were never able to build a conquering army and get creativity started by warfare, nor were they able to carry out the massive public works projects so characteristic of the Old Kingdom, probably because of lack of funds. These relatively weak pharaohs were forced to share their power with the growing bureaucracy of priests, and that limited the ability of the pharaohs to effect major changes in the society. Pyramids were built, but they were smaller and unimpressive. The capital was moved to Thebes, a location south of Memphis, where a temple complex was begun, but not finished.

The Middle Kingdom ended with an invasion from the East, which precipitated the Second Intermediate Period. The invaders, called the **Hyksos** or the Shepherd Kings, were a Semitic people. They were disliked by the Egyptians because of their foreignness, but were able to rule for several hundred years—until 1550 B.C.

Many scholars believe that the time of the rule of the Hyksos was the time when Joseph, son of Jacob in the Bible, was sold into Egypt. Joseph was recognized for his abilities at interpreting dreams and was then made the second-in-command over all Egypt. This high rank for an Israelite would be possible if other Semitic people, such as the Hyksos, were ruling the country. The favorable environment for Semitic people during the Second Intermediate Period may have facilitated the movement of Jacob and his many descendents into Egypt. Note that, according to the Bible, this is a time of great wealth followed by years of famine. Although Joseph saw this in a dream and was able to store food during the good times and therefore help Egypt and the surrounding area cope with the later famine, the very presence of the famine meant that the traditional flooding pattern of the Nile was disrupted. That must have led the native Egyptians to believe that the invading Hyksos were not demi-gods and therefore did not have the favor of the many deities who controlled the natural patterns. Many years later there arose a pharaoh "which knew not Joseph" (Exodus 1:8) who enslaved the Israelites. This new pharaoh may have been the first of the next native-Egyptian kingdom—the New Kingdom.

New Kingdom

Although never achieving the magnificence and originality of the Old Kingdom, the creative works of the New Kingdom were certainly impressive. The New Kingdom lasted from 1550 B.C. to 1050 B.C. and the capital, for most of that time, was at Thebes. It was during this period that the great temples at Thebes (Luxor and Karnak) were completed. This was also the time when the elaborately decorated and furnished tombs of the pharaohs and their families were dug in the Valley of the Kings and the Valley of the Queens. Figure 3.5 shows four aspects of the enormous temple complex at Karnak. Many pharaohs contributed individual and adjoining temples to the Karnak complex. Statues, obelisks, and hieroglyphs memorialize the pharaoh's accomplishments. Some temples were also highly religious containing an outer court, inner court, and a holy of holies.

The building of the temples and tombs demonstrated the power of the pharaohs but, because so many of these structures are religious, we can't tell if the priests shared that power and cooperated with the pharaohs. We do see, however, the strength of a few of the pharaohs during this time in the military conquests of Egypt over their neighbors, largely the fringes of the Mesopotamian Empire, but also some kingdoms to the south and west, across the deserts. The might of Egypt was not as great as in the Old Kingdom, but clearly was stronger under some New Kingdom pharaohs than in the Middle Kingdom.

Three very strong pharaohs of the New Kingdom are especially interesting. One fascinating pharaoh of the New Kingdom was **Hatshepsut,** a woman. She was the queen, chief wife of the pharaoh, when her husband died. Because the next pharaoh was still quite young, she became the regent to the crown and began to make the major decisions in the government. (According to normal rules in such cases, a man, such as an uncle, would be chosen as the regent.) She liked ruling as regent and wanted to retain the power even though the young pharaoh would eventually take control. She realized that only men could be pharaoh, so she began to dress in men's clothes and had her picture depicted as a man (even with a beard). She had a beautiful temple built between the Valley of the Kings and the Valley of the Queens and, as was the custom, she decorated the outside of the temple with hieroglyphs that told of her exploits and glory. Some experts say that when the young pharaoh came of age, he resented that he was not the pharaoh and fought against his mother, defeated her, and killed her. In his anger, he decided to wipe out all records containing Hatshepsut's name. This step was especially significant because, as indicated previously, the Egyptians believed that a critical requirement for a person to continue to live in the afterlife was that some record of that person should persist on earth. Thus, by eliminating all references to Hatshepsut, he would deny her an afterlife. You can still see the places on the walls of Hatshepsut's temple where her name has been obliterated. However, you can also see a place, deep within the temple in a small, dark room with a stone bench, where the name of Hatshepsut remains, carved into the wall below the bench. She lives! Other experts say that she died naturally but a later pharaoh was embarrassed over her reign and he rubbed out her name.

Another pharaoh was originally named Amenhotop. He became convinced that rather than worship the multitude of Egyptian gods, only one god, Aton the god of the sun, should be worshiped. He then changed his name to **Akhenaton** (servant of Aton). The exclusive worship of Aton was not possible in Thebes, the site of temples to so many other gods. Therefore, Akhenaton built a new city that was dedicated solely to Aton and required the change in religion throughout Egypt. The priests and other government officials dutifully moved to the new city, but resentments were high and only a few years after the opening of the new city, Akhenaton died; perhaps murdered. A new pharaoh was chosen—the boy king Tutonkhamen (King Tut). He died after a short reign and was succeeded by his advisor. At about this time the city of Aton was abandoned and the entire government bureaucracy

Figure 3.5 ■ Four different scenes from Karnak Temple: **A)** Entry promenade, **B)** Obelisk, **C)** Columns and hieroglyphs, **D)** Statues. *A) © 2010 by ligio. Used under license of Shutterstock, Inc. B) © 2010 by Jeffrey Liao. Used under license of Shutterstock, Inc. C) © 2010 by Maxim Kulko. Used under license of Shutterstock, Inc. D) © 2010 by Jeff Schultes. Used under license of Shutterstock, Inc.*

was returned to Thebes. The possible murders of the pharaohs clearly demonstrate the power of the priests who, if they did not murder the pharaohs themselves, certainly sanctioned the killings.

The third of the very interesting pharaohs of the New Kingdom was **Ramses II.** He was the pharaoh who is often associated with Moses and the exodus of the Israelites, although some experts believe that Akhenaton was the pharaoh of the exodus, and point to his support of a monotheistic god as evidence of his being forced to accept the god of the Israelites because of the plagues. This scenario is, however, held by a minority. Most others believe that Ramses II was the pharaoh who interacted with Moses.

Ramses II was strong, especially at the beginning of his reign. We see several great statues of Ramses II, and we have indications that he fought some foreign battles, although his success in the battles is unsure. In Egypt the records (which he made) contain glowing reports of the victories, but in other countries such as Assyria, the records suggest that, at best, the battles were a draw. (Similar situations have probably occurred throughout history, even today, where a ruler exaggerates the facts to create a better image. This is called today "putting a spin on the information.") We have no obvious Egyptian record of a person named Moses or of a mass exodus of slaves, but then we would not expect any such negative story to be told, especially by Ramses II. Furthermore, Moses might have been called by some other name and so we might not recognize him in the hieroglyphic record. We do see, however, that the Egyptian army was reduced in strength at the end of Ramses' reign and afterwards for many generations. According to the Bible, that reduction in strength would have occurred because of the miraculous parting of the Red Sea to allow the children of Israel to pass over, and then the subsequent closing of the waters to trap the Egyptian army.

Not too many years after Ramses II, the New Kingdom fell to outside invaders, and the Third Intermediate Period began. It was characterized by foreign rulers and internal fighting, which lasted until about 700 B.C. when the Late Period commenced.

Late Period

Although some Egyptians were to regain control of the government following the Third Intermediate Period, that control lasted for only about a hundred years. The reign was characterized by battles between the pharaohs and the priests who, at times, wanted different capitals for the country. Clearly the priests had gained at least as much control as the pharaohs by this time.

That brief reign by Egyptian natives was followed by a series of foreign occupations from the Libyans, Persians, and Greeks, who conquered Egypt under Alexander the Great. Upon the death of Alexander, his empire was divided among his generals; Egypt was given to Ptolemy, whose family ruled Egypt until its conquest by the Romans. The last of the Ptolemy family was Cleopatra, who ruled until she and Mark Anthony committed suicide in 31 B.C. under threat from Octavian (Caesar Augustus). Little Egyptian creative value came from the Late Period.

It is interesting to note that the decline of the Egyptian state coincided with the emergence of the strong priestly class and the simultaneous decline of the pharaohs. The lack of creativity during such times is not surprising because, in general, priests are conservators of tradition, and hate change. Since creativity is associated with change, the priests would naturally attempt to suppress such creativity. The glory of the Old Kingdom was never regained.

Timeline—Important Dates

Date	Event
3500 B.C.	*Pre-dynastic civilization begins*
3100–2200 B.C.	*Old Kingdom*
2200–2000 B.C.	*First Intermediate Period*
2000–1800 B.C.	*Middle Kingdom*
1800–1550 B.C.	*Second Intermediate Period*
1550–1050 B.C.	*New Kingdom*
1050–700 B.C.	*Third Intermediate Period*
700–31 B.C.	*Late Period*
332 B.C.	*Greek period begins with Alexander and then the Ptolemies*
31 B.C.	*Roman domination*

Suggested Readings

Boorstin, Daniel J., *The Creators,* Vintage, 1993.

Lewinter, Marty and William Widulski, *The Saga of Mathematics,* Prentice Hall, 2002.

Phillips, Graham, *Atlantis and the Ten Plagues of Egypt,* Bear & Company, 2003.

India and China
Creativity Continues to Flow

> Therefore the sage says:
> I practice non-assertion, and the people of themselves reform.
> I love quietude, and the people of themselves become righteous.
> I use no diplomacy, and the people of themselves become rich.
> I have no desire, and the people of themselves remain simple.
>
> —*Lao-Tzu,* Tao Te Ching

India

Around the year 2500 B.C., a third river valley civilization developed along the banks of the Indus River, which flows through modern-day India and Pakistan. A map of the Indus River area is given in Figure 4.1.

Compared to the other ancient river valley civilizations, relatively little is known about the people who based their lives on the life-giving waters of the Indus River. This civilization was unknown until modern archaeologists stumbled upon it in the 1920s. Furthermore, many of the mysteries of the lives of these people remain unknown, as modern scholars have not as yet been able to decipher their written, picture-based alphabet.

What is known is that the early inhabitants, called **Dravidians,** built two large cities, Harappa and Mohenjo-daro. Each city had a population in excess of fifty thousand people (based on the number of houses, etc.), making them the largest cities in the world at the time. The cities had a logical city grid, and buildings made of oven-dried bricks (versus the sun-dried bricks of Mesopotamia). With these stronger bricks the Dravidians built large-scale buildings, including a Great Assembly Hall and a very large public bath with spacious dressing rooms (suggesting possible ritual cleansing). An amazing achievement is that the cities had an extensive sanitation system. Each house had a bathroom connected to a large, brick, central drainage system that existed under the main streets of town. Such systems were not seen again until the Roman period.

Around 2000 B.C. the Dravidian empire's gradual expansion reached the apex of its size.

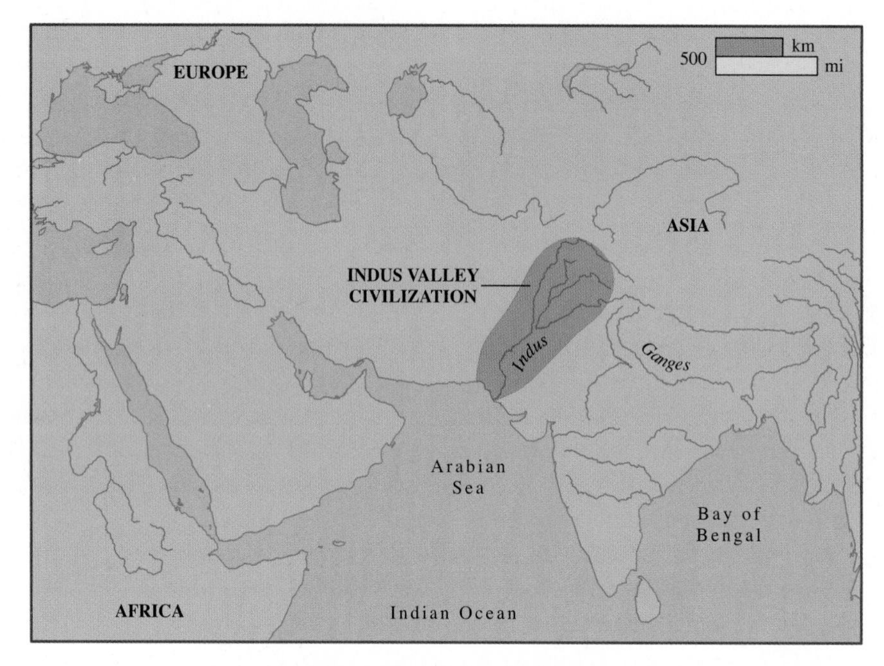

Figure 4.1 ■ *Map of the Indus River area.*

There is a kind of cohesive unity that existed throughout the empire, suggesting strong leadership. The Dravidian writing system was a standardized, picture-based, written language that seems to have been used throughout the entire area. The Dravidians also developed a standard system of weights and measures that ensured uniformity in amounts and trade. Pottery was also mass-produced and then distributed throughout the Indus River valley.

The one thing that seems to be missing from this civilization with such a large population and an obvious skill for large-scale building projects are defenses. The cities are strangely unfortified, lacking weapons, and other defensive measures. The Dravidians obviously had the knowledge and labor to construct defenses, yet they did not. There is also little evidence of a sizable army of any kind, despite having a population large enough to support one. Possibly the Dravidians had little fear of invasion or attack, as it is very likely that they had known relative peace and security on the Indian subcontinent, surrounded and protected by large deserts and the massive Himalayan mountain range. Whatever the reasons, the Dravidians were not prepared when a warlike Indo-European people, the **Aryans,** crashed down on them from the north and west around 1500 B.C. There is little evidence that there even was a battle, and it is possible the Dravidians simply surrendered, as the Aryans had bronze weaponry and tools and the Dravidians only stone. Centuries of isolation and peace seem to have slowed the Dravidians' creative process and stagnated their civilization enough that, at least in this regard, they had fallen technologically behind even the nomadic barbarians, and thus became easy prey.

The Aryans soon adopted many aspects of the generally more advanced Dravidian culture as their own, but also forced some of their beliefs and systems on the Dravidians. The Aryan language, Sanskrit, became the dominant language of India. Under Aryan rule, there was a growth of villages as the principal societal unit (rather than large cities), administered in regions under Aryan rulers or rajas (kings). This movement to villages probably occurred for two reasons. First, with the arrival of the Aryans, there were even more mouths to feed and more land had to be planted with crops. Fortunately, the Aryans had brought with them the metal tools to accomplish this task. Second, it is very likely that the Aryans, who for centuries had roamed the vast steppes to the northwest and were masters of the horse, simply felt uncomfortable with the enclosed feeling that existed in large cities.

The Aryans introduced the caste system, a hierarchical system of order that exists even in modern India. Ancient history is littered with a myriad of civilizations being conquered and then ruled by others, and most ruling cultures have developed some method to assist them in keeping the conquered peoples in their place. However, as a tool of control and oppression, the Aryan-devised caste system is creatively ingenious, as its precepts are strongly reinforced by various aspects of society. It is, of course, also highly discriminatory.

The caste system was originally based on skin color, as the Aryans were lighter skinned than the Dravidians (the word "caste" means "color"). The caste system was divided into four main castes, although each of the four castes was then subdivided into hundreds of subcastes. The uppermost caste, the Brahmins, who were the priests and advisors to the kings, were light-skinned Aryans. Below them was a second class of Aryans, and they worked doing the functions of government as aristocrats and warriors. Underneath them was the much larger peasant class made up of Dravidians. These were the farmers and shopkeepers, and this caste eventually developed into the middle class. Finally, the lowest caste were the serfs, or Sudras—Dravidians who did hard manual labor and other difficult work for the upper classes. Below them was a smaller group of people who, through some violation of ritual, were considered to be without any caste and therefore deemed as "outcasts" or "untouchables," and were often given no work other than begging, or were given work that no one else would perform.

The caste system became so rigid that even the oppressed and downtrodden lower castes grew to depend on the social stability that came from the system. For example, each caste was associated with certain types of occupations, and those occupations were restricted to those born in that caste, so that, for example, only those born Brahmins could be priests, and that was all they could be. Thus, the caste system practically eliminated any kind of social mobility, because of occupation as well as skin color. Furthermore, people were "polluted" by many features of the environment around them: their food, their homes, people they might associate with. However, the lower your caste, the more polluted you were; thus, people of different classes avoided interaction as much as possible, and social advancement through marriage was difficult, because if a person married someone of a lower caste, that would pollute the marriage and result in both people becoming members of the lower caste. Finally, the caste system was reinforced by religion.

Hinduism, the dominant religion of India, grew out of the thinking of the Brahmin caste, and incorporated the caste system into its reasoning, thus strengthening the caste system by adding to it religious doctrine. Hinduism teaches a belief in reincarnation, or that at death the soul is reborn into a new body, and Hindu doctrine says that the caste of the new body is dependent upon how well a person lived during his or her previous life. Those living a righteous and generous life can expect to be reincarnated into a higher caste, while the wicked and evil can expect to serve their next life in a lower caste. To question or complain about one's situation in life is pointless to a Hindu, because their situation is based on their caste, which is determined, they believe, by their own previous actions. Furthermore, attempts to break out of your caste are seen as wrong, and can be punished both in the current life and in the next. Therefore, there was a strong religious deterrent to challenging the caste system.

In addition to the concepts of the caste system, the Aryans also contributed a foundation for other beliefs that grew into Hinduism. Hinduism adopted the Aryan gods and the poems and other writings about the gods, which are called *Vedas* and are written in Sanskrit. (Sometimes the Aryan period is called the Vedic period because of these *Vedas.*) **Asceticism,** or self-denial of earthly pleasures, was adopted as a way for some Hindus to commune with nature and find true reality, thus drawing closer to the gods. Hindus believe that the foremost of the gods is Brahman, who is spirit only and is never represented in a tangible form. Brahman's spirit is, however, present in all people, and is called *Atman.* When a person grows in spirituality, following the moral code (which is called *dharma*), accepting and living peacefully with fate (which is called *karma*), and practicing other god-like attributes, their spirit draws closer to the ideal of Brahman. When a person's *Atman* unites with Brahman, that state is called *Nirvana,* which is the goal of human existence and the fulfillment of life. Hindu temples are beautiful locals where the many Hindu gods and goddesses are represented. The interior of a Hindu temple is shown in Figure 4.2.

Further Hindu concepts are taught in some epic poems, which include the travels of gods who come to earth and teach humans. One such epic poem is the *Mahabharata,* which contains one very well known section called the *Bhagavad-Gita,* the story of the travels and teachings of Krishna, one of the gods. These epics continue to play an important role in the ethics and culture of the Indian people.

Jainism is a religion closely associated with Hinduism. The Jains believe that history is not linear but, rather, is divided into six periods, which repeat throughout history. The first three ages are descending in complexity, and life is simple and basically nomadic. Life in the last three stages is ascending in complexity, and is based on highly developed societies, civilization, and culture. When the sixth stage has ended, the cycle runs backwards. People are born again and again throughout the periods (reincarnation). The fourth stage is when human development is at its very best. At one of these times a number of great religious teachers blazed a path to perfection (Nirvana), which Jains now follow because it leads them, ultimately, out of reincarnation and to Nirvana.

The Jains believe strongly in non-violence and are strict vegetarians. This belief in non-violence closed some occupations to Jains (soldiers, butchers, tanners, and even farmers) and so the Jains have become shopkeepers, bankers, and other service providers. As a result, the Jains are influential beyond their number, even today, in the business community of India.

Figure 4.2 ■ Interior of a Hindu temple. *© 2010 by ostill. Used under license of Shutterstock, Inc.*

Another religion, Buddhism, grew out of India and the Hindu tradition. Buddhism grew out of the enlightenment (understanding) gained by **Gautama Siddhartha,** who lived from 563 to 483 B.C. He was born in what is present-day Nepal near the Indian border to a wealthy warrior-caste family and was raised in a very sheltered environment where he never experienced pain or displeasure. One day, however, when he was a young adult (having married and fathered a child), he went out of the compound in which he lived to see the outer world. That day he saw four things that raised his awareness and changed his life. He saw an old man and learned of old age; he saw a sick man and learned of disease; he saw a corpse and learned of death; and he saw a monk and learned of the contentment of abandoning the delights of this world to seek a higher truth. At the age of 29 he renounced his position and left his wife and baby to join with a group of monks who wandered India and practiced asceticism (self-denial of pleasure).

One day he met a wise woman who suggested that he was not reaching his full potential by living the monkish life. She said that he needed to give up all desires, even the desire to be holy. This idea struck him with such great force that he immediately sat down under a Bo tree (a kind of fig or banyan tree) and began to contemplate what she had said. After many days of contemplation he had worked out the basic tenets of what he believed was a better pathway to achieving Nirvana. He had become enlightened. He began to tell others about the pathway and many agreed with him and embraced, with him, this new way of living. They called him the "enlightened one" or Buddha. Figure 4.3 is a statue of Buddha showing his serenity as a representation of the state of enlightenment which he achieved.

Buddhism is built on a foundation of Hinduism, retaining some of the same beliefs, but it has added some important new concepts. Buddhism is based on the fundamental principle that people should seek the Middle Way—neither excesses in self-denial nor self-indulgence. Buddhists realize Four Noble Truths: 1. Suffering or conflict is with us throughout life; 2. suffering and conflict originate from cravings for personal wants; 3. cessation of suffering can be achieved by rooting out these wants; and 4. suffering can best be eliminated by following the Eight Fold Path. Without going into too much detail, the Eight Fold Path helps people find the best way of living by practicing the following:

- Right understanding or view—knowledge of the Four Noble Truths
- Right intention, thought, or aim—overcoming ignorance and understanding self-sacrifice
- Right speech—honoring others
- Right conduct or action—giving love and compassion
- Right living—working in whatever job we have with sincerity
- Right endeavor or effort—trying to be your best
- Right mindfulness—thinking eternal thoughts
- Right meditation or concentration—taking time to contemplate

Buddha preached for 40 years and gained many adherents. Missionaries carried the message throughout Asia; many years later, some Asian

Figure 4.3 ■ Statue of Buddha. *© 2010 by Galina Barskaya. Used under license of Shutterstock, Inc.*

rulers adopted Buddhism as the religion of their state, thus making it the dominant religion in some areas, especially southeast Asia and China. Eventually, some Indian rulers came to power who resented the power of the Buddhists and desired more homogeneity among the Indian people. These rulers persecuted Buddhists and, to a large extent, Buddhism is now absent from India.

Little creativity emerged from India during the years following the death of Buddha until the first century B.C., the end of the period we are examining in this chapter. In retrospect, ancient India's most lasting areas of creativity from the ancient period seem to be in religion and ethical living. That heritage would prove to be tremendously important in directing many of the most creative and influential leaders of our modern day.

China

The fourth of the ancient river valley civilizations is that of the Yellow River, in China. The Yellow River, like Egypt's Nile, has a high silt content, as much as 40 percent of its volume, and therefore when it floods it lays down a rich, new layer of fertile topsoil excellent for farming. Unfortunately, unlike Egypt's Nile, the Yellow River's flooding is unpredictable, and often has a destructive power equaled only by its capacity to give life. Beginning around 2200 B.C., the first of many dynasties to rule this fertile, yet volatile, river region came to power. That society gradually spread southward into the Yangtze River valley. Figure 4.4 shows the Yellow and Yangtze River valleys in China.

Like Egypt, China was largely isolated from the outside world both because of deserts and distance, and further because of the fortification of the Great Wall, which effectively kept out invaders for many years. Therefore, China, much like Egypt, was ruled by a series of dynasties. Changes from one dynasty to another were usually because of internal warfare rather than external conquering, with only a few exceptions.

Like the Egyptian culture, the Chinese began with great creativity, probably associated with the rigors of developing a new society and ensuring its survival against tribes and others who would overthrow it. Therefore, great creativity occurred

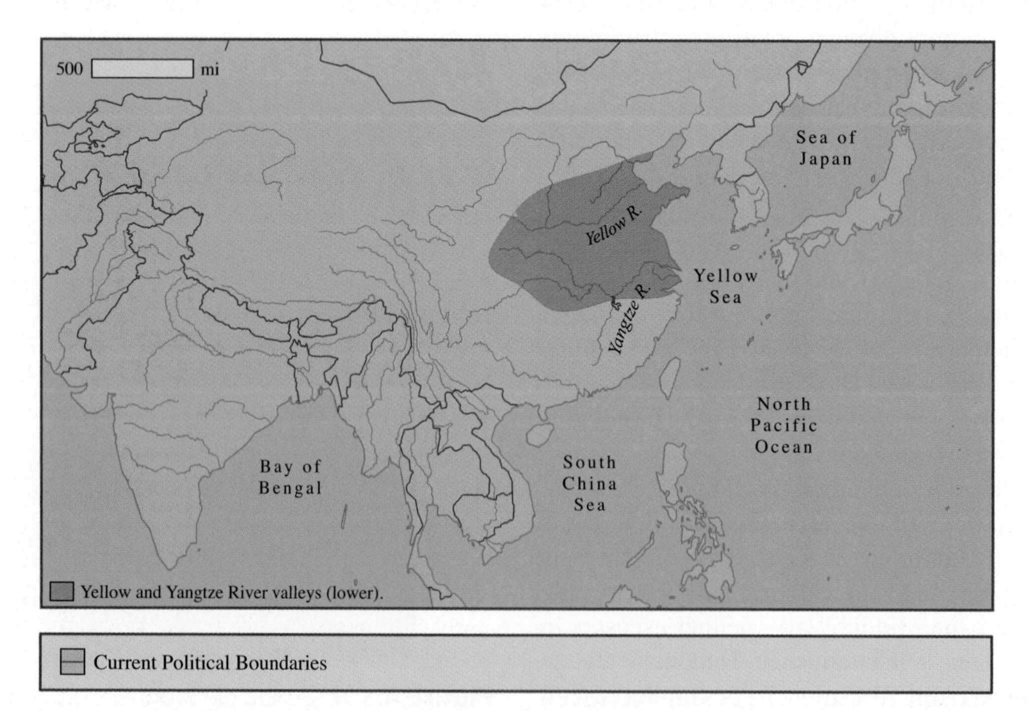

Figure 4.4 ■ *Map of Yellow and Yangtze River areas in China.*

when warfare was coupled with strong, dynamic leaders. At other times, however, several warring tribes simply fought to little advantage, and creativity seemed to be swallowed up by the chaos that reigned because of the lack of strong leadership among these tribes.

The earliest dynasty, *Hsia* or *Xia* (2200 B.C. to 1700 B.C.) made some lasting contributions to Chinese culture such as the domestication and use of the horse, the development of bronze weapons and tools, and the expansion of territory. The people were, however, largely tribal during this period, and had only a few settlements of any consequence.

The *Shang* dynasty (from about 1700 to 1000 B.C.) gave some stability to the warlike nature of early China, and bequeathed a legacy of ancestral worship that has been very important throughout Chinese history. However, the *Shang* dynasty is best known for its development of the Chinese writing system. This system uses logograms or pictographs, of which there are over 50,000, although good literacy requires knowledge of only about 5,000. Some of the characters represent concrete ideas or words, and others represent sounds. The Chinese writing system has been very influential throughout Asia, serving as the basic writing system for many of the Asian cultures, such as Japanese and early Korean. Interestingly, the Chinese writing system does not seem to have been developed over an extended period but, rather, appeared suddenly in a nearly complete form (although, of course, new characters have been steadily added over time). This writing system has given the Chinese great stability in communications over the centuries, and has been a unifying influence, although sometimes overridden by military divisions.

A very powerful class developed because of the writing system. This class, the only people who could read and write the complex system, began to emerge as government bureaucrats. These people continued to gain control over the many years and different dynasties, eventually becoming, as were the priests of Egypt, a conservative brake on creativity.

Even though the writing system was developed during this period, the real focus of the rulers was survival amidst the many wars from neighboring, and occasionally distant, tribes. As a result, some additional creative developments during the *Shang* dynasty were the horse-drawn chariot and improved bronze weapons. The development of these items is somewhat later in history than occurred for the same development in Mesopotamia. This later development probably reflects the isolation of China from the more dynamic Mesopotamian cultures characteristic of this period.

The *Zhou* (or *Chu*) dynasty (770 to 221 B.C.) created a strong feeling of divine destiny for China. During this period the emperors enunciated the concept of the Mandate of Heaven. For the Chinese, heaven was not a place but rather a state of being, in which the perfect plan was in effect. Heaven had power to favor a ruler who lived and ruled according to the perfect plan. This is called having the Mandate of Heaven. If a ruler violated these basic laws of peace and prosperity, then the Mandate of Heaven could be withdrawn. In this regard, the Chinese were similar to the Egyptians, who also believed that their rulers had the approval of heaven as evidenced by the regular patterns of flooding of the Nile and the prosperity that it brought. In both cases, this concept seemed to have contributed to the longevity of the dynasties.

The *Zhou* leaders believed (also close to the concepts of the pharaohs) that the Mandate of Heaven could be reflected in buildings and cities. Therefore, the *Zhou* kings constructed a new capital, Xi'an, which was laid out on a perfectly square pattern with a massive protective wall and straight streets, all oriented along the cardinal directions. On the northern side of the enclosure was the king's palace. The southern side was the place where commoners' homes and shops were built. When other capital cities were built in later dynasties, the pattern of Xi'an was often followed.

The creativity and order of the early *Zhou* dynasty declined as provincial warlords assumed greater independence from the *Zhou* king in Xi'an. These minor rulers eventually began to call themselves kings and take on the trappings and rituals that were formerly reserved for the main king. Inevitably, this breakdown in order led to wars among the minor kings and divisions of the kingdom into small states, eventually totaling over 250. China was in chaos. The central *Zhou* kings continued to rule in Xi'an but they had little power beyond their immediate area. Then, gradually, the minor kingdoms began to consolidate as some minor kings conquered their neighbors. This process continued for many years and finally resulted, near the end of the *Zhou* period, in about 20 states. These continued to fight each other but with little overall change for many years. This is called the period of the warring states.

It was also during the *Zhou* dynasty that two of the most important thinkers of Chinese history lived and taught. These thinkers, and many others at the same time, were concerned about the loss of the wonderful society that existed in the beginning of the *Zhou* dynasty. In these thinkers and their subsequent philosophies, we see another important impetus to creativity: the loss of a period of peace and prosperity and a desire to regain the glories of the past. It is, in essence, a negative reaction to war and chaos in which humans creatively struggle to define a system of society in which peace will reign and war will be eliminated. The first of the great thinkers was **Confucius** and the second was Lao Tzu. We will look briefly at each of them.

The name Confucius is an Anglicanized rendition of Kung Fu-Tzu, the phonetic spelling of the title Master Kung. This man lived from 551 to 479 B.C. He was born into a family of minor bureaucrats, thus affording him a good education and directing him toward a life of service to government. He worked for several governments, traveling among many of the warring states, and devised a system of good government founded on principles of life that engendered honesty, dependability, hard work, and loyalty. These qualities could obviously be applied to people who worked in the government, but were also appropriate for all people, regardless of their occupation.

Confucius contemplated the loss of the Mandate of Heaven from the early *Zhou* dynasty to the time of the warring states. He believed that virtue could be achieved if five critical relationships were cared for properly. The five critical relationships were: ruler to subject, father to son, husband to wife, older brother to younger brother, and friend to friend. Note that three of the relationships concern the family—a direct reflection of the importance of the family in Chinese life, and probably a residue of the time when ancestral worship was a key to Chinese belief.

Confucius noted that all these key relationships were hierarchal; that is, one person is above the other in some way. (This is even true for the friend-to-friend relationship, since at any one moment, one of the friends is, at least in some way, superior to the other.) The caring of these relationships required that both of the parties properly perform their expected duties in the relationship. For instance, the subject must respect the ruler and follow the ruler's dictates, but the ruler must provide a situation in the country that fosters peace and prosperity. In essence, the ruler must seek the Mandate of Heaven and then the subjects must not usurp or disobey the ruler's prerogatives. This same pattern of reciprocity would be true in each of the relationships.

The concept of taking care of the relationships needed a direct demonstration to be continually reinforced and validated. This demonstration was given by rituals. The rituals might be simple—as when a subject bowed to a leader or when two friends greeted each other with a handshake—or the rituals might be very elaborate, as when a king is crowned or a father bestows a formal blessing on his children. (Note the interesting parallel to the rituals of Medieval Europe, such as the all-night vigil and the touching of sword to shoulders when a king made a loyal subject a knight.) Confucius believed that the breakdown in the *Zhou* dynasty began when the minor lords stopped performing the rituals they owed to the central king and began to require these same rituals for themselves. Confucius believed that all of these relationships and the accompanying rituals were specific, but that, by analogy, they could be extended to all relationships in society.

Confucius wanted to return to the peace and prosperity of the early *Zhou* period, and advocated a reactionary change. After the Mandate of Heaven was reestablished, this strongly held belief resisted further change. Therefore, the teachings of Confucius inevitably led to a resistance to further creative change. However, it would be many years before his teachings were widely implemented. Confucius was accepted by only a small group of disciples during his lifetime, but his teachings were recorded by those students and then taught by them to others. Gradually the teachings grew in recognition and were eventually adopted by one of the later rulers (in the *Han* dynasty) as the code of conduct for the entire country. It became so widespread that the term "scholar" was synonymous with Confucius.

The teachings of Confucius were conveyed as a series of short statements that gave the principles of behavior he hoped to teach. A few of these statements are, for example, "A clever tongue and a fine appearance are rarely the signs of goodness" and "To guide a state of one thousand chariots, be respectful in your handling of affairs and display trustworthiness; be frugal in your expenditures and cherish others; and employ the common people only at the proper times."[1] These teachings have affected the Chinese mentality ever since. Confucianism is not a religion in the traditional sense, but is clearly a collection of moral teachings that have the same kind of effect on people's lives as would a traditional religion.

The other great Chinese moral teacher, **Lao Tzu,** lived about the same time as Confucius. Some even think that these two great moral leaders may have met. Like Confucius, Lao Tzu taught a small group of dedicated disciples who wrote down his teachings in what we now know as the *Tao Te Ching,* translated as *The Way.* Taoist teachings suggest that Nature is a great teacher that gives examples of how we can find the correct path in life if we are only observant of the world around us. For instance, we are told that yielding will eventually overcome force, and are given water and stone as examples. Stone is harder than water; thus, water yields to stone by flowing around it. Eventually, however, water will wear away the stone quite naturally, suggesting that, in the end, water, the material that yielded but was persistent, is more enduring than stone.

Taoism identifies two contrasting natures in people and in all living and inanimate things. These two natures are called *Yin* and *Yang. Yin* is characterized by the following traits: female, dark, earth, water action, strongest in autumn and winter. *Yang* is characterized by: male, light, heaven, aggressive action, strongest in summer. Each of us must learn to balance properly the two natures within us, so that we can achieve our unique unity with our true nature.

In 221 B.C. the *Zhou* dynasty was overthrown and a new dynasty, the ***Qin*** or ***Ch'in*** (from whose name the word "China" is derived), truly united the entire region for the first time. The first *Ch'in* king adopted the title "first sovereign emperor" and went about the task of joining these different peoples and consolidating the lands he held. He was a powerful and feared ruler who was creative and dynamic.

The *Ch'in* emperor understood the value of good roads, for trade, communication, and (maybe most importantly) unity for his empire, and he set his people to work building an elaborate system of roads. One of those roads, the Silk Road, went from his capital, Xi'an, to the Black Sea. This road became the principal route for trade between Europe and China. Eventually it was expanded to new capital cities of Beijing (in China) and Constantinople (in the Byzantine Empire). The Silk Road was still used throughout the Middle Ages, and was the route traveled by Marco Polo when he visited China in the thirteenth century A.D. The route of the Silk Road is given in Figure 4.5.

Like the Egyptians and Dravidians before him, the *Ch'in* emperor also realized the need to keep his peasant masses busy so that they would not have time to complain and foment revolt. When his road system was complete, China's surplus labor was turned to an even larger undertaking, possibly the largest construction ever undertaken in the history of mankind: the Great Wall of China. Like India and, to an even greater extent, Egypt, China was quite isolated by deserts and the Himalayas, except on the northern border, where nomadic, Eurasian steppe peoples (Mongolians and others) had successfully been raiding Chinese

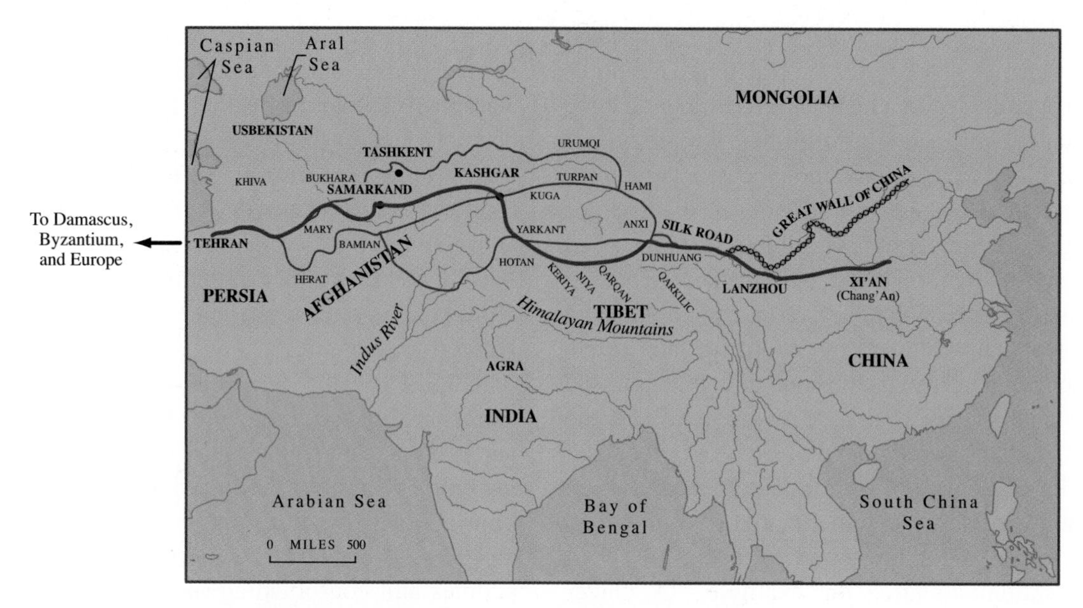

Figure 4.5 ■ *The Great Wall and the Silk Road.*

lands for centuries. So the emperor put hundreds of thousands to work improving and completing the wall begun by the previous *Zhou* dynasty. When it was finished, the Great Wall far surpassed the simple series of defensive walls the Zhou emperors had envisioned. The wall, when it reached its full length in the Ming Dynasty, stretched over 1,500 miles, from the Pacific Ocean in the east all the way to the Tibetan mountains in the southwest, and was wide enough to march armies along the top, thus serving as both a barricade and a road.

The *Ch'in* emperor, however, took the consolidation and unification of his empire one step further, by abolishing the traditional feudal system and requiring all of the aristocracy and feudal warriors to abandon their lands and move to his capital city, where he could keep an eye on them. This was an unpopular move among the nobility, but fear of his large and tested standing army made them comply. The nobility's feudal lands were then turned over to the peasants, who were then heavily taxed on those lands by the emperor. The old feudal system was then replaced with strong central authority and a new government bureaucracy where men were appointed based on merit, not heredity (as was dictated by Confucian teachings).

Standardization was viewed as being critical to the success of the *Ch'in* dynasty. During the *Zhou* dynasty, especially when there were over 250 separate kingdoms, many different types of money, measures of length and weight, laws, and government procedures were introduced. The *Ch'in* emperor standardized all of these and, to a large extent, the new standards remained. He even standardized dimensions such as the axle length of wagons, so that the ruts would be the same throughout his empire and thus facilitate travel from one region to another.

The concept of standardization and uniformity was, however, taken to the extreme under this powerful regime. The *Ch'in* emperor wanted all thought to be the same. He therefore declared that any book that taught concepts contrary to his way should be burned. If a person were found to have a prohibited book, that person would be burned. Then, when the emperor realized that many scholars had committed the books to memory, he decided to eliminate even the possibility of their remaking the books, and he buried hundreds of scholars alive. This program proved to be so successful that we have very few books that date from before the end of the *Ch'in* period.

The *Ch'in* emperor also built the incredible complex of terracotta warriors at Xi'an, the capital of the dynasty. These warrior statues were discovered in 1974 by a farmer who uncovered parts

Figure 4.6 ■ Terracotta warriors in Xian, China. *© 2010 by Jarno Gonzalez Zarraonandia. Used under license of Shutterstock, Inc.*

of one of the statues as he was plowing his field. To date, the area that has been uncovered is about 1,000 yards by 1,000 yards, with smaller excavations nearby. Thousands of warriors have been uncovered, each full size and each portraying a different person (with differing facial characteristics and different body girth and other features). Another excavation was begun about 2,000 yards away; there, some beautiful bronze carts and horses were uncovered. The second location lies between the first dig and the tomb of the emperor, which raises the possibility that the entire area surrounding the emperor's tomb might be guarded by thousands upon thousands of warriors, carts, and other military figures, all arrayed in careful order and procession. This is surely one of the most significant and creative sites of the ancient world. The extent and detailed artisanship of the first archeological site can be appreciated from the picture shown in Figure 4.6.

When the first *Ch'in* emperor died, his son inherited the throne, but he was weak and ineffective. Civil war broke out and lasted for four years, with many groups seeking to take control. One group was headed by a former general of the *Zhou* dynasty. He was very powerful, and also an excellent warrior. Most people believed that he would eventually be the new emperor. However, smaller warrior leaders contested his dominance, and each of them had to be eliminated. The story of one of these minor warrior leaders is important to consider.

This minor leader, **Liu Bang,** was actually a jailer under the *Ch'in* dynasty, in charge of transporting prisoners between prisons as the need arose because of crowding, and so on. On one of his trips, he had a large group of prisoners under his control. The trip took several days, and on one of the mornings, he awoke to find that several of the prisoners had escaped. He knew the emperor's harshness and feared that he would be punished severely, perhaps even executed. Therefore, he creatively developed a plan. He offered freedom to the remaining prisoners if they would join with him in a quest to become the emperor. The prisoners agreed and formed the core of the army that he then recruited by traveling around the country. He must have been very persuasive in his vision of China as he gradually gained a great army and became the only remaining rival to the great former general of the *Zhou* dynasty. The two armies finally met and the general defeated the jailer. However, the jailer was able to withdraw from the battle in good order. In his retreat, the jailer conquered a city in which a large granary was located. He fed his troops with the grain and then enticed many other soldiers to come to that city to be fed and to join with him. After two years he gained sufficient strength to again battle with the general. This time, the jailer was able to surround the general. That night, as the general was in his tent, the jailer's surrounding troops sang songs of their homelands, which were many, as the jailer had gathered his army from all parts of China. When the general heard songs from his own land, he realized that the jailer had widespread support and that he did not. The general then decided all was lost. He killed the concubine with whom he had been visiting and then jumped on a horse and rode wildly away from his camp. He rode into the lines of the surrounding troops, where he was cut down and killed. Thus, the jailer emerged as the sole leader of China. He established a new ruling family, which he named the *Han* dynasty, after the ethnic group to which over 90 percent of the Chinese belong. This level of ethnic purity, quite unusual in the world today, reflects the relative isolation of China.

The *Han* dynasty lasted from 206 B.C. to 220 A.D. The *Han* rulers modified many of the harsher rules of the previous dynasty, and established Confucian and Taoist concepts as the basis of the civil service. This amalgamation of philosophies has been called the Han Synthesis. In this system, the concepts of Confucius were made the basis of how the government was to treat the people and, hopefully, how the people were to treat each other. The concepts of kindness and reciprocity were key to the government's new position. However, they still needed to administer justice and enforce the laws. The Synthesis used the legal system of the *Ch'in* dynasty, which required absolute equality under the law and also harsh and immediate penalties, but softened it with Confucian ideas. That meant that some consideration would be given for extenuating circumstances. The combination of Confucian concepts with the legalism of the *Ch'in* dynasty gave a reasonable day-to-day method of governance, but didn't give a long range and cosmic view of the world from which they could develop strategic plans. This wider view was provided by Taoism. The bureaucratic class embraced the new Synthesis because it gave great power to those who understood the law and administered it. With time, this bureaucratic class ruled China whenever the emperor was weak or conditions were confused. The *Han* Synthesis proved to fit the needs of the Chinese government and people so well that the principles on which it was built persisted for 2,000 years.

The *Han* dynasty is chiefly known for its military prowess. These leaders expanded control along the Silk Road so that trade would be unimpeded, and expanded Chinese control over areas as distant as Viet Nam and Korea. To control such a vast territory, the government gave great power to a class of local leaders who were, as much as possible, members of the ruling family. These local leaders established a feudal society. As the local leaders grew in power, they would occasionally compete with the central authority much as would occur a few centuries later in feudal Europe.

Creativity flourished under the *Han* rulers. Paper was invented and became the principle medium for recording writing. (The Chinese previously used bones, bronzes, and bamboo as the medium on which writing was placed.) Great canals were dug to link rivers and provide improved transportation and trade. Art, especially bronze statues and other implements, became highly developed during the *Han* period.

We will return to consider China's history later in this book, and will also consider other Asian countries, including India and Japan. However, it is now appropriate to review the societies where civilization began and then to continue with the history of the Mediterranean area, in the next few chapters, where some interesting developments occurred.

Summary—River Societies

It is easy to see why the four river societies we have examined—Mesopotamia, Egypt, India, and

China—were the first great civilizations. They were blessed by rivers that nurtured agriculture and, because of favorable weather, yielded sufficient food for many people to work in occupations other than farming. This led to the development of cities. Civilization had begun.

Despite their similar beginnings, these societies were quite different. The Mesopotamian society was dominated by strong kings and numerous invasions. That combination led to many innovations in language, commerce, military implements, materials, mathematics, and governmental systems. The continual conquest of the area seemed to give continual renewal of the creative spark, so that creativity seemed to continue throughout the ancient period. This was like the annual renewal of the rivers that provided nutrients to the land.

Egyptian society was also initially dominated by strong kings (pharaohs); during that time called the Old Kingdom, creativity was very strong. The Old Kingdom produced the pyramids, Egyptian religion, hieroglyphics, papyrus, art, calendars, number systems, and a feeling of superiority and glory that would be the goal of later Egyptian rulers. Those later rulers believed that only by achieving and then maintaining the conditions that had existed in the Old Kingdom could the glory of the past be recaptured. That conservatism was reinforced by the priests, so that the entire Egyptian society shifted from aggressive change to passive conservatism. Occasional individual rulers were able to add to the creative culture and progress of Egypt, but their efforts seemed to be quickly absorbed and then suffocated by the domination of the priests. Eventually the Egyptians came under foreign domination but, rather than adopt the culture and creativity of the foreign rulers, the Egyptians tried to maintain their unique society, and the changes that might have occurred from the foreign interaction were squelched.

The Indian society was initially progressive, reflecting the needs of developing a civilization. However, that society soon settled into a comfortable pattern that resisted change. They were easily conquered by European invaders, the Aryans, who gave a spurt to creativity but then settled into the same relaxed and change-resistant pattern. One product of the Aryan invasion was the caste system, which illustrates how a conquered society can be effectively controlled, but also shows that creativity is not necessarily beneficial. While this stability may have slowed creativity in most areas, one particular segment of civilization seems to have benefited from the patterns of life developed in India. That segment is religion. Hinduism, Jainism, Buddhism and other lesser known religions, all have their origins in India. These religions have not only created a way of life for countless millions over the centuries, but they have also provided the world with innovative thinking methods and value systems.

The Chinese society took many years to begin to develop a strongly innovative society, probably because tribal societies were so strong in the vast area of China. But, when strong leaders and urban society finally emerged, the creativity was astounding. The Chinese developed strong ethical systems, which were institutionalized in a government that became one of the most efficient of the ancient world. Amazing works like the Great Wall, the terracotta warriors, and the Silk Road were matched in creativity, if not in size, by the invention of paper, Chinese character writing, bronze weaponry, and other implements. Eventually Chinese society, like the Egyptian, became isolated and dominated by a very conservative class, the bureaucrats, who, like the priests of Egypt, resisted change. Only when an overpowering leader emerged did Chinese society regain its creativity, and then only for brief periods.

Creativity seems to engender and thrive on change. That change may come from invasions or desires of strong leaders to improve the country. When segments of society that have a vested interests in maintaining the current situation are in power, such as priests and government bureaucrats, creativity suffers. We will see this same pattern in other societies throughout history. However, even with the lack of creativity during some times in some of the great river societies, the legacy of development that came from these four great civilizations was astounding. Civilization was certainly on firm ground because of the river societies.

Timeline—Important Dates

Date	Event
2500 B.C.	*Indian civilization established in the Indus River Valley*
2200 B.C.	*Chinese civilization established in the Yellow River Valley*
2200 B.C. to 1700 B.C.	*Hsia or Xia dynasty in China*
1700–1000 B.C.	*Shang dynasty in China*
1500 B.C.	*Aryan conquest of the Indus River civilization*
770–221 B.C.	*Zhou dynasty in China*
563–483 B.C.	*Life of Gautama Siddhartha (Buddha)*
551–479 B.C.	*Life of Confucius*
About 550–470 B.C.	*Life of Lao Tzu*
221–210 B.C.	*Ch'in or Qin dynasty*
210–206 B.C.	*Civil war*
206 B.C.–220 A.D.	*Han dynasty*

Notes

1. Edward Slingerland (trans.), *Confucius Analects* (Indianapolis: Hackett), 2003.

Suggested Readings

Humphreys, Christmas (trans.), *The Wisdom of Buddha,* Harper and Row, 1960.

Lao-Tzu, *The Tao Te Ching,* Paul Carus (trans.), St. Martin's Press, 1913.

Slingerland, Edward (trans.), *Confucius Analects,* Hackett, 2003.

Sun Tzu, *The Art of War,* Samuel B. Griffith (trans.), Oxford University Press, 1971.

Article 3
The Wisdom of Buddha

Introduction

Gautama Siddhartha (563–483 BC) was born in Northern India (Nepal) to a wealthy warrior caste family. He was raised to never see pain or experience displeasure. But one day he saw an old man, a sick man, a corpse, and a monk. That day, he first learned of agedness, sickness, death, and ascetics. He learned that life has painful experiences but that these can be conquered through a religious lifestyle. He decided to dedicate his life to discovering truth and left his family to live with a group of monks. One day he was met by a woman who suggested that his method of finding truth in life was not correct. He listened and then sat under a tree for a long period to evaluate what the path to truth and happiness might really be. Through this experience he became enlightened and realized how one can completely rid himself of suffering. Siddhartha achieved this condition, which is termed "Nirvana," and became the Buddha (the "Enlightened One").

After attaining Nirvana, Buddha began a life of traveling and teaching his Road to Happiness. He first traveled to Benares and there gave his "First Sermon" ("The Turning of the Wheel") that founded Buddhism. It is considered his most famous sermon on the "Middle Way." It reveals the Four Noble Truths and the Noble Eightfold Path that leads to the cessation of suffering. These core teachings of Buddha show the "Middle Way" to enlightenment—a compromise between complete asceticism and worldly pleasures. The ancient Buddhist text of this sermon is presented here.

Buddha's Teaching

Cease to do evil;
Learn to do good;
Cleanse your own heart;
This is the teaching of the Buddha.

The First Sermon

Thus have I heard: once the Exalted One was dwelling near Benares, at Isipatana, in the Deer-Park.

Then the Exalted One thus spake unto the company of five monks. "Monks, these two extremes should not be followed by one who has gone forth as a wanderer. What two?

"Devotion to the pleasures of sense, a low practice of villagers, a practice unworthy, unprofitable, the way of the world (on the one hand); and (on the other) devotion to self-mortification, which is painful, unworthy and unprofitable.

"By avoiding these two extremes the Tathagata [another name for Buddha] has gained knowledge of that middle path which giveth vision, which giveth knowledge, which causeth calm, special knowledge, enlightenment, Nirvana.

"And what, monks, is that middle path which giveth vision . . . Nirvana?

"Verily it is this Ariyan eightfold way, to wit: Right view, right aim, right speech, right action, right living, right effort, right mindfulness, right concentration. This, monks, is that middle path

Humphrus, Christmas (tr.), *The Wisdom of Buddha,* Harper and Row, 1960.

which giveth vision, which giveth knowledge, which causeth calm, special knowledge, enlightenment, Nirvana.

"Now this, monks, is the Ariyan truth about Ill:

"Birth is Ill, decay is Ill, sickness is Ill, death is Ill: likewise sorrow and grief, woe, lamentation and despair. To be conjoined with things which we dislike: to be separated from things which we like,—that also is Ill. Not to get what one wants—that also is Ill. In a word, this body, this fivefold mass which is based on grasping—that is ill.

"Now this, monks, is the Ariyan truth about the arising of Ill:

"It is that craving that leads back to birth, along with the lure and the lust that lingers longingly now here, now there: namely, the craving for sensual pleasure, the craving to be born again, the craving for existence to end. Such, monks, is the Ariyan truth about the arising of Ill.

"And this, monks, is the Ariyan truth about the ceasing of Ill:

"Verily it is the utter passionless cessation of, the giving up, the forsaking, the release from, the absence of longing for this craving.

"Now this, monks, is the Ariyan truth about the practice that leads to the ceasing of Ill:

"Verily it is this Ariyan eightfold way, to wit: Right views, right aim, right speech, right action, right living, right effort, right mindfulness, right concentration.

Article 4
Confucius: Analects

Introduction

Kung Fuci or Kung Fu-Tzu (551–479 BC), whose honorific title was translated into English as "Confucius," was born into a poor Chinese family of minor nobility. Through his education and personal creative reasoning, he developed many theories on good government and individual ethical behavior.

His principles, such as governing with benevolence and example, not by killing, were ahead of his time. He spent his life working for various governments and also by wandering through Asia looking for a ruler who would accept him as an advisor and adopt his teachings. He had many adherents, however, who traveled with him and eventually transcribed his teachings in *Analects.* Many years after his death, the Han dynasty adopted the principles in *Analects* as official guidelines of the state. "Confucianism" remains today a foundation of eastern thinking.

These *Analects* are considered to be the most reliable examples of his teachings and discussion of his life. They teach strict personal conduct, respect for elders, filial (towards one's parents) piety, and practicing one's education. He also proposed that all people should base their lives on the five virtues of kindness, uprightness, decorum, wisdom, and faithfulness.

Book One

One of the central themes of this Book is that learning (xue) has more to do with actual behavior than academic theory, and that virtuous public behavior as an adult is rooted in such basic familial virtues as filial piety (xiao) and respect for elders (ti) (lit. "being a good younger brother").[1]

1.1 The Master said, "To learn and then have occasion to practice what you have learned—is this not satisfying? To have friends arrive from afar—is this not a joy? To be patient even when others do not understand—is this not the mark of the gentleman?"

1.2 Master You said, "A young person who is filial and respectful of his elders rarely becomes the kind of person who is inclined to defy his superiors, and there has never been a case of one who is disinclined to defy his superiors stirring up rebellion.

"The gentleman applies himself to the roots. 'Once the roots are firmly established, the Way will grow.' Might we not say that filial piety and respect for elders constitute the root of Goodness?"

1.3 The Master said, "A clever tongue and fine appearance are rarely signs of Goodness."

1.4 Master Zeng said, "Every day I examine myself on three counts: in my dealings with others, have I in any way failed to be dutiful? In my

---

Confusius, Analects, translated by Edward Slingerland (Hackett 2003), ISBN 9780872206359, pp 1–7 excerpts.

[1]Although the literal meaning of the term is something like "being a good younger brother," *ti* often refers more generally to showing respect and being obedient to one's elders, and the more general rendering will be used throughout to maintain consistency.

interactions with friends and associates, have I in any way failed to be trustworthy? Finally, have I in any way failed to repeatedly put into practice what I teach?"

1.5 The Master said, "To guide a state of one thousand chariots, be respectful in your handing of affairs and display trustworthiness; be frugal in your expenditures and cherish others; and employ the common people only at the proper times."

1.6 The Master said, "A young person should be filial when at home and respectful of his elders when in public. Conscientious and trustworthy, he should display a general care for the masses but feel a particular affection for those who are Good. If he has any strength left over after manifesting these virtues in practice, let him devote it to learning the cultural arts (*wen*)."

1.7 Zixia said, "Imagine someone who recognizes and admires worthiness and therefore changes his lustful nature, who is able to fully exhaust his strength in serving his parents and extend himself to the utmost in serving his lord, and who is trustworthy in speech when interacting with friends and associates. Even if you said of such a person, 'Oh, but he is not learned (*xue*),' I would still insist that it is precisely such qualities that make one worthy of being called 'learned.' "

1.8 The Master said, "If a gentleman is not serious, he will not inspire awe, and what he learns will be grasped only superficially.

Let your actions be governed by dutifulness and trustworthiness, and do not accept as a friend one who is not your equal. If you have committed a transgression, do not be afraid to change your ways."[2]

1.13 Master You said, "Trustworthiness comes close to rightness, in that your word can be counted upon. Reverence comes close to ritual propriety, in that it allows you to keep shame and public disgrace at a distance. Simply following these virtues, never letting them out of your sight—one cannot deny that this is worthy of respect."

1.14 The Master said, "The gentleman is not motivated by the desire for a full belly or a comfortable abode. He is simply scrupulous in behavior and careful in speech, drawing near to those who possess the Way in order to be set straight by them. Surely this and nothing else is what it means to love learning."

1.15 Zigong said, "Poor without being obsequious, rich without being arrogant—what would you say about someone like that?"

The Master answered, "That is acceptable, but it is still not as good as being poor and yet joyful, rich and yet loving ritual."

Zigong said, "An ode says,

'As if cut, as if polished;
As if carved, as if ground.'

Is this not what you have in mind?"

The Master said, "Zigong, you are precisely the kind of person with whom one can begin to discuss the *Odes*. Informed as to what has gone before, you know what is to come."

1.16 The Master said, "Do not be concerned about whether or not others know you; be concerned about whether or not you know others."

[2]The second paragraph is repeated in 9.25.

Article 5
Lao-Tzu: Tao Te Ching

Introduction

According to legend, Lao Tzu ("Old Master") was the archives-keeper of an imperial court in China of the 5th Century BC. At the age of 80 he left the court and set out eastward across China, disappointed in the unwillingness of men to follow the way to goodness or the "Tao." The gatekeeper of Tibet stopped him and told him to write down his teachings, which his disciples did. Their writings became the book we know today as the *Tao Te Ching* ("The Way and Its Power").

The *Tao Te Ching* is the basis of the philosophy of Taoism, a major component of Eastern thought. Taoism is not religious in the sense of discussing god. Rather, it is a set of ethical principles that people should use in their lives. Often combined in ethical thinking with that of Confucius, Taoism has become so embedded in Chinese thought that the principles of Taoism have become inseparable from Chinese culture.

The backbone of Taoism is that by yielding, one can overcome force. To Western minds, this concept is contradictory. But, if we realize that by trying to overcome something, we will bring discord with nature, then submitting will maintain the balance of nature and, ultimately, will lead to success. Taoism teaches that if we are without ambition, we cannot fail. That is, we always succeed and thus we are all-powerful.

1. Reason's Realisation

The reason that can be reasoned is not the eternal Reason.
The name that can be named is not the eternal Name.
The Unnameable is of heaven and earth the beginning.
The Nameable becomes of the ten thousand things the mother.
Therefore it is said:

'He who desireless is found
The spiritual of the world will sound.
But he who by desire is bound
Sees the mere shell of things around.'

These two things are the same in source but different in name.
Their sameness is called a mystery.
Indeed, it is the mystery of mysteries.
It is the door of all spirituality.

8. Easy By Nature

Superior goodness resembles water.
Water's goodness benefits the ten thousand things,
yet it does not quarrel.

Karus, Paul (tr.), *The Teachings of Lao-Tzu: The Tao Te Ching,* St. Martin's Press, 1913.

Water dwells in the places
which the multitudes of men shun;
therefore it is near to the eternal Reason.

The dwelling of goodness is in lowliness.
The heart of goodness is in commotion.
When giving, goodness shows benevolence.
In words, goodness keeps faith.
In government goodness stands for order.
In business goodness exhibits ability.
The movements of goodness keep time.

It does not quarrel.
Therefore it is not rebuked.

11. The Function of the Non-Existent

Thirty spokes unite in one nave
and, on that which is non-existent [the hole in the nave]
depends the wheel's utility.
Clay is moulded into a vessel
and, on that which is non-existent [its hollowness]
depends the vessel's utility.
By cutting out doors and windows we build a house
and, on that which is non-existent [the empty space within]
depends the house's utility.

Therefore, existence renders actual
but non-existence renders useful.

31. Quelling War

Even victorious arms are unblest among tools,
and people had better shun them.
Therefore the one who has Reason does not rely on them.

When residing at home
the superior man honours the left.
When using arms, he honours the right.

Arms are unblest among tools
and not the superior man's tools.
Only when it is unavoidable does he use them.
Peace and quietude he holds high.

He conquers but does not rejoice.
Rejoicing at a conquest
means to enjoy the slaughter of men.
He who enjoys the slaughter of men
will most assuredly not obtain his will in the empire.

57. Simplicity In Habits

With integrity one governs the state;
with craftiness one leads the army;
with non-diplomacy one takes the empire.
How do I know that it is so?
Through IT.

The more restrictions and prohibitions are in the empire,
the poorer grow the people.
The more weapons the people have,
the more troubled is the state.
The more there is cunning and skill,
the more startling events will happen.
The more mandates and laws are enacted,
the more there will be thieves and robbers.

Therefore the sage says:
I practise non-assertion,
and the people of themselves reform.
I love quietude,
and the people of themselves become righteous.
I use no diplomacy,
and the people of themselves become rich.
I have no desire,
and the people of themselves remain simple.

63. Consider Beginnings

Assert non-assertion.
Practise non-practice.
Taste the tasteless.
Make great the small.
Make much the little.

Requite hatred with virtue.

Contemplate a difficulty when it is easy.
Manage a great thing when it is small.

The world's most difficult undertakings
necessarily originate while easy,
and the world's greatest undertakings
necessarily originate while small.

Therefore the sage to the end
does not venture to play the great,
and thus he can accomplish his greatness.

Rash promises surely lack faith,
and many easy things surely involve many difficulties.

Therefore, the sage regards everything as difficult,
and thus to the end encounters no difficulties.

78. Trust In Faith

Nothing in the world is tenderer
and more delicate than water.
In attacking the hard and the strong
nothing will surpass it.
There is nothing that herein takes its place.

The weak conquer the strong,
the tender conquer the rigid.
In the world there is no one who does not know it,
but no one will practise it.

Therefore the sage says:
'He who the country's sin makes his,
We hail as priest at the great sacrifice.
He who bears the curse of the country's failing.
As king of the empire we are hailing.'

True words seem paradoxical.

Minoan and Mycenaean Cultures
Trading Creativity

> A huge industrial development was required to produce the metals, cloth, pottery, oil, and wine, which Greece . . . exported in exchange [for food]. Fifth-century Attic [Greek] vases have been found in the Rhineland and on the banks of the Marne. . . . Industrialized to an extent which was then a novelty, and which was facilitated by the fact that the mother-city of democracy had a population that was about one-half slave, Athens would have starved but for the continuing reputation of its pottery, bronzes and the other metalwork, and furniture, which brought the cornships to the Piraeus [port of Athens].
>
> —*T. K. Derry and T. I. Williams,* A Short History of Technology

A Unique Type of Civilization

Ancient Greece was a geographically small, thinly populated region, comprised of a collection of bickering city-states that were deemed so unimportant by the various ancient empires that they avoided notice until the Persians attacked in 490 B.C., roughly 1,500 years after the first civilizations rose on the Aegean islands and peninsula. However, from this rocky point on the edge of the civilized world came one of the largest explosions of knowledge and creativity the world has ever known. The impact of this creative explosion was so great that it still shapes and directs much of thought and learning in the twenty-first century.

Undoubtedly many aspects of the physical and socio-political environments led to the development of this unique Greek civilization, but some of the most obvious are that Greece has no major rivers and has insufficient fertile soil and rainfall on which to build a strong agriculturally based society as did the Mesopotamians, Egyptians, Indians, and Chinese before them. Some new system for supporting the population had to be developed if a powerful civilization was to occupy the rocky hills of Greece. The basis of that new system was trade.

From the moment of her entrance onto the stage of the world, Greece survived by trade, and trading issues seemed to lie at the heart of much of Greek history. The Greeks established colonies throughout the Mediterranean, and beyond, to facilitate their trade. The colonies learned from the areas around them, especially Mesopotamia and Egypt, but also from the tribal peoples in areas surrounding colonies around the Black Sea and on the coasts of Western Europe. Then, when ships from the city-states of the Greek homeland visited these far-flung ports, goods and information were exchanged. The Greeks in the homeland gathered and filtered this information and grew from it. They received new ideas that sparked their imaginations and gave them seeds of creativity that created the dynamic and fruitful society that reached its full glory in the Golden Age of Greece, around the fifth century B.C.

In addition to the borrowing of knowledge and new ideas from the areas surrounding their trading partners, the Greeks had a new way of thinking—a way that led to creativity that was unique and astounding. We will look at the factors that might have contributed to that thinking, which is part of the legacy of Greece lasting even until today. We begin our study of Greece by looking at the first inhabitants of Greek territory, the Minoan civilization on Crete.

Minoans

The original inhabitants of Crete, who settled there perhaps as early as 2000 B.C., may have come from Phoenicia (the coastal part of Mesopotamia now known as Lebanon) or maybe from the colonization of a group known as the Sea People, whose origin is still unknown. A map of the Eastern Mediterranean showing Crete, the Greek mainland, Mesopotamia, and Egypt is given in Figure 5.1. As the Sea People and the Phoenicians grew in power, reaching their zenith about 1200 B.C., so did the people of Crete. These groups probably competed for trade, but may have worked together to enhance each other's array of goods that could be traded. We know little of their interaction, if there was any, but this we do know: The people of Crete were successful traders and, from that trade, lived a good life.

This early Cretan people are called today the Minoans, named after their most important king, Minos. The capital city was called Knossos. The people of Minos seemed to have lived relatively peaceful lives, as is indicated by the absence of military fortifications and defenses around their cities. Being an island society was useful, as it

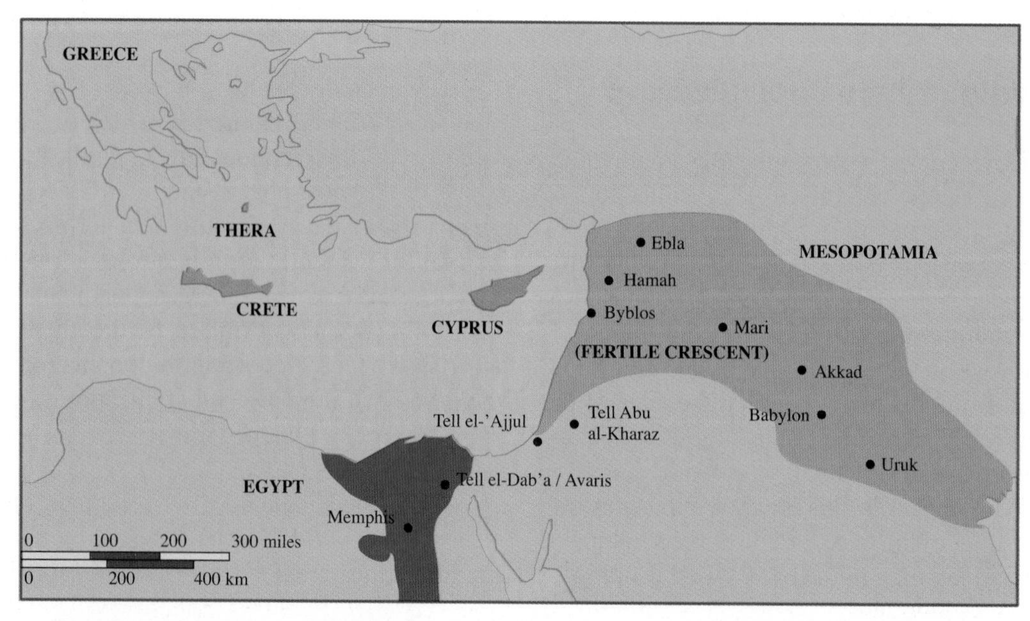

Figure 5.1 ■ *Map showing Crete, the Greek mainland, Mesopotamia, and Egypt.*

provided a natural defense against enemies and invasion.

The Minoan culture possessed all of the required traits for a stable civilization: a means of producing sufficient food (trading in this case), specialization of labor (as shown by the many types of skills demonstrated in their cities), an ordered hierarchy (as shown by the types of buildings), and a system of writing (which is called today Linear A and has not yet been deciphered, although it has some rudimentary similarity to cuneiform).

We can judge the lifestyle by the luxury of the infrastructure and buildings in Knossos. We see aqueducts to bring in fresh water and sewers to take used water out of the city. There were large grain storage facilities, which reflected the effectiveness of their trade. Many of the buildings were constructed so that they would be cool in the summer but could be heated in the winter (although the temperatures of the seasons don't vary much on Crete, so this task was relatively easy). There were palaces for the nobility and lesser homes arranged around them for aristocrats. Homes for the poor were further removed. There were open, public courtyards and rooms for public assemblies, religious ceremonies, and administrative offices.

The Minoan palaces were laid out with obvious planning, with divisions between private, governmental, religious, and public sections. Beautiful wall paintings (frescoes) depicted scenes of nature and Minoan life, showing men and women relaxing and being entertained. The women wore nice clothes and had fancy hairdos and cosmetics.

Minoans seemed to place an importance on art, not in a religious context or for glory of the ruler, as was generally the case with the Mesopotamians and Egyptians, but art just for the sake of enjoyment. Minoan art also has a vitality and creativity that separates it from the stagnant art of the Egyptians and other peoples of this period. Evidently, the Minoans had time for leisure. This lifestyle became a lost ideal for Greek societies throughout their history. The palace at Knossos has beautiful artwork depicting this love of art as shown in Figure 5.2.

Minoans seemed to have leisure time. Men were depicted playing sports, such as boxing and leaping over bulls (as shown in Figure 5.3). The bull seems to have had a special significance for Minoans. Not only are bulls depicted on the walls of their buildings, but legend also associates bulls with the Minoans. Actually, the legend is not about a bull but, rather, a Minotaur—half bull and half human. (The word "minotaur" comes from a combination of "Minoan" and "Taurus," the name for bull in Greek.) According to the legend, the people of mainland Greece were required to pay a regular tribute of seven boys and seven girls to King Minos at Knossos. According to the story, the fourteen youths who were delivered yearly were placed in a labyrinth that was the home of the Minotaur. The

Figure 5.2 ■ Palace at Knossos. *© 2010 by Karel Gallas. Used under license of Shutterstock, Inc.*

Figure 5.3 ■ *Minoan frescos from palaces in Knossos. Image from Corel.*

youths always became lost in the labyrinth and were caught and then devoured by the Minotaur. One year, a hero named Theseus (son of the king of Athens) volunteered to go to Minos and attempt to stop the bloody tribute. With the help of Minos' daughter, Ariadne who could spin webs like a spider, he was successful in killing the Minotaur and finding his way out of the labyrinth, using a cord of weblike silk.

Myths, of course, are fictitious stories, and it is obvious that these events never really occurred (unless one believes Minotaurs once lived on Earth); however, many myths are rooted in truth. It is very likely that the myth of Theseus and the Minotaur contains a core of true history, even if its Greek authors didn't realize it. Historians and archaeologists are unsure what caused the demise of Minoan society; it mysteriously ceased to exist about 1400 B.C., and the Greek myth does not answer that question. If one looks at its core, however, the myth does symbolically show the collapse of Minoan power in favor of mainland Greek control. In the story the Greek mainland is politically dominated by Minos, and has to offer tribute to the island nation (it may or may not actually have been their youth). Eventually something caused the balance of power to shift, and mainland Greece gained the upper hand in the region. This is symbolized by Theseus, the Greek hero, killing the Minotaur, which is the symbol of Minos. It is possible that the more warlike Greek mainlanders eventually just destroyed the Minoans.

Another possibility proposed for the demise of the Minoan civilization has been that a large volcano erupted nearby, polluting the air and soil of Crete with its soot and ash, and making life on Crete deadly. This explanation is strengthened because about the time of the fall of the Minoan culture, an island called Thera (now called Santorini) did explode and scatter ash and deadly gases. The proximity of Thera to Crete suggests that Crete would have been strongly affected. (Some scholars have even suggested that the explosion of Thera and the subsequent scattering of ash might have caused the Nile to turn red, and that might have led to the death of fishes, frogs leaving the river, increase in lice and flies, disease, death of animals, boils, and other events associated with the Biblical plagues of Egypt. However, no natural explanation has been given for the last plague—the death of the firstborn in houses that were not properly marked.)

The explosion of Santorini and its possible connection with the Minoan society brings to light another very interesting theory. Some scholars have equated this event with the legendary destruction of the island of Atlantis, which was reported by Plato. These scholars suggest that when Plato reported the date, location, and size of the island, he was off by a factor of ten. (The Greek numbering system, which used common Greek alphabet characters to represent numbers, was notoriously difficult to use and could have easily been misinterpreted either by Plato or his source.) These scholars believe that if the distance from the Greek mainland is corrected, along with the size of the island and the time, the disappearance of Atlantis would correspond closely with the eruption of Thera (Santorini). Hence, Atlantis may be a true legend, and the supposedly wonderful civilization that it represents was, in fact, the Minoans.

Whatever the reason, Minoan civilization died out very suddenly, probably about 1600 B.C., and the vacuum of power in the Aegean was filled by the mainland Greeks. These early mainland Greeks were given a special name to distinguish them from the Greeks of the Golden Age, which followed many centuries later. The first mainland Greeks were called the Mycenaeans.

Mycenaeans

The Mycenaeans are named for Mycenae, a city on the Greek mainland that seemed to be the most powerful of the loosely associated small kingdoms collectively known as the Mycenaean civilization. The Mycenaeans were immensely important in Greek history. They were the people who fought the Trojan War and interacted with the gods of Olympus. The Mycenaean period is sometimes called the Heroic Period. Much like the Minoans, the Mycenaeans represented an ideal for the later Greeks, but this second ideal was rooted in war. As we will see, later Greek society became an interesting combination of the Minoan and Mycenaean cultures. From the Minoans came a love of peace, beauty, and leisure. From the Mycenaeans came religion, warfare, and the traits of heroes (bravery, sacrifice for country, honor, etc.), which became the basis of Greek drama, sports, and literature.

Mycenaean society competed with the older Minoan culture that had developed on Crete. However, all evidence suggests that the Mycenaeans were culturally and politically dominated by the Minoans during these early years. The Mycenaeans adopted the Minoan palace as the design for their urban centers, and decorated their new palaces with frescoes and murals that were similar in style to those found on Crete. However, unlike the Minoans, the Mycenaeans were not isolated on an island, and the Mycenaeans had to worry constantly about attack by barbarians from the north. Therefore, Mycenaean palaces were built with strong fortifications and massive walls (up to 15 feet thick and 50 feet high) to help in their defense. The walls of Mycenae and the famous Lion Gate are shown in Figure 5.4. Furthermore, Mycenaean art might have adopted the medium and style of Minos, but the images were much more somber in color, tone, and topic. (Mycenaean murals often dealt with subjects such as war and death, whereas Minoan murals depicted nature and relaxation.)

Figure 5.4 ■ Walls and gate in Mycenae. *© 2010 by Kardmar. Used under license of Shutterstock, Inc.*

With the explosion of Thera (or whatever event resulted in the demise of the Minoan culture), the Mycenaeans began to develop their own identity. As time went on, the Mycenaeans developed a feudal-like society, with kings and champions. Like the Minoans before them, the Mycenaeans had to rely on trade rather than agriculture to survive, because of relatively poor local growing conditions and the lack of a major river. The Mycenaeans took over the Minoan colonies and trade routes, but seemed to use military force to suppress any colonial problems and to guarantee their dominance of the trade routes.

It was probably over control of these trade routes that the Mycenaeans went to war with the city of Troy (Ilium) around 1200 B.C. The Trojans were a neighboring civilization just across the Aegean Sea, and Troy may have been a Greek colony. (See the map of the Aegean Sea in Figure 5.5.) Troy was strategically located at the entrance to the series of waterways connecting the Mediterranean Sea with the Black Sea. (The most western waterway is called the Hellespont or, today, the Dardanelles, with other waterways moving toward the Black Sea called the Propontis or, today, the Sea of Marmara and the Bosporus.) Because much of the Greek trade was into the Black Sea area, control of the entrance way was critical. Hence, if problems arose with Troy, the stability of Black Sea trade was in jeopardy, and the Mycenaeans would have fought mightily to restore order.

However, that is not what legend says. According to legend, the Trojan War began with a dispute amongst the goddesses of Olympus over who was the most beautiful. When a young mortal, Paris, was asked to decide, he chose Aphrodite (Venus, in the Roman religion), who rewarded him with the most beautiful mortal woman, Helen. However, Helen was already married to Menelaus, the king of Sparta and brother to Agamemnon, king of Mycenae. When Helen was taken by Paris to his home city, Troy, the Mycenaean Greeks decided to join together to force Helen's return. The ten-year Trojan War was the result.

You can decide whether the Trojan War was over trade or love, but whichever you decide, the

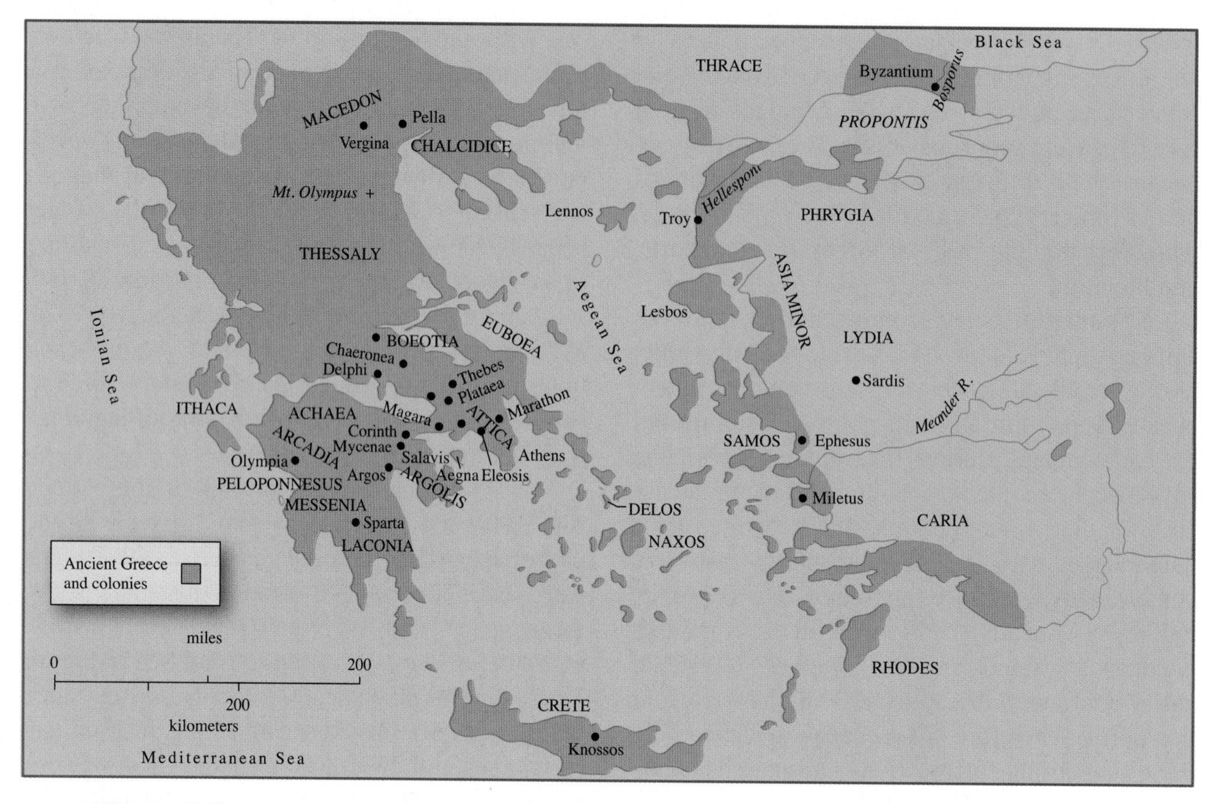

Figure 5.5 ■ *Map of the Greek colonies in the Aegean Sea, showing the location of Troy.*

result is going to be uncertain. Like the very existence of Minos and Mycenae, the Trojan War was considered to just be a Greek myth for hundreds of years. Modern archaeological evidence has shown that the Trojan War did actually occur and that this was indeed a defining moment for the Mycenaean culture. However, most of what we know of the war comes to us through literature that was written much later, and so the facts surrounding the Trojan War are still shrouded in myth and fable.

We could discuss the Trojan War in more detail at this point, but we prefer to do that later when we meet Homer, the principal author of the books that describe the Trojan War. You see, the writing of the Mycenaeans, which was called Linear B and seems to be a derivative of the Minoan Linear A, was intended for accounting and was not well suited to telling stories. Therefore, the events of the Trojan War were not recorded by the Mycenaeans but, rather, were preserved as oral stories that were finally written hundreds of years later. When they were written, we see both the Mycenaean time and also details that were characteristic of the time it was written. Hence, to get the full appreciation of the story, it is best to wait until later when we discuss a new written method (the Greek alphabet), when the story could be written with feeling and beauty.

The later Mycenaean period, after the Trojan War, continued to be a time that was rich in legend. Many later Greek dramas use events that were taken from the post-war period (whether real or invented by the dramatist, we can't say). But the legends continued. Eventually, however, the Mycenaean culture died out. When it disappeared, a period began in which no records were kept, and we know little of the history that occurred during this new period. What we know or can infer, we will discuss as the "Dark Age" of Greece.

The "Dark Age" of Greece

Around 1000 B.C., Dorian invaders (a barbarian people from Europe, probably possessing iron weapons and possibly related to the Aryans who conquered India) defeated the Mycenaeans, who had fallen to fighting among themselves and thus became relatively easy prey in spite of their strong fortifications. Greece then fell into a dark age of culture and diminished creativity that lasted several hundred years. Greece, however, eventually emerged from this dark time and began one of the most creatively explosive periods in human history.

The Greek "Dark Age" was not a time wholly without merit or creativity, however. With the fall of the Mycenaean civilization we see the birth of ancient Greece, as many of the elements that comprise what we think of as "ancient Greece" began during this time. First, the relative political unity of the Mycenaeans scattered across the Aegean ended when their civilization was destroyed and each of the dominant cities of the area—Athens, Sparta, Thebes, Corinth, and so on—became separate political entities that governed themselves and a small amount of territory around them. Thus, from the death of Mycenae we get the rise of the Greek *polis,* or city-state.

The city-state proved to be both Greece's greatest blessing and biggest curse. The city-state was beneficial because, by keeping the government on a local level, it allowed Greece's leaders and great thinkers to worry only about themselves and their city, not the governing of a large empire. This created an environment where experimentation in politics, philosophy, and many other areas could flourish (although it generally did not begin to do so until Greece emerged from its Dark Ages). The curse of the city-state was the constant warfare that arose between these independently governed political entities.

An example of the benefit of city-states is seen with the invention of a concept like that of democracy in Athens. The Athenian city-state was a small political entity; only in that type of self-governing city could true democracy—where the people vote directly on all governmental decisions—really work. Even today, the modern United States, which proclaims itself as democracy's shining beacon and champion throughout the world, falls short of a true democracy. (It is actually a representative republic where citizens choose others to make governmental decisions for them.) The problem of the United States, or almost any other political entity that wants to practice *real* democracy, is size. Modern states are simply too large to allow direct participation of all the qualified voters. Imagine the difficult logistics in getting the people to vote regularly on every law that is enacted. It is also impossible for citizens of even a moderately large country to make informed policy decisions for all areas of the country. Democracy is just one example, but it is indicative of how the small, Greek city-state helped create the new type of government that would soon occur.

The development of the city-state was, however, also the curse of Greece. The various city-states were the centers of political, social, religious, and artistic activity in their region. Each city-state developed its own variations in art, religious myths, systems of government, and lifestyle. Intense rivalries developed among the differing city-states, and the Greeks saw themselves first as Athenians or Spartans or Corinthians, before they viewed themselves as Greeks. Over time, local pride developed into bitter jealousies and hatreds as the city-states tried to outdo each other in constructing the greatest temples, training the best athletes to compete at contests like the Olympics, and controlling trade in the region. This division led to near constant fighting among themselves, and made Greece seem weak to potential conquerors. Therefore, while Greece developed many of the great ideas of history, they were not always able to enjoy the fruits of their labors, as they were almost constantly at war. The inability of the Greeks to unify into one people eventually proved to play a major role in the downfall of an independent Greek empire as well.

One of the most important and warlike of the city-states was Sparta. They developed a culture that was an extreme representation of military focus and reflected the turmoil and warlike atmosphere that was characteristic of the Dark Ages. This Spartan culture seemed to have arisen because their lifestyle depended on their domination of some small cities that surrounded them. The military focus permeated all of Spartan life. At the age of seven, all Spartan boys were taken to a residential barracks to learn military skills. The young boys lived in the barracks at least until they were 20, when they became frontline soldiers. They remained on active duty, whether actually at war or just as guards over their captive states, until the age of 30. They then were sent back to Sparta, where they formed the home guard. At this point in their lives, they could marry and have children, although many men chose to still live in the barracks and just occasionally visit with their wives.

Even though they lived in the barracks, the young boys could still enjoy the companionship of the older men at dinner time, as all men ate communally. This continued until the men finished their military obligation at the age of 60. Their food reflected the military nature of their life. They ate roasted meat with vegetables, which was all covered with a broth made from pork cooked in blood, vinegar, and salt. (Some have said that the broth must have tasted terrible and that is why the Spartans were not afraid to die.)

The women focused on bearing sons, and seemed willing to allow deformed sons to be taken away and killed or exposed so that they died. The women participated with the men in many military exercises. We have no Spartan art from this period, presumably because everyone was so fixed on warfare that there was no inclination or time for artistic pursuits.

The Spartans continued this same militaristic culture long after the Greek Dark Ages were over, while other city-states, especially Athens, emerged to a new type of culture. We will examine the forces that led to the establishing of Athenian culture when we look at the Archaic Period or, as we prefer to call it, the Formative Period.

Timeline—Important Dates

Date	Event
2000 B.C.	*Establishment of the Minoan civilization on Crete*
1600 B.C.	*End of the Minoan culture*
1600–1000 B.C.	*Mycenaean culture*
1200 B.C.	*Trojan War*
1000–800 B.C.	*Greek Dark Ages*

Suggested Readings

Berlitz, Charles, *Atlantis: The Eighth Continent,* Fawcett, 1985.

Cahill, Thomas, *Sailing the Wine-Dark Sea,* Nan A. Talese, 2003.

Derry, T. K. and T. I. Williams, *A Short History of Technology,* Oxford University Press, 1960.

Galanopoulos, A. G. and Edward Bacon, *Atlantis,* Bobbs-Merrill, 1969.

Phillips, Graham, *Atlantis and the Ten Plagues of Egypt,* Inner Traditions International, 2003.

Sarmast, Robert, *Discovery of Atlantis,* Origin Press, 2004.

Greek Archaic or Formative Period
Unique Concepts

> How foolish men are! It is their lot to suffer, but because of their folly they bring upon themselves sufferings over and above what is fated for them. And then they blame the gods.
>
> —*Homer,* The Odyssey

What a Difference Writing Makes

The Greek Dark Ages began about 1000 B.C. and lasted until about 800 B.C. After these dark days, we aren't sure what political or sociological events occurred to begin a new burst of creativity, but we do know the specific event that led directly to the new cultural awareness. That event was the creation of the Greek alphabet. We don't know if the Greek alphabet was invented by a single person and then widely adopted, or if it evolved over considerable time. What is clear, however, is that when it became widely known throughout the Greek world, it made major changes in the nature of Greek civilization. It led directly to Homer's writings, which served as a foundation of Greek civilization for many years to come. The creation of the Greek alphabet also led to Aesop's fables, which helped define Greek ethics, and to Hesiod's writings, which defined Greek religion. Greek science, which began shortly after the invention of the alphabet, was also dependent on the new form of writing and thinking that the Greek alphabet enabled.

In one sense the Greek alphabet was just a minor extension beyond the alphabet developed by the Phoenicians of coastal Mesopotamia. But in another sense, the Greek alphabet permitted something that previous alphabets—Phoenician, Egyptian, Chinese, Mesopotamian—did not allow. That new something was the ability to write in full phonetic detail—to put down all of the sounds of the spoken language. What a difference it proved to make!

All writing systems prior to the Greeks communicated *ideas,* and only rarely tried to communicate *sounds.* The pictogram languages of Egyptian hieroglyphs and Chinese characters are the most obvious in this regard. While richly representing an idea, these writing systems required that new symbols be created to express new ideas. That symbol-invention requirement limited the creation of new ideas, however subtle the restriction. Moreover, the number of symbols rapidly increased, requiring the memorization of a tremendous number of symbols. Thus, only those with much time to dedicate to learning the vocabulary could do it. Chiefly, the priests or the bureaucrats were the only classes of society that had the time. Moreover, the pictographs were inherently difficult to execute, thus requiring great skill and, therefore, practice. Again, this meant that only the privileged could spend the time to accomplish it.

In contrast, the Greek system simply represented the *sounds* of the language, which could be done using 24 simple symbols (letters) and a few simple rules for pronunciation. Hence, with their new alphabet as a tool, the Greeks were able to write as they thought, without the restriction of needing to invent new symbols for new concepts. The Greeks simply recorded the sounds of whatever new words were used to represent the new ideas. It can also be said that words represent ideas, either alone or in combination. Therefore, if a language allows new words to be created easily, as does English, then it also allows new ideas to be created easily. This was the case with Greek.

A further advantage of the Greek writing system over the pictogram systems of the Egyptians and Chinese was the ease of learning how to write. The symbols were easy to write and the rules were simple to learn. Therefore, any person could learn to write with only a brief introduction to the rules of the language and minimal training in the actual writing skills. Therefore, language became a tool for the masses or, using the Greek term, it became *demotic*. The obvious result was an empowerment of the masses, which ultimately led to the establishment of democratic government.

Another advantage of the Greek alphabet can be seen in a comparison with the Semitic languages from which the Greeks took the original alphabet concept. The Semitic languages, such as Hebrew and Phoenician, did not represent all the sounds in their alphabet. They ignored the vowels (the English letters a, e, i, o, and u) when writing words, perhaps because Semitic languages were consonant-intensive; that is, the consonants were more important than the vowels. Hence, in Semitic languages, combinations of letters could stand for several words, since it is possible, even common, to have the same consonants in two or more words. Common examples in English would be "man," "men," "mean," "main," "mane," and "omen," which would all have been represented as "mn" in the old Semitic writing systems. This type of confusion must have been troubling and confusing for the ancients and, in more modern times, has resulted in some interesting and amusing problems in translating ancient Semitic texts. A famous example is the translation of Exodus when Moses came down from Mount Sinai. The original Hebrew text said that Moses had light emitting from his head because of the glory of God. Jerome, in the fifth century A.D., read the Hebrew word for "light" as "horns" because these two words—light and horns—were the same three Hebrew consonants (k, r, and n in their English equivalents) and the vowels, which make the words different, were not included. Therefore, in the Jerome version of the Bible (called the Vulgate), he said that Moses coming down from Mt. Sinai had horns from his head. Picking up on this mistake, Michelangelo represented Moses with horns in the great sculpture he carved for the tomb of Pope Julius II, which can be seen today in the church of St. Peter in Chains (San Pietro in Vincolo) in Rome.

Greek, which is part of the Indo-European language group, is just the opposite of the Semitic languages. Greek is a vowel-intensive language. Therefore, the Greeks were forced to invent letters to represent vowels, which they simply added to the Phoenician consonants (with some changes in letter characters for simplicity) and created the first fully phonetic alphabet. Therefore, another advantage of the new Greek alphabet was the way in which it could communicate with less ambiguity than even the alphabet-based Semitic languages.

Combining their ability to express new ideas with the practices they learned from the Egyptians and Mesopotamians in recording data, the Greeks were able to describe the natural world around them as never before. This ability grew into what we now call science. However, the invention of science required another creative breakthrough as well, and we will discuss that later.

Still another advantage of the Greek alphabet was the facility that it gave to *record* spoken language. The beauty of the language and its subtleties expressed in stories and oral histories finally became recordable in a permanent form. The written language and the spoken language became, as it were, mirror images of each other. This characteristic led directly to the recording of the words of the blind poet Homer, who gave us the greatest of Greek literary works, the *Iliad* and the *Odyssey.*

Homer

During the eighth century B.C., someone recorded the epic poems narrated by a blind poet named Homer. We know little about Homer and nothing about the scribe, but the effects of that collaboration can be felt in our own time. Some literary critics have judged the two works that were created—*Iliad* and *Odyssey*—to be the greatest literary works ever, at least in terms of their impact on society. This is only partly because they are so old and had a strong effect on the important Greek civilization that was then arising. They also defined the epic genre, which has been used by so many great authors throughout history. Furthermore, these books defined basic values for the Grecian society that followed, becoming almost like a religious text in the way Greeks read (memorized) them and adhered to their principles. (This was especially true since the Greeks did not have a religion in which the gods gave commandments on what should be done by humankind, as did the God of the Old Testament.) Later on, the role of defining what mankind should do (that is, ethics) was taken on by the philosophers.

Homer's *Iliad* and *Odyssey* were unifying and universally powerful to the ancient Greeks, regardless of their local loyalties, because the poems dealt with a theme that all could be proud of, regardless of their city of origin—the glory of Mycenaean Greece, a common ancestor to all city-states. The poems discussed the Greeks' victorious exploits during and after the Trojan War. The title *"Iliad"* comes from Homer's word for Troy, Ilium. In the book the Greeks are called Achaeans, for a region of the Grecian peninsula, and might also be called by other place names of regions around the Aegean Sea, like Attica (around Athens) and Peloponnesus (around Sparta). The title of the sequel, Odyssey, comes from the Greek name of the hero, Odysseus, usually given as Ulysses in English.

To the pre-literate Greeks of Homer's time, the kingdom of Mycenae and its exploits during the Trojan War had already been mostly lost to the shadows and mists of history. It is generally believed that the Greeks themselves thought of these people and events as myths, and it is only much later in history that the reality of the core of these epic poems has come to be established as truth. However, Homer (who himself is also mostly lost to the shadows and mists of history) was able to compose these two great stories of ancient Greece, which serve not only as the mythical beginnings of Greek history and a unifying force to the Greek people and language, but as the beginning of the Western literary tradition.

Not much is actually known about Homer himself. He was a bard, or professional storyteller. He is almost universally described as being blind, so that also is probably true. During the Greek Dark Ages the Greeks had not yet become literate, so Homer almost certainly could not read or write (especially if he was blind), but simply told his tales orally. Furthermore, nearly every Greek polis of any size claimed it was the birthplace of the great Homer, so where he lived and worked is also unknown. It is also uncertain if Homer was the author of the two great poems or more of a compiler of several shorter stories into an elaborate and unified whole. Finally, it is not known for a certainty even if the same person or two different "Homers" composed the *Iliad* and the *Odyssey,* as the tone and style of the two works are quite different. Regardless of the details of who Homer was, the two poems were eventually written down and became the great works that we can appreciate today.

Before we examine the books themselves in more detail, let's discuss the genre of the epic style. Epics, which are often but not always poems, are characterized by the following traits:

- Larger than life
- Often written in a poetic form
- Long story with many events over many years
- Heroes and, often, gods
- Wrestling with problems and also with life itself

The concept "larger than life," when applied to epics, usually means that the events described in the epic are colossal in scope and may affect the entire world or society. The poetic style is often used because it tends to elevate language and make the work seem more significant. In Homer's case, the poetic form would also come from the frequent use of poetry by the ancient bards because rhyme and rhythm help the memory. Both of Homer's poems cover long periods. The Trojan War lasted ten years and the journeys of Odysseus (Ulysses) also lasted ten years. However, strictly speaking, the *Iliad* really covers only a portion of the last year of the Trojan War, but, nevertheless, the time is certainly longer than the few days of many stories or even novels. "Epic" also means that the lessons learned can apply to many people in many periods of time. Several heroes emerge in the *Iliad,* and Odysseus is clearly a hero in the *Odyssey;* in each, there are many interactions with many different gods and other marvelous and interesting characters and creatures. Finally, both Homeric poems talk about the problems of life, and how those problems are confronted and ought to be solved. The quotation at the beginning of this chapter gives, as well as any single statement, Homer's message about troubles. It states that humans are meant to have troubles in this life, but, through their own folly, they bring more troubles upon themselves than are necessary. And then we mortals blame the gods for the additional troubles.

The focus of the *Iliad* is two-fold. First is the interaction between Achilles, the greatest of the Greek warriors, and the other Greeks. Because Achilles feels slighted by actions taken by Agamemnon, the leading Greek king, Achilles retreats to his tent and sulks. This sulking goes on for a very long time, and only ends when Achilles' best friend is killed in personal battle with Hector, the greatest of the Trojan warriors. The interactions between Greek and Trojan heroes is the other focus of the *Iliad.*

Throughout the book the Greek heroes are concerned about doing things that will bring them *arête,* a Greek word that includes the concepts of glory, excellence, and virtue. It can also be rendered as "being the best you can." Some of the most interesting and touching moments in the book are the battle sequences between the various heroes, especially the scene in which Achilles and Hector meet. You might think that because Homer was a Greek, the Trojans would be vilified, but that is not the case. Hector is presented as a fine and upstanding family man who tries to do the right thing for his city. In the end, Hector is killed by Achilles, the superior warrior. Then, in an act of wanton revenge, Achilles desecrates Hector's body by dragging it behind his chariot. This leads to another touching scene in which Hector's father, Priam the king of Troy, sneaks into the tent of Achilles by night and pleads with Achilles for Hector's body. Priam pleads as a father and reminds Achilles of his own father. Achilles' heart is softened and he gives Hector's body to Priam. There are, of course, many other wonderful parts of the book but these are some of the best.

An interesting comparison can be made between the battle scenes in the *Iliad* and those in the Bible. In many ways the stories of armies battling and, especially, the choosing and combat of heroes, are similar. Compare, for example, the battles between the Israelites and the Philistines, especially the battle between David and Goliath as given in I Samuel 17. The fighting style, armor, equipment, tactics, and other details are similar to those described by Homer in the *Iliad.* This similarity confirms, for us at least, the historical authenticity of both the Biblical and the Homeric accounts.

The *Odyssey* is about the travels of Odysseus (Ulysses) when he is trying to get back to his home following the war. The tone of the *Odyssey* is much lighter than the *Iliad,* and emphasizes the cleverness and determination of Odysseus rather than his heroic acts. There is a maturing of Odysseus during the book as he overcomes the many obstacles and, in the end, conquers those who would take his place as husbands of Penelope, his wife, and as rulers of his kingdom, Ithaca.

From the standpoint of creativity, the treatment of Odysseus in both the *Iliad* and the *Odyssey* is an interesting study. From our first encounter with Odysseus in the *Iliad,* we see that the Greeks are impressed with his cleverness. We see, however, some distrust and, perhaps, even ridicule of Odysseus, because his cleverness is also seen as attempts to circumvent what is right and correct. It seems that the Greeks feel he is too clever for his own good. We might characterize that behavior as "tricky" or "conniving"—both of which carry negative meanings. Later in the stories of the Trojan War, Odysseus is given credit for his brilliant plan involving the Trojan Horse. In this case his cleverness is praised. That same positive light is generally given to his ability to overcome difficulties during his trip home. We only catch a slight feeling of the negative in the incident with the Sirens, when his curiosity and cleverness put the ship and himself in danger. Looking at the entire scope of treatment of Odysseus, we can see that these sentiments suggest that there are two sides to cleverness, which can be related to creativity. One aspect represents a positive side, where the creativity is used to benefit society in general. The other is negative, and is associated with creativity in self-interest and with negative impact on society in general. This study suggests, as we have noted elsewhere, that creativity involves acceptance and value by the community or peers. Negative attitudes toward the acts will discount the creativity, and force others to seek for another term to describe the action; perhaps a term with negative connotations. Figure 6.1 shows Odysseus returning to his home—Ithaca. Odysseus must face the changed situation that exists in his home because of his long absence. Homer includes an element of impending disaster as Odysseus finds that his wife has been surrounded by suitors during the years of his absence. All assume that he is dead. However, his wife has delayed the suitors but the suitors are forcing his wife to choose one of them as a husband. Odysseus rectifies the situation through cleverness and physical prowess.

Figure 6.1 ■ Odysseus returning to Ithaca. © *2010 by Maria Yfanti. Used under license of Shutterstock, Inc.*

These two great epics became fixed as part of Greek culture almost from the time they were written. They were read widely and often. Many people memorized them and they were quoted as often as sayings from the Bible or from Shakespeare are quoted today—maybe even more, since the ancient Greeks had so few other great works to quote. Because they became so dominant throughout the Greek world, the language they were written in became the standard Greek language. Just as Shakespeare and the King James Version of the Bible solidified English, so too did the Homeric books solidify ancient Greek. (Dante's *Divine Comedy* and Luther's Bible did much the same for Italian and German, respectively.)

We learn something about the world of Homer through the many similes and epithets found in the books. Homer used these devices to convey understanding of details, so the comparisons must have come from everyday life in Homer's time. Some examples are: "Anger swarms like smoke inside a man's heart"; "The bronze-armored Achaeans"; and "Like flies buzzing around pails of milk." These are not only beautifully descriptive, but they also tell us something about smoky fires, bronze armor, and milking pails in the time of Homer.

The Trojan War was the subject of many other works of literature and drama throughout the history of Greece. Many of these other works do not tie directly to events related in the Homeric books. For example, several Greek dramas, written and performed more than two hundred years after Homer, tell stories of the return home of other Greek heroes. One example is the story of Agamemnon's return to his unfaithful wife. Yet another is the story of Agamemnon's son and his problems following his father's death. These continuation stories are much like the stories of King Arthur and the Knights of the Round Table, which have been written over many centuries and are clearly invented by the various authors (although probably some are based in actual facts).

Religion

The Homeric epics are full of interactions between the Olympian gods and mortals. Some of the gods favor the Greeks and others favor the Trojans, thus complicating the events of the war. (For instance, Aphrodite whisks Paris away from battle just as he is about to be killed.) The famous Greek myths are not, however, found in the Homeric works. These myths were retold by another Greek writer, **Hesiod,** who lived about 700 B.C., a few decades after Homer. Hesiod's principal work, called the *Theogony,* traces the descent of the gods. A chart derived from *Theogony* is given in Figure 6.2.

In this work he identifies the Greek gods as a separate race of beings from humans; gods had the characteristic of being immortal. They did not represent all good or evil, but merely acted with human-like passions and motives. They were not patterns for proper living. They were, however, explanations for events that could not be readily understood. For example, the story of Demeter, goddess of agriculture, explains how the seasons came about, since her daughter, Persephone, was forced to leave earth and live in the Underworld of the Dead for several months each year with the king of the Underworld, Hades (Pluto). The months when she was absent were the barren months, because her mother grieved for her. When Persephone returned, Demeter was happy and the world reawakened.

Hesiod also wrote a book entitled *Work and Days,* which described his own time but related it to the activities of the gods and to past events. For example, he relates troubles in the world to the story of Pandora and her box.

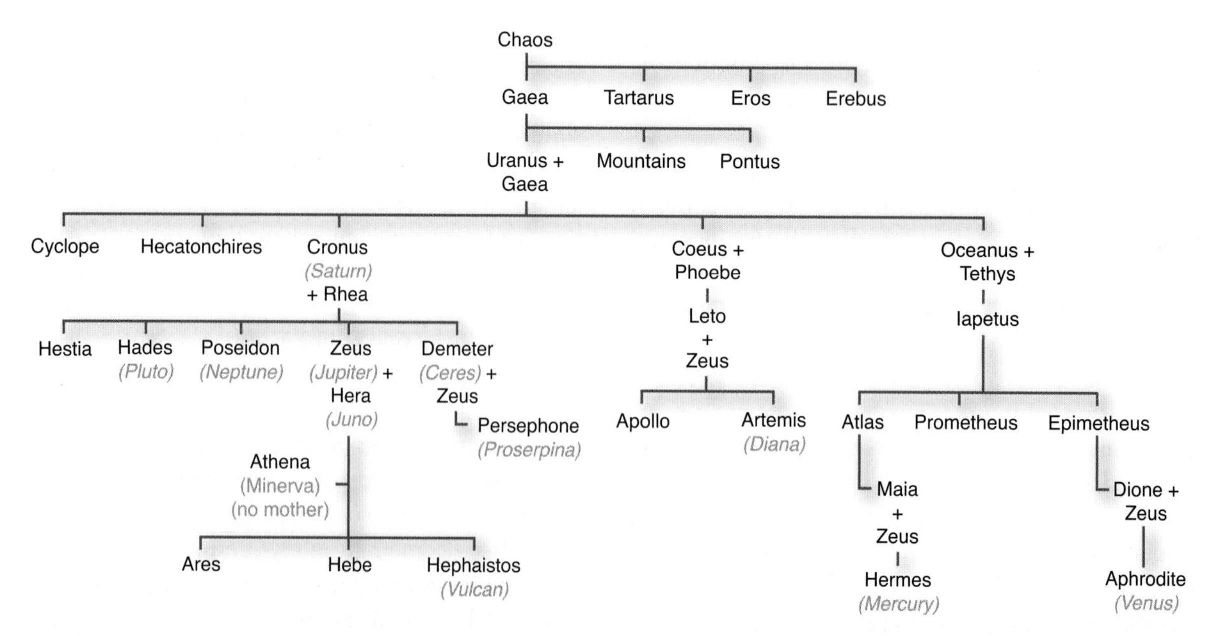

Figure 6.2 ■ *Lineage chart of the Greek gods.*

Figure 6.3 ■ Ancient Olympic stadium. *© 2010 by Mike Liu. Used under license of Shutterstock, Inc.*

Around the same time as Homer and Hesiod, the Greeks began a sporting event and festival to honor Zeus, the greatest of the gods. This sporting event took place in Olympia (not the same place as Mount Olympus) and continued for over a thousand years. Initially there were only a few events, such as foot racing, boxing, and wrestling. A few other events were added over time, such as javelin throwing, long jump, and discus. These events were very popular, as can be seen from the size of the sports complex in Olympia today (which is in ruins but still impressive). The stadium where the races were held is shown in Figure 6.3. In the current stadium are grassy areas that were large seating area and, interestingly, the people from the various city-states seemed to have sat together in certain sections. (We can tell this because coins from the various city-states have been found in the seating area and the coins are mostly congregated by city-state.) The ancient Olympics stopped in the Byzantine period, but the modern Olympics were revived in 1896.

Morals

Around the year 550 B.C., a slave named **Aesop** wrote several enjoyable and meaningful short stories, which we now call fables. Through their characters, usually animals, Aesop made points about how to live a good life. We still tell many of the stories today, such as "The Lion and the Mouse," "The Dog in the Manger," "The Greedy Dog," "The Cicada and the Fox," "The Ant and the Grasshopper," "The Fox and the Grapes," and the "Tortoise and the Hare." At the end of each story is a moral; some of the most famous are: Don't bite the hand that feeds you; it is best to prepare for the days of necessity; plodding wins the race; one good turn deserves another; and any fool can despise what he cannot get (i.e., sour grapes).

Science

Possibly the first great Greek thinker was **Thales,** a man who lived around 625 B.C. in a Greek colony on the western coast of Asia Minor (present-day Turkey) in a region called Ionia in the city of Miletus. (He is sometimes called Thales of Miletus, and the group of other thinkers who followed him are sometimes called the Ionians.) Thales is often considered to be the first philosopher and first scientist (until the nineteenth century A.D., science was called natural philosophy). In addition to his thoughts about philosophy and natural phenomena, Thales made many lasting contributions to other fields of knowledge, including mathematics and astronomy.

Because Thales lived in Ionia rather than on the Greek mainland, he had more interactions with the great Eastern empires of his day, and it is very likely that he learned mathematics and astronomy from the Babylonians in Mesopotamia. It is also likely that he studied with the Egyptians, and learned geometry from them. It is believed he actually developed some of the ideas and proofs that later were included in Euclid's great math text, *The Elements*.

However, Thales' greatest insight was not in mathematics but, rather, in the way he thought about the world; his concepts would have far-reaching consequences in both the fields of philosophy and science. Before Thales, the common view of unexplained phenomena in the ancient world could be summarized as, "I do not know why this happened; therefore, it must have been caused by a god." Thales, however, created a different view of unexplained events. Thales said, "All events, even extraordinary ones, can be explained in natural terms that can be understood by humans." What a revolutionary thought! Quite possibly Thales was the first human to suggest that the world was not a plaything of the gods that could be affected at their whim, but an orderly machine that can be understood by humans. With this one thought, a human went from being a pawn of the gods, to a potential god of the earth himself! After all, what separates man and god except knowledge? This paradigm shift in thought provided the blueprint for the explosion of Greek thought and creativity that was shortly to come to pass. Many Greeks accepted this concept wholeheartedly, helping to create a cultural environment where the Greeks felt that they could discover the cause of everything, and that mankind could be as knowledgeable as the gods.

Besides the far-reaching effects of Thales' thought on the culture of Greece, the new idea also laid the foundation for science and philosophy. The beginnings of science are found in this thought, because Thales proposed that humans can discover the causes of events and that all happenings can be explained in natural terms, not just religious ones. That thought is the essence of science.

How this idea provides the basis for philosophy is a little more complex, but basically can be summed up with this statement: "Underlying all the change in the world (the area that science probes), there is a fundamental order and unity that does not change." Philosophy is the study of this realm of underlying, fundamental, unchanging truths.

Thales believed that there was an unchanging element that served as a reference or anchor for all other things. He felt that this unchanging element was an actual physical substance. Sometimes this element can be expressed in different forms, but it is still the same basic material. For example, he saw that water existed in many forms (ice, snow, liquid, steam). Moreover, he saw that water rose by evaporation and became clouds, and that these clouds eventually caused rain. The rain gathered into rivers, which washed away dirt and also sunk into the ground. He realized that water makes up much of many natural materials like lettuce, fruits, animals, and even human beings. Therefore, the many forms of water suggested to Thales that water is the basic substance from which all other things are made.

Another early Greek thinker was **Pythagoras,** the inventor of mathematics. Much of modern mathematics can be attributed to the work of Pythagoras, who developed a system for expressing equations (such as $2 + 2 = 4$) and established the value of quantitative calculations. Pythagoras, like most Greek thinkers, believed in the basic ideas of Thales—that some unchanging fundamental element lies beneath everything else. For Pythagoras, that underlying unchanging element was not a physical material but was the abstract unity and organization that can be gained by small, whole numbers. He believed that, through math and geometry, all truth could be expressed. For him, numbers were unchanging and everything else was transient. For example, Pythagoras would proclaim that "$2 + 2 = 4$" was absolutely unchanging, and would give a myriad of other examples of mathematical fundamental statements. This, of course, differed from Thales, because the unchanging thing was not physical for Pythagoras, but he felt that math could describe physical things and could dictate how physical things must be constructed, thus giving substance to the ideas of pure math.

Pythagoras started a school for developing the relationship between mathematics and life. Within his school Pythagoras discovered many important mathematical truths, such as the Pythagorean theorem (the sum of the squares of the legs, the sides opposite the small angles, of a right triangle equals the sum of the square of the hypotenuse, the side opposite the right angle) and discovered that any triangle inscribed on the diameter of a circle is a right triangle, which led to the eventual development of trigonometry.

He may have also discovered the Golden Rectangle and the Golden Triangle, whose proportions appeared to be visually balanced and pleasing, and served as much of the basis of Greek art and architecture. Many other scientists and artists have explored the nature of these shapes and have found that both the Golden Rectangle and the Golden Triangle are related. The ratios of certain key dimensions in both of them have the same value, approximately 1.618 or, expressed as a percentage, 61.8 percent. This value, which is called the Golden Ratio, the Golden Mean or, sometimes, phi (φ), has also been found in numerous other pleasing shapes and throughout Nature.

> The Golden Mean defines the proportions of the Parthenon, the shape of playing cards and credit cards, and the proportions of the General Assembly Building at the United Nations in New York. The horizontal member of most Christian crosses separates the vertical member by just about the same ratio: the length above the crosspiece is 61.8% of the length below it. The Golden Mean also appears throughout nature—in flower patterns, the leaves of an artichoke, and the leaf stubs on a palm tree. It is also the ratio of the length of the human body above the navel to its length below the navel (in normally proportioned people, that is). The length of each successive bone in our fingers, from tip to hand, also bears this ratio.
>
> —*Peter L. Bernstein, Against the Gods, 1996, XXVI*

A line divided according to the Golden Ratio is shown in Figure 6.4. Diagrams of the human body showing various ratios of body parts are also shown in Figure 6.4. By comparing a few of the dimensions, you can discover how many are governed by the Golden Ratio.

The Golden Ratio can be used to create a series of rectangles in which one side of the rectangle is the length a+b and the other side is the length a. Such a rectangle is shown in Figure 6.5. The Golden Ratio has been used in buildings, such as the Parthenon, throughout history. Figure 6.5 also shows the Golden Triangle that is defined by the Golden Ratio and which defines a Golden Pentagon. The Golden Pentagon was used as a symbol for a secret society begun by Pythagoras and his followers.

The Golden Ratio also defines a spiral (called the Golden Spiral) that is illustrated in Figure 6.6. This spiral shape is commonly found in Nature, such as the shape of ram's horns, sea shells, and flower patterns. It is also the shape of the Milky Way. Some of these are shown in Figure 6.7.

Pythagoras was creative in the exploration of these golden shapes, but was also creative in relating them to numbers and then expanding the list of similar shapes by investigating all sorts of things that seemed to have pleasing shapes. Later, about the year 1250 A.D., an Italian scientist, Fibonacci, discovered that the Golden Ratio arose naturally from studies of natural reproduction rates, thus suggesting that the shape of plants, star systems, cellular structures, and living beings all seem to be governed by this wonderful ratio. Later mathematicians have discovered that the Golden Ratio can be obtained from several very interesting mathematical formulations. Some patterns suggesting the Golden Ratio have been found in stock market fluctuations and other seemingly random phenomena.

Another example of Pythagoras' ability to discover mathematical truths and then extend their application to daily life was his discovery that music is based in mathematics. The story is told that Pythagoras was walking down the street and he heard pleasing notes of different pitches as he passed by a blacksmith shop. Pythagoras stopped to investigate and found that metal strips of different lengths had pleasing sounds when the lengths were in whole number ratios. He developed the principles of harmonic vibrations from his experiments, and showed that plucked strings of different lengths also yielded different tones, based on numeric ratios (2:1 is an octave, 3:2 is a fifth, and 4:3 is a fourth), all chosen because they are pleasing to the ear. (Just as with the Golden Ratio, the beauty of the ratio is one of the key points for Pythagoras.) An entire musical scale can be obtained using Pythagorean ratios. However, it should be pointed out that when creating a scale using Pythagorean ratios, the notes obtained by strict adherence to the ratios will not always be pleasing in all musical keys. This became especially troublesome in the

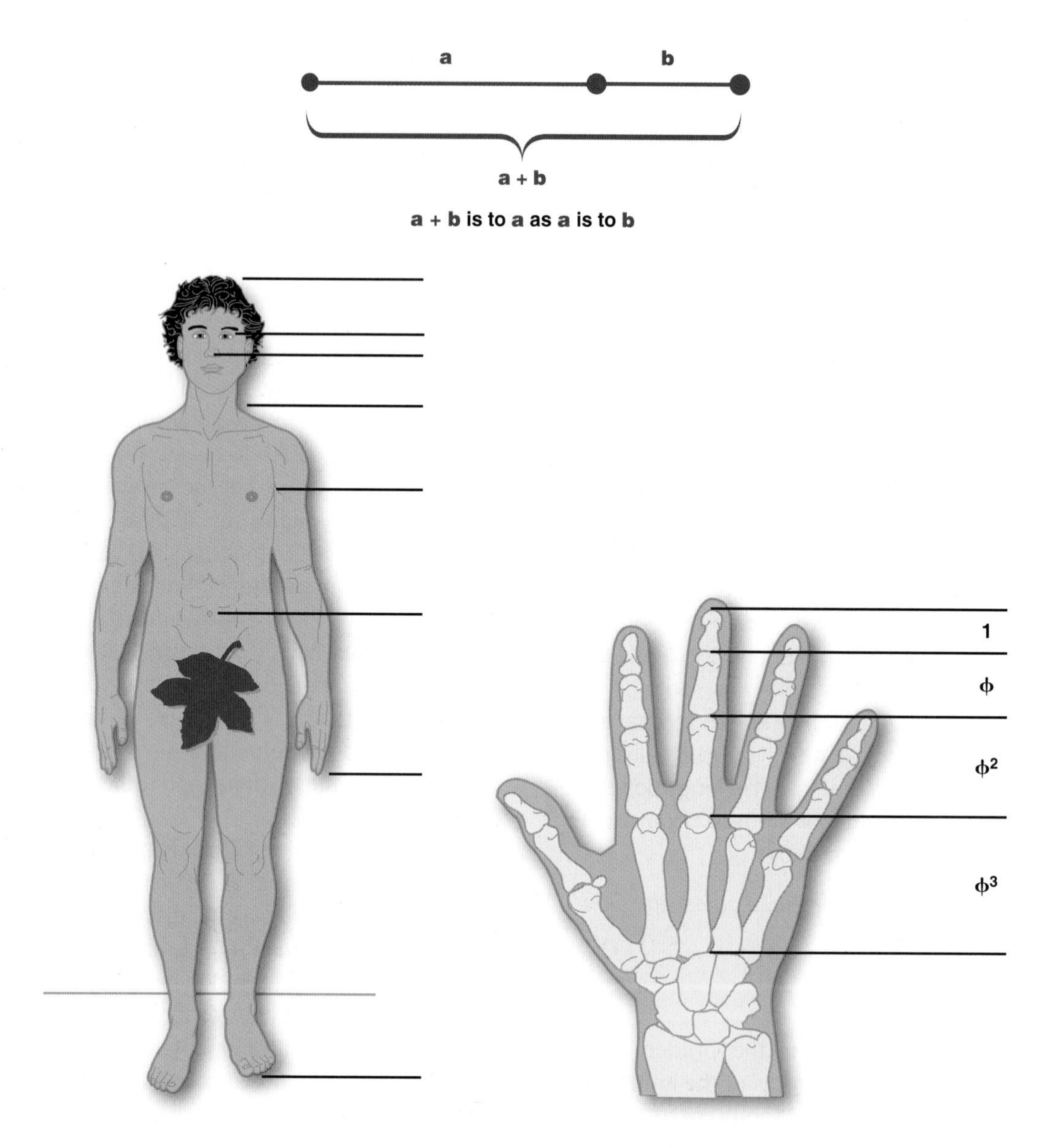

Figure 6.4 ■ *The Golden Ratio.*

seventeenth century A.D. when keyboard instruments like the harpsichord and piano were made. They found that compromises needed to be made to the strictly Pythagorean ratios if the pleasing sound was to be maintained. Therefore, the ratios were modified over the entire musical scale so that all notes sounded pleasing and so that the intervals between notes was constant. This modification was called tempering.

Pythagoras also came to many other conclusions concerning the relationship between math and life. He concluded that things were numbers and numbers were things. For example, Pythagoras believed that the number 10 was justice because the numbers 4, 3, 2, and 1 sum to 10 and can be arranged in a highly symmetric pattern according to relative areas, which implied, to him, the balance needed for justice.

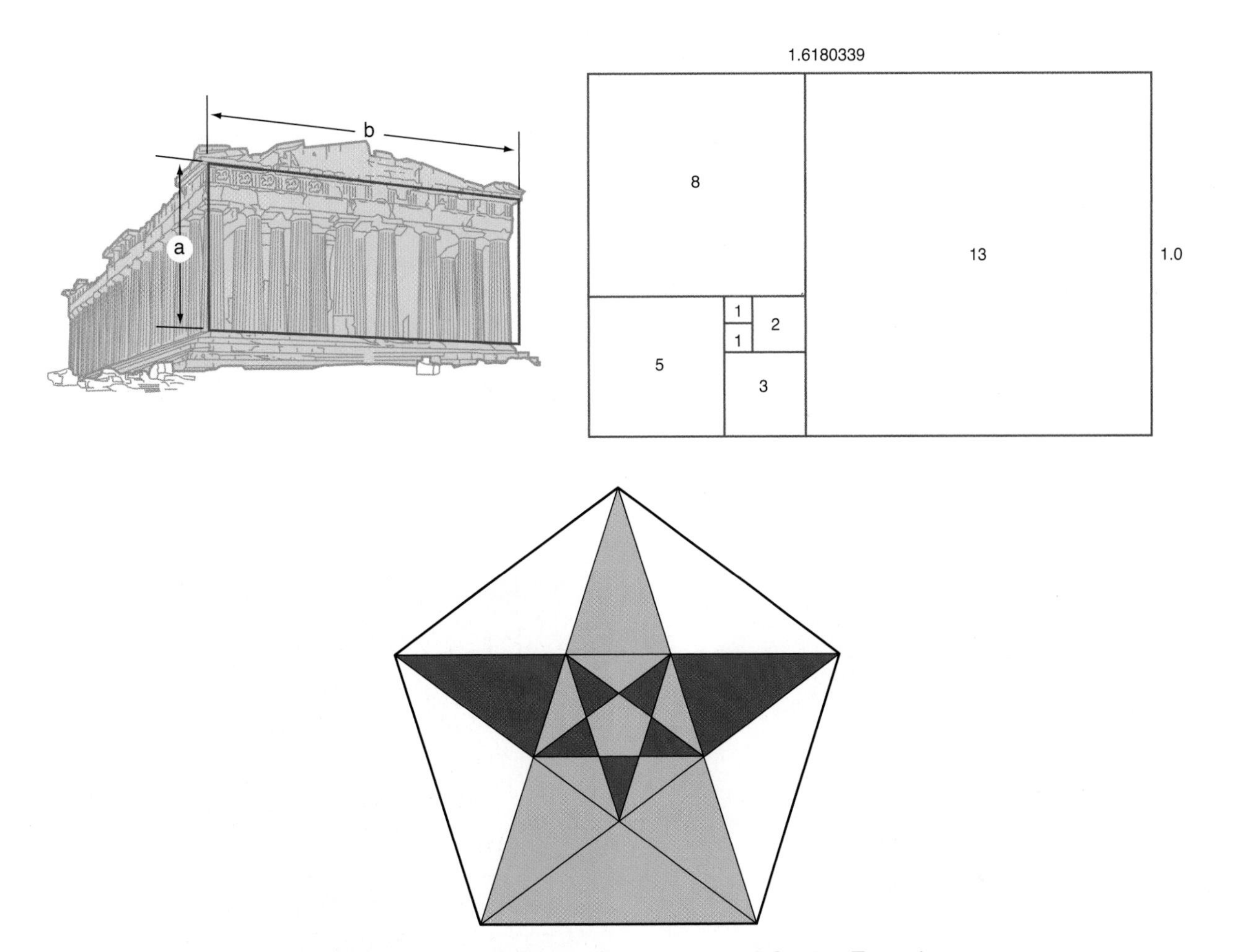

Figure 6.5 ■ *The Golden Rectangle and Golden Triangle.*

Pythagoras then went on to say that numbers must provide the basis for all natural systems, and applied his connection of math and music to health care. Pythagoras proposed that sickness occurred because of a "disharmony" in the bodily elements that caused the body to become "out of tune." He then claimed to be able to cure illness with his music, because music could restore or take way appetites, passions, pains, and afflictions.

There was one difficult problem that Pythagoras was unable to work out or even propose a theory on: Not all triangles have side ratios that are simple whole numbers. An example is the equilateral right triangle with integer length sides, that is, both sides are lengths such as 1 or 2 or 3. The hypotenuse of such a triangle cannot be given as a simple, whole number. Another example would be found in a triangle with sides equal to 1, resulting in a hypotenuse length equal to the square root of 2. The Pythagoreans found that the square root of 2 was not even a rational number (that is, it could not be expressed as the ratio of any two whole numbers). It therefore must be an irrational number. This had great and potentially dangerous consequences to people who believed that numbers are real and can be related to physical entities. This was frightening because they believed, as did Thales, that the human mind could understand all Nature; but if that were so, then Nature must be partly irrational and therefore unintelligible, hence, the paradox. This problem was so disconcerting to Pythagoras and

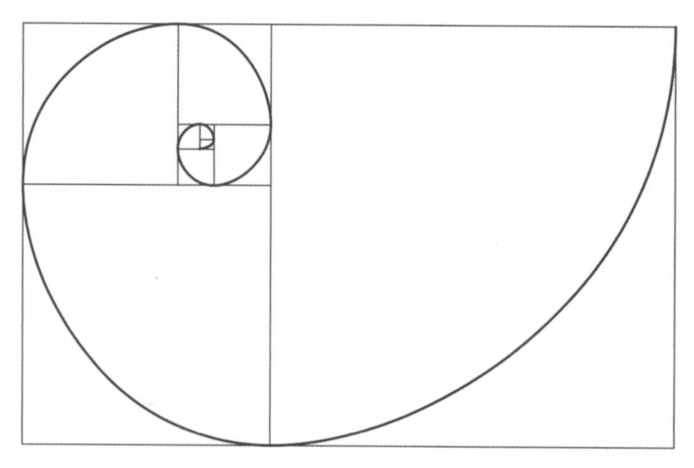

Figure 6.6 ■ *The Golden Spiral.*

Figure 6.7 ■ The Golden Spiral as seen in shells, flowers, ram's horns, and the Milky Way. *A) © 2005 PhotoDisc B) © 2006 JupiterImages Corporation C) © 2006 JupiterImages Corporation D) Corel.*

his closest followers that they called irrational numbers *arrhtos,* which means unspeakable. When one of Pythagoras' disciples eventually revealed the existence of irrational numbers, Pythagoras had him punished with death.

Questionable claims about the relationship between math and life made Pythagoras himself a divisive figure even in his own day. He had a loyal and dedicated school of followers who worked with him and believed like him that numbers were the underlying force of the world. Furthermore, for a certainty, many of Pythagoras' mathematical discoveries were not only correct, but amazing. Others, however, believed that not everything Pythagoras said was correct; and even more people were driven away from the man because of his extreme arrogance (which was legendary throughout Greece). However, 200 years later another great Greek mathematician, Euclid, would base much of his work on the foundation established by Pythagoras, and the text written by Euclid based on much of Pythagoras' work was used as a primary math text for nearly 2,000 years. Perhaps even more important was the adoption of Pythagorean thinking by Plato. But we shall talk more of that later in this book.

Modern people tend to ridicule Pythagoras' belief that all matter depends on numbers and that numbers dictate how matter must be arranged. However, modern quantum chemistry states that certain small whole numbers strictly describe the energy levels allowed for electrons and, therefore, determine the shapes of electron orbitals and, by extension, the shapes of molecules. We might want to rethink our too-easy dismissal of Pythagoras' fundamental concept of numbers.

Other important Greek thinkers followed in the search for fundamentals begun by Thales and then Pythagoras. A student of Thales, **Anaximander,** proposed that fire was the fundamental element. One of the most interesting of these scholars was **Heraclitus.** He said that the fundamental concept underlying everything was change. That is, only dynamic change is constant (if we can envision such a paradox). His famous statement was that "No one can step into the same river twice." This is obviously true in one sense, because the river has flowed between entries and is not, therefore, exactly the same river.

A rather troubling thinker of the early Greek period was Xeno. He reasoned that if we are facing a wall and want to move to the wall, we must go halfway to the wall before we can go the entire distance. (We would all agree that this is logical.) He then said that if we wanted to go just halfway to the wall, we would have to go half of that distance first, that is, cover one-fourth of the distance before going one-half. We would also have to go one-eighth before going one-fourth, and so on. By Xeno's reasoning, we would have to go one-half of any distance before we could move at all but that would be prevented because we would always have to go halfway first. Hence, according to Xeno, any movement was impossible. This is called Xeno's dilemma.

Xeno's dilemma was solved by **Democritus.** He said that as we examine matter at an ever smaller focus, we will eventually reach a point where we encounter a particle of matter that cannot be divided further. He called these smallest particles "atoms" which, in Greek, literally means "not divided." Therefore, at this atomic level, Xeno was wrong. You would eventually encounter a distance (the diameter of an atom) that cannot be divided and so you must go the entire way. At that level you would move all of it at once. That being done, you now have a way to move and Xeno's dilemma is overcome.

Democritus did not, of course, propose his atomic theory just to solve Xeno's dilemma—he believed that atoms were, in fact, the fundamental of Nature. While some later thinkers continued to accept the atomic concept of matter, some very important philosophers, especially Plato and Aristotle, disagreed and ridiculed the concept, even going so far as to burn Democritus' books. Therefore, atomic theory fell by the wayside for several decades. However, it was picked up again by a philosophical movement called the Epicureans and then, of course, was reinstated in the nineteenth century A.D. as part of the modern atomic theory.

The creativity of the early Greek scientists is truly astounding. They began a tradition that carried on for the rest of human history, especially gaining strength in our modern era. They also made some assertions that have proven to be amazingly accurate. Some have been ridiculed over time but, with greater scientific inquiry, have again been accepted. We still search for the fundamental stuff of the universe (quarks?, energy?) and still believe that human knowledge and investigation are capable of understanding everything. Some say that humans can learn all that knowledge by themselves. Others believe that humans have limitations in what they can discover, but with God's help, they are certainly capable of understanding everything. Whichever is your opinion, and it might be yet another, humans have been richly rewarded because some ancient Greeks began to think new kinds of creative thoughts.

Democracy

The beginning of democracy probably occurred about the year 620 B.C. when a tyrannical ruler (which means "one-man rule") of Athens, Draco, agreed to write and then post the laws of the city-state so that everyone could see them. The laws he established were viewed as very harsh because, among other things, the laws mandated that the state itself should seek out and execute a proven murderer rather than rely on the offended parties or their family members to seek revenge. (Even today, harsh laws are called "draconian" no matter what their particular subject might be.) By publicly posting the laws, Draco tacitly agreed to apply the same rules in every case he decided. In other words, he established the rule of law. From this time forward, Greek legal systems respected the written law and applied it evenly, at least within a particular class of people. By this respect for law, the Greek society gained a stability that allowed other creative innovations in government to occur.

The next step in government development in Greece was the change from rule by a single, hereditary ruler to a system in which land-holding families governed the city-state through a council that elected leaders who served at the pleasure of the families. The ruling council, called *Areopagus,* which in English means Council of Elders, was the basis for subsequent concepts of rule such as congresses and parliaments. A particular place in Athens was designated as the meeting location for the council. (In the Bible, when Paul visited Athens, he spoke on the Areopagus, which was a small mound at the foot of Mar's Hill. See Acts 17:19.)

A few years after Draco, the ruling families of Athens elected a man named **Solon,** who is known today as the Father of Democracy. He was asked to solve a critical problem in the city-state. The small farmers were losing money because of some adverse weather and market conditions, and their land was being purchased by the large landholders. This meant that the small farmers would no longer own land and, therefore, according to the then-existing laws of Athens, they would no longer be able to vote on the *Areopagus.* Solon was sympathetic to their worries. He wanted as many people as possible to vote in the elections, thus increasing his mandate and broadening the power base on which the city-state operated. Solon also realized that, because Athens depended so heavily on trade for its survival, the merchants in the city-state also deserved to participate in the ruling council, even though they did not generally own land. But, he noted, they did control significant wealth and were critical to the well-being of the city-state.

Solon, therefore, proposed a new system, in which four classes of citizens were recognized. The classes differed according to the amount of land they owned, but their wealth was also recognized. This system allowed the old families to retain some prestige, but also gave the new merchant class some rights of citizenship that they had never had before. (A similar system was set up in sixteenth-century Holland when the Dutch Republic was formed.) Solon also modified the legal system to allow some of the citizens to adjudicate the guilt or innocence of people brought before them. This was, of course, the beginnings of the jury system.

Solon made other reforms, such as establishing a strong currency system, during his fruitful years in leading Athens, which gave Athens a strong economic position in the Greek world. But his major contribution to history was to put in place the institutions and rules for democracy. With his innovations, the atmosphere in Athens was changed. People began to think of their city-state in a different way. They had power, and with that power came a freedom of thought and action. The climate for one of the greatest and most creative periods in history was laid. This was the legacy of Solon and the other great thinkers of the Formative Period. However, one other problem needed to be solved before Athens could really flourish. This problem was related to external politics. Greece was being threatened by invasion from the most powerful empire the world had known up to that time—the Persians, who we have already discussed in the chapter on Mesopotamia. It is to the confrontation of the Persians and the Greeks that we now direct our attention.

Persian Wars

Eventually the mighty Persian Empire took notice of Greece. Initially the Persians only conquered the Greek cities that had been established on the shores of western Asia (that is, in Ionia in present-day Turkey), and showed little interest in the Greek mainland. However, in 499 B.C. some of the conquered Greek cities, with help from Athens, revolted against their Persian masters. The Persians quickly crushed the small revolt and then turned their attention to the mainland Greeks to punish them for their interference. The Greeks, realizing their mistake in attracting the attention of mighty Persia, began preparations for a war that seemed unwinnable. Greece was still a loose collection of bickering city-states that were constantly hounded by barbarians. Persia was one of the greatest and most powerful empires the world had ever known. Greece was outnumbered and had inferior technology and strategy, and would soon be facing the best army in the world, led by the mighty King Darius.

Darius arrived with his army but, against all odds, the Greeks were victorious at the Battle of Marathon in 490 B.C., because the Greek battle tactics allowed them to encircle the Persians and attack from many sides. There were over 20,000 Persians in the army; about 6,000 died in the battle. The Greek forces numbered about 11,000 and only 192 Greeks died. (This is when the messenger ran the 26 miles from Marathon to Athens to tell the news of the battle. When he arrived at Athens, he shouted *"nike,"* which means "victory" and then collapsed and died.) Shocked and humiliated, Darius and the Persians withdrew and the Greeks had a short respite.

Ten years later Darius' son, Xerxes, returned with an even larger army (estimated to be 150,000 and 600 ships) to restore Persia's honor and force Greece into the Persian Empire. This time the strength of the Persian army was shown as they defeated the Spartans (Greece's most warlike city-state) at Thermopylae and then marched on and sacked the city of Athens as well. The Athenians, however, took to their ships and destroyed the Persian navy at the battle of Salamis (a strait near Athens).

A year later a unified Greek force defeated the Persian army (at Plataea) and forced the Persians to return home. In this battle and others a creative battle formation devised by the Greeks was instrumental in defeating the better-armed and more powerful Persians. This battle formation was the **phalanx,** which is pictured in Figure 6.8. In this formation the Greeks were arranged in a massed assembly that was about 20 rows wide and 20 rows long. Each heavily armored Greek soldier (called **hoplites**) had a shield and a very long (about 18 feet) spear. When the phalanx moved, the spears of the first few rows were lowered so that it became an impenetrable body. If they were attacked by chariots, the spears would kill or disable the horses. If they were attacked by infantry, the solid mass of men would withstand the attack and, as the front rows became disorganized during the attack, the rear rows lowered their spears and continued to move forward. If they were attacked by archers, they raised their shields to withstand the arrows. On relatively flat land, such as Plataea, the formation was devastating. It was one of the creative innovations of the Greeks that proved to be very effective. Some have postulated that the phalanx was successful, in part, because the Greek hoplites were disciplined enough to hold the formation, even during direct attack. Some have said that men who are individually responsible and yet are convinced of their strength as a unit are the most likely to achieve such success. The Greeks were such individually responsible men. (We will later see how the Romans improved on the Greek phalanx and, also, used the independence and initiative of individuals to bring about battlefield success.)

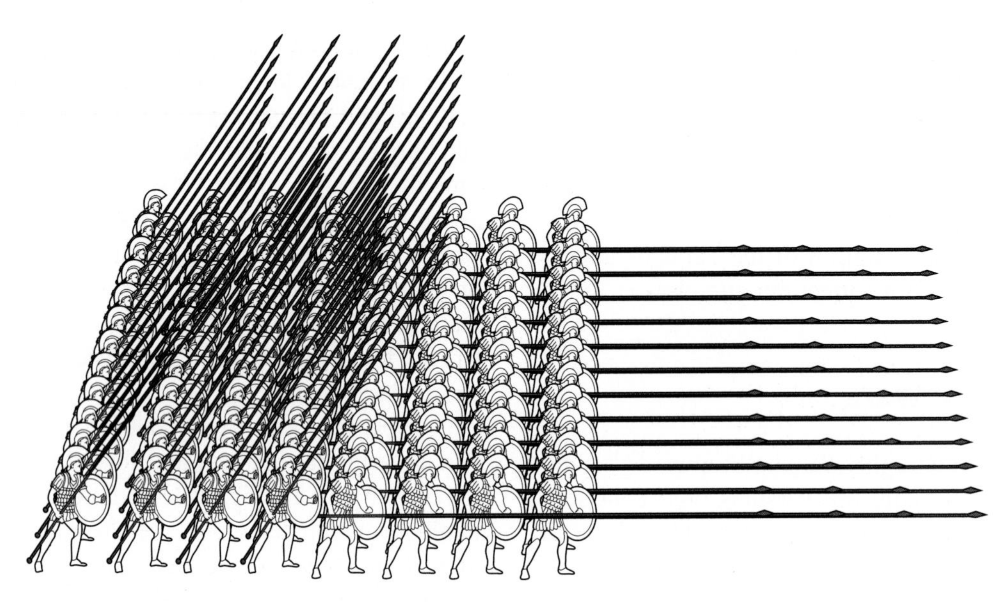

Figure 6.8 ■ *The Greek phalanx.*

After the Persians were defeated, they retreated to Asia Minor. The Greeks were able to re-establish their colonies on the islands of the Aegean Sea and in other parts of the Mediterranean. These colonies would prove to be of great benefit in financing the growth and beautification of Athens, the city-state that emerged as the greatest cultural center of the Greeks.

Finally, against their greatest threat ever, the Greeks had united. Even so, the victory over the Persians was almost incomprehensible; even the Greeks had believed the Persians undefeatable, yet somehow the Greeks had won. The victory over the Persians had renewed Greek confidence and displayed a new military might, paving the way for Greece's emergence from its Dark Age and marking the dawn of the Golden Age of Greece, when Greek ideas would explode onto the scene and would forever change the world.

Timeline—Important Dates

Date	Event
1000–800 B.C.	*Greek Dark Ages*
About 780 B.C.	*Homer dictates* Iliad *and* Odyssey
776 B.C.	*The Olympic games are initiated*
About 700 B.C.	*Hesiod writes* Theogony
625 B.C.	*Thales initiates scientific thought*
620 B.C.	*Draco establishes rule by law for a whole community*
594 B.C.	*Solon becomes the leader of Athens*
550 B.C.	*Aesop writes his fables*
About 500 B.C.	*Pythagoras promotes numbers as fundamentals*
490 B.C.	*The Battle of Marathon—Greeks defeat the Persians*
480 B.C.	*Spartans defeated by the Persians at Thermopylae*
479 B.C.	*Persians defeated and withdraw from mainland Greece*

Suggested Readings

Bakewell, Charles M., *Source Book in Ancient Philosophy,* Scribner, 1909.

Cardwell, Donald, *Technology,* Norton, 1995.

Gatti, Anne (retold), *Aesop's Fables,* Pavillion, 1992.

Hesiod, *Theogony,* Dorothea Wender (trans.), Penguin Classics, 1976.

Homer, *The Iliad,* Robert Fagles (trans.), Penguin Classics, 1990.

Homer, *The Odyssey,* Robert Fitzgerald (trans.), Anchor, 1963.

Van Doren, Charles, *The History of Knowledge,* Ballantine, 1991.

Article 6
Homer: Iliad

Introduction

On an average evening in the 9th Century BC in ancient Greece, a community would get together and listen to bards recant their tales of the Trojan War and other events about the Heroic Age of Greece (roughly in the 12th and 11th Centuries BC—several hundred years earlier). Many considered a blind poet named Homer to be the best of these tellers of tales. Legends say Homer could recite ten epic poems about that war and its aftermath; each one long enough to keep everyone awake late into the night. During the days of Homer, the Greek people developed their own written language—a unique and creative innovation that differed from other writing systems in some important ways. Instead of being a writing system of pictures (like Hieroglyphs of the Egyptians) or of just consonants (like the Semitic alphabets of the Hebrews and Phoenicians), the new Greek alphabet contained both vowels and consonants. This provided an alphabet that was truly able to represent the Greek language as it was spoken. And the Greeks began to use it profitably. One of the first uses was to write down the tales of the Heroic Age as told by Homer.

Homer's poems became a critical part of Greek culture; defining ethics and values. The characters in Homer's tales were heroic men and gods who had lived more than 200 years prior to the time of Homer. Their exploits were the legends of Greek people, much like King Arthur legends were for the English. The tales of Homer also involved the Greek gods. These gods were not the perfect beings of Hebrew and later Christian thinking, but represented a special race that was characterized by immortality and great power but also had moral weaknesses and human-like traits such as envy, lust, and anger. In essence, the tales of Homer and others writing about the gods and heroes became the foundation of Greek culture, especially its ethics and values. Greek children were taught the verses and were encouraged to live life looking for the glory and fame that the Homeric heroes died for. With memorization being as common as it was, the language Homer used, as recorded in his books, was accepted as the standard for Greek language. These stories of the first unification of Greece in a common goal became the source of Greek pride and unity for the rest of their history.

Three millennia after their creation, the two surviving Homeric epics, the *Iliad* and the *Odyssey,* are still commonly read and enjoyed. The selections from the *Iliad* presented here are classic examples of the "larger than life" style of epic poetry that makes it so entertaining even today. But these passages are truly remarkable from their treatment of emotions, such as Priam's pleading for the dead body of his son, and comparison of types of motivation between Achilles and Hector. Note how the warfare of the Trojans was similar to that of David and Goliath. Both events occurred about the same time, giving historical legitimacy to the stories of Troy and those of the Bible.

Book One: The Rage of Achilles

Rage—Goddess, sing the rage of Peleus' son Achilles, murderous, doomed, that cost the Achaeans countless losses, hurling down to the House of Death so many sturdy souls, great fighters' souls, but made their bodies carrion, feasts for the dogs and birds, and the will of Zeus was moving toward its end. Begin, Muse, when the two first broke and clashed, Agamemnon lord of men and brilliant Achilles.

What god drove them to fight with such a fury? Apollo the son of Zeus and Leto. Incensed at the king he swept a fatal plague through the army—men were dying and all because Agamemnon spurned Apollo's priest. Yes, Chryses approached the Achaeans' fast ships to win his daughter back, bringing a priceless ransom and bearing high in hand, wound on a golden staff, the wreaths of the god, the distant deadly Archer. He begged the whole Achaean army but most of all the two supreme commanders, Atreus' two sons, "Agamemnon, Menelaus—all Argives geared for war! May the gods who hold the halls of Olympus give you Priam's city to plunder, then safe passage home. Just set my daughter free, my dear one . . . here, accept these gifts, this ransom. Honor the god who strikes from worlds away—the son of Zeus, Apollo!"

And all ranks of Achaeans cried out their assent: "Respect the priest, accept the shining ransom!" But it brought no joy to the heart of Agamemnon. The king dismissed the priest with a brutal order ringing in his ears: "Never again, old man, let me catch sight of you by the hollow ships! Not loitering now, not slinking back tomorrow. The staff and the wreaths of god will never save you then. The girl—I won't give up the girl. Long before that, old age will overtake her in *my* house, in Argos, far from her fatherland, slaving back and forth at the loom, forced to share my bed! Now go, don't tempt my wrath—and you may depart alive."

The old man was terrified. He obeyed the order, turning, trailing away in silence down the shore where the battle lines of breakers crash and drag. And moving off to a safe distance, over and over the old priest prayed to the son of sleek-haired Leto, lord Apollo, "Hear me, Apollo! God of the silver bow who strides the walls of Chryse and Cilla sacrosanct—lord in power of Tenedos—Smintheus, god of the plague! If I ever roofed a shrine to please your heart, ever burned the long rich bones of bulls and goats on your holy altar, now, now bring my prayer to pass. Pay the Danaans back—your arrows for my tears!"

His prayer went up and Phoebus Apollo heard him. Down he strode from Olympus' peaks, storming at heart with his bow and hooded quiver slung across his shoulders. The arrows clanged at his back as the god quaked with rage, the god himself on the march and down he came like night. Over against the ships he dropped to a knee, let fly a shaft and a terrifying clash rang out from the great silver bow. First he went for the mules and circling dogs but then, launching a piercing shaft at the men themselves, he cut them down in droves—and the corpse-fires burned on, night and day, no end in sight.

Nine days the arrows of god swept through the army. On the tenth Achilles called all ranks to muster—the impulse seized him, sent by white-armed Hera grieving to see Achaean fighters drop and die. Once they'd gathered, crowding the meeting grounds, the swift runner Achilles rose and spoke among them: "Son of Atreus, now we are beaten back, I fear, the long campaign is lost. So home we sail . . .
if we can escape our death—if war and plague are joining forces now to crush the Argives.

But wait: let us question a holy man, a prophet,
even a man skilled with dreams—dreams as
well can come our way from Zeus—come,
someone to tell us why Apollo rages so,
whether he blames us for a vow we failed, or
sacrifice. If only the god would share the
smoky savor of lambs and full-grown goats, 90
Apollo might be willing, still, somehow, to save
us from this plague."

So he proposed
and down he sat again as Calchas rose among
them, Thestor's son, the clearest by far of all the
seers who scan the flight of birds. He knew all
things that are, all things that are past and all
that are to come, the seer who had led the
Argive ships to Troy with the second sight that
god Apollo gave him. For the armies' good the 100
seer began to speak: "Achilles, dear to Zeus . . .
you order me to explain Apollo's anger, the
distant deadly Archer? I will tell it all. But strike
a pact with me, swear you will defend me with
all your heart, with words and strength of hand.
For there is a man I will enrage—I see it now—
a powerful man who lords it over all the
Argives, one the Achaeans must obey . . .
A mighty king, raging against an inferior, is too
strong. Even if he can swallow down his wrath 110
today, still he will nurse the burning in his chest
until, sooner or later, he sends it bursting forth.
Consider it closely, Achilles. Will you save me?"

And the matchless runner reassured him:
"Courage! Out with it now, Calchas. Reveal
the will of god, whatever you may know. And I
swear by Apollo dear to Zeus, the power you
pray to, Calchas, when you reveal god's will to
the Argives—no one, not while I am alive and
see the light on earth, no one will lay his 120
heavy hands on you by the hollow ships. None
among all the armies. Not even if you mean
Agamemnon here who now claims to be, by
far, the best of the Achaeans."

The seer took heart
and this time he spoke out, bravely: "Beware—
he casts no blame for a vow we failed, a
sacrifice. The god's enraged because
Agamemnon spurned his priest, he refused to
free his daughter, he refused the ransom. That's 130
why the Archer sends us pains and he will send
us more and never drive this shameful
destruction from the Argives, not till we give
back the girl with sparkling eyes to her loving
father—no price, no ransom paid—and carry a
sacred hundred bulls to Chryse town. Then we
can calm the god, and only then appease him."

So he declared and sat down. But among
them rose the fighting son of Atreus, lord of
the far-flung kingdoms, Agamemnon—furious, 140
his dark heart filled to the brim, blazing with
anger now, his eyes like searing fire. With a
sudden, killing look he wheeled on Calchas
first: "Seer of misery! Never a word that works
to my advantage! Always misery warms your
heart, your prophecies—never a word of profit
said or brought to pass. Now, again, you divine
god's will for the armies, bruit it about, as fact,
why the deadly Archer multiplies our pains:
because I, I refused that glittering price for the 150
young girl Chryseis. Indeed, I prefer *her* by far,
the girl herself, I want her mine in my own
house! I rank her higher than Clytemnestra, my
wedded wife—she's nothing less in build or
breeding, in mind or works of hand. But I am
willing to give her back, even so, if that is best
for all. What I really want is to keep my people
safe, not see them dying. But fetch me another
prize, and straight off too, else I alone of the
Argives go without my honor. That would be a 160
disgrace. You are all witness, look—*my* prize is
snatched away!"

But the swift runner
Achilles answered him at once, "Just how,
Agamemnon, great field marshal . . . most
grasping man alive, how can the generous
Argives give you prizes now? I know of no
troves of treasure, piled, lying idle, anywhere.
Whatever we dragged from towns we
plundered, all's been portioned out. But collect 170

it, call it back from the rank and file? *That*
would be the disgrace. So return the girl to the
god, at least for now. We Achaeans will pay
you back, three, four times over, if Zeus will
grant us the gift, somehow, someday, to raze
Troy's massive ramparts to the ground."

But King Agamemnon countered, "Not so
quickly, brave as you are, godlike Achilles—
trying to cheat *me.* Oh no, you won't get past
me, take me in that way! What do you want? To 180
cling to your own prize while I sit calmly by—
empty-handed here? Is that why you order me to
give her back? No—if our generous Argives *will*
give me a prize, a match for my desires, equal to
what I've lost, well and good. But if they give
me nothing I will take a prize myself—your
own, or Ajax' or Odysseus' prize—I'll
commandeer her myself and let that man I go to
visit choke with rage! Enough. We'll deal with
all this later, in due time. Now come, we haul a 190
black ship down to the bright sea, gather a
decent number of oarsmen along her locks and
put aboard a sacrifice, and Chryseis herself, in
all her beauty . . .
we embark her too. Let one of the leading
captains take command. Ajax, Idomeneus,
trusty Odysseus or you, Achilles, you—the most
violent man alive—so you can perform the rites
for us and calm the god yourself."

A dark glance 200
and the headstrong runner answered him in
kind: "Shameless—armored in
shamelessness—always shrewd with greed!
How could any Argive soldier obey your
orders, freely and gladly do your sailing for
you or fight your enemies, full force? Not I,
no. It wasn't Trojan spearmen who brought me
here to fight. The Trojans never did *me*
damage, not in the least, they never stole my
cattle or my horses, never in Phthia where the 210
rich soil breeds strong men did they lay waste
my crops. How could they? Look at the endless
miles that lie between us . . . shadowy
mountain ranges, seas that surge and thunder.
No, you colossal, shameless—we all followed
you, to please you, to fight for you, to win your
honor back from the Trojans—Menelaus and
you, you dog-face! What do *you* care?
Nothing. You don't look right or left. And now
you threaten to strip me of my prize in 220
person—the one I fought for long and hard,
and sons of Achaea handed her to me.

My honors never equal yours,
whenever we sack some wealthy Trojan
stronghold—my arms bear the brunt of the
raw, savage fighting, true, but when it comes
to dividing up the plunder the lion's share is
yours, and back I go to my ships, clutching
some scrap, some pittance that I love, when I
have fought to exhaustion. 230

No more now—
back I go to Phthia. Better that way by far, to
journey home in the beaked ships of war. I have
no mind to linger here disgraced, brimming
your cup and piling up your plunder."

But the lord of men Agamemnon shot back,
"*Desert,* by all means—if the spirit drives you
home! I will never beg you to stay, not on *my*
account. Never—others will take my side and do
me honor, Zeus above all, whose wisdom rules 240
the world. You—I hate you most of all the
warlords loved by the gods. Always dear to your
heart, strife, yes, and battles, the bloody grind of
war. What if you are a great soldier? That's just a
gift of god. Go home with your ships and
comrades, lord it over your Myrmidons!

You *are* nothing to me—you and your
overweening anger! But let this be my warning
on your way: since Apollo insists on taking my
Chryseis, I'll send her back in my own ships with 250
my crew. But I, I will be there in person at your
tents to take Briseis in all her beauty, your own
prize—so you can learn just how much greater I
am than you and the next man up may shrink
from matching words with me, from hoping to
rival Agamemnon strength for strength!"

He broke off and anguish gripped
Achilles. The heart in his rugged chest was
pounding, torn . . . Should he draw the long
sharp sword slung at his hip, thrust through 260
the ranks and kill Agamemnon now?—or
check his rage and beat his fury down? As his
racing spirit veered back and forth, just as he
drew his huge blade from its sheath, down
from the vaulting heavens swept Athena, the
white-armed goddess Hera sped her down:
Hera loved both men and cared for both alike.
Rearing behind him Pallas seized his fiery
hair—only Achilles saw her, none of the other
fighters—struck with wonder he spun around, 270
he knew her at once, Pallas Athena! the
terrible blazing of those eyes, and his winged
words went flying: "Why, why now? Child of
Zeus with the shield of thunder, why come
now? To witness the outrage Agamemnon just
committed? I tell you this, and so help me it's
the truth—he'll soon pay for his arrogance
with his life!"

Her gray eyes clear, the goddess Athena
answered, "Down from the skies I come to 280
check your rage if only you will yield.
The white-armed goddess Hera sped me
down: she loves you both, she cares for
you both alike. Stop this fighting, now.
Don't lay hand to sword. Lash him with
threats of the price that he will face. And
I tell you this—and I *know* it is the
truth—one day glittering gifts will lie
before you, three times over to pay for
all his outrage. Hold back now. Obey us both." 290

So she urged
and the swift runner complied at once: "I
must—when the two of you hand down
commands, Goddess, a man submits though
his heart breaks with fury. Better for him by
far. If a man obeys the gods they're quick to
hear his prayers."

And with that
Achilles stayed his burly hand on the silver hilt
and slid the huge blade back in its sheath. He 300
would not fight the orders of Athena. Soaring
home to Olympus, she rejoined the gods aloft
in the halls of Zeus whose shield is thunder.

But Achilles rounded on Agamemnon
once again, lashing out at him, not relaxing his
anger for a moment: "Staggering drunk, with
your dog's eyes, your fawn's heart! Never once
did you arm with the troops and go to battle or
risk an ambush packed with Achaea's picked
men—you lack the courage, you can see death 310
coming. Safer by far, you find, to foray all
through camp, commandeering the prize of
any man who speaks against you. King who
devours his people! Worthless husks, the men
you rule—if not, Atrides, this outrage would
have been your last. I tell you this, and I swear
a mighty oath upon it . . . by this, this scepter,
look, that never again will put forth crown and
branches, now it's left its stump on the
mountain ridge forever, nor will it sprout new 320
green again, now the brazen ax has stripped its
bark and leaves, and now the sons of Achaea
pass it back and forth as they hand their
judgments down, upholding the honored
customs whenever Zeus commands—This
scepter will be the mighty force behind my
oath: someday, I swear, a yearning for Achilles
will strike Achaea's sons and all your armies!
But then, Atrides, harrowed as you will be,
nothing you do can save you—not when your 330
hordes of fighters drop and die, cut down by
the hands of man-killing Hector! Then—then
you will tear your heart out, desperate, raging
that you disgraced the best of the Achaeans!"

Down on the ground
he dashed the scepter studded bright with
golden nails, then took his seat again. The son
of Atreus smoldered, glaring across at him, but
Nestor rose between them, the man of winning
words, the clear speaker of Pylos . . . Sweeter 340
than honey from his tongue the voice flowed
on and on. Two generations of mortal men he
had seen go down by now, those who were

born and bred with him in the old days, in Pylos' holy realm, and now he ruled the third. He pleaded with both kings, with clear good will. "No more—or enormous sorrow comes to all Achaea! How they would exult, Priam and Priam's sons and all the Trojans. Oh they'd leap for joy to hear the two of you battling on 350 this way, you who excel us all, first in Achaean councils, first in the ways of war.

Stop. Please.

Listen to Nestor. You are both younger than I, and in my time I struck up with better men than you, even you, but never once did they make light of me. I've never seen such men, I never will again . . . men like Pirithous, Dryas, that fine captain, Caeneus and Exadius, and Polyphemus, royal prince, and Theseus, Aegeus' 360 boy, a match for the immortals. They were the strongest mortals ever bred on earth, the strongest, and they fought against the strongest too, shaggy Centaurs, wild brutes of the mountains—they hacked them down, terrible, deadly work. And I was in their ranks, fresh out of Pylos, far away from home—they enlisted me themselves and I fought on my own, a free lance, single-handed. And none of the men who walk the earth these days could battle with those 370 fighters, none, but they, they took to heart my counsels, marked my words. So now you listen too. Yielding is far better . . . Don't seize the girl, Agamemnon, powerful as you are—leave her, just as the sons of Achaea gave her, his prize from the very first. And you, Achilles, never hope to fight it out with your king, pitting force against his force: no one can match the honors dealt a king, you know, a sceptered king to whom great Zeus gives glory. Strong as you 380 are—a goddess was your mother—he has more power because he rules more men. Atrides, end your anger—look, it's Nestor! I beg you, cool your fury against Achilles. Here the man stands over all Achaea's armies, our rugged bulwark braced for shocks of war."

But King Agamemnon answered him in haste, "True, old man—all you say is fit and proper—but this soldier wants to tower over the armies, he wants to rule over all, to lord it 390 over all, give out orders to every man in sight. Well, there's one, I trust, who will never yield to him! What if the everlasting gods have made a spearman of him? Have they entitled him to hurl abuse at *me?*"

"Yes!"—blazing Achilles broke in quickly—"What a worthless, burnt-out coward I'd be called if I would submit to you and all your orders, whatever you blurt out. Fling them at others, don't give me commands! 400 Never again, *I* trust, will Achilles yield to *you.* And I tell you this—take it to heart, I warn you—my hands will never do battle for that girl, neither with you, King, nor any man alive. You Achaeans gave her, now you've snatched her back. But all the rest I possess beside my fast black ship—not one bit of it can you seize against my will, Atrides. Come, try it! So the men can see, that instant, your black blood gush and spurt around my spear!" 410

Once the two had fought it out with words, battling face-to-face, both sprang to their feet and broke up the muster beside the Argive squadrons. Achilles strode off to his trim ships and shelters, back to his friend Patroclus and their comrades. Agamemnon had a vessel hauled down to the sea, he picked out twenty oarsmen to man her locks, put aboard the cattle for sacrifice to the god and led Chryseis in all her beauty amidships. 420 Versatile Odysseus took the helm as captain.

All embarked,

the party launched out on the sea's foaming lanes while the son of Atreus told his troops to wash, to purify themselves from the filth of plague. They scoured it off, threw scourings in the surf and sacrificed to Apollo full-grown bulls and goats along the beaten shore of the fallow barren sea and savory smoke went swirling up the skies. 430

So the men were engaged throughout the camp. But King Agamemnon would not stop the quarrel, the first threat he hurled against Achilles. He called Talthybius and Eurybates briskly, his two heralds, ready, willing aides: "Go to Achilles' lodge. Take Briseis at once, his beauty Briseis by the hand and bring her here. But if he will not surrender her, I'll go myself, I'll seize her myself, with an army at my back—and all the worse for him!" 440

He sent them off with the strict order ringing in their ears. Against their will the two men made their way along the breaking surf of the barren salt sea and reached the Myrmidon shelters and their ships. They found him beside his lodge and black hull, seated grimly—and Achilles took no joy when he saw the two approaching. They were afraid, they held the king in awe and stood there, silent. Not a word to Achilles, not 450 a question. But he sensed it all in his heart, their fear, their charge, and broke the silence for them: "Welcome, couriers! Good heralds of Zeus and men, here, come closer. You have done nothing to me. You are not to blame. No one but Agamemnon—he is the one who sent you for Briseis. Go, Patroclus, Prince, bring out the girl and hand her to them so they can take her back. But let them both bear witness to my loss . . . in the face of blissful gods and 460 mortal men, in the face of that unbending, ruthless king—if the day should come when the armies need *me* to save their ranks from ignominious, stark defeat. The man is raving—with all the murderous fury in his heart. He lacks the sense to see a day behind, a day ahead, and safeguard the Achaeans battling by the ships."

Patroclus obeyed his great friend's command. He led Briseis in all her beauty 470 from the lodge and handed her over to the men to take away. And the two walked back along the Argive ships while she trailed on behind, reluctant, every step. But Achilles wept, and slipping away from his companions, far apart, sat down on the beach of the heaving gray sea and scanned the endless ocean. Reaching out his arms, again and again he prayed to his dear mother: "Mother! You gave me life, short as that life will be, so at least Olympian Zeus, 480 thundering up on high, should give me honor—but now he gives me nothing. Atreus' son Agamemnon, for all his far-flung kingdoms—the man disgraces me, seizes and keeps my prize, he tears her away himself!"

So he wept and prayed and his noble mother heard him, seated near her father, the Old Man of the Sea in the salt green depths. Suddenly up she rose from the churning surf like mist and settling down 490 beside him as he wept, stroked Achilles gently, whispering his name, "My child—why in tears? What sorrow has touched your heart? Tell me, please. Don't harbor it deep inside you. We must share it all."

And now from his depths the proud runner groaned: "You know, you know, why labor through it all? You know it all so well . . . We raided Thebe once, Eetion's sacred citadel, we ravaged the place, hauled all 500 the plunder here and the armies passed it round, share and share alike, and they chose the beauty Chryseis for Agamemnon. But soon her father, the holy priest of Apollo the distant deadly Archer, Chryses approached the fast trim ships of the Argives armed in bronze to win his daughter back, bringing a priceless ransom and bearing high in hand, wound on a golden staff, the wreaths of the god who strikes from worlds away. He begged the 510 whole Achaean army but most of all the two supreme commanders, Atreus' two sons, and all ranks of Achaeans cried out their assent, 'Respect the priest, accept the shining ransom!' But it brought no joy to the heart of Agamemnon, our high and mighty king dismissed the priest with a brutal order ringing in his ears. And shattered with anger, the old man withdrew but Apollo heard his prayer—he loved him, deeply—he loosed his shaft at 520 the Argives, withering plague, and now the troops began to drop and die in droves, the arrows of god went showering left and right, whipping through the Achaeans' vast encampment. But the old seer who knew the cause full well revealed the will of the archer god Apollo. And I was the first, mother, I urged them all, 'Appease the god at once!' That's when the fury gripped the son of Atreus. Agamemnon leapt to his feet and 530 hurled his threat—his threat's been driven home. One girl, Chryseis, the fiery-eyed Achaeans ferry out in a fast trim ship to Chryse Island, laden with presents for the god. The other girl, just now the heralds came and led her away from camp, Briseus' daughter, the prize the armies gave me. But you, mother, if you have any power at all, protect your son! Go to Olympus, plead with Zeus, if you ever warmed his heart with a word or any action . . . 540

Time and again I heard your claims in father's halls, boasting how you and you alone of all the immortals rescued Zeus, the lord of the dark storm cloud, from ignominious, stark defeat . . . That day the Olympians tried to chain him down, Hera, Poseidon lord of the sea, and Pallas Athena—you rushed to Zeus, dear Goddess, broke those chains, quickly ordered the hundred-hander to steep Olympus, that monster whom the immortals call 550 Briareus but every mortal calls the Sea-god's son, Aegaeon, though he's stronger than his father. Down he sat, flanking Cronus' son, gargantuan in the glory of it all, and the blessed gods were struck with terror then, they stopped shackling Zeus.

Remind him of that, now, go and sit beside him, grasp his knees . . . persuade him, somehow, to help the Trojan cause, to pin the Achaeans back against their 560 ships, trap them round the bay and mow them down. So all can reap the benefits of their king—so even mighty Atrides can see how mad he was to disgrace Achilles, the best of the Achaeans!"

And Thetis answered, bursting into tears, "O my son, my sorrow, why did I ever bear you? All I bore was doom . . . Would to god you could linger by your ships without a grief in the world, without a torment! Doomed to a 570 short life, you have so little time. And not only short, now, but filled with heartbreak too, more than all other men alive—doomed twice over. Ah to a cruel fate I bore you in our halls! Still, I shall go to Olympus crowned with snow and repeat your prayer to Zeus who loves the lightning. Perhaps he will be persuaded.

But you, my child, stay here by the fast ships, rage on at the Achaeans, just keep clear of every foray in the 580 fighting. Only yesterday Zeus went off to the Ocean River to feast with the Aethiopians, loyal, lordly men, and all the gods went with him. But in twelve days the Father returns to Olympus. Then, for your sake, up I go to the bronze floor, the royal house of Zeus—I'll grasp his knees, I think I'll win him over."

With that vow his mother went away and left him there, alone, his heart inflamed for the sashed and 590 lovely girl they'd wrenched away from him against his will. Meanwhile Odysseus drew in close to Chryse Island, bearing the splendid sacrifice in the vessel's hold. And once they had entered the harbor deep in bays they furled and stowed the sail in the black ship, they lowered the mast by the forestays, smoothly, quickly let it down on the forked mast-crutch and rowed her into a mooring under oars. Out went the bow-stones—cables 600

fast astern—and the crew themselves swung
out in the breaking surf, leading out the
sacrifice for the archer god Apollo, and out of
the deep-sea ship Chryseis stepped too. Then
tactful Odysseus led her up to the altar,
placing her in her loving father's arms, and
said, "Chryses, the lord of men Agamemnon
sent me here to bring your daughter back and
perform a sacrifice, a grand sacrifice to
Apollo—for all Achaea's sake—so we can 610
appease the god who's loosed such grief and
torment on the Argives."

With those words he left her in Chryses'
arms and the priest embraced the child he
loved, exultant. At once the men arranged the
sacrifice for Apollo, making the cattle ring his
well-built altar, then they rinsed their hands
and took up barley. Rising among them
Chryses stretched his arms to the sky and
prayed in a high resounding voice, "Hear me, 620
Apollo! God of the silver bow who strides the
walls of Chryse and Cilla sacrosanct—lord in
power of Tenedos! If you honored me last time
and heard my prayer and rained destruction
down on all Achaea's ranks, now bring my
prayer to pass once more. Now, at last, drive
this killing plague from the armies of Achaea!"

His prayer went up and Phoebus Apollo
heard him. And soon as the men had prayed
and flung the barley, first they lifted back the 630
heads of the victims, slit their throats, skinned
them and carved away the meat from the
thighbones and wrapped them in fat, a double
fold sliced clean and topped with strips of
flesh. And the old man burned these over dried
split wood and over the quarters poured out
glistening wine while young men at his side
held five-pronged forks. Once they had
burned the bones and tasted the organs they
cut the rest into pieces, pierced them with 640
spits, roasted them to a turn and pulled them
off the fire. The work done, the feast laid out,
they ate well and no man's hunger lacked a
share of the banquet. When they had put aside
desire for food and drink, the young men
brimmed the mixing bowls with wine and
tipping first drops for the god in every cup
they poured full rounds for all. And all day
long they appeased the god with song, raising
a ringing hymn to the distant archer god who 650
drives away the plague, those young Achaean
warriors singing out his power, and Apollo
listened, his great heart warm with joy.

Then when the sun went down and night
came on they made their beds and slept by the
stern-cables . . . When young Dawn with her
rose-red fingers shone once more, they set sail
for the main encampment of Achaea. The
Archer sent them a bracing following wind,
they stepped the mast, spread white sails wide, 660
the wind hit full and the canvas bellied out and
a dark blue wave, foaming up at the bow, sang
out loud and strong as the ship made way,
skimming the whitecaps, cutting toward her
goal. And once offshore of Achaea's vast
encampment they eased her in and hauled the
black ship high, far up on the sand, and shored
her up with timbers. Then they scattered, each
to his own ship and shelter.

But *he* raged on, grimly camped by his 670
fast fleet, the royal son of Peleus, the swift
runner Achilles. Now he no longer haunted the
meeting grounds where men win glory, now
he no longer went to war but day after day he
ground his heart out, waiting there, yearning,
always yearning for battle cries and combat.

But now as the twelfth dawn after this
shone clear the gods who live forever marched
home to Olympus, all in a long cortege, and
Zeus led them on. And Thetis did not forget 680
her son's appeals. She broke from a cresting
wave at first light and soaring up to the broad
sky and Mount Olympus, found the son of
Cronus gazing down on the world, peaks apart
from the other gods and seated high on the

topmost crown of rugged ridged Olympus. And crouching down at his feet, quickly grasping his knees with her left hand, her right hand holding him underneath the chin, she prayed to the lord god Zeus, the son of Cronus: "Zeus, Father Zeus! If I ever served you well among the deathless gods with a word or action, bring this prayer to pass: honor my son Achilles!— doomed to the shortest life of any man on earth. And now the lord of men Agamemnon has disgraced him, seizes and keeps his prize, tears her away himself. But you—exalt him, Olympian Zeus: your urgings rule the world! Come, grant the Trojans victory after victory till the Achaean armies pay my dear son back, building higher the honor he deserves!" 690 700

She paused but Zeus who commands the storm clouds answered nothing. The Father sat there, silent. It seemed an eternity . . . But Thetis, clasping his knees, held on, clinging, pressing her question once again: "Grant my prayer, once and for all, Father, bow your head in assent! Or deny me outright. What have *you* to fear? So I may know, too well, just how cruelly *I* am the most dishonored goddess of them all." 710

Filled with anger Zeus who marshals the storm clouds answered her at last: "Disaster. You will drive me into war with Hera. She will provoke me, she with her shrill abuse. Even now in the face of all the immortal gods she harries me perpetually, Hera charges *me* that I always go to battle for the Trojans. Away with you now. Hera might catch us here. I will see to this. I will bring it all to pass. Look, I will bow my head if that will satisfy you. That, I remind you, that among the immortal gods is the strongest, truest sign that I can give. No word or work of mine—nothing can be revoked, there is no treachery, nothing left unfinished once I bow my head to say it shall be done." 720

So he decreed. And Zeus the son of Cronus bowed his craggy dark brows and the deathless locks came pouring down from the thunderhead of the great immortal king and giant shock waves spread through all Olympus. 730

So the two of them made their pact and parted. Deep in the sea she dove from radiant Mount Olympus. Zeus went back to his own halls, and all the gods in full assembly rose from their seats at once to meet the Father striding toward them now. None dared remain at rest as Zeus advanced, they all sprang up to greet him face-to-face as he took his place before them on his throne. But Hera knew it all. She had seen how Thetis, the Old Man of the Sea's daughter, Thetis quick on her glistening feet was hatching plans with Zeus. And suddenly Hera taunted the Father, son of Cronus: "So, who of the gods this time, my treacherous one, was hatching plans with you? Always your pleasure, whenever my back is turned, to settle things in your grand clandestine way. You never deign, do you, freely and frankly, to share your plots with me—never, not a word!" 740 750

The father of men and gods replied sharply, "Hera—stop hoping to fathom all my thoughts. You will find them a trial, though you are my wife. Whatever is right for you to hear, no one, trust me, will know of it before you, neither god nor man. Whatever I choose to plan apart from all the gods—no more of your everlasting questions, probe and pry no more." 760

And Hera the Queen, her dark eyes wide, exclaimed, "Dread majesty, son of Cronus, what are you saying? Now surely I've never probed or pried in the past. Why, you can scheme to your heart's content without a qualm in the world for me. But now I have a terrible fear that she has won you over. Thetis, the Old Man of the Sea's daughter, Thetis with her glistening feet. I know it. Just at dawn she knelt down beside you and grasped your knees 770 and I suspect you bowed your head in assent to her—you granted once and for all to exalt Achilles now and slaughter hordes of Achaeans pinned against their ships."

And Zeus who marshals the thunderheads returned, "Maddening one . . . you and your eternal suspicions—I can never escape you. Ah but tell me, Hera, just what can you *do* about all this? Nothing. Only estrange yourself from me a little more—and all the worse for 780 you. If what you say is true, that must be my pleasure. Now go sit down. Be quiet now. Obey my orders, for fear the gods, however many Olympus holds, are powerless to protect you when I come to throttle you with my irresistible hands."

He subsided but Hera the Queen, her eyes wider, was terrified. She sat in silence. She wrenched her will to his. And throughout the halls of Zeus 790 the gods of heaven quaked with fear. Hephaestus the Master Craftsman rose up first to harangue them all, trying now to bring his loving mother a little comfort, the white-armed goddess Hera: "Oh disaster . . . that's what it is, and it will be unbearable if the two of you must come to blows this way, flinging the gods in chaos just for mortal men. No more joy for us in the sumptuous feast when riot rules the day. I urge you, mother—you know that I am 800 right—work back into his good graces, so the Father, our beloved Father will never wheel on us again, send our banquets crashing! The Olympian lord of lightning—what if he would like to blast us from our seats? He is far too strong. Go back to him, mother, stroke the Father with soft, winning words—at once the Olympian will turn kind to us again."

Pleading, springing up with a two-handled cup, he reached it toward his loving mother's 810 hands with his own winning words: "Patience, mother! Grieved as you are, bear up, or dear as you are, I have to see you beaten right before my eyes. I would be shattered—what could I do to save you? It's hard to fight the Olympian strength for strength. You remember the last time I rushed to your defense? He seized my foot, he hurled me off the tremendous threshold and all day long I dropped. I was dead weight and then, when the sun went 820 down, down I plunged on Lemnos, little breath left in me. But the mortals there soon nursed a fallen immortal back to life."

At that the white-armed goddess Hera smiled and smiling, took the cup from her child's hands. Then dipping sweet nectar up from the mixing bowl he poured it round to all the immortals, left to right. And uncontrollable laughter broke from the happy gods as they watched the god of fire breathing hard and 830 bustling through the halls.

That hour then and all day long till the sun went down they feasted and no god's hunger lacked a share of the handsome banquet or the gorgeous lyre Apollo struck or the Muses singing voice to voice in choirs, their vibrant music rising.

At last, when the sun's fiery light had set, each immortal went to rest in his own house, the splendid high halls Hephaestus built for 840 each with all his craft and cunning, the famous crippled Smith. And Olympian Zeus the lord of lightning went to his own bed where he had always lain when welcome sleep came on him. There he climbed and there he slept and by his side lay Hera the Queen, the goddess of the golden throne.

Book Seven: Ajax Duels with Hector

Vaunting, aflash in arms, Hector swept through the gates with his brother Paris keeping pace beside him. Both men bent on combat, on they fought like wind when a god

sends down some welcome blast to sailors
desperate for it, worked to death at the
polished oars, beating the heavy seas, their
arms slack with the labor—so welcome that
brace of men appeared to the Trojans
desperate for their captains. 10

Each one killed his man.
Paris took Menesthius, one who had lived in
Arne, a son of King Areithous lord of the
war-club and his lady Phylomedusa with large
lovely eyes. Hector slashed Eioneus' throat
with a sharp spear, ripped him under the
helmet's hammered bronze rim—his legs
collapsed in death.

Quick in the jolting onset
Lycia's captain Glaucus son of Hippolochus 20
skewered Dexius' son Iphinous just as he leapt
behind his fast mares—he stabbed his shoulder,
hard, and down from his car Iphinous crashed
to earth and his limbs went slack with death.

Rampaging Trojans!
Yes, but as soon as fiery-eyed Athena marked
them killing Argive ranks in this all-out
assault, down she rushed from the peaks of
Mount Olympus straight for sacred Troy. But
Phoebus Apollo spotting her from Pergamus 30
heights—the god grim set on victory for the
Trojans—rose to intercept her . . .
As the two came face-to-face beside the great
oak, lord Apollo the son of Zeus led off,
"What next?—what is the mighty Zeus's
daughter blazing after now? Down from
Olympus, what heroics stir your heart? No
doubt you'll hand your Argives victory soon,
you'll turn the tide of battle! You have no
mercy, none for dying Trojans. Come, listen to 40
me—my plan is so much better: let us halt the
war and the heat of combat now, at least for
today. They'll fight again tomorrow, until they
win their way to the fixed doom of Troy, since
that is your only passion—you two goddesses—
to plunder Troy to rubble."

Athena's eyes lit up
and the goddess said, "So be it, archer of the
sky! Those were my very thoughts, winging
down from Olympus into the midst of Trojans 50
and Achaeans. But tell me, how do you hope
to stop the men from fighting?"

"Hector!"—lord Apollo the son of Zeus
replied—"We'll spur his nerve and strength,
that breaker of horses, see if he'll challenge
one of the Argives man-to-man and they will
duel in bloody combat to the death. Achaeans
armed in bronze will thrill to his call, they'll
put up a man to battle shining Hector."

So Apollo staged the action. Her eyes 60
afire the goddess Pallas did not resist a
moment. She flashed the word in Helenus'
mantic spirit—the son of Priam sensed what
pleased the immortals hatching instant plans,
and coming up to Hector advised him quickly,
"Hector, son of Priam, a mastermind like
Zeus, listen to me now—let your brother guide
you. Have all Trojans and Argives take their
seats, and you, you challenge Achaea's bravest
man to duel in bloody combat to the death. It's 70
not the hour to meet your doom, not yet. I
heard a voice of the gods who live forever."

When Hector heard that challenge he
rejoiced and right in the no man's land along
his lines he strode, gripping his spear mid-haft,
staving men to a standstill while Agamemnon
seated his Argives geared for combat. And
Apollo lord of the silver bow and Queen
Athena, for all the world like carrion birds, like
vultures, slowly settled atop the broad towering 80
oak sacred to Zeus whose battle-shield is thunder, relishing those men. Wave on wave of
them settling, close ranks shuddering into a
dense, bristling glitter of shields and spears
and helmets—quick as a ripple the West Wind
suddenly risen shudders down the sea and the
deep sea swell goes dark beneath its force—
so settling waves of Trojan ranks and Achaeans

rippled down the plain . . . And Hector rose and spoke between both sides: "Hear me— Trojans, Achaeans geared for combat! I'll speak out what the heart inside me urges. Our oaths, our sworn truce—Zeus the son of Cronus throned in the clouds has brought them all to nothing and all the Father decrees is death for both sides at once. Until you Argives seize the well-built towers of Troy or you yourselves are crushed against your ships.

But now, seeing the best of all Achaeans fill your ranks, 100 let one whose nerve impels him to fight with me come striding from your lines, a lone champion pitted against Prince Hector. Here are the terms that I set forth—let Zeus look down, my witness! If that man takes my life with his sharp bronze blade, he will strip my gear and haul it back to his ships. But give my body to friends to carry home again, so Trojan men and Trojan women can do me honor with fitting rites of fire once I am dead. But if I kill 110 *him* and Apollo grants me glory, I'll strip his gear and haul it back to sacred Troy and hang it high on the deadly Archer's temple walls. But not his body: I'll hand it back to the decked ships, so the long-haired Achaeans can give him full rites and heap his barrow high by the broad Hellespont. And someday one will say, one of the men to come, steering his oar-swept ship across the wine-dark sea, 'There's the mound of a man who died in the old days, 120 one of the brave whom glorious Hector killed.' So they will say, someday, and my fame will never die."

A hushed silence went through all the Achaean ranks, ashamed to refuse, afraid to take his challenge . . . But at long last Menelaus leapt up and spoke, lashing out at them, groaning, heartsick: "Oh no—your threats, your bluster—women, not men of Achaea! What disgrace it will be—shame, 130 cringing shame if not one Danaan now steps up to battle Hector. You can all turn to earth 90 and water—rot away! Look at each of you, sitting there, lifeless, lust for glory gone. I'll harness up, I'll fight the man myself. The gods on high—*they* hold the ropes of victory in their hands!"

With that he began to don his handsome gear. And then and there, Menelaus, the death-stroke would have blazed before your eyes— 140 dead at the hands of Hector, a far stronger man—if Argive kings had not leapt up and caught you. And Atreus' son himself, powerful Agamemnon seized your right hand, shouting out your name: "You're mad, my Prince! No need for such an outburst—get a grip on yourself, distraught as you are. Just for the sake of rivalry, soldier's pride, don't rush to fight with a better man, with Hector the son of Priam. Many others shrink before him. Even Achilles 150 dreads to pit himself against him out on the battle lines where men win glory—Achilles, far and away a stronger man than you. Go back. Sit down with the comrades you command. We'll put up another champion to go against this Hector. Fearless, is he? and never sated with fighting? He'll gladly sink to a knee and rest, I'd say, if the man comes through alive from the fight he begs for, dueling to the death."

Again the iron warrior brought his brother 160 round—good counsel, fitting too. Menelaus yielded at once. His aides, elated, lifted the armor off his shoulders. And then lord Nestor rose and spoke among the men: "No more— or enormous sorrow comes to all Achaea! How he would groan at this, the old horseman Peleus, that fine speaker, the Myrmidons' famed commander. How he rejoiced that day, questioning me in his halls, when he learned the blood and birth of all the Argives. Now if 170 he heard how all cringe in the face of Hector, time and again he'd stretch his hands to the gods and pray that life breath would quit his limbs and sink to the House of Death.

Oh if only—
Father Zeus, Athena, Apollo—I were young
again! Fresh as the day we fought by
Celadon's rapids, our Pylians in platoons
against Arcadian spearmen under Phia's
ramparts, round the Iardanus' banks. When 180
Arcadia's champion Ereuthalion strode forth,
a man like a god for power, his shoulders
decked with King Areithous' armor, massive
Areithous . . . the Great War-club, so they
called that hulk, his men-at-arms and their
sashed and lovely women. He would never
fight with a bow or long spear, no, with his
giant iron club he'd break battalions open.
That monster—Lycurgus cut him down by
stealth, not force at all, on a footpath so 190
cramped his iron club was useless fending
off his death. There—before he could heft it—
a sudden lunge and Lycurgus' spear had run
him through the guts. Flat on his back he
went, slamming against the ground and his
killer stripped the armor brazen Ares gave
him. He donned it himself, for years of
grueling war, but then, when Lycurgus grew
too old in his halls, he passed it on to a
favorite henchman, Ereuthalion, and sporting 200
that gear he challenged all our best. And they,
they shook from head to foot, terrified, none
with the nerve to face him then. Only I—my
hardened courage drove me to fight the man
in a hot burst of daring, and I the youngest
trooper of us all . . . I took him on and
Athena gave me glory. By heaven, Ereuthalion
was the biggest, strongest man I ever killed,
the huge lumbering sprawl of him stretching
far and wide! Oh make me young again, and 210
the strength inside me steady as a rock! Hector
with that flashing helmet would meet his
match in combat in a moment. You, the bravest
of all Achaeans—and not one with the spine to
battle Hector face-to-face!"

The old man's taunts brought nine men to
their feet. First by far Agamemnon lord of
men sprang up and following him Tydides,
powerful Diomedes, next the Great and Little
Ajax armed in fury, Idomeneus after them and 220
Idomeneus' good aide, Meriones, a match for
the butcher god of war, Eurypylus after them,
Euaemon's gallant son, Thoas son of
Andraemon, Odysseus out for exploit: all were
roused to go up against Prince Hector. Once
more the fine old horseman gave commands:
"Now shake the lots for all, the first to the last
man—we'll see who wins. He's the one to do
his Achaean comrades proud, do himself
proud too, if he comes through alive from the 230
fight that waits him, dueling to the death."

And each soldier scratched his mark on a
stone and threw it into Atrides Agamemnon's
helmet. Fighters prayed. Stretching hands to
the gods a man would murmur, scanning the
wide sky, "Father Zeus, let Ajax win, or
Tydeus' son or the proud king himself of all
Mycenae's gold!"

So they prayed as the old horseman shook
the lots and one leapt from the helmet, the one 240
they wanted most—Great Ajax' lot it was. And
the herald took it round through all the ranks,
left to right for luck, and showed it to all
Achaea's bravest men. None of them knew it,
each denied the mark. But once he'd passed it
round and reached the man who had scratched
the stone and thrown it in the helmet—Ajax
bent on glory—out went his hand to take it,
the herald pausing beside him dropped it in
and Ajax knew his mark and thrilled to see it, 250
flung it down at his feet and shouted,
"Friends—the lot is mine and it fills my heart
with joy! I know I can overpower this dazzling
Hector. But come, while I strap my battle-
armor on, all of you pray to Cronus' son,
almighty Zeus. Pray to yourselves in silence,
so Trojans cannot hear—no, pray out loud! No
one at all to fear. No one can rout *me*—his
will against my will—not by force, god
knows, and not by a sly maneuver either. I'm 260
not such a raw recruit, I like to think, born and
bred on Salamis."

So Great Ajax vaunted
and men prayed to the son of Cronus, King
Zeus. They'd call out, scanning the wide sky,
"Father Zeus—ruling over us all from Ida, god
of greatness, glory! Now let Ajax take this
victory, shining triumph! But if you love
Hector, if you hold him dear, at least give both
men equal strength and glory." 270

So they prayed
as Ajax harnessed himself in burnished,
gleaming bronze and once he had strapped his
legs and chest in armor, out he marched like
the giant god of battle wading into the wars of
men when Zeus drives them hard to clash and
soldier on with heart-devouring hate. So giant
Ajax marched, that bulwark of the
Achaeans—a grim smile curling below his
dark shaggy brows, under his legs' power 280
taking immense strides, shaking his spear
high, its long shadow trailing. The men of
Argos exulted at the sight of him there but
terrible tremors shook each Trojan fighter's
knees—Hector himself, his heart pounding
against his ribs. But how could he shrink
before the enemy, slip back into a crowd of
cohorts now? He was the challenger, he with
his lust for battle. Ajax strode on, closing,
bearing his huge body-shield like a rampart, 290
heavy bronze over seven layers of oxhide.
Tychius made it for him, laboring long, the
finest leather-smith by far: over in Hyle
where the master had his home he crafted that
famous gleaming shield for Ajax, layering
seven welted hides of sturdy well-fed bulls
and hammered an eighth layer of bronze to
top it off. And now holding that great shield
before his chest Telamonian Ajax marched
right up to Hector, threatening with his deep 300
resounding voice, "Hector, now you'll learn,
once and for all, in combat man-to-man, what
kind of champions range the Argive ranks,
even besides Achilles, that lionheart who
mauls battalions wholesale. Off in his beaked
seagoing ships Achilles lies, raging away at
Agamemnon, marshal of armies—but here we
are, strong enough to engage *you,* and plenty
of us too. Come—lead off, if you can, with all
your fighting power!" 310

A flash of his helmet as rangy Hector
shook his head: "Ajax, royal son of Telamon,
captain of armies, don't toy with me like a
puny, weak-kneed boy or a woman never
trained in works of war! War—I know it well,
and the butchery of men. Well I know, shift to
the left, shift to the right my tough tanned
shield. That's what the real drill, defensive
fighting means to me. I know it all, how to
charge in the rush of plunging horses—I know 320
how to stand and fight to the finish, twist and
lunge in the War-god's deadly dance.

On guard!
Big and bluff as you are, I've no desire to hit
you sniping in on the sly—I'd strike you out in
the open, strike you now!"

He hurled—
his spear's long shadow flew and it struck
Ajax' shield, that awesome seven-layered
buckler, right on the eighth, the outside layer 330
of bronze that topped it off, through six hides
it tore but the seventh stopped the relentless
brazen point.

But Great Ajax next—
dear to the gods he hurled and his spear's
shadow flew and the shaft hit Hector's round
shield, hit full center—straight through the
gleaming hide the heavy weapon drove,
ripping down and in through the breastplate
finely worked, tearing the war-shirt, close by 340
Hector's flank it jabbed but the Trojan swerved
aside and dodged black death. Both seized
their lances, wrenched them from the shields
and went for each other now like lions rending
flesh or a pair of wild boars whose power
never flags. Hector stabbed at the buckler, full
center too, not smashing through, the brazen
point bent back—and Ajax lunged at him,
thrusting hard at his shield and the shaft

punched through, rammed him back in his fury and grazed his neck and the dark blood gushed forth. But not even then did Hector quit the battle . . . backing, helmet flashing, his strong hand hefting a rock from the field, dark, jagged, a ton weight—he hurled it at Ajax, struck the gigantic shield, seven oxhides thick, struck right on the jutting boss and the bronze clanged, echoing round and round as Ajax hoisting a boulder—far larger—wheeled and heaved it, putting his weight behind it, tremendous force—and the rock crashed home, Hector's shield burst in, hit by a millstone—and Hector's fine knees buckled, flat on his back he went, his shield crushing down on him swept him off his feet. But Apollo quickly pulled him up—and now they'd have closed with swords, hacked each other if heralds of Zeus and men had not come rushing in, one from the Trojans, one from the armed Achaeans, Talthybius and Idaeus, both with good clear heads. Parting them, holding their staffs between both men, the herald Idaeus, cool, skilled in tactics, urged, "No more, my sons—don't kill yourselves in combat! Zeus who marshals the storm cloud loves you both. You're both great fighters—we all know that full well. The night comes on at last. Best to yield to night."

But the giant Ajax answered briskly, "Wait, Idaeus, tell Hector here to call the truce. Mad for a fight, he challenged all our bravest. Let him lead off. I'll take his lead, you'll see."

His helmet flashed as Hector nodded: "Yes, Ajax, since god has given you power, build and sense and you are the strongest spearman of Achaea, let us break off this dueling to the death, at least for today. We'll fight again tomorrow, until some fatal power decides between our armies, handing victory down to one side or another. Look, the night comes at last. Best to yield to night. So you will bring some joy to Achaea's forces camped beside their ships, and most of all to your own troops, the comrades you command. But I'll go back to the great city of King Priam and bring some joy to the men of Troy and Trojan women trailing their long robes. Thankful for my return they'll go to meet the gods and sing their praises.

Come, let us give each other gifts, unforgettable gifts, so any man may say, Trojan soldier or Argive, 'First they fought with heart-devouring hatred, then they parted, bound by pacts of friendship.'"

With that he gave him his silver-studded sword, slung in its sheath on a supple, well-cut sword-strap, and Ajax gave his war-belt, glistening purple. So both men parted, Ajax back to Achaea's armies, Hector back to his thronging Trojans—overjoyed to see him still alive, unharmed, striding back, free of the rage and hands of Ajax still unconquered. They escorted him home to Troy—saved, past all their hopes—while far across the field the Achaean men-at-arms escorted Ajax, thrilled with victory, back to Agamemnon.

Soon as they had gathered within the warlord's tents he sacrificed an ox in their midst, a full-grown ox, five years old, to the towering son of Cronus, Zeus. They skinned the animal quickly, butchered the carcass, expertly cut the meat into pieces, pierced them with spits, roasted them to a turn and pulled them off the fire. The work done, the feast laid out, they ate well and no man's hunger lacked a share of the banquet. But the lord of far-flung kingdoms, hero Agamemnon, honored giant Telamonian Ajax first and last with the long savory cuts that line the backbone. And when they had put aside desire for food and drink the old man began to weave his counsel among them: Nestor was first to speak—from the early days his plans and tactics always seemed the best. With good will to the lords he rose and spoke: "King Agamemnon, chief of all the Argives—how many long-haired Achaeans lie here dead! And now Ares the slashing god of war has swirled their dark blood in Scamander's deep clear stream and their souls have drifted down to the House of Death. So at dawn you must call a halt to fighting by Achaeans, form your units, bring on wagons, gather up the dead and wheel the corpses back with mules and oxen. Then, at a decent distance from the ships, we burn the bodies, so every soldier here can carry back the bones to a dead man's sons when he sails home again. And let us heap a single great barrow over the pyre, one great communal grave stretched out across the plain and fronting it throw up looming ramparts quickly, a landward wall for ships and troops themselves. And amidst the wall build gateways fitted strong to open a clear path for driving chariots through. And just outside the wall we must dig a trench, a deep ditch in a broad sweeping ring to block their horse and men and break their charge—then these headlong Trojans can never rush our armies."

So he advised. All the warlords sounded their assent. And now the Trojans collected high on the crest of Troy. They were shaken, distracted men at Priam's gates but the clearheaded Antenor opened up among them: "Hear me, Trojans, Dardans, all our loyal allies, I must speak out what the heart inside me urges. On with it—give Argive Helen and all her treasures back to Atreus' sons to take away at last. We broke our sworn truce. We fight as outlaws. True, and what profit for us in the long run? Nothing—unless we do exactly as I say."

So he pressed the point, then took his seat. But among them stood magnificent Paris now, fair-haired Helen's lord, and he came back with a winging burst in answer: "Stop, Antenor! No more of your hot insistence—it repels me. You must have something better than this to say. But if you are serious, speaking from the heart, the gods themselves have blotted out your senses. Now *I* say this to our stallion-breaking Trojans, I say *No,* straight out—I won't give up the woman! But those treasures I once hauled home from Argos, I'll return them all and add from my own stores."

With that concession the prince sat down again. Then Priam the son of Dardanus rose among them, a man who could match the gods for strong advice, and with good will toward all he swayed his people: "Hear me, Trojans, Dardans, all our loyal allies—*I* must speak out what the heart inside me urges. Now take your evening meal throughout the city, just as you always have, and stand your watches, each man wide awake. And then, at first light, let the herald Idaeus go to the beaked ships and tell the Atridae, Agamemnon and Menelaus, the offer of Paris who caused our long hard campaign. Let Idaeus add this too, a good sound proposal: see if they are willing to halt the brutal war until we can burn the bodies of our dead. We'll fight again tomorrow . . . until some fatal power decides between us both, handing victory down to our side—or the other."

His people hung on his words and all obeyed the king. They took their meal by ranks throughout the army. At first light Idaeus went to the beaked ships and out on the meeting grounds he found the Argives, veterans close by the stern of Agamemnon's ship. Taking his stand, right in the milling troops, the herald called out in a high, firm voice, "Son of Atreus! Captains of all Achaeans! Priam and noble Trojans command me to report, if it proves acceptable, pleasing to one and all, the offer of Paris who caused our long hard campaign. All the treasures that filled his hollow ships and the prince hauled home to Troy—would to god he'd drowned before that day!—he'll return them all and add from his own stores. But the lawful wife of

Menelaus, renowned Menelaus, he will not give her up, Paris makes that clear, though all Troy commands him to do precisely that. They tell me to add this too, a good sound proposal: if you are willing, come, we'll halt the brutal war until we can burn the bodies of our dead. We'll fight again tomorrow—until some fatal power decides between us both, handing victory down to one side or the other."

So he spoke and a hushed silence went through all the ranks. Finally Diomedes lord of the war cry shouted out, "No one touch the treasures of Paris, Helen either! It's obvious—any fool can see it. Now, at last, the neck of Troy's in the noose—her doom is sealed."

All the Achaean soldiers roared out their assent, stirred by the stallion-breaking lord's reply, and King Agamemnon rounded on Idaeus: "There, there's the Achaeans' answer, Idaeus—a declaration—you can hear for yourself. It is my pleasure too. But about the dead, I'd never grudge their burning. No holding back for the bodies of the fallen: once they are gone, let fire soothe them quickly. That is my sworn pledge. Zeus my witness now. Hera's lord whose thunder drums the sky!"

With that oath he raised his scepter high in the eyes of all the gods and Idaeus turned, trailing back to sacred Troy. There they sat in assembly, Trojans, Dardans, all collected together, waiting long and tense for the herald to return. And home Idaeus came, delivered his message standing in their midst and they fell to making hurried preparations, dividing the labors quickly—two detachments, one to gather the bodies, one the timber. And far on the other side Achaean troops came streaming out of the well-benched ships, some to gather the bodies, some the timber.

Just as the sun began to strike the plowlands, rising out of the deep calm flow of the Ocean River to climb the vaulting sky, the opposing armies met. And hard as it was to recognize each man, each body, with clear water they washed the clotted blood away and lifted them onto wagons, weeping warm tears. Priam forbade his people to wail aloud. In silence they piled the corpses on the pyre, their hearts breaking, burned them down to ash and returned to sacred Troy. And just so on the other side Achaean men-at-arms piled the corpses on the pyre, their hearts breaking, burned them down to ash and returned to the hollow ships.

Then with the daybreak not quite risen into dawn, the night and day still deadlocked, round the pyre a work brigade of picked Achaeans grouped. They heaped a single great barrow over the corpse-fire, one great communal grave stretched out across the plain and fronting it threw up looming ramparts quickly, a landward wall for ships and troops themselves, and amidst the wall built gateways fitted strong to open a clear path for driving chariots through. And against the fortress, just outside the wall, the men dug an enormous trench, broad and deep, and drove sharp stakes to guard it.

So they labored, the long-haired Achaeans, while the gods aloft, seated at ease beside the lord of lightning, Zeus, gazed down on the grand work of Argives armed in bronze. Poseidon the god whose breakers shake the land began, "Father Zeus, is there a man on the whole wide earth who still informs the gods of all his plans, his schemes? Don't you see? Look there—the long-haired Achaeans have flung that rampart up against their ships, around it they have dug an enormous deep trench and never offered the gods a hundred splendid bulls, but its fame will spread as far as the light of dawn! And men will forget those ramparts I and Apollo reared for Troy in the old days—for the hero Laomedon—we broke our backs with labor." 610

But filled with anger, Zeus who marshals the thunderheads let loose now: "Unbelievable! God of the earthquake, you with your massive power, why are you moaning so? Another god might fear their wall—their idle whim—one far weaker than you in strength of hand and fury. Your *own* fame goes spreading far as the light of dawn. Come now, just wait till these long-haired Achaeans 620 sail back in their ships to the fatherland they love, then batter their wall, sweep it into the salt breakers and pile over the endless beach your drifts of sand again, level it to your heart's content—the Argives' mighty wall."

So they conferred together, building their resolve. The sun went down. The Argives' work was finished. They slew oxen beside the tents and took their meal. And the ships pulled in from Lemnos bringing wine, a big convoy 630 sent across by Euneus, Jason's son whom Hypsipyle bore the seasoned lord of armies. An outright gift to Atrides Agamemnon and Menelaus. Euneus gave a shipment of wine, a thousand measures full. From the rest Achaean soldiers bought their rations, some with bronze and some with gleaming iron, some with hides, some with whole live cattle, some with slaves, and they made a handsome feast. Then all that night the long-haired Achaeans 640 feasted as Trojans and Trojan allies took their meal in Troy. Yes, but all night long the Master Strategist Zeus plotted fresh disaster for both opposing armies—his thunder striking terror—and blanching panic swept across the ranks. They flung wine from their cups and wet the earth and no fighter would dare drink until he'd poured an offering out to the overwhelming son of Cronus. Then down they lay at last and took the gift of sleep. 650

Book 16: Patroclus Fights and Dies

And then and there the Achaeans might have taken Troy, her towering gates toppling under Patroclus' power heading the vanguard, storming on with his spear. But Apollo took his stand on the massive rampart, his mind blazing with death for him but help for Troy. Three times Patroclus charged the jut of the high wall, three times Apollo battered the man and hurled him back, the god's immortal hands beating down on the gleaming shield. Then at 10 Patroclus' fourth assault like something superhuman, the god shrieked down his winging words of terror: "Back—Patroclus, Prince, go back! It is not the will of fate that the proud Trojans' citadel fall before your spear, not even before Achilles—far greater man than you!"

And Patroclus gave ground, backing a good way off, clear of the deadly Archer's wrath.

But now Hector, reining his high-strung team at the Scaean 20 Gates, debated a moment, waiting . . . should he drive back to the rout and soldier on? Or call his armies now to rally within the ramparts? As he turned things over, Apollo stood beside him, taking the shape of that lusty rugged fighter Asius, an uncle of stallion-breaking Hector, a blood brother of Hecuba, son of Dymas who lived in Phrygia near Sangarius' rapids. Like him, Apollo the son of Zeus incited Hector: "Hector, why stop fighting? Neglecting your 30 duty! If only I outfought *you* as you can outfight *me,* I'd soon teach you to shirk your work in war—you'd pay the price, I swear. Up with you—fast! Lash those pounding stallions straight at Patroclus—you might kill him still—Apollo might give you glory!"

And back Apollo strode, a god in the wars of men while glorious Hector ordered skilled Cebriones, "Flog the team to battle!" Apollo

pressed on, wading into the ruck, hurling 40
Argives back in chaos and handing glory to
Hector and all the Trojan forces. But Hector
ignored the Argive masses, killing none, he
lashed his pounding stallions straight at
Patroclus. Patroclus, over against him, leapt
down from his car and hit the ground, his left
hand shaking a spear and seized with his right
a jagged, glittering stone his hand could just
cover—Patroclus flung it hard, leaning into the
heave, not backing away from Hector, no, and 50
no wasted shot. But he hit his driver—a
bastard son of famed King Priam. Cebriones
yanking the reins back taut—right between the
eyes. The sharp stone crushed both brows, the
skull caved in and both eyes burst from their
sockets, dropping down in the dust before his
feet as the reinsman vaulted, plunging off his
well-wrought car like a diver—Cebriones' life
breath left his bones behind and you taunted
his corpse, Patroclus O my rider: "Look what 60
a springy man, a nimble, flashy tumbler! Just
think what he'd do at sea where the fish
swarm—why, the man could glut a fleet,
diving for oysters! Plunging overboard, even
in choppy, heaving seas, just as he dives to
ground from his war-car now. Even these
Trojans have their tumblers—what a leap!"

And he leapt himself at the fighting driver's
corpse with the rushing lunge of a lion struck in
the chest as he lays waste pens of cattle—his 70
own lordly courage about to be his death. So
you sprang at Cebriones, full fury, Patroclus, as
Hector sprang down from his chariot just across
and the two went tussling over the corpse as
lions up on the mountain ridges over a fresh-
killed stag—both ravenous, proud and
savage—fight it out to the death. So over the
driver here and both claw-mad for battle,
Patroclus son of Menoetius, Hector ablaze for
glory strained to slash each other with ruthless 80
bronze. Hector seized the corpse's head, would
not let go—Patroclus clung to a foot and other
fighters clashed, Trojans, Argives, all in a
grueling, maiming onset.

As the East and South Winds fight in
killer-squalls deep in a mountain valley
thrashing stands of timber, oak and ash and
cornel with bark stretched taut and hard and
they whip their long sharp branches against
each other, a deafening roar goes up, the 90
splintered timber crashing—so Achaeans and
Trojans crashed, hacking into each other, and
neither side now had a thought of flight that
would have meant disaster. Showers of
whetted spears stuck fast around Cebriones,
bristling winged arrows whipped from the
bowstrings, huge rocks by the salvo battering
shields on shields as they struggled round the
corpse. And there he lay in the whirling dust,
overpowered in all his power and wiped from 100
memory all his horseman's skills.

So till the sun bestrode the sky at high
noon the weapons hurtled side-to-side and
men kept falling. But once the sun wheeled
past the hour for unyoking oxen, then the
Argives mounted a fiercer new attack, fighting
beyond their fates . . . They dragged the hero
Cebriones out from under the pelting shafts
and Trojans' piercing cries and they tore the
handsome war-gear off his back and Patroclus 110
charged the enemy, fired for the kill. Three
times he charged with the headlong speed of
Ares, screaming his savage cry, three times he
killed nine men. Then at the fourth assault
Patroclus like something superhuman—then,
Patroclus, the end of life came blazing up
before you, yes, the lord Apollo met you there
in the heart of battle, the god, the terror!
Patroclus never saw him coming, moving
across the deadly rout, shrouded in thick mist 120
and on he came against him and looming up
behind him now—slammed his broad
shoulders and back with the god's flat hand
and his eyes spun as Apollo knocked the
helmet off his head and under his horses' hoofs
it tumbled, clattering on with its four forged
horns and its hollow blank eyes and its plumes
were all smeared in the bloody dust. Forbidden
before this to defile its crest in dust, it guarded

the head and handsome brow of a god, a man
like a god, Achilles. But now the Father gave it
over to Hector to guard his head in war since
Hector's death was closing on him quickly.
Patroclus though—the spear in his grip was
shattered, the whole of its rugged bronze-shod
shadow-casting length and his shield with
straps and tassels dropped from his shoulders,
flung down on the ground—and lord Apollo
the son of Zeus wrenched his breastplate off.
Disaster seized him—his fine legs buckling— 140
he stood there, senseless—

And now,
right at his back, close-up, a Dardan fighter
speared him squarely between the shoulder
blades with a sharp lance. Panthous' son
Euphorbus, the best of his own age at spears
and a horseman's skill and speed of foot, and
even in this, his first attack in chariots—just
learning the arts of war—he'd brought down
twenty drivers off their cars. He was the first to 150
launch a spear against you, Patroclus O my
rider, but did not bring you down. Yanking out
his ashen shaft from your body, back he dashed
and lost himself in the crowds—the man would
not stand up to Patroclus here in mortal combat,
stripped, defenseless as he was. Patroclus
stunned by the spear and the god's crushing
blow was weaving back to his own thronging
comrades, trying to escape death . . .

Hector waiting, watching 160
the greathearted Patroclus trying to stagger free,
seeing him wounded there with the sharp bronze
came rushing into him right across the lines and
rammed his spearshaft home, stabbing deep in
the bowels, and the brazen point went jutting
straight out through Patroclus' back. Down he
crashed—horror gripped the Achaean armies.
As when some lion overpowers a tireless wild
boar up on a mountain summit, battling in all
their fury over a little spring of water, both 170
beasts craving to slake their thirst, but the lion
beats him down with sheer brute force as the
boar fights for breath—

130 so now with a close thrust Hector the son of
Priam tore the life from the fighting son of
Menoetius, from Patroclus who had killed so
many men in war, and gloried over him, wild
winging words: "Patroclus—surely you must
have thought you'd storm my city down, you'd
wrest from the wives of Troy their day of 180
freedom, drag them off in ships to your own
dear fatherland—you fool! Rearing in their
defense my war-team, Hector's horses were
charging out to battle, galloping, full stretch.
And I with my spear, Hector, shining among my
combat-loving comrades, I fight away from
them the fatal day—but you, the vultures will
eat your body raw!

Poor, doomed . . .
not for all his power could Achilles save you 190
now—and how he must have filled your ears
with orders as you went marching out and the
hero stayed behind; 'Now don't come back to
the hollow ships, you hear?—: Patroclus,
master horseman—not till you've slashed the
shirt around his chest and soaked it red in the
blood of man-killing Hector!' So he must have
commanded—you maniac, you obeyed."

Struggling for breath, you answered,
Patroclus O my rider, "Hector! Now is your 200
time to glory to the skies . . . now the victory
is yours. A gift of the son of Cronus, Zeus—
Apollo too—they brought me down with all
their deathless ease, *they* are the ones who tore
the armor off my back. Even if twenty Hectors
had charged against me—they'd all have died
here, laid low by my spear. No, deadly fate in
league with Apollo killed me. From the ranks
of men, Euphorbus. You came third, and all you
could do was finish off my life . . . One more 210
thing—take it to heart, I urge you—you too,
you won't live long yourself, I swear. Already I
see them looming up beside you—death and
the strong force of fate, to bring you down at
the hands of Aeacus' great royal son . . .
Achilles!"

Death cut him short. The end closed in
around him. Flying free of his limbs his soul
went winging down to the House of Death,
wailing his fate, leaving his manhood far 220
behind, his young and supple strength. But
glorious Hector taunted Patroclus' body, dead
as he was, "Why, Patroclus—why prophesy
my doom, my sudden death? Who knows?—
Achilles the son of sleek-haired Thetis may
outrace me—struck by *my* spear first—
and gasp away his life!"

With that he planted a heel against
Patroclus' chest, wrenched his brazen spear
from the wound, kicked him over, flat on his 230
back, free and clear of the weapon. At once he
went for Automedon with that spear—quick as
a god, the aide of swift Achilles—keen to cut
him down but his veering horses swept him
well away—magnificent racing stallions, gifts
of the gods to Peleus, shining immortal gifts.

Book 22: The Death of Hector

No more words—he dashed toward the city,
heart racing for some great exploit, rushing on
like a champion stallion drawing a chariot full
tilt, sweeping across the plain in easy, tearing
strides—so Achilles hurtled on, driving legs
and knees.

And old King Priam was first to see him
coming, surging over the plain, blazing like the
star that rears at harvest, flaming up in its
brilliance,—far outshining the countless stars in 10
the night sky, that star they call Orion's Dog—
brightest of all but a fatal sign emblazoned on
the heavens, it brings such killing fever down
on wretched men. So the bronze flared on his
chest as on he raced—and the old man moaned,
flinging both hands high, beating his head and
groaning deep he called, begging his dear son
who stood before the gates, unshakable, furious
to fight Achilles to the death. The old man
cried, pitifully, hands reaching out to him, "Oh 20
Hector! Don't just stand there, don't, dear child,
waiting that man's attack—alone, cut off from
friends! You'll meet your doom at once, beaten
down by Achilles, so much stronger than you—
that hard, headlong man. Oh if only the gods
loved him as much as I do . . . dogs and
vultures would eat his fallen corpse at once!—
with what a load of misery lifted from my
spirit. That man who robbed me of many sons,
brave boys, cutting them down or selling them 30
off as slaves, shipped to islands half the world
away . . . Even now there are two, Lycaon and
Polydorus—I cannot find them among the
soldiers crowding Troy, those sons Laothoë
bore me, Laothoë queen of women. But if they
are still alive in the enemy's camp, then we'll
ransom them back with bronze and gold. We
have hoards inside the walls, the rich dowry old
and famous Altes presented with his daughter.
But if they're dead already, gone to the House of 40
Death, what grief to their mother's heart and
mine—we gave them life. For the rest of Troy,
though, just a moment's grief unless you too are
battered down by Achilles. Back, come back!
Inside the walls, my boy! Rescue the men of
Troy and the Trojan women—don't hand the
great glory to Peleus' son, bereft of your own
sweet life yourself.

Pity me too!—
still in my senses, true, but a harrowed, broken 50
man marked out by doom—past the threshold
of old age . . . and Father Zeus will waste me
with a hideous fate, and after I've lived to look
on so much horror! My sons laid low, my
daughters dragged away and the treasure-
chambers looted, helpless babies hurled to the
earth in the red barbarity of war . . . my sons'
wives hauled off by the Argives' bloody
hands! And I, I last of all—the dogs before my
doors will eat me raw, once some enemy 60
brings me down with his sharp bronze sword
or spits me with a spear, wrenching the life
out of my body, yes, the very dogs I bred in

my own halls to share my table, guard my
gates—mad, rabid at heart they'll lap their
master's blood and loll before my doors.

Ah for a young man
all looks fine and noble if he goes down in
war, hacked to pieces under a slashing bronze
blade—he lies there dead . . . but whatever 70
death lays bare, all wounds are marks of glory.
When an old man's killed and the dogs go at
the gray head and the gray beard and mutilate
the genitals—that is the cruelest sight in all
our wretched lives!"

So the old man groaned
and seizing his gray hair tore it out by the roots
but he could not shake the fixed resolve of
Hector. And his mother wailed now, standing
beside Priam, weeping freely, loosing her robes 80
with one hand and holding out her bare breast
with the other, her words pouring forth in a
flight of grief and tears: "Hector, my child!
Look—have some respect for *this!* Pity your
mother too, if I ever gave you the breast to
soothe your troubles, remember it now, dear
boy—beat back that savage man from safe
inside the walls! Don't go forth, a champion
pitted against him—merciless, brutal man. If he
kills you now, how can I ever mourn you on 90
your deathbed?—dear branch in bloom, dear
child I brought to birth!—Neither I nor your
wife, that warm, generous woman . . . Now far
beyond our reach, now by the Argive ships the
rushing dogs will tear you, bolt your flesh!"

So they wept, the two of them crying out to
their dear son, both pleading time and again but
they could not shake the fixed resolve of Hector.
No, he waited Achilles, coming on, gigantic in
power. As a snake in the hills, guarding his hole, 100
awaits a man—bloated with poison, deadly
hatred seething inside him, glances flashing fire
as he coils round his lair . . .
so Hector, nursing his quenchless fury, gave no
ground, leaning his burnished shield against a
jutting wall, but harried still, he probed his
own brave heart: "No way out. If I slip inside
the gates and walls, Polydamas will be first to
heap disgrace on me—he was the one who
urged me to lead our Trojans back to Ilium just 110
last night, the disastrous night Achilles rose in
arms like a god. But did I give way? Not at all.
And how much better it would have been! Now
my army's ruined, thanks to my own reckless
pride, I would die of shame to face the men of
Troy and the Trojan women trailing their long
robes . . . Someone less of a man than I will
say, 'Our Hector—staking all on his own
strength, he destroyed his army!' So they will
mutter. So now, better by far for me to stand up 120
to Achilles, kill him, come home alive or die at
his hands in glory out before the walls. But
wait—what if I put down my studded shield
and heavy helmet, prop my spear on the
rampart and go forth, just as I am, to meet
Achilles, noble Prince Achilles . . . why, I
could promise to give back Helen, yes, and all
her treasures with her, all those riches Paris
once hauled home to Troy in the hollow
ships—and they were the cause of all our 130
endless fighting—Yes, yes, return it all to the
sons of Atreus now to haul away, and then, at
the same time, divide the rest with all the
Argives, all the city holds, and then I'd take an
oath for the Trojan royal council that we will
hide nothing! Share and share alike the hoards
our handsome citadel stores within its depths
and—Why debate, my friend? Why thrash
things out? I must not go and implore him.
He'll show no mercy, no respect for me, my 140
rights—he'll cut me down straight off—
stripped of defenses like a woman once I have
loosed the armor off my body. No way to
parley with that man—not now—not from
behind some oak or rock to whisper, like a boy
and a young girl, lovers' secrets a boy and girl
might whisper to each other . . . Better to
clash in battle, now, at once—*see* which fighter
Zeus awards the glory!"

So he wavered, 150
waiting there, but Achilles was closing on
him now like the god of war, the fighter's
helmet flashing, over his right shoulder
shaking the Pelian ash spear, that terror, and
the bronze around his body flared like a
raging fire or the rising, blazing sun. Hector
looked up, saw him, started to tremble,
nerve gone, he could hold his ground no
longer, he left the gates behind and away he
fled in fear—and Achilles went for him, 160
fast, sure of his speed as the wild mountain
hawk, the quickest thing on wings, launching
smoothly, swooping down on a cringing dove
and the dove flits out from under, the hawk
screaming over the quarry, plunging over
and over, his fury driving him down to beak
and tear his kill—so Achilles flew at him,
breakneck on in fury with Hector fleeing
along the walls of Troy, fast as his legs
would go. On and on they raced, passing the 170
lookout point, passing the wild fig tree
tossed by the wind, always out from under
the ramparts down the wagon trail they
careened until they reached the clear running
springs where whirling Scamander rises up
from its double wellsprings bubbling
strong—and one runs hot and the steam goes
up around it, drifting thick as if fire burned
at its core but the other even in summer
gushes cold as hail or freezing snow or water 180
chilled to ice . . . And here, close to the
springs, lie washing-pools scooped out in the
hollow rocks and broad and smooth where
the wives of Troy and all their lovely
daughters would wash their glistening robes
in the old days, the days of peace before the
sons of Achaea came . . . Past these they
raced, one escaping, one in pursuit and the
one who fled was great but the one pursuing
greater, even greater—their pace mounting 190
in speed since both men strove, not for a
sacrificial beast or oxhide trophy, prizes
runners fight for, no, they raced for the life
of Hector breaker of horses. Like powerful
stallions sweeping round the post for
trophies, galloping full stretch with some
fine prize at stake, a tripod, say, or woman
offered up at funeral games for some brave
hero fallen—so the two of them whirled
three times around the city of Priam, 200
sprinting at top speed while all the gods
gazed down, and the father of men and gods
broke forth among them now:
"Unbearable—a man I love, hunted round
his own city walls and right before my eyes.
My heart grieves for Hector. Hector who
burned so many oxen in my honor, rich cuts,
now on the rugged crests of Ida, now on
Ilium's heights. But now, look, brilliant
Achilles courses him round the city of Priam 210
in all his savage, lethal speed. Come, you
immortals, think this through. Decide. Either
we pluck the man from death and save his
life or strike him down at last, here at
Achilles' hands—for all his fighting heart."

But immortal Athena,
her gray eyes wide, protested strongly:
"Father! Lord of the lightning, king of the
black cloud, what are you saying? A man, a
mere mortal, his doom sealed long ago? You'd 220
set him free from all the pains of death?

Do as you please—
but none of the deathless gods will ever
praise you."

And Zeus who marshals the thunderheads
replied, "Courage, Athena, third-born of the
gods, dear child. Nothing I said was meant in
earnest, trust me, I mean you all the good will
in the world. Go. Do as your own impulse bids
you. Hold back no more." 230

So he launched Athena already poised for
action—down the goddess swept from
Olympus' craggy peaks.

And swift Achilles kept on coursing
Hector, nonstop as a hound in the mountains

starts a fawn from its lair, hunting him down
the gorges, down the narrow glens and the
fawn goes to ground, hiding deep in brush but
the hound comes racing fast, nosing him out
until he lands his kill. So Hector could never 240
throw Achilles off his trail, the swift racer
Achilles—time and again he'd make a dash for
the Dardan Gates, trying to rush beneath the
rock-built ramparts, hoping men on the
heights might save him, somehow, raining
spears but time and again Achilles would
intercept him quickly, heading him off, forcing
him out across the plain and always sprinting
along the city side himself—endless as in a
dream . . . when a man can't catch another 250
fleeing on ahead and he can never escape nor
his rival overtake him—so the one could never
run the other down in his speed nor the other
spring away. And how could Hector have fled
the fates of death so long? How unless one last
time, one final time Apollo had swept in close
beside him, driving strength in his legs and
knees to race the wind? And brilliant Achilles
shook his head at the armies, never letting
them hurl their sharp spears at Hector— 260
someone might snatch the glory, Achilles
come in second. But once they reached the
springs for the fourth time, then Father Zeus
held out his sacred golden scales: in them he
placed two fates of death that lays men low—
one for Achilles, one for Hector breaker of
horses—and gripping the beam mid-haft the
Father raised it high and down went Hector's
day of doom, dragging him down to the strong
House of Death—and god Apollo left him. 270
Athena rushed to Achilles, her bright eyes
gleaming, standing shoulder-to-shoulder,
winging orders now: "At last our hopes run
high, my brilliant Achilles—Father Zeus must
love you—we'll sweep great glory back to
Achaea's fleet, we'll kill this Hector, mad as he
is for battle! No way for him to escape us now,
no longer—not even if Phoebus the distant
deadly Archer goes through torments, pleading
for Hector's life, groveling over and over before 280
our storming Father Zeus. But you, you hold
your ground and catch your breath while I run
Hector down and persuade the man to fight you
face-to-face."

So Athena commanded
and he obeyed, rejoicing at heart—Achilles
stopped, leaning against his ashen spearshaft
barbed in bronze. And Athena left him there,
caught up with Hector at once, and taking the
build and vibrant voice of Deiphobus stood 290
shoulder-to-shoulder with him, winging
orders: "Dear brother, how brutally swift
Achilles hunts you—coursing you round the
city of Priam in all his lethal speed! Come, let
us stand our ground together—beat him back."

"Deiphobus!"—Hector, his helmet
flashing, called out to her—"dearest of all my
brothers, all these warring years, of all the sons
that Priam and Hecuba produced! Now I'm
determined to praise you all the more, you who 300
dared—seeing me in these straits—to venture
out from the walls, all for *my* sake, while the
others stay inside and cling to safety."

The goddess answered quickly, her eyes
blazing, "True, dear brother—how your father
and mother both implored me, time and again,
clutching my knees, and the comrades round
me begging me to stay! Such was the fear that
broke them, man for man, but the heart within
me broke with grief for you. Now headlong on 310
and fight! No letup, no lance spared! So now,
now we'll *see* if Achilles kills us both and hauls
our bloody armor back to the beaked ships or
he goes down in pain beneath your spear."

Athena luring him on with all her immortal
cunning—and now, at last, as the two came
closing for the kill it was tall Hector, helmet
flashing, who led off: "No more running from
you in fear, Achilles! Not as before. Three
times I fled around the great city of Priam—I 320
lacked courage then to stand your onslaught.
Now my spirit stirs me to meet you face-to-face.
Now kill or be killed! Come, we'll swear to the

gods, the highest witnesses—the gods will
oversee our binding pacts. I swear I will never
mutilate you—merciless as you are—if Zeus
allows me to last it out and tear your life away.
But once I've stripped your glorious armor,
Achilles, I will give your body back to your
loyal comrades. Swear you'll do the same." 330

A swift dark glance
and the headstrong runner answered, "Hector,
stop! You unforgivable, you . . . don't talk to
me of pacts. There are no binding oaths
between men and lions—wolves and lambs
can enjoy no meeting of the minds—they are
all bent on hating each other to the death. So
with you and me. No love between us. No
truce till one or the other falls and gluts with
blood Ares who hacks at men behind his 340
rawhide shield. Come, call up whatever
courage you can muster. Life or death—now
prove yourself a spearman, a daring man of
war! No more escape for you—Athena will
kill you with my spear in just a moment. Now
you'll pay at a stroke for all my comrades'
grief, all you killed in the fury of your spear!"

With that,
shaft poised, he hurled and his spear's long
shadow flew but seeing it coming glorious 350
Hector ducked away, crouching down,
watching the bronze tip fly past and stab the
earth—but Athena snatched it up and passed it
back to Achilles and Hector the gallant captain
never saw her. He sounded out a challenge to
Peleus' princely son: "You missed, look—the
great godlike Achilles! So you knew nothing
at all from Zeus about my death—and yet how
sure you were! All bluff, cunning with words,
that's all you are—trying to make me fear you, 360
lose my nerve, forget my fighting strength.
Well, you'll never plant your lance in my back
as I flee *you* in fear—plunge it through my
chest as I come charging in, if a god gives you
the chance! But now it's for you to dodge *my*
brazen spear—I wish you'd bury it in your
body to the hilt. How much lighter the war
would be for Trojans then if you, their greatest
scourge, were dead and gone!"

Shaft poised, he hurled and his spear's 370
long shadow flew and it struck Achilles'
shield—a dead-center hit—but off and away it
glanced and Hector seethed, his hurtling spear,
his whole arm's power poured in a wasted
shot. He stood there, cast down . . . he had no
spear in reserve. So Hector shouted out to
Deiphobus bearing his white shield—with a
ringing shout he called for a heavy lance—

but the man was nowhere near him,
vanished— 380

yes and Hector knew the truth in his
heart and the fighter cried aloud, "My time
has come! At last the gods have called me
down to death. I thought he was at my side,
the hero Deiphobus—he's safe inside the
walls, Athena's tricked me blind. And now
death, grim death is looming up beside me, no
longer far away. No way to escape it now.
This, this was their pleasure after all, sealed
long ago—Zeus and the son of Zeus, the 390
distant deadly Archer—though often before
now they rushed to my defense. So now I meet
my doom. Well let me die—but not without
struggle, not without glory, no, in some great
clash of arms that even men to come will hear
of down the years!"

And on that resolve
he drew the whetted sword that hung at his
side, tempered, massive, and gathering all his
force he swooped like a soaring eagle 400
launching down from the dark clouds to earth
to snatch some helpless lamb or trembling
hare. So Hector swooped now, swinging his
whetted sword and Achilles charged too,
bursting with rage, barbaric, guarding his chest
with the well-wrought blazoned shield, head
tossing his gleaming helmet, four horns strong
and the golden plumes shook that the god of
fire drove in bristling thick along its ridge.
Bright as that star amid the stars in the night 410
sky, star of the evening, brightest star that rides

the heavens, so fire flared from the sharp point of the spear Achilles brandished high in his right hand, bent on Hector's death, scanning his splendid body—where to pierce it best? The rest of his flesh seemed all encased in armor, burnished, brazen—*Achilles'* armor that Hector stripped from strong Patroclus when he killed him—true, but one spot lay exposed, where collarbones lift the neckbone off the shoulders, 420 the open throat, where the end of life comes quickest—*there* as Hector charged in fury brilliant Achilles drove his spear and the point went stabbing clean through the tender neck but the heavy bronze weapon failed to slash the windpipe—Hector could still gasp out some words, some last reply . . . he crashed in the dust—

godlike Achilles gloried over him: "Hector—surely you thought when you 430 stripped Patroclus' armor that you, you would be safe! Never a fear of me—far from the fighting as I was—you fool! Left behind there, down by the beaked ships his great avenger waited, a greater man by far—that man was I, and I smashed your strength! And you—the dogs and birds will maul you, shame your corpse while Achaeans bury my dear friend in glory!"

Struggling for breath, Hector, his helmet 440 flashing, said, "I beg you, beg you by your life, your parents—don't let the dogs devour me by the Argive ships! Wait, take the princely ransom of bronze and gold, the gifts my father and noble mother will give you—but give my body to friends to carry home again, so Trojan men and Trojan women can do me honor with fitting rites of fire once I am dead."

Staring grimly, the proud runner Achilles answered, "Beg no more, you fawning dog— 450 begging me by my parents! Would to god my rage, my fury would drive me now to hack your flesh away and eat you raw—such agonies you have caused me! Ransom? No man alive could keep the dog-packs off you, not if they haul in ten, twenty times that ransom and pile it here before me and promise fortunes more—no, not even if Dardan Priam should offer to weigh out your bulk in gold! Not even then will your noble mother lay you on your deathbed, mourn 460 the son she bore . . . The dogs and birds will rend you—blood and bone!"

At the point of death, Hector, his helmet flashing, said, "I know you well—I see my fate before me. Never a chance that I could win you over . . . Iron inside your chest, that heart of yours. But now beware, or my curse will draw god's wrath upon your head, that day when Paris and lord Apollo—for all your fighting heart—destroy you at the Scaean Gates!" 470

Death cut him short. The end closed in around him. Flying free of his limbs his soul went winging down to the House of Death, wailing his fate, leaving his manhood far behind, his young and supple strength. But brilliant Achilles taunted Hector's body, dead as he was, "Die, die! For my own death, I'll meet it freely—whenever Zeus and the other deathless gods would like to bring it on!"

With that he wrenched his bronze spear 480 from the corpse, laid it aside and ripped the bloody armor off the back. And the other sons of Achaea, running up around him, crowded closer, all of them gazing wonder-struck at the build and marvelous, lithe beauty of Hector. And not a man came forward who did not stab his body, glancing toward a comrade, laughing: "Ah, look here—how much softer he is to handle now, this Hector, than when he gutted our ships with roaring fire!" 490

Standing over him, so they'd gloat and stab his body. But once he had stripped the corpse the proud runner Achilles took his stand in the midst of all the Argive troops and urged them on with a flight of winging orders: "Friends—lords of the Argives, O my captains! Now that the gods have let me kill this man who caused us agonies, loss on crushing loss—more than the rest of all their men combined—come, let us ring their walls in armor, test them, see what recourse the Trojans still may have in mind. Will they abandon the city heights with this man fallen? Or brace for a last, dying stand though Hector's gone? But wait—what am I saying? Why this deep debate? Down by the ships a body lies unwept, unburied—Patroclus . . . I will never forget him, not as long as I'm still among the living and my springing knees will lift and drive me on. Though the dead forget their dead in the House of Death, I will remember, even there, my dear companion.

Now, come, you sons of Achaea, raise a song of triumph! Down to the ships we march and bear this corpse on high—we have won ourselves great glory. We have brought magnificent Hector down, that man the Trojans glorified in their city like a god!"

So he triumphed and now he was bent on outrage, on shaming noble Hector. Piercing the tendons, ankle to heel behind both feet, he knotted straps of rawhide through them both, lashed them to his chariot, left the head to drag and mounting the car, hoisting the famous arms aboard, he whipped his team to a run and breakneck on they flew, holding nothing back. And a thick cloud of dust rose up from the man they dragged, his dark hair swirling round that head so handsome once, all tumbled low in the dust—since Zeus had given him over to his enemies now to be defiled in the land of his own fathers.

Book 24: Achilles and Priam

With that urging Hermes went his way to the steep heights of Olympus. But Priam swung down to earth from the battle-car and leaving Idaeus there to rein in mules and team, the old king went 500 straight up to the lodge where Achilles dear to Zeus would always sit. Priam found the warrior there inside . . . many captains sitting some way off, but two, veteran Automedon and the fine fighter Alcimus were busy 10 serving him. He had just finished dinner, eating, drinking, and the table still stood near. The majestic king of Troy slipped past the rest and kneeling down beside Achilles, clasped his knees and kissed his hands, those terrible, 510 man-killing hands that had slaughtered Priam's many sons in battle. Awesome—as when the grip of madness seizes one who murders a man in his own fatherland and flees abroad to foreign shores, to a wealthy, noble 20 host, and a sense of marvel runs through all who see him—so Achilles marveled, beholding majestic Priam. His men marveled too, trading startled glances. But Priam prayed his heart out to Achilles: "Remember your own father, great godlike Achilles—as old as *I* 520 am, past the threshold of deadly old age! No doubt the countrymen round about him plague him now, with no one there to defend him, beat away disaster. No one—but at least he hears 30 you're still alive and his old heart rejoices, hopes rising, day by day, to see his beloved son come sailing home from Troy. But I—dear god, my life so cursed by fate . . . I fathered hero sons in the wide realm of Troy and now not a single one is left, I tell you. Fifty sons I had when the sons of Achaea came, nineteen 530 born to me from a single mother's womb and the rest by other women in the palace. Many, most of them violent Ares cut the knees from 40 under. But one, one was left me, to guard my walls, my people—the one you killed the other day, defending his fatherland, my Hector! It's all for him I've come to the ships now, to win him back from you—I bring a priceless ransom. Revere the gods, Achilles! Pity me in my own right, remember your own father! I deserve more pity . . . I have endured what no one on earth has ever done before—I put to my lips the hands of the man who killed my son." 50

Those words stirred within Achilles a deep desire to grieve for his own father. Taking the old man's hand he gently moved him back. And overpowered by memory both men gave way to grief. Priam wept freely for man-killing Hector, throbbing, crouching before Achilles' feet as Achilles wept himself, now for his father, now for Patroclus once again, and their sobbing rose and fell throughout the house. Then, when brilliant Achilles had had his fill 60 of tears and the longing for it had left his mind and body, he rose from his seat, raised the old man by the hand and filled with pity now for his gray head and gray beard, he spoke out winging words, flying straight to the heart: "Poor man, how much you've borne—pain to break the spirit! What daring brought you down to the ships, all alone, to face the glance of the man who killed your sons, so many fine brave boys? You have a heart of iron. Come, 70 please, sit down on this chair here . . . Let us put our griefs to rest in our own hearts, rake them up no more, raw as we are with mourning. What good's to be won from tears that chill the spirit? So the immortals spun our lives that we, we wretched men live on to bear such torments—the gods live free of sorrows. There are two great jars that stand on the floor of Zeus's halls and hold his gifts, our miseries one, the other blessings. When Zeus who loves 80 the lightning mixes gifts for a man, now he meets with misfortune, now good times in turn. When Zeus dispenses gifts from the jar of sorrows only, he makes a man an outcast—brutal, ravenous hunger drives him down the face of the shining earth, stalking far and wide, cursed by gods and men. So with my father, Peleus. What glittering gifts the gods rained down from the day that he was born! He excelled all men in wealth and pride of place, 90 he lorded the Myrmidons, and mortal that he was, they gave the man an immortal goddess for a wife. Yes, but even on him the Father piled hardships, no powerful race of princes born in his royal halls, only a single son he fathered, doomed at birth, cut off in the spring of life—and I, I give the man no care as he grows old since here I sit in Troy, far from my fatherland, a grief to you, a grief to all your children . . . And you too, old man, we hear 100 you prospered once: as far as Lesbos, Macar's kingdom, bounds to seaward, phrygia east and upland, the Hellespont vast and north—that entire realm, they say, you lorded over once, you excelled all men, old king, in sons and wealth. But then the gods of heaven brought this agony on you—ceaseless battles round your walls, your armies slaughtered. You must bear up now. Enough of endless tears, the pain that breaks the spirit. Grief for your son will do 110 no good at all. You will never bring him back to life—sooner you must suffer something worse."

But the old and noble Priam protested strongly: "Don't make me sit on a chair. Achilles, Prince, not while Hector lies uncared-for in your camp! Give him back to me, now, no more delay—I must see my son with my own eyes. Accept the ransom I bring you, a king's ransom! Enjoy it, all of it—return 120 to your own native land, safe and sound . . . since now you've spared my life."

A dark glance—and the headstrong runner answered, "No more, old man, don't tempt my wrath, not now! My own mind's made up to give you back your son. A messenger brought me word from Zeus—my mother, Thetis who bore me, the Old Man of the Sea's daughter. And what's more, I can see through you, Priam—no hiding the fact from me: one of the 130 gods has led you down to Achaea's fast ships. No man alive, not even a rugged young fighter, would dare to venture into our camp. Never—how could he slip past the sentries unchallenged? Or shoot back the bolt of my gates with so much ease? So don't anger me now. Don't stir my raging heart still more. Or under my own roof I may not spare your life, old man—suppliant that you are—may break the laws of Zeus!" 140

The old man was terrified. He obeyed the order. But Achilles bounded out of doors like a lion—not alone but flanked by his two aides-in-arms, veteran Automedon and Alcimus, steady comrades, Achilles' favorites next to the dead Patroclus. They loosed from harness the horses and the mules, they led the herald in, the old king's crier, and sat him down on a bench. From the polished wagon they lifted the priceless ransom brought for Hector's corpse 150 but they left behind two capes and a finely-woven shirt to shroud the body well when Priam bore him home. Then Achilles called the serving-women out: "Bathe and anoint the body—bear it aside first. Priam must not see his son." He feared that, overwhelmed by the sight of Hector, wild with grief, Priam might let his anger flare and Achilles might fly into flesh rage himself, cut the old man down and break the laws of Zeus. So when the maids had 160 bathed and anointed the body sleek with olive oil and wrapped it round and round in a braided battle-shirt and handsome battle-cape, then Achilles lifted Hector up in his own arms and laid him down on a bier, and comrades helped him raise the bier and body onto the sturdy wagon . . . Then with a groan he called his dear friend by name: "Feel no anger at me, Patroclus, if you learn—even there in the House of Death—I let his father have Prince 170 Hector back. He gave me worthy ransom and you shall have your share from me, as always, your fitting, lordly share."

So he vowed and brilliant Achilles strode back to his shelter, sat down on the well-carved chair that he had left, at the far wall of the room, leaned toward Priam and firmly spoke the words the king had come to hear: "Your son is now set 180 free, old man, as you requested. Hector lies in state. With the first light of day you will see for yourself as you convey him home. Now, at last, let us turn our thoughts to supper. Even Niobe with her lustrous hair remembered food, though she saw a dozen children killed in her own halls, six daughters and six sons in the pride and prime of youth. True, lord Apollo killed the sons with his silver bow and Artemis showering arrows killed the 190 daughters. Both gods were enraged at Niobe. Time and again she placed herself on a par with their own mother, Leto in her immortal beauty—how she insulted Leto: 'All you have borne is two, but I have borne so many!' So, two as they were, they slaughtered all her children. Nine days they lay in their blood, no one to bury them—Cronus' son had turned the people into stone . . . then on the tenth the gods of heaven interred them. And Niobe, 200 gaunt, worn to the bone with weeping, turned her thoughts to food. And now, somewhere, lost on the crags, on the lonely mountain slopes, on Sipylus where, they say, the nymphs who live forever, dancing along the Achelous River run to beds of rest—there, struck into stone, Niobe still broods on the spate of griefs the gods poured out to her.

So come—we too, old king, must think of food. Later you can mourn your beloved son 210 once more, when you bear him home to Troy, and you'll weep many tears."

Never pausing, the swift runner sprang to his feet and slaughtered a white sheep as comrades moved in to skin the carcass quickly, dress the quarters well. Expertly they cut the meat in pieces, pierced them with spits, roasted them to a turn and pulled them off the fire. Automedon brought the bread, set it out on the board in ample wicker baskets. Achilles 220 served the meat. They reached out for the good things that lay at hand and when they had put aside desire for food and drink, Priam the son of Dardanus gazed at Achilles, marveling now at the man's beauty, his magnificent build—face-to-face he seemed a deathless god . . . and Achilles gazed and marveled at Dardan Priam, beholding his noble looks, listening to his words. But once they'd had their fill of gazing at each other, the 230 old majestic Priam broke the silence first:

"Put me to bed quickly, Achilles, Prince. Time to rest, to enjoy the sweet relief of sleep. Not once have my eyes closed shut beneath my lids from the day my son went down beneath your hands . . . day and night I groan, brooding over the countless griefs, groveling in the dung that fills my walled-in court. But now, at long last, I have tasted food again and let some glistening wine go down my throat. Before 240 this hour I had tasted nothing."

He shook his head as Achilles briskly told his men and serving-women to make beds in the porch's shelter, to lay down some heavy purple throws for the beds themselves and over them spread some blankets, thick woolly robes, a warm covering laid on top. Torches in hand, they left the hall and fell to work at once and in no time two good beds were spread and made. Then 250 Achilles nodded to Priam, leading the king on with brusque advice: "Sleep outside, old friend, in case some Achaean captain comes to visit. They keep on coming now, huddling beside me, making plans for battle—it's their duty. But if one saw you here in the rushing dark night he'd tell Agamemnon straightaway, our good commander. Then you'd have real delay in ransoming the body. One more point. Tell me, be precise about it—how many days 260 do you need to bury Prince Hector? I will hold back myself and keep the Argive armies back that long."

And the old and noble Priam answered slowly, "If you truly want me to give Prince Hector burial, full, royal honors, you'd show me a great kindness, Achilles, if you would do exactly as I say. You know how crammed we are inside our city, how far it is to the hills to haul in timber, and our Trojans are afraid to 270 make the journey. Well, nine days we should mourn him in our halls, on the tenth we'd bury Hector, hold the public feast, on the eleventh build the barrow high above his body—on the twelfth we'd fight again . . . if fight we must."

The swift runner Achilles reassured him quickly: "All will be done, old Priam, as you command. I will hold our attack as long as you require."

With that he clasped the old king by the 280 wrist, by the right hand, to free his heart from fear. Then Priam and herald, minds set on the journey home, bedded down for the night within the porch's shelter. And deep in his sturdy well-built lodge Achilles slept with Briseis in all her beauty sleeping by his side.

Now the great array of gods and chariot-driving men slept all night long, overcome by gentle sleep. But sleep could never hold the running Escort—Hermes kept on turning it 290 over in his mind . . . how could he convoy Priam clear of the ships, unseen by devoted guards who held the gates? Hovering at his head the Escort rose and spoke: "Not a care in the world, old man? Look at you, how you sleep in the midst of men who'd kill you—and just because Achilles spared your life. Now, yes, you've ransomed your dear son—for a king's ransom. But wouldn't the sons you left behind be forced to pay three times as much 300 for *you* alive? What if Atrides Agamemnon learns you're here—what if the whole Achaean army learns you're here?"

The old king woke in terror, roused the herald. Hermes harnessed the mules and team for both men, drove them fast through the camp and no one saw them.

Once they reached the ford where the river runs clear, the strong, whirling Xanthus sprung of immortal Zeus, Hermes went his way to the 310 steep heights of Olympus as Dawn flung out her golden robe across the earth, and the two men, weeping, groaning, drove the team toward Troy and the mules brought on the body. No one saw them at first, neither man nor woman, none before Cassandra, golden as goddess Aphrodite. She had climbed to

Pergamus heights and from that point she saw her beloved father swaying tall in the chariot, flanked by the herald, whose cry could rouse the city. And Cassandra saw *him* too . . . drawn by the mules and stretched out on his bier. She screamed and her scream rang out through all Troy: "Come, look down, you men of Troy, you Trojan women! Behold Hector now—if you ever once rejoiced to see him striding home, home alive from battle! He was the greatest joy of Troy and all our people!" 320

Her cries plunged Troy into uncontrollable grief and not a man or woman was left inside the walls. They streamed out at the gates to meet Priam bringing in the body of the dead. Hector—his loving wife and noble mother were first to fling themselves on the wagon rolling on, the first to tear their hair, embrace his head and a wailing throng of people milled around them. And now, all day long till the setting sun went down they would have wept for Hector there before the gates if the old man, steering the car, had not commanded, "Let me through with the mules! Soon, in a moment, you can have your fill of tears—once I've brought him home." 330 340

So he called and the crowds fell back on either side, making way for the wagon. Once they had borne him into the famous halls, they laid his body down on his large carved bed and set beside him singers to lead off the laments, and their voices rose in grief—they lifted the dirge high as the women wailed in answer. And white-armed Andromache led their songs of sorrow, cradling the head of Hector, man-killing Hector gently in her arms: "O my husband . . . cut off from life so young! You leave me a widow, lost in the royal halls—and the boy only a baby, the son we bore together, you and I so doomed. I cannot think he will ever come to manhood. Long before *that* the city will be sacked, plundered top to bottom! Because you are dead, her great guardian, you who always defended Troy, who kept her loyal wives and helpless children safe, all who will soon be carried off in the hollow ships and I with them— 350 360

And you, my child, will follow me to labor, somewhere, at harsh, degrading work, slaving under some heartless master's eye—that, or some Achaean marauder will seize you by the arm and hurl you headlong down from the ramparts—horrible death—enraged at *you* because Hector once cut down his brother, his father or his son, yes, hundreds of armed Achaeans gnawed the dust of the world, crushed by Hector's hands! Your father, remember, was no man of mercy . . . not in the horror of battle, and that is why the whole city of Troy mourns you now, my Hector—you've brought your parents accursed tears and grief but to me most of all you've left the horror, the heartbreak! For you never died in bed and stretched your arms to me or said some last word from the heart I can remember, always, weeping for you through all my nights and days!" 370 380

Her voice rang out in tears and the women wailed in answer and Hecuba led them now in a throbbing chant of sorrow: "Hector, dearest to me by far of all my sons . . . and dear to the gods while we still shared this life—and they cared about you still, I see, even after death. Many the sons I had whom the swift runner Achilles caught and shipped on the barren salt sea as slaves to Samos, to Imbros, to Lemnos shrouded deep in mist! But you, once he slashed away your life with his brazen spear he dragged you time and again around his comrade's tomb, Patroclus whom you killed—not that he brought Patroclus back to life by that. But I have you with me now . . . fresh as the morning dew you lie in the royal halls like one whom Apollo, lord of the silver bow, has approached and shot to death with gentle shafts." 390 400

Her voice rang out in tears and an endless wail rose up and Helen, the third in turn, led their songs of sorrow: "Hector! Dearest to me of all my husband's brothers—my husband, Paris, magnificent as a god . . . he was the one who brought me here to Troy—Oh how I wish I'd died before that day! But this, now, is the twentieth year for me since I sailed here and forsook my own native land, yet never once did I hear from *you* a taunt, an insult. But if someone else in the royal halls would curse me, one of your brothers or sisters or brothers' wives trailing their long robes, even your own mother—not your father, always kind as my own father—why, you'd restrain them with words, Hector, you'd win them to my side . . . you with your gentle temper, all your gentle words. And so in the same breath I mourn for you and me, my doom-struck, harrowed heart! Now there is no one left in the wide realm of Troy, no friend to treat me kindly—all the countrymen cringe from me in loathing!" 410 420

Her voice rang out in tears and vast throngs wailed and old King Priam rose and gave his people orders: "Now, you men of Troy, haul timber into the city! Have no fear of an Argive ambush packed with danger—Achilles vowed, when he sent me home from the black ships, not to do us harm till the twelfth dawn arrives." 430

At his command they harnessed oxen and mules to wagons, they assembled before the city walls with all good speed and for nine days hauled in a boundless store of timber. But when the tenth Dawn brought light to the mortal world they carried gallant Hector forth, weeping tears, and they placed his corpse aloft the pyre's crest, flung a torch and set it all aflame. 440

At last, when young Dawn with her rose-red fingers shone once more, the people massed around illustrious Hector's pyre . . . And once they'd gathered, crowding the meeting grounds, they first put out the fires with glistening wine, wherever the flames still burned in all their fury. Then they collected the white bones of Hector—all his brothers, his friends-in-arms, mourning, and warm tears came streaming down their cheeks. They placed the bones they found in a golden chest, shrouding them round and round in soft purple cloths. They quickly lowered the chest in a deep, hollow grave and over it piled a cope of huge stones closely set, then hastily heaped a barrow, posted lookouts all around for fear the Achaean combat troops would launch their attack before the time agreed. And once they'd heaped the mound they turned back home to Troy, and gathering once again they shared a splendid funeral feast in Hector's honor, held in the house of Priam, king by will of Zeus. 450 460

And so the Trojans buried Hector breaker of horses. 470

Article 7
Aesop: Fables

Introduction

Aesop was a slave in the Greek city of Samos who lived in the 6th Century BC. Just as with Homer, he lived before the Golden Age of Greece and probably had a profound effect on the ethical thinking of the Greeks of later ages. However, Aesop may have received his greatest recognition in modern times when his fables have been widely read and used as the basis of numerous movies, cartoons, and children's books.

Aesop probably devoted his life to the study of ethics and made up fables to teach others his moral principles. These fables, though short and uncomplicated, are powerful teaching tools. Children in classrooms across the world are still taught the fables of *The Tortoise and the Hare, The Fox and the Grapes,* and many others. The longevity of short stories created by a slave in ancient Greece is testament to his creativity and to the applicability of his works to all times.

The Dog in the Manger

One day an ill-tempered dog was sniffing around a manger full of barley. The dog didn't like barley and was about to leave when a hungry zebra came by. Suddenly the dog decided not to leave; instead he barked fiercely and threatened the zebra.

MORAL

The greatest selfishness is to stop others having what you yourself cannot enjoy.

The Wise Cicada

For a long time a cicada sat chirping in a tree while a hungry fox sat below, thinking up a plan to catch and eat her. Finally the fox looked up at the cicada and spoke to her, showering her with compliments about her musical voice. Then he suggested that the cicada should come down so that he could see how beautiful she was.

The cicada, however, was too clever to fall into the fox's trap. Instead she broke a leaf off the tree and dropped it. Thinking it was the cicada herself, the fox dashed forward to catch it. Too late, he realized he has been tricked.

"I knew you were hoping to eat me," said the cicada. "You see, I've been on my guard against foxes ever since the day I saw cicadas' wings in a fox's droppings."

MORAL

Wise people learn from their neighbors' mistakes.

The Greedy Dog

A dog was crossing a river with a piece of meat in his mouth when, looking down, he saw his reflection in the water. Thinking the reflection was another dog carrying another piece of meat in its mouth, the dog dropped his meat and made a grab for the other dog's piece. But, of course, he ended up with nothing. His own piece fell into the water and was swept away by the river, and the other piece disappeared with it.

MORAL
Greedy people end up with less.

The Tortoise and the Hare

A tortoise and a hare once got into an argument about who could run faster. They decided that the best way to settle the matter was to have a race, so they fixed a time and a place to meet and then went their separate ways.

The hare was so confident that he was going to win that he didn't bother to start at the agreed time. Instead he decided to take a nap. He told himself that when he woke, he could easily overtake the tortoise and win the race.

The tortoise, however, set off on time. He plodded along, going slowly, but not stopping for a single rest. On and on he went. Eventually, just as the hare was waking up, the tortoise crossed the finish line. The tortoise had won the race.

MORAL
Slow and steady wins the race.

Article 8

Democritus: Fragments

Introduction

Very few writings survive from the ancient school of Greek philosopher-scientists called "the Atomists." We have only fragments, that is, small portions of primary texts, usually quoted by subsequent authors. This is partly due to the rejection of their theories by the later Greeks. The Atomists were part of the Greek tradition of natural philosophy that combined science and philosophy. These early Greek thinkers were called Sophists and today are referred to as the Pre-Socratics. After Socrates, Plato and Aristotle, the Pre-Socratics were held in low esteem and their teachings largely ignored. Their works did, however, achieve a revival in some of the ethical philosophies of the Hellenistic period, as we will discover when we read the works of Epicurus.

The Atomists proposed that all matter and even immaterial things are made up of tiny indivisible particles called "atoms" which circulated in empty space called a "void." This idea was unbelievable and even offensive to many of the philosophers, such as Aristotle, who believed that these concepts violated other explanations for matter and who abhorred the concept of a void (or vacuum). Aristotle's success at turning the majority opinion against the Atomists limited their ability to pass literature on through the years, making it impossible to know just how much they understood about the basis of modern atomic theory.

Democritus (460–370 BC) was the champion of the Atomists; it was he who proposed most of the theories the Atomists are still known for. From the biographical writings of his contemporaries, we know that he was a well-rounded scholar; he wrote books on ethics, mathematics, physics, music, literature, medicine, history, and prognostication. What is amazing about him was how far he was ahead of his time in understanding what has become the basis of modern studies of chemistry and physics.

Of the short surviving fragments of his works, here are a few selections that speak of his atomic theory and hint at his many interests. These should be compared to the concepts given by Aristotle.

The Fragments

6.* Man should know from this rule that he is cut off from truth.

7. This argument too shows that in truth we know nothing about anything, but every man shares the generally prevailing opinion.

8. And yet it will be obvious that it is difficult to really know of what sort each thing is.

10. Now, that we do not really know of what sort each thing is, or is not, has often been shown.

Bakewell, Charles M., *Source Book in Ancient Philosophy,* Charles Schribner's Sons, 1909.

*The numbering of the fragments is that of Diels, and we follow his text.

117. Verily we know nothing. Truth is buried deep.
9. In fact we do not know anything infallibly, but only that which changes according to the condition of our body and of the [influences] that reach and impinge upon it.
11. There are two forms of knowledge, one genuine, one obscure. To the obscure belong all of the following: sight, hearing, smell, taste, feeling. The other form is the genuine, and is quite distinct from this. (And then distinguishing the genuine from the obscure, he continues:) Whenever the obscure [way of knowing] has reached the *minimum sensibile* of hearing, smell, taste, and touch, and when the investigation must be carried farther into that which is still finer, then arises the genuine way of knowing, which has a finer organ of thought.

* * *

0. [Democritus] says: By convention sweet is sweet, by convention bitter is bitter, by convention hot is hot, by convention cold is cold, by convention color is color. But in reality there are atoms and the void. That is, the objects of sense are supposed to be real and it is customary to regard them as such, but in truth they are not. Only the atoms and the void are real.
2. Of practical wisdom these are the three fruits: to deliberate well, to speak to the point, to do what is right.
3. He who intends to enjoy life should not be busy about many things, and in what he does should not undertake what exceeds his natural capacity. On the contrary, he should have himself so in hand that even when fortune comes his way, and is apparently ready to lead him on to higher things, he should put her aside and not o'erreach his powers. For a being of moderate size is safer than one that bulks too big.

Classical Greece
Living Creatively

> Our constitution does not copy the laws of neighbouring states; we are rather a pattern to others than imitators ourselves. Its administration favours the many instead of the few; this is why it is called a democracy . . . The freedom which we enjoy in our government extends also to our ordinary life . . . Further, we provide plenty of means for the mind to refresh itself from business. We celebrate games and sacrifices all the year round, and the elegance of our private establishments forms a daily source of pleasure and helps to banish the spleen; while the magnitude of our city draws the produce of the world into our harbour, so that to the Athenian the fruits of other countries are as familiar a luxury as those of his own . . . Nor are these the only points in which our city is worthy of admiration. We cultivate refinement without extravagance and knowledge without effeminacy; wealth we employ more for use than for show, and place the real disgrace of poverty not in owning to the fact but in declining the struggle against it. Our public men have, besides politics, their private affairs to attend to, and our ordinary citizens, though occupied with the pursuits of industry, are still fair judges of public matters; for, unlike any other nation, regarding him who takes no part in these duties not as unambitious but as useless, we Athenians are able to judge at all events if we cannot originate, and, instead of looking on discussion as a stumbling-block in the way of action, we think it an indispensable preliminary to any wise action at all.
>
> *—Pericles' Funeral Oration (Thucydides, Peloponnesian War 2.34–46. Trans. Richard Crawley.)*

What Does Classical Mean?

The word **classical** has several meanings. One usage says that something classical is a standard against which other things are judged or evaluated. Another related meaning uses "classic" as the best or greatest. Still another meaning uses classic as something that endures. In architecture and design, "classic" is a particular style, perhaps one that is thought to be the best or enduring, but that has specific characteristics besides those comparative qualities. Classical music is an entire genre of music that is contrasted to other genres like popular music, country music, rock and roll, and so on. (These are the divisions of music that are found in most music stores.) "Classical" can also refer to a particular period of time or a particular style. The Classical Period of music was that period in which Mozart and Haydn composed (during the eighteenth century), and their style is called the Classical Style (which is, of course, part of the entire genre called classical music). The "classics" in literature are those works that have endured and become great. Today, some scholars are called classicists; they study a particular time of ancient history, which is the subject of this chapter.

The time of Classical Greece was from the fifth to the fourth centuries B.C. In some ways it is the combination of the other meanings of "classic." This period in Greece was a marvelous and creative time that many consider to be the "best" and the most "enduring" of all historical times. Classical Greece defined art and architecture that, when used in later years, are also called classical, not only in the comparative sense but in the period sense. For example, many of the government buildings in Washington D.C. look like ancient Greek buildings, and so the style of Washington is called the "classical style." The Classical Period of music when Mozart and Haydn lived was characterized by adherence to specific forms and patterns that were deemed to be especially lovely and enduring, just as the art from this time of ancient Greece is lovely and enduring. People appreciated symmetry, beauty, form, grace, and other enduring qualities. Therefore, nearly all of the senses of the word "classical" can be found in Classical Greece. Let's investigate some of the details of that wonderful time. The glory of this time is reflected in the alternate name for the Classical Period of Greece: The Golden Age.

Politics

After the defeat of the Persians and their withdrawal to Asia Minor, the Greek city-states were free of threat from foreign invaders. Barbarians in the north were not likely to attack an area that had just defeated the greatest army in the world, and there were no other empires that might look to Greece as a target. With that confidence and security, the Greek city-states began to expand their areas of influence and to focus attention and creative energy on their own separate interests, rather than a combined Greek interest.

Athens, the major seaport of Greece, seized this opportunity to greatly expand its navy and trading zone. Athens established colonies throughout the Aegean Sea and into the Black Sea, and began to dominate the already existing trading cities in that region. The Athenians so dominated this area that their influence is sometimes referred to as the Athenian Empire, although the alternate name, the Delian League (named after one of the existing trading cities that was typical of those being dominated), is more common. The Delian League was very successful. Athens dominated trade throughout the area and exacted taxes from all the areas within the Delian League, thus providing the economic power that Athenian governmental officials needed to create the architecture, art, and public works that were so important to the Golden Age.

One ruler of Athens is particularly noteworthy in his abilities to control the Delian League and for the impact he had on the culture and magnificence of Athens. That ruler is **Pericles,** who ruled Greece from 461 B.C. to 429 B.C. Many consider Pericles to be the "ideal ruler" of a city-state. He created an atmosphere in the city that stimulated creativity in many areas—drama, music, art, architecture, and literature—all of which we will consider in some detail. Like the pharaohs of ancient Egypt, Pericles seemed to realize that great public works would be important to the overall creative atmosphere. Therefore, he commissioned and supervised the building of the Acropolis, a collection of sacred buildings, mostly temples to various gods and goddesses, erected on a hill in the center of the city of Athens. A picture of the Acropolis (which means "high city") is given in Figure 7.1. The crowning glory of the Acropolis is the temple to Athena, the patron goddess of the city of Athens. This building, called the Parthenon, can be seen at the top of the hill.

The building of great temples involved many artistic efforts. Not only were architects needed, but

Figure 7.1 ■ *The Acropolis of Athens. Image © ML Sinibaldi/Corbis.*

many beautiful statues were placed in and around the buildings. Further, the outside walls of the buildings were covered with marble **reliefs** (sculpture that is not freestanding or fully three-dimensional, but rather, projects from a surface) and **friezes** (the decorative pattern around the top of the building just above the columns), which were beautifully carved. The most famous statues and reliefs were removed from the Parthenon in the nineteenth century by Lord Elgin of Great Britain, who feared for their safety during the war between the Greeks and Turks that was occurring at the time. Those reliefs and friezes, now located in the British Museum, are called the Elgin Marbles.

Pericles also sponsored festivals, such as the Festival of Dionysus, during which the arts were promoted. Drama competitions were especially important. Artists were recognized as important contributors to the daily life of Athens; some received large salaries and prizes. This feeling of cooperation between government and artists, which was so typical of Classical Athens, was also sought (and largely achieved) during the Renaissance in Florence (about 1500 A.D.).

However, not everything was rosy for Athens during the time of Pericles. The inability of Greece to continue in its unity following the defeat of the Persians brought out rivalries and, eventually, internal war. Each city-state wanted to prove its superiority to the others and to be recognized as the leading city of the region. The two cities that were most insistent on their role of leadership were Athens and Sparta. A natural rivalry had long existed between them; with the rise of Athens as head of the Delian League, that rivalry intensified.

There were also economic pressures over trading areas. For example, while Athens dominated the Aegean Sea, the Black Sea and the eastern end of the Mediterranean, Corinth, another Greek city-state, was attempting to create a trading zone in the Adriatic (the sea on the western side of the Grecian peninsula). When Athens attempted to establish trading regions in the western sea, Corinth became angry and sought a way to block Athenian advances.

These problems led to the uniting of Sparta and Corinth in a coalition against Athens and, eventually, to the war called the Peloponnesian

War, named after the southern region of Greece where Sparta was dominant. The war lasted 27 years (431–404 B.C.) and most of the male citizens of Athens, Sparta and Corinth (plus some from allied cities) were involved. Pericles himself was a soldier, as was Socrates, the great philosopher whom we will discuss in the next chapter.

The war was eventually won by Sparta/Corinth, and briefly Athens was ruled by a group of Spartan appointees. Soon, however, Sparta began its own quest for empire and, as they tried to conquer new territories, lost control over Athens. Even after the war, however, the Golden Age continued in Athens, although somewhat diminished, perhaps because Pericles had died in 429 B.C. (of disease). A further dampening of the spirit of free and creative thought must have occurred when Socrates, a well known citizen of Athens was accused of corrupting the youth of the city through his teaching, and then executed.

The simultaneity of the Golden Age and the Peloponnesian War raises an interesting question: What is the effect of a war on creativity? In the case of Athens, creativity seemed to keep going *in spite of* the war. Of course, we can't tell whether the creative achievements might have been even greater had there not been a war, but at least we can certainly say that the war did not result in a termination of creative activity.

Looking at modern situations, we can see that war seems to spur some creative work. Obviously, weaponry is advanced as one side tries to counter the technological weapons being used by the other side. Other war-support functions also seem to develop faster. For example, radar was developed as a support for the aircraft and defenses of Great Britain during the Battle of Britain when German bombing was so devastating. Codes and code-breaking were advanced on both sides of WWII. Production methods for all types of war materials were improved so that high volumes of goods could be supplied. Economies boomed, and that led to greater wealth, which led eventually to support of the arts.

On the other side, however, we see that leisure time was reduced, and so some of the creative endeavors that depended on leisure were diminished. Surely some creative people, established or potential, were killed in the war and could not realize their potential. Money was focused toward the war effort, and so during the war little support for the arts could be had. In general, however, it seems that war and creativity can co-exist, and that creativity may even be helped by the war, but the breadth of creativity is reduced.

Daily Life

Ancient Greece never could rely solely on its own ability to produce sufficient food for the entire Greek population, as the soil and water supply of the area are not well suited for extensive agriculture. Therefore, the Greeks relied on trade as their principal economic enterprise. This trade created a large merchant class, especially in Athens, the leading trade city. These merchants became wealthy and powerful. The nature of their work, coupled with the extensive slave population in Athens (as many as 200,000 of a total population of 300,000), gave the merchants and important landowners considerable leisure time that they could devote to creative pursuits and, as we have seen, to politics.

Even though the public buildings on the Acropolis and at other important places were very beautiful, the common Greek home seemed to be quite simple. It was surrounded by a wall, with an atrium around which the living quarters were arranged. Cooking was done over a hearth in the house; baking was done in ovens, often in a corner of the inner patio. The foods were simple: grains, lentils, olives, figs, grapes and occasionally vegetables, chicken, fish, and wild game (rabbits, boar, deer). The principal flavorings were onion and garlic. Wine was the usual drink.

Women ruled in the house, but were given little chance for participation in the governance of the community. However, because the law provided that Greek citizenship could only be granted to the male children of a Greek mother, the women had considerable behind-the-scenes power. For example, children born of a husband to some other woman than his wife, whether Greek or foreign, were considered illegitimate and could not be recognized as citizens. Also, even if a divorce occurred, women benefited from their ability to keep the dowry that was paid at the time of marriage.

Greeks had few material possessions. A list of goods of one of the rulers of Athens during the Golden Age listed only chests, beds, couches, tables, screens, stools, baskets, and mats as household goods. We also know that Greeks had pottery, metal utensils for cooking, tools, and some luxury items such as jewelry and fine clothes. Still, the total amount of goods was relatively small.

Religion was an important aspect of life but took little time. Small offerings were made to household and family gods to ask for prosperity. Temple rituals entailed taking an offering, usually annually, to the temple and giving it to a priest, who then burned the offering in a set ritual pattern. The concept of religion was that the gods were in charge of everything from war to specific items of nature. Each god had control over some aspect of human life and, if the people wanted to succeed in that aspect of life, they needed to appease the appropriate god. For example, a farmer would surely give an offering to Demeter, goddess of the harvest, to ensure that the crop would be bountiful. This concept leads to the interesting custom, reported in Acts 17:23, where the Athenians gave devotions to an "unknown god" who, evidently, might control some aspect of their life but was not identified to them explicitly.

Drama

Most Greek dramas were presented at the annual competition held during the Festival of Dionysus in Athens. The competing playwrights each submitted four plays—three were related tragedies and one was a satyr play (a play of farce, much like modern burlesque). The most important dramas were the trilogy of tragedies, whose themes were usually drawn from mythology or from stories associated with the time of heroes (either the Trojan War or the years immediately before or after). The plays generally assumed that the audience was familiar with the basic story of the Trojan War (which occurred about seven centuries previously but was familiar from books by Homer and others) and with the characters in the war; this is similar to the modern assumption that audiences are familiar with the stories of Adam and Eve, Noah, Abraham, and even King Arthur and George Washington.

The competition was fierce and the reputation of the playwrights rose or fell with their success. The playwrights were often responsible for writing, directing, making the costumes and scenery, and performing one of the lead roles. The money for the production came from rich benefactors who might also share in the prize money. Winning playwrights were assured a nice income for the ensuing year and good funding for the next play.

Most Greek cities of any size had an amphitheater where the plays were performed. A typical amphitheater is shown in Figure 7.2. These amphitheaters usually had a stage area (called the **orchestra**) and a small building behind the stage (called the **skene,** the origin of our word "scenery") where some offstage action might occur. (Interestingly, most deaths occurred in the *skene* and were simply reported onstage.) The acoustics in some of the amphitheaters was amazingly good. Even today, I (Strong) have gone to an amphitheater and spoken in a normal speaking voice with normal volume and could be heard clearly by someone sitting on the top row of the amphitheater. The good acoustics are likely due to the semi-circular shape and related sound reflections.

The plays were usually presented with only a few actors (all men) who wore masks indicating either happiness or sadness. Recent scholarship has suggested that megaphones were built into the mouthpieces of the masks worn by the characters, thus further adding to the amplification, especially where the amphitheater did not have the semi-circular feature. They may have changed masks to represent different characters, as a single actor often played more than one part. The plays also had

Figure 7.2 ■ *A Greek theater at Epidaurus, Greece.* *Image © Paul A. Souders/Corbis.*

a chorus of a few people (probably about 12 to 15) whose lines either commented on the developments in the play as a narrator or who took the view of the audience.

Greek drama defined the art form that, even today, has many features directly descended from ancient Greece. The genre of tragedy was first developed by a Greek playwright named Thespis, who lived around the year 534 B.C. His creative innovation was to introduce an actor separate from the chorus. This innovation allowed Thespis to focus on changes that occurred in the life of the character. Tragedy is defined as the presentation of changes in a character due to difficulties in his or her life. Since changes from difficulties are usually sad, most tragedies end with unhappiness; some, but not all, involve death. Most of the plays discussed issues of human frailties, ethics, divided loyalties, or human interactions with circumstances beyond human control. Because of the important and fundamental position of Thespis in the development of drama, actors and actresses today are sometimes called **thespians.**

The genre of comedy, which means a play that ends happily (not necessarily funny), was defined many years later. We will discuss the greatest of the ancient Greek comedy writers, Aristophanes, a little later in this chapter.

Three great playwrights dominated the drama competitions for about 100 years. Those three stand out as some of the best writers of tragedy in the history of the theater. Sadly, we have only a few of the hundreds of plays written by these men and only one complete trilogy. These three writers were Aeschylus, Sophocles, and Euripides. We will discuss the creative contributions of each.

Aeschylus (525–456 B.C.), who lived just before the rule of Pericles and not long after Thespis, seemed to be deeply aware of human weaknesses, and wrote about deep-seated anger and revenge. Aeschylus creatively used two speaking actors, thus giving a dimension to the action beyond just the interaction of a single actor with the chorus and audience. Our only complete trilogy is from Aeschylus and represents stories of the House of Atria (named after the forefather of the family, Atreus), one of the main families involved in the Trojan War. The three plays, together called the *Oresteia,* are titled *Agamemnon, The Libation Bearers,* and *The Eumenides.*

The plot of *Agamemnon* focuses on the return of this king, the son of Atreus and leader of the Greek forces during the Trojan War. Agamemnon and his wife, Clytemnestra, have become estranged because of his action at the beginning of the war concerning their daughter. The estrangement occurred when Greek ships were trapped in the harbor by unfavorable winds. According to an oracle, favorable winds would return only when Agamemnon's daughter was sacrificed to the gods. Reluctantly Agamemnon agreed to allow his daughter to be killed, which embittered Clytemnestra against the war and Agamemnon. During the war Clytemnestra took a lover and they decided to kill Agamemnon upon his return. Then, to make matters worse, Agamemnon brings a concubine, Cassandra, back to his kingdom after the war. Clytemnestra begins to follow her plan of murder when Agamemnon returns. Even though Cassandra can see the future disasters to befall Agamemnon, and tries to warn him, she is frustrated by his refusal to listen; eventually she also becomes a victim of the situation. Agamemnon is killed by Clytemnestra, who then arranges for her lover to assume the kingship of the city.

The Libation Bearers, the sequel to *Agamemnon,* is about Agamemnon's son, Orestes, who had fled Mycenae as a boy to avoid the dangers he might encounter from the new king, Clytemnestra's lover. When Orestes becomes an adult, he returns to Mycenae. With the encouragement of his sister Electra, Orestes kills his mother, Clytemnestra, and her lover the king. However, his punishment follows immediately: he is driven mad by the Furies, goddesses of vengeance.

The Eumenides tells the story of the tormented wandering of Orestes. Finally, hoping to end the torments, Orestes seeks a trial in Athens (at the Areopagus). The trial is presided over by Athena, the prosecutors are the Furies, and the defense is by Apollo, god of reason. Orestes is acquitted, which, interestingly, gives happiness to the ending of the story and also gives some additional meaning to the name of the play, which is "the kindly ones," referring to the Furies who, when seen in hindsight, actually bring benefits to Orestes.

Sophocles (496–406 B.C.), a personal friend of Pericles, gained great prestige and wealth during the Golden Age of Greece. When Sophocles began to compete in the Festival of Dionysius, he seemed to have been a consistent winner, indicating that in ancient Greece he was considered to be the best of the playwrights. In addition to the depth of drama in his plays, he is also credited with the innovation of adding a third speaking actor. This increased the interactions possible and greatly increased the complexity of the drama that could be presented.

Lists of plays indicate that Sophocles wrote 123, but only 7 survive. If we can judge from the few plays we have, Sophocles was less anxious to end his plays happily than was Aeschylus. Sophocles explored something that was new to drama: the critical defect within the principal character (the protagonist) that led to the difficulties encountered. That is, there was a **tragic flaw** in personality, such as pride or excessive anger or blind devotion to duty. This flaw led to a sequence of events that ultimately caused great suffering and sadness. Today we call this type of "defective" protagonist a "Sophoclean hero." This creative concept strongly engaged the audience in the play, because many could identify directly with the protagonist with feelings of both sympathy and disdain. The audience would see the problems, which seemed beyond the ability of the protagonist to change, yet also see that if the protagonist could change, the problems might be solved. This dual vision of the protagonist's situation has proven to be very powerful, and was identified as especially creative by Aristotle (in his work *Poetics*), who discussed at length the plays of Sophocles.

Sophocles' use of multiple actors enriched the dramatic possibilities of the plays because actors could play off one another to develop more meaningful emotions. Many experts have considered Sophocles the greatest of the Greek playwrights.

Two of the most famous and important works by Sophocles are *Oedipus Rex (Oedipus the King)* and *Antigone,* both of which relate to a single family; however (unlike the plays of Aeschylus we discussed), the two by Sophocles were not tied together in a trilogy, since they were written at different times.

The story of *Oedipus Rex* concerns two royal families, the rulers of Thebes and of Corinth. The protagonist is Oedipus, king of Thebes, who freed the people of Thebes from a terrible plague 12 years previously. Since the previous king of Thebes, Laius, had just been killed on the road, the people of Thebes asked Oedipus, a stranger at the time but the person who had freed them from the plague, to be their new king. Laius' wife, Jocasta, became Oedipus' new queen.

Now a new plague is upon Thebes and Oedipus has asked Creon, the brother of Jocasta, to go to the oracle of Apollo and inquire about the cause of the plague and how it might be lifted. Creon returns as the play opens and announces that all will be well if the killer of Laius, the former king, is found and exiled from the city. Oedipus decrees that the murderer should be so punished and, in his attempt to find the murderer, sends for a blind seer who might be able to name the murderer. With great reluctance, the seer names Oedipus as the murderer. Oedipus is outraged and says it is merely a plot to make Creon the king. Jocasta says that she doesn't believe in seers or oracles anyway, and cites as an example the false prophecy that said her own son would kill his father and have children by his mother. She confesses that she prevented this from happening by abandoning her own infant in the mountains many years ago; as for Laius, he was believed to have been killed by robbers at the junction of three roads while on a trip to Delphi.

Oedipus is disturbed by his wife's information because he recalls killing a man many years ago at the very spot identified by Jocasta as the place where Laius was killed. At that moment, a messenger arrives bearing the information that the king of Corinth, a man Oedipus believes to be his father, has died and, because Oedipus was raised as the prince of Corinth, Oedipus has now been declared to be king of Corinth. Oedipus refuses to accept the kingship, however, because the queen of Corinth is not yet dead and Oedipus is afraid of an old prophecy concerning him—that he would kill his father and marry his mother. His fear of this prophecy led to his original flight from Corinth to Thebes many years ago. The messenger from Corinth then assures Oedipus that he had nothing to worry from that old prophecy because he, Oedipus, was not the blood child of the king and queen of Corinth. He was a foundling who had been brought to them because they could not have children. The messenger's statement is confirmed by the shepherd to whom Jocasta gave her infant many years ago, assuming that the shepherd would abandon the child. Jocasta then realizes the horrible situation: Oedipus is in fact the child she abandoned long ago, and the old prophecy has been fulfilled in every detail. She flees from the room and hangs herself above her bed. Oedipus then realizes what has happened; he blinds himself with a pin from Jocasta's gown and condemns himself to exile as he originally proclaimed as the punishment for the killer of Laius.

This compelling story teaches that fate (or the will of the gods) cannot be thwarted by humans, even though, like Oedipus, humans assume that they are powerful enough to overthrow that divine will. This feeling is really false pride (which is the tragic flaw in Oedipus' life). Note the strong ethical prohibition of patricide and, of course, incest. Like a modern mystery story, the plot unfolds in small steps, with hints and clues arising as the plot advances and, like the mystery, a final scene reveals the entire story and leads to the punishment of those who committed the crimes. A subtle feature of the play is the frequent contrast of light and dark, culminating in the light of understanding that Oedipus receives, and then the darkness of blindness that he then imposes on himself.

The story of *Antigone* follows the conclusion of *Oedipus Rex* by a few years. When Jocasta's brother, Creon, became king upon the exile of Oedipus, the son of Oedipus, Polyneices, fled Thebes but has now returned with an army to battle the king. However, Polyneices and his own brother, who has remained loyal to Creon, both die in the battle. Creon orders that the loyal brother is to be buried and afforded all the honors of a hero, but commands that the body of Polyneices is to remain unburied and left to rot in the open. If anyone tries to bury or otherwise honor Polyneice's body, that person is to be killed. A guard is placed over the body to ensure that the king's commands are obeyed.

When Antigone hears of the fate of her brother's body, she gives him the burial honor that she believes he deserves, even at the threat of the king's punishment. She believes that family and religious duties are higher than duty to the king.

Even though others plead for the life of Antigone, including Creon's own son (who is betrothed to Antigone), King Creon is adamant and Antigone is led away to the dungeon to die of starvation. A seer enters and tells Creon that the gods are displeased over his prideful actions, but Creon dismisses the seer with scorn. Shortly thereafter, a messenger tells Creon that Antigone has committed suicide and that his son has joined her in suicidal death. Creon goes to the dungeon and confirms the deaths. He picks up his son's body and returns to the main chamber, where Creon's wife sees the bloody corpse and flees the room. Shortly thereafter, Creon is told that his wife has also committed suicide over the loss of her son. Creon, distraught and deeply saddened that he has caused such a holocaust, commands his guard to slay him as the murderer of his son, wife, and intended daughter-in-law. The play ends with a restatement of the sadness of the plot and an identification of Creon's tragic flaw.

Man's highest blessedness
In wisdom chiefly stands;
And in the things that touch upon the gods
'Tis best, in word or deed,
To shun unholy pride.
Great words of boasting bring great
punishments,
And so to the gray-haired age
Teach wisdom at last.[1]

The third of the great Greek tragedians is **Euripides** (484–406 B.C.), who was a contemporary of Sophocles. Euripides seemed to acknowledge the power of the gods, especially in fate, but did not respect the gods and was accused of impiety, a serious crime in ancient Athens. Euripides created strong protagonists who were able to overcome many obstacles because of their own determination and wit. However, these protagonists were not able to overcome fate, which failure seemed to be attributed negatively to the gods.

Perhaps the play that most clearly illustrates Euripides' style and feelings is *Medea.* The protagonist is Medea, a barbarian princess who falls in love with Jason, a Greek who has journeyed to her land in search of the Golden Fleece. Medea is forced to leave her family and land because of her choice to help Jason obtain the fleece and then to go with him to Greece. They are married and have two children.

After some years in Greece, Jason rejects Medea in favor of Glauce, a daughter of Creon the king of the city. Medea, outraged, creates a stormy scene, whereupon Creon sentences her to exile. Medea sets her heart on revenge. She makes a gown that poisons any who put it on. The gown is given to Glauce as a wedding dress; just as Medea intended, Glauce dies a horribly painful death. But Medea's revenge was not yet fulfilled. To strike the hardest possible blow at Jason, Medea leads her own children into their house and there she takes their lives. At that moment Jason returns to his house seeking to revenge the death of Glauce. Jason confronts Medea and learns of her actions; he is devastated. Then, a chariot of fire descends and takes up Medea and the bodies of her children. Medea is being transported by a favorable god to safe haven in Athens, where she will bury her children and continue her life. Thus is the revenge of Medea complete, but at what price? The depth of anguish and suffering related by Euripides is far greater than what was shown by either Aeschylus or Sophocles, and this may be his greatest contribution to drama.

One other playwright should be mentioned. **Aristophanes,** unlike the others we have discussed, wrote comedies. He poked fun at the other playwrights and most of the other events of Athens during his time. His life overlapped Sophocles' and Euripides' (450–385 B.C.), extending past theirs well into the time of the Spartan rule of Athens following the end of the Peloponnesian War.

Aristophanes resented warfare and ridiculed the Greek focus on war in two of his greatest works, *The Birds* and *Lysistrata.* In the first, two men escape from Athens and build a home with the birds in mid-air. Their home cuts off contact between the gods and men and, therefore, the gods have to make peace with them in order to have everything return as it was. Zeus gives them his scepter of power.

In the second, Lysistrata convinces her fellow women in Athens to not make love to their husbands until peace is negotiated. The men give in, and envoys are sent to Sparta. The play ends with Athenians and Spartans dancing together for joy at the new peace.

Greek drama is one of the most enduring legacies of ancient Greece. Creativity was exhibited in early tragedies and comedies and then expanded, in steps, through plot innovations and enrichment of drama through character additions. These innovations came over several years by a handful of people whose names are linked to drama and to the concepts of creativity.

Music

Although methods for writing music were principally developed from the Middle Ages onward, scholars since at least the Renaissance have believed that many, if not all, of the Greek plays contained music. Some of those Renaissance scholars, intent on re-creating the music of Greek dramas, met regularly in sixteenth-century Florence to pool their studies and discuss ways to represent ancient music. They called their efforts **opera,** from the Italian word for "work." Our modern operas are direct descendents of their efforts to capture the full impact of the Greek dramas.

Some fragments of evidence suggest that the Greeks did, in fact, have a notation system for their music, and that at least the choruses of the Greek plays were usually sung or chanted to the accompaniment of flutes, lyres, pipes, cymbals, or similar ancient instruments. Our word for music that can be sung, **lyric,** comes from the concept that it was accompanied by a lyre. Another music-related word derived from the Greeks is **harmony.** For us, this is a pleasing combination of music in a vertical sense; that is, the notes at any one moment all sound good together. For the Greeks, harmony was more likely to be associated with a linear arrangement; that is, the instruments and voices all were in the same rhythm and overall pattern. Such music would, of course, also be harmonious in our sense, but the Greek understanding gives additional insights into the meaning of harmony.

The Greeks had various modes (somewhat like the modern major and minor modes) that conveyed various feelings with the music. Some modes were simple, and probably sounded somewhat like the Gregorian chants of the Middle Ages. This chanting style was useful in the Greek dramas because, through chanting, the unified voices of the chorus could be projected well. Other Greek modes were associated with martial (military) feelings, contentment, and allurement. These contentment and allurement modes might have been like the late Medieval and Renaissance troubadour songs or the madrigals.

Whatever the Greek music sounded like, both Plato and Aristotle believed that music was an important element of the ideal state. Plato believed in the power of music to influence people's lives. He thought that music molded the soul. Aristotle, following Pythagoras and Plato, believed that music was an important indicator of the universe, and that the planets actually had vibrations (music) associated with their orbits. It is likely that music instruction was an important part of the ancient curriculum, just as it became one of the seven courses of instruction in the liberal arts curriculum of the Middle Ages.

Art and Sculpture

The frescos of the Minoan and Mycenaean civilizations have already been identified as one of the most important art forms of ancient Grecian culture. These frescos reveal clothing styles, personal body characteristics like hair arrangements and the absence of facial hair, leisure and work activities, and many other details of early Greek life. They also show that the techniques of fresco painting were well developed even in the far antiquity and that the methods have, in many cases, proven to be capable of communicating brilliant colors and good image retention over hundreds of years.

Art in the Formative Period was mostly limited to pottery and some simple sculptures. An example of the pottery is shown in Figure 7.3. The decorations usually show either Greek domestic life or Greek warfare. From these we can get excellent ideas of what the styles of dress and armor were like, as well as everyday activities and the methods of warfare.

Since the pottery was clearly functional, that is, was used as containers, we could ask why the maker of the pottery took the time to decorate it. Was there some economic value to a decorated vessel or, perhaps, was it merely a way for the artist to show expression? Perhaps we shall never know, but it is clear that the figures are presented in a dynamic and interesting way, often with considerable skill.

Pre-classical sculpture was reminiscent of Egyptian sculpture—the representation was in a standard, fixed pose without dynamic action, and was generic; that is, it did not represent a real person. An example of early Greek sculpture is shown in Figure 7.4.

Later Greek sculpture departed from the Egyptian mode, as shown in Figure 7.5. Initially the figures showed just hand and leg movements. Eventually, especially in the Golden Age, the entire body was involved in the action as depicted in the famous discus thrower. The Greeks were learning to show greater realism.

Perhaps the most famous of all Greek sculptures is the Venus de Milo, located in the Louvre in Paris. This sculpture is especially important because it represents the Greek idea of beauty, and involves all aspects of the Greek concept of beauty—facial loveliness, symmetry, and body proportions suggested by the Golden Mean. Combined with these physical characteristics was an attempt to convey inner qualities. The Greeks realized that no real person represented perfect beauty, but believed that artificial representations of beauty, such as sculpture, might approach perfection. This perfection could be obtained only when sculpture was done with great technical capability, expressed reality in pose and dynamics, contained the correct elements of beauty (propor-

Figure 7.3 ■ *Greek vase (red and black). Image from Corel.*

Figure 7.4 ■ *Early Greek sculpture (kore). Image from Corel.*

Figure 7.5 ■ **A** and **B)** *Greek sculptures. Images from Corel.*

tion, symmetry, and loveliness), and expressed the inner qualities that radiated beauty. These were the contributions of Greek sculpture. They were seldom achieved, but often sought, and they became a standard for beauty throughout the ages.

Architecture

One of the most common modern expressions of ancient Greek culture is in architecture. That style was not only used extensively throughout the ancient Greek world, but it has been copied by several other cultures throughout history. Romans used the essential elements of the Greek style in their most important governmental and religious buildings. Later, the builders of the Renaissance used key features of Greek architecture. The Greek style was renewed again in the Neoclassical period, around the later part of the eighteenth century, and then, from time to time, continuing on to the present, where classic Greek columns are ubiquitous, especially in governmental settings such as Washington, D.C. This profusion of the Greek style and the similarities of the different periods are shown in Figure 7.6. The Greek style seems to convey stability, democracy, and beauty—attributes which are, of course, highly valued in the seat of government, but also in settings such as law courts and conservative businesses. The enduring nature of this style certainly confirms a creativeness, but what, we might ask, is the underlying nature of the creativity of this style?

Some historians and, we suppose, experts in architecture have suggested that the Parthenon is the most perfect building in the world, and so we might start with that building to discover the nature of the creativity of Greek architecture. The Parthenon was built during the Greek Golden Age under the direction of Pericles as a temple to Athena Parthenos (the virgin), the patron goddess of Athens. The name of the building is derived from the descriptor term of Athena. A gigantic statue of Athena (about 38 feet high) inside the central room (called the *cella*) served as the center of worship to this goddess.

Figure 7.6 ■ **A)** *Ancient Greek style in Roman temple.* Image from Corel. **B)** *Ancient Greek style in United States Supreme Court.* *Image © 2005 by PhotoDisc.*

The dimensions of the building were based on the Golden Ratio. The ratio of the overall length to the overall width is the famous ratio: 1.62:1. So too approximately, are the ratios of the width of the front face to the height of the front face. Subdivisions of the building, such as the ratios of sections along the frieze and of sections of columns to their height, also follow the Golden Ratio.

The building was constructed so that it would have the appearance of perfect symmetry and proportion when viewed from a distance. For example, the horizontal lines of the building, such as the floor, are actually slightly convex, so that when viewed from afar the horizontal lines will appear to be straight. (I, Strong, have personally sighted along the top of the steps on the side of the Parthenon and confirmed the existence of this bow.) In a similar way, the tops of the columns tip slightly, to give the impression of perfect straightness when viewed with distant parallax. The columns are slightly thicker about one-third of the way up, to give the impression of perfect straightness. The columns near the corners are slightly thicker overall, and spaced more closely than are those in the center of the building, to compensate for the way the eye tends to make evenly spaced vertical lines appear closer together and thicker in the middle of the viewing area. Clearly the Greeks who built the building understood how symmetry and exact proportions could be conveyed to the human eye.

When originally built, the Parthenon was decorated with beautiful sculptures and reliefs, in the **pediments** (the triangular areas at the ends, just underneath the roof) and on the **frieze** (the decorated border that goes around the building above the columns). Phidias, one of the greatest of ancient Greek sculptors, was the artistic director for the Parthenon. He reportedly said that he alone had seen the actual image of the gods, and that he was revealing it to mankind. Another of his works was the colossal statue of Zeus at Olympia (no longer in existence), which has been named one of the seven wonders of the ancient world.

The Parthenon sculptures and reliefs were removed in 1806 by Thomas Bruce, Seventh Earl of

Elgin. They are now called the Elgin Marbles. Lord Elgin went to Athens to sketch the Parthenon decorations and to make plaster casts of them. When he arrived, he found that the Parthenon was being used as a munitions storage facility in the war between the Greeks and the Ottoman Turks. Some shelling had already occurred, and the building was clearly being severely damaged, as can be seen today. Lord Elgin bought the sculptures, removed them from the building, and shipped them to London. Other parts of the building's decorations, including much of the frieze, were sold to the British government in 1816. All these parts of the Parthenon are beautifully displayed in the British Museum. The Greek government disputes this story and has requested the return of the decorations, but, so far, to no avail.

Perhaps the most obvious elements of the Greek style are pillars supporting a lintel in a generally rectangular building. Three different types or orders of pillar designs are traditional—Doric, Ionic, and Corinthian—and these are shown in Figure 7.7. Each order has unique characteristics, such as differences in the tops (called the **capitals**), the nature of the shaft (shape and surface textures), the nature of the base of the column, and other details of the building, such as the frieze and the cornice (areas above the columns). The choice of style seemed to be up to the architect, as we see temples of several styles in the same general location and built in the same general timeframe. For example, the Parthenon is in the Doric style, but nearby on the Acropolis is the temple of Athena Nike ("victorious"), which is in the Ionic style. Another interesting columnar type is the caryatid—columns in the shape of women. This style can also be seen on the Acropolis in the Erechtheion, a temple near the Parthenon, shown in Figure 7.8.

Figure 7.7 ■ *Doric, Ionic, and Corinthian columns.*

Figure 7.8 ■ *Caryatids on the Erechtheion temple on the Acropolis. Image © 2006 Jupiter Images Corporation.*

History

The Greeks began the process of systematically and (we hope) accurately recording current and past events—the very basis of modern historical studies. Two great historians are generally considered to be the founders of this discipline. They are **Herodotus** and **Thucydides,** both of whom lived in the fifth century B.C. during the time of Pericles.

Herodotus attempted to tell the story of the great Greek victory over the Persians, with a beginning, middle, and end, as well as an explanation of why things happened the way they did. For example, he said that the Persians were defeated because of their *hubris* (excessive prideful ambition), overconfidence, and arrogance. He then cited historical examples and interesting anecdotes to prove his points. For example, he said that when Xerxes was on his way to attack Greece, he became angry when he reached the Hellespont because the waves were so high. Xerxes therefore commanded that the water be whipped, just as if it were a disobedient servant.

In addition to his retelling of the Persian wars, Herodotus traveled widely and gave us detailed descriptions of the Persian Empire, Egypt, and many parts of Greece. He interviewed eminent people, including these interviews in the careful notes he took describing his travels.

The other great historian, Thucydides, advanced the subject of history by telling of the final years of the Peloponnesian Wars, concentrating on the military part of the history, since he was a military man. The contribution of Thucydides is that he told the story objectively. In spite of the fact that Thucydides was on the losing side and that he was exiled from his home in Athens for losing an important battle, Thucydides tells his tale and gives his reasoning without taking sides, or giving it a personal or Athenian slant. Thucydides reported on the words of famous people (for example, Pericles' funeral tribute), but was criticized because he could not have been at all of the places to hear the great men speak. He admitted that this was so, but said that he had investigated the facts as deeply as possible and believed his efforts reflected what could have been said.

Medicine

Greek medicine was an interesting blend of the practices of the Egyptians and Mesopotamians combined with the science and philosophy of the Greeks. The Egyptians and Mesopotamians had experimented with quite sophisticated surgery, even brain surgery, which, combined with the knowledge of the body that arose from the mummification process, gave a strong foundation for understanding the body. That information was then used as the basis for medicine in Greece, but three different approaches evolved. Those who followed the first approach were the rationalists—they tried to apply to medicine the methods of natural philosophy (science), which led to a speculative and theoretical medicine. These rationalists tied medicine to the four elements and the four conditions (which will be discussed in the next chapter when we examine the teachings of Aristotle), and declared that the body had four fluids or humors—blood, yellow bile, black bile, and phlegm—which must be kept in balance for health to be maintained. If the body shows a fever, for example, that means that the bodily fluid associated with heat, the blood, would be in excess and therefore needs to be reduced. These physicians would, therefore, advocate blood-letting as a cure for fever.

The second group of medical authorities was the empiricists—those who believed that only visible symptoms and visible causes should be considered in treatment. They also believed that treatments should be based on past proven success. They believed that attempts to understand the workings of the body were a waste of time.

The third approach, called the methodists, saw the body as a system, and believed that sickness occurred when the system was not correct. Therefore, tenseness and laxness of the body were indications of problems, which could be solved by various drugs and physical remedies. Opium was known to the Greeks and used by this group as a way to treat some illnesses. The methodists generally viewed the rationalist and the empiricist approaches as unnecessarily complicated.

During the latter period of Pericles' rule in Athens, a medical physician of great importance established a broad program of medical practice that redefined Greek medicine and became a legacy for medicine even to the present day. This physician was Hippocrates (460–370 B.C.). His teachings suggested that natural explanations should be sought for natural phenomena, and that medicine was not magic, nor was it dependent on the whims of the gods, thus extending the teachings of Thales to medicine. **Hippocrates** also believed in the four bodily humors and the need for balance among them. In these aspects of his medicine he supported the rationalists, but he also believed that medical diagnoses should be based on observations of the sick person, and therefore supported the empiricists. He also studied the importance of diet and rest, investigated the action of various medicines, and suggested that surgery be used only as a last resort. He even studied the hereditary nature of some diseases. These concepts supported the basic concepts of the methodists.

The unification of the three approaches was not only a valuable contribution to medical practice and science, but it also gave a basis for Hippocrates' assertion that medicine deserved to be considered a craft separate from philosophy, with appropriate training and recognition for its practitioners. He then proposed a code of behavior and ethics, which was adopted in his lifetime and is still recited at the medical school graduations. This code is, of course, the Hippocratic Oath.

Creativity

After this examination of living in the Classical Period of Greece, we might pause one more time to consider why this period was one of the most creative in human history. First, let's remember a few things about what this time *was not.* It was not a time of peace. It was not a time of stability. It was neither a worldwide phenomenon nor even a Greek-wide phenomenon. It happened principally in the city of Athens.

We believe that the factors leading to this burst of creativity include the following:

- Past Greek history had developed a culture of creative inquiry even from the time of Thales, Pythagoras, and Democritus.
- The Greek language and alphabet facilitated creative inquiry, analysis, science, and literature. Furthermore, the ease of writing enabled literacy over many economic and social classes, leading to a general high level of education and an appreciation of new ways of thinking.
- Athens had developed a system of government that encouraged individual responsibility and involvement, thus empowering the people.

- The middle class in Athens shared in the governance of the city, which both fostered their creative contributions and brought in their substantial resources in money and time. Remember that this class of people is often the very group of artisans, technicians, and thinkers who are the leaders in creativity.
- Acceptance of the rule of law gave an overall stability to the city, even in light of the war. Justice was not always correct (as we shall see in the next chapter when we discuss Socrates), but the system of justice was constant. (That same concept also applies to the judicial system in the United States today.)
- The large slave population afforded much leisure time, which could be used for creative efforts.
- The government actively supported the arts, architecture, drama, and other creative activities.
- The general population supported artistic efforts and rewarded creative excellence with both money and prestige.
- Multiple areas of creativity were pursued. Often, the creativity in one discipline encouraged and assisted creativity in another. For example, architecture and sculpture were synergistic, as were mathematics and science.
- The wealth and culture of Athens provided markets and means for the creators to benefit economically from their work.
- The entire culture seemed abuzz with creative energy.

Somehow, in this wonderful milieu of creative endeavor, three men stood out as intellectual leaders in the city. They were not always liked, but they seemed to have been respected. They created an atmosphere of learning and critical thinking that directed much of the attitudes toward life, perhaps all aspects of life, of the Athenian population. These three—teacher to pupil then teacher to pupil again—formed the basis of critical thinking for the remainder of western history (certainly until today); their importance cannot be over emphasized. We will now examine these three, but that takes a whole new chapter.

Timeline—Important Dates

Date	Event
534 B.C.	*Thespis defines Greek drama, and plays begin*
525–456 B.C.	*Aeschylus, the first of the great playwrights*
496–406 B.C.	*Sophocles, the second of the great playwrights*
484–406 B.C.	*Euripedes, the third of the great playwrights*
484–420 B.C.	*Herodotus, historian*
461–429 B.C.	*Pericles rules Athens*
460–400 B.C.	*Thucydides, historian*
460–370 B.C.	*Hippocrates, physician*
450–385 B.C.	*Aristophones, the fourth of the great playwrights, comedies*
431–404 B.C.	*Peloponnesian War*

Notes

1. Sophocles, *The Complete Works of Sophocles,* Sir Richard Claverhouse Jebb (trans.), Bantam, 1967.

Suggested Readings

Hippocrates, *The Theory and Practice of Medicine,* Emerson Crosby Kelley (Introduction), Philosophical Library, 1964.

Sophocles, *The Complete Works of Sophocles,* Sir Richard Claverhouse Jebb (trans.), Bantam, 1967.

Sophocles, *Oedipus Rex,* Dover, 1991.

Article 9

Sophocles: Oedipus Rex

Introduction

Life in the fifth century B.C. in Athens was special. The economy, based on trade throughout the Mediterranean, was thriving and brought much wealth and sophistication to the people of the city. The government of the city was progressive, having instituted a democratic system to give power to the landholders and the merchants, and also to establish the rule of law. The cultural environment was the most active and sophisticated of any place in the world at the time (and for many years thereafter). All of these factors contributed to create a Golden Age that has been the envy of many later civilizations.

One of the most important aspects of the Golden Age was drama. During a yearly festival, several playwrights competed with a series of four plays, three related tragedies and a satyr. The entire city became involved in the festival and the winner was lauded for the rest of the year, and beyond. (The concept is similar to the Academy Awards for best motion picture.) The foremost of the dramatists and consistent winner was Sophocles. He was not the inventor of Greek drama, nor was he the developer of tragedy, nor was he the first to innovate with multiple actors on stage simultaneously, but he combined all of these previous innovations with his own concepts of more than two actors, showy stage effects, captivating plots, compelling characters, and excellent writing style to create the best plays of his age and, perhaps, any other age until the time of the Renaissance when Shakespeare emerged. Sophocles, like Shakespeare, was also an actor and producer of the plays he wrote.

Sophocles was recognized by no less authority than Aristotle as the greatest of the playwrights, and used Sophocles as the model for explaining what makes a tragedy great. Aristotle stated that the play should show how a main character encountered difficulties and tried to cope with them. Because of a tragic character flaw that the main character possesses, the difficulties cannot be resolved happily and so the play ends tragically. The character flaw has sometimes been called a "Sophoclean defect" because Sophocles was so adept in depicting these flaws realistically and powerfully in his characters.

Those features are all present in the best known of the plays of Sophocles—*Oedipus Rex* (sometimes called Oedipus the King). The main character, Oedipus, is a good person who tries to avoid the prophecy that he would kill his father and marry his mother. Sadly, in spite of all his efforts, Oedipus realizes that he has committed the very acts which he sought to avoid. Much has been written about the nature of his Sophoclean or tragic flaw, but the causes of his difficulties and his responses to them are open to your own interpretation. Analyzing his situation is an important part of reading and appreciating *Oedipus Rex.* Other features of the play include the nature of illumination of truth and then, somewhat by analogy, the use of light and dark in both plot and staging. (For instance, when Oedipus finally realizes the truth of his situation, he blinds himself because, apparently, he cannot stand the "light" of the truth.) Such are the subtleties of this play that you should look for and enjoy.

Oedipus Rex

Persons Represented

OEDIPUS, *King of Thebes*
PRIEST *of Zeus*
CREON, *brother to Jocasta the Queen*
TIRESIAS, *a Prophet, with the title of King*
A Messenger from Corinth
An old Shepherd.
A Second Messenger, servant of Oedipus' household.
JOCASTA *the Queen, wife to Oedipus, formerly married to Laius the last King.*
ANTIGONE, ISMENE, } *daughters to Oedipus and Jocasta*
The CHORUS *is composed of Senators of Thebes.*
Inhabitants of Thebes, Attendants.
A Boy leading Tiresias.

Scene, before the Royal Palace at Thebes. Enter OEDIPUS; *to him the Priest of Zeus, and Inhabitants of Thebes.*

OEDIPUS Children, you modern brood of Cadmus* old,
What mean you, sitting in your sessions here,
High-coronalled with votive olive-boughs,
While the whole city teems with incense-smoke,
And paean hymns, and sounds of woe the while?
Deeming unmeet, my children, this to learn
From others, by the mouth of messengers,
I have myself come hither, Oedipus,
Known far and wide by name. Do thou, old man,
Since 'tis thy privilege to speak for these,
Say in what case ye stand; if of alarm,
Or satisfaction with my readiness
To afford all aid; hard-hearted must I be,
Did I not pity such petitioners.

PRIEST Great Oedipus, my country's governor,
Thou seest our generations, who besiege
Thy altars here; some not yet strong enough
To flutter far; some priests, with weight of years
Heavy, myself of Zeus; and these, the flower
Of our young manhood; all the other folk
Sit, with like branches, in the market-place,
By the Ismenian hearth oracular**
And the twin shrines of Pallas.*** Lo, the city
Labours—thyself art witness—over-deep
Already, powerless to uprear her head
Out of the abysses of a surge of blood;
Stricken in the budding harvest of her soil,
Stricken in her pastured herds, and barren travail
Of women; and He, the God with spear of fire,
Leaps on the city, a cruel pestilence,
And harries it; whereby the Cadmean home
Is all dispeopled, and with groan and wail
The blackness of the Grave made opulent.
Not that we count thee as the peer of Heaven,
I, nor these children, seat us at thy hearth;
But as of men found foremost in affairs,
Chances of life and shifts of Providence;
Whose coming to our Cadmean town released
The toll we paid, of a hard Sorceress, ****
And that, without instruction or advice
Of our imparting; but of Heaven it came
Thou art named, and known, our life's establisher.
Thee therefore, Oedipus, the mightiest head
Among us all, all we thy supplicants
Implore to find some way to succour us,
Whether thou knowest it through some voice from heaven,
Or, haply of some man; for I perceive
In men experienced that their counsels best
Find correspondence in things actual.
Haste thee, most absolute sir, be the state's builder!

---

* Founder of Thebes.

** Referring to Ismene, a legendary Theban woman.

*** Athena.

**** The Sphinx, whose riddle Oedipus guessed.

Haste thee, look to it; doth not our country now
Call thee deliverer, for thy zeal of yore?
Never let us remember of thy rule
That we stood once erectly, and then fell;
But build this city in stability!
With a fair augury didst thou shape for us
Our fortune then; like be thy prowess now!
If thou wilt rule this land (which thou art lord of),
It were a fairer lordship filled with folk
Than empty; towers and ships are nothingness,
Void of our fellow men to inhabit them.

OEDIPUS Ah my poor children, what you come to seek
Is known already—not unknown to me.
You are all sick, I know it; and in your sickness
There is not one of you so sick as I.
For in your case his own particular pain
Comes to each singly; but my heart at once
Groans for the city, and for myself, and you.
Not therefore as one taking rest in sleep
Do you uprouse me; rather deem of me
As one that wept often, and often came
By many ways through labyrinths of care;
And the one remedy that I could find
By careful seeking—I supplied it. Creon,
Menoeceus' son, the brother of my queen,
I sent to Pytho, to Apollo's house,
To ask him by what act or word of mine
I might redeem this city; and the hours
Already measured even with today
Make me solicitous how he has sped;
For he is longer absent than the time
Sufficient, which is strange. When he shall come,
I were a wretch did I not then do all
As the God shews.

PRIEST In happy time thou speak'st;
As these, who tell me Creon is at hand.

OEDIPUS Ah King Apollo, might he but bring grace,
Radiant in fortune, as he is in face!

PRIEST I think he comes with cheer; he would not, else,
Thus be approaching us with crown on brow,
All berries of the bay.

OEDIPUS We shall know soon;
He is within hearing.

Enter CREON, *attended.*

My good lord and cousin,
Son of Menoeceus,
What answer of the God have you brought home?

CREON Favourable; I mean, even what sounds ominously,
If it have issue in the way forthright,
May all end well.

OEDIPUS How runs the oracle?
I am not confident, nor prone to fear
At what you say, so far.

CREON If you desire
To hear while these stand near us, I am ready
To speak at once—or to go in with you.

OEDIPUS Speak before all! My heavy load of care
More for their sake than for my own I bear.

CREON What the God told me, that will I declare.
Phoebus our Lord gives us express command
To drive pollution, bred within this land,
Out of the country, and not cherish it
Beyond the power of healing.

OEDIPUS By what purge?
What is the tenor of your tragedy?

CREON Exile, or recompense of death for death;
Since 'tis this blood makes winter to the city.

OEDIPUS Whose fate is this he signifies?

CREON My liege,
We had a leader, once, over this land,
Called Laius—ere you held the helm of state.

OEDIPUS So I did hear; I never saw the man.

CREON The man is dead; and now, we are clearly bidden
To bring to account certain his murderers.

OEDIPUS And where on earth are they? Where shall be found
This dim-seen track-mark of an ancient crime?

CREON "Within this land," it ran. That which is sought,

That may be caught. What is unheeded
scapes us.

OEDIPUS Was it at home, afield, or anywhere
Abroad, that Laius met this violent end?

CREON He went professedly on pilgrimage;
But since he started, came back home no
more.

OEDIPUS Nor any messenger nor way-fellow
Looked on, from whom one might have
learnt his story
And used it?

CREON No, they perished, all but one;
He fled, affrighted; and of what he saw
Had but one thing to say for certain.

OEDIPUS Well,
And what was that? one thing might be the
means
Of our discovering many, could we gain
Some narrow ground for hope.

CREON Robbers, he said,
Met them, and slew him; by no single strength,
But multitude of hands.

OEDIPUS How could your robber
Have dared so far—except there were some
practice
With gold from hence?

CREON Why, it seemed probable.
But, Laius dead, no man stood up to help
Amid our ills.

OEDIPUS What ill was in the way,
Which, when a sovereignty had lapsed like
this,
Kept you from searching of it out?

CREON The Sphinx
With her enigma forced us to dismiss
Things out of sight, and look to our own
steps.

OEDIPUS Well, I will have it all to light again.
Right well did Phoebus, yea and well may
you
Insist on this observance toward the dead;
So shall you see me, as of right, with you,
Venging this country and the God together.
Why, 'tis not for my neighbours' sake, but
mine,
I shall dispel this plague-spot; for the man,
Whoever it may be, who murdered him,
Lightly might hanker to serve me the same.
I benefit myself in aiding him.
Up then, my children, straightway, from the
floor;
Take up your votive branches; let some other
Gather the tribes of Cadmus hitherward;
Say, I will make clean work. Please Heaven,
our state
Shall soon appear happy, or desperate.

PRIEST Come children, let us rise; it was for
this,
Which he himself proclaims, that we came
hither.
Now may the sender of these oracles.
In saving and in plague-staying, Phoebus,
come!

[*Exeunt* CREON, PRIEST *and* THEBANS.
OEDIPUS *retires.*

Enter THEBAN SENATORS, as Chorus.

Chorus

I. 1.

O Prophecy of Jove, whose words are sweet,
With what doom art thou sent
To glorious Thebes, from Pytho's gilded seat?
I am distraught with fearful wonderment,
I thrill with terror, and wait reverently—
Yea, Io Paean, Delian lord,* on thee!
What matter thou wilt compass—either
strange,
Or once again recurrent as the seasons
change,
Offspring of golden Hope, immortal Oracle,
Tell me, O tell!

I. 2.

Athena first I greet with invocation,
Daughter of Jove, divine!
Next Artemis thy sister, of this nation
Keeper, high seated in the encircling shrine,

* Apollo.

Filled with her praises, of our market-place,
And Phoebus, shooting arrows far through
space;
Appear ye Three, the averters of my fate!
If e'er before, when mischief rose upon the
state,
Ye quenched the flames of evil, putting them
away,
Come—come to-day!

II. 1.

Woe, for unnumbered are the ills we bear!
Sickness pervades our hosts;
Nor is there any spear of guardian care,
Wherewith a man might save us, found in all
our coasts.
For all the fair soil's produce now no longer
springs;
Nor women from the labour and loud cries
Of their child-births arise;
And you may see, flying like a bird with
wings,
One after one, outspeeding the resistless brand,
Pass—to the Evening Land.

II. 2.

In countless hosts our city perisheth.
Her children on the plain
Lie all unpitied—pitiless—breeding death.
Our wives meanwhile, and white-haired
mothers in their train,
This way and that, suppliant, along the
altar-side
Sit, and bemoan their doleful maladies;
Like flame their paeans rise,
With wailing and lament accompanied;
For whose dear sake O Goddess, O Jove's
golden child,
Send Help with favour mild!

III. 1.

And Ares the Destroyer, him who thus—
Not now in harness of brass shields, as
wont—
Ringed round with clamour, meets us front to
front
And fevers us,
O banish from our country! Drive him back,
With winds upon his track,
On to the chamber vast of Amphitrite,**
Or that lone anchorage, the Thracian main;
For now, if night leave bounds to our annoy,
Day levels all again;
Wherefore, O father, Zeus, thou that dost
wield the might
Of fire-fraught light,
Him with thy bolt destroy!

III. 2.

Next, from the bendings of thy golden string
I would see showered thy artillery
Invincible, marshalled to succour me,
Lycean King!*
Next, those flame-bearing beams, arrows
most bright,
Which Artemis by night
Through Lycian highlands speeds her
scattering;
Thou too, the Evian, with thy Maenad band,
Thou golden-braided patron of this land
Whose visage glows with wine,
O save us from the god whom no gods
honour! Hear,
Bacchus! Draw near,
And light thy torch of pine!

Enter OEDIPUS, *attended.*

OEDIPUS You are at prayers; but for your
prayers' intent
You may gain help, and of your ills relief,
If you will minister to the pestilence,
And hearken and receive my words, which I—
A stranger to this tale, and to the deed
A stranger—shall pronounce; for of myself
I could not follow up the traces far,
Not having any key. But, made since then
A fellow-townsman to the townsmen here,
To all you Cadmeans I thus proclaim;
Whichever of you knows the man, by whom

** The sea.

* Apollo.

Laius the son of Labdacus was slain,
Even if he is afraid, seeing he himself
Suppressed the facts that made against himself,
I bid that man shew the whole truth to me;
For he shall suffer no disparagement,
Except to quit the land, unscathed. Again,
If any knows another—say some stranger
To have been guilty, let him not keep silence;
For I will pay him the reward, and favour
Shall be his due beside it. But again,
If you will hold your peace, and any man
From self or friend in terror shall repel
This word of mine, then—you must hear me say
What I shall do. Whoe'er he be, I order
That of this land, whose power and throne are mine,
None entertain him, none accost him, none
Cause him to share in prayers or sacrifice
Offered to Heaven, or pour him lustral wave,
But all men from their houses banish him;
Since it is he contaminates us all,
Even as the Pythian oracle divine
Revealed but now to me. Such is my succour
Of him that's dead, and of the Deity.
And on the guilty head I imprecate
That whether by himself he has lain covert,
Or joined with others, without happiness,
Evil, in evil, he may pine and die.
And for myself I pray, if with my knowledge
He should become an inmate of my dwelling,
That I may suffer all that I invoked
On these just now. Moreover all these things
I charge you to accomplish, in behalf
Of me, and of the God, and of this land,
So ruined, barren and forsaken of Heaven.
For even though the matter were not now
By Heaven enjoined you, 'twas unnatural
For you to suffer it to pass uncleansed,
A man most noble having been slain, a king too!
Rather, you should have searched it out; but now,
Since I am vested with the government
Which he held once, and have his marriage-bed,
And the same wife; and since our progeny—
If his had not miscarried—had sprung from us
With common ties of common motherhood—
Only that Fate came heavy upon his head—
On these accounts I, as for my own father,
Will fight this fight, and follow out every clue,
Seeking to seize the author of his murder—
The scion of Labdacus and Polydore
And earlier Cadmus and Agenor old;
And such as disobey—the Gods I ask
Neither to raise them harvest from the ground
Nor children from the womb, but that they perish
By this fate present, and yet worse than this;
While you, the other Cadmeans, who approve,
May succouring Justice and all Gods in heaven
Accompany for good for evermore!

1 SENATOR Even as thou didst adjure me, so, my king,
I will reply. I neither murdered him,
Nor can point out the murderer. For the quest—
To tell us who on earth has done this deed
Belonged to Phoebus, by whose word it came.

OEDIPUS Your words are just; but to constrain the Gods
To what they will not, passes all men's power.

1 SENATOR I would say something which appears to me
The second chance to this.

OEDIPUS And your third, also—
If such you have—by all means tell it.

1 SENATOR Sir,
Tiresias above all men, I am sure,
Ranks as a seer next Phoebus, king with king;
Of him we might enquire and learn the truth
With all assurance.

OEDIPUS That is what I did;
And with no slackness; for by Creon's advice
I sent, twice over; and for some time, now,

'Tis strange he is not here.
1 SENATOR Then all the rest
Are but stale words and dumb.
OEDIPUS What sort of words?
I am weighing every utterance.
1 SENATOR He was said
To have been killed by footpads.
OEDIPUS So I heard;
But he who saw it is himself unseen.
1 SENATOR Well, if his bosom holds a grain of fear,
Curses like yours he never will abide!
OEDIPUS Whom the doing awes not, speaking cannot scare
1 SENATOR Then there is one to expose him: here they come,
Bringing the godlike seer, the only man
Who has in him the tongue that cannot lie.

Enter TIRESIAS, *led by a boy.*

OEDIPUS Tiresias, thou who searchest everything.
Communicable or nameless, both in heaven
And on the earth—thou canst not see the city,
But knowest no less what pestilence visits it,
Wherefrom our only saviour and defence
We find, sir king, in thee. For Phoebus—if
Thou dost not know it from the messengers—
To us, who sent to ask him, sent word back,
That from this sickness no release should come,
Till we had found and slain the men who slew
Laius, or driven them, banished, from the land.
Wherefore do thou—not sparing augury,
Either through birds, or any other way
Thou hast of divination—save thyself,
And save the city, and me; save the whole mass
By this dead corpse infected; for in thee
Stands our existence; and for men, to help
With might and main is of all tasks the highest.
TIRESIAS Alas! How terrible it is to know,
Where no good comes of knowing! Of these matters
I was full well aware, but let them slip me;
Else I had not come hither.
OEDIPUS But what is it?
How out of heart thou hast come!
TIRESIAS Let me go home;
So shalt thou bear thy load most easily—
If thou wilt take my counsel—and I mine.
OEDIPUS Thou hast not spoken loyally, nor friendly
Toward the State that bred thee, cheating her
Of this response!
TIRESIAS Because I do not see
Thy words, not even thine, going to the mark;
So, not to be in the same plight—
1 SENATOR For Heaven's sake,
If thou hast knowledge, do not turn away,
When all of us implore thee suppliant!
TIRESIAS Ye
Are all unknowing; my say, in any sort,
I will not say, lest I display thy sorrow.
OEDIPUS What, you do know, and will not speak? Your mind
Is to betray us, and destroy the city?
TIRESIAS I will not bring remorse upon myself
And upon you. Why do you search these matters?
Vain, vain! I will not tell you.
OEDIPUS Worst of traitors!
For you would rouse a very stone to wrath—
Will you not speak out ever, but stand thus
Relentless and persistent?
TIRESIAS My offence
You censure; but your own, at home, you see not,
And yet blame me!
OEDIPUS Who would not take offence,
Hearing the words in which you flout the city?
TIRESIAS Well, it will come, keep silence as I may.
OEDIPUS And what will come should I not hear from you?
TIRESIAS I will declare no further. Storm at this,
If't please you, to the wildest height of anger!
OEDIPUS At least I will not, being so far in anger,
Spare anything of what is clear to me:

Know, I suspect you joined to hatch the deed;
Yea, did it—all but slaying with your own hands;
And if you were not blind, I should aver
The act was your work only!

TIRESIAS Was it so?
I charge you to abide by your decree
As you proclaimed it; not from this day forth
Speak word to these, or me; being of this land
Yourself the abominable contaminator!

OEDIPUS So shamelessly set you this story on foot,
And think, perhaps, you shall go free?

TIRESIAS I am
Free! for I have in me the strength of truth.

OEDIPUS Who prompted you? for from your art it was not!

TIRESIAS Yourself! You made me speak, against my will.

OEDIPUS Speak! What? Repeat, that I may learn it better!

TIRESIAS Did you not understand me at first hearing,
Or are you tempting me, when you say "Speak!"

OEDIPUS Not so to say for certain; speak again.

TIRESIAS I say that you are Laius' murderer—
He whom you seek.

OEDIPUS Not without chastisement
Shall you, twice over, utter wounds!

TIRESIAS Then shall I
Say something more, that may incense you further?

OEDIPUS Say what you please; it will be said in vain.

TIRESIAS I say you know not in what worst of shame
You live together with those nearest you,
And see not in what evil plight you stand.

OEDIPUS Do you expect to go on revelling
In utterances like this?

TIRESIAS Yes, if the truth
Has any force at all.

OEDIPUS Why so it has,
Except for you; it is not so with you;
Blind as you are in eyes, and ears, and mind!

TIRESIAS Fool, you reproach me as not one of these
Shall not reproach you, soon!

OEDIPUS You cannot hurt me,
Nor any other who beholds the light,
Your life being all one night.

TIRESIAS Nor is it fated
You by my hand should fall; Apollo is
Sufficient; he will bring it all to pass.

OEDIPUS Are these inventions Creon's work, or yours?

TIRESIAS Your bane is no-ways Creon, but your own self.

OEDIPUS O riches, and dominion, and the craft
That excels craft, and makes life enviable,
How vast the grudge that is nursed up for you,
When for this sovereignty, which the state
Committed to my hands, unsought-for, free,
Creon, the trusty, the familiar friend,
With secret mines covets to oust me from it,
And has suborned a sorcerer like this,
An engine-botching crafty cogging knave,
Who has no eyes to see with, but for gain,
And was born blind in the art! Why, tell me now,
How stand your claims to prescience? How came it,
When the oracular monster was alive,
You said no word to set this people free?
And yet it was not for the first that came
To solve her riddle; sooth was needed then,
Which you could not afford; neither from birds,
Nor any inspiration; till I came,
The unlettered Oedipus, and ended her,
By sleight of wit, untaught of augury—
I whom you now seek to cast out, in hope
To stand upon the steps of Creon's throne!
You and the framer of this plot methinks
Shall rue your purge for guilt! Dotard you seem,
Else by experience you had come to know
What thoughts these are you think!

1 SENATOR As we conceive,
His words appear (and, Oedipus, your own,)

To have been said in anger; now not such
Our need, but rather to consider this—
How best to interpret the God's oracle.

TIRESIAS King as you are, we must be peers at least
In argument; I am your equal, there;
For I am Loxias'* servant, and not yours;
So never need be writ of Creon's train.
And since you have reproached me with my blindness,
I say—you have your sight, and do not see
What evils are about you, nor with whom,
Nor in what home you are dwelling. Do you know
From whom you are? Yea, you are ignorant
That to your own you are an enemy,
Whether on earth, alive, or under it.
Soon from this land shall drive you, stalking grim,
Your mother's and your father's two-edged curse,
With eyes then dark, though they look proudly now.
What place on earth shall not be harbour, then,
For your lamenting? What Cithaeron-peak**
Shall not be resonant soon, when you discern
What hymen-song was that, which wafted you
On a fair voyage, to foul anchorage
Under your roof? and multitudes besides
Of ills you know not of shall level you
Down to your self—down to your children! Go,
Trample on Creon, and on this mouth of mine;
But know, there is not one of all mankind
That shall be bruised more utterly than you.

OEDIPUS Must I endure to hear all this from him?
Hence, to perdition! quickly hence! begone
Back from these walls, and turn you home again.

TIRESIAS But that you called me, I had not come hither.

OEDIPUS I did not know that you would utter folly;
Else I had scarce sent for you, to my house.

TIRESIAS Yea, such is what we seem, foolish to you,
And to your fathers, who begat you, wise.

OEDIPUS What fathers? Stop! Who was it gave me being?

TIRESIAS This day shall give you birth and death in one.

OEDIPUS How all too full of riddles and obscure
Is your discourse!

TIRESIAS Were you not excellent
At solving riddles?

OEDIPUS Ay, cast in my teeth
Matters in which you must allow my greatness!

TIRESIAS And yet this very fortune was your ruin!

OEDIPUS Well, if I saved this city, I care not.

TIRESIAS Well,
I am going; and you, boy, take me home.

OEDIPUS Ay, let him.
Your turbulence impedes us, while you stay;
When you are gone, you can annoy no more.

[Retires.

TIRESIAS I go, having said that I came to say;
Not that I fear your frown; for you possess
No power to kill me; but I say to you—
The man you have been seeking, threatening him,
And loud proclaiming him for Laius' murder,
That man is here; believed a foreigner
Here sojourning; but shall be recognized
For Theban born hereafter; yet not pleased
In the event; for blind instead of seeing,
And poor for wealthy, to a foreign land,
A staff to point his footsteps, he shall go.
Also to his own sons he shall be found
Related as a brother, though their sire,
And of the woman from whose womb he came

* Apollo's.

** Mountain associated with many myths.

Both son and spouse; one that has raised up
seed
To his own father, and has murdered him.
Now get you in, and ponder what I say;
And if you can detect me in a lie,
Then come and say that I am no true seer.

[*Exeunt* Tiresias *and Boy.*

Chorus

I. 1.

Who is he, who was said
By the Delphian soothsaying rock
To have wrought with hands blood-red
Nameless unspeakable deeds?
Time it were that he fled
Faster than storm-swift steeds!
For upon him springs with a shock,
Armed in thunder and fire,
The Child of Jove, at the head
Of the Destinies dread,
That follow, and will not tire.

I. 2

For a word but now blazed clear
From Parnassus' snow-covered mound,*
To hunt down the Unknown!
He, through the forest drear,
By rocks, by cavernous ways,
Stalks, like a bull that strays,
Heartsore, footsore, alone;
Flying from Earth's central seat,
Flying the oracular sound
That with swift wings' beat
For ever circles him round.

II. 1.

Of a truth dark thoughts, yea dark and fell,
The augur wise doth arouse in me,
Who neither assent, nor yet gainsay;
And what to affirm, I cannot tell;
But I flutter in hope, unapt to see
Things of to-morrow, or to-day.

Why in Polybus' son** they should find a
foe,
Or he in the heirs of Labdacus,
I know no cause, or of old, or late,
In test whereof I am now to go
Against the repute of Oedipus,
To avenge a Labdakid's unknown fate.

II. 2.

True, Zeus indeed, and Apollo, are wise,
And knowers of what concerns mankind;
But that word of a seer, a man like me,
Weighs more than mine, for a man to prize,
Is all unsure. Yea, one man's mind
May surpass another's in subtlety;

But never will I, till I see the rest,
Assent to those who accuse him now.
I saw how the air-borne Maiden came
Against him, and proved him wise, by the test,
And good to the state; and for this, I trow,
He shall not, ever, be put to shame.

Enter Creon.

Creon I am come hither, fellow citizens,
Having been told that Oedipus the king
Lays grievous accusations to my charge,
Which I will not endure. For if he fancies
He in our present troubles has endured
Aught at my hands, either in word or deed,
Tending to harm him, I have no desire
My life should be prolonged, bearing this
blame.
The injury that such a word may do
Is no mere trifle, but more vast than any,
If I am to be called a criminal
Here in the town, and by my friends, and you.

* Mount Parnassus is also associated with Apollo.

** Oedipus.

1 SENATOR Nay, the reproach, it may be, rather came
Through stress of anger, than advisedly.
CREON But it was plainly said, by my advice
The prophet gave false answers.
1 SENATOR It was said;
But how advised I know not.
CREON Was this charge
Of a set mind, and with set countenance
Imputed against me?
1 SENATOR I do not know.
I have no eyes for what my masters do.
But here he comes, himself, forth of the palace.

Enter OEDIPUS.

OEDIPUS Fellow, how cam'st thou hither? Dost thou boast
So great a front of daring, as to come
Under my roof, the assassin clear of me,
And manifest pirate of my royalty?
Tell me, by heaven, did you detect in me
The bearing of a craven, or a fool,
That you laid plans to do it; or suppose
I should not recognize your work in this,
Creeping on slily, and defend myself?
Is it not folly, this attempt of yours,
Without a following, without friends, to hunt
After a throne, a thing which is achieved
By aid of followers and much revenue?
CREON Do me this favour; hear me say as much
As you have said; and then, yourself decide.
OEDIPUS You are quick to talk, but I am slow to learn
Of you; for I have found you contrary
And dangerous to me.
CREON Now, this same thing
First hear, how I shall state it.
OEDIPUS This same thing
Do not tell me—that you are not a villain!
CREON If you suppose your arrogance weighs aught
Apart from reason, you are much astray.
OEDIPUS If you suppose you can escape the pain
Due for a kinsman's wrong, you are astray!
CREON You speak with justice; I agree! But tell me,
How is it that you say I injured you?
OEDIPUS Did you persuade me that I ought to send
To fetch that canting soothsayer, or no?
CREON Why yes, and now, I am of the same mind, still.
OEDIPUS How long is it since Laius—
CREON What? I know not.
OEDIPUS Died—disappeared, murdered by violence?
CREON Long seasons might be numbered, long gone by.
OEDIPUS Well, did this seer then practise in the craft?
CREON Yes, just as wise, and just as much revered.
OEDIPUS And did he at that time say one word of me?
CREON Well, nowhere in my presence, anyhow.
OEDIPUS But did not you hold inquest for the dead?
CREON We did, of course; and got no evidence.
OEDIPUS Well then, how came it that this wiseacre
Did not say these things then?
CREON I do not know.
In matters where I have no cognizance
I hold my tongue.
OEDIPUS This much, at least, you know,
And if you are wise, will say!
CREON And what is that?
For if I know it, I shall not refuse.
OEDIPUS Why, that unless he had conspired with you
He never would have said that Laius' murder
Was of my doing!
CREON If he says so, you know.
Only I claim to know that first from you,
Which you put now to me.
OEDIPUS Learn anything!
For I shall not be found a murderer.
CREON Well then; you have my sister to your wife?
OEDIPUS There's no denying that question.
CREON And with her

Rule equal, and in common hold the land?
OEDIPUS All she may wish for she obtains of me.
CREON And make I not a third, equal with you?
OEDIPUS Ay, there appears your friendship's falsity.
CREON Not if you reason with yourself, as I.
And note this first; if you can think that any
Would rather choose a sovereignty, with fears,
Than the same power, with undisturbed repose?
Neither am I, by nature, covetous
To be a king, rather than play the king,
Nor any man who has sagacity.
Now I have all things, without fear, from you;
Reigned I myself, I must do much I hated.
How were a throne, then, pleasanter for me
Than painless empire and authority?
I am not yet so blinded as to wish
For honour, other than is joined with gain.
Now am I hail-fellow-well-met with all;
Now every man gives me good-morrow; now
The waiters on your favour fawn on me;
For all their prospering depends thereby.
Then how should I exchange this lot for yours?
A mind well balanced cannot turn to crime.
I neither am in love with this design,
Nor, in a comrade, would I suffer it.
For proof of which, first, go to Pytho; ask
For the oracles, if I declared them truly;
Next, if you can detect me in the act
Of any conjuration with the seer,
Then, by a double vote, not one alone,
Mine and your own, take me, and take my life;
But do not, on a dubious argument,
Charge me beside the facts. For just it is not,
To hold bad men for good, good men for bad,
To no good end; nay, 'twere all one to me
To throw away a friend, a worthy one,
And one's own life, which most of all one values.
Ah well; in time, you will see these things plainly;
For time alone shews a man's honesty,
But in one day you may discern his guilt.

1 SENATOR His words sound fair—to one who fears to fall;
For swift in counsel is unsafe, my liege.
OEDIPUS When he who plots against me in the dark
Comes swiftly on, I must be swift in turn.
If I stay quiet, his ends will have been gained,
And mine all missed.
CREON What is it that you want?
To expel me from the country?
OEDIPUS Not at all.
Your death I purpose, not your banishment.
CREON Not without shewing, first, what a thing is jealousy!
OEDIPUS You talk like one who will not yield, nor heed.
CREON Because I see you mean injuriously.
OEDIPUS Not to myself!
CREON No more you ought to me!
OEDIPUS You are a traitor!
CREON What if you are no judge?
OEDIPUS I must be ruler.
CREON Not if you rule badly.
OEDIPUS City, my city!
CREON The city is mine too,
And not yours only.
1 SENATOR Good my lords, have done,
Here is Jocasta; in good time, I see her
Come to you from the palace; with her aid
'Twere meet to appease your present difference.

Enter JOCASTA.

JOCASTA Unhappy men, what was it made you raise
This senseless broil of words? Are you not both
Ashamed of stirring private grievances,
The land being thus afflicted? Get you in—
And, Creon, do you go home; push not mere nothing
On to some terrible calamity!
CREON Sister, your husband Oedipus thinks fit
To treat me villainously; choosing for me
Of two bad things, one; to expatriate me,
Or seize and kill me.
OEDIPUS I admit it, wife;

For I have found him out in an offence
Against my person, joined with treachery.

CREON So may I never thrive, but perish, banned
Of Heaven, if I have done a thing to you
Of what you charge against me!

JOCASTA Oedipus!
O in Heaven's name believe it! Above all
Revere this oath in heaven; secondly
Myself, and these, who stand before you here.

1 SENATOR Hear her, my king! With wisdom and goodwill
I pray you hear!

OEDIPUS What would you have me grant?

1 SENATOR Respect his word; no bauble, heretofore;
And by this oath made weighty.

OEDIPUS Do you know
For what you ask?

1 SENATOR I do.

OEDIPUS Say what you mean, then!

1 SENATOR That you expel not, ever, with disgrace,
The friend, who has abjured it, on a charge
Void of clear proof.

OEDIPUS Now, understand it well;
Seek this, you seek my death or exile!

1 SENATOR Nay,
By the Sun-god, first of all Gods in heaven!
So may I perish, to the uttermost,
Cut off from Heaven, without the help of men,
If I have such a thought! But the land's waste
Will break my heart with grief—and that this woe,
Your strife, is added to its former woe.

OEDIPUS Well, let him go, though I get slain outright,
Or thrust by force, dishonoured, from the land;
Your voice, not his, makes me compassionate,
Pleading for pity; he, where'er he be,
Shall have my hatred.

CREON You display your spleen
In yielding; but, when your wrath passes bound,
Are formidable! Tempers such as yours
Most grievous are to their own selves to bear,
Not without justice.

OEDIPUS Leave me; get you gone!

CREON I go; you know me not; these know me honest.

[*Exit.*

1 SENATOR Lady, what hinders you from taking him
Into the house?

JOCASTA I would know how this happened.

1 SENATOR A blind surmise arose, out of mere babble;
But even what is unjust inflicts a sting.

JOCASTA On part of both?

1 SENATOR Yes truly.

JOCASTA And what was said?

1 SENATOR Enough it seems, enough it seems to me,
Under the former trouble of the land,
To leave this where it lies.

OEDIPUS Do you perceive
How far you are carried—a well-meaning man!
Slurring my anger thus, and blunting it?

1 SENATOR I said it, O my king, not once alone—
But be assured, I should have shewn myself
Robbed of my wits, useless for work of wit,
Renouncing thee! who didst impel the sails
Of my dear land, baffled mid straits, right onward,
And it may be, wilt waft her safely now!

JOCASTA For Heaven's sake tell me too, my lord, what was it
Caused you so deep an anger?

OEDIPUS I will tell you;
For I respect you, lady, more than these;
'Twas Creon—at plots which he has laid for me.

JOCASTA If you will charge the quarrel in plain terms,
Why speak!

OEDIPUS He says that I am Laius' slayer.

JOCASTA Of his own knowledge, or on hearsay?

OEDIPUS Nay,
But by citation of a knavish seer;
As for himself, he keeps his words blame-free.

JOCASTA Now set you free from thought of that you talk of;
Listen and learn, nothing in human life
Turns on the soothsayer's art. Tokens of this
I'll show you in few words. To Laius once
There came an oracle, I do not say
From Phoebus' self, but from his ministers,
That so it should befall, that he should die
By a son's hands, whom he should have by me.
And him—the story goes—robbers abroad
Have murdered, at a place where three roads meet;
While from our son's birth not three days went by
Before, with ankles pinned, he cast him out,
By hands of others, on a pathless moor.
And so Apollo did not bring about
That he should be his father's murderer;
Nor yet that Laius should endure the stroke
At his son's hands, of which he was afraid.
This is what came of soothsayers' oracles;
Whereof take thou no heed. That which we lack,
If a God seek, himself will soon reveal.

OEDIPUS What perturbation and perplexity
Take hold upon me, woman, hearing you!

JOCASTA What stress of trouble is on you, that you say so?

OEDIPUS I thought I heard you say Laius was slain
Where three roads meet!

JOCASTA Yes, so the rumour ran,
And so runs still.

OEDIPUS And where might be the spot
Where this befell?

JOCASTA Phocis the land is named;
There are two separate roads converge in one
From Daulia and Delphi.

OEDIPUS And what time
Has passed since then?

JOCASTA It was but just before
You were installed as ruler of the land,
The tidings reached the city.

OEDIPUS God of Heaven!
What would'st thou do unto me!

JOCASTA Oedipus,
What is it on your mind?

OEDIPUS Ask me not yet.
But Laius—say, what was he like? what prime
Of youth had he attained to?

JOCASTA He was tall;
The first white flowers had blossomed in his hair;
His figure was not much unlike your own.

OEDIPUS Me miserable! It seems I have but now
Proffered myself to a tremendous curse
Not knowing!

JOCASTA How say you? I tremble, O my lord,
To gaze upon you!

OEDIPUS I am sore afraid
The prophet was not blind; but you will make
More certain, if you answer one thing more.

JOCASTA Indeed I tremble; but the thing you ask
I'll answer, when I know it.

OEDIPUS Was he going
Poorly attended, or with many spears
About him, like a prince?

JOCASTA But five in all;
One was a herald; and one carriage held
Laius himself,

OEDIPUS O, it is plain already!
Woman, who was it told this tale to you?

JOCASTA A servant, who alone came safe away.

OEDIPUS Is he perchance now present, in the house?

JOCASTA Why no; for after he was come from thence,
And saw you governing, and Laius dead,
He came and touched my hand, and begged of me
To send him to the fields and sheep-meadows,
So he might be as far as possible
From eyesight of the townsmen; and I sent him;
For he was worthy, for a slave, to obtain
Even greater favours.

OEDIPUS Could we have him back
Quickly?
JOCASTA We could. But why this order?
OEDIPUS Wife,
I fear me I have spoken far too much;
Wherefore I wish to see him.
JOCASTA He shall come!
But I am worthy, in my turn, to know
What weighs so heavily upon you, Sir?
OEDIPUS And you shall know; since I have passed so far
The bounds of apprehension. For to whom
Could I impart, passing through such a need,
Greater in place—if that were all—than you?
—I am the son of Polybus of Corinth,
And of a Dorian mother, Merope.
And I was counted most preëminent
Among the townsmen there; up to the time
A circumstance befell me, of this fashion—
Worthy of wonder, though of my concern
Unworthy. At the board a drunken fellow
Over his cups called me a changeling;
And I, being indignant—all that day
Hardly refrained—but on the morrow went
And taxed my parents with it to their face;
Who took the scandal grievously, of him
Who launched the story. Well, with what they said
I was content; and yet the thing still galled me;
For it spread far. So without cognizance
Of sire or mother I set out to go
To Pytho.* Phoebus sent me of my quest
Bootless away; but other terrible
And strange and lamentable things revealed,
Saying I should wed my mother, and produce
A race intolerable for men to see,
And be my natural father's murderer.
When I heard that, measuring where Corinth stands
Even thereafter by the stars alone,
Where I might never think to see fulfilled
The scandals of ill prophecies of me,
I fled, an exile. As I journeyed on,
I found myself upon the self-same spot
Where, you say, this king perished. In your ears,
Wife, I will tell the whole. When in my travels
I was come near this place where three roads meet,
There met me a herald, and a man that rode
In a colt-carriage, as you tell of him,
And from the track the leader, by main force,
And the old man himself, would thrust me. I,
Being enraged, strike him who jostled me—
The driver—and the old man, when he saw it,
Watching as I was passing, from the car
With his goad's fork smote me upon the head.
He paid, though! duly I say not; but in brief,
Smitten by the staff in this right hand of mine,
Out of the middle of the carriage straight
He rolls down headlong; and I slay them all!
But if there be a semblance to connect
This nameless man with Laius, who is now
More miserable than I am? Who on earth
Could have been born with more of hate from heaven?
Whom never citizen or stranger may
Receive into their dwellings, or accost,
But must thrust out of doors; and 'tis no other
Laid all these curses on myself, than I!
Yea, with embraces of the arms whereby
He perished, I pollute my victim's bed!
Am I not vile? Am I not all unclean?
If I must fly, and flying, never can
See my own folk, or on my native land
Set foot, or else must with my mother wed,
And slay my father Polybus, who begat
And bred me? Would he not speak truly of me
Who judged these things sent by some barbarous Power?
Never, you sacred majesties of Heaven,
Never may I behold that day; but pass
Out of men's sight, ere I shall see myself
Touched by the stain of such a destiny!
1 SENATOR My liege, these things affect us grievously;
Still, till you hear his story who was by,
Do not lose hope!
OEDIPUS Yea, so much hope is left,

* The Pythian oracle at Delphi.

Merely to wait for him, the herdsman.
JOCASTA Well,
Suppose him here, what do you want of him?
OEDIPUS I'll tell you; if he should be found to say
Just what you said, I shall be clear from harm.
JOCASTA What did you hear me say, that did not tally?
OEDIPUS You were just telling me that he made mention
Of "robbers"—"men"—as Laius' murderers.
Now if he shall affirm their number still,
I did not slay him. One cannot be the same
As many. But if he shall speak of one—
One only, it is evident this deed
Already will have been brought home to me.
JOCASTA But be assured, that was the word, quite plainly!
And now he cannot blot it out again.
Not I alone, but the whole city heard it.
Then, even if he shift from his first tale,
Not so, my lord, will he at all explain
The death of Laius, as it should have been,
Whom Loxias declared my son must slay!
And after all, the poor thing never killed him,
But died itself before! so that henceforth
I do not mean to look to left or right
For fear of soothsaying!
OEDIPUS You are well advised.
Still, send and fetch the labourer; do not miss it.
JOCASTA I will send quickly. Now let us go within.
I would do nothing that displeases you.
[*Exeunt* OEDIPUS *and* JOCASTA.

Chorus

I. 1.

Let it be mine to keep
The holy purity of word and deed
Foreguided all by mandates from on high
Born in the ethereal region of the sky,
Their only sire Olympus; them nor seed
Of mortal man brought forth, nor Lethe cold
Shall ever lay to sleep;
In them Deity is great, and grows not old.

I. 2.

Pride is the germ of kings;
Pride, when puffed up, vainly, with many things
Unseasonable, unfitting, mounts the wall,
Only to hurry to that fatal fall,
Where feet are vain to serve her. But the task
Propitious to the city GOD I ask
Never to take away!
GOD I will never cease to hold my stay.

II. 1.

But if any man proceed
Insolently in word or deed,
Without fear of right, or care
For the seats where Virtues are,
Him, for his ill-omened pride,
Let an evil death betide!
If honestly his gear he will not gain,
Nor keep himself from deeds unholy,
Nor from inviolable things abstain,
Blinded by folly.
In such a course, what mortal from his heart
Dart upon dart
Can hope to avert of indignation?
Yea, and if acts like these are held in estimation,
Why dance we here our part?

II. 2.

Never to the inviolate hearth
At the navel of the earth,*
Nor to Abae's fane, in prayer,
Nor the Olympian, will I fare,
If it shall not so befall
Manifestly unto all.
But O our king—if thou art named aright—
Zeus, that art Lord of all things ever,
Be this not hid from Thee, nor from Thy might
Which endeth never.
For now already men invalidate
The dooms of Fate
Uttered for Laius, fading slowly;

* The oracle at Delphi.

Apollo's name and rites are nowhere now
kept holy;
Worship is out of date.

Enter JOCASTA, *attended.*

JOCASTA Lords of the land, it came into my heart
To approach the temples of the Deities,
Taking in hand these garlands, and this
incense;
For Oedipus lets his mind float too light
Upon the eddies of all kinds of grief;
Nor will he, like a man of soberness,
Measure the new by knowledge of the old,
But is at mercy of whoever speaks,
If he but speak the language of despair.
I can do nothing by exhorting him.
Wherefore, Lycean Phoebus, unto thee—
For thou art very near us—I am come.
Bringing these offerings, a petitioner
That thou afford us fair deliverance;
Since now we are all frighted, seeing him—
The vessel's pilot, as 'twere—panic-stricken.

Enter a Messenger.

MESSENGER Sirs, might I learn of you, where is
the palace
Of Oedipus the King? or rather, where
He is himself, if you know, tell me.

1 SENATOR Stranger,
This is his dwelling, and he is within;
This lady is his children's mother, too.

MESSENGER A blessing ever be on hers and her,
Who is, in such a perfect sort, his wife!

JOCASTA The like be with you too, as you
deserve,
Sir, for your compliment. But say what end
You come for, and what news you wish to
tell.

MESSENGER Good to the house, and to your
husband, lady.

JOCASTA Of what sort? and from whom come
you?

MESSENGER From Corinth.
In that which I am now about to say
May you find pleasure! and why not? And yet
Perhaps you may be sorry.

JOCASTA But what is it?
How can it carry such ambiguous force?

MESSENGER The dwellers in the land of Isthmia.
As was there said, intend to appoint him king.

JOCASTA What! Is not Polybus, the old prince,
still reigning?

MESSENGER No, truly; he is Death's subject, in
the grave.

JOCASTA How say you, father? Is Polybus no
more?

MESSENGER I stake my life upon it, if I lie!

JOCASTA Run, girl, and tell your master
instantly.

[*Exit an attendant.*

O prophecies of Gods, where are you now!
Oedipus fled, long since, from this man's
presence,
Fearing to kill him; and now he has died
A natural death, not by his means at all!

Enter OEDIPUS.

OEDIPUS O my most dear Jocasta, wife of mine,
Why did you fetch me hither from the house?

JOCASTA Hear this man speak! Listen and mark,
to what
The dark responses of the God are come!

OEDIPUS And who is this? What says he?

JOCASTA He's from Corinth,
To tell us that your father Polybus
Lives no more, but is dead!

OEDIPUS What say you, sir?
Tell your own tale yourself.

MESSENGER If first of all
I must deliver this for certainty,
Know well, that he has gone the way of
mortals.

OEDIPUS Was it by treason, or some chance
disease?

MESSENGER A little shock prostrates an aged
frame!

OEDIPUS Sickness, you mean, was my poor
father's end?

MESSENGER Yes, and old age; his term of life
was full.

OEDIPUS Heigh ho! Why, wife! why should a man regard
The oracular hearth of Pytho, or the birds
Cawing above us, by whose canons I
Was to have slain my father? He is dead,
And buried out of sight; and here am I,
Laying no finger to the instrument,
(Unless, indeed, he pined for want of me,
And so, I killed him!) Well, Polybus is gone;
And with him all those oracles of ours
Bundled to Hades, for old songs, together!

JOCASTA Did I not say so all along?

OEDIPUS You did;
But I was led astray by fear.

JOCASTA Well, now
Let none of these predictions any more
Weigh on your mind!

OEDIPUS And how can I help dreading
My mother's bed?

JOCASTA But why should men be fearful,
O'er whom Fortune is mistress, and foreknowledge
Of nothing sure? Best take life easily,
As a man may. For that maternal wedding,
Have you no fear; for many men ere now
Have dreamed as much; but he who by such dreams
Sets nothing, has the easiest life of it.

OEDIPUS All these things would have been well said of you,
Were not my mother living still; but now,
She being alive, there is all need of dread;
Though you say well.

JOCASTA And yet your father's burial
Lets in much daylight!

OEDIPUS I acknowledge, much.
Still, her who lives I fear.

MESSENGER But at what woman
Are you dismayed?

OEDIPUS At Merope, old man,
The wife of Polybus.

MESSENGER And what of her
Causes you terror?

OEDIPUS A dark oracle,
Stranger, from heaven.

MESSENGER May it be put in words?
Or is it wrong another man should know it?

OEDIPUS No, not at all. Why, Loxias declared
That I should one day marry my own mother,
And with my own hands shed my father's blood.
Wherefore from Corinth I have kept away
Far, for long years; and prospered; none the less
It is most sweet to see one's parents' face.

MESSENGER And in this apprehension you became
An emigrant from Corinth?

OEDIPUS And, old man,
Desiring not to be a parricide.

MESSENGER Why should I not deliver you, my liege—
Since my intent in coming here was good—
Out of this fear?

OEDIPUS Indeed you would obtain
Good guerdon from me.

MESSENGER And indeed for this
Chiefest I came, that upon your return
I might in some sort benefit.

OEDIPUS But I
Will never go, to meet my parents there!

MESSENGER O son, 'tis plain you know not what you do!

OEDIPUS How so, old man? in Heaven's name tell me!

MESSENGER If
On this account you shun the journey home!

OEDIPUS Of course I fear lest Phoebus turn out true.

MESSENGER Lest through your parents you incur foul stain?

OEDIPUS Yes, father, yes; that is what always scares me.

MESSENGER Now do you know you tremble, really, at nothing?

OEDIPUS How can that be, if I was born their child?

MESSENGER Because Polybus was nought akin to you!

OEDIPUS What, did not Polybus beget me?

MESSENGER No,
No more than I did; just so much as I!

OEDIPUS How, my own sire no more than—nobody?
MESSENGER But neither he begat you, nor did I.
OEDIPUS Then from what motive did he call me son?
MESSENGER Look here; he had you as a gift from me.
OEDIPUS And loved me then, so much, at second hand?
MESSENGER Yes, his long childlessness prevailed on him.
OEDIPUS And did you find or purchase me, to give him?
MESSENGER I found you in Cithaeron's wooded dells.
OEDIPUS How came you to be journeying in these parts?
MESSENGER I tended flocks upon the mountains here.
OEDIPUS You were a shepherd, and you ranged for hire?
MESSENGER But at the same time your preserver, son!
OEDIPUS You found me in distress? What was my trouble?
MESSENGER Your ankle joints may witness.
OEDIPUS O, why speak you
Of that old evil?
MESSENGER I untied you, when
You had the soles of both your feet bored through.
OEDIPUS A shameful sort of swaddling bands were mine.
MESSENGER Such, that from them you had the name you bear.*
OEDIPUS Tell me, by heaven! at sire's or mother's hand—
MESSENGER I know not: he who gave you knows of that
Better than I.
OEDIPUS You got me from another?
You did not find me?
MESSENGER No, another shepherd
Gave you to me.
OEDIPUS Who was he? are you able
To point him out?
MESSENGER They said that he was one
Of those who followed Laius, whom you know.
OEDIPUS Him who was once the monarch of this land?
MESSENGER Precisely! This man was his herdsman.
OEDIPUS Now
Is this man still alive for me to see?
MESSENGER You must know best, the people of the place.
OEDIPUS Is any here among you bystanders,
Who knows the herdsman whom he tells us of,
From seeing him, either in the fields or here?
Speak! it were time that this had been cleared up.
1 SENATOR I think he is no other than that peasant
Whom you were taking pains to find, before;
But she could say as well as any one—
Jocasta.
OEDIPUS Lady, you remember him
Whose coming we were wishing for but now;
Does he mean him?
JOCASTA Why ask who 'twas he spoke of?
Nay, never mind—never remember it—
'Twas idly spoken!
OEDIPUS Nay, it cannot be
That having such a clue I should refuse
To solve the mystery of my parentage!
JOCASTA For Heaven's sake, if you care for your own life,
Don't seek it! I am sick, and that's enough!
OEDIPUS Courage! At least, if I be thrice a slave,
Born so three-deep, it cannot injure you!
JOCASTA But I beseech you, hearken! Do not do it!
OEDIPUS I will not hearken—not to know the whole.
JOCASTA I mean well; and I tell you for the best!
OEDIPUS What you call best is an old sore of mine.
JOCASTA Wretch, what thou art O might'st thou never know!

* By a folk etymology, the name Oedipus is taken to mean "swollen feet."

OEDIPUS Will some one go and fetch the herdsman hither?
She is welcome to her gilded lineage!

JOCASTA O
Woe, woe, unhappy! This is all I have
To say to thee, and no word more, for ever!

[Exit

1 SENATOR Why has the woman vanished, Oedipus,
Driven so wild with grief? I am afraid
Out of her silence will break forth some trouble.

OEDIPUS Break out what will, I shall not hesitate,
Low though it be, to trace the source of me.
But she, perhaps, being, as a woman, proud,
Of my unfit extraction is ashamed.
—I deem myself the child of Fortune! I
Shall not be shamed of her, who favours me;
Seeing I have her for mother; and for kin
The limitary Moons, that found me small,
That fashioned me for great! Parented thus,
How could I ever in the issue prove
Other—that I should leave my birth unknown?

Chorus

1.

If I am a true seer,
My mind from error clear,
Tomorrow's moon shall not pass over us,
Ere, O Cithaeron, we
Shall magnify in thee
The land, the lap, the womb of Oedipus;
And we shall hymn thy praises, for good things
Of thy bestowing, done unto our kings.
Yea, Phoebus, if thou wilt, amen, so might it be!

2.

Who bare thee? Which, O child,
Over the mountain-wild
Sought to by Pan of the immortal Maids?
Or Loxias—was he
The sire who fathered thee?
For dear to him are all the upland glades.
Was it Cyllene's lord* acquired a son,
Or Bacchus, dweller on the heights, from one
Of those he liefest loves, Oreads** of Helicon?

Enter Attendants with an Old Man, a Shepherd.

OEDIPUS If I may guess, who never met with him,
I think I see that herdsman, Senators,
We have long been seeking; for his ripe old age
Harmoniously accords with this man's measure;
Besides, I recognize the men who bring him
As of my household; but in certainty
You can perhaps exceed me, who beheld
The herdsman formerly.

1 SENATOR Why, to be sure,
I recognize him; for he was a man
Trusty as any Laius ever had
About his pastures.

OEDIPUS You I ask the first,
The Corinthian stranger; do you speak of him?

MESSENGER Yes, him you see.

OEDIPUS Sirrah, old man, look here;
Answer my questions. Were you Laius' man?

OLD MAN Truly his thrall; not bought, but bred at home.

OEDIPUS Minding what work, or in what character?

OLD MAN Most of my time I went after the flocks.

OEDIPUS In what directions, chiefly, were your folds?

OLD MAN There was Cithaeron; and a bit near by.

* Hermes.

** Mountain nymphs.

*** The constellation Bootes.

OEDIPUS Do you know this man, then? Did you see him there?
OLD MAN Him? After what? What man do you mean?
OEDIPUS This fellow
Here present; did you ever meet with him?
OLD MAN Not so to say off-hand, from memory.
MESSENGER And that's no wonder, sir; but beyond doubt
I will remind him, though he has forgotten,
I am quite sure he knows, once on a time,
When in the bit about Cithaeron there—
He with two flocks together, I with one—
I was his neighbour for three whole half years
From spring-tide onward to the Bear-ward's day;
And with the winter to my folds I drove,
And he to Laius' stables. Are these facts,
Or are they not—what I am saying?
OLD MAN Yes,
You speak the truth; but it was long ago.
MESSENGER Come, say now, don't you mind that you then gave me
A baby boy to bring up for my own?
OLD MAN What do you mean? Why do you ask it me?
MESSENGER This is the man, good fellow; who was then
A youngling!
OLD MAN Out upon you! Hold your peace!
OEDIPUS Nay, old man, do not chide him; for your words
Deserve a chiding rather than his own!
OLD MAN O best of masters, what is my offence?
OEDIPUS Not telling of that boy he asks about.
OLD MAN He says he knows not what! He is all astray!
OEDIPUS You will not speak of grace—you shall perforce!
OLD MAN Do not for God's sake harm me, an old man!
OEDIPUS Quick, some one, twist his hands behind him!
OLD MAN Wretch,
What have I done? What do you want to know?
OEDIPUS Did you give him that boy he asks about?
OLD MAN I gave it him. Would I had died that day!
OEDIPUS Tell the whole truth, or you will come to it!
OLD MAN I am undone far more, though, if I speak!
OEDIPUS The man is trifling with us, I believe.
OLD MAN No, no; I said I gave it, long ago!
OEDIPUS Where did you get it? At home, or from some other?
OLD MAN It was not mine; another gave it me.
OEDIPUS Which of these citizens? and from what roof?
OLD MAN Don't, master, for God's sake, don't ask me more!
OEDIPUS You are a dead man, if I speak again!
OLD MAN Then—'twas a child—of Laius' household.
OEDIPUS What,
Slave-born? or one of his own family?
OLD MAN O, I am at the horror, now, to speak!
OEDIPUS And I to hear. But I must hear—no less.
OLD MAN Truly it was called his son; but she within,
Your lady, could best tell you how it was.
OEDIPUS Did she then give it you?
OLD MAN My lord, even so.
OEDIPUS For what?
OLD MAN For me to make away with it.
OEDIPUS Herself the mother? miserable!
OLD MAN In dread
Of evil prophecies—
OEDIPUS What prophecies?
OLD MAN That he should kill his parents, it was said.
OEDIPUS How came you then to give it to this old man?
OLD MAN For pity, O my master! thinking he
Would carry it away to other soil,

---

* The Danube.

** A river emptying into the Black Sea.

From whence he came; but he to the worst of harms
Saved it! for if thou art the man he says,
Sure thou wast born destined to misery!

OEDIPUS Woe! woe! It is all plain, indeed! O Light,
This be the last time I shall gaze on thee,
Who am revealed to have been born of those
Of whom I ought not—to have wedded whom
I ought not—and slain whom I might not slay!

[*Exit.*

Chorus

I. 1.

O generations of mankind!
How do I find
Your lives nought worth at all!
For who is he—what state
Is there, more fortunate
Than only to seem great,
And then, to fall?
I having thee for pattern, and thy lot—
Thine, O poor Oedipus—I envy not
Aught in mortality;
For this is he

I. 2.

Who, shooting far beyond the rest,
Won wealth all-blest,
Slaying, Zeus, thy monster-maid,
Crook-taloned, boding; and
Who did arise and stand
Betwixt death and our land,
A tower of aid;
Yea for this cause thou hast been named our king,
And honoured in the highest, governing
The city of Thebae great
In royal state.

II. 1.

And now, who lives more utterly undone?
Who with sad woes, who with mischances rude
Stands closer yoked by life's vicissitude?
O honoured head of Oedipus, for whom
Within the same wide haven there was room
To come—child, to the birth—
Sire, to the nuptial bower,
How could the furrows of thy parent earth—
How could they suffer thee, O hapless one,
In silence, to this hour?

II. 2.

Time found thee out—Time who sees everything—
Unwittingly guilty; and arraigns thee now
Consort ill-sorted, unto whom are bred
Sons of thy getting, in thine own birth-bed.
O scion of Laius' race,
Would I had never never seen thy face!
For I lament, even as from lips that sing
Pouring a dirge; yet verily it was thou
Gav'st me to rise
And breathe again, and close my watching eyes.

Enter a second MESSENGER.

2 MESSENGER O you most honoured ever of this land,
What deeds have you to hear, what sights to see,
What sorrow to endure, if you still cherish
The house of Labdacus with loyalty?
For Ister* I suppose or Phasis'** wave
Never could purge this dwelling from the ills
It covers—or shall instantly reveal,
Invited, not inflicted; of all wounds,
Those that seem wilful are the worst to bear.

1 SENATOR There was no lack, in what we knew before,
Of lamentable; what have you more to say?

2 MESSENGER The speediest of all tales to hear and tell;
The illustrious Jocasta is no more.

1 SENATOR Unhappy woman! From what cause?

2 MESSENGER Self-slain.

Of what befell the saddest part is spared;
For you were not a witness. None the less
So far as I can tell it you shall hear
Her miserable story. When she passed
So frantically inside the vestibule,
She went straight onward to the bed-chamber,
With both her hands tearing her hair; the doors
She dashed to as she entered, crying out
On Laius, long since dead, calling to mind
His fore-begotten offspring, by whose hands
He, she said, died, and left to his own seed
Its mother's most unnatural bearing-bed.
Nor did she not bewail that nuptial-couch
Where she brought forth, unhappy, brood on brood,
Spouse to her spouse, and children to her child.
And then—I know no further how she perished;
For Oedipus brake in, crying aloud;
For whom it was impossible to watch
The ending of her misery; but on him
We gazed, as he went raging all about,
Beseeching us to furnish him a sword
And say where he could find his wife—no wife,
Rather the mother-soil both of himself
And children; and, as he raved thus, some Power
Shews him—at least, none of us present did.
Then, shouting loud, he sprang upon the doors
As following some guide, and burst the bars
Out of their sockets, and alights within.
There we beheld his wife hanging, entwined
In a twined noose. He seeing her, with a groan
Looses the halter; then, when on the ground
Lay the poor wretch, dreadful it was to see
What followed; snatching from her dress gold pins
Wherewith she was adorned, he lifted them,
And smote the nerves of his own eyeballs, saying
Something like this—that they should see no more
Evils like those he had endured or wrought;
Darkling, thereafter, let them gaze on forms
He might not see, and fail to recognize
The faces he desired! Chanting this burden,
Not once, but many times, he raised his hand
And stabbed his eyes; so that from both of them
The blood ran down his face, not drop by drop,
But all at once, in a dark shower of gore.
—These are the ills that from a two-fold source,
Not one alone, but in both wife and spouse,
Mingled together, have burst forth at once.
Their former pristine happiness indeed
Was happiness before; but in this hour
Shame—lamentation—Atè*—death—of all
That has a name of evil, nought's away!

1 SENATOR And does he stand in any respite now
Of misery, poor soul?

2 MESSENGER He calls aloud
For some one to undo the bolts, and shew
To all the Cadmeans him, his father's slayer—
His mother's—uttering words unhallowed—words
I may not speak; that he will cast himself
Forth of the land, abide no more at home
Under the curse of his own cursing. Nay,
But he lacks force, and guidance; for his sickness
Is more than man can bear. See for yourself;
For these gates open, and you will straight behold
A sight—such as even he that loathes must pity!

Enter OEDIPUS *blind.*

---

* Doom caused by guilt and ignorance.

Chorus

O sorrow, lamentable for eyes to see!
Sorest of all past ills encountering me!
What frenzy, O wretch, is this, that came on thee?

What Deity was it that with a leap so great—
Farther than farthest—sprang on thy sad fate?
Woe is me, woe is me for thee—unfortunate!

Fain would I gaze at thee, would ask thee much,
Many things learn of thee, wert thou not such
As I may not even behold, as I shudder to touch.

OEDIPUS Me miserable! Whither must I go?
Ah whither flits my voice, borne to and fro?
Thou Power unseen, how hast thou brought me low!
1 SENATOR To ills, intolerable to hear or see.
OEDIPUS Thou horror of thick darkness overspread,
Thou shadow of unutterable dread
Not to be stemmed or stayed, fallen on my head—
Woe's me once more! How crowd upon my heart
Stings of these wounds, and memories of woe!
1 SENATOR No marvel if thou bear a double smart
And writhe, so stricken, with a two-fold throe!
OEDIPUS Still art thou near me—ready still to tend
And to endure me, faithful to the end,
Blind as I am, with kindness, O my friend!
For strange thou art not; but full well I know
That voice of thine, all darkling though I be.
1 SENATOR Rash man, how could'st thou bear to outrage so
Thine eyes? What Power was it, that wrought on thee?
OEDIPUS Apollo, Apollo fulfils,
O friends, my measure of ills—
Fills my measure of woe;
Author was none, but I,
None other, of the blow;
For why was I to see,
When to descry
No sight on earth could have a charm for me?
1 SENATOR It was even as thou sayest.
OEDIPUS What was there left for sight?
What, that could give delight?
Or whose address,
O friends, could I still hear with happiness?
Lead me to exile straight;
Lead me, O my friends, the worst
Of murderers, of mortals most accurst,
Yea and to Gods chief object of their hate.
1 SENATOR Of cunning hapless, as of hapless fate,
I would that I had never known thy name!
OEDIPUS May he perish, whoe'er 'twas drew me
Out of the cruel gyve
That bound my feet, on the lea!
He who saved me alive,
Who rescued me from fate,
Shewing no kindness to me!
Sorrow so great,
Had I died then, had spared both mine and me.
1 SENATOR Fain were I too it had been so.
OEDIPUS Not then had I become
My father's murderer,
Nor wedded her I have my being from:
Whom now no God will bless,
Child of incestuousness
In her that bare me, being the spouse of her;
Yea if aught ill worse than all ill be there,
That Oedipus must bear.
1 SENATOR I know not how to say thou hast done well;
For it were better for thee now to die,
Than to live on in blindness.
OEDIPUS Tell me not—
Give me no counsel now, that what is done
Has not been done thus best. I know not how
With seeing eyes I could have looked upon
My father—coming to the under-world,
Or my poor mother, when against them both
I have sinned sins, worse than a halter's meed.

Or do you think that children were a sight
Delectable for me to gaze at, born
As they were born? Never with eyes of mine!
No, nor the city, nor the citadel,
Nor consecrated shrines of deities,
From which, to my most utter misery,
I, of all other men in Thebes the man
Most bravely nurtured, cut myself away,
And of my own mouth dictated to all
To thrust out me, the impious—me, declared
Abominable of Heaven, and Laius' son,
Was I, who in myself made evident
So dark a stain, with unaverted eyes
To look on these? That least of all! Nay
rather,
If there were any way to choke the fount
Of hearing, through my ears, I would have
tried
To seal up all this miserable frame
And live blind, deaf to all things; sweet it
were
To dwell in fancy, out of reach of pain.
—Cithaeron! wherefore didst thou harbour
me!
Why not at once have slain me? Never then
Had I displayed before the face of men
Who and from whom I am! O Polybus,
And Corinth, and the old paternal roof
I once called mine, with what thin film
of honour,
Corruption over-skinned, you fostered me,
Found ill myself, and from ill parents, now!
O you, the three roads, and the lonely brake,
The copse, and pass at the divided way,
Which at my hands drank blood that was
my own—
My father's—do you keep in memory
What in your sight I did, and how again
I wrought, when I came hither?
Wedlock, wedlock,
You gave me being, you raised up seed again
To the same lineage, and exhibited
In one incestuous flesh son—brother—sire,
Bride, wife and mother; and all ghastliest
deeds
Wrought among men! But O, ill done,
ill worded!
In Heaven's name hide me with all speed
away,
Or slay me, or send adrift upon some sea
Where you may look on me no longer!
Come,
Touch, if you will, a miserable man;
Pray you, fear nothing; for my misery
No mortal but myself can underbear.

1 SENATOR Creon is at hand; he is the man you need,
Who must decide and do; being, after you,
The sole protector left us, for the land.

OEDIPUS Ah Heaven, what language shall I hold to him?
What rightful credit will appear in me?
For I have been found wholly in the wrong
In all that passed between us heretofore!

Enter CREON.

CREON Not as a mocker come I, Oedipus,
Nor to reproach for any former pain.
But you—even if you reverence no more
Children of men,—at least so far revere
The royal Sun-god's all-sustaining fire,
Not to parade, thus flagrant, such a sore
As neither earth nor day can tolerate,
Nor dew from Heaven! Take him in instantly!
That kindred only should behold and hear
The griefs of kin, fits best with decency.

OEDIPUS In Heaven's name, seeing that you transported me
Beyond all hope, coming, the first of men,
To me the last of men, grant me one boon!
'Tis for your good, not for my own, I say it.

CREON What is it that you crave so eagerly?

OEDIPUS Out of this country cast me with all speed,
Where I may pass without accost of men.

CREON So had I done, be sure, had I not wished
To learn our duty, first, at the God's mouth.

OEDIPUS Surely his oracle was all made plain,
Me, the profane, the parricide, to slay!

CREON So was it said; but in our present need
'Tis better to enquire what we must do.

OEDIPUS Will ye seek answer for a wretch like me?

Creon Even you might trust what the God answers, now.

Oedipus Ay, and I charge thee, and will beg of thee,
Order thyself such burial as thou wilt,
For her who lies within; seeing it is meet
Thou do so, for thine own. But never more
Be this my native town burdened with me
For living inmate; rather suffer me
To haunt the mountains—where my mountain is,
Cithaeron, which my mother and my sire,
Living, appointed for my sepulchre,
That as they meant, my slayers, I may expire.
Howbeit this much I know, neither disease
Nor aught beside can kill me; never else
Had I been rescued from the brink of death,
But for some dire calamity. Ah well,
Let our own fate wag onward as it may;
And for my sons, Creon, take thou no care
Upon thee; they are men, so that they never
Can lack the means to live, where'er they be;
But my two girls, wretched and pitiable,
For whose repast was never board of mine
Ordered apart, without me, but in all
That I partook they always shared with me,
Take care of them; and let me, above all else,
Touch them with hands, and weep away my troubles!
Pardon, my lord; pardon, illustrious sir;
If but my hands could feel them, I might seem
To have them still, as when I still could see.

Antigone *and* Ismene *are brought in.*

—What do I say? In Heaven's name, do I not
Hear my two darlings, somewhere shedding tears?
And can it be that Creon, pitying me,
Sends me my dearest, my two daughters, hither?
Is it so indeed?

Creon Yes, it is I vouchsafed this boon, aware
What joy you have and long have had of them.

Oedipus Why then, good luck go with thee, and Providence
Be guardian to thee, better than to me,
In payment for their coming!—Children dear,
Where are you? Come, come hither to my arms—
To these brotherly arms—procurers that
The eyes—that were your sire's—once bright—should see
Thus! who am shewn, O children, to have been
Author of you—unseeing—unknowing—in
Her bed, whence I derived my being! You
I weep for; for I cannot gaze on you;
Knowing what is left of bitter in the life
Which at men's hands you needs must henceforth live.
For to what gatherings of the citizens
Will you resort, or to what festivals,
Whence you will not, in place of holiday,
Come home in tears? Or when you shall have grown
To years of marriage, who—ah, who will be
The man to abide the hazard of disgrace
Such as must be the bane, both of my sons,
And you as well? For what reproach is lacking?
Your father slew his father, and became
Father of you—by her who bare him. So
Will they reproach you; who will wed you then?
No one, my children; but you needs must wither,
Barren—unwed. But thou, Menoeceus' son,
Since thou art all the father these have left them,
For we, the two that were their parents, now
Are both undone, do not thou suffer them
To wander, vagabond and husband-less,
Being of thy kin; nor let them fall so low
As are my fortunes; but have pity on them,
Seeing them so tender, and so desolate
Of all friends, but for thee. Give me thy hand,
Good sir, and promise this.—To you, my girls,
If you were old enough to understand,
I should have much to say; but as it is,
This be your prayer; in some permitted place
That you may breathe; and have your lot in life

Happier than his, who did engender you.
CREON Get thee in; thou hast bewailed thee enough, in reason.
OEDIPUS Though it be bitter, I must do it.
CREON All's good, in good season.
OEDIPUS Do you know how to make me?
CREON Say on, and I shall know.
OEDIPUS Banish me from this country.
CREON That must the God bestow.
OEDIPUS But to Gods, above all men, I am a mark for hate.
CREON And for that same reason you will obtain it straight.
OEDIPUS Say you so?
CREON Yes truly, and I mean what I say.
OEDIPUS Lead me hence then, quickly.
CREON Go; but let the children stay.
OEDIPUS Do not take them from me!
CREON Think not to have all at thy pleasure;
For what thou didst attain to far outwent thy measure.

CREON, *the Children, etc. retire.* OEDIPUS is led in.

Chorus

Dwellers in Thebes, behold this Oedipus,
The man who solved the riddle marvellous,
A prince of men,
Whose lot what citizen
Did not with envy see,
How deep the billows of calamity
Above him roll.
Watch therefore and regard that supreme day;
And of no mortal say
"That man is happy," till
Vexed by no grievous ill
He pass Life's goal.

[*Exeunt omnes.*

Article 10

Hippocrates: Theory and Practice of Medicine

Introduction

Hippocrates (460–370 BC) was a Greek physician in the days when medicine, philosophy and superstition were intertwined. Medicine was very unreliable in its ability to cure and was wrapped in many beliefs that, today, seem just as likely to harm as to cure. Hippocrates' regular success at healing, therefore, became famous through the ancient world. He became known as the founder of modern medicine and was regarded as the greatest physician of his time.

Hippocrates was successful because of his pioneering of many medical principles. He sought natural explanations for the natural phenomena associated with sickness. He based his medical diagnoses on empirical knowledge (observations) and not the "magic" that his contemporaries used. He also separated medicine from philosophy by declaring that medicine was its own special craft. Hippocrates also developed an oath of ethics for physicians to follow. This oath (somewhat modified) is still taken by physicians today at the beginning of their medical practice.

The Oath of Hippocrates

I swear by Apollo the physician, and Æsculapius, and Health, and All-heal, and all the gods and goddesses, that, according to my ability and judgment, I will keep this Oath and this stipulation—to reckon him who taught me this Art equally dear to me as my parents, to share my substance with him, and relieve his necessities if required; to look upon his offspring in the same footing as my own brothers, and to teach them this art, if they shall wish to learn it, without fee or stipulation; and that by precept, lecture, and every other mode of instruction, I will impart a knowledge of the Art to my own sons, and those of my teachers, and to disciples bound by a stipulation and oath according to the law of medicine, but to none others. I will follow that system of regimen which, according to my ability and judgment, I consider for the benefit of my patients, and abstain from whatever is deleterious and mischievous. I will give no deadly medicine to any one if asked, nor suggest any such counsel; and in like manner I will not give to a woman a pessary to produce abortion. With purity and with holiness I will pass my life and practice my Art. I will not cut persons laboring under the stone, but will leave this to be done by men who are practitioners of this work. Into whatever houses I enter, I will go into them for the benefit of the sick, and will abstain from every voluntary act of mischief and corruption; and, further, from the seduction of females or males, of freemen and slaves. Whatever, in connection with my professional practice or not, in connection with it, I see or hear, in the life of men, which ought not

Hippocrates, *The Theory and Practice of Medicine,* Philosophical Library, 1964.

to be spoken of abroad, I will not divulge, as reckoning that all such should be kept secret. While I continue to keep this Oath unviolated, may it be granted to me to enjoy life and the practice of the art, respected by all men, in all times! But should I trespass and violate this Oath, may the reverse be my lot!

Theory and Practice of Medicine

For the art of Medicine would not have been invented at first, nor would it have been made a subject of investigation (for there would have been no need of it), if when men are indisposed, the same food and other articles of regimen which they eat and drink when in good health were proper for them, and if no others were preferable to these. But now necessity itself made medicine to be sought out and discovered by men, since the same things when administered to the sick, which agreed with them when in good health, neither did nor do agree with them. But to go still further back, I hold that the diet and food which people in health now use would not have been discovered, provided it had suited with man to eat and drink in like manner as the ox, the horse, and all other animals, except man, do of the productions of the earth, such as fruits, weeds, and grass; for from such things these animals grow, live free of disease, and require no other kind of food. And, at first, I am of opinion that man used the same sort of food, and that the present articles of diet had been discovered and invented only after a long lapse of time. For when they suffered much and severely from this strong and brutish diet, swallowing things which were raw, unmixed, and possessing great strength, they became exposed to strong pains and diseases, and to early deaths. It is likely, indeed, that from habit they would suffer less from these things then than we would now, but still they would suffer severely even then; and it is likely that the greater number, and those who had weaker constitutions, would all perish; whereas the stronger would hold out for a longer time, as even nowadays some, in consequence of using strong articles of food, get off with little trouble, but others with much pain and suffering. From this necessity it appears to me that they would search out the food befitting their nature, and thus discover that which we now use: and that from wheat, by macerating it, stripping it of its hull, grinding it all down, sifting, toasting, and baking it, they formed bread; and from barley they formed cake (maza), performing many operations in regard to it; they boiled, they roasted, they mixed, they diluted those things which are strong and of intense qualities with weaker things, fashioning them to the nature and powers of man, and considering that the stronger things Nature would not be able to manage if administered, and that from such things pains, diseases, and death would arise, but such as Nature could manage, that from them food, growth, and health, would arise. To such a discovery and investigation what more suitable name could one give than that of Medicine? since it was discovered for the health of man, for his nourishment and safety, as a substitute for that kind of diet by which pains, diseases, and deaths were occasioned.

Classical Greek Philosophy
The Form of Creativity

> The only useful knowledge is that which betters us.
>
> —*Socrates*

Introduction

Creativity can be defined as "A way of thinking and doing that brings unexpected and original ideas to fruition." This definition suggests that creativity is more than just creative thinking. It also involves doing things that bring the ideas into some real or actual condition. For engineers, artists, sculptors, playwrights, and even musicians, the reduction of the idea into something physical is not only expected, but it is the essence of the profession. For scientists, the reduction to actuality is more abstract, but it could be a confirming experiment or a carefully structured proof that receives the review of peers. But what is the method of actualization for a philosopher?

Philosophers might argue that reduction to practice occurs with a well organized proof that receives the review of peers, much like a mathematical proof. Others might say that practicality is achieved when a book or paper is written about the idea, much like a literary work. Still others might say that the real proof of the idea is its implementation, which would certainly be appropriate for an idea in ethics.

Classical Greek philosophy, especially, has been reduced to actuality in all of those ways. It has received the review of peers for hundreds of years, and is generally recognized as the basis of all Western philosophy. Greek philosophy was written by either the philosophers themselves or by those who heard the philosophers directly. Many of the important concepts have been implemented in actual lives and, in some cases, have spawned ethical belief systems followed by millions of people. As Socrates said in the quotation given at the beginning of this chapter, the greatest truth helps humankind. The many adherents to the philosophical concepts of the Classical Greeks and the importance of their thinking even in today's world suggest a tremendous legacy of acceptance, and confirm the creativity of the great philosophers of ancient Greece.

Classical Greek thought reached its apex between 470 B.C. and 322 B.C., when three of the greatest philosophers the world has ever known—Socrates, Plato, and Aristotle—lived and thought and taught in Greece. **Philosopher** literally means "lover of wisdom," and these men were philosophers in the truest sense of the word. They devoted their lives to a search for what was good and beautiful and true. It did not matter whether those truths existed in government, science, art, or religion, or in the realm of philosophy itself. They were believers in the revolutionary idea of Thales—that man could understand this world—and they set themselves to the task of understanding those underlying, constant truths that they felt must exist beneath the chaos and change of daily life.

Socrates (470–399 B.C.)

The first of these great thinkers was **Socrates,** an unpretentious man of humble origins, the son of a stonemason and a midwife, who supported his family as a stonemason himself. He was not handsome (many said he was ugly) and he dressed poorly, in stark contrast to the fixation of Athenians on beauty. He was married to a shrewish wife, but seemed to provide for her adequately. He served honorably in the Peloponnesian War. In spite of these humble and ordinary characteristics, at the time of his death, one comment on his life said he was "The best and wisest and most righteous man of our time." Over two thousand years later, it was said that he was "The noblest man who ever lived." Surely these comments indicate that this was a man whose life is worth studying.

In many ways Socrates was the anti-philosopher. Socrates believed that the key to wisdom was not an extensive knowledge of other people and things, but that wisdom was acquired through a close and careful examination and understanding of oneself. Two of the most famous Socratic quotations concern this belief: "Know thyself" and "The unexamined life is not worth living."

Socrates believed that most of the **sophists** (the men who considered themselves the great thinkers of Socrates' day) taught knowledge, but not thinking. Unlike many of the sophists who felt there were no absolute truths in the world, Socrates felt truth was inherent to the world, but it had to be discovered. Socrates dedicated his life to searching for the truth.

Socrates was also atypical among the "great thinkers" (the sophists) because of his attitude toward the use of knowledge. The sophists were generally an arrogant and proud lot who believed that they knew more than they probably did, and loved to show off their knowledge and ability to reason. They often taught for pay, and modified their conclusions to agree with the preconceived ideas of their benefactors. Socrates, on the other hand, felt that he was not wise, and never took money for teaching.

A legendary story regarding Socrates is that a friend of his went to the Great Oracle at Delphi and asked "Who is the wisest man in Athens?" The oracle replied that Socrates was the wisest man in Athens. The friend then returned to Athens and told Socrates what the oracle had said. Socrates doubted the words of the oracle and decided that he would prove the oracle wrong by finding, for himself, the wisest man in Athens. Socrates went about Athens questioning all of the city's noted thinkers, politicians, military leaders and other leading citizens to try and find the real wisest man. After questioning all who he could find, Socrates finally conceded that he, himself, might indeed be the wisest man in Athens because he knew that he didn't know, whereas all the others did not know that they didn't know. This story highlights what Socrates felt about his own knowledge, the knowledge of others, and the pursuit of truth.

Socrates disliked the hypocrisy of an over-elevated opinion of one's own wisdom. He therefore continued his questioning of the city's leading citizens. He wanted them to think about the really important concepts regarding their own life and, if they were hypocritically shallow in their thinking, to make them appear ridiculous as they tried to defend their knowledge. He would do this by repeatedly posing questions of a critical nature to the position of the citizen and then questioning the answers given—a tactic known now as the Socratic Method or the dialectic method. Some examples: To a politician he might ask, "What is liberty?" or to a military leader he might ask, "What is duty?" If you are a student in the arts, he might have asked you, "What is beauty?" or to a student in business, "What is ethics?" At the end of every conversation, he was able to show that the people did not really understand the concept at the heart of their profession.

Socrates was respected, but not loved, in his day. Some have given him the name of "gadfly" because of his ability to bother incessantly. His methods were seen as eccentric and humiliating to those "great people" he often discredited. Furthermore, he had a group of followers, mostly young people from the city, whom he would talk with and teach. Many believed that these young followers were being corrupted by Socrates' teachings. Of course, these youths respected Socrates and imitated his methods. Before long there was a small host of troublesome thinkers wandering the city, questioning others, and generally making the citizens look ridiculous.

Eventually, Socrates (with some help from his followers) made enough enemies in the city that they were able to put him on trial for a variety of crimes. Among the charges were accusations of corrupting the youth of Athens, and disbelieving in the traditional gods. His guilt on the charge of corrupting the youth depends on your point of view. His guilt on the charge of disbelieving in the traditional gods was true, as Socrates believed in a single, all-powerful god. In this disbelief, Socrates was not alone, as many of the educated citizens of Athens did not actually believe in the traditional Greek gods in the day, although most continued to offer the sacrifices required.

When Socrates was placed on trial, the timing played an important part in the outcome, as Athens had just recently lost a war with her rival city-state, Sparta, and Socrates was seen as being overly friendly toward Alcibiades, the Athenian general whose fateful decision to invade Sicily cost Athens the war. Alcibiades later became a traitor to Athens and helped the Spartans, making Socrates' friendship with him even more suspect.

Socrates did little to help himself at his trial. Many of the jurors were sympathetic toward him and he probably would have been exonerated, or at the very least given a lighter sentence, if Socrates had played along with the charade of the trial. However, Socrates refused to do so and did not defend himself. In the absence of a defense, he was convicted. In the sentencing phase of the trial, his enemies suggested that Socrates be executed, perhaps thinking that they could register a strong protest with such a ridiculous sentence. Once again, Socrates proved to be obstinate and difficult. Instead of suggesting a minor punishment for himself that could have led to an agreeable "slap on the hands," he suggested the city reward him for his "crimes" by giving him free meals for life at the gymnasium, among other honors. The rules of Athenian law dictated that the sentence must come from among the alternatives offered. The citizens were left with few options and, feeling mocked, they sentenced Socrates to death by drinking poison hemlock. Socrates was given one final chance at life when one of his followers offered him an opportunity to escape, but Socrates rejected this offer as well. On the fateful day, Socrates met with his family, spoke with his pupils, drank the hemlock, and walked around until the poison took effect. His last words were about the delights he would have meeting the great people of the past in the afterlife, whom he anticipated seeing soon.

Socrates died without ever writing anything that has come to us through history. All that we know of him was recorded by his students, chiefly Plato. We now turn our attention to Plato's life and teachings.

Plato (427–347 B.C.)

Following the death of Socrates, his premier student, **Plato,** left Athens and traveled for several years. Plato returned to Athens in 387 B.C. and felt that the concepts of Socrates and his own needed to be taught in a more formal way than had previously been done. Plato established his school and named it the Academy. The level of teaching and type of instruction would qualify the Academy as the world's first university. The focus of Plato and his Academy was on philosophy, math, law, and political theory. The purpose of his work, however, was to shift people's thinking to the deeper meanings of life, especially ethics and the ultimate nature of reality. Plato reported the words of Socrates to teach basic principles of both truth and method. (It is from Plato that we get almost all our knowledge of Socrates.) However, it is on Plato's conception of reality and the fundamentals of the universe (remember the concepts of Thales and Pythagoras) that we will begin our examination of Plato's work, for it is this concept that is at the heart of all else that he taught.

Plato was a strong believer in many of the concepts proposed by Pythagoras, which is seen in the emphasis on mathematics in the Academy (which had as a motto: "Let no one ignorant of geometry enter here") and in the nature of the fundamental reality that Plato proposed. He called this fundamental reality the **Form.** The concept is a bit strange for us today, and so we need to discuss it in some detail.

Imagine a right triangle, something that Plato would have discussed in great detail because of his love of Pythagorean teachings. By definition, that right triangle contains one angle that is *exactly* 90°. If that triangle is drawn on the whiteboard or paper for all to see, there is a minor problem. You will not be able to draw the right angle to be exactly 90°. You may even use a carpenter's square or protractor or even a draftsman's triangle, but each of these devices has been made on equipment and by methods that do not allow them to be *exactly* 90°. If you were to examine under a microscope the angle that you have drawn, you would find that some minor deviation had occurred. And, even if you could see no deviation with the microscope you are using, if you were to get a microscope with higher magnification, you would surely find some deviation on the exactness of the angle. We can, therefore, conclude in general that no actual physical representation of an *exact* 90° angle is possible and so, of course, no physical representation of a right triangle is possible. But, does that mean that the Pythagorean law of right triangles is invalid? Of course not. It is valid, but only in the theoretical world—just as the only right triangle that really, *exactly,* exists is the one that we imagined at the beginning of our exercise. It is this theoretical and exact version of the right triangle that Plato calls the Form of the right triangle. But, because the Form of the thing is constant, unchanging, and eternal, it is more real than the physical version of the thing, which is imperfect and changeable. Therefore, to Plato and his followers, the theoretical or mental was more real than the physical. (Later Christian writers like St. Augustine will equate the theoretical and mental aspects of things with the spiritual and godlike and adopt many of Plato's ideas into Christianity.) To Plato, the physical, material world we can see and touch was an illusion—it wasn't real. It was just a corrupted version of the immaterial spiritual world, where all things existed in their perfect Form.

The exactness of the Form and the inexactness of the real representation of the Form hold for all geometrical figures. Notice that we intuitively recognize this fact because we can identify right angles, right triangles, circles, and so on, even when they are not accurately drawn (which is always the case). There is something about these figures that allows us to recognize them as perfect even though they actually have major or minor discrepancies. Plato says that the reason these inexact things can still be recognized is because we see in them the Form of what they ought to be. They are merely representations of the true Form, but they are close enough for us to recognize and understand them. Other terms for the Form (*eidos* in Greek) are: fundamental, idea, essence, transcendent first principle, universal, changeless absolute, immortal deity, and archetype.

We can understand another aspect of the Forms of things by considering several types of chairs, perhaps like those depicted in Figure 8.1. The first chair is quite standard, and we easily say that is has the characteristics that we expect a chair to have. The next chair is less standard and we still recognize it as a chair. In Plato's terms, those fundamental characteristics that allow us to tie the depicted chairs together, and all other chairs in the world, for that matter, are called the Form of a chair. We might also call it "Chairness,"

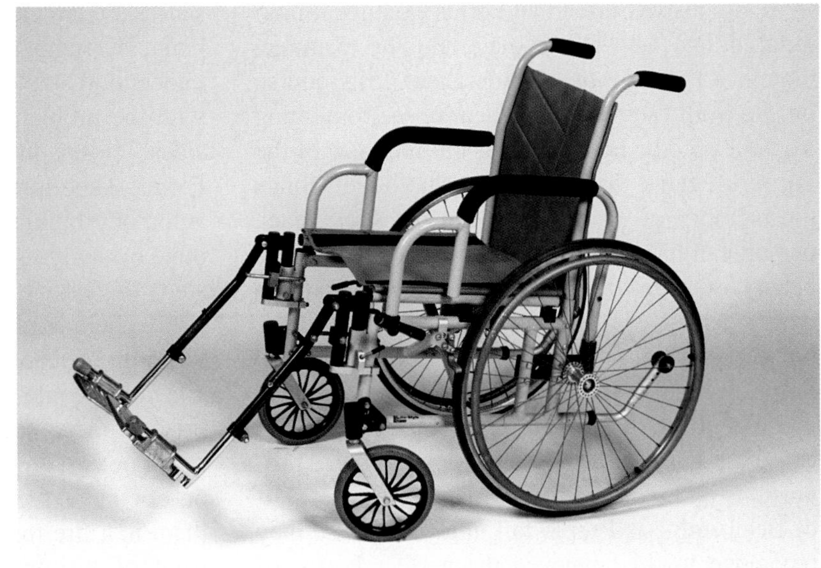

Figure 8.1 ■ *Different types of chairs, illustrating the Form of chairs (Chairness). Image © 2005 by PhotoDisc.*

meaning the characteristics that make the thing a chair.

A brief exercise might convince you that while Chairness seems easy to identify—that is, when we see a chair we recognize it—the definition of Chairness is not so easy. We might try to define the fundamental characteristics of a chair by saying that a chair is something that we sit on. However, we sit on many things, such as tables, the floor, even the seat of our pants, but merely our sitting on them doesn't change their nature. They don't become chairs just by our sitting on them. Moreover, a chair is still a chair even when no one is sitting on it. You will find that all attempts to define a chair by its purpose are inadequate. Likewise, you might attempt to define a chair by its shape (for example: flat area with a back and supports to the floor). You will find, however, that exceptions will occur in every case. For instance, the chair might not have a back, or the flat area might not be flat, or the supports might be from the side or even the top. In the end, you are likely to conclude that the fundamental characteristics of a chair are best expressed simply by saying that the chair is identified and defined by its Chairness—the Form of a chair in Plato's terms.

In terms of people, we might say that even though every person in the world is different, we can still see the Form of "person" in them. To some extent, the separation of animals and plants into species or genera or some other biological division is an attempt to identify the Form of each group of animals or plants. Humans innately seem to want to classify things according to patterns or, alternately, to discover patterns by organization. These may be attempts to use and understand the Forms.

The next question you might ask is "How do I recognize the Form of something?" Plato answers this question by asserting that before we came to this world we visited the World of Forms, that is, the place where the true Forms are located. We saw what the Form of things looked like. Then, when we came here to the physical world, we still had a memory of the Forms that we saw previously, and we recognize the elements or approximations of the Forms in the physical things around us.

Plato also asserted that Forms exist for immaterial things as well as material. For example, there is a Form for beauty, goodness, love, and so on. He would suggest that when we see something we believe to be beautiful, it is our memory of the Form of beauty that leads us to that belief. Since the memory of all people is not the same, each person can have his or her own opinion as to the beauty of a particular object. That may explain why a person who is beautiful to one of us may not be beautiful to you. However, symmetry and proportion seem to be beautiful to everyone (remember the Golden Ratio), but that is only because the Form of beauty must possess these proportions and we have merely discovered that part of Beautifulness. People fall in love because they recognize in their beloved the perfect Forms of beauty, compassion, charity, and so on.

Plato's understanding of the Form led to his discussion of how the world was created. He believed that a powerful being, a Demi-god or, as it was sometimes called, a Demi-urge, wanted to create the world. This Demi-god had access to the World of Forms and also to physical matter. The Demi-god shaped the physical matter into the various shapes that were like the Forms, but matter, being imperfect, was not able to hold the perfect shape of the Form. The matter became the world we live in. Therefore, the world is only an approximation of the World of Forms. That approximation arises, not from the weakness of the Demi-god, but from the innate nature of imperfect matter. A similar situation exists for immaterial things like beauty. These are all influenced by physical things and so they are also only approximations of true Forms.

Clearly, for Plato, the world is not fundamental. The world is an approximation of true reality. This observation leads to Plato's depreciation of physical and worldly things. He believes, for example, that true love is best expressed in a non-physical sense, because that more closely approximates the true Form of love. Today, when two people share a non-physical love, we call it "platonic love," named after Plato.

Plato also asserted that Forms could not be fully understood using the senses. He said that the senses are too closely associated with the physical body. He suggested that the Forms could best be understood by the mind. The mind is less involved with the problems of physical matter and is, besides, closer to memory, which has seen the Forms. Therefore, Plato encouraged us all to develop our thinking. He believed that could best be done by studying philosophy, and so he made that study the basis of the Academy.

To help explain his ideas to others, Plato devised the Allegory of the Cave. According to the allegory, people are like prisoners in a cave. The prisoners are bound so that they cannot move much or turn around and see what is behind them or, of course, see the entrance to the cave. Behind them is a fire that casts its light onto the wall in front of the prisoners. Occasionally images of things, like a model of a chair, for instance, are moved between the fire and the backs of the prisoners. The prisoners can see the shadows of these images of things on the wall of the cave and, because they have never seen anything else, the prisoners believe that the shadows are reality.

However, if some of the prisoners are released and allowed to turn around, they would see that they had only been looking at shadows. They would not, however, be able to tell whether the images were the real things or just images because, even turning around, they would not have any experience with the real things (like a chair).

Then, suppose that some of the released prisoners are allowed to actually move about and they find the entrance to the cave. They will, of course, be initially blinded by the bright light in the open. Eventually, however, their eyes will become accustomed to the light and they will perceive the world. In this world they will see a chair that is more than just an image. These people are, therefore, those who have been able to see reality.

Plato says that the prisoners who have been released are like the philosophers, and that moving out of the cave is like moving into the World of Forms, something that can only be done in this life through mental understanding. Nevertheless, those who can understand the real Forms should be the leaders of all people, because only they can understand reality.

Plato wrote his idea of a perfect society in his book *The Republic.* In that perfect society, the philosophers who could understand the World of Forms would be the leaders. Children would be separated according to their ability to think, and those who proved to be most adept at thinking would eventually become the leaders. Plato's vision of this perfect society is quite complex, but is well worth your detailed analysis.

Plato's concept of the Form and his rigid disbelief in the reality of the material or physical world were not without its critics. While Plato's explanation of the Form was nearly the ultimate explanation of Thales' problem of what is the underlying truth from the philosophical point of view, it was virtually useless from a scientific point of view, because it completely discounted the reality of the material world and the ability of mankind to study and understand that world through the senses. In one famous exchange between Plato and a critic of his belief in the Form, the critic said, "I see horses, but not horseness" and Plato replied "That is because your eyes have no intelligence." Unfortunately, not all of Plato's critics could be as easily silenced; foremost among them being his top pupil, Aristotle.

Aristotle (384–322 B.C.)

Aristotle was the son of a physician in Macedonia, a northern province on the edge of what was considered Greece proper (the Macedonians considered themselves Greeks, but the Greeks considered the Macedonians little better than barbarians). Despite being considered an outsider in many respects, Aristotle went to Athens to be educated, and soon found himself the leading student at Plato's Academy.

Aristotle, however, did not agree with his mentor on some of his basic concepts. When Plato died and Plato's son took over the Academy, Aristotle left Athens and traveled for 12 years. During his travels he set up schools in many cities, married the daughter of a king, and spent three years as personal tutor to a young prince from his home in Macedonia, named Alexander. Alexander would later become known to the world as Alexander the Great, and would spread Greek ideas across the known Earth. After serving as Alexander's tutor, Aristotle returned to Athens, where he formed his own school, the Lyceum, to compete with the Academy.

The most basic disagreement between Plato and Aristotle concerned their opinions on what was the ultimate nature of things. Plato said that only the Form was real and all physical nature was of much lower importance. Aristotle said that all things consist of two parts: their matter, called a potential, and their Form. In Aristotle's view, a piece of marble would be matter and exist in a particular Form (such as a block), but it had the potential to be changed into a different Form (such as a statue) because the matter could be modified (that is, some of the matter could be removed). If it were a bronze statue, the matter could be melted and reshaped; thus, the matter would be changed by a different physical process. Aristotle also saw a potential, of a slightly different but related kind, in animate things. For example, he saw that seeds have the potential to become a plant, or an acorn to become an oak tree. In these cases, no external force was needed to effect the change in the matter (that is, to realize its potential).

For Aristotle, there were obvious differences between animate and inanimate things. These differences served as the basis of classification that Aristotle invented and that has served as the basis for our modern biological classification system into species, genera, classes, and so on.

Aristotle's Lyceum focused more on the exploration of the natural sciences (although Aristotle still dealt extensively with more traditional philosophy) than did the Academy. The difference in emphasis between the two schools illustrates the difference in ideology that existed between Aristotle and his mentor, Plato. This difference was depicted by Raphael in his fresco *The School of Athens,* painted in the early sixteenth century A.D. during the Italian Renaissance. In this painting Plato is pointing upward, reflecting his concern for the World of Forms (which lies above the earth), and Aristotle is pointing downward, reflecting his interest in the earthly world.

This may all seem like a theoretical argument with little practical purpose or application, but to Plato and Aristotle the difference had great consequences, because it affected how they should search for truth. To Plato, who believed that the Form was immaterial truth, the real nature of things could only be discovered by using the mind and the soul; thus, truth was revealed through philosophy. For Aristotle, the true nature of things could be extrapolated from sensory observations in the everyday world, and therefore could be understood by what we would call a **scientific method.**

Aristotle developed a scientific method that was based on asking four critical questions about things in the world. The questions are answered both by observation (that is, through the senses) and by rational means. These questions can, perhaps, best be understood by applying them to a representative case. Let's apply them to a common field mouse.

1. Material question: What is it made of? This question would be answered by a chemical analysis of the mouse. We could find that the answer is various chemical compounds.
2. Efficient question: What caused it? The mouse was caused by a birth process and would be determined by observing clues such as the presence of a belly button, the similarity of this mouse to other mice, and our familiarity with the birth of other mice.
3. Formal question: What is its essence? This question asks us to think about the Form of the mouse. We would investigate the characteristics of the mouse that are not discoverable by physical or chemical analysis. (Remember that Aristotle believed that everything had two natures—material and Form—and that those would be discovered using different methods.) In Aristotle's time, the Form would be perceived by rationalization of the similarities of this mouse to others and of the extent to which we would see changes occurring in the mouse but still perceive this mouse as a mouse. Today, we have an interesting additional insight in the Form of a mouse. We know that DNA dictates the characteristics of a mouse. The DNA is the information that controls the specialization of the cells and other growth processes. This concept is inherent in our understanding of the word "information," which could be rewritten as in-Form-ation, thus emphasizing that Form is really about information.
4. What is its purpose? The answer would rely on a set of standards of behavior for the animal in light of a plan that would apply to the entire world. This mouse could have as its purpose the dissemination of seeds, thus helping trees reproduce. It could also be food for a fox or snake, which integrates it into the food chain. It might be just a vehicle for our study, thus fulfilling its purpose in our examination. In general, modern science, especially from the 17th to 19th centuries A.D., rarely asked the final question. Sir Isaac Newton, for example, said that it was not his purpose to give the cause, purpose, or origin of gravity but, rather, to just describe its effects. Today, some scientists are again asking the purpose of things, just as was done by Aristotle. For example: What is the purpose of an appendix? What is the purpose of the earth? What is the purpose of a ritual conducted by a primitive tribe? Admittedly, these are questions more commonly asked by social scientists today, but some physical scientists are also contemplating deep questions in some areas. Religious thinkers and philosophers have always asked these questions.

Aristotle's interests led to his personal investigation of the nature of the physical world. He indicated that all matter is composed of four elements—fire, earth, water, and air. These elements were confined to the earthly realm. There was, in addition, a heavenly realm that surrounded the earth. In that realm were the moon, the sun, the planets, and the stars. Aristotle believed that everything above the earth was perfect, and therefore unchanging. Since it was unchanging, it must be composed of a different material. This substance is called **quintessence** (literally meaning the fifth material) which, in modern English, means the essence of something in its most perfect form.

The four earthly elements can also be associated with fundamental qualities of matter from which all other qualities are derived. Those linkages are given in Figure 8.2 and, as shown, the qualities come from a combination of the elements: cold comes from water and earth, for example. Furthermore, the elements and qualities have a relationship with human bodies and medicine, as explained by Hippocrates, the father of medicine, whom we discussed in the last chapter, and a contemporary of Plato's. He believed that the body contains four fluids or humors—blood, phlegm, black bile, and yellow bile. Illness came when these humors were out of balance (a very Greek idea), so when we are sick, we need to adjust the balance. For example, if a person has a fever, that must be due to an excess of the humor associated with heat—blood. The remedy would be, therefore, to let the excess blood out of the body; this thinking led to the practice of blood-letting. Hippocrates declared that medicine was its own craft; he separated it from philosophy and installed an oath for all those who would practice that craft. Medical doctors still take that oath today.

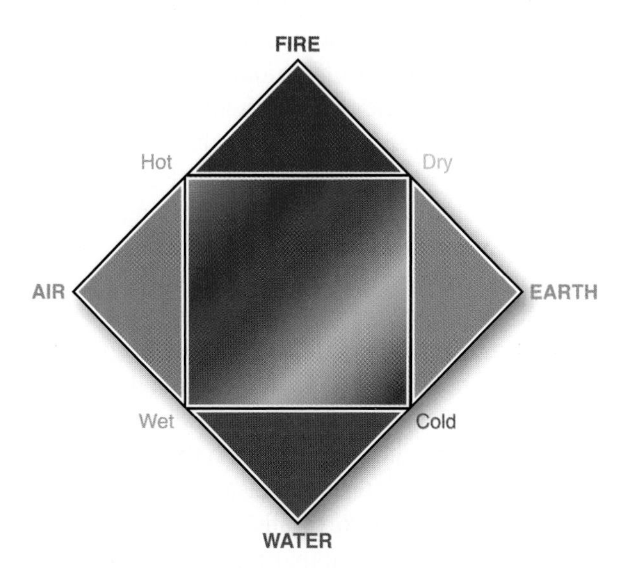

Figure 8.2 ■ *Aristotle's representation of the elements and the qualities.*

Aristotle also studied the motion of bodies. He said that the most stable condition for a body composed of earth-like material would be on the earth. Therefore, rocks fall to earth. He reasoned that bigger rocks would have more of a tendency to fall because they had more of the earth-like material. Therefore, the rate of falling of a body would be proportional to the size of the body. However, from experiments done by Galileo in the Renaissance, we know that Aristotle was wrong in his description of motion. We might ask, why didn't Aristotle simply go out to a high tower and do the experiment himself? Aristotle believed that if the investigator becomes involved in the phenomena being observed, as would be the case if an experiment were being performed (as opposed to simply an observation of naturally occurring conditions), then the results could not be trusted. He said, in essence, that if we interfere with nature, we can't really describe nature. We have observed something that is not natural and our observation is limited only to the special case we have observed. We see, therefore, that Aristotle had a different understanding from modern science regarding the nature of cause and effect. (We should note, however, that in twentieth century physics, Heisenberg stated that merely measuring the position or speed of a particle will change the result—essentially reconfirming Aristotle's belief about experimentation.)

Aristotle's influence was so strong that his ideas, right and wrong, were the only ones accepted throughout the Middle Ages. Little by little a new type of scientist, one dependent on experimentation, began to emerge and refute some of Aristotle's assertions, but this did not happen until the 16th century A.D.

Just as Plato dreamed of and described a perfect society, so too did Aristotle. However, the approach was different. Where Plato simply built the vision of his republic on theoretical ideas, Aristotle gathered information about existing societies and evaluated what was already being done. He assembled 158 constitutions and compared them, and then selected features that he felt were the best from each. He said that three types of government existed and that, in each case, both good and bad governments were possible. Those three types of government were:

- Rule by one man: Good = monarchy; bad = tyranny
- Rule by a few: Good = aristocracy; bad = oligarchy
- Rule by the many: Good = polity (constitution guides actions of the people); bad = democracy (each person acting on his/her own without a general guide)

In each case, the bad form of government occurred because the ruler or ruling group was self-interested. The good ruler(s) was interested in the good of the people as a whole. Aristotle believed that the middle class (today's phrase, not his) should be the ultimate rulers of the society. Therefore, the best of all the forms of government would be the polity.

Aristotle also wrote about ethics. He suggested that people should act so as to achieve happiness, but he specified that the happiness must be overall and extended in time, and not just some focused and short-lived pleasure. Aristotle suggested that there are three levels of happiness, which can guide us in our ethical behavior. These three types of happiness differ in motivation and in the type of person who seeks each type. According to Aristotle, they are:

- Happiness based on pleasure (which is the goal of the vulgar man)
- Happiness based on honor (which is the goal of the cultivated man)
- Happiness based on true principles of truth and virtue (which is the highest form of happiness and comes from contemplation and philosophy)

Religious teachers today generally teach that happiness comes from the last of the types, and they associate this ultimate happiness with the concept of joy. They say that joy can be understood by studying and living God's revealed principles of truth and virtue. Aristotle himself summarized other aspects of ethics by suggesting that people follow the Golden Mean, which for him meant to avoid extremes.

One more area of interest for Aristotle was rhetoric, that is, the methods that can be employed to influence others. Again, Aristotle gives a list of rhetorical methods, which guide us in our use of rhetoric:

- **Ethos** is the power of persuasion created by the character of the speaker. An example would be Lincoln's *Gettysburg Address.*
- **Pathos** is the power of persuasion created by the passion of the speaker. An example would be Patrick Henry's "Give Me Liberty or Give Me Death" speech.
- **Logos** is the power of persuasion contained within the speech itself, usually because of logic or reason. An example would be a speech employing syllogisms to make the points such as the following: Our taxes are insufficient to pay for repair of our roads. But, without the roads, our economy will falter and taxes will decrease further. Therefore, we should increase taxes to repair the roads.

Aristotle advocated the use of *logos* as the principal method that should be used to influence people. He wrote a treatise on syllogisms and other methods of logic to help ensure that the rules of logic used in *logos* would be followed properly.

In addition to all of the other areas we have mentioned, Aristotle was a literary and drama critic. He analyzed the nature of drama and then commented on what he thought had been done well. For example, he defined tragedy, and illuminated the use of tragic flaws by Sophocles, citing in particular *Oedipus Rex.* As with other areas of interest for Aristotle, his well organized mind and penchant for making lists were applied to drama. Aristotle believed that good drama must develop a **catharsis** in the audience. Catharsis means purging or cleansing and has to do with the need to resolve the pity and fear which are often part of tragedy. In *Oedipus Rex* catharsis was achieved when Jocasta and Oedipus recognized their odious relationship and took appropriate steps to resolve it—death in her case, blindness and exile in his. According to Aristotle, catharsis is achieved, and good drama created, when various factors are present in the play and properly executed. These are the factors of drama that Aristotle identified, and the order in which he believed they were important to good drama:

- Plot. Here Aristotle was most interested in the way the incidents of the story are arranged for the audience. These may be linked by a strong story, but the importance of the story is merely to carry the action among the three essential parts of the plot: the initiation of the action (with cause and effect clearly shown), the climax (which must result from the earlier actions), and the resolution.
- Character. This is where Aristotle points out the importance of a tragic flaw or mistake. He also gives a set of characteristics that must be possessed by the main characters: They must be fine (that is noble or high-ranking) characters, true to life and believable, and true to themselves.
- Thought. This is a discussion of how the characters should reveal themselves and the plot through their speeches. This factor is related to his work on rhetoric.
- Diction. This is the expression of the meaning of the words, which should be correct, both in terms of language and in terms of the character.
- Melodic element. Aristotle believed that the chorus should be fully integrated into the play, thus requiring that the music fit the mood of the play.
- Spectacle. This is dependent more on the mechanic than the poet but, in the days of Sophocles, the two functions may have been done by the same person, or at least supervised by him. Today, spectacle remains important in the staging of a play. We have, for example, been amazed at the deep underground labyrinth of *Phantom of the Opera,* and the complex barricade of *Les Miserables,* and the arrival on stage of a helicopter in *Miss Saigon.*

Creativity in Greek Classical Philosophy

Few people would doubt the depth of the ideas of Socrates, Plato, and Aristotle. Likewise, few would question the significance and wide-ranging effects of those ideas. To that extent, therefore, these three clearly satisfy the requirement that creative ideas be valued and influential. We might also ask whether their ideas were unique. Some of their ideas were certainly based on the previous ideas of others as, for example, the ideas of Plato on the Form and the concepts of Pythagoras on math, and Aristotle's obvious dependence on Plato's ideas in the nature of objects. However, even in those areas where ideas clearly had an origin with someone else, the treatment of the ideas was unique. Plato's Forms were much more than math, and Aristotle's description of the nature of matter went beyond, and conflicted with, Plato's ideas. We believe, therefore, that the ideas of each of these three great philosophers were unique and valued.

We might also ask if their ideas had both depth and breadth—elements often associated with creativity. We believe that both aspects are obvious. The depth is shown in the way philosophy, the discipline in which they were involved, has continued to wrestle with ideas that are almost completely demarcated by the concepts of these ancient Greeks. Socrates, Plato, and Aristotle plumbed the depth of their disciplines.

As for breadth, few people have ever written as extensively or as widely as Plato and Aristotle. While it is true that science and philosophy were not separate disciplines in their day, still we are impressed with their discussions of biology, physics, astronomy, and other scientific fields. We are also impressed with their discussions on government, ethics, method, literary criticism, education, and a host of other areas.

To conclude, we have just examined the work and lives of three of the most influential men in history. We will refer back many times to them and their teachings. For us, there is no doubt about the excellence of their creativity.

Timeline—Important Dates

Date	Event
470–399 B.C.	*Socrates*
427–347 B.C.	*Plato*
384–322 B.C.	*Aristotle*

Suggested Readings

Archer-Hind, R. D. (trans.), *The Timaeus of Plato,* Arno Press, 1973.

Hardie, R. P. and R. K. Gaye, *The Works of Aristotle,* Oxford University Press, 1953.

Howe, Paul, *Classics in Translation,* vol. 1, University of Wisconsin Press, 1952.

Lindberg, David C., *The Beginnings of Western Science,* University of Chicago Press, 1992.

McClellan, James E. III and Harold Dorn, *Science and Technology in World History,* Johns Hopkins University Press, 1999.

McDeon, Richard (ed.), *The Basic Works of Aristotle,* Random House, 1941.

Palmer, Donald, *Does the Center Hold?,* Mayfield, 1991.

Rouse, W. H. D., *Great Dialogues of Plato,* Dutton Signet, 1984.

Tarnas, Richard, *The Passion of the Western Mind,* Ballantine, 1991.

Plato: Apology, Phaedo, The Republic, Timaeus

Introduction

Greece in the 5th and 4th Centuries BC was the intellectual and political center of the world. This was the period called Greece's Golden Age. A democratic government was ruling the principle Greek city, Athens, and great buildings and other works of art were being created. Drama, historical writing, and sculpture were developing creative methods that would be standards for the rest of history. But, perhaps the most important of the innovations during the Golden Age was the organized thinking that was done chiefly by three great philosophers. The first was Socrates, then Plato, and finally Aristotle.

Plato (427–347 BC) was the foremost student of Socrates. After Socrates' execution Plato traveled the countryside writing down the teachings of Socrates, developing his own theories, and teaching anyone who would listen. Eventually Plato returned to Athens where he created a school, the Academy, which lasted over 1000 years. While Plato's teachings are complex and extensive, we can summarize some of the basic points. Plato became the champion of "the Form"—the perfect essence of a thing (it can be either material or virtual) that exists eternally but can only be perceived by the mind. He also taught that the intellectual is higher than the physical. Also, Plato believed, as did some other Greek philosophers like Pythagoras, that reality is highly organized and can be represented by small whole numbers. His teachings, although highly abstract even today, are a major component of the study of philosophy.

The *Apology* is Plato's retelling of Socrates' own defense of the philosopher's lifestyle spoken in front of the jury accusing him (Socrates) of corrupting the youth of Athens. We have almost no teachings of Socrates except through Plato's writings.

The *Phaedo* is Plato's account of the last hours of Socrates, just before he commits suicide by order of the state. Fittingly, most of the dialogue is concerned with the immortal nature of the soul. When reading here of the importance of spiritual values over material ones, later Christian doctrine comes to mind. Several early Christian teachers, such as St. Augustine, were avowed Platonists and used Plato's teachings to supplement and explain Christian doctrine.

The Republic was Plato's proposal for an ideal society. He proposed that because mankind is generally unable to comprehend the Forms, they are limited in what they can rightly understand about many issues. Plato suggested an allegory that depicts this confused state of mankind. The "Allegory of the Cave" illustrates how only those who are able to perceive the true nature of the Forms will be able to find truth. The philosophers are able to break their chains of ignorance and misperception to finally emerge from the cave of shadows into the true light of reality. Hence, we should look to philosophers as our leaders.

Timaeus is one of Plato's later works. It discusses the origin of the world which was created by the "Demiurge," a god-like force that is the personification of reason, who united Forms with matter to make the world. However, matter, being imperfect, was not able to exactly replicate the Forms and so the actual world we live in is not a true representation of the Forms. To early Christians, this concept of the creation sounded very much like the concept of God creating the world using a spiritual existence as a Form. Because of this closeness to Christianity, the *Timaeus* was translated into Latin and was the only work of Plato available in Europe throughout the Middle Ages.

Article 11
Apology

[Socrates is speaking]
Consider now why I tell you this; I am going to explain to you the source of the slander against me. When I had heard the answer of the oracle, I said to myself: "What in the world does the god mean, and what is this riddle? For I realize that I am wise in nothing, great or small; what then does he mean by saying that I am the wisest? Surely, he does not lie; that is not in keeping with his nature." For a long time I was perplexed; then I resorted to this method of inquiry. I went to one of those men who were reputed to be wise, with the idea of disproving the oracle and of showing it: "Here is one wiser than I; but you said that I was the wisest." Well, after observing and talking with him (I don't need to mention his name; but he was a politician), I had this experience: the man seemed in the opinions of many other men, and especially of himself, to be wise; but he really wasn't. And then I tried to show him that he thought he was wise, but really wasn't; so I found myself disliked by him and by many of those present. So I left him, and said to myself: "Well, I am wiser than this man. Probably neither of us knows anything noble; but he thinks he knows, whereas he doesn't, while I neither know nor think I know. So I seem to have this slight advantage over him, that I don't think I know what I don't know." Next I went to another man who was reputed to be even wiser, and in my opinion the result was the same; and I got myself disliked by him and by many others.

After that I went to other men in turn, aware of the dislike that I incurred, and regretting and fearing it; yet I felt that God's word must come first, so that I must go to all who had the reputation of knowing anything, as I inquired into the meaning of the oracle. And by the Dog! gentlemen, for I must tell you the truth, this is what happened to me in my quest: those who were in greatest repute were just about the most lacking, while others in less repute were better off in respect to wisdom. I really must expound to you my wanderings, my Herculean labors to test the oracle. After the politicians, I went to the poets, tragic, dithyrambic, and the rest, with the expectation that there I should be caught less wise than they. So picking up those of their poems which seemed to me to be particularly elaborated, I asked them what they meant, so that at the same time I might learn something from them. Now I am ashamed to tell you the truth, but it must be spoken; almost every one present could have talked better about the poems than their authors. So presently I came to know that the poets, too, like the seers and the soothsayers, do what they do not through wisdom but through a sort of genius and inspiration; for the poets, like them, say many fine things without understanding what they are saying. And I noticed also that they supposed because of their poetry that they were wisest of men in other matters in which they were not wise. So I left them, too, believing that I had the same advantage over them that I had over the politicians.

Finally I went to the craftsmen; for I knew that I knew hardly anything, but that I should find them knowing many fine things. And I was not deceived in this; they knew things that I did not know, and in this way they were wiser than I. But even good craftsmen seemed to me to have the same failing as the poets; because of his skill in his craft each one supposed that he excelled also in other matters of the greatest importance; and this lapse obscured their wisdom. So I asked myself whether I would prefer to be as I was, without their wisdom and without their ignorance, or to have both their wisdom and their ignorance; and I answered myself and the oracle that I was better off just as I was.

From this inquiry many enmities have arisen against me, both violent and grievous, as well as many slanders and my reputation of being "wise." For those who are present on each occasion suppose that I have the wisdom that I find wanting in others; but the truth is that only God is wise, and that by that oracle he means to show that human wisdom is worth little or nothing. And by speaking of "Socrates" he appears to use me and my name merely as an example, just as if he were to say, "Mortals, he of you is wisest who, like Socrates, knows that in truth his wisdom is worth nothing." That is why I go about even now, questioning and examining in God's name any man, citizen or stranger, whom I suppose to be wise. And whenever I find that he is not wise, then in vindication of the divine oracle I show him that he is not wise. And by reason of this preoccupation I have no leisure to accomplish any public business worth mentioning or any private business, but I am in extreme poverty because of my service to the god.

Besides this, the young men who follow me about of their own accord, well-to-do and with plenty of leisure, take delight in hearing men put to the test, and often imitate me and put others to test; and then, I believe, they find no lack of men who suppose they know something but who know little or nothing. Then the people who are quizzed by them are angry with me, not with themselves, and say, "There is one Socrates who is a rascal and who corrupts the young." And when any one asks them what this Socrates does or teaches, they don't know and have nothing to say, but so as not to seem to be at a loss they repeat the ready-made charges made against all philosophers, about things celestial and things subterranean, and not believing in gods, and making the worse appear the better case. They wouldn't like to admit the truth, I suppose, which is that they have been shown up as pretenders to knowledge that they do not possess. Now since they are ambitious and energetic and numerous, and are well marshalled and persuasive, they have filled your ears with vehement and oft-repeated slander.

Article 12
Phaedo

[Socrates is speaking.] "Now then, I want to give the proof at once, to you as my judges, why I think it likely that one who has spent his life in philosophy should be confident when he is going to die, and have good hopes that he will win the greatest blessings in the next world when he has ended: so Simmias and Cebes my judges, I will try to show how this could be true.

"The fact is, those who tackle philosophy aright are simply and solely practicing dying, practicing death, all the time, but nobody sees it. If this is true, then it would surely be unreasonable that they should earnestly do this and nothing else all their lives, yet when death comes they should object to what they had been so long earnestly practicing."

Simmias laughed at this, and said, "I don't feel like laughing just now, Socrates, but you have made me laugh. I think the many if they heard that would say, 'That's a good one for the philosophers!' And other people in my city would heartily agree that philosophers are really suffering from a wish to die, and now they have found them out, that they richly deserve it!"

"That would be true, Simmias," said Socrates, "except the words 'found out.' For they have not found out in what sense the real philosophers wish to die and deserve to die, and what kind of death it is. Let us say good-bye to them," he went on, "and ask ourselves: Do we think there is such a thing as death?"

"Certainly," Simmias put in.

"Is it anything more than the separation of the soul from the body?" said Socrates. "Death is, that the body separates from the soul, and remains by itself apart from the soul, and the soul, separated from the body, exists by itself apart from the body. Is death anything but that?"

"No," he said, "that is what death is."

"Then consider, my good friend, if you agree with me here, for I think this is the best way to understand the question we are examining. Do you think it the part of a philosopher to be earnestly concerned with what are called pleasures, such as these—eating and drinking, for example?"

"Not at all," said Simmias.

"The pleasures of love, then?"

"Oh no."

"Well, do you suppose a man like that regards the other bodily indulgences as precious? Getting fine clothes and shoes and other bodily adornments—ought he to price them high or low, beyond whatever share of them it is absolutely necessary to have?"

"Low, I think," he said, "if he is a true philosopher."

"Then in general," he said, "do you think that such a man's concern is not for the body, but as far as he can he stands aloof from that and turns towards the soul?"

"I do."

"Then firstly, is it not clear that in such things the philosopher as much as possible sets free the soul from communion with the body, more than other men?"

"So it appears."

"And I suppose, Simmias, it must seem to most men that he who has no pleasure in such things and takes no share in them does not deserve to live, but he is getting pretty close to death if he does not care about pleasures which he has by means of the body."

"Quite true, indeed."

"Well then, what about the actual getting of wisdom? Is the body in the way or not, if a man takes it with him as companion in the search? I mean, for example, is there any truth for men in their sight and hearing? Or as poets are forever dinning into our ears, do we hear nothing and see nothing exactly? Yet if these of our bodily senses are not exact and clear, the others will hardly be, for they are all inferior to these, don't you think so?"

"Certainly," he said.

"Then," said he, "when does the soul get hold of the truth? For whenever the soul tries to examine anything in company with the body, it is plain that it is deceived by it."

"Quite true."

"Then is it not clear that in reasoning, if anywhere, something of the realities becomes visible to it?"

"Yes."

"And I suppose it reasons best when none of these senses disturbs it, hearing or sight, or pain, or pleasure indeed, but when it is completely by itself and says good-bye to the body, and so far as possible has no dealings with it, when it reaches out and grasps that which really is."

"That is true."

"And is it not then that the philosopher's soul chiefly holds the body cheap and escapes from it, while it seeks to be by itself?"

"So it seems."

"Let us pass on, Simmias. Do we say there is such a thing as justice by itself, or not?"

"We do say so, certainly!"

"Such a thing as the good and beautiful?"

"Of course!"

"And did you ever see one of them with your eyes?"

"Never," said he.

"By any other sense of those the body has did you ever grasp them? I mean all such things, greatness, health, strength, in short everything that really is the nature of things whatever they are: Is it through the body that the real truth is perceived? Or is this better—whoever of us prepares himself most completely and most exactly to comprehend each thing which he examines would come nearest to knowing each one?"

"Certainly."

"And would he do that most purely who should approach each with his intelligence alone, not adding sight to intelligence, or dragging in any other sense along with reasoning, but using the intelligence uncontaminated alone by itself, while he tries to hunt out each essence uncontaminated, keeping clear of eyes and ears and, one might say, of the whole body, because he thinks the body disturbs him and hinders the soul from getting possession of truth and wisdom when body and soul are companions—is not this the man, Simmias, if anyone, who will hit reality?"

"Nothing could be more true, Socrates," said Simmias.

"Then from all this," said Socrates, "genuine philosophers must come to some such opinion as follows, so as to make to one another statements such as these: 'A sort of direct path, so to speak, seems to take us to the conclusion that so long as we have the body with us in our enquiry, and our soul is mixed up with so great an evil, we shall never attain sufficiently what we desire, and that, we say, is the truth. For the body provides thousands of busy distractions because of its necessary food; besides, if diseases fall upon us, they hinder us from the pursuit of the real. With loves and desires and fears and all kinds of fancies and much rubbish, it infects us, and really and truly makes us, as they say, unable to think one little bit about anything at any time. Indeed, wars and factions and battles all come from the body and its desires, and from nothing else. For the desire of getting wealth causes all wars, and we are compelled to desire wealth by the body, being slaves to its culture; therefore we have no leisure for philosophy, from all these reasons. Chief of all is that if we do have some leisure, and turn away from the body to speculate on something, in our searches it is everywhere interfering, it causes confusion and disturbance, and dazzles us so that it will not let us see the truth; so in fact we see that if we are ever to know anything purely we must get rid of it, and examine the real things by the soul alone; and then, it seems, after we are dead, as the reasoning shows, not while we live, we shall possess that which we desire, lovers of which we say we are, namely wisdom. For if it is impossible in company with the body to know anything purely, one thing of two follows: either knowledge is possible nowhere, or only after death; for then alone the soul will be quite by itself apart from the body, but not before. And while we are alive, we shall be nearest to knowing, as it seems, if as far as possible we have no commerce or communion with the body which is not absolutely necessary, and if we are not infected with its nature, but keep ourselves pure from it, until God himself shall set us free. And so, pure and rid of the body's foolishness, we shall probably be in the company of those like ourselves, and shall know through our own selves complete incontamination, and that is perhaps the truth. But for the impure to grasp the pure is not, it seems, allowed.' So we must think, Simmias, and so we must say to one another, all who are rightly lovers of learning; don't you agree?"

"Assuredly, Socrates."

"Then," said Socrates, "if this is true, my comrade, there is great hope that when I arrive where I am travelling, there if anywhere I shall sufficiently possess that for which all our study has been pursued in this past life. So the journey which has been commanded for me is made with good hope, and the same for any other man who believes he has got his mind purified, as I may call it."

"Certainly," replied Simmias.

"And is not purification really that which has been mentioned so often in our discussion, to separate as far as possible the soul from the body, and to accustom it to collect itself together out of the body in every part, and to dwell alone by itself as far as it can, both at this present and in the future, being freed from the body as if from a prison?"

"By all means," said he.

"Then is not this called death—a freeing and separation of soul from body?"

"Not a doubt of that," said he.

"But to set it free, as we say, is the chief endeavor of those who rightly love wisdom, nay of those alone, and the very care and practice of the philosophers is nothing but the freeing and separation of soul from body, don't you think so?"

"It appears to be so."

"Then, as I said at first, it would be absurd for a man preparing himself in his life to be as near as possible to death, so to live, and then when death came, to object?"

"Of course."

"Then in fact, Simmias," he said, "those who rightly love wisdom are practicing dying, and death to them is the least terrible thing in the world. Look at it in this way: If they are everywhere at enmity with the body, and desire the soul to be alone by itself, and if, when this very thing happens, they shall fear and object—would not that be wholly unreasonable? Should they not willingly go to a place where there is good hope of finding what they were in love with all through life (and they loved wisdom), and of ridding themselves of the companion which they hated? When human favorites and wives and sons have died, many have been willing to go down to the grave, drawn by the hope of seeing there those they used to desire, and of being with them; but one who is really in love with wisdom and holds firm to this same hope, that he will find it in the grave, and nowhere else worth speaking of—will he then fret at dying and not go thither rejoicing? We must surely think, my comrade, that he will go rejoicing, if he is really a philosopher; he will surely believe that he will find wisdom in its purity there and there alone. If this is true, would it not be most unreasonable, as I said just now, if such a one feared death?"

"Unreasonable, I do declare," said he.

. . . [He] got up and retired into another room for the bath, and Criton went after him, telling us to wait. So we waited discussing and talking together about what had been said, or sometimes speaking of the great misfortune which had befallen us, for we felt really as if we had lost a father and had to spend the rest of our lives as orphans. When he had bathed, and his children had been brought to see him—for he had two little sons, and one big—and when the women of his family had come, he talked to them before Criton and gave what instructions he wished. Then he asked the women and children to go, and came back to us. It was now near sunset, for he had spent a long time within. He came and sat down after his bath, and he had not talked long after this when the servant of the Eleven came in, and standing by him said, "O Socrates! I have not to complain of you as I do of others, that they are angry with me, and curse me, because I bring them word to drink their potion, which my officers make me do! But I have always found you in this time most generous and gentle, and the best man who ever came here. And now too, I know well you are not angry with me, for you know who are responsible, and you keep it for them. Now you know what I came to tell you, so farewell, and try to bear as well as you can what can't be helped."

Then he turned and was going out, with tears running down his cheeks. And Socrates looked up at him and said, "Farewell to you also, I will do so." Then, at the same time turning to us, "What a nice fellow!" he said. "All the time he has been coming and talking to me, a real good sort, and now how generously he sheds tears for me! Come along, Criton, let's obey him. Someone bring the potion, if the stuff has been ground; if not, let the fellow grind it."

Then Criton said, "But, Socrates, I think the sun is still over the hills, it has not set yet. Yes, and I know of others who, having been told to drink the poison, have done it very late; they had dinner first and a good one, and some enjoyed the company of any they wanted. Please don't be in a hurry, there is time to spare."

But Socrates said, "Those you speak of have very good reason for doing that, for they think they will gain by doing it; and I have good reasons why I won't do it. For I think I shall gain nothing by drinking a little later, only that I shall think myself a fool for clinging to life and sparing when the cask's empty. Come along," he said, "do what I tell you, if you please."

And Criton, hearing this, nodded to the boy who stood near. The boy went out, and after spending a long time, came in with the man who was to give the poison carrying it ground ready in a cup. Socrates caught sight of the man and said, "Here, my good man, you know about these things; what must I do?"

"Just drink it," he said, "and walk about till your legs get heavy, then lie down. In that way the drug will act of itself."

At the same time, he held out the cup to Socrates, and he took it quite cheerfully, Echecrates, not a tremble, not a change in color or looks; but looking full at the man under his brows, as he used to do, he asked him, "What do you say about this drink? What of a libation to someone? Is that allowed, or not?"

He said, "We only grind so much as we think enough for a moderate potion."

"I understand," he said, "but at least, I suppose, it is allowed to offer a prayer to the gods and that must be done, for good luck in the migration from here to there. Then that is my prayer, and so may it be!"

With these words he put the cup to his lips and, quite easy and contented, drank it up. So far most of us had been able to hold back our tears pretty well; but when we saw him begin drinking and end drinking, we could no longer. I burst into a flood of tears for all I could do, so I wrapped up my face and cried myself out; not for him indeed, but for my own misfortune in losing such a man and such a comrade. Criton had got up and gone out even before I did, for he could not hold the tears in. Apollodoros had never ceased weeping all this time, and now he burst out into loud sobs, and by his weeping and lamentations completely broke down every man there except Socrates himself. He only said, "What a scene! You amaze me. That's just why I sent the women away, to keep them from making a scene like this. I've heard that one ought to make an end in decent silence. Quiet yourselves and endure."

When we heard him we felt ashamed and restrained our tears. He walked about, and when he said that his legs were feeling heavy, he lay down on his back, as the man told him to do; at the same time the one who gave him the potion felt him, and after a while examined his feet and legs; then pinching a foot hard, he asked if he felt anything; he said no. After this, again, he pressed the shins; and, moving up like this, he showed us that he was growing cold and stiff. Again he felt him, and told us that when it came to his heart, he would be gone. Already the cold had come nearly as far as the abdomen, when Socrates threw off the covering from his face—for he had covered it over—and said, the last words he uttered, "Criton," he said, "we owe a cock to Asclepios; pay it without fail."

"That indeed shall be done," said Criton. "Have you anything more to say?"

When Criton had asked this, Socrates gave no further answer, but after a little time, he stirred, and the man uncovered him, and his eyes were still. Criton, seeing this, closed the mouth and eyelids.

This was the end of our comrade, Echecrates, a man, as we would say, of all then living we had ever met, the noblest and the wisest and most just.

Article 13
The Republic

Allegory of the Cave

"Next, then," I said, "take the following parable of education and ignorance as a picture of the condition of our nature. Imagine mankind as dwelling in an underground cave with a long entrance open to the light across the whole width of the cave; in this they have been from childhood, with necks and legs fettered, so they have to stay where they are. They cannot move their heads round because of the fetters, and they can only look forward, but light comes to them from fire burning behind them higher up at a distance. Between the fire and the prisoners is a road above their level, and along it imagine a low wall has been built, as puppet showmen have screens in front of their people over which they work their puppets."

"I see," he said.

"See, then, bearers carrying along this wall all sorts of articles which they hold projecting above the wall, statues of men and other living things, made of stone or wood and all kinds of stuff, some of the bearers speaking and some silent, as you might expect."

"What a remarkable image," he said, "and what remarkable prisoners!"

"Just like ourselves," I said. "For, first of all, tell me this: What do you think such people would have seen of themselves and each other except their shadows, which the fire cast on the opposite wall of the cave?"

"I don't see how they could see anything else," said he, "if they were compelled to keep their heads unmoving all their lives!"

"Very well, what of the things being carried along? Would not this be the same?"

"Of course it would."

"Suppose the prisoners were able to talk together, don't you think that when they named the shadows which they saw passing they would believe they were naming things?"

"Necessarily."

"Then if their prison had an echo from the opposite wall, whenever one of the passing bearers uttered a sound, would they not suppose that the passing shadow must be making the sound? Don't you think so?"

"Indeed I do," he said.

"If so," said I, "such persons would certainly believe that there were no realities except those shadows of handmade things."

"So it must be," said he.

"Now consider," said I, "what their release would be like, and their cure from these fetters and their folly; let us imagine whether it might naturally be something like this. One might be released, and compelled suddenly to stand up and turn his neck round, and to walk and look towards the firelight; all this would hurt him, and he would be too much dazzled to see distinctly those things whose shadows he had seen before. What do you think he would say, if someone told him that what

---

he saw before was foolery, but now he saw more rightly, being a bit nearer reality and turned towards what was a little more real? What if he were shown each of the passing things, and compelled by questions to answer what each one was? Don't you think he would be puzzled, and believe what he saw before was more true than what was shown to him now?"

"Far more," he said.

"Then suppose he were compelled to look toward the real light, it would hurt his eyes, and he would escape by turning them away to the things which he was able to look at, and these he would believe to be clearer than what was being shown to him."

"Just so," said he.

"Suppose, now," said I, "that someone should drag him thence by force, up the rough ascent, the steep way up, and never stop until he could drag him out into the light of the sun, would he not be distressed and furious at being dragged; and when he came into the light, the brilliance would fill his eyes and he would not be able to see even one of the things now called real?"

"That he would not," said he, "all of a sudden."

"He would have to get used to it, surely, I think, if he is to see the things above. First he would most easily look at shadows, after that images of mankind and the rest in water, lastly the things themselves. After this he would find it easier to survey by night the heavens themselves and all that is in them, gazing at the light of the stars and moon, rather than by day the sun and the sun's light."

"Of course."

"Last of all, I suppose, the sun; he could look on the sun itself by itself in its own place, and see what it is like, not reflections of it in water or as it appears in some alien setting."

"Necessarily," said he.

"And only after all this he might reason about it, how this is he who provides seasons and years, and is set over all there is in the visible region, and he is in a manner the cause of all things which they saw."

"Yes, it is clear," said he, "that after all that, he would come to this last."

"Very good. Let him be reminded of his first habitation, and what was wisdom in that place, and of his fellow-prisoners there; don't you think he would bless himself for the change, and pity them?"

"Yes, indeed."

"And if there were honors and praises among them and prizes for the one who saw the passing things most sharply and remembered best which of them used to come before and which after and which together, and from these was best able to prophesy accordingly what was going to come—do you believe he would set his desire on that, and envy those who were honored men or potentates among them? Would he not feel as Homer says, and heartily desire rather to be serf of some landless man on earth and to endure anything in the world, rather than to opine as they did and to live in that way?"

"Yes indeed," said he, "he would rather accept anything than live like that."

"Then again," I said, "just consider; if such a one should go down again and sit on his old seat, would he not get his eyes full of darkness coming in suddenly out of the sun?"

"Very much so," said he.

"And if he should have to compete with those who had been always prisoners, by laying down the law about those shadows while he was blinking before his eyes were settled down—and it would take a good long time to get used to things—wouldn't they all laugh at him and say he had spoiled his eyesight by going up there, and it was not worthwhile so much as to try to go up? And would they not kill anyone who tried to release them and take them up, if they could somehow lay hands on him and kill him?"

"That they would!" said he.

"Then we must apply this image, my dear Glaucon," said I, "to all we have been saying. The world of our sight is like the habitation in prison, the firelight there to the sunlight here, the ascent and the view of the upper world is the rising of the soul into the world of mind; put it so and you will not be far from my own surmise, since that is what you want to hear; but God knows if it is really true. At least, what appears to me is, that in the world of the known, last of all, is the idea of the good, and with what toil to be seen! And seen, this must be inferred to be the cause of all right and beautiful things for all, which gives birth to light and the king of light in the world of sight, and, in the world of mind, herself the queen produces truth and reason; and she must be seen by one who is to act with reason publicly or privately."

"I believe as you do," he said, "insofar as I am able."

"Then believe also, as I do," said I, "and do not be surprised, that those who come thither are not willing to have part in the affairs of men, but their souls ever strive to remain above; for that surely may be expected if our parable fits the case."

"Quite so," he said.

"Well then," said I, "do you think it surprising if one leaving divine contemplations and passing to the evils of men is awkward and appears to be a great fool, while he is still blinking—not yet accustomed to the darkness around him, but compelled to struggle in law courts or elsewhere about shadows of justice, or the images which make the shadows, and to quarrel about notions of justice in those who have never seen justice itself?"

"Not surprising at all," said he.

"But any man of sense," I said, "would remember that the eyes are doubly confused from two different causes, both in passing from light to darkness and from darkness to light; and believing that the same things happen with regard to the soul also, whenever he sees a soul confused and unable to discern anything he would not just laugh carelessly; he would examine whether it had come out of a more brilliant life, and if it were darkened by the strangeness; or whether it had come out of greater ignorance into a more brilliant light, and if it were dazzled with the brighter illumination. Then only would he congratulate the one soul upon its happy experience and way of life, and pity the other; but if he must laugh, his laugh would be a less down right laugh than his laughter at the soul which came out of the light above."

Article 14
Timaeus

What is that which is eternally and has no becoming, and again what is that which comes to be but is never? The one is comprehensible by thought with the aid of reason, ever changeless; the other opinable by opinion with the aid of reasonless sensation, becoming and perishing, never truly existent. Now all that comes to be must needs be brought into being by some cause: for it is impossible for anything without a cause to attain to birth. Of whatsoever thing then the Artificer, looking ever to the changeless and using that as his model, works out the design and function, all that is so accomplished must needs be fair: but if he look to that which has come to be, using the created as his model, the work is not fair. Now as to the whole heaven or order of the universe—for whatsoever name is most acceptable to it, be it so named by us—we must first ask concerning it the question which lies at the outset of every inquiry, whether did it exist eternally, having no beginning of generation, or has it come into being, starting from some beginning? It has come into being: for it can be seen and felt and has body; and all such things are sensible, and sensible things, apprehensible by opinion with sensation, belong, as we saw, to becoming and creation. We say that what has come to be must be brought into being by some cause. Now the maker and father of this All it were a hard task to find, and having found him, it were impossible to declare him to all men. However we must again inquire concerning him, after which of the models did the framer of it fashion the universe, after the changeless and abiding, or after that which has come into being? If now this universe is fair and its Artificer good, it is plain that he looked to the eternal; but if—nay it may not even be uttered without impiety—then it was to that which has come into being. Now it is manifest to every one that he looked to the eternal: for the universe is fairest of all things that have come to be, and he is the most excellent of causes. And having come on this wise into being it has been created in the image of that which is comprehensible by reason and wisdom and changes never. Granting this, it must needs be that this universe is a likeness of something. Now it is all-important to make our beginning according to nature: and this affirmation must be laid down with regard to a likeness and its model, that the words must be akin to the subjects of which they are the interpreters: therefore of that which is abiding and sure and discoverable by the aid of reason the words too must be abiding and unchanging, and so far as it lies in words to be incontrovertible and immovable, they must in no wise fall short of this; but those which deal with that which is made in the image of the former and which is a likeness must be likely and duly corresponding with their subject: as being is to becoming, so is truth to belief. If then, Socrates, after so many men have said divers things concerning the gods and the generation of the universe, we should not prove able to render an account everywhere and in all respects consistent and accurate, let no one be surprised; but if we can produce one as probable as any other, we must be content, remembering that I

Archer-Hind, R. D. (ed.) *The Timaeus of Plato,* Arno Pass, 1973.

who speak and you my judges are but men: so that on these subjects we should be satisfied with the probable story and seek nothing further.

In the first place, what we now have named water, by condensation, as we suppose, we see turning to stones and earth; and by rarefying and expanding this same element becomes wind and air; and air when inflamed becomes fire: and conversely fire contracted and quenched returns again to the form of air; also air concentrating and condensing becomes cloud and mist; and from these yet further compressed comes flowing water; and from water earth and stones once more: and so, it appears, they hand on one to another the cycle of generation. Thus then since these several bodies never assume one constant form, which of them can we positively affirm to be really *this* and not another without being shamed in our own eyes? It cannot be: it is far the safest course when we make a statement concerning them to speak as follows. What we see in process of perpetual transmutation, as for instance fire, we must not call *this,* but *such-like* is the appellation we must confer on fire; nor must we call water *this,* but always *such;* nor must we apply to anything, as if it had any stability, such predicates as we express by the use of the terms *this* and *that* and suppose that we signify something thereby. For it flees and will not abide such terms as *this* and *that* and *relative to this,* and every phrase which represents it as stable. The word *this* we must not use of any of them; but *such,* applying in the same sense to all their mutations, we must predicate of each and all: fire we must call that which universally has that appearance; and so must we name all things such as come into being. That wherein they come to be severally and show themselves, and from whence again they perish, in naming that alone must we use the words *that* and *this;* but whatever has any quality, such as white or hot or any of two opposite attributes, and all combinations of these, we must denote by no such term.

But we must try to speak yet more clearly on this matter. Suppose a man having moulded all kinds of figures out of gold should unceasingly remould them, interchanging them all with one another, it were much the safest thing in view of truth to say that it is gold; but as to the triangles or any other shapes that were impressed on it, never to speak of them as existing, seeing that they change even as we are in the act of defining them; but if it will admit the term *such* with any tolerable security, we must be content. The same language must be applied to the nature which receives into it all material things: we must call it always the same; for it never departs from its own function at all. It ever receives all things into it and has nowhere any form in any wise like to aught of the shapes that enter into it. For it is as the substance wherein all things are naturally moulded, being stirred and informed by the entering shapes; and owing to them it appears different from time to time. But the shapes which pass in and out are likenesses of the eternal existences, being copied from them in a fashion wondrous and hard to declare.

Is there an absolute idea of fire, and do all those absolute ideas exist to which in every case we always ascribe absolute being? Or do those things which we actually see or perceive with any other bodily sense alone possess such reality? and is it true that there are no manner of real existences beyond these at all, but we talk idly when we speak of an intelligible idea as actually existent, whereas it was nothing but a conception? Now it does not become us either to dismiss the present question unjudged and undecided, simply asserting that the ideas exist, nor yet must we add to our already long discourse another as long which is subordinate. But if we could see our way to a great definition couched in brief words, that would be most seasonable for our present purpose. Thus then do I give my own verdict: if reason and true opinion are of two different kinds, then the ideas do surely exist, forms not perceptible by our senses, the objects of thought alone; but if, as some hold, true opinion differs nothing from reason, then all that we apprehend by our bodily organs we must affirm to be the most real existence. Now we must declare them to be two, because they are different in origin and unlike in nature. The one is engendered in us by instruction, the other by persuasion; the one is ever accompanied by right understanding, the other is without understanding; the one is not to be moved by persuasion, the other yields to persuasion; true opinion we must admit is shared by all men, but reason by the gods alone and a very small portion of mankind. This being so, we must agree that there is first the unchanging idea, unbegotten and imperishable, neither receiving aught into itself from without nor itself entering into aught else, invisible, nor in any wise perceptible—even that whereof the contemplation belongs to thought. Second is that which is named after it and is like to it, sensible, created, ever in motion, coming to be in a certain place and again from thence perishing, apprehensible by opinion with sensation. And the third kind is space everlasting, admitting not destruction, but affording place for all things that come into being, itself apprehensible without sensation by a sort of bastard reasoning, hardly matter of belief. It is with this in view that dreaming we say that all which exists must be in some place and filling some space, and that what is neither on earth nor in heaven anywhere is nought. All these and many kindred fancies have we even concerning that unsleeping essence and truly existing, for that by reason of this dreaming state we become impotent to arouse ourselves and affirm the truth; namely, that to an image it belongs, seeing that it is not the very model of itself, on which itself has been created, but is ever the fleeting semblance of another, in another to come into being, clinging to existence as best it may, on pain of being nothing at all; but to the really existent essence reason in all exactness true comes as an ally, declaring that so long as one thing is one and another thing is other, neither of them shall come to be in the other, so that the same becomes at once one and two.

Aristotle: Physics, Poetics

Introduction

Aristotle (384–322 BC) was a student at Plato's Academy and became the intellectual successor to Plato although, in some important points, Aristotle differed from is teacher. After Plato's death, Aristotle formed his own school in Athens, the Lyceum, wherein he taught his own views. Whereas Plato's beliefs centered on mathematics and the Forms, Aristotle focused on the natural world. He believed in a dynamic relationship between Forms and matter. In essence Aristotle believed that reality could best be understood through living systems which, he said, had a life force that propelled the development of all things towards their ultimate purpose which was, in most cases, the Form.

Aristotle's teachings, though in competition with Plato's, became just as popular and some are still taught today. He developed an empirical experimental method that acquired a canonical status during the Middle Ages as the basis of natural philosophy (science).

The passages provided here show his unique viewpoint on the nature of existence, as well as his breadth of study. Indeed, glancing over the titles of his works proves that he knew a lot about a lot.

Aristotle's *Physics* contains the dynamic view of nature that Aristotle was famous for. In these excerpts, he speaks of causation—the basis of exploratory science. In it he describes his system of "knowing" as the four causes—the material, formal, efficient, and the final cause. The discovery of these four causes became the method used by science from the times of Aristotle until the scientific reawakening in the 17th Century AD. Some modern scientists believe that science may have gone too far in dropping Aristotle's methods. Perhaps we should still inquire about the causes of things, especially the final cause. That is, for what final purpose does a thing exist?

Classical Greek tragedy was very popular in Aristotle's day; most Greeks knew the works of the great Greek playwrights—Aeschylus, Sophocles, and Euripides. *Poetics* is Aristotle's proof of his love for tragedy-poetry, and his commentary on it. In this passage, he gives the guidelines for what type of person the tragic hero should be, and what the tragic deed and the other characters should be. This passage shows that the Greeks were interested in the psychological side of these tragedies.

Article 15
Physics

Again, since the stars are spherical, as our opponents assert and we may consistently admit, inasmuch as we construct them out of the spherical body, and since the spherical body has two movements proper to itself, namely rolling and spinning, it follows that if the stars have a movement of their own, it will be one of these. But neither is observed. (1) Suppose them to *spin*. They would then stay where they were, and not change their place, as, by observation and general consent, they do. Further, one would expect them all to exhibit the same movement: but the only star which appears to possess this movement is the sun, at sunrise or sunset, and this appearance is due not to the sun itself but to the distance from which we observe it. The visual ray being excessively prolonged becomes weak and wavering. The same reason probably accounts for the apparent twinkling of the fixed stars and the absence of twinkling in the planets. The planets are near, so that the visual ray reaches them in its full vigour, but when it comes to the fixed stars it is quivering because of the distance and its excessive extension; and its tremor produces an appearance of movement in the star: for it makes no difference whether movement is set up in the ray or in the object of vision. (2) On the other hand, it is also clear that the stars do not *roll*. For rolling involves rotation: but the 'face', as it is called, of the moon is always seen. Therefore, since any movement of their own which the stars possessed would presumably be one proper to themselves, and no such movement is observed in them, clearly they have no movement of their own.

With regard to the shape of each star, the most reasonable view is that they are spherical. It has been shown that it is not in their nature to move themselves, and, since nature is no wanton or random creator, clearly she will have given things which possess no movement a shape particularly unadapted to movement. Such a shape is the sphere, since it possesses no instrument of movement. Clearly then their mass will have the form of a sphere. Again, what holds of one holds of all, and the evidence of our eyes shows us that the moon is spherical. For how else should the moon as it waxes and wanes show for the most part a crescent-shaped or gibbous figure, and only at one moment a half-moon? And astronomical arguments give further confirmation; for no other hypothesis accounts for the crescent shape of the sun's eclipses. One, then, of the heavenly bodies being spherical, clearly the rest will be spherical also.

Its shape must necessarily be spherical. For every portion of earth has weight until it reaches the centre, and the jostling of parts greater and smaller would bring about not a waved surface, but rather compression and convergence of part and part until the centre is reached. The process should be conceived by supposing the earth to come into being in the way that some of the natural philosophers describe. Only they attribute the downward movement to constraint, and it is better to keep to the truth and say that the reason of this motion is that a thing which possesses weight is naturally endowed with a centripetal movement. When the mixture, then, was merely potential, the things that

---

Hardie, R. P. and R. K. Goye, *The Works of Aristotle,* Oxford University Press, 1953.

were separated off moved similarly from every side towards the centre. Whether the parts which came together at the centre were distributed at the extremities evenly, or in some other way, makes no difference. If, on the one hand, there were a similar movement from each quarter of the extremity to the single centre, it is obvious that the resulting mass would be similar on every side. For if an equal amount is added on every side the extremity of the mass will be everywhere equidistant from its centre, i.e. the figure will be spherical.

Again, our observations of the stars make it evident, not only that the earth is circular, but also that it is a circle of no great size. For quite a small change of position to south or north causes a manifest alteration of the horizon. There is much change, I mean, in the stars which are overhead, and the stars seen are different, as one moves northward or southward. Indeed there are some stars seen in Egypt and in the neighbourhood of Cyprus which are not seen in the northerly regions; and stars, which in the north are never beyond the range of observation, in those regions rise and set. All of which goes to show not only that the earth is circular in shape, but also that it is a sphere of no great size: for otherwise the effect of so slight a change of place would not be so quickly apparent. Hence one should not be too sure of the incredibility of the view of those who conceive that there is continuity between the parts about the pillars of Hercules and the parts about India, and that in this way the ocean is one. As further evidence in favour of this they quote the case of elephants, a species occurring in each of these extreme regions, suggesting that the common characteristic of these extremes is explained by their continuity. Also, those mathematicians who try to calculate the size of the earth's circumference arrive at the figure 400,000 stades. This indicates not only that the earth's mass is spherical in shape, but also that as compared with the stars it is not of great size.

Article 16
Poetics

The next points after what we have said above will be these: (1) What is the poet to aim at, and what is he to avoid, in constructing his Plots? and (2) What are the conditions on which the tragic effect depends?

We assume that, for the finest form of Tragedy, the Plot must be not simple but complex; and further, that it must imitate actions arousing fear and pity, since that is the distinctive function of this kind of imitation. It follows, therefore, that there are three forms of Plot to be avoided. (1) A good man must not be seen passing from happiness to misery, or (2) a bad man from misery to happiness. The first situation is not fear-inspiring or piteous, but simply odious to us. The second is the most untragic that can be; it has no one of the requisites of Tragedy; it does not appeal either to the human feeling in us, or to our pity, or to our fears. Nor, on the other hand, should (3) an extremely bad man be seen falling from happiness into misery. Such a story may arouse the human feeling in us, but it will not move us to either pity or fear; pity is occasioned by undeserved misfortune, and fear by that of one like ourselves; so that there will be nothing either piteous or fear-inspiring in the situation. There remains, then, the intermediate kind of personage, a man not preeminently virtuous and just, whose misfortune, however, is brought upon him not by vice and depravity but by some error of judgement, of the number of those in the enjoyment of great reputation and prosperity; e.g. Oedipus, Thyestes, and the men of note of similar families. The perfect Plot, accordingly, must have a single, and not (as some tell us) a double issue; the change in the hero's fortunes must be not from misery to happiness, but on the contrary from happiness to misery; and the cause of it must lie not in any depravity, but in some great error on his part; the man himself being either such as we have described, or better, not worse, than that. Fact also confirms our theory. Though the poets began by accepting any tragic story that came to hand, in these days the finest tragedies are always on the story of some few houses, on that of Alcmeon, Oedipus, Orestes, Meleager, Thyestes, Telephus, or any others that may have been involved, as either agents or sufferers, in some deed of horror. The theoretically best tragedy, then, has a Plot of this description. The critics, therefore, are wrong who blame Euripides for taking this line in his tragedies, and giving many of them an unhappy ending. It is, as we have said, the right line to take. The best proof is this: on the stage, and in the public performances, such plays, properly worked out, are seen to be the most truly tragic; and Euripides, even if his execution be faulty in every other point, is seen to be nevertheless the most tragic certainly of the dramatists. After this comes the construction of Plot which some rank first, one with a double story (like the *Odyssey*) and an opposite issue for the good and the bad personages. It is ranked as first only through the weakness of the audiences; the poets merely follow their public, writing as its wishes dictate. But the pleasure here is not that of

From *Oxford Translation of Aristotle,* edited by W.D. Ross, 1925. Reprinted by permission of Oxford University Press, Ltd.

Tragedy. It belongs rather to Comedy, where the bitterest enemies in the piece (e.g. Orestes and Aegisthus) walk off good friends at the end, with no slaying of any one by any one.

The tragic fear and pity may be aroused by the Spectacle; but they may also be aroused by the very structure and incidents of the play—which is the better way and shows the better poet. The Plot in fact should be so framed that, even without seeing the things take place, he who simply hears the account of them shall be filled with horror and pity at the incidents; which is just the effect that the mere recital of the story in *Oedipus* would have on one. To produce this same effect by means of the Spectacle is less artistic, and requires extraneous aid. Those, however, who make use of the Spectacle to put before us that which is merely monstrous and not productive of fear, are wholly out of touch with Tragedy; not every kind of pleasure should be required of a tragedy, but only its own proper pleasure.

This will explain why our tragedies are restricted (as we said just now) to such a small number of families. It was accident rather than art that led the poets in quest of subjects to embody this kind of incident in their Plots. They are still obliged, accordingly, to have recourse to the families in which such horrors have occurred.

On the construction of the Plot, and the kind of Plot required for Tragedy, enough has now been said.

In the Characters there are four points to aim at. First and foremost, that they shall be good. There will be an element of character in the play, if (as has been observed) what a personage says or does reveals a certain moral purpose; and a good element of character, if the purpose so revealed is good. Such goodness is possible in every type of personage, even in a woman or a slave, though the one is perhaps an inferior, and the other a wholly worthless being. The second point is to make them appropriate. The Character before us may be, say, manly; but it is not appropriate in a female Character to be manly, or clever. The third is to make them like the reality, which is not the same as their being good and appropriate, in our sense of the term. The fourth is to make them consistent and the same throughout; even if inconsistency be part of the man before one for imitation as presenting that form of character, he should still be consistently inconsistent.

There should be nothing improbable among the actual incidents. If it be unavoidable, however, it should be outside the tragedy, like the improbability in the *Oedipus* of Sophocles. But to return to the Characters. As Tragedy is an imitation of personages better than the ordinary man, we in our way should follow the example of good portrait-painters, who reproduce the distinctive features of a man, and at the same time, without losing the likeness, make him handsomer than he is. The poet in like manner, in portraying men quick or slow to anger, or with similar infirmities of character, must know how to represent them as such, and at the same time as good men, as Agathon and Homer have represented Achilles.

All these rules one must keep in mind throughout, and, further, those also for such points of stage-effect as directly depend on the art of the poet, since in these too one may often make mistakes. Enough, however, has been said on the subject in one of our published writings.

Hellenism
Creativity for the World

> Eureka!
>
> —*Archimedes*

Hellenism—Alexander Spreads Greek Culture

The words **Hellenism** and **Hellenistic Period** are taken from the Greek word for Greece—*Hellas.* The Hellenistic Period describes the time between the fall of the Golden Age of Greece and the establishment of the Roman Empire. As we will see, when Classical Greece was brought to a close, Greek culture did not die. Just the contrary—it was carried throughout much of the civilized world and largely adopted by the various peoples in that vast area. We call this time the Hellenistic Period because we want to distinguish it from the Classical Greek period that we have just discussed. Even though the Hellenistic culture was based on the Classical Greek culture, there are some important differences. One obvious difference is that the cultural centers of Hellenism ceased to be focused within the territory of Greece itself. Other locations, spread from Egypt to Persia, became important, sometimes surpassing even Greece. In this chapter and the next we will examine how Classical Greece culture evolved into the Hellenistic Age, and look at some of the differences that emerged from the mingling of Greek culture and the rest of the world. First, however, we will look at the people who made it happen.

In 359 B.C., **Philip** II came to power in the northern semi-Greek kingdom **of Macedonia.** Philip spoke Greek and was enamored with all things Greek (thus his hiring of fellow-Macedonian Aristotle as a tutor for his son Alexander). Philip considered himself part of the greater Greek culture, even though the Greeks thought he was an uncouth barbarian. Nevertheless, Philip began to expand the role of Macedonia within the greater Greek-speaking world. Over time, and in spite of resistance from Athens, which had traditionally been the leading city in Greece, Philip was able to unite the various Greek city-states into a single political entity via diplomacy and warfare. He was resented by the Greeks, but there was little they could do in light of his overpowering army. (One of Greece's greatest orators, Demonsthenes, spoke against Philip, but was eventually silenced.) The beginning of Philip's rule over Greece traditionally marks the end of the age of Classical Greece and the beginning of the Hellenistic Age. While Phillip was on the throne, little expansion outside the Greek world had yet occurred. But that ended when Philip was assassinated in 336 B.C.

Philip was succeeded by his son, age 20, who was not only Philip's heir, but also one of the leading Macedonian generals. **Alexander,** like his father, dreamed of greatness. As a child Alexander is known to have wept bitterly, saying, "My father will get ahead of me in everything, and will leave nothing great for me to do." Alexander's boyhood fear couldn't have been more wrong. His father may have conquered and unified Greece, but Alexander conquered and unified most of the known world, and in the process spread Greek thinking and culture throughout that empire.

Alexander was able to achieve his dreams largely because of his creativity in leadership. That creativity was based on the principle of planning and then executing that plan with determined diligence. His plans seem to have arisen from a combination of his unquenchable desire for greatness coupled with incredible organization for bringing about his goals. We are struck with the thought that Alexander's organizational capabilities might have been the product of his early education at the hand of Aristotle who, as we have seen in the last chapter, was incredibly organized. We see other traits of Aristotle in the young Alexander (such as a love of biology), so it is not far-fetched to think that Aristotle's organizational capability was also passed on. Whatever the origin, Alexander's planning, coupled with intense desires for accomplishment, led to his greatness.

Even before he became king, Alexander proved to be an adept and creative leader. At 16 he became one of his father's generals and was a strong participant in the battles to unite Macedonia, prior to his father's conquest of Greece. He also served as his father's ambassador to Athens. He then was a general in the decisive battle that brought all of Greece under his father's control.

His youthful energy and personality seemed to have instilled confidence in his men. He wisely and creatively demonstrated these traits to all those around him. Alexander represented the ideal qualities of the "perfect" Greek. He was handsome, he was well educated (by Aristotle), he respected and knew the great Greek past (he memorized and carried with him a copy of the *Iliad*), he was adept at rhetoric and diplomacy (serving as his father's ambassador to Athens), he was a respected military leader (having won several battles during his father's conquest of Greece), he was athletic (competing regularly throughout his life), and he pursued strong interests in geography, animals, plants, and other natural phenomena. He took scientists with him on his military campaigns. (Napoleon later tried to emulate many of these traits and actions, and achieved similar successes.)

After ascending the throne, Alexander quickly demonstrated his abilities to execute his plans for greatness. He sensed that there were rivals in the Macedonian court (especially since his father had been assassinated by a personal guard), and ruthlessly had all of these potential rivals killed. Later, one of the Greek cities, Thebes, which was then very powerful, decided to revolt from the confederation controlled by the young king. Alexander attacked and conquered Thebes and then, to discourage any other cities from rebelling, sold 30,000 Thebians into slavery and destroyed the city (saving only the temples and the home of Pindar the poet—a nice touch to perpetuate his image as the "perfect Greek"). These actions assured that there would be no further revolts from the Greek city-states, even though Alexander was out of Greece for the rest of his life.

Alexander then began the execution of his plan for world domination. His first target was the Persian Empire. Alexander mobilized the combined Macedonian/Greek army and attacked Greece's main nemesis, the Persians, who had backed away from any military confrontation with the Greeks after being defeated in Persia's attempts to conquer Greece, but remained the major imperial power in the world. Persia remained a threat to Greek colonies, if not to Greece itself. The Persian Empire was rich and, at the time of Alexander, was governed by a relatively weak emperor. Alexander saw the riches and realized that the empire was ripe for conquest. The Greeks wanted to expand their trading dominion, and the Persians were their chief rivals. Besides, Alexander and the Greeks were still angry over the original attacks of the Persians many years before. There was also, of course, the issue of Alexander's desire for greatness.

Alexander's plan for conquering the Persian Empire was masterful. He realized that the Persian fleet was much stronger than his own. Therefore, even if he were to be successful in his penetration of Persian territory, he would be vulnerable to the Persians' landing a large army behind him and then attacking him from the rear and, moreover, cutting off his supplies and path of reinforcements. He therefore decided to attack and disable the Persian ports as he entered Persian territory. His first battles were along the Ionian coast, and all were very successful.

Alexander's army was eventually confronted by a relatively large Persian army at the Granicus River near where it empties into the sea. Alexander sent his cavalry across the river very early in the morning, realizing that the Persian religion prevented the Persian army from moving until they had made sacrifices to the gods. By the time the sun came up and the sacrifices had been made, Alexander's cavalry had crossed the river and was upon the unprepared Persians. A total victory ensued because of Alexander's creative strategy.

Alexander then went to the city of Gordium where there was a famous knot. This knot tied a yoke onto the tongue of a wagon. The knot was very complex and, as legend had it, anyone who could untie the knot would rule the world. Alexander either knew or was told the legend and, upon seeing the knot, simply took out his sword and cut the knot in twain. His troops were astonished and elated. They believed that they were being led by a man who was destined to rule the world. (Alexander's creative manipulation of people is clearly evident in this incident.)

Alexander's next creative moment came when he was finally confronted by the entire Persian army, led by the Persian emperor himself, Darius III. This battle occurred near the city of Issus, which is near the easternmost tip of the Mediterranean Sea, where the seacoast turns southward. The Greek army was outmanned by at least 3 to 1; some say it was 10 to 1. The battle commenced with an attack by the Greek phalanx into the center of the Persian line, with the Greek cavalry attempting to skirt the ends of the Persian line, hoping to begin an attack from behind. However, the size and strength of the Persian army resisted the Greek attack, and no advantage could be seen on either side. At that point, Alexander again showed his creative leadership. He personally led a frantic attack into the center of the Persian line, directly at the location where Darius himself stood. The presence of Alexander, and the fury of the attack, gave the Greeks courage. They broke through the Persian line and threatened Darius' position. Darius fled and with his departure the Persian defense collapsed.

Not only had Alexander's creative leadership led directly to the victory, but he then showed creative skill in the aftermath. When Darius had fled so quickly, his wife and mother had been left behind and were captured. Even though Alexander had shown ruthlessness in other situations, in this case he ordered that the wife and queen be given all the respect and privileges of royalty. This act impressed the many captured Persians. Alexander then offered the captured Persians an opportunity to join the Greek army and march toward Egypt, where the spoils of war would be theirs. Many of the captives readily agreed.

As seen in the map given in Figure 9.1, the route to Egypt was a logical path on his quest to conquer the world. Whatever was left of the Persian army was in disarray, and Darius had lost his will to fight. Therefore, the Persians were little risk to the Greeks, so an attack on Egypt was not only safe but also inviting, because of the recently acquired reinforcements of the Persian captives and the promise of riches. Alexander therefore continued along the Mediterranean coast, heading toward Egypt. Along the way he came to the island city of Tyre, a major trading center of the Phoenicians and, of course, a rival of the Greeks in trade. Alexander besieged the city, but Tyre proved to be a difficult conquest. Eventually,

Alexander creatively built a causeway from the shore to the island city and succeeded in conquering the city. In actions reminiscent of Thebes, Alexander destroyed the city, killed 8,000 Tyrians, and sold another 30,000 into slavery. Later, Gaza also resisted the Greek attack, and was destroyed. All other cities in the area, including Jerusalem, surrendered without a battle.

When Alexander reached Egypt, he was greeted as a hero. The Egyptians were then ruled by non-Egyptians, and the people probably felt little love for their rulers. Alexander was proclaimed a pharaoh. He was told a legend about a holy place in the Libyan desert where the holy oracle of Ammon dwelt, who might recognize Alexander's special descent from the gods. Alexander visited the oasis site and was declared to be the son of the god Ammon, thus further strengthening the mystique he wanted to create of being invincible. While in Egypt, Alexander founded the city of Alexandria, at the mouth of the Nile River. (This was one of over 70 cities founded by Alexander—most of them also called Alexandria; however, the one in Egypt was the only one that grew into great importance.)

After just a year in the western region, Alexander again turned eastward and entered Persian territory again. This time, Darius also had a plan. He chose a site where he felt that the Persian chariots would have a major advantage in the battle. This area, the plain of Gaugamela, was on the eastern side of the Tigris River—deep in Persian territory. To ensure that Alexander would move to this site, Darius left the pathway to Gaugamela relatively unguarded, but placed troops along both sides of the way, thus forming a type of corridor to Gaugamela. Alexander took the bait, but when he got to the site, he delayed the attack. The Persian troops were confused at the ease of Alexander's progress and were upset that he was so deep in

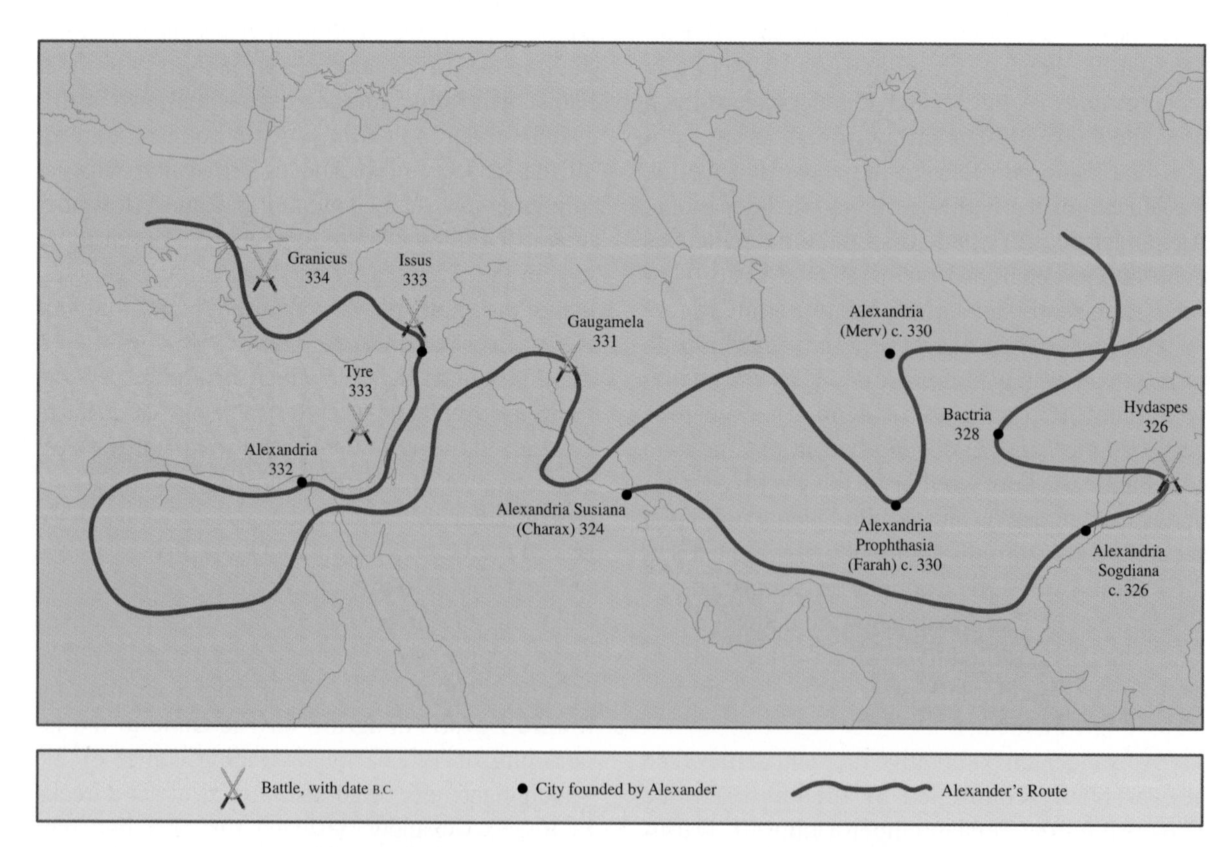

Figure 9.1 ■ *Map of Alexander's battles and route.*

Persian territory. Then, on the first night after Alexander crossed over the Tigris (viewed by the Persians as an especially critical moment), there was an eclipse of the moon. The Persians were distraught—they believed that such an omen marked the end of an era and naturally assumed that the ending era was the Persian rule. The Persians were further perplexed when Alexander did not attack the next day. The next night, when a meteor shower occurred, the Persians took this to be a negative omen as well. Alexander delayed his attack for yet another day, and on the ensuing night there were still more meteors. By this time the Persians were so upset that they could hardly contain themselves. Alexander finally attacked on the next day and, in keeping with his plan, went straight for Darius. As before, Darius withdrew when he was personally in danger. That act, coupled with the apprehensions of the Persians, resulted in the complete collapse of the Persian army and the victory for Alexander. The fleeing Darius was killed by his own troops. There is no doubt that Alexander's creative leadership led directly to the final victory over the Persians. We don't know, however, if Alexander knew about the celestial activities beforehand (from astronomical observations), but whether he did or not, he certainly knew how to exploit them to his advantage.

Alexander then decided to complete his conquest of the Persian Empire. He met little resistance as he swept all of eastern Persia under his control. In this process he captured great stores of gold and silver, some of which he divided among his army. He established cities, which became administrative centers from which the various provinces were ruled for many decades. When he reached the farthest borders of Persia, he continued eastward, conquering territory that is today part of Afghanistan and Pakistan. He married a princess from this territory, who eventually bore him a son.

Along the way, however, he lost the support of his troops. They were tired, and yearned for the conquest to be over. In the midst of this discontent, Alexander killed one of his closest advisors in a drunken brawl, further alienating the soldiers. There were even several attempts on his life, and several generals were executed for their involvement. Eventually the army refused to go further eastward. It may have been the heavy rains of the monsoon season or the swollen rivers from the melt of the Himalayan snows, but whatever the reason, Alexander had lost the allegiance of the army. He reluctantly agreed to return.

When Alexander returned to Persia, he began the integration of the Greeks and the Persians. He had established a Greek administration of the territories he had conquered and now wanted to combine the cultures of the two peoples so that the Greek rule would be secure. Toward this end, he sponsored the marriage of 10,000 Greek soldiers to Persian wives. He even took a Persian wife himself.

Alexander died in 323 B.C. at the age of 33. He became sick after swimming in the river, possibly contracting malaria or cholera. His body was displayed for his troops who, even after the problems of the eastern campaign, filed by his body in great reverence and honor. Following that homage, he was taken to Alexandria, Egypt, where his body was cremated.

The Empires after Alexander

Alexander's conquests were a key event in the history of the world. These military occupations mark a shift to the Greek way (or Western way) of thinking, even in the great river societies that had been the basis of so much of civilization up to that time. The paradigm shift that had occurred in mainland Greece four centuries earlier, and which had allowed for the explosion of Greek thought, was now taking place, because of Alexander, on a much larger scale.

Of course, just as Greek culture influenced the conquered peoples of the Hellenic Empire, even so the cultures of the conquered peoples also affected the Greeks. One of the best examples of the conquered Eastern cultures affecting the Greek way of life can be seen in the person of Alexander himself. As Alexander came into more and more contact with the empires of the East, he found that they had ideas that appealed to his vanity as a leader. We have already noted how he visited the oracle of Ammon in the Libyan desert, where he was told that he was the son of a god. Alexander became enamored with this idea and instructed his subjects to treat him as a deity, similar to the way that the Egyptians viewed their pharaohs. Initially, to his Greek soldiers, this was a silly idea, as they had known Alexander's father, and because the Greek gods were far from being perfect, honorable, and all-powerful. However, the longer Alexander lived, the more he aspired to be treated like an Eastern-style demigod, as opposed to a Western-style king.

Upon the death of Alexander, his principal generals divided the kingdom, and each assumed control over part of the territory. These Greek generals began dynasties that continued to rule their particular territory until the conquest of the entire area by the Romans many generations later. As indicated in the map shown in Figure 9.2, a general named Ptolemy took over the Egyptian region, Seleucus took over in Persia and eastward, Attalid ruled in Pergamum, and a combination of four generals ruled the combined area of Macedonia and Greece.

The division of Alexander's empire actually sped up the process of Hellenization, as each king imported Greeks to their land to help run the bureaucracy. As more and more Greeks came, the influence of Greek culture on the conquered peoples became greater. The Greeks were not hard masters; non-Greek youths could even look for advancement and glory within Greek society, and most abandoned the traditions of their fathers and adopted a Greek lifestyle. Over time, nearly all of the subjugated peoples adopted Greek culture, at

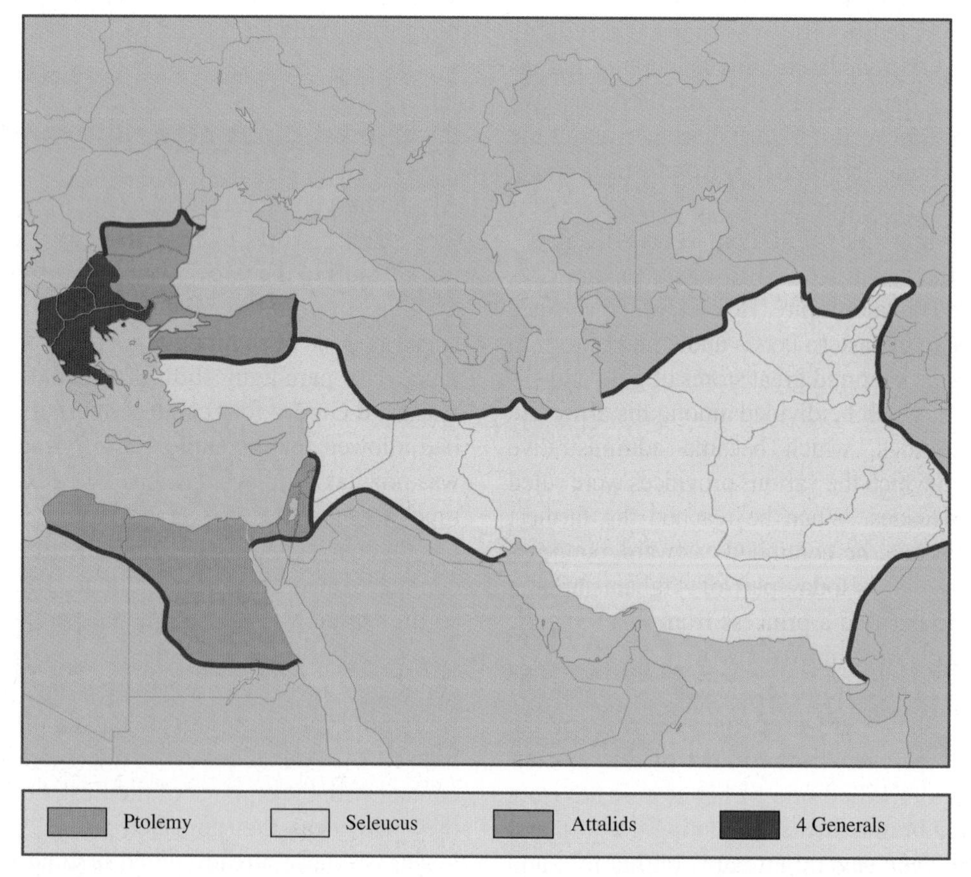

Figure 9.2 ■ *Map of the division of the Hellenistic Empire following the death of Alexander.*

least to some extent, and the spread of the Greek way of thinking continued. Greek became the language of culture and trade, and continued so even throughout the Roman period. Even today we can see the evidence of Greek amphitheaters and public buildings throughout the territory. An example is the treasury building in Petra, now located in Jordan, depicted in Figure 9.3. The Greek influence is obvious from the columns and other architectural features. At this and many other sites, the Greek influence is seen by other Greek buildings such as temples, public baths, gymnasiums, stadiums, theaters, and fountains.

The constant drain of people away from Greece weakened the Greek mainland, and in 202 B.C. Greece itself was conquered by the Romans, who would dominate that area for the next 700 years. However, even the mighty Roman Empire could not escape the attraction of Hellenism, and the wonders of Greece became the blueprint for Roman culture. But that is a story we will discuss later.

Hellenistic Art and Architecture

Either from the natural evolution of Greek art or from interactions with the conquered peoples, classical Greek art became ever more realistic and emotional. (We will see this same evolution—of a classical period into a more realistic and emotional period—several more times throughout history.) In this case, the change in artistic style can be seen in two very famous sculptures: *Victory at Samothrace* and *Laocoön and His Sons.*

The moving and beautiful *Victory (Nike) at Samothrace* is located in the Louvre in Paris. It is shown in Figure 9.4. This sculpture shows wonderful movement, especially in the way the folds of the dress are swept by the wind and stretched as the figure is striding forward.

Laocoön and His Sons, shown in Figure 9.5, depicts the story of a Trojan priest who, along with his sons, tried to warn the Trojans not to accept the horse. ("Beware of Greeks bearing gifts.") Poseidon, who hated the Trojans, did not want the plan

Figure 9.3 ■ *The treasury in Petra, in modern-day Jordan, showing the Greek influence. Image © Jose Fuste Raga/Corbis.*

Figure 9.4 ■ *Victory (Nike) at Samothrace. Image © Paul Almasy/Corbis.*

Figure 9.5 ■ *Laocoön and His Sons. Image © 2006 Jupiter Images Corporation.*

of the Greeks to be foiled, so he sent poisonous snakes to kill Laocoön and his sons. The statue shows great emotion and action—typical of the Hellenistic style at its fullest development.

In keeping with the spread of Greek culture throughout the civilized world, some of the most important buildings were the libraries that were built in the capitals of the various Hellenistic kingdoms. The most famous was at Alexandria, Egypt, but others that eventually grew to rival Alexandria's were in Antioch, Syria, and Pergamum, capital of the Attalid kingdom. These libraries became very aggressive in obtaining documents. In Alexandria, for example, every ship entering the port was required to allow inspection of the ship for the intent of finding documents. If any document was found, the owner was required to allow the library to copy the document.

Alexandria was well known for its lighthouse, a tower over 400 feet high located on a small island at the entrance to the port. A light on the top was intensified by reflectors, thus enabling the light to be seen miles at sea. This lighthouse was so impressive that it has been designated as one of the wonders of the ancient world.

Pergamum, a Hellenistic city located in present-day Turkey, was the chief rival city to Alexandria. A temple in Pergamum, which contained a massive statue of Zeus, was regarded as the most beautiful temple in the world.

The competition between Pergamum and Alexandria led to one of the most creative inventions of the ancient period. The people in Alexandria decided that they would stop the growth of the library in Pergamum by refusing to ship any papyrus out of Egypt. Since Egypt was the only source of papyrus, they believed that their action would prevent Pergamum from making new books. Ancient scribes report that the scholars in Pergamum, however, created a new type of writing material—split and appropriately tanned animal skins (which we now call **parchment**). This seemed to solve the problem, except that the skins could not be rolled like papyrus because they eventually hardened in their rolled form and then became difficult to unroll. Again, the creativity of the Pergamum scholars was seen when they decided that they would leave the skins flat and simply bind one edge so that the skins would not get out of order. This invention became, of course, books. (A handwritten book of the type created in Pergamum is called a codex.)

Hellenistic Science

Although Hellenistic science was widespread throughout the Hellenistic empires, two men were so influential, both in their time and continuing for many years thereafter, that we will focus on their works as examples of Hellenistic science. Those two were Euclid and Archimedes.

Euclid (330–260 B.C.) lived in Alexandria, Egypt. He assembled all that was then known about geometry and then set out the principles of this science in a logical system. He began with certain basic assumptions such as (1) the shortest distance between two points is a straight line; (2) parallel lines do not meet; and (3) two non-parallel straight lines cross at one and only one point.

The textbook that he wrote, *Elements of Geometry,* became the standard textbook for the study of geometry, and was widely used until about 1900. Euclidean geometry was the basis for Newton's laws of motion.

Archimedes (287–212 B.C.) lived in the Greek colony of Syracuse on the island of Sicily, which at the time of Archimedes was the largest Greek-speaking city in the world. Archimedes traveled throughout the Hellenistic world; when he was in Alexandria, he was taught by a pupil of Euclid. Archimedes made significant contributions in mechanics, hydraulics, warfare, mathematics, and astronomy. His importance can be judged from the words of Newton, who said that he used the principles of Archimedes as his starting point. Archimedes is probably the most important scientist before Newton.

Archimedes had a fascination with very large numbers, but struggled with the awkward Greek system for expressing numbers. (The Greeks used their letters as representations of the numbers. The largest number the Greeks could express was 10,000, which they called a *myriad.*) In one of his exercises of interest, Archimedes wanted to approximate the total number of sand particles in the world. Obviously he needed to be able to use a number larger than 10,000, and so he devised a system utilizing powers of ten to represent large numbers. This system, still widely in use, is called **scientific notation.**

Archimedes was also fascinated with various geometrical shapes like cones, spheres, and circles. He found, for example, a very interesting relationship between the surface area of a sphere and the cylinder in which it can be inscribed, as represented in Figure 9.6. The surface areas are in the ratio of 3:2. He also noted that the volumes of the sphere and cylinder are also in the ratio of 3:2. He then noted that the ratios of the volumes and areas of cones, spheres, and cylinders are 9:6:4. This ratio is reminiscent of Pythagorean concepts and, in keeping with Archimedes' Greek education, he considered these geometrical discoveries to be his finest achievements. He even requested that they be inscribed on his tomb.

In his studies of these figures, the value of π became very important. At the time, that value could not be determined well because of difficulties in determining the circumference of a circle. Archimedes set out to calculate the value of π to a much greater accuracy. He knew how to precisely calculate the perimeter of a multi-sided figure (a polygon) from Euclidean geometry. Therefore, he reasoned, if he put a polygon *inside* a circle and also another, slightly larger polygon, *outside* the circle, he would know that the true value for the circumference of the circle must lie between the values of the perimeters of the polygons. This situation is represented in Figure 9.7. Archimedes noted that there were small areas between the circle and the polygon, and realized that these areas represented errors and therefore meant that the

Figure 9.6 ■ *A sphere inscribed in a cylinder—a figure of great interest to Archimedes.*

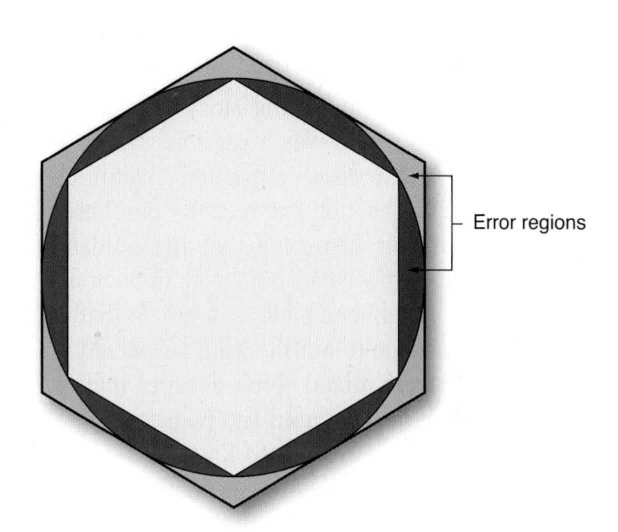

Figure 9.7 ■ *Archimedes' method of determining the circumference of a circle, and therefore π, by using two polygons whose perimeters can be calculated.*

value of π was not accurate. However, he also realized that as he increased the number of sides in the polygons, the size of these small areas decreased and, therefore, the perimeters became better approximations to the circumference. He reported the value of π calculated by this method for polygons with 70 and 71 sides. Much later, Newton used the same concept of error minimization as the basis of calculus. The concept today is called **reducing the error to the limit.**

Archimedes was also interested in mechanics. In particular, he studied levers and pulleys. The basic relationships he worked out are still taught in physics classes. He realized the power of levers, and once said, "Give me a lever long enough and a place to stand, and I can move the earth."

Although these relationships are intriguing, another discovery by Archimedes is much better known and has an interesting story. One day the king of Syracuse, who was a personal friend and admirer of Archimedes, presented Archimedes with a problem. The king had recently purchased a golden crown, but suspected that the goldsmith who made the crown had not been fully honest. The goldsmith had been paid for a crown that was supposedly pure gold, but the king suspected that the goldsmith had mixed some cheaper material, probably silver, into the gold and pocketed the excess gold. The king wanted to know for sure but did not want the crown to be harmed in any way. For many days Archimedes struggled with how to determine if the crown was pure gold. Then, just as Archimedes was entering a pool for his daily bath, he noticed that the water in the bathtub rose as he lowered his body into the water. He realized that if he were to dip the crown into a bath of water, the volume of water displaced would be the same as the volume of the crown. Then, he could determine the density (weight divided by volume) of the crown and compare it with the density of pure gold. If the crown were lower in density, the thievery of the goldsmith would be confirmed. When Archimedes discovered this principle, he was so excited that he jumped from the bathtub and ran naked down the street crying "Eureka!" or "I have found it!" By the way, we are told that the goldsmith was dishonest and was executed by the king. The scientific principle found by Archimedes is called the **buoyancy principle.**

Several years later, the king of Syracuse came to Archimedes with another problem. This time it affected the future of the city of Syracuse itself. Because of some political issues between Rome and Carthage, a city on the northern rim of Africa, Syracuse became involved in a war with Rome. The Roman fleet and army were on their way toward Syracuse. The king requested that Archimedes do something, anything, to delay the Romans. The king hoped to solve the problem and avoid being conquered by the Romans. Archimedes accepted the challenge and prepared several surprises for the Romans.

When the Roman fleet entered the harbor at Syracuse, they had to pass close to a cliff that overlooked the entrance. Archimedes had built a large crane with a hook or claw on the end, which could be used to latch onto the Roman ships and, we are told, could flip the ships over or, at least, upset them. This caused the Roman general, Marcellus, great consternation, at least until he was able to attack the cliff and destroy the giant lever.

After the Roman fleet finally was able to enter the harbor, Archimedes revealed his next surprise. He supposedly arranged some soldiers around the harbor in a parabolic formation and instructed them to orient their shiny shields so that the rays of the sun reflected on the sails of the Roman ships. We are told that this tactic caused the sails to ignite. (Doubters have said that this is impossible, but supporters have claimed that the experiment has been repeated in Syracuse as late as the 19th century. Doubters still don't believe it, but the principle involved is certainly true.)

In another incident, Archimedes used his levers to catapult large stones onto the Roman ships. Reportedly, he could hurl stones weighing over one-quarter ton. This obviously sank many of the Roman ships. Similarly, when the Roman soldiers finally began their assault on the walls of Syracuse, Archimedes' catapults were used to hurl all types of missiles onto the soldiers. Tradition reports that the Roman soldiers became so worried over these counter-attacks that if anything were to be hurled over the wall, they would retreat in terror. (This is probably unlikely in light of the courage and discipline of the Roman army, but it makes a good story.)

When the Romans finally were able to breach the walls and enter the city, the Roman general gave orders that Archimedes was not to be harmed. However, when a soldier came to Archimedes' house, he walked right into the courtyard and disturbed the place where Archimedes was drawing some geometric figures on the sand. Archimedes became angry and scolded the soldier, who promptly killed Archimedes. Thus ended the life of, perhaps, the most creative scientist of the ancient world. He certainly is a favorite of ours.

Summary of Hellenistic Creativity

The Hellenistic Period changed the course of the world because of the creativity of the Greeks. Alexander's creative leadership brought nearly the entire Mediterranean world under Greek domination. When the Greeks moved into the conquered territories as administrators and merchants, the people in those territories found the Greek culture and lifestyle to be very inviting. They therefore adopted Greek ways, along with the Greek language. In most cases they retained their own language, but Greek became the language of commerce and culture.

Art in the Hellenistic Period was characteristically Greek, but showed greater emotion and movement than the Classical style. Some of the art pieces of the Hellenistic Period are more emotional and dramatic than any others would be for over 1,000 years, until the Baroque Period. The spread of Greek architecture came to represent the standard of style for the entire world and has, again, persisted until today.

Science in the Hellenistic time continued the acceleration begun in the days of Thales. Some of the greatest of all ancient scientists contributed knowledge that has been instrumental in establishing the basis of science even today. Newton, in particular, gave reverence to Archimedes and Euclid, both of whom gave a basis for scientific principles that Newton used to develop his own fundamental laws. Truly we can say that Hellenistic creativity has endured.

Timeline—Important Dates

Date	Event
359 B.C.	*Philip II becomes king in Macedonia*
336 B.C.	*Alexander becomes king of Macedonia and Greece*
323 B.C.	*Death of Alexander*
330–260 B.C.	*Euclid*
287–212 B.C.	*Archimedes*

Suggested Readings

Burke, James, *Connections,* Little, Brown, 1978.

Hanson, Victor Davis, *Carnage and Culture,* Anchor Books, 2001.

Hellenistic Philosophy and Religion

Ethics, Truth, and Beauty

> Now while Paul waited for them in Athens, his spirit was stirred in him, when he saw the city wholly given to idolatry. Therefore disputed he in the synagogue with the Jews, and with the devout persons, and in the market daily with them that met with him. Then certain philosophers of the Epicureans, and of the Stoicks, encountered him. And some said, What will this babbler say? Other some, He seemeth to be a setter forth of strange gods: because he preached unto them Jesus, and the resurrection.
>
> —*Acts 17:16–18*

The Legacies of Classical Philosophy

By the end of the Golden Age, the Greeks had largely abandoned belief in the gods of Olympus, even though social customs and some residual superstitions dictated that offerings still be made to those gods. The offerings, when done in the early days of the Greek civilization, were thought of as ways to placate the gods so that they would be favorable to a person. For example, an offering could be given to Demeter, the goddess of the harvest, so that she would help a particular farmer have a good harvest. The gods were also remembered so that catastrophes would be avoided for the entire community. When an unexplainable disaster struck, the people would assume that the gods were angry, and would offer sacrifices to correct the problem. Sometimes people who had failed to offer the correct sacrifice were blamed for the disaster. But, with the growing understanding of science, the Greeks had developed a rational approach to most natural phenomena, so the old assumption of an angry god was no longer seen as correct.

The gods of Olympus were never considered to be examples of ethical behavior. The stories of the Olympian gods were viewed as interesting and explanatory of unknown and seemingly supernatural events, but were recognized as little more than myths. Therefore, the ethical behavior derived from the myths had little more effect than would a legend or, today, a fairy tale.

This situation left the Greeks in need of ethical standards that could be used to govern everyday living. Ethics had come from the traditions of the ancient heroes through epics like the *Iliad* and the *Odyssey,* along with the dramas of Aeschylus, Sophocles, Euripides, and other playwrights who expanded the hero legends. However, these works were clearly of human origin and, although they communicated ethics, they seemed to be confusing, because they did not have any strong basis that tied them all into a coherent belief system. They were just incidents without any coherent vision.

Philosophy seemed to be the answer to satisfy the needs of the Greeks for systematic ethical standards. Initially the pre-Socratic sophists tried to give the Greeks that ethical foundation, but their teachings were largely discounted because of their tendency to change the ethical standard according to the whims of the person for whom they worked.

When Socrates, Plato, and Aristotle entered the Greek world, there was a vacuum in ethical standards; sensing this need, the three great philosophers all dedicated significant energy and time to establishing ethical systems that could serve as standards for living. However, because of the differences between Plato and Aristotle, the standards took on different characteristics, depending on which of the philosophers a person might have wanted to follow. These differences eventually led to two very different systems of ethical behavior, which became important in the Hellenistic period and continued in their importance throughout the Roman period. The two systems of ethical behavior became known as the Epicureans and the Stoics. As seen from the Biblical quotation at the beginning of the chapter, the apostle Paul encountered both of them in his visit to Athens in the first century A.D. Neither group agreed with Paul, but, as we shall see, they eventually had a profound impact on Christian ethics and doctrine.

Descent of Ethical Systems from Plato

One group of Greeks who tried to follow Plato found themselves in a difficult intellectual quandary. Because they accepted Plato's rejection of sensory information as being only a shadowy perception of the truth of things, these Platonists could not accept knowledge known only through the senses. However, their use of only rational knowledge to discover truth proved to be confusing, because they could not agree either on the basic questions of life or on the details of everyday actions that would be ethical. This irresolution led to the philosophical position of suspension of judgment. That meant that they could not know anything for sure, and they suspended knowing for sure until an absolute knowledge could be acquired, which never came. This Plato-derived philosophy is called Skepticism or Cynicism.

These **Skeptics and Cynics** were an unhappy group. Because of their rejection of the physical side of life, they sought very little. Life for them became very pessimistic; since they could never know anything for sure; they doubted everything, which led them to always look on the negative side.

An interesting story is told about one of their leaders, **Diogenes.** The story says that Diogenes was visited by Alexander, who admired him. Diogenes was sunning himself at the time of Alexander's visit. Alexander approached but Diogenes did not rise to greet him or, indeed, move at all. Somewhat taken aback, Alexander nevertheless wanted to express his admiration of Diogenes in some tangible way, and offered to give Diogenes anything he desired. Without stirring, Diogenes only asked that Alexander move out of the sunlight, as he was casting a shadow that was interfering with the sunning.

The emptiness of Skepticism and Cynicism did not attract many who wanted to use Skepticism as a basis for their lives. However, many people still admired Plato's principles and wished to find a system of living that would give a more positive view of life. These people modified the thinking of the Skeptics and Cynics and, as we will see, developed a powerful and popular ethical system. The new group were called Stoics.

The **Stoics** began at a school founded in Athens by Zenos (335–262 B.C.). The term comes from the Greek word *stoa,* which means colonnade, and describes the school building and garden where Zeno taught. The Stoics accepted Plato's depreciation of the physical state but, unlike the Skeptics and Cynics, did not totally reject the value of experience and sensory information. Instead, they suggested that life would best approach the ideal set by Plato if people lived simply, shunning luxury and complexity while retaining some value of sensory perceptions. This concept is sometimes called **asceticism.** (The monks whom Buddha joined before his enlightenment were ascetics, as are many of the monks and nuns in Christian monasteries.) As much as possible, the Stoics sought to live according to Plato's perfect society as described in *The Republic.*

The simple life allowed the Stoics time and energy to grow close to and understand ultimate truth. Pure reason was their way to find the ultimate truth, but sensory information could be passed to and processed by the brain so that pure reason can gain from the sensory information. However, the Stoics recognized that emotions lie between the senses and the brain, and can distort the pathway, thus also distorting the truth. Therefore, for Stoics, emotions should be eliminated or, if not, at least strongly controlled. Emotions are the opposite of a rational approach to life. The word they used to describe this absence and control of emotion is *apathea,* from which, obviously, we get the word "apathy." Today, when a person is intentionally apathetic, we might say they are being "stoical."

Stoics believed that there was a Divine Will, which they called the *Logos.* They felt that the Divine Will controlled all the events of the world. This Divine Will was probably directly related to Plato's concept of the Demi-urge and the Form. Stoics believed that happiness comes when people align their lives, and especially their thinking and emotions, with the Divine Will. This situation will bring inner peace, which is the ultimate goal of a Stoic.

The Divine Will *(Logos)* permeated all beings and all parts of nature. Because of its divine nature, the *Logos* was perfectly organized. It therefore governed all things according to a perfect "natural law" which, if someone were properly attuned, could be rationally perceived and followed. Those who were properly attuned were reminiscent of Plato's concept of the philosophers as the only ones who could perceive the world of Forms.

For some Stoics, the *Logos* was just a pervasive energy that controlled nature. We might compare it to the force of Mother Nature or, perhaps, the natural organization of the laws of Nature, like the laws of motion or the laws of thermodynamics. For others Stoics, however, the *Logos* took on a rational and intelligent feeling like Plato's Demigod. In other words, they believed in a god and identified that god as the *Logos,* a purely rational being. Some Stoics believed that Nature was the body of that ethereal god. They accepted an interaction between humans and the *Logos,* and suggested that those interactions could be detected as a wind or whisper or, at other times, could be sensed as a fiery impression.

As we will see in more detail in a later chapter, the Stoics had a profound influence on Christian thinking. For Christians who adopted Stoic thinking, God was identified with the Divine Will, whose attributes were associated with the Holy Ghost. Christ was also associated with the *Logos.* In fact, the book of John, in the Greek, uses the word "logos" in Chapter 1 verse 1 when it refers to "the Word" which was "with God" and "was God." The close connection between the Stoical concepts of Divine Will, *Logos* and their manifestation as wind or fire led to the concept of the Trinity.

Stoical thinking became very important within the Hellenistic world and grew in importance under Rome. Several characteristics of Stoicism seemed to coincide with Roman values, so there was a natural tendency of the Romans to adopt Stoicism as their personal ethical system. (Because the early Roman religion was much like the early Greek religion, the Romans had the same lack of moral and ethical basis for their lives; hence, the Romans were looking for a viable ethical system.) Romans believed that the world was logical, and readily accepted the concept that all was controlled by a Divine Will or *Logos.* The Romans strongly believed in rule by an elite group (them) and so they readily accepted the Platonic concepts of *The Republic* in which philosopher elites were given leadership. The Romans did not consider themselves philosophers, but they felt that with proper diligence, they could discover the underlying principles of the world and, therefore, would be fit to rule. The Romans believed in cool and calculated actions; that view agreed with the Stoical view of suppression of emotions.

The Romans had strong beliefs in the value of the family, freedom (for themselves), rational and participative government, loyalty, perseverance, bravery, and self-sacrifice for the greater good of the society. All these were reinforced by Stoical concepts of the underlying orderliness and logic of the world.

Most of our record of Stoical thinking comes from Roman writers who were trying to develop the principles of Stoicism and unite them into an ethical system that would fit within the Roman world. Some of these ethical thinkers were high Roman officials. In fact, one of them, Marcus Aurelius, was a Roman emperor.

In modern times another interesting connection has been made with an entity similar to the Stoical concept of Divine Will or *Logos.* That is "The Force" of *Star Wars* movies. Note that those who are able to use "The Force," such as Yoda, also exhibit the other attributes associated with Stoics, that is, unemotional behavior, deep concentration, belief in the rationality and consistency of Nature, and a confidence in an ultimate good.

The descent of ethical systems from Plato is summarized in Figure 10.1. This is not meant to say that the descent encompasses all the people who believed in Plato's thinking, nor is it meant to say that Christian doctrine only came from Plato. It does, however, illustrate the connections among the various ethical and religious systems.

Figure 10.1 ■ *Descent of ethical systems from Plato.*

Descent of Ethical Systems from Aristotle

Those who followed the teachings of Aristotle focused on his acceptance of sensory perceptions. Aristotle believed that the senses were a legitimate source of knowledge and that truth came from understanding (logically) the information gained from the senses. The Aristotelians were also sometimes called **Peripatetics,** which means "those who wander around," because they wandered about the world seeking knowledge—and also from Aristotle's habit of wandering around the Lyceum when he lectured. They valued observations of the real world and the use of that sensory knowledge to construct a logical view of the world. Such thinking is clearly scientific and, as we have seen, great science was done in the Hellenistic Period. The center for that science was Alexandria, Egypt and so the Hellenistic scientists are sometimes referred to as the **Alexandrian scientists.**

Ultimately, the observational emphasis of the Aristotelians was a problem for the development of a usable ethical system. Some thinking needed to be done to give these scientists a way to guide future actions, a very difficult problem in light of their emphasis on mere observation. That linkage of science with ethical behavior was provided by a man named **Epicurus,** who lived in Athens between 340 B.C. and 270 B.C. and wrote over 300 treatises defining his ethical system.

Those who followed the ethical system developed by Epicurus were called the **Epicureans.** They strongly supported the idea of gaining knowledge through the senses, but added to it a belief that the emotions were valid as a way to interpret sensory information. Hence, the Stoics denied and suppressed the emotions, whereas the Epicureans sought out and promoted the emotions. In fact, the core of Epicurean belief was that we should follow our emotional interpretation of sensory data in such a way that we always strive for that action that will bring us the most pleasure. Pleasure was defined as "freedom from pain and fear." Clearly this definition also has a strong element of happiness within it. They believed that happiness or pleasure flowed to people naturally as they did things that were right or ethical.

Like Aristotle, they believed that this pleasure or happiness comes from a pursuit of the Golden Mean, that is, avoidance of extremes in life. Pleasure could not be obtained from extreme behavior. For example, if a person received pleasure from eating a nice meal, that pleasure would disappear if the eating was to excess. Likewise, too little food would result in a non-pleasurable state. Therefore, with respect to eating, a person should seek to eat a moderate amount of fine food.

Sexual pleasure should be similarly moderated. While some might seek excessive sexual stimuli, the long-term effects can be decidedly non-pleasurable. For example, if sexual pleasure is sought outside normal limits, venereal disease can result; also, families can be destroyed. Both of these consequences could lead to unhappiness and pain. Thus, according to Epicurus, these excesses should be avoided.

The Epicureans believed that laws governed nature but, unlike the Stoics, the Epicureans did not believe in any Divine Will or *Logos* that guided or established the fundamental laws. The Epicureans believed the atomic theory of **Democritus** (wherein they differed from Aristotle's view of the four elements). The atomic theory, they believed, operated on laws that were independent of any will, either from a person or a divine entity. Therefore, the Epicureans did not have any belief in a god or supernatural power. They rejected religion, which they viewed as based on ignorance. They believed that life began by spontaneous generation and ended absolutely with death.

Epicureans cared little for ultimate truth. Theirs was a system that seemed satisfied with the knowledge that their actions would give the best pleasure and happiness. Because of the potential for negative interactions with the rest of the world in pursuing this pleasurable happiness, Epicureans would often withdraw from the world to enclaves where they could be happy in a solitary existence.

Important elements of the Epicurean system were adopted by many Romans, especially late in the Roman Empire period. These Romans were not very concerned with the basic values that were being taught and practiced by the Roman Stoics. Rather, the Roman Epicureans, who had been conditioned to a life of idleness and entertainment, saw the pursuit of pleasure as the ultimate good in life. However, in direct contrast to the concepts of Epicurus, the Romans did not confine their pursuit to moderation. They didn't seem to accept the reasoning that long-term pleasure comes from moderation but, rather, focused only on short-term maximization of pleasure. This corruption of the Epicurean philosophy is called **Hedonism** (from the Greek *hedone* = "pleasure"). It survives today in the lives of those who constantly seek short-term satisfaction and are not concerned about moderation.

Modern secular and atheistic science has much in common with Epicurean beliefs. In both systems, God and religion are rejected. They view life as being spontaneously generated and see no possibility for an afterlife existence. The laws of nature—in this case, the mechanistic laws of the atomic theory—control our total existence, and we are happiest when our lives conform to those natural laws.

The descent of Aristotelian concepts to the Peripatetics or Alexandrian scientists and then on to the Epicureans is shown in Figure 10.2. That chart also shows the extension of Epicureanism

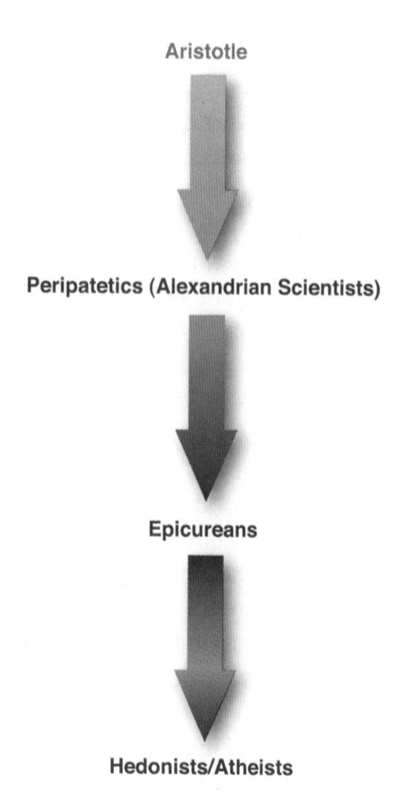

Figure 10.2 ■ *Descent of ethical systems from Aristotle.*

to Hedonism, which is the view taken by many in the later Roman period and also by some in modern days.

A Unique Type of Religion

The expansion of Greek culture throughout the known world brought about an interesting interaction in religious beliefs. That interaction was between those who accepted Greek culture and the Jews. The interaction was centered in the Levant, that area at the eastern end of the Mediterranean Sea that is occupied by modern Israel, Lebanon, Syria, and Palestine, but it was also seen throughout the Hellenistic world, because the Jewish people had been scattered throughout the Persian Empire following their capture by the Babylonians at the beginning of the sixth century B.C.

As we discussed in the chapter in Mesopotamia, the Jews are really remnants of the Hebrews, a nomadic people who had first entered history in Ur, a city in Mesopotamia, and had subsequently moved to the Levant. There they lived a hard and lonely life as shepherds, wandering through the wilderness seeking food and water for their herds and themselves, and fending off raids from other groups who wanted their animals and women. The Hebrews developed a closeness with their God, Jehovah (or, as some render the name, Yahweh), both as a calling from God but also as a means of dealing with the difficult circumstances in which they found themselves. Knowing the will of God was often difficult, however, as the Hebrews were a loose collection of various nomadic family clans who rarely came together to hear their leader relate to them what God would have them do. Furthermore, nearly all of the Hebrews were illiterate, and so little of God's word was, as yet, recorded. Within the Hebrew religion developed the tradition of prophets—righteous men who learned from God via visions, dreams, or direct communication, and then related what they had learned to their followers. Most of their teachings were retained as oral transmissions and then written later.

Unique among the desert nomadic tribes (and probably the world at this time) was the Hebrew belief that their God was not just another god, but the only God—an all-powerful Creator that had chosen the Hebrews as His people. This belief served as both blessing and curse for the Hebrews. Their complete devotion to Jehovah and their strict belief in monotheism served as a unifying force for the Hebrews as they struggled to survive the many obstacles they would face as a people, but this same devotion to Jehovah, and their reluctance to recognize the gods of their neighbors, made them outsiders and enemies, and thus brought many of their struggles on them.

Another difficulty the Hebrews faced was location. The lands they wandered and eventually settled in were nearly always nestled between the great powers of the ancient world. To the south was the powerful Egyptian Empire, and in the north were the various empires of Mesopotamia.

Thus, the land the Hebrews called home was both the crossroads for commerce and the buffer zone for wars between these empires. This unfortunate fact meant that the Hebrews not only had to contend with their own neighbors because of their unique religious convictions, but they were almost always hopelessly involved in the conflicts between empires.

Relatively early in the history of the Hebrews (about 1600 B.C.) we find the powerful Egyptians enslaving them and using them as forced labor in their empire-building; while much later the Babylonians (587 B.C.) destroyed the independent Hebrew kingdom of Judah and took the Jews into slavery and captivity in Babylon. In the thousand years between these two periods of enslavement, the Hebrews were invaded and politically dominated repeatedly by each power in turn. Only for a very brief time under the leadership of the kings David and Solomon did the Hebrews have the political unity and military strength to ward off the neighboring empires and effectively govern themselves, and even then it is only over a relatively small territory.

The Babylonian Captivity of the Hebrews, however, was very different from their enslavement under the Egyptians, and in many ways was a hidden blessing for the desert people. The Hebrews were taken into Babylon as an uneducated, semi-barbaric people, with limited spiritual or political unity. However, while in Babylon, the Jews were educated and modernized. It is most likely during their time in Babylon that the Jewish scriptures were assembled as a collection of books containing the Pentateuch, or first five books of the modern Bible, along with other Jewish writings now found in the Old Testament, such as Kings, Psalms, and Proverbs and made publicly available. The Jews were also taught about government, art, and civilization while living in Babylon.

The Jewish religion changed in Babylon. In their homeland, the temple in Jerusalem was the center of worship. The Jews were commanded to offer sacrifices to Jehovah at various times of the year and when various personal events occurred. However, when they were taken to Babylon and were cut off from the temple in Jerusalem, the Jews needed to find another way to worship Jehovah. Because of previous rivalries with the northern ten tribes of Israel, the Jews, who lived in a separate kingdom of Judah, believed that only the temple in Jerusalem was a worthy and acceptable place for sacrifice. (The Israelites in the north had begun to offer sacrifices in groves of trees and on mountain tops—places that the Jews believed were condemned by Jehovah.) Therefore, the priests, who were responsible for the sacrifices, became largely irrelevant for religious purposes, although they retained positions of influence as Jewish leaders. This is the time that rabbis (teachers) became important in the Jewish religion as local teachers of the word of God.

Therefore, when the Persians overtook Babylon and King Cyrus allowed the Jews to return to Jerusalem to rebuild their temple and city in 538 B.C., it was an educated and politically self-conscious people who returned. (In spite of the benefits that came from their Babylonian Captivity, the Jews have traditionally viewed this period with disdain. A similar attitude was displayed by Catholics in the fourteenth century A.D. when the French king moved the center of the Catholic Church from Rome to Avignon, France. For the Catholics, this was like being cut off from their holy places, just as the Jews were cut off from the temple. Therefore, the Catholics named the period when the headquarters of the Church was in France a "Babylonian Captivity.")

But only a small group of Jews elected to go back to Jerusalem; most stayed in Mesopotamia, while others eventually migrated to places such as Egypt. The Jews who returned to Jerusalem may have gained some ability to renew their homeland, but they did not regain their independence. They remained under the domination of the Persians and, with Alexander's conquest of the Persian Empire, became part of the post-Alexandrian kingdom of the Seleucids, centered in Syria. They continued under the Seleucids for many generations.

Throughout this period we see a steady growth of Hellenism among the Jews, with many adopting Greek culture and customs, including not circumcising male children (which had been the unique method of identification for the Hebrew boys). Eventually even the Jewish high priests adopted

Greek names and manners, and encouraged the people to accept Greek ways.

Like so many others, the culture of the Jews was slowly being overtaken by that of the Greeks; and the Jews might have been completely Hellenized except for the actions of the Syrian king, **Antiochus IV.** Antiochus believed the time had come to completely Hellenize and unite the various peoples of his empire, and ordered the end to the worship of any gods other than Zeus and the other gods of the Greek pantheon. The worship of Jehovah in Jerusalem and all of the other towns of Judea was strictly forbidden. The Jewish temple and shrines were converted into temples to Zeus, and any person found worshipping Jehovah or possessing any object distinctly Jewish was to be put to death.

This pronouncement served as a wake-up call to the wayward Jews, but resistance seemed nearly impossible in the face of such strict penalties. However, in a small community not far from Jerusalem, an aged priest named **Mattathias** refused to accept the decree. The courage of Mattathias inspired other Jews, and he slowly gathered a following that openly rebelled against the decree of Antiochus. At the death of Mattathias, his son **Judas Maccabeus** took his place and led the rebellious Jews to a series of military victories that have become known to history as the Maccabean revolt. The revolt reached its apex in 165 B.C., when the Maccabees captured Jerusalem and cleansed the Temple. (The Jewish festival of Hanukkah celebrates this rededication of the temple, and commemorates the miraculous burning of the temple menorah for eight days, even though the Maccabees could only find and use enough oil for one day.)

The revolt continued, with leadership passing from Judas to his brother Jonathan, who was recognized as leader (High Priest) of the Jews by the Syrian crown, and the Jews were given some degree of independence. Another brother, Simon, took Jonathan's place when a disgruntled Syrian general had Jonathan captured and killed. Under Simon, the Jews finally gained their independence, and the Jews governed themselves for about a century, until they were conquered by the Romans.

This was not, however, a time for Jewish unity. Several factions developed within the Jewish community. The most prominent faction was governed by the ruling priest class, called the **Sadducees.** These Sadducees believed that the survival of the Jewish people depended on their accommodation with the Greeks who ruled them. As a result, the Sadducees accepted Greek ways and advocated that others do likewise. They had seen the change in the Jewish religion during the Babylonian Captivity, and believed that further change was both inevitable and desirable if the Jewish people themselves were to continue.

The Sadducees were opposed by a vocal and powerful group that resisted any accommodation with the Greek rulers. This latter group was known as the **Pharisees.** Having gained power as a result of the Maccabean revolt, they resisted all changes to the religion, and believed that adoption of foreign cultures would inevitably result in religious changes. Therefore, the Pharisees resisted Hellenization.

This internal bickering made the Jews easy prey for the Roman Empire, which conquered Judea in 63 B.C. Roman rule, at least in the beginning, was relatively unobtrusive. The Jews looked to Caesar as their earthly ruler and paid his taxes, but for the most part governed themselves locally and practiced their religion in peace.

Relative self-government was to last for only a short time, however, as **Julius Caesar** came to power in Rome. In the rush to solidify his hold on the far-flung empire and to reward friends who had supported his coup, Julius awarded offices and positions. One of the people who benefited from Julius' bestowal of position was **Antipater,** a leader of the **Idumaeans,** a people that lived in the Levant and had interacted with the Jews (usually as enemies) for centuries. Antipater gave his son **Herod** the governorship of Jerusalem and from this position Herod later acquired the throne of the Jews in 37 B.C.

Already hated by the Jews because he was supported by the Romans, Herod soon gained a reputation as a tyrant because he murdered many of the people attached to the Maccabean dynasty. Herod attempted to win support of the Jews by refurbishing and enlarging the temple. A model of this Herodian-modified temple is shown in Figure 10.3.

Figure 10.3 ■ Model of Jewish temple. *© 2010 by Stasys Eidejus. Used under license of Shutterstock, Inc.*

Later in life Herod became more paranoid and felt even less secure in his position; he instituted another series of purges, killing thousands of innocent Jews. Finally, just years before his death, Herod heard of the birth of the legal heir to the throne of the Jews, and ordered a final purge to kill all male children under the age of two. This true heir to the political throne of the Jews was Jesus of Nazareth, saved by his parents when they fled to Egypt. Jesus would never sit on the throne that was his by right, but would go on to play a much larger role in history than that of a vassal king in a backward corner of the Roman Empire.

As the next fifty years passed, the Jews lost more and more political and religious control. Upon the death of Herod, Caesar Augustus revoked his family's right to rule directly and placed a Roman procurator in charge of Jerusalem. It was the procurator **Pontius Pilate** who crucified Jesus. Later procurators were more and more oppressive, and life for the Jews got steadily worse, leading to more frequent instances of open rebellion. As the rebellions against Roman rule became more troublesome for Rome, the Jews began to draw the attentions of the Caesars. By 70 A.D. the Roman legions had moved into Jerusalem and destroyed the Temple. They then took the Jews prisoners and scattered them throughout the empire so that the Jews could no longer unite and cause trouble. This punishment implemented by Rome proved to be extremely effective, as the Jews did not return to Jerusalem as a people until the mid-20th century; the Temple at Jerusalem has yet to be rebuilt.

Throughout their history, the Jews have effectively adapted their religion and culture and shown an amazing ability to survive in the face of great adversity. The Jews would have to do so once again during the **Diaspora** (the name given to the scattering of the Jews by the Romans). The Jews, scattered across Europe, Africa, and Asia, found it difficult to have a central governing body the way they had at Jerusalem, so Judaism lost much of its central authority and had to rely more and more on local rabbis to interpret the scriptures and direct the flock. This condition eventually led to the creation of several different branches of Judaism with different beliefs, as well as the closure of the Jewish canon of scripture and an end to revelation as part of the Jewish religion. Furthermore, because of the destruction of the Temple and the inability of the Jews to go to the Temple to make sacrifices, prayer began to play a more prominent role in the Jewish religion in place of Temple sacrifice.

Eventually within Rome, and later in Europe, the Jews found themselves living in an area dominated by Christianity, often hated and persecuted as the people who had crucified Jesus. In order to be needed, and to prosper in the face of restrictions such as the denial of the right to own land, Jews took up trades that required special training or that were forbidden to Christians, becoming artisans and moneylenders. Even with their efforts to make themselves needed and useful, persecution has plagued the history of the Jews during the Diaspora. It has often only been their faith in God and His promise—that they will one day be delivered—that has given them the hope to continue through the dark times such as the Medieval Crusades, the Russian pogroms, and the death camps of Nazi Germany. Judaism has proven to be a religion that has adapted to its various circumstances, and this creative adaptation has allowed both itself and its adherents to survive great difficulties. Jewish creativity can also be seen in the great religious literary texts of their faith—the **Torah** and other writings of the Old Testament prophets, and the **Talmud,** the rabbinical commentaries that assist in understanding the Torah.

In spite of the modifications and changes that Judaism has made throughout history, some fundamentals of the Jewish faith have remained constant. These unchanged characteristics of the faith are often quite different from those of the surrounding, largely Christian, community in which the Jews have lived for 2,000 years. Many of these characteristics contrast sharply with Christian values. These contrasts may have subtly led to much of the persecution of the Jews. Interestingly, the Jewish concepts or characteristics are far closer to the typical Eastern concepts, as shown in Eastern religions and philosophy, than to Western thinking as expressed in Christianity and Greek philosophy. These contrasts are worth commenting on, and are summarized in Figure 10.4. The chart is obviously a gross simplification, but it has concepts that are generally descriptive of the two ways of thinking that have distinguished both the Western/Christian thinking and Eastern/Jewish thinking. An understanding of these differences helps give toleration for each other, and can also help Christians understand better the Old Testament, which is, of course, a Jewish book written with Jewish values and philosophies.

The methods of learning in a Christian-oriented school system or, equivalently, in a typical secular (public) school in the Christian West are much different from the Jewish-oriented school or, equivalently, schools in the Orient. The Western school emphasizes experience and reason (empiricism and logic), whereas the Eastern school emphasizes rote learning. The Western schools seem to value individualism in learning, whereas the Eastern schools value the experience of elders who lived and learned in the past.

For Western minds, facts are absolute and unchanging. They are, simply, the way they are. The Eastern mind sees facts as always depending on humans for discovery, interpretation, or transmission; therefore, the prejudices and paradigms of the individuals involved unavoidably skew the facts. Moreover, for those in the Eastern world, God is viewed as a powerful being who can change the facts as His plan may require.

The typical Western book about ethics and religion is logical, much like the thinking of Aristotle. It is to be well organized and should lead from one conclusion to another. History is viewed as linear. In contrast, the Eastern book is poetic, especially in religion and philosophy. Note how the writings of Lao Tzu, Confucius, and Isaiah possess a poetic quality and are not intended to be logical. They are understood best by feelings rather than by logic. This difference of writing style is undoubtedly one of the reasons that many Christians have trouble understanding Isaiah.

Freedom is not the same in the Western and Eastern cultures. For Westerners, freedom is linked to the individual and the rights of the individual, which should be protected and guaranteed by the society. Democracy, which is the right of the individual to dictate the government, is paramount for freedom to exist. For Eastern societies,

Cultural Characteristic	Western	Eastern
Methods of learning	Experience and reason.	Rote learning.
View of the nature of facts	Facts are absolute.	Facts can be transitory and subject to Divine Will.
Typical writing types	Aristotle's well-reasoned works.	Isaiah's poetical and image-filled exhortations.
Politics	Freedom of the individual is paramount and should be guaranteed by society.	Individuals are secondary to the state. Individual freedom can exist even when the state is not democratic.
Family	Open and not structured.	Patriarchal.
Loyalty	To the state or society.	To the leader.
Religion	Tends to be cerebral.	Tends to be emotional and mystical.
View of man	Man is the ultimate being and is lord of the earth by right of reason.	Man is a subject of God and should seek to do His will.
Cultural	The body is the most glorious creation and should be a focus of life through art, exercise, leisure, and pursuit of pleasure.	People should be modest and cover their body. No statues or art to depict bodies (no graven images), only minor efforts to ensure personal comfort.

Figure 10.4 ■ *Western (Greek) versus Eastern (Jewish) cultures and thought.*

individuals are secondary to the welfare of the group; therefore, the emphasis is on the good of the society, and individual freedom can exist even when the society is not democratic.

The differences of emphasis on individuals versus groups can also be seen in the structures of the Western and Eastern families. In the West, the individual is the most important entity, so children are given much choice and are catered to by the parents. In the Eastern family, the parents are revered to a greater extent, and the children have far fewer choices.

The concepts of loyalty also have a basis in the differences we have noted over individuality and groups. For the Westerner, loyalty is given to the state itself, simply because the state is the entity that guarantees freedom for the individual. For the Easterner, loyalty is given to the *leader* of the state, who, like a kind father, dictates what is best for all the people.

Just as writing in the West is logical, so too is religion. There is a strong tendency to focus on doctrine and the logical nature of religion. In the East the emphasis is on mystical experiences and feelings. Although these religious experiences are not absent in Western religions, the religions that emphasize such experiences are viewed as slightly different from mainstream Christianity.

In light of the previous discussion, we would expect that the views of mankind in the West and

East are quite different. In the West, man is the ultimate being, and is lord of the earth by right of reason. In the East, man is subject to God, and should seek God's will.

The Western emphasis on man leads to a cultural focus on the human body as the greatest of God's creations; it should be the focus of art, exercise, leisure, and pursuit of pleasure. In Eastern thinking, the body should not be shown. Modesty is paramount. No statues or art should depict bodies, and only minor efforts should be given to ensure personal physical comfort.

What Is Ethics, Beauty, Truth?

Sometimes we can benefit from an overall comparison, even though that comparison presents the material in an overly simplified way. In hopes that such a comparison will be useful, we have created several tables that summarize information from this chapter and some of the previous chapters. These data illustrate several aspects of civilization that were especially important in the Hellenistic Period, and so they are presented in this chapter.

A table summarizing the concept of "What is ethical?" for various philosophical and religious systems is presented in Figure 10.5. We have included brief snippets of information on the following ethical systems: Plato/Stoics, Aristotle/Epicureans, Jews, Christians, Buddhists, and Confucists/Taoists.

One of the most fundamental questions of any ethical system is "How should we find happiness?" For the Platonists/Stoics, happiness comes from living in conformity with the plan of Divine Will (*Logos*). That concept is not too different from the Jewish and Christian injunction that happiness comes from living according to the will of God. For Aristotle and the Epicureans, happiness should be the focus of existence, and it comes when pleasure is found. The Confucists/Taoists view is surprisingly similar to the Epicureans, since for the Confucists/Taoists, happiness comes through finding your own role in the world and then living according to that role. Buddhists seem to be between the others. They see happiness coming from enlightenment, which is individual in nature, but also from finding the correct path, which suggests that a preferred way can be known, much like the feeling obtained when a person trusts God or a Divine Will to show the way.

Whereas finding happiness is a goal for most ethical systems, the pathway along which we should travel is equally important for most ethical systems to define. For Plato and the Stoics, the pathway was defined by reason; emotions were carefully circumscribed, as they often interfere with reason. That path should, however, also include helping others, as it is important to be in conformance with Divine Will, which seeks to improve the lives of all people. Aristotle and the Epicureans were able to simplify the pathway by suggesting that extremes should be avoided. They called this middle ground the Golden Mean. Buddhists, like the Epicureans, see moderation as the way to act. Buddhists call their pathway the Middle Way. Jews take a very stringent view of the pathway. For them, it is defined by God's laws, and each person must keep those laws as the primary activity in life. Although Christians also believe that God has given the path, that pathway is less well defined than for Jews. The Christian emphasizes charity and love as motivations and attitudes that should direct actions. Confucists/Taoists are close to the Christians in their recognition of deeper attitudes as motivators and instigators of actions. Patience and acceptance, over the long term, are viewed as attitudes that should govern actions.

Each of the ethical systems is concerned about thinking, ideas, attitudes, and the mind. For Stoics, the attitude that governs the mind should be acceptance of whatever happens and control the emotions. Stoics are strongly influenced by a feeling of fate. The Aristotelians and Epicureans believe in science and the ultimate validity of empirical knowledge, that is, knowledge gained from sensory experience. For the Jews, our minds should accept the knowledge that is given to us by prophets, supplemented by reading and thinking about that prophetic knowledge. The Christians must think in terms of salvation and realize that

	Platonists/ Stoics	Aristotelians /Epicureans	Jews	Christians	Buddhists	Confucists/ Taoists
Happiness	Conform to the plan of divine reason (the Form or *Logos*).	Happiness is found through pleasure (no pain).	Obedience to God brings happiness.	Live according to the laws of Christ.	Happiness from achieving Nirvana (enlightenment).	Each person has a role and happiness comes from finding and fulfilling that role.
How to live	Use reason and diminish emotions. Help others.	Live the Golden Mean (avoid extremes).	Keep the law at all costs.	Charity and love.	Seek the Middle Way—neither excessive self-denial nor excessive self-indulgence.	Be like water (patience and acceptance).
Ideas and mind	Accept whatever happens. Accept fate.	Science and empirical knowledge are the key to truth.	God's law is known by ancient inspiration and tradition (Torah and Talmud).	Judgment will come to all men and only those with righteous actions and/or feelings will be saved.	Life will repeat at higher or lower levels depending on how virtuously one lived in this life.	Balance Yin and Yang.
Living with the world	Government by an elite. Live simply.	Government not very important. Live separately and avoid conflicts.	Keep separate as a chosen people.	Involvement in community is a way to show love and charity.	Focus on individual and inner progress.	Avoid force. Seek inner peace through the Tao.

Figure 10.5 ■ *What Is Ethical?*

all they do and feel will affect their salvation, so they should have proper feelings and actions. The Buddhists think about the transitory and repeating nature of life, thus gaining a very long perspective. For the Taoists, the conflicts between Yin and Yang should be foremost in their mind, and they should always strive to balance these opposing forces.

Some ethical systems, like the Stoics, encourage strong participation in the world. As a result, Stoics have been politicians and other public figures, in part, because they could improve the lives of others. The Christians believe even more strongly that they should be involved, as that is a way in which charity and love can best be shown. The Jews were happy to be isolated, since they felt they were God's chosen people and isolation was acceptable, although they should still be examples to others, but that could be done from afar. The Epicureans also felt that isolation was acceptable. For them, the isolation allowed a person to live the simple, pleasurable life. Buddhists focused on their inner selves and found that they could best do that in isolation, at least for a portion of the day. The Taoists also sought inner peace, and felt that could be achieved in isolation, but the Confucists believed that involvement in the community was a higher goal. Hence, the typical person who follows both Taoism and Confucianism will have some time alone and some time in the community.

Beauty is a concept that was very important for the Greeks. The assimilation of Greek culture by the Hellenistic world led to some interesting clashes over this concept as the Jews and then later the Christians interacted with this Hellenistic culture. Figure 10.6 summarizes the views of the Greeks, Jews, and Christians toward the concepts of Beauty.

For Greeks, physical beauty was an expression of perfection because it captured some of the Form of beauty. The mathematical nature of the Greeks suggested that beauty would be symmetrical and dimensionally correct. The Greeks felt that the human body was one of the best representations of beauty, and should be openly appreciated. This could be done through art in which nudes were common. Symmetry and dimension could and should also be shown in buildings and other manmade creations.

The Jews believed that all of God's creations were beautiful, but did not attempt to understand the nature of God through a detailed study and categorization of those creations. With respect to the human body, it should be covered modestly. This modesty came from God's encouragement of sexual restraint and also from His commandment to avoid graven images. This all led to a belief that simplicity was generally closely linked to beauty.

Christians believed that beauty comes from God through the Holy Spirit and, therefore, any-

	Greeks	Jews	Christians
Underlying principle	Dimensional perfection. Attempt to capture the Form of beauty that is within.	God's creations are all beautiful.	Beauty is found in both God's creations and also in human creations.
The human body	The human body is the most perfect creation and should be seen and honored.	No graven images. Modesty in revealing the human body.	All art should lift the spiritual life of mankind. Nudity may be uplifting or may be degrading.
Additional concepts	All art, especially buildings, should have symmetry and balance.	Simplicity is best.	Beauty comes from the spirit or goodness that is inside.

Figure 10.6 ■ *What Is Beauty?*

	Plato	Aristotle	Jews/Christians
The nature of truth	The Form is true and unchanging.	The senses lead to an understanding of the true nature of things.	Truth is known to God.
How truth is perceived	Reason.	Empiricism.	Humans can find truth on their own or by revelation.
Human understanding of truth	Humans know truth in their memory of previous lives.	Humans understand truth through nature.	Conflicts between human knowledge and God's will be resolved in God's favor.

Figure 10.7 ■ *What Is Truth?*

thing that elevates the spirit of mankind can be beautiful. Man's creations could, therefore, be just as beautiful as God's. If artwork is uplifting and inspirational, then it can be beautiful, and that includes portrayals of the human body.

Truth is a concept that is just as hard to define as beauty, but one that has been at the heart of Greek, Jewish, and Christian thought. Because of their fundamental differences on this issue, we have given the views of both Plato and Aristotle on the nature of truth. Since the Jews and the Christians are much alike in their views, we have combined them in Figure 10.7.

For Plato, truth is the Form. It is perceived through Reason and cannot be perceived in any other way. Humans understand the truth of things because of memory from a preexistence in which they saw the true Forms.

For Aristotelians (and modern secular scientists), truth is discovered from empirical knowledge, that is, through the senses. It is understood and shaped by reason. Humans understand the truth, therefore, through investigations of Nature.

Christians and Jews believe that truth is known to God. He may reveal that truth to humans either through revelation or directly by investigating God's creations. If conflicts arise between God's revealed truth and human perception of truth, God's revealed truth will prevail.

Summary

Some people have thought of the Hellenistic Period as merely a brief transition between the Golden Age of Greece and the rise of the Roman Empire. In truth, the Hellenistic Age was much more than that. It was a time of great change in the cultures of the various people who were conquered by Alexander and, therefore, became subject to the nearly overwhelming influence of Greek culture. That culture appealed strongly to the desires for beauty, art, and elevation of the mind of individuals. Greek culture emphasized individualism and fostered individual growth and development. These concepts and practices were naturally appealing and were, therefore, widely adopted. Other aspects of Greek culture were often adopted simultaneously. (In the modern world, American culture and values are having a similar impact.)

Conservatives among the conquered peoples often resisted the adoption of Greek culture and its accompanying values. Nowhere was the conflict more pronounced than in the land of the Jews. This conflict gave rise to the separation of the Jewish people according to their toleration for and acceptance of Greek culture. The conflicts between these two groups would later lead to strong opinions about the message of Jesus of Nazareth.

Some believed he advocated non-Jewish ideas and, therefore, was to be rejected. This feeling eventually led to his death and to the dissemination of his ideas into the non-Jewish world. But that is a story for another chapter.

Timeline—Important Dates

Date	Event
538 B.C.	*Jews allowed to return to Jerusalem from Babylon*
335–262 B.C.	*Zenos founds the Stoics*
340–270 B.C.	*Epicurus founds the Epicureans*
332 B.C.	*Greek control of Palestine under the Seleucids*
175 B.C.	*Maccabean revolt*
63 B.C.	*Romans conquer Palestine*
37 B.C.	*Herod becomes king of the Jews*
70 A.D.	*Romans destroy Jerusalem to end a revolt*

Suggested Readings

Epictetus, *Moral Discourses,* Elizabeth Carter (trans.), Dent, 1957.

Mitchell, Richard, *The Gift of Fire,* A Common Reader Edition, 1999.

O'Connor, Eugene (trans.), *The Essential Epicurus,* Prometheus Books, 1993.

Epicurus: The Atoms, Golden Maxims

Introduction

Epicurus (340–270 BC) was a major philosopher of the Hellenistic Period, when Greeks controlled the Eastern Mediterranean and eastward to India following the military successes of Alexander the Great. This was a period when Greek teachings, culture and language became the standard of the Mediterranean world. During the Hellenistic Period, Greek life was modified from the standards of the Golden Age to meet the needs of a worldwide society. Art became much more expressive, science became more technical and practical, and philosophy became more relevant to daily living. Two major schools of philosophical teachings and ethics developed during the Hellenistic period. One of those ethical systems was Epicureanism and the other was Stoicism. Both of these had major impacts on later civilizations and will be examined through key writers from each of these ethical schools.

Epicurus, our spokesman for Epicureanism, taught a lifestyle based on empiricism (science) and the pursuit of happiness through a search for pleasure (avoidance of pain). The Epicureans taught that the world was made up of atoms which strictly obeyed natural laws. The selected readings from *The Atoms* explain the basis of these beliefs. Epicurus used this atomic theory to explain all natural phenomena. He obviously had access to the writings of Democritus and other Atomists. While he differed from Aristotle on the nature of matter, his reliance on knowledge of the physical world through the senses suggests that he was a philosophical descendent of Aristotle. He rejected religion and Plato's Forms and believed that all knowledge comes from the experience of the senses.

Epicurus also taught that only actions that bring pleasure are intrinsically good. He asserted the *Golden Maxims* as a way of life for those who would seek true happiness. For this purpose, he personally sought to avoid politics and other interactions with the world. He lived a quiet, secluded life free from the complications of worldly living. Epicurus' philosophy of pleasure and freedom of pain was very popular. He also taught that God has never existed. Many communities of Epicureans existed long after his death. Later societies, such as the Romans of the late empire, adopted some of the concepts of Epicurus and distorted them to be hedonistic in nature. Epicurus would not have been pleased. He taught and practiced a simple life in which extremes were avoided and pleasure was thought of in purely psychological terms.

Article 17

The Atoms

And, furthermore, we must consider that atoms exhibit none of the qualities belonging to visible things except shape, mass, and size, and whatever is necessarily related to shape. For every quality changes; but the atoms do not change, since, in the dissolution of compound substances, there must remain something solid and indestructible, which causes changes not into the nonexistent, nor from the nonexistent, but as a result of the transpositions of some particles and the approach or departure of others. Therefore, it is necessary that these shifting particles be everlasting and not share in the nature of what is changeable, but rather possess their own mass and configurations. For they must needs remain permanent. Even among things perceptible to us that change their configurations by loss of matter, there is still perceived an inherent shape; the other qualities do not remain in the object as it changes, just as shape survives, but they are removed from the entire body. These properties that are left behind are enough to cause the differences in compound substances, since it is necessary that some at least remain and are not destroyed into the nonexistent.

O'Connor, Eugene (tr.), *The Essential Epicurus,* Prometheus Books, 1993.

Article 18
Golden Maxims

Pleasure is an original and natural good, but we do not choose every pleasure. Sometimes we avoid pleasures when a greater pain follows them; and many pains we consider preferable to pleasure when they lead eventually to a greater pleasure. Self-sufficiency is to be sought. Luxuries are hard to get, but natural things are easy and give us much pleasure.

When we say pleasure is the purpose of life, we do not mean the pleasures of the sensually self-indulgent, as some assert, but rather freedom from bodily pain and mental disturbance. The life of pleasure does not come from drinking or revels, or other sensual pleasures. It comes from sober thinking, the sensible investigation of what to choose and to avoid, and getting rid of ideas which agitate the soul. Common sense is our best guide. It tells us that we cannot live happily unless we live wisely, nobly, and justly without being happy. The virtues are inseparably linked with pleasure. For whom do you rate higher than the man who has correct beliefs about God, who has no fear of death, who has understood the purpose of Nature, who realizes that pain does not last long, and that Necessity, which some people consider the directing force of the world, is partly a matter of luck, and partly in our power?

* * *

Accustom yourself to think that death means nothing to us. For what is good and bad is a matter of sensation, and death is an end of sensation. Grasping this principle makes human life pleasant, not by giving us any promise of immortality, but by freeing us from any desire for immortality. For there is nothing in life to be afraid of for a man who understands that he need not be afraid of its extinction. So death, usually regarded as the greatest of calamities, is actually nothing to us; for while we are, death is not, and when death is here, we are not. So death means nothing to either the living or the dead, for it has nothing to do with the living and the dead do not exist.

Article 19

Epictetus: Moral Discourses

Introduction

Although he lived in the 2nd Century AD, we will discuss the writings of Epictetus in the post-classical Greek period, often called the Hellenistic period—from the 4th to the 2nd century BC. This will provide a good comparison between the Epicureans and the Stoics. The Greek world and then the subsequent Roman world, which included all of the Greek world plus much more, had become polarized between the Greek ethical traditions of Stoicism and Epicureanism. Whereas Epicureans believed that the world ran strictly according to natural laws that existed without any guiding spirit or force, Stoics taught that the world was guided by purpose and that happiness could be found by alignment with that purpose. To Stoics it would be futile to fight against Nature. But, discovering Nature takes work and diligence. Then, once discovered, adhering to natural principles requires some effort. However, if Nature is not well understood, then mankind might suffer. These sufferings are to be accepted without emotion and complaint. They are all part of the purpose that rules the world. We get our modern term "stoical" from this acceptance of difficulties.

One of the Roman champions of Stoicism was Epictetus who was born a slave but earned his freedom and then devoted his life to teaching the traditional Stoic curriculum of logic, physics, and ethics. He began his own school where he emphasized ethics and the philosopher life.

Epictetus is most famous for description of "a calm and disciplined life." He taught that one must accept a lack of control over external events or circumstances and learn to always be happy by accepting things exactly as they are. This attitude is taught most clearly in *Moral Discourses* where Epictetus describes the Stoics' view of death.

How to Face Death

I must die: if instantly, I will die instantly; if in a short time, I will dine first; and when the hour comes, then I will die. How? As becomes one who restores what is not his own.

When you have had enough to-day, you sit weeping about to-morrow, how you shall get food. Why, if you have it, wretch, you will have it: if not, you will go out of life. The door is open: why do you lament? What room doth there remain for tears? What occasion for flattery? Why should any one person envy another? Why should he be struck with awful admiration of those who have great possessions, or are placed in high rank? Especially if they are powerful and passionate? For what will they do to us? The things which they can do we do not regard: the things which we are concerned about they cannot do. Who then, after all, shall command a person thus disposed?

Do not admire your clothes, and you will not be angry with the thief. Do not admire the beauty

Epictetus, *Moral Discourses,* Elizabeth Carder (tr.), J. M. Dent & Sons, Ltd., 1957.

of your wife, and you will not be angry with an adulterer. Know that a thief and an adulterer have no place in the things that are properly your own; but in those that belong to others, and which are not in your power. If you give up these things, and look upon them as nothing, with whom will you any longer be angry? But while you admire them, be angry with yourself rather than with others. Consider only: You have a fine suit of clothes, your neighbour has not. You have a window, you want to air them. He knows not in what the good of man consists, but imagines it is in a fine suit of clothes; the very thing which you imagine too. Must not he, then, of course, come and take them away? When you show a cake to greedy people, and are devouring it all yourself, would not you have them snatch it from you? Do not provoke them. Do not have a window. Do not air your clothes. I, too, the other day, had an iron lamp burning before my household deities. Hearing a noise at the window, I ran. I found my lamp was stolen. I considered, that he who took it away did nothing unaccountable. What then? To-morrow, says I, you shall find an earthen one; for a man loses only what he hath. *I have lost my coat. Ay, because you had a coat. I have a pain in my head. Why, can you have a pain in your horns? Why, then, are you out of humour? For loss and pain can be only of such things as are possessed.*

Do not you know that both sickness and death must overtake us? At what employment? The husbandman at his plough; the sailor on his voyage. At what employment would you be taken? For, indeed, at what employment ought you to be taken? If there is any better employment at which you can be taken, follow that. For my own part, I would be taken engaged in nothing, but in the care of my own faculty of choice; how to render it undisturbed, unrestrained, uncompelled, free. I would be found studying this, that I may be able to say to God, "Have I transgressed thy commands? Have I perverted the powers, the senses, the preconceptions which thou hast given me? Have I ever accused thee, or censured thy dispensations? I have been sick, because it was thy pleasure; and so have others, but I willingly. I have been poor, it being thy will, but with joy. I have not been in power, because it was not thy will; and power I have never desired. Hast thou ever seen me out of humour upon this account? Have I not always approached thee with a cheerful countenance, prepared to execute thy commands and the significations of thy will? Is it thy pleasure that I should depart from this assembly? I depart. I give thee all thanks that thou hast thought me worthy to have a share in it with thee; to behold thy works, and to join with thee in comprehending thy administration." Let death overtake me while I am thinking, while I am writing, while I am reading such things as these.

All things happen by virtue of necessity, the vortex being the cause of the creation of all things, and this he calls necessity. The end of action is tranquillity, which is not identical with pleasure, as some by a false interpretation have understood, but a state in which the soul continues calm and strong, undisturbed by any fear or superstition or any other emotion. This he calls well-being and many other names. The qualities of things exist merely by convention; in nature there is nothing but atoms and void space. These, then, are his opinions.

Roman Republic
Governmental Creativity

Many a time, gentlemen, have I spoken at length in this House; many a time have I reproached our fellow citizens for their self-indulgence and greed—and by so doing have made many enemies; for as I had never, in my own conscience, excused myself for any wrongdoing, I found it hard to pardon the sins which other men's passions led them to commit. . . . Now, however, it is not the question whether our morals are good or bad, nor is it the size and grandeur of the Roman empire that we have to consider. The issue is whether that empire, whatever we may think of it, is going to remain ours, or whether we and it together are to fall into the hands of enemies. In such a crisis does anyone talk to me of clemency and compassion?

—Cato's words to the Senate condemning conspirators who sought to overthrow the Republic; as quoted by Sallust, The Conspiracy of Cataline, *52.*

Founding of the Roman People and Then the City of Rome

Just as the Greeks looked with pride on their ancient past, so too did the Romans (perhaps because of the example of the Greeks). The Romans wanted to believe that they were descended from a noble race of heroes who had established a people or race and had built a great city where their civilization had been implemented. That civilization of the past needed to embody the same values that the Romans held so dear. The Romans created that desired-for ancient past; it gave their society great pride and, moreover, solidified the values that they felt were so important. However, this is not to suggest that the ancient, heroic past was totally a fabrication. Both archeological evidence and oral history give data confirming much of what the founding legends say, at least in general terms. These legends are probably as accurate as the stories of the heroic past for the Greeks as related in the Homeric legends. Like the Greeks, the Romans expanded and enhanced the legends over time and, like the Greeks, the ethics and values of the heroes became the ethics and values of the Romans in the days of their own Golden Age.

Legend says that the Roman race was founded in the years immediately following the Trojan

War, as a direct result of the consequences of that famous war. This is the tale of Aeneas, the son of the goddess Venus and her mate, the brother of the king of Troy. Aeneas is, therefore, a cousin to Hector and Paris, at least in his mortal heredity. His story was written most completely in the first century B.C. by the Roman poet **Virgil,** but some portions of the legend existed in the sixth century B.C.; archeological evidence shows that the region in which the Roman people lived was inhabited by Greek-like people as early as the eleventh century B.C.—just right for the legend to be true.

Virgil's epic book, called the *Aeneid,* relates the story of the exploits of **Aeneas,** who, as one of the most admired of the Trojan heroes, is discussed in other books and legends about the war. Virgil's book tells of the Trojan horse and the subsequent fall of Troy. The story tells that as the city is being destroyed by the Greeks, Aeneas flees carrying his aged father and the household gods on his back and leading his wife and son. They board ships but, sadly, his wife becomes lost and dies before boarding the ship. Figure 11.1 shows a statue of Aeneas carrying his father and leading his son. This statue wonderfully shows details that are amazingly real. For example, the skin texture of Aeneas' father is like old wrinkled leather whereas the skin of Aeneas' son is soft and pliant, and Aeneas' skin is firm and shows straining muscles underneath.

Figure 11.1 ■ Aeneas carrying his father and leading his son (by Bernini). *© Gianni Dagli Orti/Corbis*

Aeneas has been told by the gods that his destiny is to found a noble people. The gods even told him that he was to begin this society in Italy. However, the goddess Juno (Hera in the Greek pantheon) hates the Trojans and, therefore, she does not want Aeneas to succeed. She sends many trials that complicate and delay his arrival at the land where the Roman people would come to be.

One of the best-known incidents in the wanderings of Aeneas is his encounter with Dido, the queen of Carthage. Aeneas and his band of Trojans are cast ashore on the coast of northern Africa, near the city of Carthage. There he encounters queen Dido, who desperately falls in love with Aeneas. They live a happy existence for many days but, eventually, Jupiter (Zeus to the Greeks) becomes angry that Aeneas is not fulfilling his destiny, and sends Mercury to chastise Aeneas and urge him to immediately leave Carthage for Italy. Aeneas is faced with a choice of duty or love. He chooses duty and tells his men to prepare the ship. When Dido discovers his intent to leave, she is outraged and brokenhearted. She attempts to stop Aeneas, but when that fails, she commits suicide. (Aeneas' devotion to duty in the face of love is just one of many incidents in which Aeneas acts in a way that reflects the values of the Romans of the first century B.C.)

Later in the legend, Aeneas is taken to the world of spirits where he again sees Dido. She refuses to acknowledge his presence, indicating the continuing animosity between herself and Aeneas. (It is interesting that the most important of the early Roman wars were against Carthage and, of course, the story of Aeneas and Dido anticipates the problems between these two cities.)

Eventually Aeneas reached Italy. There he meets King Latinus, with whom he forms an alliance. The king offers his daughter, Lavinia, to

Aeneas as his wife. However, Lavinia's former suitor becomes angry over this occurrence and sets out to drive the Trojans from the land. After many battles, the Trojans are victorious, in part because of the bravery of Aeneas in personal combat. At the end of his life, Aeneas is deified at the urging of his mother, Venus, and in recognition of his piety in following the destiny given to him.

The story of Aeneas seems to be a combination of the *Iliad* and the *Odyssey,* only in reverse order; that is, for Aeneas the wanderings came first and the war afterward. Like the Homeric epics, the *Aeneid* both tells a story and defines the personal qualities that should be emulated by the people. After the *Aeneid,* the Romans could point to their native epic and say that their history was just as great and just as old as that of the Greeks.

After the Roman race was founded by the Trojans and the local Italians, their descendents lived in the general area of central Italy, but did not specifically occupy the area now known as the city of Rome. The legend concerning the founding of the city of Rome is, perhaps, more commonly known than the story of Aeneas, although there has been no great literary epic that addresses this story. It comes from legends, but also has some archeological support.

According to the legend, the area of central Italy was ruled by a series of Latin kings who were descended from Aeneas and Lavinia. The last of these Latin kings had no male children and no grandchildren. Therefore, the kingship was given to another family. The Latin king did, however, have a daughter, Rhea Silvia, who was a Vestal virgin (a priestess of the cult of Vesta) and could not, therefore, have sexual relations. However, Rhea Silvia was raped by the god Mars and she bore twin sons, **Romulus and Remus.** The king who had succeeded the old Latin king ordered that the twins be drowned in the river, because he was afraid that they would eventually become rivals for the throne. Miraculously, they were washed ashore and found by a she-wolf who suckled them until they were later discovered by a shepherd who raised them. (Statues such as Figure 11.2 showing a she-wolf suckling two infant boys are placed throughout the city of Rome today.)

Figure 11.2 ■ Romulus and Remus suckled by a she-wolf as a symbol of Rome. *© 2010 by Andrei Nekrassov. Used under license of Shutterstock, Inc.*

When grown, the twins decided to found a city where they could live in safety. They built the city, with appropriate fortifications, on hills along the banks of the Tiber River. Strife arose between the brothers when Remus mocked the short height of the walls. In the ensuing fight Remus was killed. Romulus then became the first king of the city, which he named Rome, in his own honor.

To encourage population growth, King Romulus allowed all people to live in the city, including escaped slaves, robbers, and misfits. There were few women and so the men of the city looked to the neighboring tribes for brides. There were many women among the neighboring Sabines (a tribe from the hill area not too far from Rome), but the Sabine elders refused to allow their daughters to marry into such a mean and rough group. However, the Sabines did agree to a joint religious festival in Rome; during the festival, the Roman men raped (carried off) the Sabine daughters. The Sabine elders were furious, and returned home to their villages to prepare for war. However, when they returned to Rome to take back their daughters by force, the Sabine elders found that the daughters had reconciled with their

Roman mates and had settled into comfortable domesticity. These Sabine daughters stopped the battle by placing themselves between the attacking Sabine army and the Roman men, a moment depicted in a famous painting by Jacques-Louis David. With this act of interfering bravery, the war was concluded and the Romans and Sabines reconciled and became allies.

Historical and archeological evidence for the legend of the founding of the city of Rome is quite good. A city *was* built on the hills of Rome and dates from the eighth century B.C., which coincides well with the traditional date for the founding of Rome: 753 B.C. Today, you can see a small, very old hut, reputed to be the home of Romulus, nestled among the later Roman ruins on the top of the Palatine Hill in Rome. The hut dates from the appropriate period.

Romulus, the first of the Roman kings, began a period of over 200 years when Rome was ruled by a series of seven kings. This was called the Regal Period. Some of the kings, like Romulus, were from the Latin (Roman) tribe. Others were from the Sabine tribe, and still others were Etruscans, from the north (the current Italian province of Tuscany). This variety of kings shows that during the Regal Period the city of Rome was occasionally ruled by outsiders. Historical evidence is quite strong that the Romans were ruled by other tribes and that the Roman civilization borrowed from the surrounding cultures.

The last king in the Regal Period, Lucius Tarquinius Superbus was a murderer, usurper of the throne, and unbearably oppressive. He was overthrown by the citizens of Rome. Because of the strongly negative impression that this king left on the minds of the Romans, they decided to found a new kind of government—one that would be organized so that no king would ever be able to come to power again. Therefore, in the year 509 B.C., the Romans founded the world's first republic. This has proven to be one of history's most creative tasks. The form of the Roman government did not happen suddenly but, rather, evolved over many years. For simplicity, however, we will focus on the amazing result of this long effort to found a lasting and efficient republican government.

Government

As was the case in so many areas of Roman life, ancient Greece may have been the blueprint Rome used for its government. (The establishment of democratic government in Athens dates from the time of Solon, about 100 years prior to the traditional founding date of the Roman Republic.) Although both Greek (Athenian) and Roman models were based on the principle of rule by the people, the Greek model used direct voting by all the qualified citizens, whereas the Roman model used a series of both direct and representational voting groups. Hence, one is called a democracy and the other is a republic.

Using the Greek system as a model, if indeed the Romans did, and with some time to observe the Greek system, the Romans may have gained clues to avoid some of the problems of the Greeks. For example, the Greeks never had a unified code of laws that applied throughout Greece or, even when Athens had a trading empire, to all of the subservient cities. It is very likely that this lack of legal and governmental order led many of the great philosophers of Greece to deal with the topic of good government. Moreover, the concept of democracy was absolute in Athens, occasionally resulting in decisions that were highly suspect—like the decision to convict Socrates. The Romans might also have observed the unwieldy nature of the Greek system, which required that literally hundreds of people gather together to enact even the most mundane rules of government.

By choosing to adopt the Athenian concept of democracy, Rome was also, it seemed, forcing itself to make another important and difficult choice—a choice between freedom and stability. One of the great factors of democracy was that it allowed all people deemed citizens to have a voice in the government, thus making each man free and independent. However, one difficulty with freedom is that very quickly two people decide that they want to exercise their freedom in contradictory ways, thus leading to conflict. Greece, as it was wont to do, strove for the ideal, and almost always placed the idea of freedom ahead of the idea of peace and stability. Thus, Greek citizens had their freedom, but at the high cost of near constant conflict.

In the end Rome developed a unique system of government that achieved both individual freedom and governmental stability. It was done by combining the rule of the people (freedom) with stability from dividing governmental power among a series of governing institutions with appropriate checks and balances to prevent excessive power in any one of the institutions. The symbol of Rome, SPQR, stands for *"Senatus Populusque Romanum"* ("Senate and People of Rome"), which expresses the sharing of power by both the Senate and the population as a whole. This concept is still represented in modern Rome as illustrated in Figure 11.3. This concept is still represented in modern Rome as illustrated in Figure 11.3.

Stability also came because the Romans recognized that both of the major population groups needed to be represented in the government. These two groups were the land holders, called **patricians,** and everyone else, called **plebians.** (Slaves were not counted in either group.) The plebians (or plebs) consisted of the artisans, merchants, soldiers, tenant farmers, and other common people within Rome. While not as powerful or as wealthy as the patricians, the plebs certainly represented an important economic and cultural group that needed to feel they could affect the direction and policies of the government. This concept of allowing governmental participation to the non-land holders was introduced by the Greeks (chiefly Solon) but was clearly expanded upon in the governmental institutions created by the Romans.

The Romans devised a series of councils, some of which existed at one time and were then merged into others. Some councils were only for patricians, some only for plebs, and some with both patricians and plebs mixed together. These councils had different authorities and different missions, but all contributed to the functioning of the government. The councils could vote on issues and could also name some operating officials, generally called **magistrates,** but given specific names depending on their duties and the council that elected them. Each of the major councils will be examined, with a focus on their composition, their duties, their limitations, and the titles of the magistrates they could elect.

Figure 11.3 ■ **A** and **B)** Ancient Roman insignia (re-created) and a modern manhole cover showing the use of SPQR. *B) © 2010 by StinjtS. Used under license of Shutterstock, Inc.*

- *Senatus*—The Senate was the best known of the councils and probably the most important to the overall operation of the government of Rome. It met in a building in the forum called the curia. The Senate was given control over foreign affairs, that is, anything outside the city of Rome. (Later, this was interpreted to mean outside the area of Italy.) In this capacity, therefore, the Senate appointed governors of the territories outside Rome. The Senate was also directly responsible for the army, since that concerned policies outside the city, but was restricted in being able to authorize a war, as will be discussed later. The Senate nominated and directed the **consuls.** The consuls were the chief executive officers of Rome. Usually there were two consuls, appointed for one-year terms. Each consul could exercise the power of veto (from the Latin word for "I forbid") over the actions of the other. They had no direct responsibilities or powers affecting the day-to-day policies of the city of Rome. Interestingly, the Senate could make no laws. However, the Senate often gave opinions and recommendations, which were usually adopted by the council that had law-making authority. The Senate did have two important rights that gave it tremendous fiscal and emergency power even over the operations within the city. The fiscal power came from its control over the treasury and the dispensing of money. The Senate could also act in emergency situations by appointing a **dictator.** This is a person, originally viewed as an experienced, older senator who was accomplished in speaking (from which the name "dictator" is derived because it means "speaker"). The dictator could assume total control of the government in emergencies; however, the granting of these emergency powers could only be for a specific term of six months, or until the specific emergency ended, whichever came first.
- *Concilium Plebes*—This council, consisting only of plebs, made all the laws of Rome—both those concerning the city of Rome and concerning foreign affairs. In this way, the laws were likely to be consistent throughout the empire (solving one of the problems of the Greeks). Because the laws were made by this Plebian Council, the laws were called **plebecites,** a name still in use in the United States, where it designates laws that are created by direct vote of the populace (as opposed to laws created by the legislature). The Plebian Council elected ten **tribunes**—officials who oversaw the running of the city of Rome. (The name "tribune" comes from the word "tribe" and probably reflected the fact that plebs were originally the people of the ten tribes who lived within the city of Rome, or it may reflect a custom of the plebs, who often arranged themselves according to their tribe when they met.) These tribunes were powerful magistrates, not only because they carried out the day-to-day running of the city, but because the Plebian Council could only consider matters if the tribunes submitted the matters to them formally. That is, the Plebian Council had no authority to raise any topic on its own initiative, but had to wait for the tribunes to bring it up. To limit the power of the tribunes, they were each given veto power; that is, any tribune who disagreed with any law could cancel the law by voting against it. The Plebian Council also elected a large group of administrators. It is instructive to note that the normal meeting place of the Plebian Council was in the Roman Forum (central gathering place of the city) directly in front of the building where the Senate met. That meant that the senators could stand on the front steps of the Senate building and oversee (and influence, at least psychologically) the actions of the Plebian Council.
- *Comitia Senturiata*—This council consisted of both plebs and patricians and was linked to their service as soldiers and as taxpayers. This council was able to commit the military power of Rome, called the *emporium* (from which we get the words "imperial" and "empire"). The *emporium* could be granted for a specific length of time or for a specific purpose (such as to put down a revolt in a particular territory). It

could also be given, and usually was, as a part of an office, such as a governor. The governors needed this power to enforce their decrees. This council also elected major magistrates (consuls, judges, **censors.**) These censors were magistrates who were responsible for guarding the moral values of Rome and for conducting a census of the people, during which they could judge whether a person should be raised from the status of pleb to patrician.

- *Pontifex Maximus*—This was the chief religious official of Rome. He was elected by the patricians, usually as an action of the Senate. His election was for one year and, during that time, he would set the religious calendar, select priests, select vestal virgins, and, if necessary, conduct judicial proceedings against members of the priesthood.

Note that the Romans had a formal separation of government into branches, which could be grouped as executive, legislative, and judicial. While not perfect, the system of multiple councils devised by the practical Romans came close to providing a fair way to allow the voices of rich and poor to be heard. The wealthy patricians chose their consuls to govern the far-flung empire; the poorer plebs elected their tribunes to serve as the local leaders, and over it all was the Senate which, though it was composed of wealthy and aristocratic families, was generally believed to be looking out for the good of the city of Rome. (The root of the word "patrician" is the same as the root of "father" and the people generally thought of the senators as fathers of the city.) For many years, the plebs and their elected tribunes had little real power, because of the economic and psychological power of the Senate. However, the consuls and Senate were wise enough to realize that they could only rule by keeping the masses happy, and therefore wisely relied on the tribunes to keep their fingers on the pulse of the general populace.

The Romans, by electing consuls and tribunes, in essence created the idea of representative government, or a government where the general populace chooses others to represent them in matters of government. Republics are much more practical and realistic in the demands that they place on the citizenry than was the direct democracy of the Greeks. This is a good example of Roman adaptation of a novel Greek idea to make it more practical, if less "perfect."

The Roman government was the model for the government of the United States. Some of the most obvious similarities include the separation of governmental functions into different branches with a system of checks and balances between them, including the veto power, to prevent any branch from overpowering the others. The office of Roman consul was clearly like the U.S. presidency, with the exceptions that two consuls were elected and they were not directly responsible for domestic affairs. The Roman Senate was like the U.S. Senate and the Plebian Council was like the House of Representatives. The granting of *emporium* by a separate entity was preserved in the United States by the requirement that war could only be declared by the Senate, and could not be assumed by the president alone.

When it was initially formed, the focus of the Roman Republic was on protecting itself from the invasions of neighboring tribes. Eventually the Roman population grew large enough and powerful enough that it began to expand the territory that it controlled. This expansion continued until Rome grew to be the most powerful empire that the world has known, and the most long-lived. Let's examine how the Republic accomplished that tremendous feat.

Defense, Conquest, and Expansion

The new Roman Republic seemed to be an easy target for the kings of the tribes surrounding the city of Rome. The Republic had no strong leader and, in the eyes of the tribal kings, that equated directly with weakness and indecision. Therefore, for decades, the major task of the Republic was self-preservation. During this time, some heroes rose to help in the defense of the Republic. These heroes usually illustrated principles valued by the Romans. In this regard, the Roman heroes might be compared to the heroes of early American history, like Paul Revere, John Paul Jones, Davy Crockett, and Francis Marion (the swamp fox).

One of the most interesting of the heroes, named **Horatio,** lived during a time when the Etruscans were attempting to overthrow the Republic. The Roman army had met the Etruscans on the plains outside the city of Rome but was losing the battle and was being driven back toward the city. As the army approached the wooden bridge that was the only way to cross over the Tiber, one of the Roman leaders, Horatio, realized that if the bridge were to be destroyed, the army would be safe behind the river and the fortifications surrounding the Roman hills. Horatio instructed the others in the army to cross over the bridge and begin its destruction. He would stand on the far side of the bridge and hold off the Etruscans. Horatio's bravery impressed a few of the other Roman soldiers, and they joined him in battling the Etruscan advance. Eventually these Roman defenders felt the shaking of the bridge, indicating that the task of destruction was nearly complete, and all but Horatio turned and fled to safety before the bridge collapsed. Horatio stood alone at the bridge, fighting to save Rome. When the bridge finally collapsed, Horatio fell into the water but was miraculously saved by being swept to the Roman shore. Today, a famous saying is that a brave person, who is determined in his defense of a seemingly insurmountable task, is like "Horatio at the bridge."

Another story that teaches the values of the Romans involves three brothers (triplets) of the Roman family **Horatii.** (This incident actually occurred during the Regal Period, but the principle of using heroes to illustrate Roman values is the same.) At this time, Rome had been challenged by a neighboring tribe to a duel of champions and the three Horatii brothers were to fight against another set of triplets from the tribe of the **Curiatii.** The Horatii took an oath that they would defend the city of Rome to the death, an act immortalized in a painting by Jacques-Louis David. The battle between the two sets of brothers was fierce and two of the Horatii were killed. However, the remaining brother was able to escape and, while the Curiatii were chasing him, the Curiatii became separated and the remaining Horatii was able to kill all of the Curiatii, one at a time. He then returned home as a hero. However, when he went to his home and told his family about the events, one of his sisters became distraught. He asked her why, and she indicated that she was crying for one of the dead Curiatii, to whom she was betrothed. The last of the Horatii brothers went over to her, drew his sword and slew her, with the comment that no Roman woman should grieve for a slain foe of Rome. Again, the moral lesson is that Rome and her interests come before personal interests.

As Rome matured, the government realized the importance of a strong military, and began to creatively reorganize their method of conducting war. They had previously fought first as tribal units, generally without detailed plans or organized groups. These units were, in most senses, relatively small groups of chaotic warriors who won because of personal courage and determination. In this method the Romans were like the tribes who surrounded them and, to a large degree, like most other tribal societies throughout history.

Eventually the Romans learned of the disciplined army of the Greeks and how larger armies, like those of the Persians, had been defeated through the organization and formation of the Greek phalanxes. This organization appealed to Roman practicality, but the Greek system had some problems for the Romans. The first problem was the difficulty of fighting with phalanxes in the hilly and confined terrain of central Italy. The phalanxes were large units that proved to be unwieldy for the Roman conditions. The second problem was the method of command. Phalanxes worked best when directed from afar, that is, from a central command that could see the overall battlefield and direct the movement of the phalanxes accordingly. This, however, was difficult in confined areas and, furthermore, removed the responsiveness that the Romans were accustomed to when fighting as tribes.

Therefore, the Romans created an organization that used the best of the tribal and Greek systems. The tribal concept was preserved by forming, as the smallest unit of the Roman army, *centuries*. Each century, consisting of a hundred men, was headed by a **centurion,** an experienced fighter who had come up through the ranks and had shown great personal bravery and dedication to Roman values. Hence, the centuries preserved the flexibility and emphasis of personal courage that were characteristic of the tribal fighting units.

The next larger unit of the Roman army was called a **maniple** (from the root of a "hand full"). The maniples were heavily armed units of two or three centuries, about half as large as a phalanx and therefore much more maneuverable; each had a unit commander (called a **military tribune**) who was given much more authority than any leader of a similar size unit in the Greek army (or any other highly structured army). The title "tribune," like the office elected by the Plebian Council, probably came from its association with tribes. In the military case, the maniples may have been thought of as a collection of tribes, and may have originally been organized by tribe, hence the use of the tribune name.

The Romans then combined groups of maniples, together with supporting light cavalry, into what the Romans called a **legion** (from the root word for "chosen"). Legions were typically about 6,000 men total. The units within the legions could act jointly, as would be required in overall battle plans, but the Roman system still allowed for some command judgment at the maniple level. This proved to be very successful, for instance, when the Romans fought the Greeks.

The story is told of a battle in which the Romans and the Greeks were assembling themselves early in the morning in anticipation of the day's fighting. One of the Roman maniples was especially quick in getting into their assigned position and, when they arrived at the appointed place, the tribune heading the maniple noted that the Greeks were still trying to assemble themselves into a phalanx. In the midst of the hurrying around and general confusion of this pre-organized stage of the Greek formation, the Roman tribune gave the order to attack. He had no higher authority to do so, and would have been severely reprimanded in any other army (if the army would have even had a commander at that level), but in the Roman army he was empowered to act on his own best judgment. The Roman maniple devastated the ill-prepared phalanx and created a severe weakness in the line of Greek defense, which the Roman generals, who headed the legion, were able to exploit for an easy victory. In essence, the Romans combined the unity of the Greeks with the flexibility of the tribes. The current American army has sought to have these same characteristics by giving commanders of small units the same type of empowerment that the Roman tribunes practiced so well.

The Roman soldiers were renowned for their bravery and determination. Undoubtedly those traits came from their acceptance of the values of the Roman people, but the army leaders had other methods to ensure that bravery and obedience were maintained. If a soldier were ever to show gross cowardice or disobedience, such as by running away in the midst of a battle, that person would be punished by being beaten to death by his comrades in arms. The reasoning was that the act of cowardice or disobedience most endangered his comrades and so they should be the ones to exact punishment.

If an entire unit showed cowardice or disobedience, a different system of punishment was used. In this case, the unit would be lined up and then a military commander would walk along the row and choose every tenth man to be executed, usually on the spot. This procedure was called "decimation," from the root word for one-tenth.

Through great courage, dogged determination, superior military organization, and perhaps fear, Rome eventually became strong enough that when neighboring tribes, such as the Etruscans, fought the Romans, the Romans were able to conquer them and occupy their territory. In the minds of the Romans, they never conquered a territory through desire for expansion; rather, they viewed the expansion as a way to defend themselves. This view held throughout the entire history of the Roman Republic and the Roman Empire. From the perspective of the citizens of Rome, they never fought a war of aggression.

This territorial expansion presented the Roman citizens with an interesting problem, which they solved in one of the most creative political decisions ever made and one that proved to be extremely important to the long-term stability and strength of the Roman state. The problem had to do with the rights of the people in the newly conquered territories. To what extent should Rome extend the rights of Roman citizenship to these conquered people, and under what conditions might those rights change? Until the Roman time, and for many years later in other societies, the conquered people had no rights. They might be enslaved or, at the least, they might be allowed to stay in place but were subjected to arbitrary laws and rulings from the conquerors. Only the Romans tried a different system.

The Romans decided that conquered people could earn full Roman citizenship. This citizenship carried certain privileges, so enticing that the conquered people were highly motivated to fulfill the requirements for gaining that citizenship. For example, Roman citizens paid no taxes. Also, any Roman citizen convicted of a crime in any court in the Roman Empire had the right to appeal his conviction directly to the head of the Roman state, which was a consul in the days of the Republic and later was the emperor. (Remember that in Acts 25:10 Paul, a citizen of Rome, appealed to Caesar following the judgment of Felix, which Paul believed to be in error.) Roman citizens could, of course, also vote to determine the nature of the government. Rights of land ownership and economic benefit also followed citizenship.

The conquered people were told that when they had demonstrated loyalty to Rome and exhibited the values that Rome esteemed, then their case could be reviewed and they could be granted citizenship. To further motivate the conquered people, the Romans often granted citizenship to the leaders of these people immediately after occupying the territory. This act was seen as benevolent; it also assured the loyalty of the leaders while letting people see the value of Roman citizenship and suggesting a pattern for them to follow. A further advantage was that other peoples, not yet conquered by the Romans, could see the advantages of working with the Romans rather than against them, thus lowering some of the barriers to joining with the Romans. Eventually, all of the people throughout the entire Italian peninsula were granted Roman citizenship.

The value of this system can be seen in the story of the invasion of Italy by **King Pyrrhus,** a Greek monarch intent on expansion during the time when Rome was still just consolidating its control over all of Italy. King Pyrrhus' army invaded Italy and, when met by the Roman army, proved to be so superior in size that it was able to defeat the Romans after a long and difficult campaign that lasted for all of the summer and early fall. When winter came, the Roman army withdrew and the Greeks settled into a winter camp. Because of his devastation of the Roman army, King Pyrrhus anticipated that in the spring he would be able to march easily into the city of Rome and assume control over all the Roman-held territory. However, when spring arrived, King Pyrrhus was surprised to find he was confronted by a new Roman army—larger than the one he had fought the previous year. There followed a series of costly battles that, again, lasted from spring into the fall. King Pyrrhus was again able to defeat the Romans, who withdrew from the battlefield. Due to the lateness of the season, King Pyrrhus again established a winter camp, with the expectation that he would easily occupy Rome the following year. He was even more confident this time, because he was sure that the Roman population was not sufficient to supply another army. However, in the spring a new Roman army entered the battlefield. For a third time the Greek army fought costly battles but emerged triumphant. By this time, however, the Greek army was severely depleted and, although victorious, King Pyrrhus sailed home to Greece. He could not be sure whether another Roman army would confront him the next spring. In the end, the victories proved to be too costly for King Pyrrhus. Even today, a victory that costs more than it is worth is called a "pyrrhic victory."

You might ask, "How were the Romans able to find enough troops to mount so many armies against King Pyrrhus?" The answer is that the armies were not just Romans. They were augmented by troops from the conquered Italian territories who saw service in the Roman army as a way to gain Roman citizenship. Even those who had already become Roman citizens were told that if they were successful, they would be granted land, which might allow them to move from the ranks of the plebs into the class of patricians. The granting of land to soldiers proved to be even more important as the Romans began to expand outside Italy, where choice new land came under Roman control and, therefore, was an incentive to Roman soldiers desiring to move socially and economically upward.

The **Punic Wars** were the first expansion of Rome outside the Italian peninsula. These wars were dictated indirectly by economics—the Romans felt the need to increase trade—but the immediate cause of the conflict was because of Roman protection of cities within its broad area of influence (but not control). The city in question was Messana, a port in Sicily which is just off the coast of the Italian peninsula. The people of Messana, who were controlled by the Carthaginians, revolted against their rulers and sought Roman support in their revolt. Carthage was a very old and large city on the northern coast of Africa near present-day Tunis. It was established over 700 years previously, by the Phoenicians, a sea people from Mesopotamia. The Carthaginians controlled a large trading empire along the entire northern coast of Africa, into southern Spain and southern France, and covered the islands of Corsica, Sardinia, and Sicily. That Carthaginian Empire would inhibit Roman attempts to increase their own trade.

At this time Rome was a rising star, a prosperous and growing city on the Italian peninsula, that had united Italy, and a likely heir to the power and glory of Greece. However, before Rome was able to fill the vacuum of power left by a crumbling Greek empire, it had to deal with Carthage. Both cities envisioned themselves as the future power in the region, and realized that the key to Mediterranean (and possibly world) dominance was the elimination of the other, and it was this conflict between Rome and Carthage that allowed the various decaying Greek empires to retain their power for another two hundred years. War between Rome and Carthage was inevitable. Eventually, three wars would be fought between these two cities. They are called the Punic Wars after the Latin name for the Carthaginians, *poeni,* which reflects their origin in Phoenicia.

When the Carthaginians attempted to subdue the rebellion in Messana, Rome met them. Early in the conflict Carthage had the upper hand and was able to use its far superior navy to help land troops and defeat the Romans in a series of small skirmishes and minor battles. Rome realized that to win they would have to build an effective navy, and they used a captured Carthaginian ship as a model. They then improved upon the Carthaginian model by adding a spiked gangplank to their ships, which allowed the Roman ships to grapple opposing ships and to send Roman legionnaires from the Roman boat to that of the enemy. Rome built many ships using this model and became an equal naval rival of the Carthaginians and winner of the First Punic War.

However, while Rome was working to improve its navy, the Carthaginians were developing a stronger army under the direction of their famous general, **Hannibal.** Hannibal decided that crossing the Mediterranean Sea and attacking Rome from the south was a poor idea, as that would be what the Romans were expecting. In order to gain the element of surprise over the Romans, Hannibal decided to march his troops over the Alps and down the Italian peninsula, attacking an unsuspecting Rome from the north. He assembled a great army in Spain, complete with reinforcement troops from Africa and including African elephants as beasts of burden and attack vehicles. Hannibal's army marched over the Pyrenees Mountains in northern Spain and then continued over the Alps into northern Italy. A map showing Hannibal's movements is shown in Figure 11.4.

Hannibal entered Italy and fought a series of battles within Italy over several years. He was able to fight and defeat most of the Roman armies sent out to confront him, but he did not feel that his army was large enough to attack the city of Rome directly. Hannibal's plan was to recruit additional soldiers from the many conquered peoples within Italy. He assumed that these people hated the

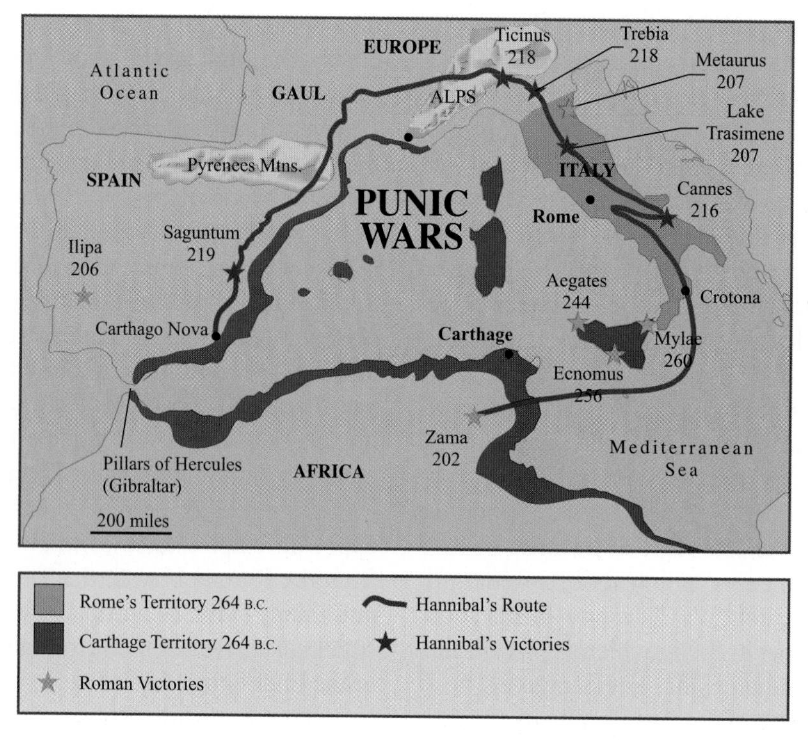

Figure 11.4 ■ *Map of the Punic Wars.*

Romans and would be anxious to overthrow them. However, Hannibal did not understand the Roman system of citizenship. He was never able to entice a large number of recruits and, therefore, was forced to wander the Italian countryside, harassed by the Roman armies.

Eventually, the Romans changed their generals, getting rid of those who were unable to defeat Hannibal, and bringing in new generals who took a fresh approach to the war. These new generals left just enough soldiers in Italy to continue the pressure on Hannibal, loaded the bulk of their army onto ships, and left to attack a virtually undefended Carthage. Upon hearing this, Hannibal gave up his intent to attack Rome and fled home to defend his own city. Hannibal arrived in time to give the Romans battle, but the exhausted and depleted Carthaginian army was unable to defeat the Roman legions and lost the deciding battle in 201 B.C. to the Roman general Scipio Africanus. Thus ended the Second Punic War.

Carthage was beaten but not defeated, and by 150 B.C. had gained sufficient strength to once again initiate hostilities with Rome. The Romans, however, were able to again defeat their ambitious southern neighbors; this time they decided to rid themselves of the Carthaginians forever. After defeating the Carthaginian army, the Roman legions marched to Carthage itself and, in 146 B.C., tore down its walls, destroyed the city.

Finally freed of the troublesome Carthaginians, Rome turned its attention toward the decayed Greek Empire. By the end of the second century before Christ, Rome had conquered Greece and many of the territories that had been ruled by Greek kings following Alexander. (Some of the minor Greek kings voluntarily surrendered because they felt that the Roman occupation was inevitable and, besides, they did not like the kings who were their overseers.)

The Greeks, however, may have had the last laugh because, during the two centuries between the death of Alexander and the Roman conquest of Greece, generation upon generation of peoples had been exposed to and accepted Greek culture and thought. So, while the new masters may have been from Rome, the culture of the empire remained Greek. As the Roman poet Horace said, "The captive Greeks got their revenge by captivating their conquerors."

After conquering Greece, the Romans continued around the Mediterranean coast and subdued all of the territories that had previously been conquered by Alexander. In one of those territories, Parthia, an interesting method of battle gave rise to a phrase that is still used in English. The Parthians used cavalry as an important part of their military system. Their cavalry, who were armed with bows and arrows, attacked the Roman army and then, after the Romans had resisted and largely overcome the attack, the Parthian cavalry retreated. The Roman cavalry, which supported the army, pursued the Parthians, but suddenly the Parthians turned in their saddles and launched one last volley of arrows into the midst of the pursuing Romans. This last volley was called a "Parthian shot" and has since then been applied to a situation where someone has been in the midst of an argument and then gives up. However, just as the person is leaving the room, they turn and hurl back a mean-spirited comment, and then quickly depart.

■ Decay of the Republic

The Romans had succeeded in building an empire. But it was not governed like an empire. The government in Italy was still based on the republican model. The Roman occupiers were less generous in offering Roman citizenship to these conquered territories outside Italy, but the treatment of these newly conquered territories was generally quite benign. The Romans wanted to control trade, receive taxes, and protect the territory from outside attacks. For most people, inclusion in the Roman Empire was not too disagreeable, and may have been substantially better than it was under the Greeks.

Back in the city of Rome, some problems began to surface concerning different approaches to the ever-increasing plebian population. Some of the patricians believed that the plebs should be given more control, as would befit their increasing numbers. This faction became known as the *Populares.* Others believed that the old rules and governmental structures were important to maintain, especially because those structures reflected the values of the Roman people as, in their opinion, they ought to be. Those values included: piety, bravery, discipline, frugality, absence of greed, never fighting wars of aggression, and never quitting in the face of adversity. This second faction was called the *Optimates.* From this time onward, these two factions would struggle for control over the Senate and the other institutions of the Roman Republic.

Around the year 130 B.C., two brothers entered the scene of Roman power. The oldest, **Tiberius Gracchus,** was angered when some treaties he had negotiated as governor in Spain were rejected by the Senate. This was, of course, greatly embarrassing for Tiberius and he attempted to overrule the Senate by becoming a tribune and then taking the treaty approval directly to the Plebian Council without first consulting the Senate. (The Senate should have considered the items first because they concerned foreign territories—the area of Senate responsibility.) However, upon the advice of Tiberius' enemies in the Senate, one of the other tribunes vetoed the measures during the meeting of the Plebian Council. Tiberius was incensed and submitted the measures again for a Plebian Council vote. When they were again defeated, Tiberius removed the other tribune by force. This unprecedented move brought violence into the Roman government, setting a precedent that would haunt the Roman people. When Tiberius sought an unprecedented second term as tribune, he was assassinated in the street.

However, the involvement of the Gracchus family was not over. Tiberius' younger brother, **Gaius,** blamed the *Optimates* for his brother's death and began a campaign of revenge. He succeeded in being elected tribune and then, from that power position, he initiated many laws that decreased the power of the Senate. Gaius forced the passage of these laws by threatening the other tribunes. Eventually, Gaius and 3,000 of his supporters were killed during a riot in the forum protesting his oppressive methods.

The Gracchus brothers were followed by another powerful leader, **Marius,** who was elected consul, in part, to solve the problem of a revolt in Africa. He then asked the Plebian Council, where he had strong support, to also appoint him commander of the army in Africa. This broke precedent because the appointment of a general in a foreign territory was the prerogative of the Senate. Nevertheless, the Plebian Council acceded to Marius' request and he was authorized to raise an army for the African campaign. Then Marius personally offered those who would join his new army riches and land in the conquered territories. Again, the granting of foreign land to soldiers as a reward for good service had always been the prerogative of the Senate. The result of Marius' action was, for the first time, a professional army and, moreover, an army that was beholden directly to their general.

Marius took his army to Africa and was successful. Then, just as he was completing the African campaign, trouble broke out on the northern border of the empire when the Germans attacked. Marius rushed to Rome and volunteered to go to Germany with his army. He insisted, however, on being elected consul for a second year, another unprecedented occurrence. However, the Senate panicked at the German attack, and complied. Because of continuing military difficulties around the empire and his gaining military strength, Marius was elected consul for a third time.

Eventually Marius made some political decisions that were so hated by the Senate that he was forced into exile. He attempted a return and was partially successful in gaining support, but was then exiled a second time. He returned yet again with an army and was made consul, but died shortly thereafter, probably of old age.

During the time of the exile of Marius, another powerful leader, **Sulla,** gained control. Whereas the Gracchus brothers and Marius were *Populares,* Sulla was the leader of the *Optimates.* Sulla pointed out the threat from Marius and, therefore, asked the Senate to appoint him dictator, which they did. However, he continued the dictatorship beyond the six-month limit, thus breaking another of the old precedents. Sulla also initiated a powerful and very destructive tool against his enemies. This tool was a "proscription list," in which he listed the names of his enemies and promised that whoever killed the people on the list would be rewarded with the land of the person they had killed. This list obviously threw fear into the hearts of all those on the list, and rightfully so, as several thousand people were killed during Sulla's regime. After Sulla had made the changes he felt were necessary in government, he resigned and then died of natural causes a year later.

Following Sulla's resignation, a power vacuum invited several people into active politics. One of those, **Cataline,** attempted to become consul but was defeated by the great **Cicero,** a powerful leader of the *Optimates.* It was at this time that **Cato,** a leader of the Senate, gave his resounding condemnation of Cataline that was quoted at the beginning of this chapter. Unwilling to accept defeat, Cataline attempted to influence the Senate to overthrow Cicero and then, when that attempt failed, Cataline tried to stage a violent overthrow of the government. He was overcome, and fled from Rome. Eventually he was arrested and killed, along with the other conspirators. Cicero was criticized for his handling of the conspiracy, especially because his rapid execution of the conspirators was said to have denied them some basic rights. **Julius Caesar** was one of those who spoke against Cicero. Caesar advocated moderation. The opposition of Caesar to Cicero was not surprising, as Caesar was a member of the *Populares* and Cicero was of the *Optimates.*

Clearly the Roman Republic was in a state of turmoil. The Senate was deeply divided, consuls had abused their office, the position of tribune had been corrupted, force had been employed to exert a person's will, and the entire checks-and-balance system seemed to have disappeared. But many senators yearned for a return to the founding values and systems of the Republic. These senators gathered their strengths together and struck a blow against what they saw as the final act of erosion of the Republic—the possibility of the reestablishment of a king. They remembered the stories told of the evils of the old kings, and how the Romans of the past had created the Republic with all its checks and balances just so that a king would never rise again. The threat of having a king was just too much for them to bear; they acted upon it on the Ides of March, 44 B.C. The person they acted upon was, of course, Julius Caesar. The people of Rome disagreed with their action and, ultimately, the conspirators paid with their lives for what they did. But, to really understand the situation surrounding their action, we need to trace the rise of Julius Caesar and then examine the circumstances in Rome that surrounded their fateful act.

Julius Caesar

The early life of Julius Caesar was not particularly outstanding. He was born (by caesarian section, a medical procedure named in his honor) into a noble family and followed the normal path of training in both the military and government that was typical of other young Roman patricians. One unusual experience in his youth occurred, however, when Caesar was on a ship that was attacked by pirates and Caesar was captured. The pirates decided to hold him for ransom. When Caesar found out the amount of ransom the pirates requested, he laughed and told them that he was worth much more than they were asking. The pirates then upped their request and, because Caesar's family was quite wealthy, the increased ransom was paid. Caesar was released and returned to Rome. There he decided to exact justice for what had happened. He assembled a crew for a ship with a contingent of soldiers and then sailed in search of the pirates. When Caesar finally found the pirates, he killed them all (by crucifixion).

Another interesting event that tells us about the personality of Caesar occurred in Spain, where he had been appointed to be a minor official. There he encountered a statue to Alexander the Great that seemed to deeply affect Caesar, in part, because Caesar was, at that moment, about the same age as Alexander when Alexander had realized so much success. Caesar noted that Alexander had conquered the known world but that he, Caesar, had accomplished very little. Caesar resolved to change his life and pattern it after the model of Alexander. Caesar immediately set about to learn military strategy, to understand the subtleties of government, and to make the personal connections that would allow him to rise in the ranks of Roman government.

When Caesar's Spanish appointment was concluded, he returned to Rome, where he participated in the actions of the *Populares* and became active in the work of the Senate. He was opposed by the current *Optimates* who were led by Cicero and Cato the younger. These two were critics of Caesar throughout their lives.

In keeping with the concept of the *Populares* that the plebs should have more power, Caesar had a bill introduced to the Plebian Council without first seeking Senate approval and comment. (Remember that the Senate could make no laws, but commented on all laws so that the Plebian Council could assess the will of the Senate.) This particular proposal would give the Plebian Council authority to appoint the Chief Magistrate of the city without Senate consultation. The bill was passed and, not coincidentally, Caesar was elected as Chief Magistrate. He did many things to favor the plebs and became very popular with them. That popularity led to his appointment as governor of a major area in Spain.

When Caesar arrived in Spain, a rebellion was underway. Caesar took personal interest in leading the army in restoring order. He worked hard at becoming a good administrator and military commander, becoming popular with both the people and the army. He devised the concept of supporting each century in the army with a contingent of engineers, thus enabling each of these small units greater capability in making decisions about crossing rivers, besieging a town, or erecting a defensive wall. When not actively engaged in warfare, Caesar kept the engineers sharp by using them to build fortifications for his various military bases, and also built structures that would help the Spanish population, such as aqueducts, roads, and bridges.

When his appointment as governor in Spain was over, Caesar returned to Rome with much honor. There he forged an alliance with the wealthy and powerful **Crassus** and used Crassus' money to bribe officials to get favors for himself and his friends. (Crassus gained his wealth by organizing Rome's only fire department and then exacting payments from homeowners and businessmen for membership in the group that would be protected by the fire department. If the payments were not made, "accidental" fires would sometimes occur in those non-member structures and, because they were not members, no firefighting unit would respond. Needless to say, most people joined. These strong-arm tactics of Crassus have been remembered in the English word "crass," which denotes a grossness of mind and a non-caring attitude.)

Crassus had also gained some credibility as the leader of the Roman army that defeated the slave revolt led by **Spartacus.** In that effort, Crassus used decimation of the army to "encourage" them to work harder in their pursuit of Spartacus. When Spartacus was finally captured, Crassus commanded that the surviving slaves (followers of Spartacus) be crucified. As a reward, Crassus was elected consul in 70 B.C. His companion consul was **Pompey,** a highly competent and popular general who had gained great fame in Asia Minor and Syria.

In 63 B.C. Cicero, the leader of the party to which Caesar was opposed, was elected consul but, in an interesting show of strength, Caesar was elected *Pontifex Maximus,* religious leader of Rome. During this year Pompey seized Jerusalem as part of his continuing conquests in the East, and Cicero had to put down the Cataline revolt, which we have already discussed and about which we have the quotation at the beginning of the chapter. There were clearly problems for Cicero and the other *Optimates.*

In 60 B.C., Caesar and Crassus united with Pompey in what has become known as the **triumvirate.** To cement their relationship, Caesar married one of Pompey's relatives and Pompey married Caesar's daughter (who was much younger than Pompey). Together, the triumvirate proved to be very powerful. In 59 B.C. Caesar was elected consul, with the support of Crassus and Pompey. These three, together, ruled Rome, although the triumvirate was strictly unofficial, since both Crassus and Pompey had already served as consul, and re-election to another term was still forbidden (although some dictators like Sulla had done so, but only at the great displeasure of the Roman Senate and people). Over the year of Caesar's consulate and even later, the triumvirate was successful in reducing the influence of their enemies in the Senate. Cicero was exiled and Cato was sent to Asia on an appointment that he could not refuse.

Caesar realized that to really gain power he would have to have the loyalty of an army, much like Pompey, who still had the Asian army at his disposal. Therefore, when his year as consul was over, Caesar had himself appointed governor of Gaul (known today as France) with full power to conduct war in that territory. Caesar stayed in Gaul for nine years, expanding the territory to include portions of Germany and Britain. He also established a highly workable administrative infrastructure. As before, he used engineers to build both military and civilian structures, thus winning the support of both the army and the people.

Crassus also sought additional power by gaining the control of an army in the wars against the Parthians in the East. However, Crassus was captured by the Parthians and killed (supposedly by pouring gold down his throat).

Upon the death of Crassus, and with Caesar in Gaul, Pompey began a move to gain total power for himself. In 52 B.C., Pompey had himself again elected consul. Caesar was very apprehensive and became convinced that Pompey would become a tyrant of the type seen earlier (that is, Marius, Sulla, etc.). Therefore, in 49 B.C., Caesar decided to take his army in Gaul and march on Rome to depose Pompey from power. At the **Rubicon River** in northern Italy, Caesar was faced with a difficult decision. Roman tradition and action of the Senate said that no general could enter Italy with his army, thus suggesting that if anyone did, it would be viewed as rebellion. On the banks of the Rubicon, Caesar contemplated this situation, but reported that he saw a vision of a giant who sounded a trumpet and then went across the river and beckoned to Caesar. Seeing this, Caesar remarked, "The die is cast," and then plunged ahead with his army into the territory of Italy. Thereafter, when someone makes a decision that is irrevocable, as was Caesar's, the decision is called "crossing the Rubicon."

Civil war between Caesar and Pompey ensued. Caesar was elected dictator and consul during this time—reflecting the popularity of Caesar and the skill of his friends in the Senate, such as **Mark Anthony.** After four years of battles in Italy, Spain, Greece, and Africa, and successive appointments of Caesar as consul and dictator, Pompey was finally killed in Egypt by the king of Egypt, **Ptolemy XIII,** who was the brother and husband of **Cleopatra VII,** his nominal co-ruler (although the two were bitter rivals). When Caesar entered Egypt four days later in pursuit of Pompey, Pompey's head was presented to Caesar. The Roman civil war was over.

Caesar desired to take over control of Egypt, the last of the Greek states not assumed under the control of Rome. He therefore asked Ptolemy to meet with him in the palace and discuss the relationship between Egypt and Rome. Cleopatra was also invited, but she feared to openly enter the palace (she had been hiding in another location for several months). She therefore rolled herself inside an oriental rug and was carried into the palace. When in Caesar's presence, the rug was unrolled and she presented herself to Caesar. The story is that their love affair began that night. A brief war between the two Egyptian factions ensued, with Rome supporting Cleopatra; in the end, Ptolemy was killed and Rome took control over Egypt, with Cleopatra remaining as ruler under Roman authority. (Because of Egyptian rules against a woman ruling alone, she was married to her younger brother, Ptolemy XIV, but that was for show only.)

When Caesar finally returned to Rome, he staged the biggest celebration the city had ever seen. Caesar was honored for his triumphs in Gaul, Greece, Asia, and Egypt. Unquestionably he was the sole ruler of Rome and the most popular and powerful leader ever.

He proved to be an excellent administrator. He enlarged the membership of the Senate from 600 to 900, thus diluting the power of the *Optimates* and increasing his own power, since he was able to name many of those who were appointed. In keeping with his desire to give more power to the plebs, he shifted several decisions from the Senate to the Plebian Council. He redistributed state-owned land in Italy (mostly to plebs, who then became patricians) and provided work projects for plebs. He also improved housing conditions, eliminated usury, and reduced corruption in government—all actions that increased the power of the plebs. He even changed the calendar from 355 days in a year to 365 1/4, and reorganized the months. He renamed some of the months, like July, which was named for himself, but did not rename others. For that reason, we have September, October, November, and December (which mean seventh, eighth, ninth, and tenth months) occurring as the ninth, tenth, eleventh and twelfth months, respectively. There is little doubt why he was again elected consul and also dictator, this time for life.

Caesar must have felt great honor at being named ruler of Rome for life. But something inside him yearned for more. Perhaps it was his youthful desire to become like Alexander. Militarily, Caesar had equaled Alexander, but, as yet, Caesar had not been crowned king or emperor as had Alexander. Therefore, one day, Caesar went to the Forum where he routinely spoke with the citizens. On this occasion, Caesar had his chief assistant, Mark Anthony, openly offer Caesar a crown. Caesar turned to the crowd and asked them what they thought. To Caesar's apparent surprise, the crowd reacted negatively. Cleverly, Caesar then turned to Mark Anthony and refused the crown. The desire to be a king must have still been strong in Caesar's life because a few weeks later, as Caesar met with the citizens, Caesar again had Mark Anthony offer him a crown. The reaction of the citizens was, again, negative. Evidently the traditions against kings were so strong that they prevailed over even Caesar's popularity. Sorely disappointed, Caesar never again attempted to receive a crown.

Those who opposed Caesar noted the drama and, fearful that Caesar would try some other method to become a king, resolved to take action. They saw Caesar as a person who was strongly leading Rome away from the traditions of the past. Caesar was obviously and unalterably in favor of increasing the power of the plebs and decreasing the power of the patricians. The Optimates faction also saw Caesar as one more in the line of rulers who flaunted the system of checks and balances. Perhaps they also saw an erosion of the old value system. In essence, they saw Caesar as the vehicle that would ultimately bring an end to the Roman Republic. (In this they were correct, but not exactly as they supposed.)

Therefore, on March 15, 44 B.C., a group of twenty opposing Senators, including Caesar's illegitimate son, Brutus, took concerted action against Caesar. They assassinated him inside the Senate chamber. Seeking the approval of their act from the Roman population, they spoke to the people and explained why they had done it. However, they allowed Caesar's closest ally, Mark Anthony, to also address the people and, after both speeches, the people's love for Caesar held sway and the conspirators were condemned. A civil war ensued, with the conspirators on one side and Mark Anthony and Caesar's heir, ***Octavian,*** on the other.

After a few years, Mark Anthony and Octavian successfully defeated the conspirators and began to rule Rome together. Then, probably in part because of his affair with Cleopatra, Mark Anthony lost the support of the Roman public and of Octavian. Another war ensued and Mark Anthony was forced to commit suicide in Egypt. Cleopatra also took her own life. Octavian then returned to Rome as the sole leader. However, as we will see in the next chapter, Octavian wanted to reform the often chaotic pattern that had prevailed for over a hundred years. He created a new system that lasted, in some modified forms, for another 500 years. That new system we call the Roman Empire.

Summary

The Roman Republic not only gained the great empire but also established the government and principles on which the Roman Empire was to be launched. These same governmental forms and principles were later adopted by other countries, including the United States. Combined with personal values of loyalty and duty, the Roman army and citizens were a powerful force in politics, war, and commerce.

The creativity of the Romans was demonstrated in their uncanny ability to foresee the consequences of their actions. They were both ruthless and kind to those they conquered. This combination was administered cleverly to unite the people of Italy within their sphere and then to gather the remainder of the civilized world into the empire. Sadly, the Roman Republic was not able to perpetuate itself, mostly because of its lack of desire to truly enforce the principles of government that were the basis of the state. The people feared the power of a single ruler, but in the end, were undone by men who gained the power that was so strongly avoided at the beginning.

Timeline—Important Dates

Date	Event
1100 B.C.	*Legendary founding of the Roman people by Aeneas*
753 B.C.	*Founding of the city of Rome by Romulus (and Remus)*
753–509 B.C.	*Regal period (7 kings)*
509 B.C.	*Founding of the Roman Republic*
264–146 B.C.	*The three Punic Wars*
146 B.C.	*Rome completes its conquest of Greece*
130 B.C.	*Gracchus brothers defy Roman rules of government*
105 B.C.	*Marius rules Rome*
86 B.C.	*Sulla rules Rome*
60 B.C.	*The triumvirate rules Rome*
44 B.C.	*Death of Caesar*

31 B.C.	*Battle of Actium (defeat of the conspirators against Caesar)*
30 B.C.	*Death of Mark Anthony and rule by Octavian*

Suggested Readings

Keyes, Clinton W. (trans.), *Cicero: Volume XVI~De Republica,* Loeb Classical Library, Vol. 273, Harvard University Press, 1928.

Lewis, C. Day (trans.), *Aeneid,* SLL/Sterling Lord Literistic, Inc., 1953.

Van Doren, Charles, *A History of Knowledge,* Ballantine Books, 1991.

Article 20

Virgil: The Aeneid

Introduction

Virgil was a Roman poet who wrote a book that defined Roman values, the *Aenid,* much as the *Iliad* and the *Odyssey* defined Greek values. Virgil lived during the time of Julius Caesar and Augustus Caesar and was a personal friend of Augustus who was instrumental in publishing the *Aenid.* Virgil also wrote works about farming life and the beauties of nature which reflected his choice to live his life in the quiet countryside as a farmer.

Virgil probably felt that the Roman state, which had expanded to encompass the entire Mediterranean region by the time Virgil was born, needed a historical past that was as glorious as that of the Greeks whom they had conquered. The *Aenid* gives Rome that history. It is the story of a prince of Troy, Aeneas, who is led by the gods to found the race of Roman people. Aeneas leaves Troy as it is being sacked by the Greeks, carrying his father on his shoulders and leading his son by the hand, and then assembles a fleet of Trojan survivors that sails throughout the Mediterranean area encountering many trials and adventures. It is, in this regard, much like the *Odyssey.* Eventually Aeneas reaches the Latinian region that became known as Rome where he battles some of the tribes and eventually marries the princess of the Latiums, thus founding the Roman race. These battles prove his abilities and values, much as the Greeks proved in the *Iliad.* Hence, the *Aenid* combines concepts from both the *Odyssey* and the *Iliad.* It also contains a section in which Aeneas visits the underworld and there he encounters people who have died and also people not yet been born, among them Augustus Caesar. These are identified to him as being noble and great.

The *Aenid* became an immediate classic and remained such throughout the Middle Ages. Dante used the *Aenid* as inspiration, even going so far as to have Virgil serve as the guide through much of his work, *The Divine Comedy.* Many others have been strongly influenced by Virgil's *Aenid,* including Chaucer, Tennyson, and Milton.

The readings tell the story of Aeneas' leaving Troy and encountering trouble because some of the gods are supporters of the Greeks and resent that other gods are favoring Aeneas. Later we read of his affair with Dido, the queen of Carthage. Note in particular Dido's poignant feelings when Aeneas must break off their relationship because the gods tell him he must continue his journey toward Italy. Finally, we read of the future of Rome as seen by Aeneas in his journey to the underworld. Clearly the glories of the days of Augustus Caesar are anticipated.

The Aenid

[The gods determine the fate of Aeneas, a Trojan who sails with other Trojan survivors toward Latinium, his land of destiny.]

I tell about war and the hero who first from Troy's frontier,
Displaced by destiny, came to the Latinian shores,
To Italy—a man much travailed on sea and land
By the powers above, because of the brooding anger of Juno
Suffering much in war until he could found a city
And march his gods into Latium, whence rose the Latin race,
The royal line of Alba and the high walls of Rome.
Where lay the cause of it all? How was her godhead injured?
What grievance made the queen of heaven so harry a man
Renowned for piety, through such toils, such a cycle of calamity? 10
Can a divine being be so persevering in anger?
There was a town of old—men from Tyre colonized it—
Over against Italy and Tiber mouth, but afar off,
Carthage, rich in resources, fiercely efficient in warfare.
This town, they say, was Juno's favorite dwelling, preferred
To all lands, even Samos: here were her arms, her chariot:
And even from the long-ago time she cherished the aim that this
Should be, if fate allowed, the metropolis of all nations.
Nevertheless, she had heard a future race was forming
Of Trojan blood, which one day would topple that Tyrian stronghold— 20
A people arrogant in war, born to be everywhere rulers
And root up her Libyan empire—so the Destiny-Spinners planned.
Juno, afraid of this, and remembering well the old war
Wherein she had championed the Greeks whom she loved against the Trojans—
Besides, she has other reasons for rage, bitter affronts
Unblotted as yet from her heart: deep in her mind rankle
The judgment of Paris, the insult of having her beauty scorned,
Her hate for Troy's origin, Ganymede taken and made a favorite—
Furious at these things too, she tossed all over the sea
The Trojans, the few that the Greeks and relentless Achilles had left, 30
And rode them off from their goal, Latium.
Many years
They were wandering round the seven seas, moved on by destiny.
So massive a task it was to found the Roman race.
They were only just out of sight of Sicily, towards deep water
Joyfully crowding on sail and driving the foam-flocks before them,
When Juno, who under her heart nursed that inveterate wound,
Soliloquized thus:—
Shall I give up? own myself beaten?
Impotent now to foil the Trojan lord from Italy?
Fate forbids me, indeed! Did not Athene burn 40
The Argive fleet and drown the crews, because one man
Had given offence? because of the criminal madness of Ajax?

Why, she herself flung down Jove's firebolt from the clouds,
Blasted that navy and capsized the sea with a storm;
And Ajax, gasping flame out of his cloven breast,
She whisked up in the whirlwind, impaled him on a crag.
But I, who walk in majesty, queen of heaven, Jove's
Sister and consort, I must feud with a single nation
For all these years. Does anyone worship my divinity
After this, or pay my altar a suppliant's homage? 50
Such were the thoughts milling round in her angry heart as the goddess
Came to the storm-cloud country, the womb-land of brawling siroccos,
Aeolia. Here in a huge cavern King Aeolus
Keeps curbed and stalled, chained up in durance to his own will,
The heaving winds and far-reverberating tempests.
Behind the bars they bellow, mightily fretting the mountain is
One immense murmur, Aeolus, aloft on his throne of power,
Scepter in hand, gentles and disciplines their fierce spirits.
Otherwise, they'd be bolting off with the earth and the ocean
And the deep sky—yes, brushing them all away into space. 60
But to guard against this the Father of heaven put the winds
In a dark cavern and laid a heap of mountains upon them,
And gave them an overlord who was bound by a firm contract
To rein them in or give them their head, as he was ordered.
Him Juno now petitioned. Here are the words she used:—

Aeolus, the king of gods and men has granted
You the rule of the winds, to lull the waves or lift them.
A breed I have no love for now sails the Tyrrhene sea,
Transporting Troy's defeated gods to Italy.
Lash fury into your winds! Whelm those ships and sink them! 70
Flail the crews apart! Litter the sea with their fragments!
Fourteen nymphs I have—their charms are quite out of the common—
Of whom the fairest in form, Deiopea, I'll join
To you in lasting marriage and seal her yours for ever,
A reward for this great favor I ask, to live out all
The years with you, and make you the father of handsome children.

Aeolus answered thus:—

O queen, it is for you to
Be fully aware what you ask: my duty is but to obey.
Through you I hold this kingdom, for what it's worth, as Jove's 80
Viceroy; you grant the right to sit at the gods' table;
You are the one who makes me grand master of cloud and storm.

Thus he spoke, and pointing his spear at the hollow mountain,
I shed at its flank: and the winds, as it were in a solid mass,
Hurl themselves through the gates and sweep the land with tornadoes.
They have fallen upon the sea, they are heaving it up from its deepest
Abysses, the whole sea—East wind, South, Sou'wester
Thick with squalls—and bowling great billows at the shore.
There follows a shouting of men, a shrilling of stays and halyards.

All of a sudden the storm-clouds are snatching the heavens, the daylight 90
From the eyes of the Trojans; night, black night is fallen on the sea.
The welkin explodes, the firmament flickers with thick-and-fast lightning,
And everything is threatening the instant death of men.
At once a mortal chill went through Aeneas and sapped him;
He groaned, and stretching out his two hands toward the stars,
Uttered these words:—

Oh, thrice and four times blessèd you
Whose luck it was to fall before your father's eyes
Under Troy's battlements! O Diomed, the bravest
Of the Greek kind, why could not I have fallen to death 100
On Ilium's plains and shed my soul upon your sword?
Fallen where Hector lies, whom Achilles slew, and tall
Sarpedon fell, and Simois our river rolls so many
Helmets and shields and heroes together down its stream?

Even as he cried out thus, a howling gust from the North
Hit the front of the sail, and a wave climbed the sky.
Oars snapped; then the ship yawed, wallowing broadside on
To the seas: and then, piled up there, a precipice of sea hung.
One vessel was poised on a wave crest; for another the waters, collapsing,
Showed sea-bottom in the trough: the tide-race boiled with sand. 110
Three times did the South wind spin them towards an ambush of rocks
(Those sea-girt rocks which Italians call by the name of "The Altars"),
Rocks like a giant spine on the sea: three times did the East wind
Drive them in to the Syrtes shoal, a piteous spectacle—
Hammering them on the shallows and hemming them round with sandbanks.
One ship, which carried in her the Lycians and faithful Orontes,
Before Aeneas' eyes is caught by an avalanche wave
And popped: her helmsman is flicked from off the deck and headlong
Sent flying; but three times the vessel is twirled around
By the wave ere the waters open and greedily gulp her down. 120
A man or two can be seen swimming the huge maelstrom,
With weapons and planks and Trojan treasure spilt on the sea.
Now Ilioneus' strong ship, now the ship of valiant Achates,
And the ships that carry Abás and aged Aletes go
Down to the gale; the ships have all sprung leaks and are letting
The enemy pour in through the loosened joints of their hulls,

Meanwhile Neptune has felt how greatly the sea is in turmoil,
Felt the unbridled storm disturbing the water even
Down to the sea-bed, and sorely troubled has broken surface;
He gazes forth on the deep with a pacific mien. 130
He sees the fleet of Aeneas all over the main, dismembered,
The Trojans crushed by waves and the sky in ribbons about them:
Juno's vindictive stratagems do not escape her brother.
He summons the East and the West winds, and then proceeds to say:—

Does family pride tempt you to such impertinence?
Do you really dare, you Winds, without my divine assent

To confound earth and sky, and raise this riot of water?
You, whom I—! Well, you have made the storm, I must lay it.
Next time, I shall not let you so lightly redeem your sins.
Now leave, and quickly leave, and tell your overlord this— 140
Not to him but to me was allotted the stern trident,
Dominion over the seas. His domain is the mountain of rock,
Your domicile, O East wind. Let Aeolus be king of
That castle and let him keep the winds locked up in its dungeon.
He spoke; and before he had finished, the insurgent sea was calmed,
The mob of cloud dispersed and the sun restored to power.
Nereid and Triton heaving together pushed the ships off
From the sharp rock, while Neptune levered them up with his trident,
And channelled a way through the sandbanks, and made the sea lie down—
Then lightly charioted off over the face of the waters. 150
Just as so often it happens, when a crowd collects, and violence
Brews up, and the mass mind boils nastily over, and the next thing
Firebrands and brickbats are flying (hysteria soon finds a missile),
That then, if they see some man whose goodness of heart and conduct
Have won their respect, they fall silent and stand still, ready to hear him;
And he can change their temper and calm their thoughts with a speech:
So now the crash of the seas died down, when Neptune gazed forth
Over their face, and the sky cleared, and the Father of ocean,
Turning his horses, wheeled away on an easy course.

* * *

[After harrowing experiences at sea, Aeneas and his men sailed toward Carthage, a Phoenician City on the North coast of Africa.]

Aeneas' men, worn out, with a last effort, make for 160
The nearest landing place; somewhere on the coast of Libya.
A spot there is in a deep inlet, a natural harbor
Formed by an island's flanks upon which the swell from the deep sea
Breaks and dividing runs into the land's recesses.
At either end of the lofty cliffs a peak towers up
Formidably to heaven, and under these twin summits
The bay lies still and sheltered: a curtain of overhanging
Woods with their shifting light and shadow forms the backdrop;
At the seaward foot of the cliffs there's a cave of stalactites
Fresh water within, and seats which nature has hewn from the stone— 170
A home of the nymphs. Here, then, tired ships could lie, and need
No cable nor the hooking teeth of an anchor to hold them.
Here, with seven ships mustered, all that was left of his convoy,
Aeneas now put in: and the Trojans, aching for dry land,
Tumbled out of their ships onto the sands they craved so,
And laid their limbs, crusted with brine, upon the shore
Then first of all Achates struck a spark from flint,

Nursed the spark to a flame on tinder, gave it to feed on
Dry fuel packed around it and made the flame blaze up there.
Sick of mischance, the men got ready the gifts and gear of 180
Ceres, setting themselves to roast on the fire and grind,
Though tainted it was with the salt water, what grain they had salvaged.
While this was going forward, Aeneas scaled a crag
To get an extensive view of the sea, hoping to sight
Some Trojan ship—Antheus perhaps, safe from the storm,
Or Capys, or the tall ship displaying the shield of Caicus.
Ship there was none in view; but on the shore three stags
Caught his eye as they wandered with a whole herd behind them,
A straggling drove of deer which browsed along the valley.
Aeneas, where he stood, snatched up the bow and arrows— 190
The weapons he had borrowed just now from faithful Achates—
And aiming first at the leaders of the herd, which carried their heads high
With branching antlers, he laid them low; then shot at the herd,
And his arrows sent it dodging all over the leafy woods.
Nor would he stop shooting until triumphantly
He had brought down seven beasts, one for each of his ships.
Then he returned to the harbor and shared them among his comrades.
And then he shared out the wine which good Acestes had casked
In Sicily and given them—a generous parting present,
And spoke these words of comfort to his sad-hearted friends:— 200

Comrades, we're well acquainted with evils, then and now.
Worse than this you have suffered. God will end all this too.
You, who have risked the mad bitch, Scylla, risked the cliffs
So cavernously resounding, and the stony land of the Cyclops,
Take heart again, oh, put your dismal fears away!
One day—who knows?—even these will be grand things to look back on.
Through chance and change, through hosts of dangers, our road still
Leads on to Latium: there, destiny offers a home
And peace; there duty tells us to build the second Troy.
Hold on, and find salvation in the hope of better things! 210

Thus spoke Aeneas; and though his heart was sick with anxiety,
He wore a confident look and kept his troubles to himself.
The Trojans set to work, preparing the game for a banquet;
Hacked the chines apart from the ribs, and exposed the guts:
Some sliced the meat into steaks which they spitted with trembling fingers,
Some set down cooking pots on the beach, and fed the fires,
Then they restored their strength with the food, and sprawling at ease
On the grass they took their fill of the wine and the rich venison.
Afterwards, hunger appeased and the meal cleared away, for a long time
They talked of their missing friends, longing to have them back, 220
Half-way between hope and fear, not knowing whether to deem them
Alive or utterly perished and far beyond human call.
True-hearted Aeneas grieved especially for the fate of
Ardent Orontes, and Amycus, and the cruel fate of Lycus,

Grieved for Gyas the brave and for the brave Cloanthus.
At last they made an end. Jupiter from high heaven
Looked down at the flights of sails on the sea, and the earth beneath him,
Its shores and its far-flung peoples: so, at the top of the morning
He stood, and presently focused his gaze on the Libyan realm.
Now, as he deeply pondered the troubles there, came Venus, 230
Sadder than is her wont, her eyes shining with tears,
And spoke to him:—

Sir, you govern the affairs of gods and men
By law unto eternity, you are terrible in the lightning:
Tell me, what wrong could my Aeneas or his Trojans
Have done you, so unforgivable that, after all these deaths,
To stop them reaching Italy they are locked out from the whole world?
Verily you had promised that hence, as the years rolled on,
Troy's renaissance would come, would spring the Roman people
And rule as sovereigns absolute over earth and sea. 240
You promised it. Oh, my father, why have you changed your mind?
That knowledge once consoled me for the sad fall of Troy:
I could balance fate against fate, past ills with luck to come.
But still the same ill fortune dogs my disaster-ridden
Heroes. Oh when, great king, will you let their ordeal end?
Antenor, slipping away through the Greek army, could safely
Sail right up the Illyrian gulf, pass by the remote
Liburnians, and pass the source of river Timavus
Where tidal water, roaring aloud below rock, spouts up
Through nine mouths, and the fields are hemmed with a sound of the sea. 250
He was allowed to found Padua, make a home for
Trojans there—could give his people a name, and nail up
His arms, could settle down to enjoy peace and quiet.
But we, your seed, for whom you sanction a place in heaven—
Our ships damnably sunk—because of one being's anger
We are cheated, and fenced afar from Italy.
Is this the reward for being true? Is it thus you restore a king?

The begetter of gods and men inclined towards her the smiling
Countenance which calms the sky and makes fair weather,
Gently kissed his daughter's mouth, and began to speak:— 260

Fear no more, Cytherea. Take comfort, for your people's
Destiny is unaltered; you shall behold the promised
City walls of Lavinium, and exalt great-hearted Aeneas
Even: the starry skies. I have not changed my mind.
I say it now—for I know these cares constantly gnaw you—
And show you further into the secret book of fate:
Aeneas, mightily warring in Italy, shall crush
Proud tribes, to establish city walls and a way of life,
Till a third summer has seen him reigning in Latium
And winter thrice passed over his camp in the conquered land. 270
His son Ascanius, whose surname is now Iulus—. . .

Ilus it was, before the realm of Ilium fell—
Ascanius for his reign shall have full thirty years
With all their wheeling mouths; shall move the kingdom from
Lavinium and make Long Alba his sure stronghold.
Here for three hundred years shall rule the dynasty
Of Hector, until a priestess and queen of Trojan blood,
With child by Mars, shall presently give birth to twin sons.
Romulus, then, gay in the coat of the tawny she-wolf
Which suckled him, shall succeed to power and found the city 280
Of Mars with his own name endow the Roman nation.
To these I set no bounds, either in space or time;
Unlimited power I give them. Even the spiteful Juno,
Who in her fear now troubles the earth, the sea and the sky,
Shall think better of this and join me in fostering
The cause of the Romans, the lords of creation, the togaed people.
Thus it is written. An age shall come, as the years glide by,
When the children of Troy shall enslave the children of Agamemnon,
Of Diomed and Achilles, and rule in conquered Argos.
From the fair seed of Troy there shall be born a Caesar— 290
Julius, his name derived from great Iulus—whose empire
Shall reach to the ocean's limits, whose fame shall end in the stars.
He shall hold the East in fee; one day, cares ended, you shall
Receive him into heaven; him also will mortals pray to.
Then shall the age of violence be mellowing into peace:
Venerable Faith, and the Home, with Romulus and Remus,
Shall make the laws; the grim, steel-welded gates of War
Be locked; and within, on a heap of armaments, a hundred
Bronzen knots tying his hands behind him, shall sit
Growling and bloody-mouthed the godless spirit of Discord. 300
So Jupiter spoke, and sent Mercury down from on high
To see that the land and the new-built towers of Carthage offered
Asylum to the Trojans, for otherwise might queen Dido,
Blind to destiny, turn them away.

* * *

[The love affair between Aeneas and Dido, queen of Carthage, which ends when the gods command Aeneas to continue his journey of destiny.]

But who can ever hoodwink a woman in love? The queen,
Apprehensive even when things went well, now sensed his deception,
Got wind of what was going to happen. That mischievous Rumor,
Whispering the fleet was preparing to sail, put her in a frenzy.
Distraught, she witlessly wandered about the city, raving
Like some Bacchante driven wild, when the emblems of sanctity
Stir, by the shouts of "Hail, Bacchus!" and drawn to Cithaeron

At night by the din of revellers, at the triennial orgies.
Finding Aeneas at last, she cried, before he could speak:—
    Unfaithful man, did you think you could do such a dreadful thing   10
And keep it dark? yes, skulk from my land without one word?
Our love, the vows you made me—do these not give you pause,
Nor even the thought of Dido meeting a painful death?
Now, in the dead of winter, to be getting your ships ready
And hurrying to set sail when northerly gales are blowing,
You heartless one! Suppose the fields were not foreign, the home was
Not strange that you are bound for, suppose Troy stood as of old,
Would you be sailing for Troy, now, in this stormy weather?
Am I your reason for going? By these tears, by the hand you gave me—
They are all I have left, to-day, in my misery—I implore you,   20
And by our union of hearts, by our marriage hardly begun,
If I have ever helped you at all, if anything
About me pleased you, be sad for our broken home, forgo
Your purpose, I beg you, unless it's too late for prayers of mine!
Because of you, the Libyan tribes and the Nomad chieftains
Hate me, the Tyrians are hostile: because of you I have lost
My old reputation for faithfulness—the one thing that could have made me
Immortal. Oh, I am dying! To what, my guest, are you leaving me?
"Guest"—that is all I may call you now, who have called you husband.
Why do I linger here? Shall I wait till my brother, Pygmalion,   30
Destroys this place, or Iarbas leads me away captive?
If even I might have conceived a child by you before
You went away, a little Aeneas to play in the palace
And, in spite of all this, to remind me of you by his looks, oh then
I should not feel so utterly finished and desolate.
    She had spoken. Aeneas, mindful of Jove's words, kept his eyes
Unyielding, and with a great effort repressed his feeling for her.
In the end he managed to answer:—
    Dido, I'll never pretend
You have not been good to me, deserving of everything   40
You can claim. I shall not regret my memories of Elissa
As long as I breathe, as long as I remember my own self.
For my conduct—this, briefly: I did not look to make off from here
In secret—do not suppose it; nor did I offer you marriage
At any time or consent to be bound by a marriage contract.
If fate allowed me to be my own master, and gave me
Free will to choose my way of life, to solve my problems,
Old Troy would be my first choice: I would restore it, and honor
My people's relics—the high halls of Priam perpetuated,
Troy given back to its conquered sons, a renaissant city   50
Had been my task. But now Apollo and the Lycian
Oracle have told me that Italy is our bourne.
There lies my heart, my homeland. You, a Phoenician, are held by

These Carthaginian towers, by the charm of your Libyan city:
So can you grudge us Trojans our vision of settling down
In Italy? We too may seek a kingdom abroad.
Often as night envelops the earth in dewy darkness,
Often as star-rise, the troubled ghost of my father, Anchises,
Comes to me in my dreams, warns me and frightens me.
I am disturbed no less by the wrong I am doing Ascanius, 60
Defrauding him of his destined realm in Hesperia.
What's more, just now the courier of heaven, sent by Jupiter—
I swear it on your life and mine—conveyed to me, swiftly flying,
His orders: I saw the god, as clear as day, with my own eyes,
Entering the city, and these ears drank in the words he uttered.
No more reproaches, then—they only torture us both.
God's will, not mine, says "Italy."

All the while he was speaking she gazed at him askance,
Her glances flickering over him, eyes exploring the whole man
In deadly silence. Now, furiously, she burst out:— 70

Faithless and false! No goddess mothered you, no Dardanus
Your ancestor! I believe harsh Caucasus begat you
On a flint-hearted rock and Hyrcanian tigers suckled you.
Why should I hide my feelings? What worse can there be to keep them for?
Not one sigh from him when I wept! Not a softer glance!
Did he yield an inch, or a tear, in pity for her who loves him?
I don't know what to say first. It has come to this,—not Juno,
Not Jove himself can view my plight with the eye of justice.
Nowhere is it safe to be trustful. I took him, a castaway,
A pauper, and shared my kingdom with him—I must have been mad— 80
Rescued his lost fleet, rescued his friends from death.
Oh, I'm on fire and drifting! And now Apollo's prophecies,
Lycian oracles, couriers of heaven sent by Jupiter
With stern commands—all these order you to betray me.
Oh, of course this is just the sort of transaction that troubles the calm of
The gods. I'll not keep you, nor probe the dishonesty of your words,
Chase your Italy, then! Go, sail to your realm overseas!
I only hope that, if the just spirits have any power,
Marooned on some mid-sea rock you may drink the full cup of agony
And often cry out for Dido. I'll dog you, from far, with the death-fires; 90
And when cold death has parted my soul from my body, my specter
Will be wherever you are. You shall pay for the evil you've done me.
The tale of your punishment will come to me down in the shades.

With these words Dido suddenly ended, and sick at heart
Turned from him, tore herself away from his eyes, ran indoors,
While he hung back in dread of a still worse scene, although
He had much to say. Her maids bore up the fainting queen
Into her marble chamber and laid her down on the bed.

But the god-fearing Aeneas, much as he longed to soothe
Her anguish with consolation, with words that would end her troubles, 100

Heavily sighing, his heart melting from love of her,
Nevertheless obeyed the gods and went off to his fleet.

* * *

[Aeneas enters the underworld where he meets people from the past, including the dead Dido.]
You gods who rule the kingdom of souls!
You soundless shades!
Chaos, and Phlegethon! O mute wide leagues of Nightland!—
Grant me to tell what I have heard! With your assent
May I reveal what lies deep in the gloom of the Underworld!
Dimly through the shadows and dark solitudes they wended,
Through the void domiciles of Dis, the bodiless regions:
Just as, through fitful moonbeams, under the moon's thin light,
A path lies in a forest, when Jove has palled the sky
With gloom, and the night's blackness has bled the world of color. 10
See! At the very porch and entrance way to Orcus
Grief and ever-haunting Anxiety make their bed:
Here dwell pallid Diseases, here morose Old Age,
With Fear, ill-prompting Hunger, and squalid Indigence,
Shapes horrible to look at, Death and Agony;
Sleep, too, which is the cousin of Death; and Guilty Joys,
And there, against the threshold, War, the bringer of Death:
Here are the iron cells of the Furies, and lunatic Strife
Whose viperine hair is caught up with a headband soaked in blood.
In the open a huge dark elm tree spreads wide its immemorial 20
Branches like arms, whereon, according to old wives' tales,
Roost the unsolid Dreams, clinging everywhere under its foliage.
Besides, many varieties of monsters can be found
Ensnarled here at the doors—Centaurs and freakish Scyllas,
Briareus with his hundred hands, the Lernaean Hydra
That hisses terribly and the flame-throwing Chimaera,
Gorgons and Harpies, and the ghost of three-bodied Geryon.
Now did Aeneas shake with a spasm of fear, and drawing
His sword, offered its edge against the creatures' onset:
Had not his learned guide assured him they were but incorporeal 30
Existences floating there, forms with no substance behind them,
He'd have attacked them, and wildly winnowed with steel mere shadows.
From here is the road that leads to the dismal waters of Acheron.
Here a whirlpool boils with mud and immense swirlings
Of water, spouting up all the slimy sand of Cocytus.
A dreadful ferryman looks after the river crossing,
Charon: Appallingly filthy he is, with a bush of unkempt
White beard upon his chin, with eyes like jets of fire;
And a dirty cloak draggles down, knotted about his shoulders.
He poles the boat, he looks after the sails, he is all the crew 40

Of the rust-colored wherry which takes the dead across—
An ancient now, but a god's old age is green and sappy.
This way came fast and streaming up to the bank the whole throng:
Matrons and men were there, and there were great-heart heroes
Finished with earthly life, boys and unmarried maidens,
Young men laid on the pyre before their parents' eyes;
Multitudinous as the leaves that fall in a forest
At the first frost of autumn, or the birds that out of the deep sea
Fly to land in migrant flocks, when the cold of the year
Has sent them overseas in search of a warmer climate. 50
So they all stood, each begging to be ferried across first,
Their hands stretched out in longing for the shore beyond the river.
But the surly ferryman embarks now this, now that group,
While others he keeps away at a distance from the shingle.
Aeneas, being astonished and moved by the great stir, said:—
    Tell me, O Sibyl, what means this rendezvous at the river?
What purpose have these souls? By what distinction are some
Turned back, while other souls sweep over the wan water?
To which the long-lived Sibyl uttered this brief reply:—
    O son of Anchises' loins and true-born offspring of heaven, 60
What you see is the mere of Cocytus, the Stygian marsh
By whose mystery even the gods, having sworn, are afraid to be forsworn.
All this crowd you see are the helpless ones, the unburied:
That ferryman is Charon: the ones he conveys have had burial.
None may be taken across from bank to awesome bank of
That harsh-voiced river until his bones are laid to rest.
Otherwise, he must haunt this place for a hundred years
Before he's allowed to revisit the longed-for stream at last.
    The son of Anchises paused and stood stock still, in deep
Meditation, pierced to the heart by pity for their hard fortune. 70
He saw there, sorrowing because deprived of death's fulfilment,
Leucaspis and Orontes, the commodore of the Lycian
Squadron, who had gone down, their ship being lost with all hands
In a squall, sailing with him the stormy seas from Troy.
    And look! yonder was roaming the helmsman, Palinurus,
Who, on their recent voyage, while watching the stars, had fallen
From the afterdeck, thrown off the ship there in mid-passage.
A somber form in the deep shadows, Aeneas barely
Recognized him; then accosted:—
    Which of the gods, Palinurus, 80
Snatched you away from us and made you drown in the midsea?
Oh, tell me! For Apollo, whom never before had I found
Untruthful, did delude my mind with this one answer,
Foretelling that you would make your passage to Italy
Unharmed by sea. Is it thus he fulfils a sacred promise?
    Palinurus replied:—
    The oracle of Phoebus has not tricked you,

My captain, son of Anchises; nor was I drowned by a god.
It was an accident: I slipped, and the violent shock
Of my fall broke off the tiller to which I was holding firmly 90
As helmsman, and steering the ship. By the wild seas I swear
That not on my own account was I frightened nearly so much as
Lest your ship, thus crippled, its helmsman overboard,
Lose steerage-way and founder amid the mountainous waves.
Three stormy nights did the South wind furiously drive me along
Over the limitless waters: on the fourth day I just
Caught sight of Italy, being lifted high on a wave crest.
Little by little I swam to the shore. I was all but safe,
When, as I clung to the rough-edged cliff top, my fingers crooked
And my soaking garments weighing me down, some barbarous natives 100
Attacked me with swords, in their ignorance thinking that I was a rich prize.
Now the waves have me, the winds keep tossing me up on the shore again.
So now, by the sweet light and breath of heaven above
I implore you, and by your father, by your hopes for growing Ascanius
Redeem me from this doom, unconquered one! Please sprinkle
Dust on my corpse—you can do it and quickly get back to port Velia:
Or else, if way there is, some way that your heavenly mother
Is showing you (not, for sure, without the assent of deity
Would you be going to cross the swampy Stygian stream),
Give poor Palinurus your hand, take me with you across the water 110
So that at least I may rest in the quiet place, in death.

Thus did the phantom speak, and the Sibyl began to speak thus:—

This longing of yours, Palinurus, has carried you quite away.
Shall you, unburied, view the Styx, the austere river
Of the Infernal gods, or come to its bank unbidden?
Give up this hope that the course of fate can be swerved by prayer.
But hear and remember my words, to console you in your hard fortune.
I say that the neighboring peoples, compelled by portents from heaven
Occurring in every township, shall expiate your death,
Shall give you burial and offer the solemn dues to your grave, 120
And the place shall keep the name of Palinurus forever.

Her sayings eased for a while the anguish of his sad heart;
He forgot his cares in the joy of giving his name to a region.

So they resumed their interrupted journey, and drew near
The river. Now when the ferryman, from out on the Styx, espied them
Threading the soundless wood and making fast for the bank,
He hailed them, aggressively shouting at them before they could speak:—

Whoever you are that approaches my river, carrying a weapon,
Halt there! Keep your distance, and tell me why you are come!
This is the land of ghosts, of sleep and somnolent night: 130
The living are not permitted to use the Stygian ferry.
Not with impunity did I take Hercules,
When he came, upon this water, nor Theseus, nor Pirithous,
Though their stock was divine and their powers were irresistible.

Hercules wished to drag off on a leash the watch-dog of Hades,
Even from our monarch's throne, and dragged it away trembling:
The others essayed to kidnap our queen from her lord's bedchamber.
The priestess of Apollo answered him shortly, thus:—
There is no such duplicity here, so set your mind at rest;
These weapons offer no violence: the huge watch-dog in his kennel 140
May go on barking for ever and scaring the bloodless dead,
Prosperpine keep her uncle's house, unthreatened in chastity.
Trojan Aeneas, renowned for war and a duteous heart,
Comes down to meet his father in the shades of the Underworld.
If you are quite unmoved by the spectacle of such great faith,
This you must recognize—
And here she disclosed the golden
Bough which was hid in her robe. His angry mood calms down.
No more is said. Charon is struck with awe to see
After so long that magic gift, the bough fate-given; 150
He turns his sombre boat and poles it towards the bank.
Then, displacing the souls who were seated along its benches
And clearing the gangways, to make room for the big frame of Aeneas,
He takes him on board. The ramshackle craft creaked under his weight
And let in through its seams great swashes of muddy water.
At last, getting the Sibyl and the hero safe across,
He landed them amidst wan reeds on a dreary mud flat.
Huge Cerberus, monstrously couched in a cave confronting them,
Made the whole region echo with his three-throated barking.
The Sibyl, seeing the snakes bristling upon his neck now, 160
Threw him for bait a cake of honey and wheat infused with
Sedative drugs. The creature, crazy with hunger, opened
Its three mouths, gobbled the bait; then its huge body relaxed
And legs sprawled out on the ground, the whole length of the cave kennel.
Aeneas, passing its entrance, the watch-dog neutralized,
Strode rapidly from the bank of that river of no return.
At once were voices heard, a sound of mewling and wailing,
Ghosts of infants sobbing there at the threshold, infants
From whom a dark day stole their share of delicious life,
Snatched them away from the breast, gave them sour death to drink. 170
Next to them were those condemned to death on a false charge.
Yet every place is duly allotted and judgment is given.
Minos, as president, summons a jury of the dead: he hears
Every charge, examines the record of each; he shakes the urn.
Next again are located the sorrowful ones who killed
Themselves, throwing their lives away, not driven by guilt
But because they loathed living: how they would like to be
In the world above now, enduring poverty and hard trials!
God's law forbids: that unlovely fen with its glooming water
Corrals them there, the nine rings of Styx corral them in. 180
Not far from here can be seen, extending in all directions,

The vale of mourning—such is the name it bears: a region
Where those consumed by the wasting torments of merciless love
Had the sequestered alleys and myrtle groves that give them
Cover; death itself cannot cure them of love's disease.
Here Aeneas descried Phaedra and Procris, sad
Eriphyle displaying the wounds her heartless son once dealt her,
Evadne and Pasiphae; with them goes Laodamia;
Here too is Caeneus, once a young man, but next a woman
And now changed back by fate to his original sex. 190
Amongst them, with her death-wound still bleeding, through the deep wood
Was straying Phoenician Dido. Now when the Trojan leader
Found himself near her and knew that the form he glimpsed through the shadows
Was hers—as early in the month one sees, or imagines he sees,
Through a wrack of cloud the new moon rising and glimmering—
He shed some tears, and addressed her in tender, loving tones:—
Poor, unhappy Dido, so the message was true that came to me
Saying you'd put an end to your life with the sword and were dead?
Oh god! was it death I brought you, then? I swear by the stars,
By the powers above, by whatever is sacred in the Underworld, 200
It was not of my own will, Dido, I left your land.
Heaven's commands, which now force me to traverse the shades,
This sour and derelict region, this pit of darkness, drove me
Imperiously from your side. I did not, could not imagine
My going would ever bring such terrible agony on you.
Don't move away! Oh, let me see you a little longer!
To fly from me, when this is the last word fate allows us!
Thus did Aeneas speak, trying to soften the wild-eyed,
Passionate-hearted ghost, and brought the tears to his own eyes.
She would not turn to him; she kept her gaze on the ground, 210
And her countenance remained as stubborn to his appeal
As if it were carved from recalcitrant flint or a crag of marble.
At last she flung away, hating him still, and vanished
Into the shadowy wood where her first husband, Sychaeus,
Understands her unhappiness and gives her an equal love.
Nonetheless did Aeneas, hard hit by her piteous fate,
Weep after her from afar, as she went, with tears of compassion.

* * *

[Aeneas fulfills his destiny.]
When Anchises had finished, he drew his son and the Sibyl
Into the thick of the murmuring concourse assembled there
And took his stand on an eminence from which he could scan the long files
Over against him, and mark the features of those who passed
Listen, for I will show you your destiny, setting forth
The fame that from now shall attend the seed of Dardanus

The posterity that awaits you from an Italian marriage—
Illustrious souls, one day to come in for our Trojan name.
That young man there—do you see him? who leans on an untipped spear,
Has been allotted the next passage to life, and first of 10
All these will ascend to earth, with Italian blood in his veins;
He is Silvius, an Alban name, and destined to be your last child,
The child of your late old age by a wife, Lavinia, who shall
Bear him in sylvan surroundings, a king and the father of kings
Through whom our lineage shall rule in Alba Longa.
Next to him stands Procas, a glory to the Trojan line;
Then Capys and Numitor, and one who'll revive your own name—
Silvius Aeneas, outstanding alike for moral rectitude
And prowess in warfare, if ever he comes to the Alban throne.
What fine young men they are! Look at their stalwart bearing, 20
The oak leaves that shade their brows—decorations for saving life!
These shall found your Nomentum, Gabii and Fidenae,
These shall rear on the hills Collatia's citadel,
Pometii, and the Fort of Inuus, Bola and Cora—
All nameless sites at present, but then they shall have these names.
Further, a child of Mars shall go to join his grandsire—
Romulus, born of the stock of Assarcus by his mother,
Ilia. Look at the twin plumes upon his helmet's crest,
Mars' cognizance, which marks him out for the world of earth!
His are the auguries, my son, whereby great Rome 30
Shall rule to the ends of the earth, shall aspire to the highest achievement,
Shall ring the seven hills with a wall to make one city,
Blessed in her breed of men: as Cybele, wearing her turreted
Crown, is charioted round the Phrygian cities, proud of
Her brood of gods, embracing a hundred of her children's children—
Heaven-dwellers all, tenants of the realm above.
Now bend your gaze this way, look at that people there!
They are your Romans. Caesar is there and all Ascanius'
Posterity, who shall pass beneath the arch of day.
And here, here is the man, the promised one you know of— 40
Caesar Augustus, son of a god, destined to rule
Where Saturn ruled of old in Latium, and there
Bring back the age of gold: his empire shall expand
Past Garamants and Indians to a land beyond the zodiac
And the sun's yearly path, where Atlas the sky-bearer pivots
The wheeling heavens, embossed with fiery stars, on his shoulder.
Even now the Caspian realm, the Crimean country
Tremble at oracles of the gods predicting his advent,
And the seven mouths of the Nile are in a lather of fright.
Not even Hercules roved so far and wide over earth, 50
Although he shot the bronze-footed deer, brought peace to the woods of
Erymanthus, subdued Lerna with the terror of his bow;
Nor Bacchus, triumphantly driving his team with vines for reins,

His team of tigers down from Mount Nysa, travelled so far.
Do we still hesitate, then, to enlarge our courage by action?
Shrink from occupying the territory of Ausonia?
Who is that in the distance, bearing the hallows, crowned with
A wreath of olive? I recognize—grey hair and hoary chin—
That Roman king who, called to high power from humble Cures,
A town in a poor area, shall found our system of law 60
And thus refound our city. The successor of Numa, destined
To shake our land out of its indolence, stirring men up to fight
Who have grown unadventurous and lost the habit of victory,
Is Tullus. After him shall reign the too boastful Ancus,
Already over-fond of the breath of popular favor.
Would you see the Tarquin kings, and arrogant as they, Brutus
The avenger, with the symbols of civic freedom he won back?
He shall be first to receive consular rank and its power of
Life and death: when his sons awake the dormant conflict,
Their father, a tragic figure, shall call them to pay the extreme 70
Penalty, for fair freedom's sake. However posterity
Look on that deed, patriotism shall prevail and love of
Honor. See over there the Decii, the Drusi, Torquatus
With merciless axe, Camillus with the standards he recovered.
See those twin souls, resplendent in duplicate armor: now
They're of one mind, and shall be as long as the Underworld holds them;
But oh, if ever they reach the world above, what warfare,
What battles and what carnage will they create between them—
Caesar descending from Alpine strongholds, the fort of Monoceus,
His son-in-law Pompey lined up with an Eastern army against him. 80
Lads, do not harden yourselves to face such terrible wars!
Turn not your country's hand against your country's heart!
You, be the first to renounce it, my son of heavenly lineage,
You be the first to bury the hatchet! . . .
That one shall ride in triumph to the lofty Capitol,
The conqueror of Corinth, renowned for the Greeks he has slain.
That one shall wipe out Argos and Agamemnon's Mycenae,
Destroying an heir of Aeacus, the seed of warrior Achilles,
Avenging his Trojan sires and the sacrilege done to Minerva.
Who could leave unnoticed the glorious Cato, Cossus, 90
The family of the Gracchi, the two Scipios—thunderbolts
In war and death to Libya; Fabricius, who had plenty
In poverty; Serranus, sowing his furrowed fields?
Fabii, where do you lead my lagging steps? O Fabias,
The greatest, you the preserver of Rome by delaying tactics!
Yet others fashion from bronze more lifelike, breathing images—
For so they shall—and evoke living faces from marble,
Others excel as orators, others track with their instruments
The planets circling in heaven and predict when stars will appear.
But, Romans, never forget that government is your medium! 100

Be this your art:—to practice men in the habit of peace,
Generosity to the conquered, and firmness against aggressors.
    They marvelled at Anchises' words, and he went on:—
    Look how Marcellus comes all glorious with the highest
Of trophies, a victor over-topping all other men!
He shall buttress the Roman cause when a great war shakes it,
Shatter the Carthaginian and rebel Gaul with his cavalry,
Give to Quirinus the third set of arms won in single combat.
    Aeneas interposed, seeing beside Marcellus
Youth of fine appearance, in glittering accoutrements, 110
But his face was far from cheerful and downcast were his eyes:—
    Father, who is he that walks with Marcellus there?
His son? Or one of the noble line of his children's children?
How the retinue murmurs around him! How fine is the young man's presence!
Yet is his head haloed by somber shade of night.
    Then father Anchises began, tears welling up in his eyes:—
    My son, do not probe into the sorrows of your kin.
Fate shall allow the earth one glimpse of this young man—
One glimpse, no more. Too puissant had been Rome's stock, ye gods,
In your sight, had such gifts been granted it to keep. 120
What lamentations of men shall the Campus Martius echo
To Mars' great city! O Tiber, what obsequies you shall see
One day as you glide past the new-built mausoleum!
No lad of the Trojan line shall with such hopeful promise
Exalt his Latin forebears, nor shall the land of Romulus
Ever again be so proud of one she has given birth to.
Alas for the sense of duty, the old-time honor! Alas for
The hand unvanquished in war! Him would no foe have met
In battle and not rued it, whether he charged on foot
Or drove his lathering steed with spurs against the enemy. 130
Alas, poor youth! If only you could escape your harsh fate!
Marcellus you shall be. Give me armfuls of lilies
That may scatter their shining blooms and shower these gifts
At least upon the dear soul, all to no purpose though
Such kindness be.
    So far and wide, surveying all,
They wandered through that region, those broad and hazy plains.
After Anchises had shown his son over the whole place
And fired his heart with passion for the great things to come,
He told the hero of wars he would have to fight one day, 140
Told of the Laurentines and the city of Latinus,
And now to evade, or endure, each crisis upon his way.
    There are two gates of Sleep: the one is made of horn,
They say, and affords the outlet for genuine apparitions:
The other's gate of brightly-shining ivory; this way
The Shades send up to earth false dreams that impose upon us.
Talking, then, of such matters, Anchises escorted his son

And the Sibyl as far as the ivory gate and sent them through it.
Aeneas made his way back to the ships and his friends with all speed,
Then coasted along direct to the harbor of Caieta. 150
The ships, anchored by the bows, line the shore with their sterns.

Article 21

Cicero: The Republic, Laws

Introduction

Marcus Tullius Cicero (106–43 BC) was a great orator, lawyer, and government official (consul) during the last years of the Roman Republic. Cicero adamantly opposed Julius Caesar's attempted self-crowning as the Emperor of Rome. He felt that the end of the Republic would begin the end of Rome. His staunch support for the values of the Republic made many enemies, and he was murdered by Mark Anthony. Despite the many people who criticized Cicero, the values he presented as the core values of the Republic were generally accepted by Romans, even through the period of the Roman Empire when many of the values were not practiced. Some compare the values of the Republic to the values of the American founding fathers and point out that today, just as in the days of the Empire, the original values are ignored.

Cicero's writings have proven to be very valuable. His discussion of the government during the Roman Republic is a glimpse of what democratic republics, including the United States of America, should be like. His philosophical writings show values deeply rooted in Stoicism and are very useful to the modern-day student of that philosophy.

Presented here are passages from his two greatest works, *The Republic* and *Laws*. They describe the ideal constitution of a government, the relationship between reason and law, and how law relates to divinity. The excerpts should be compared to Plato's Republic, the government of the United States, the works of Confucius, and ancient legal works like Exodus and the Code of Hammurabi.

Republic

In kingships the subjects have too small a share in the administration of justice and in deliberation; and in aristocracies the masses can hardly have their share of liberty, since they are entirely excluded from deliberation for the common wealth and from power; and when all the power is in the people's hands, even though they exercise it with justice and moderation, yet the resulting equality itself is inequitable, since it allows no distinctions in rank.

XXVIII. I am now speaking of these three forms of government, not when they are confused and mingled with one another, but when they retain their appropriate character. All of them are, in the first place, subject each to the faults I have mentioned, and they suffer from other dangerous faults in addition: for before every one of them lies a slippery and precipitous path leading to a certain depraved form that is a close neighbour to it.

A wise man should be acquainted with these changes, but it calls for great citizens and for a

Reprinted by permission of the publishers and the Trustees of the Loeb Classical Library from Cicero: Volume XVI—DE RE Publica. Loeb Classical Library Volume 213, translated by Clinton W. Keyes, Cambridge, MA, Harvard University Press.

man of almost divine powers to foresee them when they threaten, and, while holding the reins of government, to direct their courses and keep them under his control. Therefore I consider a fourth form of government the most commendable—that form which is a well-regulated mixture of the three which I mentioned at first.

Laws

XXII. . . . True law is right reason in agreement with nature; it is of universal application, unchanging and everlasting; it summons to duty by its commands, and averts from wrongdoing by its prohibitions. And it does not lay its commands or prohibitions upon good men in vain, though neither have any effect on the wicked. It is a sin to try to to alter this law, nor is it allowable to attempt to repeal any part of it, and it is impossible to abolish it entirely. We cannot be freed from its obligations by senate or people, and we need not look outside ourselves for an expounder or interpreter of it. And there will not be different laws at Rome and at Athens, or different laws now and in the future, but one eternal and unchangeable law will be valid for all nations and all times, and there will be one master and ruler, that is, God, over us all, for he is the author of this law, its promulgator, and its enforcing judge. Whoever is disobedient is fleeing from himself and denying his human nature, and by reason of this very fact he will suffer the worst penalties, even if he escapes what is commonly considered punishment. . . .

. . . the most learned men have determined to begin with Law, and it would seem that they are right, if, according to their definition, Law is the highest reason, implanted in Nature, which commands what ought to be done and forbids the opposite. This reason, when firmly fixed and fully developed in the human mind, is Law. And so they believe that Law is intelligence, whose natural function it is to command right conduct and forbid wrongdoing. They think that this quality has derived its name in Greek from the idea of granting to every man his own, and in our language I believe it has been named from the idea of choosing. For as they have attributed the idea of fairness to the word law, so we have given it that of selection, though both ideas properly belong to Law. Now if this is correct, as I think it to be in general, then the origin of Justice is to be found in Law, for Law is a natural force; it is the mind and reason of the intelligent man, the standard by which Justice and Injustice are measured.

. . . that animal which we call man, endowed with foresight and quick intelligence, complex, keen, possessing memory, full of reason and prudence, has been given a certain distinguished status by the supreme God who created him; for he is the only one among so many different kinds and varieties of living beings who has a share in reason and thought, while all the rest are deprived of it. But what is more divine, I will not say in man only, but in all heaven and earth, than reason? And reason, when it is full grown and perfected, is rightly called wisdom. Therefore, since there is nothing better than reason, and since it exists both in man and God, the first common possession of man and God is reason. But those who have reason in common must also have right reason in common. And since right reason is Law, we must believe that men have Law also in common with the gods. Further, those who share Law must also share Justice; and those who share these are to be regarded as members of the same commonwealth. If indeed they obey the same authorities and powers, this is true in a far greater degree; but as a matter of fact they do obey this celestial system, the divine mind, and the God of transcendent power. Hence we must now conceive of this whole universe as one commonwealth of which both gods and men are members.

Roman Empire
Creative World Dominance

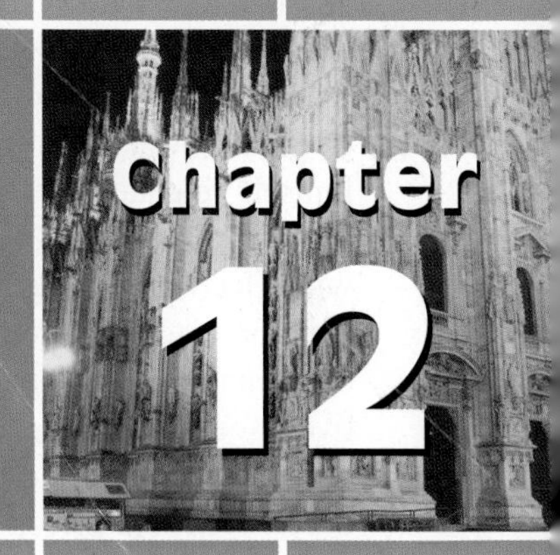

> A close study of each of these dead civilizations indicates that they usually started on their road to glory because of fortuitous circumstances exploited by a strong, inspiring leader. The nation then carried on for a period under its own momentum. Finally, creeping vanity led the people to become enamored of their undisputed superiority; they became so impressed with their past achievements that they lost interest in working for further change. Soon their sons, coddled in the use of all the great things their fathers and grandfathers had pioneered, became as helpless as new-born babes when faced with the harsh reality of an aggressive and changing world.
>
> —*Eugene K. Von Fange,* Professional Creativity

The Principate

Julius Caesar's nephew, Octavian, may have been the most creative leader of the entire ancient period, regardless of location. He was able to form the most effective and longest lasting political entity the world has ever known, the Roman Empire, and to accomplish that creative feat starting within a chaotic environment of civil war, collapsing institutional forms, fierce political rivalries, economic distress, public uncertainty on direction or goals, and personal inexperience. When he was finished, the Roman Empire was clearly the master of the known world: the government was stable and economically secure; the military was loyal and efficient; a system of civil laws was in place that would last hundreds of years, and which has served as the basis of most modern Western legal systems; the arts were flourishing; technology was not only solving the day-to-day problems of the empire, but was also creating a lifestyle that was the envy of the world; the people were united in their collective goals; and he was personally so loved that, both formally and informally, he was named "the greatest," that is, "Augustus."

Perhaps the heart of this amazing creative endeavor was the clever way in which Octavian took control of the Roman government after the 27 years of civil war following the death of Julius Caesar. He and Mark Anthony were the clear victors in the wars against the forces of the conspirators in the death of Julius Caesar, and then he had personally and individually triumphed over Mark Anthony. In the past, such complete and personal accomplishments would have led the victor to seek a position of great power and prestige, perhaps even calling himself "dictator" or "emperor" or "king," as was attempted by Julius Caesar. Such was not the case with Octavian. He realized that he must head the government, but he sought only to be called *"princeps civitatis"* or "first citizen." Moreover, he actively sought to restore (at least in appearances) the traditional checks and balances of the Roman Republic, which had been so seriously eroded and neglected over the decades just past. In taking this position of service and apparent humility, he won the hearts of the people and calmed the fears of his enemies, mostly senators of the *Optimates* party. In this environment of cooperation and trust Octavian was then able to put in place changes in the government that, in the end, would give him personal and complete control over the government without antagonizing either the people or the Senate. From his example, we see just how powerful image and perception can be. (It is of great historical interest that Napoleon initially followed the example of Octavian, but then departed from it when Napoleon took upon himself the title of emperor, and, for many, began the process of decline.)

We traditionally mark the beginning of the rule of Octavian at 27 B.C., when Octavian returned from his Egyptian victory and entered the Senate chambers to report. Many of the Senators feared that he would demand a position of power, and, frankly, they were prepared to haggle over the terms of his appointment so that they could limit his power. Instead, Octavian simply announced his retirement from public life, indicating that he would return to the comforts of his home and be a passive participant in the affairs of the state. The Senators were apparently shocked and confused. They couldn't allow Octavian to retire—who would lead the country? At the insistence of the Senate (note the irony of who is insisting on what), Octavian was appointed to a 10-year term as the head of most of the foreign territories (Spain, Gaul, Syria, Egypt, Cyprus) with a mandate *(emporium)* to conduct war against any external threat and to do whatever else would be necessary to establish a lasting peace in those territories. He would also retain the position of consul, but would act under the direction of the Senate. In essence, the Senate maintained direct control over the heart of the empire (Rome, Italy, and Greece) but gave Octavian control over the rest. This situation met Octavian's desire to appear to be a strong traditionalist and not threaten those who might fear him. A few days later, perhaps recognizing that not enough honors had been given to Octavian, the Senate met again and bestowed upon him the title of "Augustus," which has the implications of greatness in both a civil and a religious sense. Hence, they were proclaiming Octavian to be the foremost citizen, leader of the army, and savior of the state. (From this point on, we will refer to Octavian by his new title, **Augustus.**) Augustus referred to himself as *princeps civitatis,* first citizen—a term from which we get the modern word "prince." The period of the rule of Augustus is called the **principate.**

For the following three years, Augustus left Rome for a tour of the territories he was now asked to administer. (Note how well this action maintained the image he wished to convey of being a compliant servant of the people and the Senate.) While he was gone, his aides worked with the Senate and the tribunes, supervising governmental actions within Rome itself. About the time Augustus returned to Rome (in 23 B.C.), a conspiracy was discovered that evidently so disturbed the Senate that further adjustments were made in Augustus' position. First, Augustus resigned his position as consul, thus maintaining his appearance as a traditionalist and self-demeaning servant of the state. Then, Augustus was appointed to a position of **proconsul** (a new position) over all territories outside Rome. He was also given the same power as a tribune, but was specifically not named to the position of tribune. As a result, Augustus had authority over the governors in all foreign lands, and also had the authority to supervise day-to-day operations within the city of Rome. These powers were, of course, nearly total, but no worrisome title was bestowed, thus maintaining the image Augustus wanted.

Over the next several years, Augustus would resign from various positions and accept others, refuse several requests by the people that he accept titles such as "dictator for life" and yet accept other titles of honor, such as *pater patriae,* father of the country—a title he loved because it conveyed exactly the image he wished. Throughout, he maintained control over the government and kept the love and respect of the people. Perhaps his greatest accomplishment in this regard was the recognition given to his "suggestions" or "requests" by the various institutions and officials of the state. When it was learned by any official that Augustus wanted something to be done, it was done—simply because Augustus had a quality called *auctoritas,* which means prestige, power from trust, or influence. In essence, his will was done because everyone believed in him. In honor of his heritage from Julius Caesar, Augustus was also called Caesar, a name that became a title for the ruler of the empire, and was perpetuated by all the rulers who succeeded Augustus.

During the reign of Augustus, Rome was given an honest government, characterized by effective postal, police, fire, and trash removal systems. He improved the roads (extending them to over 53,000 miles) and improved the harbors. A single currency was established throughout the entire empire, thus facilitating trade and prosperity. The legal system was administered fairly (according to the standards of that day), and was accessible to the people. He refined various legal concepts relating to equity (allowing extenuating circumstances to be considered in a trial), inheritance, property ownership, obligations to slaves, family life, and citizenship.

Augustus reduced the size of the military but created a permanent, professional army and navy. He established an elite personal guard (the **Praetorian Guard**), which helped maintain stability throughout his reign. He expanded Roman territory and established defendable boundaries, as shown in Figure 12.1. He then counseled that further expansion was both unwise and unnecessary. His counsel was largely followed, with the exception of a few additional territories that were added between 110 A.D. and 140 A.D. Augustus advocated, and largely achieved, a period of peace that lasted about 400 years, and which the world has called the *Pax Romana.*

Augustus tried to establish a succession system that would allow much of the prestige and power he had enjoyed to be passed on smoothly. However, the very personal nature of his successful reign, with informal alliances and widespread consent of the people, complicated the succession process. Therefore, to Augustus, the answer was to name a successor who was both politically competent and also personally related to him. Since he had no sons who could succeed him, Augustus named the highly effective leader **Tiberius** to be his successor, and then adopted Tiberius as a nephew, thus attempting to create the personal linkage. The plan seemed to work, as the transition to Tiberius was smooth upon the death of Augustus in 14 A.D. However, as we will see, later rulers were far less successful in establishing both the competency and personal linkages necessary for effective rule and smooth succession. To a great extent, that is the story of the succeeding rulers of the Roman Empire. Rather than discuss each of the emperors individually, we can conveniently divide them into a few groups, as shown in Figure 12.2, and then discuss the characteristics of the groups, with a few specific examples to illustrate the nature of the empire during each period.

Julio-Claudians

Tiberius (r. 14–37 A.D.) was the successor to Augustus and was, by adoption, his nephew and therefore was of the family of Julio (which is the same family as Julius Caesar). Tiberius seemed to have begun well, with a significant enriching of the coffers of the state and even some honors given to him, such as the naming of the principal city in the north of Judea. After several years, however, Tiberius became estranged from the Senate, even being blamed for the death of his popular nephew and apparent successor. Tiberius increasingly withdrew from public life, and eventually retired to his estate on the Isle of Capri, leaving control of the government in the hands of the commander of the guard, Sejanus. But paranoia gripped Sejanus, who conducted a series of persecutions against supposed rivals, eventually falling to the power of

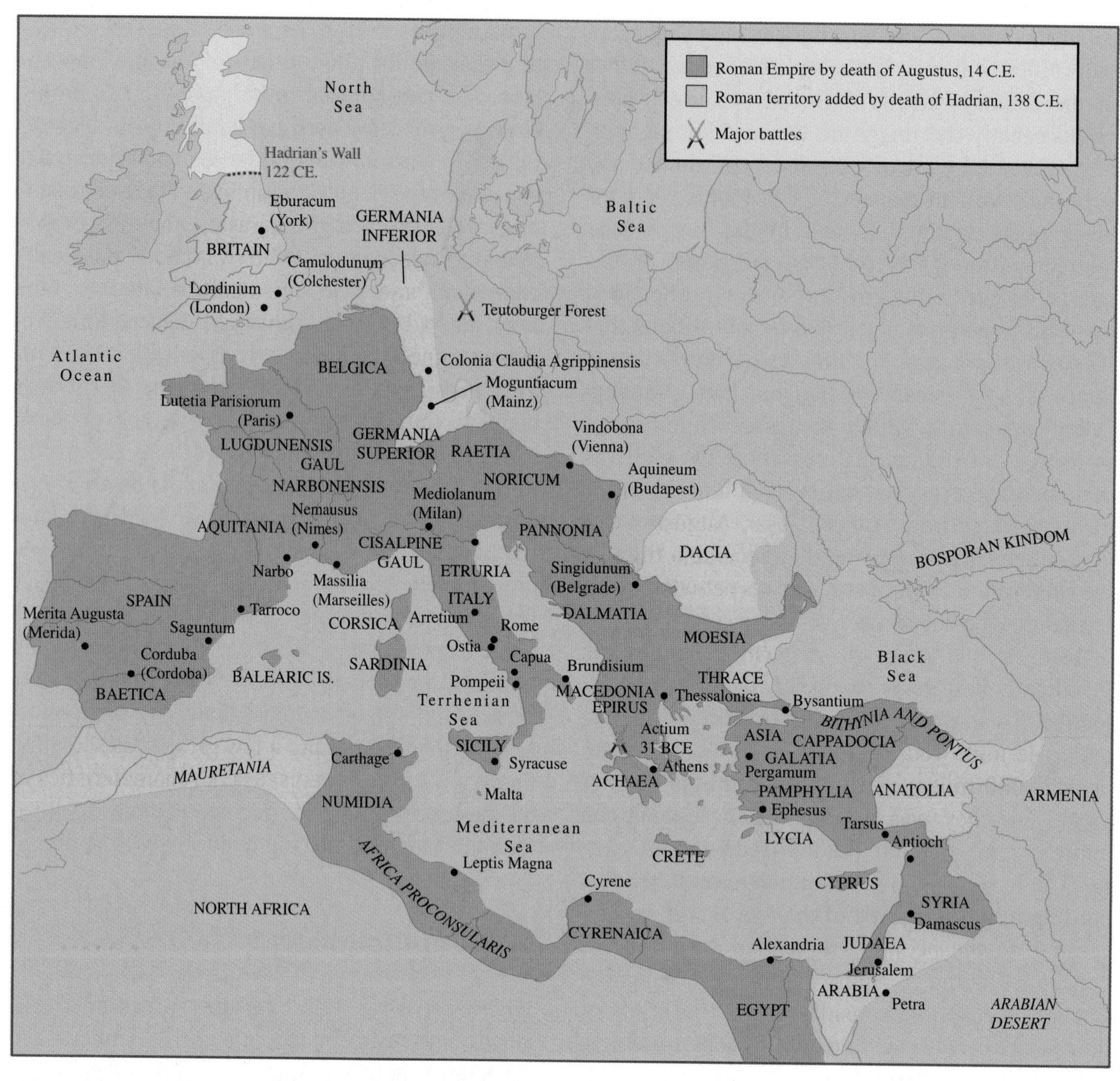

Figure 12.1 ■ *The Roman Empire.*

Tiberius himself, who was forced to leave retirement and have Sejanus executed. Tiberius died shortly thereafter amidst upheaval and controversy.

Most of the logical successors to Tiberius had been eliminated in the purges conducted by Sejanus. Therefore, of the few viable successors to Tiberius, the one named was an inexperienced grandnephew, **Gaius,** better known as **Caligula.** (Caligula is a nickname meaning "little boot," which was given to him by the soldiers of the palace guard in recognition of his attempts, when small, to act like a soldier.) Caligula started off well enough by stopping the purges, but he soon fell into problems brought on by his increasing insanity. After only four years in power, Caligula was killed by the commander of the guard, who then supported as new emperor the only remaining descendent of Tiberius, **Claudius.**

Claudius proved to be a competent administrator, but had serious domestic problems. His wife was unfaithful to him, and he therefore had her executed. He then married his niece, Agrip-

Dates	Name of Group of Emperors	Some Specific Emperors
27 B.C.–69 A.D.	Julio-Claudians	Augustus Tiberius Gaius (Caligula) Claudius Nero Year of the Four Emperors
69–96 A.D.	Flavians	Vespasian Titus Domitian
96–193 A.D.	Nervan-Antonian	Nerva Trajan Hadrian Antoninus Pius Marcus Aurelius Commodus
193–284 A.D.	Crisis during the 3rd Century	
284–308 A.D.	Tetrarchy	Diocletian
308–337 A.D.	Constantinian	Constantine the Great
337–476 A.D.	Post-Constantinian	Julian the Apostate Theodocius Romulus Augustus

Figure 12.2 ■ *Groups of Roman emperors.*

pina, who had been previously married. Agrippina had a very strong influence over Claudius but, in the end, that influence was not sufficient for Agrippina and she participated in the murder of Claudius so that her son by her previous marriage, **Nero,** could become emperor.

Initially, the 16-year-old Nero left the rule of the empire in the hands of his mother and his advisors, the chief of whom was **Seneca,** a famous Stoic writer. Nero married the daughter of Claudius, to further solidify his position as the ruler. After eight years, Nero took personal control of the empire, had his mother killed, and forced his advisors to commit suicide. Nero also divorced his wife and had her killed.

It is too bad that Nero did not follow the advice of Seneca, whose advice seems directed specifically at Nero's problems. Here are a few selections from Seneca:

- "Be harsh with yourself at times."
- "All cruelty springs from weakness."
- "If thou wishest to be loved, love."
- "To govern was to serve, not to rule."
- "You roll my log and I'll roll yours."
- "This life is only a prelude to eternity."
- "Our plans miscarry because they have no aim."
- "Luck is what happens when preparation meets opportunity."

Tradition has it that Nero played the fiddle while Rome burned. This statement, while likely not exactly true, still recognizes that Nero was indeed a performer of the lyre and, to ensure attendance while he played, would lock the doors after inviting in a large group of people. Further, it is likely that Nero had the fire started to create a place for him to build a new and ultra-elaborate palace. When the public came to believe that he might have started the fire, Nero suggested that a small, radical religious group called the Christians had actually started the fire. Nero persecuted the Christians, not for what they believed but as a way to deflect criticism from himself. Nero committed suicide in 68 A.D., just two years after killing the Christian apostles Peter and Paul. A revolt by the Jews in Judea further added to the resentment of the Roman government toward the Christians, who were, at that time, considered to be a Jewish sect. Over the next several decades, the continuation of the Jewish revolt, followed by another revolt in the 2nd century, forced the Romans to destroy the city of Jerusalem and scatter the Jews throughout the world so that they would never be able to again unite in rebellion.

Chaos followed the death of Nero and four different generals claimed the emperorship. Eventually, one of them, Vespasian, defeated the others and he began the next dynasty of emperors, which has been called the Flavians, named after Vespasian's family name.

Flavians

The three Flavian emperors—**Vespasian, Titus,** and **Domitian**—had conflicts with the Senate. Each sought to reduce the power of the Senate and increase the power of the emperorship, including the ability of the emperor to impose taxes and to name his successor. In this they were quite successful and, to a great degree, the Senate never was able to regain the position of influence it had in the Republic or even earlier in the empire.

The large treasury developed by Vespasian from the taxes he imposed allowed him to begin construction of the great Roman Colosseum. The structure was completed by Titus, his son, who celebrated with extensive games that lasted for 100 days. Titus was emperor during the eruption of Vesuvius and, because of the extensive treasury, was able to assist the surviving citizens of Pompeii in recovering from their losses.

Titus was assassinated by his brother, Domitian, who proved to be an inept ruler. The assassination of Domitian by a conspiracy of Senators marked an attempt of the Senate to reassert their authority. Throughout the early years of the empire, the role of the Senate in relation to the emperor was unclear, and this uncertainty caused tension. This may have been a negative legacy of the way Augustus ruled without a strong title, but may have also been a reflection of inferior leadership.

Nervan-Antonians

Because he was childless, elderly (62), and not from the powerful families of the city of Rome, **Nerva** seemed the ideal choice for the Senatorial conspirators as they chose a successor to Domitian. With his ascension to the emperorship, the Romans began a nearly hundred-year period of prosperity and growth that has been characterized as the Golden Age of Rome. The period is also called the time of the Five Good Emperors.

Rome was the largest city in the world, the hub of an extensive trading system that brought wealth and prosperity. The poor of the city of Rome were given a share of the prosperity through extensive games (such as chariot races, gladiator contests, and the like), as well as generous subsidies on basic foods and housing.

In an effort to unite the empire's various factions and to gain further support of the Senate, Nerva released political prisoners (most of them senators), restored their property, and returned some of the power that the Senate had lost under the Flavians. However, in so doing, Nerva angered the army; a brief revolt of the Praetorian Guard was successful in forcing Nerva to hand over those senators who had been responsible for the killing of Domitian. These men were, of course, the same group who installed Nerva himself, which angered the other senators and set up a rivalry between the Senate and the army that would prove to be a problem in later years.

Nerva recognized that the pattern of succession developed long ago by Augustus was basically sound, and so he named as his successor the most able person in the empire, **Trajan,** the successful general on the German front, who was then also adopted by Nerva. Trajan proved to be a capable successor whose military successes were popular with the army, and thus his appointment united both the military and senatorial aspects of the empire. He continued an expansive military program and conquered Dacia (present-day Romania), and also acquired some areas in Africa and Arabia. Trajan adopted a passive position toward the continuing persecution of the Christians. He suggested to the African governor, **Pliny,** that Christians should not be sought out or persecuted but, rather, ignored. Should any Christian be identified through the normal course of governance, the Christian would be urged to simply offer a sacrifice to the state gods and thus avoid punishment.

Trajan became ill during one of his military campaigns and, just before his death, named a distant relative, **Hadrian,** as his successor. Hadrian's reign was a time for consolidation of the empire's borders. He had a wall built across the northern frontier of Britain (**Hadrian's Wall**) that even today can be seen as a separator between England and Scotland. Hadrian also built extensive wooden fortifications along the Rhine and Danube Rivers. He even gave back part of the territory in Mesopotamia that Trajan had conquered, because Hadrian thought it was undefendable.

The successor to Hadrian was a highly qualified Roman aristocrat, **Antoninus Pius,** who had spent his life serving the state and had acquired great experience and knowledge. He was, in many ways, similar to the model of public service projected by Augustus. He gained power through a series of increasing responsibilities that had been practiced in the days of the Roman Republic, thus imitating Augustus. During his tenure, he was a strong promoter of the arts, sciences, and technologies.

Antoninus' successor was his son-in-law, **Marcus Aurelius.** He was the last of the Five Good Emperors. However, his reign was characterized by nearly constant warfare along the frontiers of the empire, in which he was largely successful in defending the empire's borders. Marcus Aurelius was, however, better known for his writings than for his warfare. He was a committed Stoic whose *Meditations* are some of the most insightful thoughts on the Stoic way of approaching life. Marcus Aurelius was succeeded by his son, **Commodus,** an extreme egotist who, in many experts' view, began the decline of the Roman Empire. Commodus is the emperor who infamously dressed as a gladiator in order to "experience" the thrill of combat. He also is known for attempting to "re-found" and rename Rome in his own honor as "Colonia Commodiana."

Crisis during the Third Century

Commodus was killed by the army, who could not tolerate his weak and ineffective rule. His death was followed by a series of military emperors who were constantly challenged by claimants seeking to depose them from the emperorship. Violence and revolt were constant because the emperors were typically chosen by competing military units. The erratic nature of the emperorship is revealed by the numbers. During the third century, there were 24 emperors plus 24 additional men who claimed to be emperor. Of those 48 men, 45 were assassinated, 1 died in captivity, 1 died in battle, and 1 died of plague. That is a rather abysmal situation.

These emperors were fixed on their own importance, as can be clearly seen from the inflated and grandiose title that one emperor used for himself: Emperor Caesar Galerius Valerius Maximianus Invictus Augustus, Pontifex Maximus, Germanicus Maximus, Egyptiacus Maximus, Thebaicus Maximus, Sarmaticus Maximus five times, Persicus Maximus twice, Carpicus Maximus, Holder of Tribunician Authority for the twentieth time, Imperator for the nineteenth, Consul for the eighth, Pater Patriae, Proconsul.

They were generally very poor administrators and, as a result, Rome entered a period of overwhelming inflation. To cope with the very high prices, the people were given bread and other necessary commodities. These gifts further increased the inflation, since the government further debased the money to pay for the free food.

Tetrarchy

The end of the crisis came when **Diocletian** was appointed emperor by the army and his chief rival was assassinated, thus leaving this remarkable man to head the empire. He decided that the current system of election by army units could not work. Moreover, he believed that the empire had grown so large that it must be administered in two sections—the Latin-speaking western part of the empire and the Greek-speaking eastern part. Under his plan, each of these halves would be administered by a leader who had full authority. He called these leadership positions *augustii;* that is, each was an "augustus." He became the augustus of the east and he named a faithful aide, **Maximian,** as the augustus of the west. To further improve the administration of the empire and to solve what had become a major problem of succession, he also designated a second-in-command in each of the halves of the empire and named these secondary leaders "caesars." The secondary leaders were located in separate cities from the *augustii.* The empire was actually being managed by these four leaders, each in their own capital city. Hence, the name of the system was the "Tetrarchy," which means "four leaders." The locations of the various sections of the empire are shown in Figure 12.3.

The establishment of the Tetrarchy was not the only creative administrative change made by Diocletian. He also imposed price and wage controls as a way to end the rampant inflation of the third century. Violators of the economic laws were threatened with death. The tactics worked reasonably well.

Diocletian also felt that the empire needed a unity of purpose. That unity could be promoted by a uniform religion. It is also possible that he was an extremely devout believer in the gods of the empire. Whichever the case, Diocletian imposed a mandate that all individuals within the empire must offer a sacrifice or some other public devotion to the gods of the state. Failure to do so would result in death. Most Romans were happy to comply; but not the

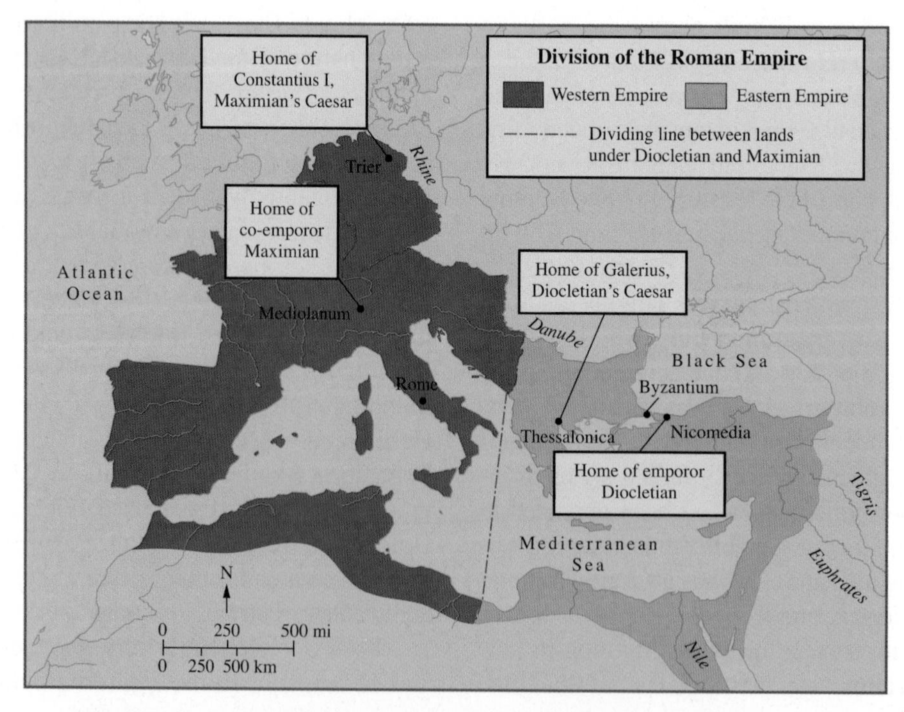

Figure 12.3 ■ *Division of the Roman Empire during the Tetrarchy.*

Christians, who by this time had grown to be about 10 percent of the population of the empire. They were large enough to be noticed but not large enough to be a voice in opposition to Diocletian's order. Therefore, the empire began a systematic persecution of the Christians, killing many in the arenas and by other methods. While many Christians must have complied with Diocletian's laws, many others chose martyrdom instead.

When most of the critical problems had been solved, Diocletian retired to his estate in present-day Croatia. He is the only emperor to retire totally on his own volition. He wrote to the other augustus and requested (demanded) that Maximian also retire. These dual retirements elevated the caesars to the positions of *augustii* and then each of them appointed another caesar to be second-in-command in their half of the empire. The Tetrarch succession system seemed to work (with a little urging from Diocletian), but when one of the new *augustii* died the next year, the entire system was thrown into chaos, with many claimants to all of the offices. Warfare ensued, with the claimants killing each other until only two were left—**Constantine** and Maxentius, who had each been ruling for several years as caesars but were also competing with each other for total control. The armies of these two met at Milvian bridge just outside Rome.

On the night before the battle, Constantine reported receiving a vision of a Christian symbol (the Chi Rho, which stands for Christ the King) in the heavens and received the impression that if he were to fight under the Christian symbol, he would be victorious. Constantine announced the vision to his troops, who painted the symbol on their shields. They were successful in the ensuing battle and Constantine became the sole ruler of the empire.

Constantine

From the moment of his victory under the Christian symbol, Constantine was friendly toward the Christian faith, eventually becoming a Christian (on his deathbed). While he was also friendly toward other religions (often building new pagan temples, personally sacrificing in them, inscribing coins with pagan images, and putting pagan inscriptions on monuments), he clearly took steps that favored the Christians. For example, he declared that all religions, no matter what their nature, would be respected (called the **Edict of Milan**). This edict ended the persecution of Christians that had begun under Diocletian. He allowed his mother, Helena, to journey to the Holy Land and identify locations where the events of Christ's life might have occurred. (Some of the sites she identified are likely the correct locations, but others are probably wrong.) Constantine built churches on several of the sites she selected.

The Christian Church began to thrive under Constantine. As it grew, several controversies over doctrine developed. Constantine decided to convene a conference in the city of Nicaea (in present-day Turkey) and resolve some of the issues of doctrine. In the end, Constantine expressed his support for the doctrinal position taken by the Bishop of Rome. This position then became the only accepted position within the empire on the points of doctrine, and in an irony of intolerance, Constantine forced compliance with the statement of belief (creed) that emerged from the Nicaean conference. The action of Constantine in convening the Nicaean Council and then enforcing the council's action is the beginning of what became known as the **Imperial Church,** that is, a church in which the emperor is the ultimate authority. (The Church of England is one example of a religion today in which the sovereign is the head of the church.) The Imperial Church continued for many years. In fact, the interplay between the authority of the church versus the authority of the emperor or of later kings was a major issue throughout the Middle Ages and into the Renaissance.

Just as Diocletian had split the empire along Latin-speaking and Greek-speaking lines for improved administration, Constantine did likewise although only informally. He retained ultimate authority over both parts of the empire, but chose to locate his headquarters in the east. He decided to build a new city at the chosen location at Byzantium, a small village on the banks of the

Bosporus in present-day Turkey. Constantine called the city Neo-Roma but after his death it was renamed Constantinople. He built the city as a Christian center, clearly anticipating his own conversion.

Post-Constantinians

After Constantine, all the Roman emperors, save one, **Julian the Apostate,** were Christians. Initially the Christian faith was favored by the emperors, but had not official recognition in the empire over other religions. Eventually, by edict of **Theodosius I,** it became the official religion of the Roman Empire, in 391 A.D. Interestingly, Theodosius I, even though strongly favoring the Christian faith, was forced to seek public forgiveness by **Ambrose,** the Bishop of Milan. The situation occurred because of a riot in the city of Thessalonica over the arrest of a favorite charioteer for being scandalously immoral. The populace stormed the prison, killed many guards and city officials, and then dismembered the officials and paraded their body parts around the city. Theodosius traveled to the city and asked the populace to meet with him in the Hippodrome, where the situation could be discussed. During the meeting, Theodosius gave a signal to his troops, who were stationed throughout the stadium as guards, and the troops killed 7,000 men, women, and children. The Roman world was shocked and, when Theodosius returned to Milan where he had his capital, the Bishop of Milan refused to allow Theodosius to enter the cathedral. After several weeks without receiving the benefits of the mass, Theodosius yielded and came to the cathedral as a penitent. The priests stripped off his insignia of rank and he was forced to ask Bishop Ambrose for forgiveness. The humble petition was accepted and Theodosius was given the sacrament of the Eucharist and his insignia returned.

Most of the emperors during the Post-Constantinian period were weak; the empire itself was weakening. The city of Rome itself was, perhaps, typically representative of the problems. It had become horribly corrupt and filthy. Disease was rampant; the infrastructure of the city, which had been so good during the Golden Age of Rome, was falling apart. Even the emperors refused to live in the city, and moved the capital of the western part of the empire elsewhere, as did Theodosius I, who had Milan as his capital. The city of Ravenna, a seaport city northeast of Rome and south of Venice on the Adriatic, emerged as the governmental headquarters for most of the emperors in this period.

Eventually, various barbarian tribes entered the empire and some of them threatened the city of Rome, which was still the big prize for the marauding and pillaging barbarians. It was sacked on at least three occasions and, on the final one, the barbarian king went on to attack and conquer Ravenna, thus deposing the seat of power of the western part of the empire. This occurred in 476 A.D. and has become the date for the final fall of the western portion of the Roman Empire. The last western emperor was **Romulus Augustus.** His insignia of office and other imperial symbols of power were transported to Constantinople, where they were given to the emperor in the east. As we will see, the power of the east was not eroded to the same extent and the eastern part of the empire persisted for many more years. However, to clearly differentiate between the time before and after the fall of the west, that eastern empire is called the **Byzantine Empire,** the subject of a later chapter.

The End of Roman Dominance

A variety of problems eventually allowed mighty Rome to be destroyed by its barbarian neighbors. Among these was the fact that the vast majority of the Roman army was no longer Roman, but a hodgepodge of conquered peoples who were Roman only in name and nominal loyalty. The empire could neither muster nor afford a fully Roman army. The size of the army had been decreasing over many years so that, over the last hundred years or so, only critical parts of the frontier were being guarded, and then only by the mixture of Romans supplemented with barbarian mercenaries. In the face of this shrinking Roman army, the people surrounding the empire were gaining in power. The Germans had united into much larger groups, such as the Visigoths, the Ostrogoths, the Franks, and the Anglo-Saxons.

A major problem occurred for the Roman Empire when the Persians conquered the Parthians on the far eastern frontier of the empire and began to threaten the Romans. The Roman army was shifted to strengthen the far-eastern frontier in Mesopotamia. That meant that Rome could no longer maintain enough troops in their farthest northwest territory—Britain. Therefore, in the early part of the fifth century, Rome withdrew from Britain. Sensing the vacuum that the Roman withdrawal created, groups of Anglos and Saxons invaded Britain from Germany and occupied eastern Britain. The Germans fought against the local Britains, mostly a series of Celtic kings. We will discuss this German invasion of Britain in a later chapter.

Not long afterward, a group of Germans, the **Franks,** attacked and settled in northern Gaul (what is today Holland, Belgium, and northern France). Again, the Roman army was not large enough to dislodge the Franks from what the Romans saw as a relatively unimportant part of the empire.

The unifications of related German tribes (the **Visigoths**) had occurred as a result of the Germans' own realization that they were more effective in larger fighting units, and also because of their fear of the **Huns,** a non-German tribe from central Asia that was attacking the Germans and pushing them against the Roman frontiers. The Huns, under their masterful leader, **Attila,** were fierce warriors who struck terror into the Germans. The Visigoths sought permission to cross the Danube River into Roman territory to avoid the onslaught of the Huns. The Roman officials agreed to allow the Visigoths to enter. However, the Romans treated the Visigoths poorly and, by so doing, encouraged the Visigoths to raid among the Roman citizenry. Eventually the Visigoths turned against the Romans and sacked the city of Rome in 410 A.D. These were the barbarian conquerors. After the sack of Rome, the Visigoths, under their leader **Alaric,** withdrew to northern Italy, where a combined Roman and Visigoth army was able to defeat Attila in 451 A.D., after which Attila retreated to Hungary, where he established his people. The Romans then directed the Visigoths over to Spain, where they were employed as mercenaries. The Visigoths took over and ruled Spain after the fall of the western empire.

Another barbarian group to enter the Roman Empire were the **Vandals.** These Germans settled in North Africa, from which they eventually also invaded Italy and sacked Rome. However, like the Visigoths, the Vandals retired afterwards and then ruled North Africa following the final defeat of the west in 476 A.D.

Yet a third German group to enter the Roman Empire were the **Ostrogoths.** Under their leader, **Odoacer,** they moved into Italy and conquered the city of Rome, and then captured the imperial capital of Ravenna. Odoacer did not retreat, but forced the last of the Roman emperors, Romulus Augustus, to resign. However, Odoacer was not the highest king of the Ostrogoths. When the highest king, **Theodoric,** became aware of what had occurred, he fought against and deposed Odoacer. Theodoric then made a covenant of non-aggression with the emperor in the east, headquartered, as we have already discussed, at Constantinople. Theordoric ruled for many years as king of the Ostrogoths in Italy under nominal control from Constantinople; in reality, he was free to do as he wished.

The lack of military power was, of course, an important factor in the fall of the Roman Empire. However, an even larger factor that contributed to Rome's demise was the inability of Rome, at least after the Republic period, to creatively solve its own problems. Rome had proven again and again that it could modify and adapt the ideas of the beloved Greeks and make them more practical and appealing. However, Rome was never able to come up with original solutions to problems, especially political ones, that the Greeks hadn't solved.

Rome may have been practical, but it was certainly not innovative in some areas; and this lack of innovation left Rome unable to solve some of its biggest problems, leading to its eventual downfall. First, the Roman Empire never devised a consistent way for its emperors to choose a successor and to transfer power. This problem led to chaos and intrigue almost every time an emperor died, and hastened the death of many an emperor. Rome could never decide if heredity, military might, imperial whim, or popular appeal should dictate who would rule next. Thus, in spite of Rome's greatness, weak, tyrannical, and/or insane men often ruled it.

This led to Rome's second problem: the government of the city of Rome itself. While the far-flung reaches of the empire were generally ruled efficiently by bureaucrats and kept in line by the military, this was never true of the city of Rome. Within the capital there was the age-old challenge of balancing stability and freedom, and of balancing the power of the Senate and the influence of the people. With the fall of the Roman Republic at the time of the death of Julius Caesar, the empire itself was brought under the institutionalized tyranny of the Caesars. In essence, the citizens gave up their freedom for stability, but within the city of Rome the balance between freedom and stability was never achieved. Yes, the emperor reigned there and was a dictator, the same as the rest of the empire, but the city of Rome was also the home of the Senate; these proud men wanted their voice to be heard, and while the emperors had no legal obligation to listen to the Senate, anyone wanting to remain in power usually did. Thus, the complex situation gave the citizens of the city of Rome a large degree of freedom, but made the stability of the government of Rome less sure, as the emperors had to constantly appease the Roman masses and also appease the Senate, or experience the threat of a murder plot from either the people or the Senate. The ruins of the ancient Roman Forum are symbolic of the problems of the Roman Empire. As seen in Figure 12.4, most of the structures that remain are religious with the exception of the senate building which is seen, largely intact, in the upper left of the photo (Figure 12.4). The senate exerted influence because it remained at the center of Roman life.

Finally, as we will discuss in detail in the next chapter, the Roman Empire struggled with mak-

Figure 12.4 ■ Ruins of the Forum in modern Rome. *© 2010 by steba. Used under license of Shutterstock, Inc.*

ing original advancements in science and technology. Rome was great at using and improving technological advancements like the column and the arch, but made very little new progress in its nearly one thousand years of dominance. Even when Roman citizens did come up with useful innovations, they were often ignored. A prime example is a Roman Greek named **Hero of Alexandria,** who invented a kind of steam engine in the first century A.D. It was a device that could have been useful in Rome's grand construction projects and in the distribution of food and supplies across the vast empire, yet it was ignored.

How Rome Succeeded Where Greece Failed

Both the Greeks and Romans were able to build huge territorial empires. Rome's ability to do so reaffirmed to them that they were indeed destined to be the inheritors of the glory of Greece. However, there is an important difference between the empire built by the Greeks and that of the Romans: the Romans were able to keep their empire, while the Greek Empire disintegrated quickly. There are reasons for this difference.

Unlike Greece, which never was able to unify itself under a single legal system, Rome had a passion for and love of law. As early as 450 B.C., 300 years prior to Rome's defeat of Carthage, Rome had codified its laws in the Twelve Tables. From this point Roman law continued in its development, becoming more complex and intricate, but always remembering that the reason for its existence was to help govern and regulate the daily lives of people. Improvement of the Roman legal system was a major factor in the Augustian period.

Roman law was one of the great gifts given by the Romans to the many peoples they conquered. Wherever Roman soldiers went and conquered, Roman law went with them. When new cities or territories were brought into the Roman Empire, Roman laws were posted in a public place so that the newly conquered peoples would know their rights within the Roman Empire, and to show them what manner of civilized people had conquered them. To the Romans, law was administered to all. It made no difference if the violator was from an aristocratic Roman family and the victim a newly conquered semi-barbarian, or vice versa. In theory, all subjects of Rome had the same rights in law (although Roman citizens did have some added benefits). In many cases the stability and fairness brought by the Romans and their laws were superior to what the conquered peoples, including the Greeks, had previously known. The Romans were able to gain the loyalty and reduce the resentment of many of their conquered subjects simply because life under Roman law was better than it had been before the Romans arrived.

A second reason the Roman Empire had such longevity, whereas the Greeks were divided and eventually conquered, is inclusion. The Greeks had never really mastered this principle while building their empire. Most Greeks believed that the people they conquered were inferior, and that intermarrying with those they conquered, or allowing conquered peoples to help in government, was both politically unwise and damaging to Greek racial purity. And while Alexander himself ignored these beliefs (possibly because he was Macedonian and not true-born Greek), those who followed him and governed his empire after his death generally followed traditional Greek practice and did not intermingle with those they conquered. Thus, the rulers often misunderstood and feared their subjects, and the subjects often resented and hated their rulers.

At first, Rome followed the pattern of Greece (and most other empires) and made those they conquered slaves. However, while spreading themselves out across the Italian peninsula, the Romans soon found that slaves were poor and unwilling workers who spent most of their energy resenting their captors or designing ways to regain their freedom. Rome's early energy and efforts were being spent controlling their slaves rather than expanding their empire and strengthening their borders. To remedy this situation, Rome decided that they would make all Italians Roman citizens and find their slaves elsewhere. Even the lowest Roman citizen, if he fought for Rome for the predetermined amount of time, would be granted land to work and build on. This decision to include the Italians energized the early Republic and allowed Rome to achieve its later greatness, as it now had an army stocked with loyal citizens who had something to gain from dedicated service. As the empire grew, peoples all over the world wanted to become Roman citizens and enjoy the rights and privileges that went with this title. Citizenship was easy for the Romans to give. It cost them nothing, and made empire-building easier. Both Greece and Rome were conquerors of nations, but Rome was able to keep their holdings by including those they conquered with citizenship, thus giving these peoples a new sense of pride and belonging.

Finally, the Romans were able to create a way of life that was incredibly appealing. It was based on the values of the Greeks, but went beyond that by expanding the comforts of Roman living to entire societies. The secret of this capability was technology. From Roman roads, which connected the empire together, to Roman medicine and science, Rome shared its knowledge with all. This sharing improved everyone's life and strengthened the empire. Let's examine Roman science, art, and technology to see how this was done.

Timeline—Important Dates

Date	Event
27 B.C.	*Reign of Octavian (Augustus) begins*
27 B.C.–69 A.D.	*Julio-Claudians*
69–96 A.D.	*Flavians*
96–193 A.D.	*Nervan-Antonians*
193–284 A.D.	*Crisis in the Third Century*
284–308 A.D.	*Tetrarchy*
308–337 A.D.	*Constantine*
337–476 A.D.	*Post-Constantinians*
476 A.D.	*Last of the western emperors resigns*

Suggested Readings

Farquharson, A. S. L. (trans.), *The Meditations of Marcus Aurelius Antoninus,* Oxford University Press, 1944.

Gaius Sallustius Crispus, *Historiae* (II Fragment 72 in *Salustii Historian Reliquae,* B. Maurenbecher (ed.), Cambridge University Press, 1893.

Gibbon, Edward, *The Decline and Fall of the Roman Empire,* A One-Volume Abridgement by Dero A. Saunders, Penguin Books, 1980.

Seneca: On Favours and Natural Questions

Introduction

Lucius Annaeus Seneca (4 BC–65 AD) was born in Spain, educated in Rome, and became famous as a philosopher, orator, and playwright. He served as tutor and advisor to the Emperor Nero for most of Nero's life and was a good influence on the young ruler. Nero eventually diverged from his education, however, and became the infamous tyrant we now remember him as. After retiring from his post with Nero, Seneca had a falling out with his former pupil, was accused of conspiracy and forced to commit suicide.

At least 8 surviving plays have been attributed to Seneca; all adapted for his audiences from previously written tragedies. Perhaps his greatest contribution to western thinking however, was his writings on the philosophy of stoicism.

In *On Favours,* he gives a thoughtful essay on how good works should be chosen for their own sake and not for the sake of reward and pleasure. This passage is worthy of any history textbook as it includes a clear comparison between the Stoic view and the Epicurean.

"What is the Principal Thing in Life" comes from Seneca's *Natural Questions.* This passage mentions the proper motivation for good works again, but only as an example of the broader picture of stoicism. Everything deemed important in this passage is immaterial; it is the direct opposite of the Epicurean's search for earthly pleasure.

[1]Gaius Sallustius Crispus, *Historiae* (II Fragment 72 in *Salustii Historian Reliquae* ed. B. Maurenbecher (Leipzig 1891–3)). Seneca cites the same phrase, without naming the author, at *On Providence* 5. 9 and *On Peace of Mind* 14.10.

Article 22
On Favours

I. (1) Nothing in all the questions that we have handled, Aebutius Liberalis, is so vital, it would seem, or 'more in need', as Sallust puts it, 'of careful discussion' than what is now before us: are doing a favour and showing gratitude in return things to be chosen for their own sake?

(2) You find people who cultivate honourable action for gain and have no liking for virtue without reward. But there is no grandeur in it, if there is anything venal. Nothing is more shameful than for anyone to calculate a good man's worth. Virtue invokes neither profit to attract nor loss to deter. So far is it from corrupting anyone by raising hopes or making promises that, on the contrary, it calls for sacrifice and is more often a matter of offerings freely made. You must trample on your own interests to approach it; you must go wherever you are summoned or sent, without regard for your property, at times without even a thought for your own blood; nor must you ever try to evade its commands. (3) 'What am I to gain by acting bravely or showing gratitude?' The gain of having done so. Nothing else is on offer. If some advantage happens to come your way, you can treat it as a bonus. Things that are honourable contain their own reward. If anything honourable is to be chosen for its own sake, and if a favour is something honourable, it can only come on the same terms, being of the same nature. And that anything honourable is to be chosen for its own sake has been often and abundantly proved.

II. (1) On this point, we are in arms against the Epicureans, that self-indulgent and sheltered crowd of dinner-party philosophers, for whom virtue is the handmaid of pleasure, obeying it, serving it, seeing it as of higher rank. 'Yet you cannot have pleasure without virtue', you may say. (2) But why put it in front of virtue? Do not think that this is simply a disagreement about precedence. The whole question of virtue and its authority is at issue. It will not be virtue at all, if it can come second. It has a right to the leading role—to go first, to give orders, to stand in the highest position. And you want it to ask for a signal before acting! (3) 'What difference does it make to you? I, too, deny that without virtue a happy life is possible. Pleasure itself, though I follow it and have made myself its slave, I repudiate and condemn, if virtue be absent. There is only one point of disagreement: is virtue the cause of the highest good or is it the highest good itself?' Suppose this alone were the question: are you thinking simply of a change of precedence? To put last things first is a real muddle, of course, an obvious lack of vision. (4) But what outrages me is not that virtue should be placed after pleasure, but that it should be placed alongside pleasure at all. It despises and hates pleasure, recoiling as far as it can from it, having more to do with the manly inconveniences of toil and pain than with this effeminate 'good' of yours.

III. (1) I had to insert these remarks, dear Liberalis, because doing a favour, which is what we are now discussing, is a function of virtue, and nothing is more shameful than doing one for any purpose other than that of doing it. For if we gave in the hope of getting back, we would give to the wealthiest, not the worthiest. As it is, I would prefer a pauper to an unsuitable rich man. It is not a favour at all if it considers a person's fortune. (2) Besides, if advantage were all that induced us to help, those who could most easily spread their favours would be under the least obligation to do so—I mean the rich and powerful, I mean monarchs with no need for aid from others. The very gods would not make the gifts that they do in such numbers, pouring them forth unceasingly day and night. In everything their own nature is enough to keep them fully provided, safe and inviolate. No one would receive any favour from them, if the one motive for doing it lay in looking to oneself and to one's own advantage. (3) You are not doing a favour, you are making an investment, if you cast your eyes around to see not where your outlay would do the most good, but where it would be the most profitable and the returns the easiest. Since the gods are far from this sort of consideration, it follows that they will not be liberal. If the one motive for benefaction is the benefactor's own advantage and a god can expect no advantage from us, there can be no motive for a god's beneficence.

Article 23

Natural Questions

11. To raise your mind above the threats and promises of fortune, to consider nothing worth hoping for. What does fortune have that you should be covetous of? Whenever you withdraw from an association with divine things and turn to human affairs you will be blinded, like the eyes of those who turn from bright sunlight to dark shade.

12. What is important? To be able to endure adversity with a cheerful mind. To bear whatever happens just as though you wanted it to happen to you. For you would have been quite right to want it, if you had known that all things happen in accordance with a decree of god. To weep, to complain, to groan is to rebel.

16. What is important? To have your breath on your very lips; this makes a man free not by right of Roman citizenship but by right of nature. A man is free who has escaped slavery to himself. Such slavery is continuous, ineluctable, pressing constantly day and night without pause, without interruption, without leave of absence.

17. To be a slave to one's self is the most grievous kind of slavery. It is easy to shake off if you cease demanding so much of yourself, if you stop searching for personal profit, if you keep before your eyes your nature and time of life—even if you are still young—and say to yourself: "Why am I a fool? Why do I pant, sweat, upset the earth and the forum? I do not need much, and only for a short time."

Article 24

Marcus Aurelius: Meditations

Introduction

The second century AD has been called the "Golden Age of Rome" due to Rome's success as a stable institution with its borders extended as far as they ever would be and the strong development of the arts and technology. This success is attributed to the rule of five powerful but benevolent emperors in succession, a streak that the Romans never enjoyed again. Marcus Aurelius Antoninus (121–180 AD) was the last and most well known of those "Five Good Emperors." He was educated by the greatest thinkers of the day and became a great intellectual leader. He was a military genius and a hero for peace at the same time. Such a large empire naturally had many challenges. Marcus Aurelius dealt with two major invasions, a great plague, and financial problems from supporting the massive army. He also suffered from a notoriously disloyal wife and an unkind son-heir with no leadership skills.

The philosophy of Stoicism helped Marcus through these challenges. His *Meditations* is like a personal diary; reading it lets one feel his desire for self-mastery and harmony with nature through reason, searching for truth, and abandonment of emotion. The introspective nature of this book was rare for its time and allows the reader to really understand a man's feelings two thousand years ago.

Book 1: speaks of not allowing ourselves to be overcome by the evils around us, and to forgive others on the basis that we all possess imperfections.

Book 2: exhorts the reader to not waste his steadily decreasing balance of days of life.

Book 3: speaks of maintaining purpose in all action and using one's inner mind as a retreat.

Book 4: speaks of the inherent justice in nature, our attitude toward death and many other adages of the Stoic lifestyle.

Book II

Written Among the Quadi on the River Gran

1. Say to yourself in the early morning: I shall meet today inquisitive, ungrateful, violent, treacherous, envious, uncharitable men. All these things have come upon them through ignorance of real good and ill. But I, because I have seen that the nature of good is the right, and of ill the wrong, and that the nature of the man himself who does wrong is akin to my own (not of the same blood and seed, but partaking with me in mind, that is in a portion of divinity), I can neither be harmed by any of them, for no man will involve me in wrong, nor can I be angry with my kinsman or hate him; for we have come into the world to work together, like feet, like hands, like eyelids, like the rows of upper and lower teeth. To work against one another therefore is to oppose Nature, and to be vexed with another or to turn away from him is to tend to antagonism.

Book III

Written in Carnuntum

1. We ought to take into account not only the fact that day by day life is being spent and a smaller balance remaining, but this further point also that, should we live longer, it is at least doubtful whether the intellect will hereafter be the same, still sufficient to comprehend events and the speculation which contributes to the understanding alike of things divine and human. For, if the mind begin to decay, there will be no failure of functions like transpiration, nutrition, sense-impression, and desire; but the right employment of ourselves, precision in regard to the related elements of duty, analysis of the indications of sense, to know just whether the time is come to take leave of life, and all questions of the kind which specially require a trained judgement—these are extinguished before the rest. Accordingly we must press forward, not only because every day we are drawing nearer to death, but also because the apprehension of events and the ability to adapt ourselves to them begin to wane before the end.

Book IV

1. The sovereign power within, in its natural state, so confronts what comes to pass as always to adapt itself readily to what is feasible and is presented to it. This is because it puts its affection upon no material of its own choice; rather it sets itself upon its objects with a reservation, and then makes the opposition which encounters it into material for itself. It is like a fire, when it masters what falls into it, whereby a little taper would have been put out, but a bright fire very quickly appropriates and devours what is heaped upon it, and leaps up higher out of those very obstacles.
2. Nothing that is undertaken is to be undertaken without a purpose, nor otherwise than according to a principle which makes the art of living perfect.
3. Men look for retreats for themselves, the country, the seashore, the hills; and you yourself, too, are peculiarly accustomed to feel the same want. Yet all this is very unlike a philosopher, when you may at any hour you please retreat into yourself. For nowhere does a man retreat into more quiet or more privacy than into his own mind, especially one who has within such things that he has only to look into, and become at once in perfect ease; and by ease I mean nothing else but good behaviour. Continually, therefore, grant yourself this retreat and repair yourself. But let them be brief and fundamental truths, which will suffice at once by their presence to wash away all sorrow, and to send you back without repugnance to the life to which you return.

Book IX

1. Whosoever does injustice commits sin; for Universal Nature having made reasonable creatures for the sake of one another, to benefit each other according to desert but in no wise to do injury, manifestly he who transgresses her will sins against the most venerable of the gods, because Universal Nature is a nature of what is, and what is is related to all that exists.
2. A wiser man's part had been to go away from men without tasting falsehood, hypocrisy, luxury, and pride; a second-best course is to breathe your last filled at least with distaste for these things.
3. Disdain not death, but be well satisfied with it, because this, too, is one of the things which Nature wills. For as are adolescence and old age, growth and maturity, development of teeth and beard and grey hair, begetting, conception, and childbearing and the rest of the natural functions which life's seasons bring, such also is actual dissolution. This, therefore, is like a man of trained reason, not to be rash or violent or disdainful in the face of death, but to wait for it as one of the natural functions; and, as you now wait for the unborn

child to come forth from your wife's womb, so expect the hour in which your soul will drop from this shell.

4. Whosoever does wrong, wrongs himself; whosoever does injustice, does it to himself, making himself evil.
5. Often he who omits an act does injustice, not only he who commits an act.
7. Wipe out imagination: check impulse: quench desire: keep the governing self in its own control.

Roman Science, Technology, and Art
Thieves or Geniuses

> The captive Greeks revenged themselves by capturing their conquerors.
>
> —*Horace (Roman writer of the first century* B.C.*)*

Acquiring and Adapting

Beginning with the earliest days of Rome, the Roman people eagerly adopted elements of technology and culture from any society they encountered. They took the arch from the Etruscans, ship technology from the Carthaginians, and the calendar from the Egyptians, but mostly they took from the Greeks. Perhaps the rough, warlike Romans saw the Greek lifestyle as the ideal for which they were striving, and so they readily adopted Greek culture. In this, the Romans were much like the Macedonians under Alexander, who also succumbed to the enticements of the Greeks. Perhaps also the Romans felt the need for a cultural heritage, and found that by adopting Greek culture, they could also adopt, as their own, the ancient traditions of the Greeks. For whatever reason, the Romans clearly made Greek culture their own, especially in the areas of art, sculpture, literature, and drama, where the Greek love of beauty, symmetry, proportion, and myth were so important. Roman sculpture was not influenced by Greece—it was Greek! Roman artists not only used Greek art as a starting point or as inspiration, but as an ideal. With only a few exceptions, Roman artists were not praised and respected for their originality, but for how closely they could copy the work of the Greeks. This adoration of Greek art was so pervasive that despite nearly a thousand years of Roman dominance there may not be a single piece of surviving Roman art that was not derived or copied from the Greeks. Furthermore, most of the sculptures we commonly consider to be "Greek" are actually Roman copies.

But the Romans retained certain differences from all the cultures they encountered, even the Greeks, and these differences were important in making Roman creativity different from and, in many ways, more enduring than the cultures of those around them. A conservative strain among the Romans constantly cried out for caution in adopting Greek values and lifestyle. Romans saw themselves as strong and powerful, and dedicated to basic principles of justice and morality that seemed inconsistent with the leisurely and self-indulgent lifestyle of the Greeks. The Greeks were also abstract, placing great importance on theory and truth. The Greeks were constantly seeking for perfection, for the "truth," for the underlying answer, for the non-tangible "Form." This constant search spurred the Greeks to great creativity, but often at the price of stability and practicality. To the Greeks, the fundamental truths and underlying Forms were all-important. The Romans did not feel the need to constantly search and question. To the Romans, stability and practicality were more important than ultimate truth. The Romans believed a smaller idea that had a practical use was more valuable than a grand theory, no matter how true it seemed. So, while Rome idolized and imitated Greece, it also adapted and changed Greek ideas to make them more useful and appealing to the masses. This difference leads to one of the ultimate questions in the history of creativity: Is the adoption and adaptation of another culture's ideas creative in itself, or is just the genesis of these ideas by the original culture a creative process? Or in this case, is Rome creative for adapting Greek ideas to make them better fit Roman society, or is it only the original Greek ideas that are creative? We will return to this question at the end of this chapter, but first we will examine the contributions of the Romans and their system of adopting and then adapting.

Examples of Roman adoption and adaptation are common. Roman architecture has Greek columns supporting Etruscan arches. The Romans saw the advantages of the vowel-containing alphabet of the Greeks, but modified it for simplicity and compatibility with Latin. The battle methods of the Greeks, especially the determination of the Spartans, were adopted by the Romans, but the units of the Roman army were made smaller and more independent, in keeping with Roman terrain and leadership values. The Greek gods were renamed and their mythology replicated; Zeus became Jupiter, Aphrodite became Venus, Poseidon was renamed Neptune, Apollo kept the same name. Finally, even Greek societal mores were adopted by most Romans as being civilized and appropriate, keeping in place the stronger values of dedication to state and family that the Romans held dear.

Literature, Drama, History

Ancient Greece's great literary works were Homer's epic poems, and Homer's great hero was that roving adventurer Odysseus. Odysseus was beloved by Greece because he was a symbol and stereotype of all things cherished by the people of ancient Greece. Odysseus loved and honored his country and his freedom; he was adventurous and impetuous; he was a risk taker who explored other lands and loved other women, always hopeful that his wife, Penelope, would remain true and faithful and await his eventual return.

It should come as no surprise, then, that when **Virgil,** the great Roman poet, decided to write his own epic poem explaining the history and founding of glorious Rome, he chose to model his own poem, the *Aeneid,* on Homer's classics. And like Homer's Odysseus, Virgil chose to make his hero, Aeneas, a wandering adventurer. However, as Rome would do with many of Greece's creative ideas, Virgil stripped away many of the excesses and extravagances of Odysseus, and made his Aeneas a reluctant adventurer with a destiny and sense of duty that dictated his actions.

Odysseus began his epic journey by leaving behind his wife and family to fight a war against distant Troy to ensure power for Greece and glory for himself. During his wanderings (which take place after the Trojan War), Odysseus spent time with many women, sought out monsters and quests, and openly defied the gods—all with the eventual goal of returning home. (It took Odysseus ten years to get home, so it is doubtful he took the most direct route home to his wife and family.) In contrast, Aeneas was forced onto his journey when his home, Troy, was destroyed. Aeneas took his aged father and young son with him (his wife had been killed) and left on a quest to find a new home for him, his people, and his gods. On the way, Aeneas stopped in Carthage, where the queen, Dido, offered herself and her country if Aeneas would stay with her and make Carthage his home. Aeneas was briefly tempted, but knew that his destiny and that of his people was to found a home of their own, and in the end he left Dido. Eventually, Aeneas landed his ships in Latium, on the western coast of Italy, and with the blessing of the local king, married his daughter and settled down in his new home.

The differences between Odysseus and Aeneas are worth pointing out, as they are indicative of the difference between the cultures of ancient Greece and Rome. Rome based its culture and creativity on that of Greece, just as Virgil based his hero, Aeneas, on Homer's Odysseus. However, Aeneas is a much more moderate character, only doing what he is forced to do by fate and circumstance. Odysseus, on the other hand, seeks out adventure and tempts fate. Similarly, Rome built its society on that of Greece, but whereas the Greeks were enthralled with the grand idea and the great discovery, the Romans were content with the simple and the practical. This relationship between the heroes of these two civilizations' legendary histories shows the pattern that Rome would use in its imitation of Greek creativity.

The Homeric epics, written early in Greek history, established the basis for Greek ethics and attitudes, at least until the time of the great Greek philosophers. In contrast, the *Aeneid* was written during the time of Augustus Caesar—half a millennium *after* the founding of the Republic and on the threshold of the Empire. Therefore, rather than *establishing* values for the Roman society, the *Aeneid reflected* values already in place. However, the style and subject of the *Aeneid* gave Rome an ancient past that was just as honorable and glorious as that of the Greeks. Virgil's book also reflected the glorious present, that is, the days of Augustus, by introducing Augustus in the *Aeneid* when Aeneas is shown the future leaders of the society he would found. Even though Virgil didn't complete the book to his satisfaction (he even left instructions that it be destroyed upon his death because it was incomplete), the direct action of Augustus in publishing the book gave it official support and the public readily adopted it as the basis of their culture. It even gained a sort of divine nature, as people would ask a question and then randomly open the *Aeneid,* read wherever they opened, and try to find an answer to their question.

As we do today, learned Romans recognized the greatness and depth of Greek philosophy. Socrates, Plato, Aristotle, Zeno, and Epicurus were part of the curriculum studied by any well educated Roman. Greek philosophy may be the pinnacle of philosophical thought (at least in the Roman period, although arguably it is still true) but it was also challenging, difficult, and for many Romans, unapproachable in real life. To the Romans, who always wanted to be like the Greeks, this was a difficult circumstance. How could they be like their beloved Greeks if they could not live as the greatest Greeks taught? The Roman remedy to this dilemma was to bring Greek philosophy down to the level of the common man, rather than to raise the common man to the level of Greek philosophy.

The writings of the great Roman orator and consul **Cicero** are a good example of the Roman adaptation of Greek philosophy. Cicero lived during the turbulent times surrounding the decline of the Roman Republic and the establishment of the Roman Empire. Cicero was always a champion of the republic and disliked Julius Caesar for his erosion of it. However, Cicero and Caesar had a mutual admiration for one another, and while they disliked and mistrusted one another, they also worked together for the good of Rome when needed. Cicero was not saddened, though, upon learning of Julius Caesar's death. Cicero valiantly, but imprudently, opposed Caesar's successors, Octavian and Mark Anthony, and eventually was murdered by Mark Anthony as a message to others who might oppose those who would succeed Caesar.

Because his strong republican political leanings found him generally out of favor with the various rulers of Rome, Cicero spent his last ten years of life in forced semi-retirement. And since he could not speak publicly, he chose to write. It is from this period of his life that we have most of his philosophical writings. In fairness to Cicero, he claimed to be only a translator and conveyor of Greek ideals, not a great philosopher. And truly he made no great discoveries and had no new wondrous philosophical insights. Cicero did set himself a difficult task, however—to make the strenuous virtue and lofty expectations of Greek philosophy applicable to the average Roman. Greek philosophy seemed to say that the key to happiness and virtue was to step out of the world; to leave the political arena. The Greeks disagreed on the best way to do this. Epicureans said it could only be done by physically withdrawing from the world. The Stoics argued that it only required strict personal control, not physical retreat. Atomists argued there was no free will; all men could do was accept their fate with courage and play out their part in life. For Cicero and the Romans, who gloried in the joys and challenges of public life and service, no kind of retreat was wholly acceptable.

Cicero's solution was to retain the Greeks' strict sense of virtue while removing the need for retreat or surrender. In essence, Cicero said to the Romans, "Participate, but do the virtuous thing—always." And what is the virtuous thing? Well, first it is obeying the law; but the law is not always fair and just, he admits, so virtue must be taken further. It is this second step that is more difficult, Cicero says. He asserts that one should be honest, kind, and fair to everyone at all times. It does not matter if one is dealing with the emperor, a senator, a slave, or a woman. It does not matter if one is rich and one is poor, one a friend and one an enemy. We should always treat people with honesty, kindness, and fairness, regardless of the circumstances. Furthermore, Cicero argued that defining what is virtuous is not subjective to each person; he claimed that all people know virtue inherently.

Cicero acted as he taught, and it possibly led to his downfall and death. Yet, in spite of being a difficult way of life, to the Roman public it at least seemed possible to live a virtuous life. This was an important distinction for the Romans, who loved and respected the Greek philosophers, yet couldn't escape the fact that it was one thing to love Socrates, and another to live like him. Cicero's explanation and example seemed to provide a difficult, but livable, way to love Greece and be Roman.

A strong sense of dedication to what is right can also be seen in the writings of the great Roman emperor-philosopher, **Marcus Aurelius.** He lived in the midst of the Roman Empire period but still retained many of the same concepts as Cicero. But, by the time of Marcus Aurelius, those concepts had become part of the Stoic philosophy. The *Meditations* of Marcus Aurelius reflect well the thinking of the Roman elite during the days of the Roman Golden Age. However, as was seen by the unethical and contrary actions of Marcus Aurelius' successor, his son, that deeply ethical thinking was either limited to a few or was easily ignored.

Two other Roman leaders who wrote well were **Augustus Caesar,** a poet and historian, and **Julius Caesar,** whose works on the conquest of Gaul and Asia are standard primers for Latin students even today. Caesar's works contain the familiar phrases "All Gaul is divided into three parts," and "Veni, Vedi, Vici" (I came, I saw, I conquered).

The pattern of adoption and adaptation can also be seen in Roman drama. The Greeks had invented drama, and Greek tragedy was masterful. The great Greek playwrights, Sophocles, Aeschylus, and Euripides, wrote elaborate tragedies of intrigue, betrayal, sex, and murder, loaded with psychological drama, and with action taking place on several levels.

The Romans, who always loved to be entertained, found the baser aspects of Greek tragedy—the murder, incest, and intrigues—to be fascinating and entertaining. However, Greek drama is as challenging as it is inspiring and entertaining, and the Romans soon grew tired of the complex psychological background and semi-religious parables and allusions characteristic of Greek tragedy. The Romans therefore wrote their own plays, which are quite inferior copies, generally lacking the psychological complexity and unexpected plot twists. Foremost among these Roman playwrights was Seneca.

Seneca was not a playwright by trade, but an intellectual and teacher to young Nero, who was later to become emperor. Nero's ascension to the throne at age 19 made Seneca one of the most powerful men in the world, as his student respected him and looked to him for advice and counsel, which we have quoted in the previous chapter. However,

Seneca's influence waned as Nero's reign went on. Nero was becoming ever more tyrannical, and eventually began to go mad. Seneca disapproved of Nero's tyranny and as his criticism of Nero increased, Nero's love for Seneca decreased. Eventually Nero suspected Seneca had been involved in a plot to kill him, and ordered Seneca put to death. Soldiers were sent to surround Seneca's house and, knowing the end that awaited him, Seneca took his own life. Sadly, Seneca was not involved in the plot to kill Nero.

Seneca left behind a collection of written works including letters to friends, philosophical treatises, and plays. The letters and philosophy are highly quotable and seem to be based on solid Roman values of ethics and prudent living. The plays of Seneca are tragedies written loosely in the Greek style. In his day Seneca was considered the great Roman tragic playwright and the successor and heir to the Greek masters. Seneca's plays may pale in comparison to the great tragedies of Greece, but that did not diminish their popularity in Rome. Seneca's successes came because he was able to do for Greek drama what so many other Romans had done to other Greek ideas. His plays stripped away the complexity and difficulty of the Greek tragedies and left just the violence, intrigue, sex, and murder. In doing so he had lost the richness of what the Greeks had created, but left what was entertaining for the masses. In a sense he had removed the art and left only the amusement. A similar thing often happens in modern entertainment when a classic novel is made into a movie. Those who labor through the novel are challenged. The experience may not always be pleasant at the time, but at the end there is a sense of the greatness of the art and a fulfillment at having had the experience. Those who only sit through the movie may be entertained, but they usually miss the greatness and depth of the novel.

Like Roman philosophy and drama, Roman historical writings were based on that of Greece. Also like Roman philosophy and drama, Roman history was made more accessible by removing some of the difficulty and austerity of Greek works and making it more accessible and interesting to the masses. Rome's great historian was named **Tacitus** and his two great works, *Histories* and *Annals,* both deal with the history of Rome. However, they differ from their Greek predecessors in their degree of objectivity and verification of truthfulness.

Greece's great historian, Thucydides, wrote of the Peloponnesian Wars between Athens and Sparta. As true history, Thucydides writings are masterful. He is almost perfectly objective, careful not to cloud what has happened with his own feelings, opinions, and point of view. This is especially noteworthy considering he was a disgraced and banished commander who had fought for the losing side. If there was ever a case for historical revision, Thucydides' may have been it. Yet, Thucydides related the history as if he were uninvolved and completely impartial, giving fair treatment to both sides and attempting to be painstakingly accurate in his details. The accuracy and objectivity of Thucydides are the blueprints of all history since that time. However, if Thucydides' history is objective and accurate, it is also dry reading, with nothing to color it or add interest for the average reader.

Tacitus took the opposite approach of Thucydides. Tacitus wanted the average Roman reader to be interested in what he wrote, and he made his history as exciting as possible. Tacitus focused on interesting and important people rather than pivotal events. Tacitus also was less concerned with objectivity than Thucydides, and often made his own feelings and opinions known. Finally, while Tacitus was a historian and wanted to tell the story as accurately as possible, he was also not above including stories based on dubious sources or unsubstantiated facts. Thus, he includes within his narrative interesting, yet doubtful stories, such as Nero playing the fiddle while he watched Rome burn. Tacitus' brand of history certainly is not as scholarly, but it was much more accessible to the Roman people. Thucydides was certainly the better historian, but Tacitus was certainly more interesting.

The inclusion of unsubstantiated facts is characteristic of another famous Roman writer, **Pliny the Elder.** He wrote a book, *Natural History,* in which he tried to collect the entire knowledge of humankind about the natural world. His subjects include cosmology, astronomy, geography, anthropology, zoology, botany, and mineralogy. While much of it is both interesting and accurate, some of the information has proven to be in error, probably because Pliny gathered his information from a variety of unproven sources. Some of the tall tales we have today came from his book, such as the story of ostriches poking their heads in the sand, and of elephants being afraid of mice. Pliny was incredibly curious about the world and, in the end, died from his curiosity when he got too close to the eruption of Mt. Vesuvius in 79 A.D.

Sculpture

Most Roman sculpture was simply copied from the Greek original, usually trying to be as exact in the copy as possible. Many Greek sculptures were famous, such as the discus thrower and Venus de Milo, and the Romans wanted to have an exact copy. This would be like someone wanting a copy of Rodin's *Thinker* or Michelangelo's *David* today. These Roman copies of Greek originals became so popular that, in many cases, the Greek sculptures that we have today in the museums of the world are generally the Roman copies.

When Roman sculptors did works that were not copies of the Greek, their approach to sculpting was quite different from the approach of the Greeks. Whereas Greek sculptors sought to depict the perfect proportions of the ideal human body, the Romans made their sculptures look realistic, often portraying a specific person and showing personal characteristics, even if the characteristic was of an imperfect form. The Roman sculptors may have done this because the client wanted a life-like appearance so that he or she could be remembered as they actually appeared. Such a sculpture is shown in Figure 13.1. Perhaps the sculptor wanted to honor the subject; for this, an accurate representation was required, so that others would know who was being depicted. In this case, symbols such as those depicting imperial power or divine origin might be included in the sculpture. The sculpture shown in Figure 13.2 shows Augustus Caesar giving a gesture of power and also shows Cupid at his feet as a remem-

Figure 13.1 ■ *Roman portrait sculpture. Image © Araldo de Luca/Corbis.*

Figure 13.2 ■ *Sculpture of emperor. Image © Araldo de Luca/Corbis.*

Figure 13.3 ■ **A)** *Triumphal arch of Titus, and the relief of the sacking of Jerusalem. Image from Corel. B) Image © Dave Bartruff/Corbis.*

brance that Augustus was supposedly descended from Venus, as was Cupid.

Romans also liked to decorate tombs and memorials with sculpture, often done in relief. An example is the triumphal **Arch of Titus,** in which the sacking of Jerusalem is shown (Figure 13.3; note the representation of carrying off the temple menorah). Many triumphal arches are scattered throughout Rome and the rest of the ancient empire. Of course, the style of triumphal arch was also used in more modern times; such as the Triumphal Arch in Paris that commemorates Napoleon's victories.

■ Architecture and Engineering

The Romans saw little difference between architecture and engineering, and taught them together in their technology schools. Likewise, Roman textbooks discussed construction, hydraulic systems, city planning, and mechanical devices all together. The Roman integration of architecture and engineering reveals, as much as any other example, the Roman emphasis on practicality over the Greek emphasis on beauty. For the Romans, architecture was a practical discipline, like engineering, whose function was to make structures that were useful. They may use Greek columns and other decorative devices, but the essence of the structure was engineering-based. The Roman approach is logical—they had an empire to control—and that required buildings and other structures that had to work in order to further the use for which they were erected. Beauty, while nice, was certainly an afterthought. It was the engineering that was important, so architecture was just one of the engineering specialties.

Roman engineers developed two technologies that proved to be critical for the successful implementation of the many structures that made the empire work. These two technologies were the perfection of the arch and the invention of concrete. Though originally developed independently, these two technologies were eventually combined into some of the most original and long-lasting structures ever built. They have served as models even to the modern era.

The use of the arch is probably the most prevalent evidence we see today of ancient Roman life. We see single arches used for memorials, like the Arch of Titus, and multiple arches in buildings, sometimes stacked several stories high. Multiple-arch structures reveal the engineering creativity of the Romans. They realized that an arch can support more weight than the post-and-lintel system used by the Egyptians and Greeks, simply because the arch transfers the weight above it onto the columns of the arch (pushing both downward and outward), whereas the weight above a lintel pushes on the middle of the lintel itself, which is not strong against that type of force. This is depicted in Figure 13.4 A and B. Tunnels could be constructed by placing a series of arches together, front to back as is shown in Figure 13.4 C. More complicated structures, like the vaults of ceilings can also be made from arches, Figures 13.4 D and E. Perhaps the most impressive of all is the dome, depicted in Figure 13.4 F. The Romans further realized that if several arches were placed side by side in an arcade, the outward portion of the force on the columns of one arch would be counteracted by the outward forces on the adjacent arch, thus canceling the outward forces for both arches. Hence, a series of arches in an arcade-type structure was found to be espe-

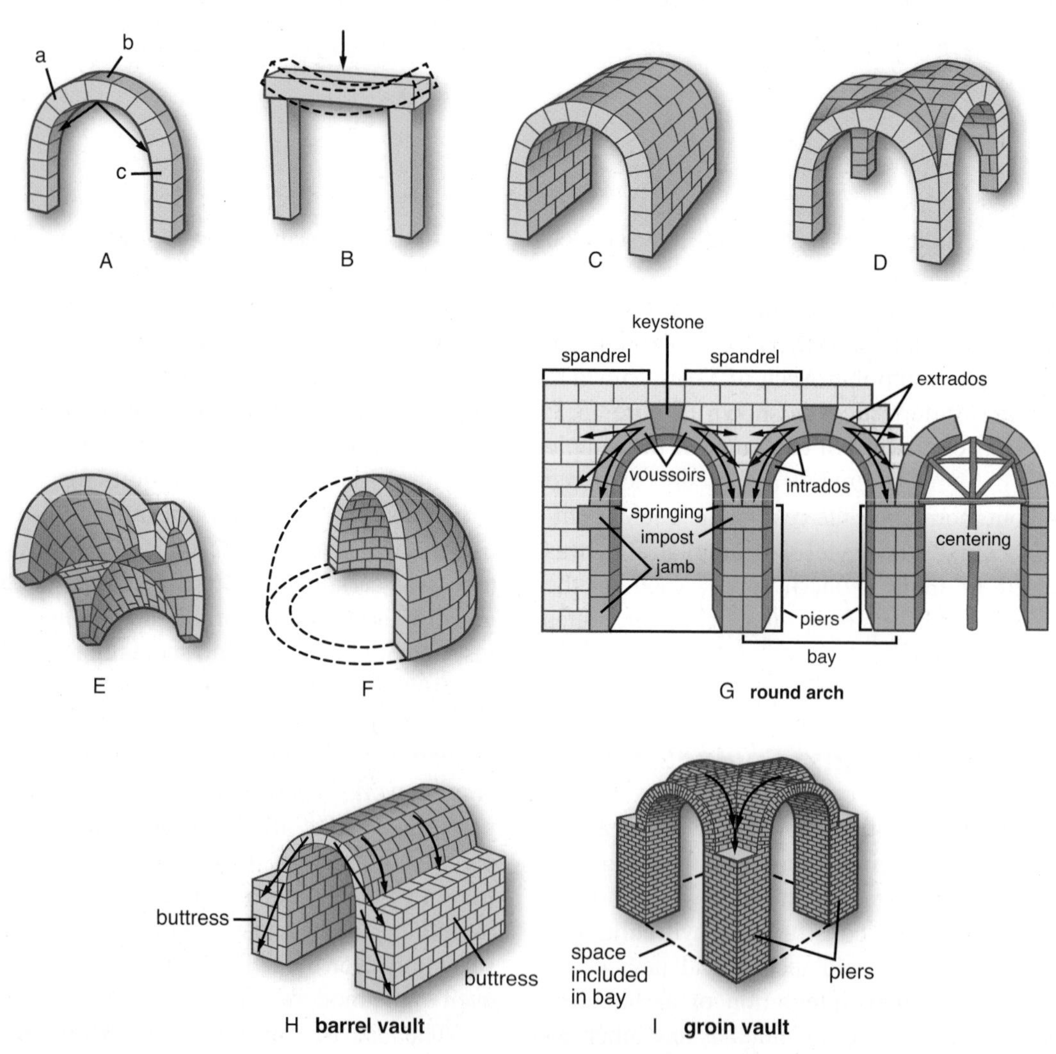

Figure 13.4 ■ *Comparison of post-and-lintel versus single and multiple-arch systems.*

cially strong; it could support very high loads. See Figure 13.4 G. If a tall structure was desired, the Romans realized that a simple way to construct such a structure would be to stack one arcade on top of another. This is the construction seen in the coliseum (Figure 13.5) and in a Roman aqueduct (Figure 13.6).

The engineering associated with the Pont du Gard, perhaps the most famous of the aqueducts, is so amazing that we should consider it in some detail. The structure crossing the Gard River today near the southern French town of Nîmes, is really just a small portion of a much larger and longer aqueduct built by the Romans in the first century B.C. to carry water from a source in the mountains to the city of Nîmes. The source of water was 30 miles distant and was only 60 feet higher than the city. There were, however, some mountains and valleys between the source and the city, forcing the Romans to build several tunnels and bridges, all the while maintaining a steady slope of no more than 3 percent overall, and less than 1 percent in any single section. The bridge over the Gard River is, for example, over 160 feet high, clearly illustrating the depth of some of the valleys that had to be traversed. The tunnels were made possible because the Romans realized that extending an arch lengthwise would result in a stable tunnel structure that could support the weight of, for example, a mountain above it. This concept is shown in Figure 13.4 H. (When free-standing, the tunnel would be built with supports on the sides and would be called a tunnel vault; it could be used as part of a building.) The aqueduct was built without mortar except for the lining of the channel that carried the water. Each of the tunnels, the bridges, and the aqueduct itself would be considered an engineering marvel, especially in light of the technology of the ancient Roman world, but taken together, they reveal an engineering sophistication and creativity that was not matched in the ancient world.

The **Coliseum** in Rome is another magnificent Roman structure. Built to accommodate 50,000 to 60,000 spectators, it has three levels of seats, all individually identified with numbers for making seat assignments according to price (just like a modern sports stadium). The stadium even had a provision for a cloth covering to be slid into place for shade. An extensive system of rooms and passageways was built below the arena floor so that animals and people could be housed prior to their entry into the arena. Today the Coliseum is in partial ruin because the Romans in the Middle Ages took the blocks to build other structures.

The best preserved ancient Roman structure in Rome is an engineering marvel that combines the concepts of the arch, taken to their logical conclusion—the dome—with the other

Figure 13.5 ■ *The Roman Coliseum, showing the use of multiple arches. Image © 2006 Jupiter Images Corporation.*

Figure 13.6 ■ Pont du Gard (Roman aqueduct). *© 2010 by Filip Fuxa. Used under license of Shutterstock, Inc.*

great engineering technology developed by the Romans—concrete. This building is the **Pantheon** (Figure 13.7) and it also deserves our detailed consideration. A sketch of the Pantheon is shown in Figure 13.8.

Figure 13.7 ■ *The Pantheon in Rome. Image © Sean Sexton Collection/Corbis.*

The dome of the Pantheon in Rome is over 140 feet in diameter. The structure is lighted by a single opening in the top, called an **oculus,** which is open to the sky. The Romans used the building as a temple to their gods (the name Pantheon means "all the gods"); it was later used as a church by the Christians, and is now a memorial tomb for some of the greatest people in the history of Italy. Although the dome structure is impressive and, incidentally, was studied as a model for the great domes of the churches of the Renaissance, the dome was made possible by the invention of concrete. It is the combination of this highly developed arch system (that is, the dome) and concrete that resulted in this magnificent structure.

Concrete was, literally and figuratively, the glue that held the Roman world together. It is interesting that in the history of the world, the most advanced material of the time often limits the culture and, as a result, the epoch is identified by that material. The Stone Age, the Bronze Age, the Iron Age, and the Plastics Age are just the most obvious examples. While history books don't generally

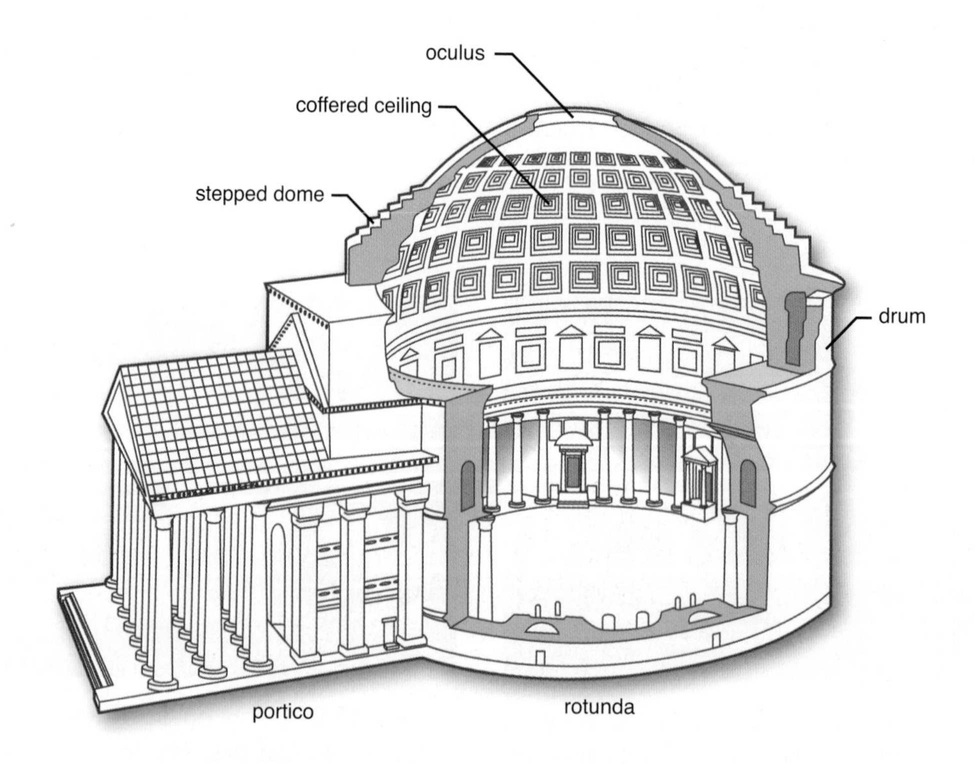

Figure 13.8 ■ *The Pantheon in Rome.* (sketch).

identify the Roman period as the Concrete Age, they should, because concrete was clearly the material that enabled much of the Roman construction, and that defined the technology of the era.

Concrete consists of powdered lime, volcanic sand, and various types of rubble (small rocks, broken pottery, etc.), which were mixed with water, causing a chemical reaction that hardened the mass together. The advantage of concrete over other building materials is that concrete could be poured into a mold of almost any shape (usually constructed of simple, small rocks or bricks) and then hardened to give a strong and lasting structure that, if it were made entirely out of stones, might require extensive shaping of the stones. Even then, it might be impossible to erect because of the span or height, both of which were easier to achieve with concrete. Concrete construction was also faster, so that even when a structure could be made out of stones, it was often made from concrete. For example, a wall could be quickly built out of concrete, as shown in Figure 13.9 (where three different construction methods are depicted). If the wall needed to be decorative, the faces of the wall could be covered with bricks, thin sheets of marble, or other stones. Many of the houses in the cities of the Roman Empire were built using concrete construction.

Concrete was also used, along with other materials, to provide many of the municipal services for the cities. For example, the aqueducts bringing water to Rome terminated in a series of large concrete pools from which pipes (usually made of lead) distributed the water throughout the city. The water usage for Rome has been estimated to be 50 to 150 million gallons a day. These pipes were supported by concrete at critical points. Also, the waste water in the sewer system was

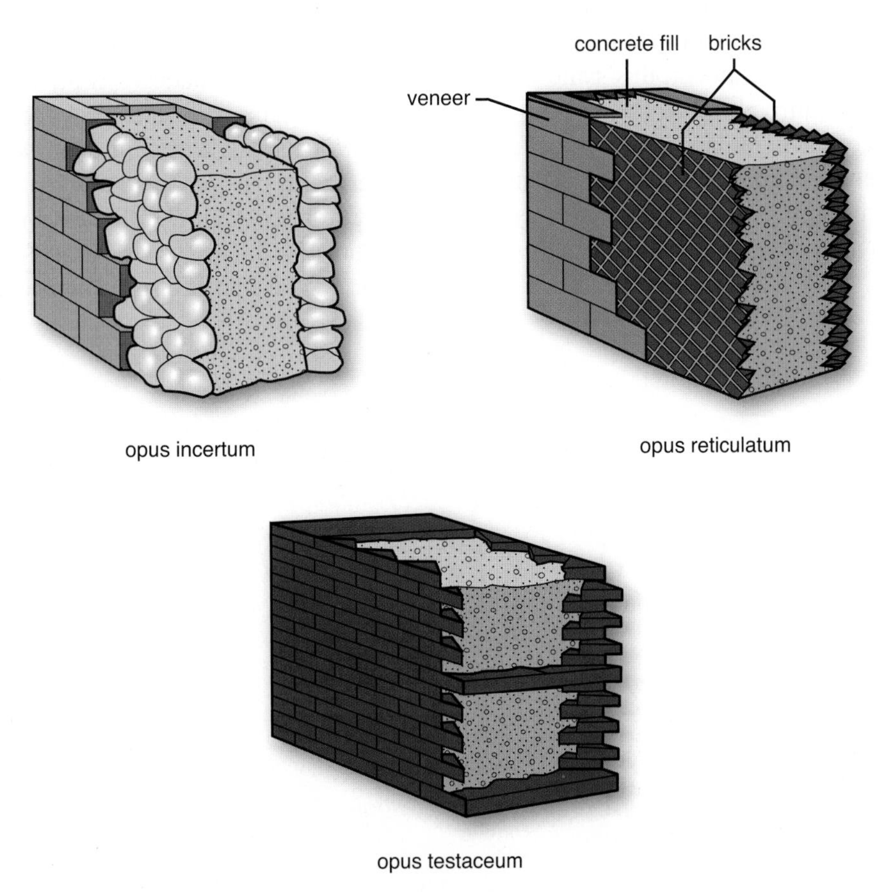

Figure 13.9 ■ *Concrete walls.*

contained within concrete sluices that ran under the streets of the city. (Before the invention of concrete, and in areas where concrete was not available, most of the baths and sewers were made of shaped stones or stones with mortar.)

Roman roads within the cities, which the Romans generally laid out in a grid pattern, sometimes used concrete under the top layer of paving stones. In the countryside, however, the roads were multi-layered structures that used different-sized stones for the paving layer, the support layers, and the drainage layers. The Roman roads were so well built that many of the roads are still in use (such as the Appian Way, just outside of the city of Rome) and were used extensively throughout the Middle Ages. Some have claimed that the extensive use of the roads resulted in grooves where the wheels rode. Since it was easier to ride in the grooves than try to stay out of them, the width of Roman vehicles was standardized to put the wheels in the grooves. Later in history, the continuing use of the Roman roads dictated that carts and other vehicles maintain this same wheel separation. When railroads were begun, the first rail vehicles were carriages, and so the wheel separation became the standard railroad track gauge. Hence, today, the strange width of the tracks of a standard railroad is derived from the width of a Roman chariot.

Science and Medicine

Because science is largely a theoretical and investigatory pursuit, as opposed to technology, which is largely an application-and-use activity, the Romans tended to let the Greeks do the science. Few Roman scientists made significant contributions. On the other hand, some of the Greeks, especially those in Alexandria, carried on the Hellenistic tradition of science, and made significant contributions, even during the Roman period.

Perhaps the most important of these Greek scientists was **Ptolemy,** who lived in Alexandria between 100 A.D. and 170 A.D. He developed an extensive astronomical system that was used, and accepted as true, until the time of the scientific awakening in the 1500s. Following the traditions of the Greeks, Ptolemy maintained that the planets, sun, and moon moved about the earth in circular orbits. However, careful observations of the movement of the planets suggested that the circular orbits were too simplistic, and that some modification must be made to explain the planetary motion. Ptolemy proposed that the planets actually moved along a general circular path, called the **deferent,** but also were obliged to follow a series of smaller circles, called epicycles, as shown in Figure 13.10. His system was able to predict the motion of the planets, sun, and moon within the

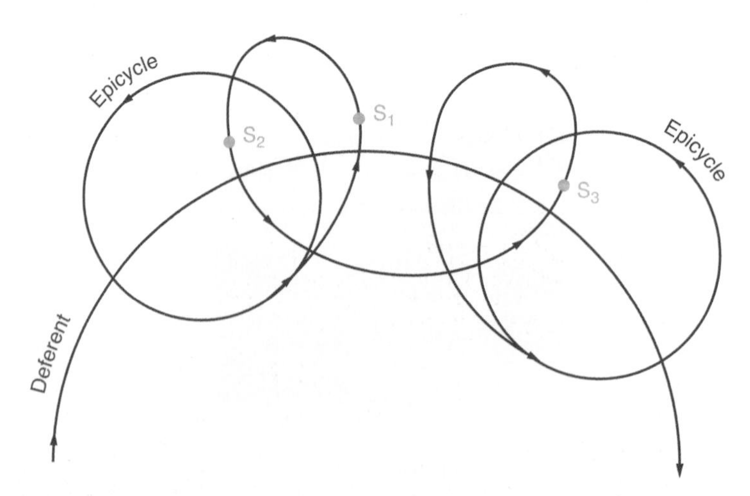

Figure 13.10 ■ *Ptolemy's view of the solar system, showing epicycles.*

level of accuracy of the times and was, therefore, considered to be correct. Ptolemy was also interested in optics, and devised many rules of reflection and refraction that are still used today.

Another Alexandrian Greek scientist of the Roman period was **Hero.** He developed a primitive steam engine that illustrated the ability of steam to supply power. However, perhaps because he was a scientist primarily and not an engineer, he did not use the steam principle for supplying power beyond just the laboratory example.

Medicine is, of course, a highly applied field and was, therefore, of great interest to the Romans. A Roman physician, **Galen,** who lived from 130 A.D. to 220 A.D., built upon the concepts of Hippocrates and further defined the methods of modern medicine, including the use of observations and notes to assist in diagnosis. He advocated that physicians have knowledge of the body and the purpose of the organs, which he personally obtained as the physician to the gladiators. (He was able to observe the inner workings of the body as he tried to treat the many deep and extensive wounds of the gladiators.) He identified most of the muscles of the body and described how they worked in groups. He discussed the importance of the spinal cord, and demonstrated how severing the cord in different places resulted in paralysis to different parts of the body. He also explained the linkage between physical and mental health.

Galen conveyed this information in 22 volumes that served as standard medical textbooks into the modern era. He also classified diseases and the normal treatments that were effective. He sought to determine the causes of diseases—a unique concept in those days. Like Hippocrates, the ancient Greek, he believed that the four bodily fluids or humors—blood, yellow bile, black bile, and phlegm—combined together to form tissues, and that those tissues combined to form the organs. If a person was ill, Galen believed that it was a result of imbalance in the humors.

Galen was recognized in his own day as Rome's leading physician. Besides his work on the gladiators, he was appointed to be personal physician to several of the emperors and other leading Roman citizens. He was truly a creative individual who exhibited well the Roman desire to make knowledge useful.

Roman Legacy

Roman society presents us with one of the most fascinating questions in the history of creativity: Is adaptation of the creative ideas of others a creative process, or is only original innovation a truly creative act? If the former is correct, then Rome was indeed creative; but if the latter is what defines creativity, then Rome was nothing more than a talented thief.

We believe that Roman society was highly creative. Their approach to knowledge was obviously different from that of the Greeks, but the approach of the Greeks was different from that of the Egyptians and Mesopotamians, from whom the Greeks received much background information. We can characterize these different approaches by suggesting that the questions asked to obtain knowledge were different for the three societies. Those questions seemed to be the following:

- By the Egyptians and Mesopotamians: What is out there?
- By the Greeks: Why does it exist?
- By the Romans: What is it good for?

The creativity of the Romans might be judged by examining their legacy. The earliest contribution of the Romans was the Latin language, which they obviously borrowed from the Latin-speaking tribes who inhabited central Italy before Rome was established. Latin is the basis for many of the languages of Europe—French, Spanish, Portuguese, Romanian, and Italian, just to name a few. It is, moreover, a major part of modern English, since English is based on German with substantial French additions, as can be seen in the many Latin-based words and phrases in our language. Some examples of Latin phrases that retain their Latin character are: *alma mater, alter ego, antebellum, habeas corpus, ignoramus, in extremis, ipso facto, persona non grata, per capita, prima facie, quid pro quo, vice versa, a.m., p.m., i.e.,* A.D., *Q.E.D., carpe diem,* and *e pluribus unum*. The alphabet we use in English and most of the European languages is Roman.

Roman government served as a model for the United States government and parts of many other modern governments. Most are republics, that is, derived from the power of the people, but with representatives rather than direct participation. The system of checks and balances among the various parts of the Roman republican government was the basis of the separation of powers outlined in the U.S. Constitution. The division of legislative power between the patricians and the plebs was the basis of the U.S. Senate and the U.S. House of Representatives. The Roman legal system, developed under the rule of Augustus, has provided key features for the legal systems of the United States and most of the countries of Western Europe.

Roman engineering and technology have been models for innumerable buildings, water and sewage systems, streets and roads, bridges, and materials usage (concrete). But, most of all, the attitude of the Romans toward knowledge was passed on, perhaps most evident in modern American society, where practicality and usefulness are strongly appreciated. Creativity requires uniqueness, but it also requires that it be valued and developed with intent and implementation excellence. The Romans succeeded in creating a valued legacy largely on the basis of their intent and implementation. It was worth much.

Timeline—Important Dates

Date	Event
126 A.D.	*Pantheon constructed*
100–170 A.D.	*Ptolemy*
130–220 A.D.	*Galen*
106–43 B.C.	*Cicero*
70–19 A.D.	*Virgil*
3 B.C.–65 A.D.	*Seneca*

Suggested Readings

Baigrie, Brian S., *Scientific Revolutions,* Prentice Hall, 2004.

Copernicus, Nicolaus, *On the Revolutions of the Heavenly Spheres,* Great Books of the Western World, Encyclopaedia Brittanica, Inc., 1952.

Kepler, Johannes, *The Harmonies of the World,* Great Books of the Western World, Encyclopaedia Brittanica, Inc., 1952.

Man, John, *Alpha Beta,* Wiley, 2001.

Ptolemy, *Almagest,* Great Books of the Western World, Encyclopaedia Brittanica, Inc., 1952.

The Builders, National Geographic Society, 1992.

Toomer, J. G., *Ptolemy's Almagest,* Princeton University Press, 1998.

Van Doren, Charles, *A History of Knowledge: Past, Present and Future,* Ballantine Books, 1991.

Article 25
Ptolemy: Almagest

Introduction

Little is known about the personal life of Ptolemy (100–170 AD). He lived in Alexandria, the great center of learning of the Roman Empire during the time when it was still largely a city of Greek (Hellenistic) culture but was ruled by the Romans. There he became highly educated and became an expert in astronomy, mathematics, geometry, and astrology. Although his name is the same as the Greek rulers of Alexandria during the Hellenistic period, we have no evidence that he was related to that dynasty.

Ptolemy's greatest contribution to science was his 13-volume *Mathematical Syntaxis,* or *The Almagest.* This work was translated into Arabic as *al-Majisti* (Great Work) which was rendered into Latin by medieval translators as *Almagesti* and has come to us as *The Almagest.*

This work is his report on the study of astronomy and the mathematical application of astronomy. In it, he presents a geocentric theory of the solar system's planets (as they were known in his day) using epicycles and eccentric circles. Although it was based on an earth-centered solar system, it predicted the position of the planets and the sun accurately to the naked eye. The Ptolemaic model of the solar system would not be improved upon until Copernicus' heliocentric view was proposed in 1543. The *Almagest* also contains conceptions, speculation, and deductions on earth, sun, moon, and star movement, eclipses, and lengths of months. It also contains a list of 48 star constellations, where the names used still today were standardized.

Selections from the *Almagest* appear here. They deal with the spherical nature of the Earth and the earth-centered model of the planets. The excerpts also explain Ptolemy's usage of epicycles and eccentrics in predicting the movement of celestial bodies.

Almagest

That also the Earth, Taken as a Whole, Is Sensibly Spherical

Now, that also the earth taken as a whole is sensibly spherical, we could most likely think out in this way. For again it is possible to see that the sun and moon and the other stars do not rise and set at the same time for every observer on the earth, but always earlier for those living towards the orient and later for those living towards the occident. For we find that the phenomena of eclipses taking place at the same time, especially those of the moon, are not recorded at the same hours for everyone—that is, relatively to equal intervals of time from noon; but we always find later hours recorded for observers towards the orient than for those towards the occident. And since the differences in the hours is found to be proportional to the distances between the places, one would reasonably suppose the surface of the earth spherical, with the result that the general uniformity of curvature would assure every part's covering those following it proportionately. But this would not happen if the figure were any other, as can be seen from the following considerations.

For, if it were concave, the rising stars would appear first to people towards the occident; and if it were flat, the stars would rise and set for all people together and at the same time; and if it were a pyramid, a cube, or any other polygonal figure, they would again appear at the same time for all observers on the same straight line. But none of these things appears to happen. It is further clear that it could not be cylindrical with the curved surface turned to the risings and settings and the plane bases to the poles of the universe, which some think more plausible. For then never would any of the stars be always visible to any of the inhabitants of the curved surface, but either all the stars would both rise and set for observers or the same stars for an equal distance from either of the poles would always be invisible to all observers. Yet the more we advance towards the north pole, the more the southern stars are hidden and the northern stars appear. So it is clear that here the curvature of the earth covering parts uniformly in oblique directions proves its spherical form on every side. Again, whenever we sail towards mountains or any high places from whatever angle and in whatever direction, we see their bulk little by little increasing as if they were arising from the sea, whereas before they seemed submerged because of the curvature of the water's surface.

That the Earth Is in the Middle of the Heavens

Now with this done, if one should next take up the question of the earth's position, the observed appearances with respect to it could only be understood if we put it in the middle of the heavens as the centre of the sphere. If this were not so, then the earth would either have to be off the axis but equidistant from the poles, or on the axis but farther advanced towards one of the poles, or neither on the axis nor equidistant from the poles.

The following considerations are opposed to the first of these three positions—namely, that if the earth were conceived as placed off the axis either above or below in respect to certain parts of the earth, those parts, in the right sphere, would never have any equinox since the section above the earth and the section below the earth would always be cut unequally by the horizon. Again, if the sphere were inclined with respect to these parts, either they would have no equinox or else the equinox would not take place midway between the summer and winter solstices. The distances would be unequal because the equator which is the greatest of those parallel circles described about the poles would not be cut in half by the horizon; but one of the circles parallel to it, either to the north or to the south, would be so cut in half. It is absolutely agreed by all, however, that these distances are everywhere equal because the increase from the equinox to the longest day at the summer tropic are equal to the decreases to the least days at the winter tropic. And if the deviation for certain parts of the earth were supposed either towards the orient or the occident, it would result that for these parts neither the sizes and angular distances of the stars would appear equal and the same at the eastern and western horizons, nor would the time from rising to the meridian be equal to the time from the meridian to setting. But these things evidently are altogether contrary to the appearances.

As to the second position where the earth would be on the axis but farther advanced towards one of the poles, one could again object that, if this were so, the plane of the horizon in each latitude would always cut into uneven parts the sections of the heavens below the earth and above, different with respect to each other and to themselves for each different deviation. And the horizon could cut into two even parts only in the right sphere. But in the case of the inclined sphere with the nearer pole ever visible, the horizon would always make the part above the earth less and the part below the earth greater with the result that also the great circle through the centre of the signs of the zodiac [ecliptic] would be cut unequally by the plane of the horizon. But this has never been seen, for six of the twelve parts are always and everywhere visible above the earth, and the other six invisible; and again when all these last six are all at once visible, the others are at the same time invisible. And so—from the fact that the same semicircles are cut off entirely, now above the earth, now below—it is evident that the sections of the zodiac are cut in half by the horizon.

And, in general, if the earth did not have its position under the equator but lay either to the north or south nearer one of the poles, the result would be that, during the equinoxes, the shadows of the gnomons at sunrise would never perceptibly be on a straight line with those at sunset in planes parallel to the horizon. But the contrary is everywhere seen to occur. And it is immediately clear that it is not possible to advance the third position since each of the obstacles to the first two would be present here also.

In brief, all the observed order of the increases and decreases of day and night would be thrown into utter confusion if the earth were not in the middle. And there would be added the fact that the eclipses of the moon could not take place for all parts of the heavens by a diametrical opposition to the sun, for the earth would often not be interposed between them in their diametrical oppositions, but at distances less than a semicircle.

On the Hypotheses Concerning Regular and Circular Movement

Since the next thing is to explain the apparent irregularity of the sun, it is first necessary to assume in general that the motions of the planets in the directions contrary to the movement of the heavens are all regular and circular by nature, like the movement of the universe in the other direction. That is, the straight lines, conceived as revolving the stars or their circles, cut off in equal times on absolutely all circumferences equal angles at the centres of each; and their apparent irregularities result from the positions and arrangements of the circles on their spheres through which they produce these movements, but no departure from their unchangeableness has really occurred in their nature in regard to the supposed disorder of their appearances.

But the cause of this irregular appearance can be accounted for by as many as two primary simple hypotheses. For if their movement is considered with respect to a circle in the plane of the ecliptic concentric with the cosmos so that our eye is the centre, then it is necessary to suppose that they make their regular movements either along circles not concentric with the cosmos, or along concentric circles; not with these simply, but with other circles borne upon them called epicycles. For according to either hypothesis it will appear possible for the ecliptic circle which is concentric with the cosmos.

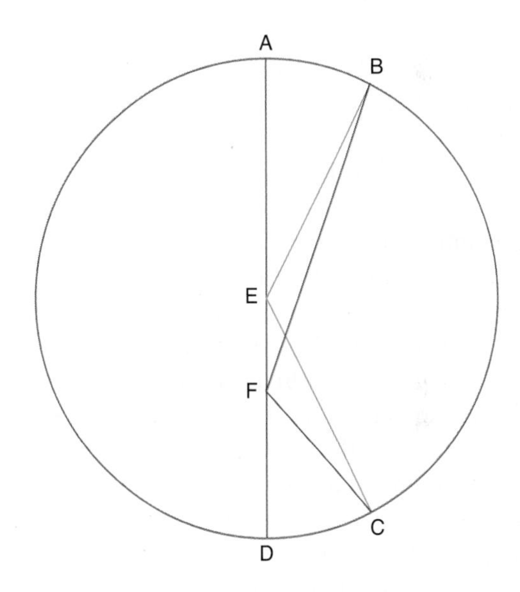

For if, in the case of the hypothesis of eccentricity, we conceive the eccentric circle *ABCD* [Fig 1] on which the star moves regularly, with *E* as center and with diameter *AED*, and the point *F* on it as your eye so that the point *A* becomes the apogee and the point *D* the perigee; and if, cutting off equal arcs *AB* and *DC*, we joint *BE*, *BF*, *CE*, and *CF*, then it will be evident that the star moving through each of the arcs *AB* and *CD* in an equal period of time will seem to have passed through unequal arcs on the circle described around *F* as a centre. For since angle *BEA* = angle *CED*, therefore angle *BFA* is less than either of them, and angle *CFD* greater.

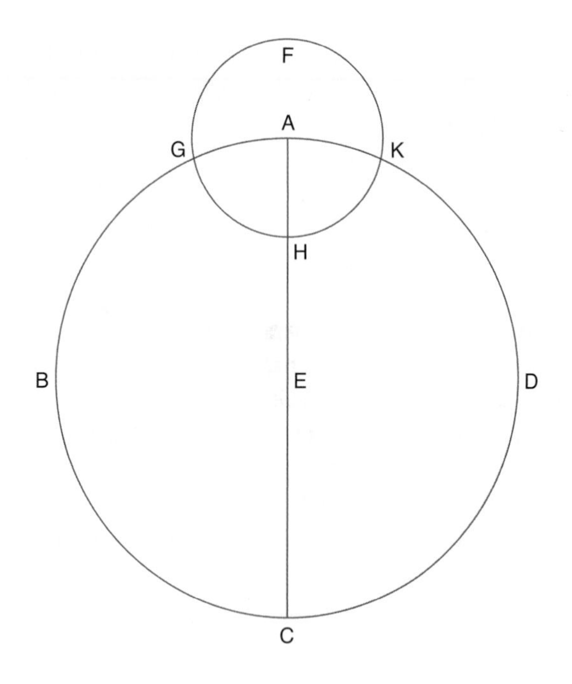

And if in the hypothesis of the epicycle we conceive the circle *ABCD* [Fig 2] concentric with the ecliptic with centre *E* and diameter *AEC,* and the epicycle *FGHK* borne on it on which the star moves, with its centre at *A,* then it will be immediately evident also that as the epicycle passes regularly along the circle *ABCD,* from *A* to *B* for example, and the star along the epicycle, the star will appear indifferently to be at *A* the centre of the epicycle when it is at *F* or *H;* but when it is at other points, it will not. But having come to *G,* for instance, it will seem to have produced a movement greater than the regular movement by the arc *AG;* and having come to *K,* likewise less by the arc *AK.*

Then with the hypothesis of eccentricity it is always the case that the least movement belongs to the apogee and the greatest movement to the perigee, since angle *AFB* is always less than angle *DFC.* But both cases can come about with the hypothesis of the epicycle. For when the epicycle moves contrary to the heavens [from west to east], for example from *A* to *B,* if the star so moves on the epicycle that it goes from the apogee again contrary to the heavens (that is, from *F* in the direction of *G*), there will result at the apogee the greatest advance, because the epicycle and the star are moving the same way. But if the movement of the star on the epicycle is in the direction of that of the heavens [from east to west], that is, from *F* towards *K,* conversely the least advance will be effected at the apogee because the star is then moving contrary to the movement of the epicycle.

With these things established, it must next be understood that, in the case of those planets which effect two anomalies, it is possible to combine both of these hypotheses, as we shall show in the chapters concerning them. But, in the case of those planets subject to only one anomaly, one of the hypotheses will suffice. And it must be understood that all the appearances can be cared for interchangeably according to either hypothesis, when the same ratios are involved in each. In other words, the hypotheses are interchangeable when, in the case of the hypothesis of epicycle, the ratio of the epicycle's radius to the radius of the circle carrying it is the same as, in the case of the hypothesis of eccentricity, the ratio of the line between the centres (that is, between the eye and the centre of the eccentric circle), to the eccentric circle's radius; with the added conditions that the star move on the epicycle from the apogee in the direction of the movement of the heavens with the same angular velocity as the epicycle moves on the circle concentric with the eye in the direction opposite to that of the heavens, and that the star move regularly on the eccentric circle with the same angular velocity also and in the direction opposite to the movement of the heavens.

And we shall briefly show in a systematic way, first by reasoning and secondly by the numbers discovered in the appearances of the sun's anomaly, that with the above assumptions the same appearances agree with either hypothesis.

I say first, then, that on either hypothesis the greatest difference between the regular movement and the apparent irregular movement (difference by which the mean passage of the stars is apprehended) occurs when the apparent angular distance cuts off a quadrant from the apogee; and that the time from the apogee to this mean passage is greater than from this mean passage to the perigee.

Therefore it results—always on the hypothesis of the eccentric circles, and on the hypothesis of the epicycle whenever their movements occur in the direction of the movement of the heavens—that the time from the least passage to the mean passage is greater than that from the mean to the greatest passage, because in each case the least progress is effected at the apogee. But on the hypothesis of the epicycles which supposes the revolutions of the stars on them in the direction contrary to that of the heavens, conversely the time from the greatest to the mean passage is greater than that from the mean to the least, because in this case the greatest progress is effected at the apogee.

Early Christianity
Creatively Coping with Change

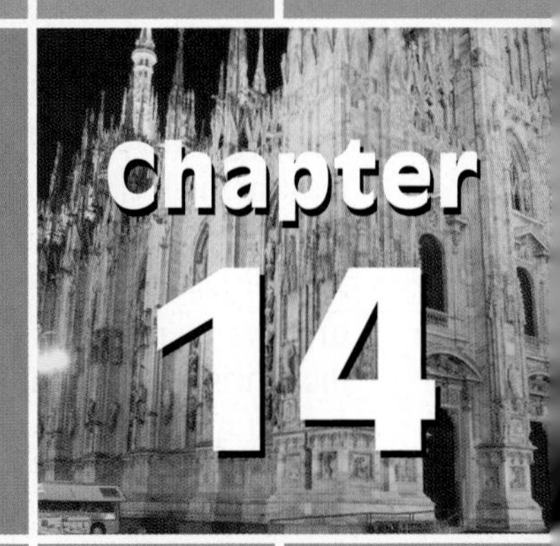

> For besides the disciplines of good behavior, and the ways to eternal happiness (which are called virtues) and besides the grace of God which is in Jesus Christ, imparted only to the sons of the promise, invention has brought forth so many and such sciences and arts that the excellence of His capacity makes the rare goodness of His creation apparent . . . What varieties has man found out in buildings, attires, husbandry, navigation, sculpture, and imagery! What perfection has he shown, in the shows of theatres, in taming, killing, and catching wild beasts! What millions of inventions has he against others, and for himself in poisons, arms, engines, stratagems, and the like! What thousands of medicines for the health, of meats for the throat, of means and figures to persuade, of eloquent phrases to delight, of verses for pleasure, of musical inventions and instruments! What excellent inventions are geography, arithmetic, astrology, and the rest! How large is the capacity of man, if we should stand upon particulars!
>
> —*St. Augustine,* In Praise of Creation

Christianity in the First Century A.D.

The origins of Christianity are inseparably entwined with the history of the Jews, which we have discussed in both the chapter on Mesopotamia and the chapter on Hellenism. The Jews always saw themselves as different from their neighbors; when under the rule of the Hellenistic Greeks, they fought to maintain that uniqueness in spite of the overwhelming enticements and occasional political pressures of the Greek lifestyle. Rather than use creativity as an agent for change, the Jews were creative in devising methods to maintain tradition. Christianity entered the Jewish world in the midst of this struggle to resist change. But, in contrast to the Greek and later Roman influences on Jewish society, the Christians were not external to Judaism. Christianity was a force for change from within, and in that regard it posed a different and potentially more serious threat to Jewish tradition, at least as viewed by the Jewish leaders of the early first century A.D. (The relationship of early Christianity to Judaism is similar to the relationship of early Protestantism to the Catholic Church, that is, one had its origin in the other.) It is not surprising that the Jewish leaders resisted and rejected the teachings of Jesus of Nazareth, who advocated, at least in their view, a dramatic change from the traditions of the past. As we will see, that rejection by Jewish leaders, and consequently by the majority of Jews themselves, led to Jewish persecution of the Christians and, ultimately, a change in the nature of the Christian Church. Specifically, the emphasis of Christian missionary work shifted from the Jews to the Gentiles. With that shift, the Christian Church was forced to confront the Greek and Roman world with a much different perspective from the perspective of the Jews. The Greek and Roman world was not outside of this broadened Christianity—it was the heritage of the majority of Christians themselves. Coping with that reality, especially in the midst of a basic transition in the nature of Christianity, required a new creativity. That creative change is the subject of this chapter.

The central person of Christianity, **Jesus of Nazareth,** known to Christians as Jesus the Christ, was himself a Jew. Relatively little is known about the childhood and early life of Jesus. Upon reaching the age of 30, the age at which a Jewish man was allowed to speak in the synagogues as a teacher, Jesus began his religious ministry. Jesus and a group of followers traveled the Judean countryside teaching a message of love, hope, and forgiveness to those who would listen. Jesus taught that the new law he was sharing was a fulfillment of the earlier Law of Moses. He also claimed that he was the Son of God and the Jews' promised deliverer, the anointed one or **Messiah** (from whence Christians derive the name *Christ,* from the Greek for anointed one), and that he had not come to free the Jews from political bonds (as many Jews understood the prophecies), but from spiritual bonds of error.

The teachings of Jesus were very controversial among the Jewish people, and there was great debate over whether or not Jesus could truly be who and what he claimed to be. In the end, both the Pharisees and Sadducees, rival doctrinal groups within Judaism, felt that their political and religious power was threatened by Jesus, and they denounced him as a fraud. However, Jesus' following among the masses continued to increase as he repeatedly worked miracles and confounded his doubters and detractors.

Despite the controversy, Jesus and his followers, from whom he had chosen twelve men to serve as apostles and help him spread his message, continued to teach those who would listen. The ministry of Jesus came to its end, however, when he and his apostles returned to the city of Jerusalem to celebrate the Passover during the third year of his teaching. While in the city, one of his apostles, Judas Iscariot, betrayed Jesus to the Jewish leaders, who arrested him on trumped-up charges. Eventually the **Sanhedrin,** the Jewish court, found Jesus guilty and took him before the Romans. Pontius Pilate, the Roman procurator (governor), thought that the Jews had overreacted, and tried to free Jesus, but eventually gave in to insistent Jewish pressure, and issued the order to crucify him. It is the central belief of Christianity that during these last days, Christ miraculously took upon himself the sins of all mankind, died on the cross, and three days later was resurrected. In so doing Jesus provided a way for mankind to repent, overcome death through resurrection, and return to the presence of God.

After Jesus' death, both the Romans and Jews anticipated that Christianity would crumble. However, Jesus' apostles continued to preach his message and perform miracles; the number of devotees to the new religion continued to increase at a rapid pace. One notable example took place on the day of Pentecost, shortly after Jesus' crucifixion, when the apostles converted over 3,000 people in one day alone (Acts 2:41). This rapid rate of growth continued and expanded when the head apostle, **Peter,** was inspired to begin preaching the message of Jesus to all people, not just the Jews (Acts 10:34–48). Once this decision was made, the majority of the apostles scattered across the known world to serve as missionaries for the new faith, going to places as far and diverse as present-day Egypt, Spain, India, Persia, Armenia, Turkey, Greece, and Rome itself.

Peter's decision to allow Christianity to be taught to all people was certainly creative. It was unique, highly valued by those who were allowed to hear the gospel, and it was intended and eventually became the central mission of the Christian Church, implemented with great excellence by Peter himself and later, especially, by **Paul** (who was previously called Saul of Tarsus). Paul was a Jew who was miraculously converted by a vision of the resurrected Jesus while on a trip to Damascus where he, Paul, was to join with some persecutors of the Christians. After his conversion, Paul became the foremost missionary to the Gentiles (non-Jews).

Peter's decision then caused many other creative decisions to be made, such as whether the Gentile converts would be required to accept and live the entire law of the Jews, or whether the teachings of the Old Testament still applied to the new Church and, if so, to what extent. An interesting question arises with respect to the origin of these ideas and the effect of that origin on the nature of creativity: Christians would agree that Peter did not take the initiative of broadening the scope of gospel teaching from within his own thinking but, rather, was inspired by God in this action. We might ask, therefore, whether Peter's action was creative, since he was not its author. In other words, can a person be creative if the origin of the creative idea is not from within himself or herself? To some extent, we have already addressed this issue in discussing the way in which the Romans took Greek ideas and (in our opinion) creatively adapted them to new circumstances and in new directions. But the idea of an inspired creative idea is still somewhat different, and it deserves a little more discussion.

Throughout history—ancient and modern—many creative individuals who believed in God would attribute their creative ideas to God's inspiration. Some obvious examples are Handel's feelings about the origins of *Messiah* and Milton's attributions of many concepts in *Paradise Lost.* In our opinion, the celestial origin of their ideas does not detract from their human creativity. Those who believe in God would say that God was enhancing, not detracting from, human creativity. Those who don't believe in God would dismiss the idea of inspiration and continue to attribute all the creativity to the individuals. Therefore, in either case, those who claim inspiration are creative. At the very least, we would say that these individuals who received divine inspiration were prepared to receive it and had the ability to recognize it. Furthermore, their implementation of the creative idea would generally qualify as creative. Peter was, therefore, creative, as was Paul, who was chiefly responsible for teaching Christianity to the Greek and Roman world, and who devised many unique and creative solutions to the problems he encountered in trying to integrate Gentile converts into a Jewish-based religion.

Christianity continued to expand across the Roman Empire and beyond. The rapid growth, however, brought with it not only devoted believers, but powerful enemies. Both the Jewish community and, eventually, the Roman Empire felt threatened by the spread of Christianity—the Jews because Christianity was a threat to its spiritual power and claims of exclusivity as God's only chosen people; and the Romans because Christianity was a threat to its political power. The Jews and the Romans would persecute Christians over the next few centuries.

Jewish leaders viewed Christianity as an aberrant version of Judaism, and rightly felt threatened by Christianity's message and its warm reception; its founding principle was that the covenants and laws God made with the Jews had been fulfilled by the teachings and acts of Jesus, thus making traditional Judaism a dead religion. Many Jews disliked the idea of resurrection, as that meant that Jesus might have actually been the Messiah. Furthermore, they resented the idea of a new covenant, as that meant they had lost the first covenant. The Jews also felt as though Christians had usurped the "messiah" concept from them. Finally, Jews disproved of the miracles being done in the name of Christ, as they believed that only God could heal. In an effort to stop the spread of Christianity, many Jews tried to dissuade or kill Christian leaders. The apostle Paul was first a persecutor of the Christians and then, after his conversion, was given forty lashes at the hands of different Jews at least five times (2 Cor 11:24). The New Testament also records that the Jews took council to kill Paul (Acts 9:23–25), and successfully stoned to death Stephen, another Christian leader (Acts 7:59–60).

Originally the Roman government took little action, only taking interest in the Christian phenomenon when others brought it to its attention, such as when the soothsayers took Paul to the authorities (Acts 16:19–20) or when the silversmiths in Ephesus grew angry because their business had been hurt by the Christian converts who did not buy statues of the gods (Acts 19:23–31). However, as time went by and Christianity continued to spread, the authorities in Rome paid it more notice and felt more threatened by it. The first serious Roman persecutions against the Christians occurred under Emperor Nero. When Rome burned in 64 A.D., Nero blamed the Christians, because they were unpopular in the city of Rome at that time anyway. It was during these persecutions that Peter and Paul were killed in Rome. At one point, Nero went so far as to crucify Christians along the **Appian Way,** the main thoroughfare into Rome, and then set them afire to provide lighting to the road. It is at this time that the Christians begin to flee to the catacombs beneath the city of Rome for safety. It is also around this time that the Christians begin to develop a system of coded symbols, such as Christ being represented by a fish, to aid in recognizing one another. Persecution of the Christians did not end with the death of Nero. When the Roman legions invaded Jerusalem in 70 A.D. and destroyed the Temple, the Christians were persecuted along with the Jews and only avoided being shipped off with the Jews into the Diaspora by fleeing to the mountains and across the Jordan (traditionally to Pella).

The Roman destruction of Jerusalem and the scattering of the Jews precipitated a change in the Christian religion. Prior to this time, the center of Christianity was in Jerusalem, although some missionary efforts, especially those of Paul, seem to have centered in Antioch, perhaps because it was a more cosmopolitan center with better transportation. Perhaps, also, the Jewish opposition in Jerusalem complicated the efforts of the Christian Church in that locale. But when the Romans destroyed Jerusalem, with fighting continuing to

Figure 14.1 ■ Appian Way (modern view).

150 A.D., the Christians had no choice but to relocate the center of the Church. Antioch was a logical alternate because of its proximity to Jerusalem and its prominence as the major Greek-speaking city in the Roman Empire. (Remember that, increasingly, Greek was becoming the principal language of the Church as the number of Greek-speaking Gentile converts grew with respect to the Jewish converts.) However, Alexandria soon became a rival to Antioch, at least in the area of Church doctrine and intellectual thought. Rome emerged as a third Christian center, largely because of its political influence.

The persecution of Christians continued off and on for the next few years, and while the adversity facing Christians may have slowed the growth of the Church, it never was successful in stopping it completely. What the Roman and Jewish animosity toward Christianity was successful in doing was changing how the Church was structured and governed. As persecution became intense, travel became more difficult for Christian leaders; often the Jews or Romans killed those leaders who ventured out. Consequently, the direction of the Church fell more and more often into the hands of local leaders rather than to the established apostolic central authority. Thus, the first-century Christian Church continued to evolve and adapt over the years in a semi-underground status, developing doctrinal divisions and leadership struggles along the way.

Christianity in the Second Century A.D.

The early years of Christianity in the second century are known from scant reliable historical records, but we can imagine that the local congregations were faced with some difficult decisions in the absence of apostolic leadership. One of the few historical records is from a book written in the fourth century A.D. in which the Christian bishop of Caesarea, **Eusebius,** passed on historical information about this early period in his comprehensive work *The History of the Church.* An early problem encountered by the local members was leadership succession. Previously, the local leaders had been chosen by the apostolic leadership, but that could no longer occur after the apostles had been killed. Eusebius noted that "When James the Righteous had suffered martyrdom like the Lord and for the same reason, Symeon the son of his uncle Clopas was appointed bishop. He being a cousin of the Lord, it was the universal demand that he should be the second."[1] The members chose their new leader because he was related to Jesus. But, what would happen when there were no relatives of Jesus in the congregation? In those circumstances, the members of the Church seemed to have continued the pattern of local selection of leaders, at least until a Church hierarchy developed.

Another problem encountered by the post-apostolic Church membership was doctrinal error. Eusebius commented on the problem as follows: "But when the sacred band of the apostles had in various ways reached the end of their life, and the generation of those privileged to listen with their own ears to the divine wisdom had passed on, then godless error began to take shape, through the deceit of false teachers, who now that none of the apostles was left they took off the mask and attempted to counter the preaching of the truth by preaching the knowledge falsely so called."[2] The problem with doctrine was that no official records of Christ's teachings were widespread. Some records had been made in the first century A.D. but those had been copied many times and, inevitably, had many errors.

Over the next several centuries, doctrinal disputes were frequent and widespread. These disputes arose from doctrinal treatises circulated throughout the Church in the same way that letters of the apostles (such as Paul's letters and those of Peter and John) were circulated during the first century. These later treatises were written by local leaders, scholars, and just interested members. Some would attempt to give authority to their writings by claiming to have direct information from the apostles, while others would forge the authorship of their letters and claim that it was written by an apostle or some other well recognized Church authority. Eusebius quotes an earlier Church leader, Dionysius, who says that even when he wrote a treatise, it was not kept as written. "When my fellow-Christians invited me to write letters to them I did so. These the devil's apostles have filled with tares, taking away some things and adding others. For them the woe is reserved. Small wonder then if some have dared to tamper even with the word of the Lord Himself, when they have conspired to mutilate my own humble efforts."[3] The result of all these writings was a confusion of doctrine.

An interesting doctrinal difficulty arose as the membership of the Church became increasingly Gentile. When these Gentile converts were faced with a doctrinal issue, they would, of course, resort to their background methods of reasoning to develop a resolution to the doctrinal issue. These converts were largely schooled in Greek philosophy, in direct contrast to the earliest of Christians who, as Jews, would rely on their background in the Jewish scriptures (Old Testament) as the method of deciding doctrine. Eusebius commented on the manipulation of Jewish scriptures when he said, "In their eagerness to find, not a way to reject the depravity of the Jewish Scriptures, but a means of explaining it away, they resorted to interpretations which cannot be reconciled or harmonized with those scriptures."[4] Eusebius also commented on the readiness of some writers, such as the church father, **Origen,** to base their teachings on Greek philosophy. "In his [Origen's] life he behaved like a Christian, defying the law: in his metaphysical and theological ideas he played the Greek, giving a Greek twist to foreign tales. He associated himself at all times with Plato, and was at home among the writings of . . . followers of Pythagoras. He made use, too, of the books of Chaeremon the Stoic and Cornutus, which taught him the allegorical method of interpreting the Greek mysteries, a method he applied to the Jewish Scriptures."[5]

One idea from Greek philosophy that was especially important in Christian thinking was the concept of *Logos.* Greek thinkers, especially the Stoics, believed in a guiding force or power, the *Logos,* that infused all matter and gave animation to all beings. The *Logos* was readily identified with Christ or the Spirit of Christ, especially since the Greek version of the Gospel of John used *Logos* in John 1:1, which the English translation renders as "word." Various Christian teachers felt that the Greek philosophers, in particular Plato, but later Aristotle, were inspired in their writings and were giving true Christian principles, but they lacked a knowledge of Christ because He had not yet been born.

In retrospect and after one of the doctrinal opinions had emerged as dominant, some of the writers of the second and later centuries were accepted as correct. These writers were given special status and called "fathers of the church." Some of the most famous of these include the following: Justin Martyr, Polycarp of Smyrna, Clement of Rome, Tertullian of Carthage, Dionysius of Corinth, Clement of Alexandria, Origen of Alexandria, Eusebius of Caesarea, and **Jerome** of Constantinople. The writings of these fathers of the church became nearly as authoritative as the scriptures, and led to the acceptance of tradition in interpreting doctrine of the Church. The doctrinal position that gradually emerged as dominant became known as **orthodox** and all conflicting views were known as **heretical.** Just as the Jews at the time of Christ viewed his doctrine as especially threatening because it was advocating change and it came from within, those who held the orthodox view viewed heretics as especially threatening and, therefore, relentlessly persecuted those Christians who held views different from their own.

Christianity in the Third Century A.D.

Leadership of the Christian Church became a critical issue in the third century. The tradition of local election of bishops by a council of local elders (called **presbyters**) was widespread throughout the Christian Church, but some of the bishops, especially those in large metropolitan areas, were giving advice and otherwise taking responsibility for directing the Church in smaller cities. Therefore, a hierarchy of bishops naturally developed. The higher bishops, who eventually became known as **archbishops** and **cardinals** (Latin Church) or **metropolitans** (Greek Church), began to try and influence the selection of bishops in the small cities in their vicinity. The major centers of the Church—Antioch, Alexandria, and Rome—openly competed against each other for the right to name bishops.

An interesting example of this competition occurred between Alexandria and Rome when a bishop of Rome died in the early third century. **Clement of Alexandria,** the leader of the highly influential Christian school in Alexandria (called the **catechetical school**), sent one of his supporters, Valentinus, to campaign for the office of Bishop of Rome. Valentinus was defeated by three votes. Then, when the Bishop of Alexandria died not too long afterwards, the Bishop of Rome sent one of his supporters, a man named Peter (not, of course, Peter the Apostle), to campaign in Alexandria. Peter was elected by the vote of the Alexandrian presbyters but was still opposed by Clement and his foremost student, Origen. Because of the influence of Clement and Origen, Peter was not accepted by the larger body of Alexandrian saints. Peter, the new bishop, was exiled from Alexandria.

But, because Peter was the legitimately elected bishop, no other bishop could serve, so the Church in Alexandria was supervised by Clement and Origen, even though they were not ordained priests but were merely presbyters and, of course, professors in the catechetical school. Upon the death of Clement, Peter returned to Alexandria and gained control. Origen was exiled from Alexandria and went to Caesarea to teach; there he was ordained a bishop by the Bishop of Antioch, but he never regained control of Alexandria.

As the power of the Bishops of Rome and Antioch increased, these two began to have so much influence that they could appoint bishops and not worry about presbyter election. From this period onward, the strength of these two Church centers began to grow rapidly, both in supervising the leadership of the Church and in doctrinal interpretation.

During the third century, groups of Christians located themselves on the shores of the Red Sea in areas where pagan hermits had been established. The desire of these Christians seemed to be to seek spiritual excellence through a separation from the world, and holiness through a life of asceticism. Soon, similar Christian communities sprang up throughout the Egyptian desert as havens for Christians fleeing the continuing persecutions of the Romans. Others sought isolation from worldly depravity.

The early Christian hermits vied with each other for greater displays of self-sacrifice. Some climbed to the top of columns to emphasize their separation from the world. One of the column sitters was renowned for touching his head to his feet for 1,244 times in succession every day for 37 years. Some of the hermits ate grass like cows. Others practiced self-torture, including acts such as standing on one leg like a crane for hours and confining themselves to small cages.

Eventually a set of rules was established to regulate and standardize the actions of the hermits, thus establishing the origins of Christian **monastic orders.** The first rules were created by **St. Anthony** in Egypt (about 305 A.D.) and many thousands flocked to join him and his sister (who directed retreats for women). He later introduced rules for Christians living in Italy, Gaul, and Libya. Rules were later established by **St. Basil** in 356, which are the principal rules governing most Orthodox Church (Greek Church) monasteries. In the sixth century **St. Benedict** conducted a religious revival and wrote new rules that established the basis of modern Roman Catholic monasticism.

Figure 14.2 ■ Monastery of St. Catherine at the foot of traditional Mount Sinai. *© 2010 by PavieMarjanovic. Used under license of Shutterstock, Inc.*

Christianity in the Fourth Century A.D.

The Romans eventually saw a threat to their political power in Christianity. The rapid spread of Christianity and the devotion of its followers to Christ (whom they saw as a resurrected king who would soon return to free them from their earthly political bonds) caused the Romans to question the allegiance of Christians to both emperor and the empire. Furthermore, Rome feared that if the leaders of the Christian Church grew too powerful, they might be able to take over the reins of power from the Caesars.

Christianity seemed to have a power within the Roman Empire far beyond its actual numbers. Scholars today estimate that in the first 300 years of Christianity, up to the reign of **Constantine,** the total number of Christians rose to about 10 percent of the Roman population. While even this percentage may seem to be a very rapid growth, especially in light of the person-by-person nature of early Christian conversions (as opposed to the wholesale conversions that followed the time of Constantine), such a growth rate is not unknown in our day. The growth of the Church of Jesus Christ of Latter-Day Saints (The Mormons) has followed about that same growth pattern over a comparable period.

In 294 A.D. the Emperor Diocletian ordered all inhabitants of Rome to sacrifice to the Roman gods or be put to death, causing many Christians to abandon Christianity, and leading to a debate within the Church regarding the status of "turn-coat" Christians. Some Christians fled the Roman Empire and lived among the barbarians; leading to the conversion of many of the barbarians to Christianity. It also further diversified the doctrine of the Church.

After the reign of Diocletian, a power struggle ensued and, as we discussed in the chapter on the Roman Empire, eventually Constantine emerged as the sole Roman emperor. Constantine's ascension to power was linked with Christianity, at least in his mind, and this proved to be a blessing and relief to the Christians within the Empire. As previously discussed, on the night before a pivotal battle Constantine had a vision in which he was told that he would conquer under the sign of Christianity. In an impressive act of faith (especially considering he was not a Christian), Constantine had a Christian symbol painted on the shields of his soldiers before they left for battle. The battle was won, and eventually the war, making Constantine emperor. Once in power Constantine issued an edict of religious tolerance, and the persecutions against Christians ended. Constantine continued to perform various pagan acts but seemed to favor Christianity over other religions, as evidenced by his personal donations of land, erection of Christian places of worship, and establishment of his new capital, Constantinople, as a Christian city. Eventually, near the end of his life, Constantine himself was baptized a Christian.

Despite its newfound status, the Christian Church suffered terribly from doctrinal differences and divisions in leadership that had developed during the centuries when Christianity had languished under state-sanctioned persecution. Among the most pressing difficulties were the already growing rift between the Christian Churches in the eastern and western halves of the empire, including the question of whether the bishop of Rome held supremacy over the other bishops or if he was simply first among equals; the nature of the Trinity; the growth of **Arian Christianity** (which decreed that Christ was only a mortal man begotten of God and reduced his role to the lesser status of a demigod—a doctrine that was especially popular among Egyptian Christians and the barbarian Christians of Europe); and the relationship between Church and state. In an effort to remedy these problems and unify the Christian Church, Constantine called a council of the Church to be held at the city of **Nicaea** (in present-day Turkey and, therefore, reasonably close to Constantinople).

The **Nicene Council,** which was documented by the church father Eusebius and overseen by Constantine himself, was successful in resolving some of the problems plaguing the Christian Church. The largest accomplishment was reaching an agreement on the nature of the Trinity and a declaration that the Arian belief was heretical. The Nicene Creed declared that God the Son was begotten of the Father's substance, that God is one object *in* Himself and three objects *to* Himself, and that the Trinity is the fundamental miracle of the world. This definition of the Trinity was the core of the Nicene Creed, and acceptance of these findings were made the test of orthodoxy. Thus, with one stroke the primary belief of Arian Christianity was ruled heretical. The Nicene Council also helped resolve the relationship between the Church and the state, because the various bishops in attendance all agreed to recognize Constantine (the emperor) as Christ's surrogate—a role the emperor would fill until the collapse of the Empire. In the western empire, the eventual collapse of effective political power and the resultant assumption of power by the Bishop of Rome resulted in the pope's claiming to be surrogate for Christ on earth, but in the eastern empire, the remaining emperors retained the ultimate authority over the Church until the fall of Constantinople in 1453.

The Nicene Creed did not solve all of the troubles within Christianity, however. It was made the official orthodox doctrine of the Christian Church, but many Christian leaders refused to accept the decision of the Nicene Council and continued to teach what they considered to be "true" Christian principles. However, those who did so were branded heretics and rebels against the faith, and eventually forced to flee, recant, or die. The force was supplied by the Roman government itself because Constantine vowed to enforce the decision of the Nicene Council. Thus, over time, the Nicene Creed became generally more accepted.

Another problem of the early Christian Church was the growing split between the eastern and western Christian Churches, and the Nicene Council only aggravated this problem. Despite having moved his capital to the eastern half of the empire, Constantine supported the doctrinal position of the Bishop of Rome. Thus, the western Church's views on doctrine, especially concerning the Trinity, were forced on the eastern bishops, who had to obey Constantine. While the Nicene Creed became the theological basis for the eastern Church as well as the western, the hatred and mistrust that grew out of the Nicene Council was poison to an already frail relationship, and contributed to the eventual split between eastern and western Churches.

■ Christianity in the Fifth Century A.D.

Near the beginning of the fifth century, a priest named Jerome moved to Rome and began a compilation and sorting of the existing manuscripts and letters that might be considered authentic works of scriptures. Dozens of such books and letters existed, many with several versions because of transmission changes, and others because of doctrinal changes. Eusebius, writing a generation before Jerome, commented on the difficulties in distinguishing the true works from the false.

> *It will be well, at this point, to classify the New Testament writings already referred to. We must, of course, put first the holy quartet of the gospels, followed by the Acts of the Apostles. The next place in the list goes to Paul's epistles, and after them we must recognize the epistle called 1 John; likewise I Peter. To these may be added, if it is thought proper, the Revelation of John, the arguments about which I shall set out when the time comes. These are classed as Recognized Books. Those that are disputed, yet familiar to most, include the epistles known as James, Jude, and 2 Peter, and those called 2 and 3 John, the work either of the evangelist or of someone else with the same name.*[6]

Eusebius further discusses the problems with the books of John.

> *By the phraseology also we can measure the difference between the Gospel and Epistle and the Revelation. The first two are written not only without any blunders in the use of Greek, but with remarkable skill as regards diction, logical thought, and orderly expression. It is impossible to find in them one barbarous word or solecism, or any kind of vulgarism . . . The other saw revelations and received knowledge and prophecy I will not deny; but I observe that his language and style are not really Greek: he uses barbarous idioms, and is sometimes guilty of solecisms. There is no need to pick these out now; for I have not said these things in order to pour scorn on him—do not imagine it—but solely to prove the dissimilarity between these books.*[7]

Further, comments about the books of Peter are also interesting.

> *Of Peter, one epistle, known as his first, is accepted, and this the early fathers quoted freely, as undoubtedly genuine, in their own writings. But the second Petrine epistle we have been taught to regard as uncanonical; many, however, have thought it valuable and have honored it with a place among the other Scriptures.*[8]

Even after these issues of authorship were reasonably decided, the number of versions was overwhelming. By some counts, there were as many corrections or changes between one version and others as there were total words in the texts. Some of the changes were, evidently, caused by those who would make the scriptures agree with their own doctrine. Eusebius reports, "So it was that they [apostates] laid hands unblushingly on the Holy Scriptures, claiming to have corrected them. . . . Either they do not believe that the inspired scriptures were spoken by the Holy Spirit—if so, they are unbelievers; or they imagine that they are wiser than He—if so, can they be other than possessed?"[9]

In spite of these difficulties, Jerome, who moved from Rome to Jerusalem, assembled a group of writings that was officially pronounced as canonical by the Bishop of Rome. Jerome's version of the Bible used a Latin translation of the Septuagint, a Greek-language version of the Old Testament created in about the third century B.C. in Alexandria, as the **Old Testament.** (It included some of the books commonly known as the **Apocrypha.**) The **New Testament** was a translation into Latin of the many books selected by Jerome as being scripture. This Latin version was called the **Vulgate** (which reflected the fact that the Bible was rendered in the common or vulgar tongue of the time: Latin).

Christianity continued to grow and evolve in its new role as the official religion of the Roman state, eventually becoming so entrenched that when the Roman Empire collapsed in the west, the Christian Church carried on as the one remaining Roman institution. However, in spite of the Church's privileged position, many non-Christians blamed Christianity's rise for the collapse of the Roman Empire. Some critics argued that Christianity and its teachings of love, brotherhood, and tolerance had made the empire weak. Others said that the Christians' denial of the traditional gods of Rome had eventually caused the Roman gods to become angry and allowed Rome to be overthrown. After a time these views began to gain some credibility, and Christians were forced to defend themselves. Many Christians would write treatises and defenses, but the most famous would be that written by **Saint Augustine.**

St. Augustine

Despite being the son of a devout Christian mother, Augustine (354 to 430 A.D.) grew up disbelieving the doctrines of Christianity, which he felt were too mystical and intellectually confusing. He pursued an education in classical Greek thought, whose logic and rationality he found appealing. Augustine eventually adopted Manichaeanism, a blending of Greek philosophy and religious principles that taught there were two forces in the universe, Good and Evil, which constantly competed with one another for supremacy. However, Augustine eventually found Manichaeanism to be too mystical as well, and he became frustrated when its teachers could not answer his questions. Finding no direction or answers to his questions, Augustine went on to lead a life he described as openly sinful. Slowly, however, through the persistence of his mother **Monica** and the work of **Ambrose,** the bishop of Milan, who became a friend and mentor to Augustine, he came to understand the divine characteristics of Christ, and Augustine converted to Christianity.

Augustine then gave up a lucrative teaching position and returned to his hometown of Tagaste, where he became a priest. Not long after, Augustine was made the bishop of Hippo, a major city near his home in north Africa. It was while serving in this position that Augustine wrote his two great works. Augustine's first major work was his *Confessions,* which related his sinful past and conversion to the gospel of Christ. However, it was his defense of Christianity in the face of the collapse of the Roman Empire, his book *The City of God,* that was Augustine's greatest work.

The City of God was more than a defense of Christianity; it was a Christian interpretation of world history, and an outline for spiritual refinement. Within *The City of God,* Augustine discusses two cities, the city of God and the city of Man, and explains that they have competed with one another for control throughout history, and would continue to do so. The city of Man was human and material in nature, and pulled mankind away from God; the city of God was spiritual in nature and lifted mankind toward God. Augustine then argued that Rome was the city of Man, and that it did not matter that Christianity was centered there, because the state itself could not be holy—it was inherently earthly. He then defended this opinion by reminding readers that Christ had warned Peter to remember the difference between what was Caesar's and what was God's.

The city of God, taught Augustine, was not any physical place or earthly city, and therefore could not be conquered by an enemy, as Rome had. The city of God was the heart and soul of every true Christian. The city of God was truth as Christ, through the Spirit, taught it to each person, and it existed wherever true Christians could be found seeking divine guidance and inspiration. The city of Man may be destroyed, because it was made by man and was imperfect. The city of God will exist forever because it was a gift given from God. True Christians, Augustine believed, did not concern themselves with what happened to the city of Man, because they lived for another goal in another life. Augustine himself was able to exemplify this point when he and his city were destroyed in a Vandal attack around 450 A.D.

Augustine's teachings lived on in Catholic doctrine. He taught that because man sinned in the Garden of Eden, all subsequent humans entered the world in a sinful state. This doctrine, called **original sin,** pervades the teachings of the Catholic Church. According to Augustine, because of original sin, humans must be saved and that salvation requires that certain ordinances be performed, such as baptism, confirmation, confession, and communion. Those can only be done by the Catholic Church, and so any who are not Catholic cannot be saved.

Augustine strongly supported the doctrine of the Bishop of Rome and gave that doctrine a strong Platonic backing which, after Augustine, became accepted as the correct or orthodox view. Augustine believed that God was present in the soul of every human being, much as the Form is present in all things. The Nicene Council had proclaimed that God was incorporeal and Augustine identified God with the non-physical Platonic Form, thus linking the god of the Nicene Creed with the god of Platonic thought. Augustine also preached against the pleasures of the flesh, again citing the Platonic teaching that the intellectual (spiritual, for Augustine) is higher than the physical. While other views continued to be expressed, the authority of Augustine seemed to overwhelm them, and they all eventually disappeared. The teachings of Augustine were the foundation of the Catholic Church throughout the Middle Ages, and continue to be influential today.

Christianity in the Sixth Century and Beyond

Disputes between the pope and other bishops, as well as disputes over doctrine, continued well into the sixth century, and beyond. In order to strengthen his position as leader of the Church, **Pope Gregory I,** who was pope in the sixth century, announced a great accommodation of the Church to pagan beliefs. He wanted to entice pagans to join the Christian Church, and was willing to accept a certain amount of pagan beliefs if the barbarians would accept the basic tenets of Christianity. Such accommodations had already occurred in the Christian Church with the adoption of various pagan festivals as Christian holidays, and acceptance of pagan rituals and symbols as part of Christian religious rites. With the strong missionary effort of Gregory I, Christianity began its dominance over paganism in Europe and the dominance of the Roman Bishop over all other leaders in the Church. Full consolidation of the Pope's power would be a long and difficult task, not being fully resolved until the mid-19th century, but clearly the position of Pope at the time of Gregory I was strong and, in the absence of other strong leaders in western Europe, dominant.

Religion and Creativity

Questions regarding the relationship between creativity and religion, and whether religions can creatively adapt or inspire individuals to do creative things, are hard to answer, as the answer depends in large part on one's own religious views. Are changes within a religion creative? That depends on whether one believes that the religion has been changed by men, and therefore corrupts what God has established, even though the change might be creative; or a change ordered by God through revelation or inspiration, in which case man may not take credit for the creativity. We have previously argued in this chapter, however, that even with inspiration, mankind's acts can be considered creative. The same argument can be made in regard to the individual who uses religion to paint, or sculpt, or write a masterpiece. Again, are the persons inspired by God to create the work, or are they praising God by creatively using their own talents? Perhaps both.

We may also ask whether the changes in the Christian Church, even if they are creative, are "good." As we noted with the Egyptians, some of the most adamant opponents to change are the priests. In the case of early Christianity, the Church leaders both resisted change, when they felt it deviated from the doctrine of Christ, and also supported change when needed for accommodation with the larger world. Some, such as the heretics, believed, however, that the doctrinal positions taken by the leaders were not the same as those originally given by Christ; that dispute has raged throughout the history of Christianity. It is interesting that Christianity is the religion most concerned about doctrine. Whereas pagan religions and most Eastern religions only worried about actions, Christianity worries about both actions and beliefs. This concern about belief expresses the Christian faith's focus on intent as well as action, and may also reflect the importance of philosophical teachings in early Christianity, especially in the way heretics were persecuted. Hence, in Christianity, thought was just as important as action.

Unquestionably, religion is responsible, in one-way or another, for many of the great intellectual and artistic advancements of mankind. Religion can breed creativity, but has, on some occasions been just the opposite, as was the case in ancient Egypt. Christian, medieval Europe produced very little creativity, for some of the same reasons that existed in Egypt—powerful and conservative clergy and a general reluctance to accept change. In addition, the medieval Church's emphasis on happiness in the next life and its belief that mysticism (revelation), not study, would lead to true enlightenment and truth seemed to diminish the importance of creativity, especially for improving life here on earth. Looking at a different aspect of creativity and religion, we note that religions themselves seem to be quite creative (again, disregarding the direct intervention of God) in their ability to adapt and remain relevant over decades and centuries and millennia of change.

Timeline—Important Dates

Date	Event
33 A.D.	*Death and resurrection of Jesus Christ*
64	*Death of Peter and Paul*
96	*Probable date of the last-written New Testament book*
100–200	*Writings of the Church Fathers*
200–300	*Wars of the bishops over control of local congregations*
200–350	*Rise of monasticism*
300	*Height of official Roman persecution*
308–337	*Constantine*
325	*Nicene Council*
406	*Jerome solidifies official canon of scripture*
420–450	*Augustine is bishop in Hippo*
476	*Fall of the western Roman Empire*
540–604	*Life of Pope Gregory I*

Notes

1. Eusebius, *History of the Church,* G. A. Williamson (trans.), Penguin Classics, 1965, p.129, orig. text ref. 4:22.7.
2. Eusebius, *History of the Church,* p. 96, orig. 3:32.6.
3. Eusebius, *History of the Church,* p. 132, orig. 4:23.11.
4. Eusebius, *History of the Church,* p. 195, orig. 6:19.4.

5. Eusebius, *History of the Church,* p. 196, orig. 6:19.4.
6. Eusebius, *History of the Church,* p. 88, orig. 3:25.1.
7. Eusebius, *History of the Church,* p. 243, orig. 7:25.11.
8. Eusebius, *History of the Church,* p. 65, orig. 3:3.3.
9. Eusebius, *History of the Church,* p.177, orig. 5:28.18.

Suggested Readings

Cahill, Thomas, *Desire of the Everlasting Hills,* Nan A. Talese/AnchorBooks, 2001.

Ehrman, Bart D., *The Orthodox Corruption of Scripture,* Oxford University Press, 1993.

Eusebius, The *History of the Church,* G. A. Williamson (trans.), Penguin Classics, 1965.

Gabel, John B., Charles B. Wheeler, and Anthony L. D. York, *The Bible as Literature,* 3rd Ed., Oxford University Press, 1996.

Griggs, C. Wilford, *Early Egyptian Christianity,* E. J. Brill, 1993.

Lunt, Gerald, *The Kingdom and the Crown,* Shadow Mountain, 2000.

St. Augustine, *City of God,* Great Books of the Western World, Encyclopaedia Brittanica, Inc., 1952.

St. Augustine, *Confessions,* Frank Sheed (trans.), Sheed and Ward, 1970.

Saint Augustine: Confessions, The City of God

Introduction

The story of Augustine of Hippo (354–430) is one of unquenchable learning and intense personal evaluation and then dedication. Born and raised in the last days of the Roman Empire in present-day Algeria, he received a classical education in Africa and then in Rome. Although his mother was a Christian, he initially followed other religious paths but eventually became converted to the Christian faith. His conversion and repentance were noticed by the church fathers and he was appointed Bishop of Hippo, a Roman city in northern Africa.

Augustine is considered the greatest writer of the Latin-Christian world. His largely Platonic theories on almost every issue in theology were the basis for 1500 years of Catholic dogma. Even the Protestant reformers appealed to his core doctrines concerning the nature of God, His will, and the imperfect nature of mankind. The Latin prose he perfected in his writing is admired and studied even today.

Confessions was perhaps the first major work dedicated to self-reflection. "I would know myself that I might know Thee," is the prayer to God that Augustine begins the book with. This book is his own recounting of his sins, misconceptions during his youth, and conversion experience. It is his testimony of his faith in God and praise for Him. The selection presented below is his story of stealing from a pear tree, the cause for such an action, and its consequences in his life. His discussion in this selection of doing evil solely for evil's sake has been a principle of self-examination ever since.

Augustine was a champion of Christianity in its early days. Anti-Christian views were still widespread throughout the Roman Empire. It was a common belief among the persecutors of Christianity that Roman tolerance for the religion was to blame for the weakness of Rome against the barbarian invasion. In his monumental work, *The City of God,* Augustine gave his response to these claims by laying down the history of the world as planned and directed by God. He described a perpetual conflict between the "City of Earth" wherein dwell those who love themselves and the "City of God" wherein dwell those who love God and their fellowmen. The book's prophetic ending narrates the eventual triumph of the City of God and restitution of all things good to the world. Beyond its theological value, this book is also the first attempt at an all-embracing history of the West.

Article 26

Confessions

The Pear Tree

I propose now to set down my past wickedness and the carnal corruptions of my soul, not for love of them but that I may love Thee, O my God. I do it for love of Thy love, passing again in the bitterness of remembrance over my most evil ways that Thou mayest thereby grow ever lovelier to me, O Loveliness that dost not deceive, Loveliness happy and abiding: and I collect my self out of that broken state in which my very being was torn asunder because I was turned away from Thee, the One, and wasted myself upon the many.

Arrived now at adolescence I burned for all the satisfactions of hell, and I sank to the animal in a succession of dark lusts: *my beauty consumed away,* and I stank in Thine eyes, yet was pleasing in my own and anxious to please the eyes of men.

My one delight was to love and to be loved. But in this I did not keep the measure of mind to mind, which is the luminous line of friendship but from the muddy concupiscence of the flesh and the hot imagination of puberty mists steamed up to becloud and darken my heart so that I could not distinguish the white light of love from the fog of lust. Both love and lust boiled within me, and swept my youthful immaturity over the precipice of evil desires to leave me half drowned in a whirlpool of abominable sins. Your wrath had grown mighty against me and I knew it not. I had grown deaf from the clanking of the chain of my mortality, the punishment for the pride of my soul: and I departed further from You, and You left me to myself: and I was tossed about and wasted and poured out and boiling over in my fornications: and You were silent, O my late-won Joy. You were silent, and I, arrogant and depressed, weary and restless, wandered further and further from You into more and more sins which could bear no fruit save sorrows.

* * *

Where then was I, and how far from the delights of Your house, in that sixteenth year of my life in this world, when the madness of lust—needing no licence from human shamelessness, receiving no licence from Your laws—took complete control of me, and I surrendered wholly to it? My family took no care to save me from this moral destruction by marriage: their only concern was that I should learn to make as fine and persuasive speeches as possible.

* * *

Your law, O Lord, punishes theft; and this law is so written in the hearts of men that not even the breaking of it blots it out: for no thief bears calmly being stolen from—not even if he is rich and the other steals through want. Yet I chose to steal, and not because want drove me to it, unless it was a want of justice and a contempt for it with an excess of iniquity.—For I stole things which I already had in plenty and of better quality. Nor had I any desire to enjoy the things I stole, but only the stealing of them and the sin. There was a pear tree near our vineyard, heavy with fruit, but fruit that was not particularly tempting either to look at or to taste. A group of young blackguards, and I among them, went out to knock down the pear and carry them off late one night, for it was our bad habit to carry on our games in the streets till very late. We carried off an immense load of pears, not to eat—for we barely tasted them before throwing them to the hogs. Our only pleasure in doing it was that it was forbidden. Such was my heart, O God, such was my heart, yet in the depth of the abyss. You had pity on it. Let that heart now tell You what it sought when I was thus evil for no object, having no cause for wrongdoing save my wrongness. The malice of the act was base and I loved it—that is to say I loved my own undoing, I loved the evil in me—not the thing for which I did the evil, simply the evil: my soul was depraved, and hurled itself down from security in You into utter destruction, seeking no profit from wickedness but only to be wicked.

* * *

Article 27

The City of God

On Christian Doctrine

ARGUMENT. Having treated in the four preceding books of the origin of the two cities, the earthly and the heavenly, Augustine explains their growth and progress in the four books which follow; and, in order to do so, he explains the chief passages of the sacred history which bear upon this subject. In this fifteenth book he opens this part of his work by explaining the events recorded in genesis from the time of Cain and Abel to the deluge.

CHAP. I. *Of the two lines of the human race which from first to last divide it*

OF the bliss of Paradise, of Paradise itself, and of the life of our first parents there, and of their sin and punishment, many have thought much, spoken much, written much. We ourselves, too, have spoken of these things in the foregoing books, and have written either what we read in the Holy Scriptures, or what we could reasonably deduce from them. And were we to enter into a more detailed investigation of these matters, an endless number of endless questions would arise, which would involve us in a larger work than the present occasion admits. We cannot be expected to find room for replying to every question that may be started by unoccupied and captious men, who are ever more ready to ask questions than capable of understanding the answer. Yet I trust we have already done justice to these great and difficult questions regarding the beginning of the world, or of the soul, or of the human race itself. This race we have distributed into two parts, the one consisting of those who live according to man, the other of those who live according to God. And these we also mystically call the two cities, or the two communities of men, of which the one is predestined to reign eternally with God, and the other to suffer eternal punishment with the devil. This, however, is their end, and of it we are to speak afterwards. At present, as we have said enough about their origin, whether among the angels, whose numbers we know not, or in the two first human beings, it seems suitable to attempt an account of their career, from the time when our two first parents began to propagate the race until all human generation shall cease. For this whole time or world-age, in which the dying give place and those who are born succeed, is the career of these two cities concerning which we treat.

Of these two first parents of the human race, then, Cain was the first-born, and he belonged to the city of men; after him was born Abel, who belonged to the city of God. For as in the individual the truth of the apostle's statement is discerned, "that is not first which is spiritual, but that which is natural and afterward that which is spiritual,"[1] whence it comes to pass that each man, being derived from a condemned stock, is first of all born of Adam evil and carnal, and becomes good and

[1] I Cor. 15. 46.

spiritual only afterwards, when he is grafted into Christ by regeneration: so was it in the human race as a whole. When these two cities began to run their course by a series of deaths and births, the citizen of this world was the first-born, and after him the stranger in this world, the citizen of the city of God, predestinated by grace, elected by grace, by grace a stranger below, and by grace a citizen above. By grace—for so far as regards himself he is sprung from the same mass, all of which is condemned in its origin: but God, like a potter (for this comparison is introduced by the apostle judiciously, and not without thought), of the same lump made one vessel to honour, another to dishonour.[2] But first the vessel to dishonour was made, and after it another to honour. For in each individual, as I have already said, there is first of all that which is reprobate, that from which we must begin, but in which we need not necessarily remain; afterwards is that which is well-approved, to which we may by advancing attain, and in which, when we have reached it, we may abide. Not, indeed, that every wicked man shall be good, but that no one will be good who was not first of all wicked; but the sooner any one becomes a good man, the more speedily does he receive this title, and abolish the old name in the new. Accordingly, it is recorded of Cain that he built a city,[3] but Abel, being a sojourner, built none. For the city of the saints is above, although here below it begets citizens in whom it sojourns till the time of its reign arrives, when it shall gather together all in the day of the resurrection; and then shall the promised kingdom be given to them, in which they shall reign with their Prince, the King of the ages, time without end.

CHAP. 17. *What produces peace, and what discord, between the heavenly and earthly cities*

But the families which do not live by faith seek their peace in the earthly advantages of this life; while the families which live by faith look for those eternal blessings which are promised, and use as pilgrims such advantages of time and of earth as do not fascinate and divert them from God, but rather aid them to endure with greater ease, and to keep down the number of those burdens of the corruptible body which weigh upon the soul. Thus the things necessary for this mortal life are used by both kinds of men and families alike, but each has its own peculiar and widely different aim in using them. The earthly city, which does not live by faith, seeks an earthly peace, and the end it proposes, in the well-ordered concord of civic obedience and rule, is the combination of men's wills to attain the things which are helpful to this life. The heavenly city, or rather the part of it which sojourns on earth and lives by faith, makes use of this peace only because it must, until this mortal condition which necessitates it shall pass away. Consequently, so long as it lives like a captive and a stranger in the earthly city, though it has already received the promise of redemption, and the gift of the Spirit as the earnest of it, it makes no scruple to obey the laws of the earthly city, whereby the things necessary for the maintenance of this mortal life are administered; and thus, as this life is common to both cities, so there is a harmony between them in regard to what belongs to it. But, as the earthly city has had some philosophers whose doctrine is condemned by the divine teaching, and who, being deceived either by their own conjectures or by demons, supposed that many gods must be invited to take an interest in human affairs, and assigned to each a separate function and a separate department—to one the body, to another the soul; and in the body itself, to one the head, to another the neck, and each of the other members to one of the gods; and in like manner, in the soul, to one god the natural capacity was assigned, to another education, to another anger, to another lust; and so the various affairs of life were assigned—cattle to one, corn to another, wine to another, oil to another, the woods to another, money to another, navigation to another, wars and victories to another, marriages to another, births and fecundity to another, and other things to other gods: and as the celestial city, on the other hand, knew that one God only was to be worshipped, and that to Him alone was due that service which the Greeks call *latreia,* and which can be given only to a god, it

[2]Rom. 9. 21.

[3]Gen. 4. 17.

has come to pass that the two cities could not have common laws of religion, and that the heavenly city has been compelled in this matter to dissent, and to become obnoxious to those who think differently, and to stand the brunt of their anger and hatred and persecutions, except in so far as the minds of their enemies have been alarmed by the multitude of the Christians and quelled by the manifest protection of God accorded to them. This heavenly city, then, while it sojourns on earth, calls citizens out of all nations and gathers together a society of pilgrims of all languages, not scrupling about diversities in the manners, laws, and institutions whereby earthly peace is secured and maintained, but recognizing that, however various these are, they all tend to one and the same end of earthly peace. It therefore is so far from rescinding and abolishing these diversities, that it even preserves and adopts them, so long only as no hindrance to the worship of the one supreme and true God is thus introduced. Even the heavenly city, therefore, while in its state of pilgrimage, avails itself of the peace of earth, and, so far as it can without injuring faith and godliness, desires and maintains a common agreement among men regarding the acquisition of the necessaries of life, and makes this earthly peace bear upon the peace of heaven; for this alone can be truly called and esteemed the peace of the reasonable creatures, consisting as it does in the perfectly ordered and harmonious enjoyment of God and of one another in God. When we shall have reached that peace, this mortal life shall give place to one that is eternal, and our body shall be no more this animal body which by its corruption weighs down the soul, but a spiritual body feeling no want, and in all its members subjected to the will. In its pilgrim state the heavenly city possesses this peace by faith; and by this faith it lives righteously when it refers to the attainment of that peace every good action towards God and man; for the life of the city is a social life.

CHAP. 30. *Of the eternal felicity of the city of God, and of the perpetual Sabbath*

How great shall be that felicity, which shall be tainted with no evil, which shall lack no good, and which shall afford leisure for the praises of God, Who shall be all in all! For I know not what other employment there can be where no lassitude shall slacken activity, nor any want stimulate to labour. I am admonished also by the sacred song, in which I read or hear the words, "Blessed are they that dwell in Thy house, O Lord; they will be still praising Thee."[1] All the members and organs of the incorruptible body, which now we see to be suited to various necessary uses, shall contribute to the praises of God; for in that life necessity shall have no place, but full, certain, secure, everlasting felicity. For all those parts[2] of the bodily harmony, which are distributed through the whole body, within and without, and of which I have just been saying that they at present elude our observation, shall then be discerned; and, along with the other great and marvellous discoveries which shall then kindle rational minds in praise of the great Artificer, there shall be the enjoyment of a beauty which appeals to the reason. What power of movement such bodies shall possess, I have not the audacity rashly to define, as I have not the ability to conceive. Nevertheless I will say that in any case, both in motion and at rest, they shall be, as in their appearance, seemly; for into that state nothing which is unseemly shall be admitted. One thing is certain, the body shall forthwith be wherever the spirit wills, and the spirit shall will nothing which is unbecoming either to the spirit or to the body. True honour shall be there, for it shall be denied to none who is worthy, nor yielded to any unworthy; neither shall any unworthy person so much as sue for it, for none but the worthy shall be there. True peace shall be there, where no one shall suffer opposition either from himself or any other. God Himself, Who is the Author of virtue, shall there be its reward; for, as there is nothing greater or better, He has promised Himself. What else was meant by His word through the prophet, "I will be your God, and ye shall be my people,"[3] than, "I shall be their satisfaction, I shall be all that men honourably desire"—life, and health,

---

[1]Ps. 84. 4.

[2]Numbers.

[3]Lev. 26. 12.

[4]I Cor. 15. 28.

and nourishment, and plenty, and glory, and honour, and peace, and all good things? This, too, is the right interpretation of the saying of the apostle, "That God may be all in all."[4] He shall be the end of our desires who shall be seen without end, loved without cloy, praised without weariness. This outgoing of affection, this employment, shall certainly be, like eternal life itself, common to all.

But who can conceive, not to say describe, what degrees of honour and glory shall be awarded to the various degrees of merit? Yet it cannot be doubted that there shall be degrees. And in that blessed city there shall be this great blessing, that no inferior shall envy any superior, as now the archangels are not envied by the angels, because no one will wish to be what he has not received, though bound in strictest concord with him who has received; as in the body the finger does not seek to be the eye, though both members are harmoniously included in the complete structure of the body. And thus, along with his gift, greater or less, each shall receive this further gift of contentment to desire no more than he has.

Neither are we to suppose that, because sin shall have no power to delight them, free will must be withdrawn. It will, on the contrary, be all the more truly free, because set free from delight in sinning to take unfailing delight in not sinning. For the first freedom of will which man received when he was created upright consisted in an ability not to sin, but also in an ability to sin; whereas this last freedom of will shall be superior, inasmuch as it shall not be able to sin. This, indeed, shall not be a natural ability, but the gift of God. For it is one thing to be God, another thing to be a partaker of God. God by nature cannot sin, but the partaker of God receives this inability from God. And in this divine gift there was to be observed this gradation, that man should first receive a free will by which he was able not to sin, and at last a free will by which he was not able to sin—the former being adapted to the acquiring of merit, the latter to the enjoying of the reward. But the nature thus constituted, having sinned when it had the ability to do so, it is by a more abundant grace that it is delivered so as to reach that freedom in which it cannot sin. For as the first immortality which Adam lost by sinning consisted in his being able not to die, while the last shall consist in his not being able to die; so the first free will consisted in his being able not to sin, the last in his not being able to sin. And thus piety and justice shall be as indefeasible as happiness. For certainly by sinning we lost both piety and happiness; but when we lost happiness, we did not lose the love of it. Are we to say that God Himself is not free because He cannot sin? In that city, then, there shall be free will, one in all the citizens, and indivisible in each, delivered from all ill, filled with all good, enjoying indefeasibly the delights of eternal joys, oblivious of sins, oblivious of sufferings, and yet not so oblivious of its deliverance as to be ungrateful to its Deliverer.

The soul, then, shall have an intellectual remembrance of its past ills; but, so far as regards sensible experience, they shall be quite forgotten. For a skillful physician knows, indeed, professionally almost all diseases; but experimentally he is ignorant of a great number which he himself has never suffered from. As, therefore, there are two ways of knowing evil things—one by mental insight, the other by sensible experience, for it is one thing to understand all vices by the wisdom of a cultivated mind, another to understand them by the foolishness of an abandoned life—so also there are two ways of forgetting evils. For a well-instructed and learned man forgets them one way, and he who has experimentally suffered from them forgets them another—the former by neglecting what he has learned, the latter by escaping what he has suffered. And in this latter way the saints shall forget their past ills, for they shall have so thoroughly escaped them all that they shall be quite blotted out of their experience. But their intellectual knowledge, which shall be great, shall keep them acquainted not only with their own past woes, but with the eternal sufferings of the lost. For if they were not to know that they had been miserable, how could they, as the Psalmist says, for ever sing the mercies of God? Certainly that city shall have no greater joy than the celebra-

[4] I Cor. 15. 28.

tion of the grace of Christ, Who redeemed us by His blood. There shall be accomplished the words of the psalm, "Be still, and know that I am God."[1] There shall be the great Sabbath which has no evening, which God celebrated among His first works, as it is written, "And God rested on the seventh day from all His works which He had made. And God blessed the seventh day, and sanctified it; because that in it He had rested from all His work which God began to make."[2] For we shall ourselves be the seventh day, when we shall be filled and replenished with God's blessing and sanctification. There shall we be still, and know that He is God; that He is that which we ourselves aspired to be when we fell away from Him, and listened to the voice of the seducer, "Ye shall be as gods,"[3] and so abandoned God, Who would have made us as gods, not by deserting Him, but by participating in Him. For without Him what have we accomplished, save to perish in His anger? But when we are restored by Him and perfected with greater grace, we shall have eternal leisure to see that He is God for we shall be full of Him when He shall be all in all. For even our good works, when they are understood to be rather His than ours, are imputed to us that we may enjoy this Sabbath rest. For if we attribute them to ourselves, they shall be servile; for it is said of the Sabbath, "Ye shall do no servile work in it."[4] Wherefore also it is said by Ezekiel the prophet, "And I gave them my Sabbaths to be a sign between me and them, that they might know that I am the Lord who sanctify them."[5] This knowledge shall be perfected when we shall be perfectly at rest, and shall perfectly know that He is God.

This Sabbath shall appear still more clearly if we count the ages as days, in accordance with the periods of time defined in Scripture, for that period will be found to be the seventh. The first age, as the first day, extends from Adam to the deluge; the second from the deluge to Abraham equalling the first, not in length of time, but in the number of generations, there being ten in each. From Abraham to the advent of Christ there are, as the evangelist Matthew calculates, three periods, in each of which are fourteen generations—one period from Abraham to David, a second from David to the captivity, a third from the captivity to the birth of Christ in the flesh. There are thus five ages in all. The sixth is now passing, and cannot be measured by any number of generations, as it has been said, "It is not for you to know the times, which the Father hath put in His own power."[6] After this period God shall rest as on the seventh day, when He shall give us (who shall be the seventh day) rest in Himself.[7] But there is not now space to treat of these ages; suffice it to say that the seventh shall be our Sabbath, which shall be brought to a close, not by an evening, but by the Lord's day, as an eighth and eternal day, consecrated by the resurrection of Christ and prefiguring the eternal repose not only of the spirit, but also of the body. There we shall rest and see, see and love, love and praise. This is what shall be in the end without end. For what other end do we propose to ourselves than to attain to the kingdom of which there is no end?

I think I have now, by God's help, discharged my obligation in writing this large work. Let those who think I have said too little, or those who think I have said too much, forgive me; and let those who think I have said just enough join me in giving thanks to God. Amen.

[1]Ps. 46. 10.

[2]Gen. 2. 2, 3.

[3]Gen. 3. 5.

[4]Deut. 5. 14.

[5]Ezek. 20. 12.

[6]Acts, I. 7.

[7]See BK. XX, Chaps. 6–10.

Byzantium
Creativity Holding On

> As it is clear that you desire war more than peace, since I cannot satisfy you either by my protestations of sincerity, or by my readiness to swear allegiance, so let it be according to your desire. I turn now and look to God alone. Should it be his will that the city be yours, where is he who can oppose it? If he should inspire you with a desire for peace, I shall be only too happy. However, I release you from all your oaths and treaties with me, and, closing the gates of my capital, I will defend my people to the last drop of my blood. Reign in happiness until the All-just, the Supreme God, calls us both before his judgment seat.
>
> —*Constantine XI (last Byzantine Emperor) to the Ottoman Turks*

What Was the Byzantine Empire?

Most people date the collapse of the Roman Empire at 476 A.D., when Romulus Augustus was forced to abdicate the throne of Rome to Germanic warlords of a tribe known as the Ostrogoths. However, this date is only a partial truth; a useful way of dividing up history into manageable parts. In reality, history is a chain of connected and interrelated events that cannot be easily separated from one another. Although the 476 date was certainly pivotal, and marked the moment when a weak and insignificant emperor recognized the power of an invading barbarian force, continuity of history would demand that we consider a larger and more complex reality. In truth, the collapse of Rome began much earlier, and was completed much later. The collapse began when the vast Roman Empire was divided into eastern and western halves nearly two hundred years earlier, in 286 A.D. The western half, especially, experienced a slow weakening and disintegration from that date forward. It is this weakened western half that surrendered in 476. The later completion of the collapse occurred nearly a millennium later, when the eastern half of the Roman Empire finally fell to the Turks in 1453. However, the eastern half of the Roman Empire that continued for a thousand years was different from the previous empire in some important ways that we will discuss. Hence, historians have designated that continuing eastern empire with a different name: the **Byzantine Empire.** If you were to live in the eastern half of the Roman Empire during the Byzantine Era, you would not have thought of yourself as being part of any empire other than the Roman Empire. In fact, the people of this period called themselves "Romans." Nevertheless, it is convenient for us to distinguish between the Roman Empire (prior to 476 A.D.) and the continuation of that empire's eastern half—the Byzantine Empire, which we will study in this chapter.

In a study of the history of creativity, the paths of these two halves of empire following the pivotal events of 476 present an interesting dichotomy. The history and learning of both the east and west were similar up to that time. In essence, both civilizations had the same building blocks to use in their quest for greatness, wealth, and political power. Yet, in the west, Europe fell into its darkest age; while in the east, Asia Minor entered a golden era—perhaps not as glorious as the days of the great emperors in the Roman Golden Age in the second century, but certainly an example of cultural brilliance. That difference invites the question of why these two halves of empire would be so different. The answer lies, in part, in the attitude, acceptance, and use of creativity within each civilization. We will discuss the nature of creativity in the eastern half of the empire in this chapter, and then discuss the nature of creativity in the western half in later chapters. (The rise of Islam, which occurred in the century following the fall of the west will be considered in an intermediate chapter.)

■ Constantinople

Just as the death of the traditional Roman Empire began with the split of the empire into two halves by Diocletian in 286 A.D., that date marks the reasonable beginning of the Byzantine Empire, although, of course, no one realized it at the time. When Constantine became emperor a few years after Diocletian, Constantine continued the division of the empire and decided to build a new city to serve as the administrative head of the empire. He called the new city *"Neo Roma"* (New Rome) but after his death, the city was renamed Constantinople in his honor.

Constantine chose the small Greek trading town of **Byzantium** as the site where he would build this new city. The location was ideal for a major city. Sitting on a peninsula jutting out from Europe toward Asia, on the banks of the **Bosporus,** the sea channel that joins the **Sea of Marmara** (a branch of the Mediterranean Sea) to the **Black Sea,** Constantinople commanded the major land and sea routes for trade between Europe and Asia. Because Constantinople was on a peninsula, it was much easier to defend than the city of Rome. Constantinople had a large outer defensive wall, which protected the only land approach. This wall, which would be enlarged into a system of walled reinforcements over the next thousand years, was nearly impregnable. It would not be successfully breached until the time of gunpowder, when explosions weakened it. A map of Constantinople is given in Figure 15.1.

There were other advantages to the site of Constantinople, including a deepwater port with a natural harbor, a large freshwater river, a warm climate, and good soil for farming in the region to support the population of a city. The design of the city was laid out by Constantine himself and patterned after Rome, containing a large square like the forum, an acropolis, hippodrome and senate house. However, the city had a strong Christian feel to it as well, as Constantine built several Christian churches, including the **Church of Holy Wisdom** (*Hagia Sophia* in Greek), which was the largest church in Christianity at the time. There were also relics enshrined throughout the city, including the crosses of the two thieves, part of the bread with which Christ fed the 5,000, and the tools Noah had used to build the ark. Constantinople was a creative effort to build the greatest city that the greatest empire could construct.

Despite its size and detail, Constantinople was ready for occupancy in just six years. Because of its location on major trading routes and its new designation as capital of the whole empire, Constantinople grew quickly of its own accord. However, Constantine took steps to increase the

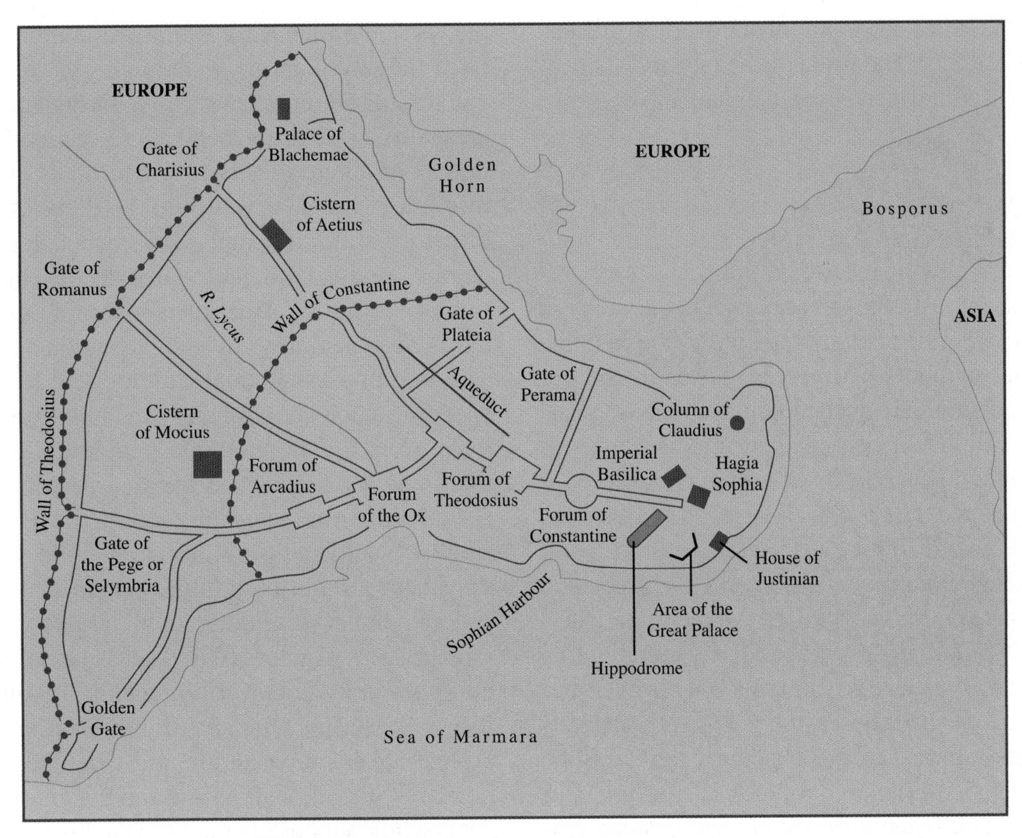

Figure 15.1 ■ *Map of Constantinople.*

population even more. For commoners, Constantine offered free food and entertainment, like the circus. For soldiers, Constantine placed his military headquarters in Constantinople. For scholars, Constantine built large libraries and stocked them with all the Latin and Greek manuscripts he could find. And for wealthy aristocrats of Rome who served as its senators, Constantine built a new Senate and promised to build new homes that were exact replicas of those the senators left behind. Constantine's effort and vision were realized, and by the end of his life Constantinople was the true capital and commercial center of the Roman Empire.

However, as the fortunes of Constantinople and the east rose, those of Rome and the west fell. Crushing poverty ruled the lives of many western Romans at this time, a situation that was only aggravated by continually spiraling inflation. The city of Rome was dirty, and living conditions unsanitary. Much of the grand construction and architecture had fallen into disrepair and ruin, many purposely destroyed by the city's own citizens so that they could use the stones and other materials to build their homes. The final insult to the greatness of the city of Rome, and the last gasp at reviving the empire in the west, occurred in 402, when the emperor Honorius decided to move the capital of the west from Rome to **Ravenna,** a seaport on the Adriatic coast. This move, while sealing the doom of the city of Rome, probably extended the life of the western empire by sixty years, as in 410 the city of Rome was sacked and destroyed by a Germanic tribe called the Visigoths. Rome was semi-rebuilt, only to be sacked again in 455 by the Vandals. This time the weak and decadent empire could not afford to rebuild its former capital, and Rome was left in ruins. A large part of Rome's mystique had been its political importance and uniqueness. This was Rome, after all, home of the world's greatest political wonder. The pride of the city and its people was also damaged beyond repair.

Between the Fall of the West and Justinian

When Romulus Augustus abdicated the western throne in 476, he actually transferred the insignia and other symbols of imperial power to the co-emperor, **Zeno,** in Constantinople, so that the barbarians would not get them. Romulus Augustus also wanted to support the continuing authority of the emperor of the east. The king of the Goths who eventually came to power (there was a brief revolt within the Gothic tribes) also seemed to recognize the ultimate power and authority of the eastern emperor. This Gothic king, **Theodoric,** entered into a treaty with the eastern Roman emperor even before the Goths had successfully captured the western empire. In that treaty, Theodoric agreed to be subservient to the emperor of the east and not to attack any lands administered by the eastern emperor (thus illustrating that the eastern and western empires were administered separately). That treaty was renewed by the emperor of the east when Theodoric came to power in the west.

In 491 the eastern emperor, Zeno, died and **Anastasius I** became the new Byzantine emperor. Anastasius was an effective ruler who strengthened the empire both militarily and financially. He realized that peaceful borders and a well-defended capital had been two of the keys to the greatness and longevity of the Roman Empire. He also realized that the Byzantine Empire's military strength was not as impressive as that of old Rome, and took steps to remedy that difference. Among the first things Anastasius did was secure his western border by reaffirming the mutual protection agreement with Theodoric the Goth, who was still ruling in the west. Anastasius also increased the size and improved the training of his army. Pains were also taken to ensure the safety of his capital city, Constantinople. The largest project undertaken to increase the fortifications of Constantinople was a new defensive wall, several miles further from the city than the walls built by Constantine when Constantinople was first built, and which were further strengthened by the emperor **Theodosius** in about 440. By the end of its construction, this new outer wall built by Anastasius was over forty miles in length, and has become known as the **Long Wall.** In spite of the increased military spending, Anastasius was able to restore fiscal responsibility to the Byzantine Empire. Through improved administration and less lavish spending habits, Anastasius was able to both reduce taxes for the common people and increase the amount of money in the treasury, helping to secure the firm financial footing the Byzantine Empire would enjoy all through its golden era.

In spite of his fiscal improvements, Anastasius was unpopular with the people, largely over religious issues (which we will discuss later). Sensing an opportunity, a powerful general, **Justin,** overthrew Anastasius and gained the imperial throne. At age 68, Justin was quite old when he came to power. Realizing that his age and the animosity of Anastasius' supporters might make his reign brief, he seized his opportunity to begin a dynasty within his family and quickly named his nephew **Justinian** as his successor. To prepare Justinian to be a great emperor, Justin had his nephew trained in classical and theological education, military science, and government. Justin's decision to name Justinian his heir and successor was his greatest accomplishment as emperor, as Justinian would lead Byzantium into its golden age.

Justin also affirmed the treaty with Theodoric the Goth but secretly had ambitions to reestablish the Roman Empire of old, with both eastern and western halves united. While technically Theodoric was subject to the emperors of the Byzantine Empire, with Italy designated as a province of Byzantium, in reality Theodoric had ignored Byzantium and had done as he pleased. However, 90 percent of Theodoric's subjects were Romans, not Goths, and this presented a problem for the Goths, especially upon the death of Theodoric, which occurred not long after Justin became emperor of the eastern realm.

Justinian and the Creation of a Revived Christian Empire

When Justin died, his nephew Justinian succeeded to the Byzantine throne without incident. On the other hand, the death of Theodoric resulted in a succession crisis for the Goths, since Theodoric had no son, and no compelling leader arose. Justinian cleverly refused to sign another treaty with the Goths, with the hope that he would be able to assert his power in Italy. But first, Justinian faced some other military threats. The most immediate problem was on the far eastern frontier where the Persians had revolted. Justinian decided to attack the Persians; for this task he selected a general, **Belisarius,** who had been a faithful bodyguard to Justinian's uncle, Justin, and was currently serving as the magistrate over Mesopotamia, an eastern Byzantine province. Belisarius proved to be a highly competent general, winning more battles than any other Roman general since Julius Caesar. He was a man of high integrity, even withstanding stoically the open unfaithfulness of his wife and occasionally taking her with him on military campaigns. Belisarius was loved by his troops and was completely loyal to Justinian. While serving Justinian in the east, Belisarius achieved several victories over the Persians and forced the Persian Shah to seek a peace accord with Justinian. This accord bought the Byzantine Empire eight years of peace from the Persians on their eastern border.

Believing his eastern frontier safe from invasion, Justinian turned his attentions to conquering parts of Africa that had been taken by the Vandals, including the ancient city of Carthage. In order to facilitate this plan, Justinian recalled Belisarius from the eastern front and brought him back to Constantinople in order to make preparations for the invasion of Africa. However, before Belisarius could leave for Africa, a more immediate crisis occurred in Constantinople.

Like the circus of the Roman Empire and the modern professional sports of today, Byzantium entertained the populace with sporting events, the most popular being chariot racing. All sizable cities within the Byzantine Empire had chariot-racing factions, that is, groups of fans who took the name of their group from the color of their favorite team. The four major teams in Constantinople were the Blues, Reds, Whites, and Greens, each of which was a professional organization responsible for fielding teams to the chariot races held at the hippodromes. Two teams, the Blues and Greens, were dominant, with Justinian known as a supporter of the Blues. Fans of the various teams were fiercely loyal; street fighting and hooliganism often broke out between supporters of rival teams.

Early in the year 532 tensions between supporters of the Blues and Greens exploded into riot conditions within Constantinople; rioters burned the palace of the prefect and made it unsafe to venture out into the city. Justinian cracked down harshly on the violence and had many of the leaders of the Blues and Greens arrested; several of them were scheduled to be hanged. In spite of the violence, Justinian continued with the planned chariot races three days later. At the races both the Blues and Greens pled with Justinian for mercy for their captured leaders. Justinian ignored their pleas and refused to reply. At the 22nd race (out of 24), the cry of "Nike!" (Greek for victory) went up in the stands and the fans started to riot anew, forcing Justinian and his court to take refuge within the palace.

For nearly a week Constantinople was ravaged by riot and revolt, with even the military unable to bring order to the city. Finally, five days later, Justinian returned to the Hippodrome, gave a public apology, and promised an amnesty. But the mob once again turned hostile and Justinian once again retreated to the palace for safety. The mob, however, found Hypatius, a nephew of a former emperor, and proclaimed him the new Byzantine Emperor right there in the Hippodrome. Justinian was ready to give in and flee the city, and would have done so if not for the courage of his wife **Theodora,** who encouraged him to stay and crush the revolt. Theodora's advice was heeded; instead of fleeing, Justinian planned a ruthless blow against the revolt. He ordered Belisarius to take the army to the next chariot races and quickly strike from both sides of the Hippodrome. The orders were obeyed and the move was unexpected. Nearly all the mob in the Hippodrome was murdered in a vicious bloodbath and the **Nike Revolt** was ended.

Belisarius was honored for his role in extinguishing the revolt and now was more popular than ever with the emperor. Justinian, however, still had designs on Africa, and soon Belisarius was sent to Africa to conquer the Vandals and gain the area for the Byzantine Empire. It was a quick, easy, and impressive victory for Belisarius and the Byzantines. It was also an important victory because it convinced Justinian that the Germanic barbarians could be defeated and military victories could be achieved in the west. It meant that Justinian's dream of seeing old Rome reunited under Byzantine rule was possible.

Emboldened by the ease with which Belisarius had conquered the Vandals in Africa, Justinian immediately sent Belisarius and his armies on to Italy to attack the Goths and reclaim the west for Byzantium. His timing could not have been better. The succession crisis following the death of Theodoric still raged and the Goths were not able to mount an effective defense against the Byzantine army. Belisarius met with little resistance as he stormed through Italy from the south. When Belisarius did meet with opposition, he discovered inventive ways to gain the upper hand, such as in Naples, where he had his troops sneak into the city by walking up the aqueduct. In Rome itself, the pope encouraged the Romans to invite Belisarius into the city, which they did. Belisarius followed the Goths north and placed Ravenna, the Goth capital, under siege. This siege lasted for three years and, although he was able to contain the Gothic armies, Belisarius was unable to breach the city's defenses and force surrender.

With the war in a virtual stalemate, the Goths decided to try a new tactic to bring an end to the war. Belisarius had known nothing but success as a general and was admired, respected, and loved by his men because of it. Ever since his quick victory over the Vandals, rumors had circulated in the army camps that Belisarius wanted to be a king, and his popularity among his men assured him support if he had made the move. Hearing these rumors (most likely just idle talk of men who loved and respected their commander), the Goths offered Belisarius a deal: They would surrender to Belisarius if he would agree to become their new king. Belisarius agreed to the deal, at least as a strategic move, and the Byzantines took Ravenna without further fighting. However, Belisarius himself never saw the inside of Ravenna, as Justinian, hearing of the plot, ordered Belisarius to return to Constantinople, which he immediately did. To the everlasting credit of Belisarius, there is no evidence that he intended to keep the throne for himself, but was simply using the ploy as a way to acquire the city for Justinian. However, Belisarius returned to Constantinople under a cloud of suspicion.

What seemed like a great victory and the realization of Justinian's dream for a reunification of east and west soon fell apart. On the eastern front, the Persians broke the treaty and invaded, while in the west the Goths reacted to the occupation of Ravenna by choosing a new king and rebelling against Byzantine rule. To make matters worse, an epidemic of **Bubonic Plague** swept across the Byzantine Empire, killing between 40 and 70 percent of the population. Whether because the relationship between Justinian and Belisarius had been mended or because Justinian realized he faced a war on two fronts and needed all the help he could get is unclear, but for one reason or another Belisarius was given a new command in the east, fighting the Persians. Once again Belisarius outwitted his opponents and gained the upper hand against the Persian army. Victory seemed near for Belisarius and the Byzantines, when Belisarius was mysteriously summoned to return to Constantinople. Circumstances regarding his summons are not completely clear, but it is known that other generals and officers were recalled at about this time because they had spoken too freely regarding who should succeed Justinian (he was very sick with plague, and many thought he would die). Some of the other officers were imprisoned for up to a year, although there is no evidence that Belisarius ever was. Whatever the reason for Belisarius' recall to Constantinople, he was kept in the capital and not given a new command for a year. When he was finally given a command, Belisarius was sent back to Italy to re-conquer what he had already once taken.

The retaking of Italy from the Goths was not as easy as the first invasion, for a variety of reasons. This time the Goths were better prepared, and expected an attack from Byzantium. Furthermore, the succession turmoil following the deaths of Theodoric had ended with the rise to power of a Gothic king who proved to be both effective and popular. Finally, conditions back in Byzantium made the war more difficult this time. The Byzantine Empire was still fighting on its eastern front against the Persians as well as in Italy, thus dividing men and resources. The plague had killed a sizable percentage of the population as well, affecting everything from finding recruits for the army to growing crops. Finally, years of warfare and elaborate building programs in Constantinople had drained much of the treasury.

The next two years saw Belisarius make small gains, but the lack of men and supplies proved a severe hindrance to his success, and overall the two forces were in stalemate. Knowing of her husband's need for supplies and men, Belisarius' wife Antonia went to Constantinople to see Empress Theodora (the two were old friends) to ask her to persuade Justinian to send more troops and equipment to Belisarius in Italy. However, upon arriving, she found Theodora dead and Justinian in mourning. With conditions in the palace changed, Antonia instead decided she had been apart from her husband for too long and petitioned for Belisarius' recall to Constantinople, perhaps hoping that Belisarius might become Justinian's chief advisor in the place of Theodora. Justinian decided to grant her request and Belisarius was sent for. Except for one brief skirmish late in life, Belisarius would not go afield again.

Soon after Belisarius left Italy, the Goths were able to recapture Rome. Justinian, who still dreamed of seeing the old Roman Empire united during his lifetime (and feeling his own mortality with the death of his wife), knew that he had to either make a final effort to take Italy or focus his attentions elsewhere. He ordered a massive army raised, and placed them under the command of general Narses. With the large and well supplied army that Belisarius was denied, Narses broke the Goths and reunited all of Italy with the eastern empire. It was a great day for Justinian, who now ruled over nearly all of the old Roman Empire (with the exception of northern Europe and Spain). In the mind of Justinian, his goal had been accomplished—ancient Rome had been restored to its greatness under the banner of Christian Byzantium.

One of the most important underpinnings of the Roman Empire, and a key factor to its success and longevity, was its emphasis on law. In general, Roman law was universally known, highly practical, and well enforced. This helped create a sense of fairness, equality, and community throughout the geographically, ethnically, and religiously vast empire. However, by the time Justinian ascended to power in the east, the Roman legal code had become a chaotic mess. Byzantium used the old Roman legal code, but many of these laws conflicted with the laws of conquered states; these conflicts had not been reconciled in over 300 years. Furthermore, since the Roman law had been established there had been great changes within the empire: Gothic conquest of the west, the creation of the Byzantine Empire in the east, and the wholesale adoption of Christianity and its infusion with the government. All of these factors made for a legal hodgepodge that was practically undecipherable even by legal scholars and those in government.

Justinian understood that if he was to effectively control an empire as large and powerful as old Rome he would have to do more than just conquer lost territory. He would have to unite peoples with great differences and effectively govern them, and this required a strong and clear legal base. Knowing this, and understanding what a daunting task fixing Byzantium's broken legal code would be, less than a year after he came to power he chose ten of the empire's foremost jurists and legal scholars to begin the task of consolidating and codifying the legal code. It took over two years to complete but the *Codex Justinianus* **(Justinian Code),** also sometimes referred to as the *Codex Constitutonum,* was completed, approved, and published in 529. After its publication, all other laws in the empire were required to be harmonious with the *Codex Justinianus,* thus ending the legal chaos in Byzantium.

The new law code was still firmly based in Roman law, but added to it a distinct Christian influence. The *Codex Justinianus* was practical—dealing with day-to-day legal matters such as property rights, inheritances, and trial and punishment of criminals. The status of women was improved, as females were given inheritance rights through the mother, and divorce was allowed under some circumstances. Rapists now were punished by death, and all of their property was confiscated and given to the victimized woman. The new law also solidified the Christian church's place at the center of the empire, by banning all heretical movements and affirming the Bishop of Rome as leader of the church (although both civil and ecclesiastical law emanated from the emperor). The Christian element also was encoded into the law by making some aspects of the law more compassionate. Slavery was allowed but governed with strict rules designed to protect the slaves; and freed slaves were now guaranteed the same rights as natural-born freemen. The *Codex Justinianus* was effective in achieving its goal of bringing order to a chaotic legal system and unity to a large empire.

Justinian's reign was truly a golden age for Byzantium. He expanded militarily and imposed a legal system as a basis of effective rule. He also reestablished other key features of the old Roman Empire. For example, commerce and trade were at a level that had not been seen in hundreds of years. Justinian traded with the Orient and, sensing the value of silk, sent monks to China, where they obtained some silk worms, eggs, and mulberry trees. (Because taking materials that would allow silk to be made in other places was illegal according to Chinese law, the monks hid the worms and eggs in hollowed-out walking sticks.) With these, Justinian established a silk industry in Constantinople that became an important part of Byzantine trade with Europe. Metal work became an important industry by combining precious jewels from throughout the world with gold and silver worked in Byzantium. Some of the most sought-after products were jewelry, icons, relic boxes, tableware, badges, and insignia. The imperial currency was accepted throughout the world, and banking was active in providing capital for new ventures. Universities were active in places such as Alexandria, Constantinople, and Antioch, but the Academy in Athens was closed and its land confiscated because of its association with paganism. Medicine, science, literature, architecture, and the arts were all fostered, and showed great progress during Justinian's reign.

Figure 15.2 ■ Hagia Sophia (external view).

One of the best examples of Justinian's support of the arts is *Hagia Sophia,* which was rebuilt by Justinian following a fire. This church featured a series of windows near the top of a great dome set over the massive central vault. Other domes were arranged around the great dome to support it and give the building a feeling of extensiveness and symmetry. Some said that the dome seemed not to rest on the masonry below it but to be suspended by a golden chain from the heavens. The overall effect was to give a feeling of lightness and elevation that invoked reverence and awe, as might be appreciated from the pictures of *Hagia Sophia* given in Figure 15.2 and 15.3.

Justinian also built a group of beautiful churches in Ravenna, the capital of the west. These churches are noted for their wonderful mosaics, showing, among other scenes, Christ as the ruler of heaven and earth, the apostles and prophets, Justinian himself, his wife Theodora, and their many courtiers. A picture of the mosaics of Theodora is given in Figure 15.4.

Figure 15.3 ■ *Hagia Sophia. Image © Adam Woolfitt/Corbis.*

Figure 15.4 ■ *Mosaics in Ravenna of Theodora, and her courtiers. Image © Archivo Iconografico, S. A./ Corbis.*

The Church in the Byzantine Empire

Just as the Christian church was important in the western half of the empire, becoming the central focus of medieval Europe (which we will discuss in a later chapter), the Christian church in the eastern half of the empire was critically important to daily life, art, and politics. The church in the east was originally united with the western church, but they eventually grew apart, although the formal break was not to occur for several hundred years. The influence of the Byzantine emperor was always important in the Greek (Eastern) Church, but was not important in the Latin (Western) Church, especially as the power of the emperor became largely irrelevant in the west after the time of Justinian. With time, the absence of a strong political force in the west gave rise to an increasingly independent and politically powerful pope, whereas the patriarch in the east was always subservient to the emperor. The history of these changes between the churches is fascinating. Now let's examine some of the interactions between the eastern and western churches.

From the time of Constantine, the church was run by local bishops who operated under the appointment and control of the emperor. There was no central control of the church separate from the empire. In spite of the efforts of the emperors to unify the faith, such as Constantine's convening of the Nicene Council, the church was torn into several factions, each with differing beliefs regarding many of the basic principles and precepts of the Christian faith. One of the doctrines being most rigorously debated within the early church concerned the nature of Jesus Christ.

The nature of Christ had been debated within the church from the death of the apostles, with one group's view being supported by some official church councils, only to later be condemned by another official council. The Nicene Council was, of course, the first attempt to deal with this problem, but with the death of Constantine and his enforcement of the official creed, disputes again broke out. In the fifth century, the main division was between two groups, the **Chalcedonians** and the **Monophysites.** The Chalcedonians believed that Christ had two separate natures, one human and one divine, and that each existed simultaneously, yet separately, within the person of the resurrected Jesus Christ. This conclusion was reached by the Christian church at the **Council of Chalcedon** in 451 and was considered to be the official (orthodox) position of the church. However, the Monophysites, who believed that the resurrected Christ had only one nature, as the divine person of Christ took over his human nature so that the human nature no longer existed, refused to accept the decision reached in Chalcedon, and thus the debate continued.[1]

The eastern emperor, Zeno, who personally sided with the Monophysites, issued a religious proclamation called the *Henotikon,* which was intended to be a compromise between the two factions. The *Henotikon* was generally accepted by the patriarchs (bishops in the Eastern Church) in the Byzantine Empire, as Monophysitism was more popular in the east. However, the bishops in the western Church, where Monophysitism was not generally believed, were appalled that the eastern patriarchs would embrace this "heretical" doctrine. In reaction, **Pope Felix III** decided to excommunicate the **Patriarch of Constantinople,** who was the symbolic head of the church in the east.[2] The eastern church had always questioned the authority of the pope over the entire Christian church, and refused to recognize the excommunication of the patriarch, and thus a schism occurred between the Christian churches in the east and west. Eventually the split within the Christian church would become official, and the Catholic and Orthodox Christian churches would grow out of it, but that did not occur for several centuries. In the meantime, the two groups drifted apart and took quite different views on several other key points. Thus, while the Byzantine Empire would have a strongly Christian tradition, it would not be the Catholic tradition of the west.

Like Zeno before him, Anastasius was a very religious man, and a Monophysite. Therefore, the contentious split between east and west continued. However, unlike his two most recent predecessors, Zeno and Anastasius, Justin was a Chalcedonian, not a Monophysite, which meant his religious leanings were more like the Christians of the west than those of the east. Justin's religious beliefs helped lessen the tensions between east and west in the Christian church, at least for a time. Justin attacked another heresy, **Arianism** (which was the type of Christianity followed by the Goths), and this attack against a common religious enemy seemed to unite the eastern and western groups.

In the early days of Justinian's reign, he vigorously pursued his policy of making Byzantium a Christian empire, by persecuting the pagans, Samaritans, "heretical" Christians, and, to a lesser extent, Jews who lived within the borders of the Byzantine Empire. Paganism was considered to be both evil and dangerous to the empire, and Justinian took steps to stamp it out. Pagans, for the first time, were barred from serving in the Byzantine civil service. Furthermore, pagan teachers and tutors throughout the empire were denied stipends from the imperial treasury, had their personal property confiscated, and were banished from the empire if they would not accept baptism. Under the weight of this decree, the Academy in Athens, founded by Plato over 900 years earlier, was forced to shut down, as it was still a stronghold of paganism.

Samaritans, who were hated by both Christian and Jew, found themselves in even more dire circumstances as Justinian's decrees regarding them were even stricter. Samaritan synagogues were destroyed and Samaritans were disallowed the right to deed their property to anyone who was not a Christian. Thus, Samaritans had to convert to Christianity in order to keep family lands. These hardships proved too much for the Samaritans to bear, and they revolted against Justinian and the Byzantine government in 529. The Samaritans initially had some success in their revolt, but were eventually defeated. As punishment, the Samaritan leader was beheaded (his head was sent to Justinian as a trophy) and over 20,000 Samaritans were sold into slavery.

Christians who were deemed heretics received the harshest treatment, however. With so many people converting to Christianity under duress, the laws against backsliding Christians were very harsh. Any baptized Christian found practicing pagan rituals or sacrificing to the gods was to be immediately put to death. "Heretical" Christians within the Byzantine Empire found themselves facing many of the same penalties and punishments as pagans and Samaritans; namely confiscation of property, banishment from the capital, the loss of their children (who would be then taught the correct variety of Christianity and baptized), and possibly death.

Nominally, the emperor was still the head of the Christian church, and the western tradition and the eastern tradition were merely different factions within the same church. That situation changed with the proclamation of the Byzantine emperor, Leo III in 726. This highly religious man came to believe that the use of icons and statues violated God's command to not make any graven images. **Icons** are paintings and holy images of religious figures, considered a window to the heavenly world, so one could speak through the image to the world of divinity and thus draw closer to God. An example of an icon is shown in Figure 15.5. Many icons were destroyed during this period and those who did the destruction were called **iconoclasts** (literally, image breakers). The word has since taken the meaning to refer to any person who attacks an established tradition, belief, or institution. The Roman church was strongly opposed to the view of Leo III, and the pope excommunicated the emperor over this issue. Because the Catholic Church still wanted to have a religious state, supported by an emperor, the western church sought alliances with various kings, eventually culminating in the recognition of the king of the Franks, **Charlemagne,** as a new Roman emperor. The title bestowed on Charlemagne by the pope was "Holy Roman Emperor," thus simultaneously challenging the position of the Byzantine Emperor as head of the church and also proclaiming that a new Roman Empire was being established in the west that would be independent of the Byzantine Empire. A compromise was worked out over the issue of icons and statues, and the emperor of the east was eventually restored to the church, but the title of Holy Roman Emperor remained with certain leaders in the west, as we will discuss in later chapters.

Figure 15.5 ■ *An example of a religious icon. Image from Corel.*

From that time on, bad feelings continued between the Orthodox and Catholic Churches and between the Byzantine Empire and Europe. Even calls by the emperor to assist in regaining the Holy Land, which led to the European crusades, resulted in broken promises and anger between the parties. Disputes over doctrine and the role of the pope led to an eventual complete break (in 1054) and the two entities formally became two different churches. Some of the major differences that exist are that the western Catholics believe that the Pope is infallible, that the Holy Ghost emanates from the Father and Son, that Mary was conceived without original sin, that there are no restrictions on types of icons used in the liturgy, and that priests should not marry. The Eastern Orthodox believe that the pope is simply one of the patriarchs, that the Holy Ghost emanates only from the Father, that there is no special significance to Mary's conception and birth (which is different from the conception and birth of Jesus), that icons used in the liturgy should only be two-dimensional, and that priests can marry.

Post-Justinian Byzantium

After Justianian's death, the western empire slipped away from his son and successor, **Justin II,** and was never to be reclaimed by Byzantium. Through a combination of elaborate spending and bad luck, the greatness of the empire faded. Near-constant warfare and border skirmishes with the Persians, Avars, and Slavs over the next 300 years kept the empire emotionally and economically exhausted. This made the Byzantine Empire ripe pickings for the **Muslims,** who, by the late seventh century, had taken most of Byzantium's African and Middle Eastern territory. (We will discuss this development in more detail in the next chapter.) Because of the loss of so much land, the gentry were disbanded; the remaining land was given to the peasants in return for their service in the military. Up until this time the Byzantine Empire had always used professional soldiers, but with the negative turns of events, commoners were needed in the army.

During the next 300 years, from about 800 to 1100, the Byzantine Empire made a recovery of sorts. The treasury was built back up and the empire was more financially secure than it had been since early in Justinian's reign. Also, the remaining territory left to the empire was solidified. The Byzantines rebuilt their empire and protected the seaward approaches to their capital with a creative discovery called **Greek Fire,** some type of petroleum product that could be sprayed on an opposing ship and ignited. It could not be readily washed off or otherwise removed, thus inevitably resulting in great damage to the opposing ship.

After this period of relative peace and stability, Byzantium was once again beset by outside invaders. The **Magyars** attacked between 1060 and 1107, taking much of Hungary and Romania (Byzantium's remaining European territory), although they were unable to take Constantinople. The Christian crusaders from Europe sacked Constantinople in 1204 while on their way to the Holy Land to fight the Muslims. The Muslims also renewed their attacks and slowly took more and more land. Finally, by 1400 Byzantium was only a small area surrounding Constantinople. In 1453 the Ottoman Turks captured Constantinople and eventually renamed it **Istanbul,** bringing an end to the eastern empire. The loss of Constantinople to the Muslim Turks forced the Christian scholars living there to flee for safety. Most of the scholars fled west to Italy, taking with them much of the knowledge lost to Europe during the Dark Ages, and helping to bring about the Renaissance.

The Byzantine Empire was an extension of the Roman Empire. It had carried on, expanded, and adapted the Roman legacy for another thousand years after the fall of western Rome. Byzantium and its leaders understood the greatness of Rome and worked to creatively adapt to their own situation the factors that caused that greatness. They kept what had worked for Rome, discarded what had not, and added their own unique touches. Over time, as had happened with Rome itself, decadence, complacency, and a resistance to change contributed to its demise. However, no empire that lasts over a millennium and controls a land area as large as that of Byzantium can be considered a failure. Was Byzantium the equal of Rome? No. Was it one of the largest and most successful empires in history? Yes. Like the Romans before them had done with the Greeks, they based their civilization on the creativity of their predecessor and used their own creative spark to make the needed adaptations to survive and improve. Yet, some feeling of failure is unavoidable when considering the Byzantine Empire. Perhaps that feeling comes because of the lack of a creative goal for the empire. Byzantium's only goal, from the beginning to the end, was to recapture the greatness of ancient Rome. And, just like the Middle and New Kingdoms of Egypt, a search for the glories of the past is not a good substitute for a forward-looking goal. Somehow the past is never completely recovered, and the accomplishments of the present, although good, are always considered to be failures. Eventually, this feeling of failure brings stagnation and loss of creative energy.

Timeline—Important Dates

Date	Event
476 A.D.	*Fall of the western Roman Empire*
474–491	*Zeno rules in Byzantium*
491–518	*Anastasium I, emperor in the east*
518–527	*Justin rules*
527–565	*Justinian I, emperor of the east*
532	*Nike Revolt*
726	*Emperor Leo III declares that icons be destroyed*
867–1081	*New prosperity for Byzantine Empire*

1024	*Formal split between the Roman and Eastern Churches*
1204	*Constantinople sacked by the Fourth Crusade*
1453	*Fall of Constantinople and end of the Byzantine Empire*

Notes

1. Bender, Elise M., "The Ecole Initiative Glossary—Monophysitism," http://cedar.evansville.edu/~ecoleweb/glossary/monophysitism.html (May 25, 2001)
2. Elton, Hugh, "De Imperatoribus Romanis—Zeno," http://www.roman-emperors.org/zeno.htm (May 25, 2001)

Suggested Readings

Thatcher, Oliver J. (ed.), *The Library of Original Sources,* "The Justinian Code," University Research Extension Co., 1907.

Article 28
The Justinian Code

Introduction

Justinian, who ruled from 527–565, was the greatest of the Byzantine Emperors. Raised with the best education available and early military leadership, he was a natural leader. Perhaps his greatest military feat was the expansion of the Byzantine borders to reclaim much of the former Roman Empire, including all of Barbarian-conquered Africa and Italy. He built many beautiful churches throughout this area and rebuilt (after it was burned down) the largest and most magnificent church of Christianity, Hagia Sofia, in Constantinople.

To be a successful leader over so many citizens of the old Roman Empire in so many different territories required creative adaptation and modification of the old government. The only universal code of laws available was the outdated Roman code which had been largely written by Augustus Caesar about 600 years previously. This earlier code of laws conflicted with many of the laws of the core states of the Byzantine Empire on the eastern Mediterranean. To end the conflicts, Justinian had a new code prepared blending old Roman law with local territorial laws, thus establishing a constitution for the entire empire to which all would adhere. It was written in Greek and not Latin, thus once and for all solidifying Greek as the official language of the Eastern Empire. Many laws were based on Christian values, further enshrining Christianity as the official religion in the Byzantine Empire and confirming the emperor's special position in leading the Eastern Church (in cooperation with the Patriarch of Constantinople).

This code should be compared to other legal writings which we have studied such as the Biblical laws given to Moses and the Hammurabi code. The Justinian Code is less retributive than the earlier codes and introduces the concept of different kinds of law—natural, common, and civil. This concept continues today in the legal system of the United States.

Book I. Of Persons

I. Justice and Law

JUSTICE is the constant and perpetual wish to render every one his due.

1. Jurisprudence is the knowledge of things divine and human; the science of the just and the unjust.
2. Having explained these general terms, we think we shall commence our exposition of the law of the Roman people most advantageously, if we pursue at first a plain and easy path, and then proceed to explain particular details with the utmost care and exactness. For, if at the outset we overload the mind of the student, while yet new to the subject and unable to bear much, with a multitude and variety of topics, one of two things will

Thatcher, Oliver J. (ed.), *The Library of Original Sources,* University Research Extension Co., 1907.

happen—we shall either cause him wholly to abandon his studies, or, after great toil, and often after great distrust to himself (the most frequent stumbling block in the way of youth), we shall at last conduct him to the point, to which, if he had been led by an easier road, he might, without great labor, and without any distrust of his own powers, have been sooner conducted.

3. The maxims of law are these: to live honestly, to hurt no one, to give every one his due.
4. The study of law is divided into two branches; that of public and that of private law. Public law regards the government of the Roman empire; private law, the interest of the individuals. We are now to treat of the latter, which is composed of three elements, and consists of precepts belonging to the natural law, to the law of nations, and to the civil law.

II. Natural, Common, and Civil Law

1. The law of nature is that law which nature teaches to all animals. For this law does not belong exclusively to the human race, but belongs to all animals, whether of the earth, the air, or the water. Hence comes the union of the male and female, which we term matrimony; hence the procreation and bringing up of children. We see, indeed, that all the other animals besides men are considered as having knowledge of this law. [Natural laws are also laws of nations.]
2. The law of the nations is common to all mankind, for nations have established certain laws, as occasion and the necessities of human life required. Wars arose, and in their train followed captivity and then slavery, which is contrary to the law of nature; for by that law all men are originally born free. Further, by the law of nations almost all contracts were at first introduced, as, for instance, buying and selling, letting and hiring, partnership, deposits, loans returnable in kind, and very many others.
3. Civil law is thus distinguished from the law of nations. Every community governed by laws and customs uses partly its own law, partly laws common to all mankind. The law which a people makes for its own government belongs exclusively to that state and is called the civil law, as being the law of the particular state. But the law which natural reason appoints for all mankind obtains equally among all nations, because all nations make use of it. The people of Rome, then, are governed partly by their own laws, and partly by the laws which are common to all mankind. We will take notice of this distinction as occasion may arise.
4. Our law is written and unwritten, just as among the Greeks some of their laws were written and others were not written. The written part consists of *leges (lex), plebiscita, senatusconsulta, constitutiones* of emperors, *edicta* of magistrates, and *responsa* of jurisprudents [*i.e.*, jurists].
6. That which seems good to the emperor has also the force of law; for the people, by the *Lex Regia,* which is passed to confer on him his power, make over to him their whole power and authority. Therefore whatever the emperor ordains by *rescript,* or decides in adjudging a cause, or lays down by edict, is unquestionably law; and it is these enactments of the emperor that are called *constitutiones.* Of these, some are personal, and are not to be drawn into precedent, such not being the intention of the emperor. Supposing the emperor has granted a favor to any man on account of his merit, or inflicted some punishment, or granted some extraordinary relief, the application of these acts does not extend beyond the particular individual. But the other *constitutiones,* being general, are undoubtedly binding on all.
9. The unwritten law is that which usage has established; for ancient customs, being sanctioned by the consent of those who adopt them, are like laws.
11. The laws of nature, which all nations observe alike, being established by a divine providence, remain ever fixed and im-

mutable. But the laws which every state has enacted, undergo frequent changes, either by the tacit consent of the people, or by a new law being subsequently passed.

III. The Law of Persons

All our law relates either to persons, or to things, or to actions. Let us first speak of persons; as it is of little purpose to know the law, if we do not know the persons for whose sake the law was made. The chief division in the rights of persons is this: men are all either free or slaves.

1. Freedom, from which men are said to be free, is the natural power of doing what we each please, unless prevented by force or by law.
2. Slavery is an institution of the law of nations, by which one man is made the property of another, contrary to natural right.
3. Slaves are denominated *servi,* because generals order their captives to be sold, and thus preserve them, and do not put them to death. Slaves are also called *mancipia,* because they are taken from the enemy by the strong hand.
4. Slaves either are born or become so. They are born so when their mother is a slave; they become so either by the law of nations, that is, by captivity, or by the civil law, as when a free person, above the age of twenty, suffers himself to be sold, that he may share the price given for him.
5. In the condition of slaves there is no distinction; but there are many distinctions among free persons; for they are either born free, or have been set free.

Book II. Of Things

I. Divisions of Things

In the preceding book we have treated of the law of persons. Let us now speak of things, which either are in our *patrimony,* or not in our *patrimony.* For some things by the law of nature are common to all; some are public; some belong to corporate bodies, and some belong to no one. Most things are the property of individuals who acquire them in different ways, as will appear hereafter.

1. By the law of nature these things are common to mankind—the air, running water, the sea, and consequently the shores of the sea. No one, therefore, is forbidden to approach the seashore, provided that he respects *habitationes,* monuments, and buildings which are not, like the sea, subject only to the law of nations.
6. Among things belonging to a corporate body, not to individuals, are, for instance, buildings in cities, theaters, race-courses, and other similar places belonging in common to a whole city.
7. Things sacred, religious, and holy belong to no one; for that which is subject to divine law is not the property of any one.
8. Things are sacred which have been duly consecrated by the pontiffs, as sacred buildings and offerings, properly dedicated to the service of God, which we have forbidden by our *constitutio* to be sold or mortgaged, except for the purposes of purchasing the freedom of captives. But, if any one consecrates a building by his own authority, it is not sacred, but profane. But ground on which a sacred edifice has once been erected, even after the building has been destroyed, continues to be sacred, as Papinian also writes.
9. Any man at his pleasure makes a place religious by burying a dead body in his own ground; but it is not permitted to bury a dead body in land hitherto pure, which is held in common, against the wishes of a co-proprietor. But when a sepulcher is held in common, any one co-proprietor may bury in it, even against the wishes of the rest. So, too, if another person has the *usufructus,* the proprietor may not, without the consent of the *usufructuary,* render the place religious. But a dead body may be laid in a place belonging to another person, with the consent of the owner; and even if the owner only ratifies the act after the dead body has been buried, yet the place is religious.

10. Holy things also, as the walls and gates of a city, are to a certain degree subject to divine law, and therefore are not part of the property of any one. The walls of a city are said to be holy, inasmuch as any offence against them is punished capitally; so, too, those parts of laws by which punishments are established against transgressors, we term sanctions.
11. Things become the property of individuals in various ways; of some we acquire the ownership by natural law, which, as we have observed, is also termed the law of nations; of others by the civil law. It will be most convenient to begin with the more ancient law; and it is very evident that the law of nature, established by nature at the first origin of mankind, is the more ancient, for civil laws could then only begin to exist when states began to be founded, magistrates to be created, and laws to be written.

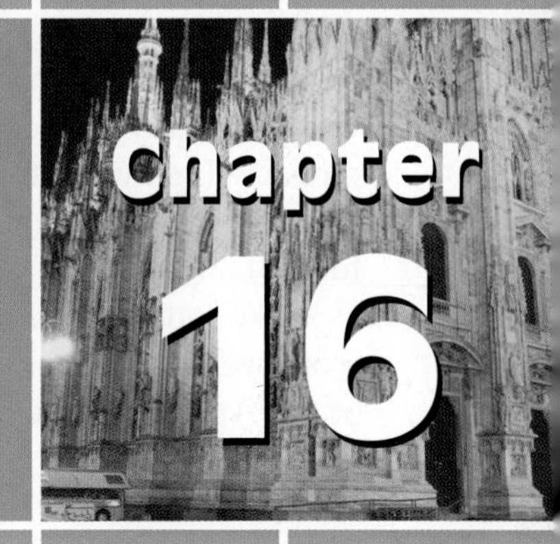

Chapter 16

Islam
Creativity in the Desert

> Seek knowledge from the cradle to the grave . . . Verily the men of knowledge are the inheritors of the prophets.
>
> —*Mohammed (from the* Hadith*)*

What Is Islam?

Islam is the most recent of the three great monotheistic faiths (Judaism, Christianity, and Islam), dating its origins in the year 610 A.D. when the prophet **Mohammed** received his first heavenly instructions. Islam is the second largest religion in the world (behind Christianity) but is the fastest growing major religion, both in converts and in births. Although Islam is practiced throughout the world, the greatest concentration is around the equatorial belt in Africa and Asia. In some of the countries in this region, the Islamic population is nearly 100 percent.

Many Westerners use the terms Arab, Islam, and Muslim interchangeably, which is incorrect and leads to confusion. **Arabs** are an ethnic group of people, and can belong to a variety of religions, although the majority of Arabs are followers of Islam, which is the religion. Since Islam began among the Arabs, the Arabs and Islam are strongly connected, but they are not the same, and the differences between an ethnic Arab and the religion of Islam should be remembered. The word **Islam** means "submission or peace," and that concept reflects the most basic tenet of the religion. The word **Muslim** (also spelled Muslim) means, simply, "one who surrenders or submits his will to Allah," so Muslims are people who believe in the religion of Islam. They can be of any race or ethnic group, and are not necessarily Arabs. For example, Indonesia is the world's largest Islamic country, but the vast majority of Indonesians are not Arabs. Some non-Muslims have referred to the religion as Mohammedanism or some similar derivative of Mohammed. Although the Prophet Mohammed was certainly important in receiving the word of Allah and leading the people in their path to obey Allah's words, Mohammed is not worshipped by Muslims, and any suggestion that he has a status of a god is entirely erroneous. In this chapter we will often comment on the creativity of Islam and also of Mohammed. That is to be interpreted as arising from inspiration or word from Allah, although it is clear that Mohammed was personally righteous, highly intelligent, and probably highly creative. Taking advantage of inspiration and expanding upon the word of God is a form of creativity.

Like Judaism and Christianity, Islam traces its roots back to the Bible, both through the ancestry of the Arabs and doctrinal beliefs that recognize the various Biblical prophets as messengers of God. The Arabs are descendents of **Abraham,** through his oldest son **Ishmael,** and **Isaac,** through Isaac's eldest son **Esau,** as well as from **Midian,** another son of Abraham. Many of the other ancient tribes of the Middle East who may or may not be descended from the Biblical patriarchs, such as the **Ammonites** and **Canaanites,** are also included in the general group now called Arabs. Furthermore, in much the same way that Christianity views itself as a fulfillment and extension of Judaism, Islam views itself as a fulfillment and extension of both Judaism and Christianity. Muslims consider Jews and Christians to be fellow "People of the Book," because they worship the same God. The name of God in Arabic, **Allah,** is the equivalent name for God in Hebrew, **YHWH,** which has been alternately rendered in English as **Jehovah.**

The Creativity of Mohammed

Islam is largely based on the teachings of the ***Holy Qur'an,*** (sometimes written as ***Koran***) which were conveyed to mankind through a man named Mohammed, who Muslims believe was the great, last prophet. Unlike Christianity, whose founder Jesus' early life is virtually unknown, the early life of Mohammed has been better documented. Mohammed was born in 570 A.D. in the Arabian town of **Mecca,** an important religious site to the pagan and tribal Arabs who occupied much of the Arabian peninsula, parts of North Africa, and the coastal region of the Middle East (the **Levant**). His father died previous to his birth and his mother died when he was only six, so his uncle, who was a chief of Mecca's ruling tribe and a successful merchant, raised Mohammed. Mohammed spent much of his youth working for his uncle as a shepherd, and never learned to read or write.

Even as a young man, several instances occurred in Mohammed's life that seemed to demonstrate both his own personal integrity and his favor in the eyes of God. The first of these incidents occurred when heavy rains damaged Mecca's holy shrine, the *Ka'ba,* which Muslims believe was the first house of worship of God or Allah, and which they believe was built by Adam. The *Ka'ba* has been reconstructed five to twelve times by other prophets such as Abraham and Ishmael. The *Ka'ba* is a cube-shaped building, approximately 48 feet by 33 feet and 30 feet high, that houses a black rock or meteorite that Arabs believed came from God and had special powers. It was perhaps the most holy of all Arab shrines. The four principal tribes of Mecca agreed that they would share the honor of rebuilding this most sacred shrine, and they cooperated while the building itself was refurbished. However, when time came to replace the black stone, a heated argument erupted over which tribe should get that singular honor. The argument went on for some time, until an old man suggested that they put it in the hands of the gods (they were pagan at this time) by allowing the decision to be made by the next person to walk in through the door of the *Ka'ba* enclosure. The tribes agreed and Mohammed was the first person through the door. This was pleasing to the tribes, as Mohammed already had earned a reputation for honesty in Mecca, and they felt he could make a fair decision. Rather than choosing one of the tribes to place the stone, Mohammed placed a cloak on the ground and placed the stone on the cloak. He then had a representative of each tribe take a corner of the cloak; all together they lifted the stone to the proper height. Mohammed himself then moved the stone from the cloak to its proper place. The tribes were pleased with their joint participation, and marveled at the creativity of Mohammed in solving the problem.

Another event from later in his youth also seemed to show that God had a role for Mohammed to play. Because of his great reputation for honesty, a widow named **Khadijah** asked him to work for her. Khadijah was a trader (merchant) who needed someone to lead her caravan of goods to Syria to be sold. Mohammed agreed to lead her caravan. While traveling to Syria, a slave on the trip, named Maysarah, claimed to have been told by a Christian hermit whom they met in the desert that Mohammed was a prophet. Maysarah also said she saw two angels protecting Mohammed from the sun with shields on the hottest days. Furthermore, the trip was a success, and Mohammed brought Khadijah home more money than she had ever made before.

Mohammed kept working for Khadijah and eventually the two fell in love and were married. Though Khadijah was fifteen years older than Mohammed, the two seemed to have an idyllic marriage and she proved to be a great support and strength to her husband. Eventually the couple had six children—two boys and four girls, although only the girls lived to adulthood.

As an adult, Mohammed was a thoughtful person who often took trips into the mountains to think and pray. One of the topics that interested him was the teachings of Jews and Christians. He was curious about their belief in only one god as opposed to the traditional polytheistic, pagan view of the contemporary Arabs. In the year 610, during the month of **Ramadan,** Mohammed retreated to a cave on **Mount Hira,** to contemplate this and other questions. After several days of prayer and meditation, the angel **Gabriel** came to Mohammed and commanded him to recite from a beautiful scroll. Mohammed protested that he was not literate and therefore could not read the scroll. Two more times Gabriel made his request, and twice more Mohammed argued that he could not. The angel Gabriel then told Mohammed that God could teach him things that could not be read; then Gabriel began to teach him. The messages that Gabriel gave to Mohammed at this time and others that came later became the *Qu'ran,* Islam's holy book.

At the end of the teaching, Mohammed returned home tired, bewildered, and unsure whether he had really experienced a divine manifestation. He related what had happened to his wife and was assured by Khadijah that he was not dreaming. Khadijah also asked a Christian friend to speak with Mohammed, and the Christian confirmed that Mohammed had received a visitation from a holy messenger, and that he had been chosen as a prophet.

Over the next several months Mohammed received several more visitations and was instructed in the basic tenets of Islam. Mohammed taught what he had learned from the angel to Khadijah and she accepted the teachings, but he did not share them with anyone else. Then, one night when **Ali** (Mohammed's young cousin and husband of Mohammed's daughter **Fatima**) saw Mohammed and Khadijah praying, he asked them what they were doing. Mohammed told Ali what he had experienced, and Ali readily accepted his message. Mohammed then understood that he had an obligation to spread the message of Islam, and began to teach the inhabitants of Mecca.

Mohammed must have been disappointed if he thought that all people would accept the message of Islam as quickly as had Khadijah and Ali. Initially Mohammed was criticized by many of the Arabs, who felt that he had learned his new religion from the Christians and Jews. This criticism turned to anger when the Arab merchants realized that if Islam were successful, pilgrims who came to worship at the *Ka'ba* and bought many idols in Mecca would not do so any longer. Mohammed was offered wealth and position to give up teaching about Islam. He refused. Others threatened to kill him, but his uncle protected Mohammed. A short time later Mohammed's uncle died and the new tribal chief let Mohammed know that he would not provide the same protection that his uncle had. For his own safety and that of his followers, Allah instructed Mohammed to leave Mecca.

The period of time between Mohammed's departure from Mecca in defeat and his eventual triumphant return is known as the *Hegira.* Mohammed and his small group of followers left Mecca in 622 and headed off to settle in the village of **Yathrib.** The Islamic calendar counts this year, 622 on the Christian calendar, as the beginning year, and so dates might be given as 1426 A.H. where the A.H. stands for "after Hegira." (The year 1426 A.H. corresponds to

2005 A.D. You should realize that the Islamic year, which is based on the moon, is eleven days shorter than the Gregorian solar year, which is the commonly used calendar in the Western World, so the number of Islamic years since the *Hegira* is greater than the number of solar years.) It is not clear why Mohammed chose Yathrib as his refuge; possibly he felt he could successfully convert the large Jewish population there. In Yathrib the message of Islam was more readily accepted, although not generally by the Jews. Eventually Mohammed and his followers had converted enough of the region's population that Yathrib was renamed **Medina,** meaning "City of the Prophet." It was in Medina that Mohammed started the first Muslim community and changed the civil laws to reflect the laws of God. Also around this time, the first mosque was built next to Mohammed's home in Medina. The word **mosque** means "place of kneeling". Originally Muslims prayed facing Jerusalem and worshipped on Saturday, possibly as a way of reaching out to potential Jewish converts. However, when the Jews in the area became unfriendly toward Islam, worship was moved to Friday, and prayer was redirected toward Mecca.

As Islam gained a larger following, Mohammed began to lead his followers in a series of religious wars. In 630 Mohammed gathered his followers and attacked Mecca. Mohammed and his followers were victorious, transforming Mecca into an Islamic community, destroying all of the idols, and turning the *Ka'ba* into a mosque. They left the stone in the *Ka'ba* in place because it represented the power of God, and today the *Ka'ba* is the holiest site in Islam; it sits in the middle of the **Grand Mosque.** The *Ka'ba* is shown in Figure 16.1. After the capture of Mecca, Islam began to gain converts very rapidly, and the last few years of Mohammed's life were rewarding to him. He died two years after the capture of Mecca, in 632.

Much of the success of Islam is because the religion is so simple and direct. Within Islam there is no hierarchal clergy or difficult doctrine. Islam is believed by its followers to be the simple religion of Abraham. The teachings of the *Qu'ran* led to the establishment of a few fundamental principles, the most important of which are the five basic pillars of Islam, that is, five fundamental beliefs and practices that all Muslims should accept. Those five pillars are:

Figure 16.1 ■ *Ka'ba* in Mecca showing Muslims preparing for prayer. *© 2010 by ayazad. Used under license of Shutterstock, Inc.*

- Believe in only one God, Allah, and Mohammed as his last and greatest prophet. This Muslim creed is often repeated as, "There is no God but Allah, and Mohammed is his prophet."
- Pray five times daily. Prayers are normally said at dawn, noon, afternoon, evening, and night, according to exact times established in each locale. In areas where Muslims are plentiful, calls to prayer are broadcast from loudspeakers located on the mosques (which have replaced actual live calls made before the time of electronics). Prayers are quite ritualized, with certain set prayers being recited while a person kneels and touches one's head to the

Figure 16.2 ■ *Dome of the Rock shrine in Jerusalem. Image © 2006 Jupiter Images Corporation.*

ground. Men and women are separated during prayers. Ritual cleansing (ablutions with water) are required before prayer, especially on Friday when the community of believers gathers at noon in the mosque to pray. Prayer is always done facing Mecca (which is identified by a nook in the wall of the mosque).

- Give alms to the needy. The alms can be given to a special fund, so that anonymity is preserved, or may be given directly. The amount of alms is one-fortieth (2½ percent) of a person's income.
- Fast during the month of Ramadan. The Muslim fast is a complete abstinence of food, water, and earthly desires (such as sexual intercourse) during daylight hours. Because the Islamic calendar is based on the lunar year (hence the crescent moon is a symbol of Islam), the month of Ramadan migrates through the solar year, occurring about eleven days earlier each year. Therefore, some years Ramadan is in the solar winter and the fasting period is quite short; in other years, when Ramadan occurs in the summer, fasting can be for well over twelve hours. If a person is sick or traveling, the fasting restrictions are relaxed. Ramadan is more than just a month for fasting. It is a time of spiritual renewal. People are especially adherent during this time and many take special time to read the *Qu'ran.* Readings of the *Qu'ran* over the radio are also common during Ramadan. When Ramadan comes to a close, a special celebration, *Eid,* is held, at which families gather to give thanks; almsgiving is especially prevalent then.
- Visit Mecca on a pilgrimage, a journey called the *Haj.* During the *Haj,* Muslims participate in a five-day ritual of spiritual cleansing and rebirth. Muslims from all over the world gather in Mecca during the last month of the Islamic calendar on their *Haj.* Undoubtedly this gathering of people, all dressed in white pilgrim robes, gives great cultural and spiritual solidarity to the Islamic people.

In addition to the acceptance of the five pillars, Muslims believe that only through personal struggle can someone draw close to Allah. The person must become contrite and submissive. This struggle is called **jihad.** The concept of *jihad* can also be collective, since the people must be united in their struggle to ensure that Allah's will is being followed. If the community of Islam is threatened, a united struggle, *jihad,* might be called for as a way to ensure that Allah's people will be free to worship Allah as they wish. It is in this sense that terrorists call their struggles by the name of *jihad.* In general, however, the terrorists fail to receive the support of the majority of the people, and they also kill innocents, both of which violate Islamic law concerning the calling of a *jihad.* Therefore, the majority of Muslims reject the idea that these terrorist acts are a *jihad.*

Islam teaches modesty in dress and behavior. In some areas, tradition and local custom dictate that women's wear have full coverage of their bodies by long dresses and veils. Traditions in other areas allow more latitude in dress. The use of head covering is quite common throughout the Islamic world, but even that is a matter of personal belief and local tradition.

The interactions among Muslims, Christians, and Jews are widely misunderstood. Muslims accept most of the Jewish prophets of the Bible, and also accept Jesus as the greatest prophet of all time prior to Mohammed. The *Qu'ran* says that Jesus was miraculously conceived by the Virgin Mary through the intervention of God, but they deny that Jesus was begotten by God. The Muslims believe that Jesus will come to earth in the last days, but believe that he will come, not as a resurrected being but rather as a translated being. Muslims do not accept that Jesus died on the cross, but believe that he was taken to heaven without dying. They do not accept that Jesus paid for our sins through his suffering (the atonement). For Muslims, both Judaism and Christianity had fallen into error by the time Mohammed was called to be a prophet. Therefore, they believe in a type of restoration of the truth through Mohammed.

Mohammed's legacy is more than just the religion of Islam. The teachings he received from Allah through Gabriel were published shortly after his death as the *Qu'ran* and were written in beautiful Arabic that has become the standard for the language. Even today, Muslims in all parts of the world believe that the *Qu'ran* is the word of Allah only in Arabic. Hence, many of the prayers and other teachings of Islam are in Arabic, even though the people might speak another language. Other teachings of Mohammed were written in a collection known as the ***Hadith,*** which is a guide in living and is not considered to have the same doctrinal weight as the *Qu'ran.* The quotation at the beginning of this chapter is from the *Hadith;* it expresses the strong commitment of Islam to knowledge.

We have already discussed the issue of creativity and inspiration, surely a question that must be answered when the creativity of Mohammed is examined. However, even those who do not believe that Mohammed was a prophet can appreciate the creative way in which the Arab people quickly changed from a backward group of nomads into a strong and dynamic force in the world. Mohammed's teachings emphasized the value of knowledge and thus set the basis for the tremendous creativity of Islam in its golden age, which we will examine later in this chapter. The history of Islam after Mohammed is really a continuation of his principles, which were spread over a tremendous area and very nearly became the religion of the world. Let's discuss how that came to be, and then examine the cultural contributions made in Islamic countries during the time that Islam was the center of creative civilization.

The Islamic Dynasties

Muslims believe that Mohammed was the last prophet, but that the message of Islam should not end with him. His successor said: "O people! Whoever worshipped Mohammed should know that Mohammed is dead. Whoever worshipped Allah (God) should know Allah is alive and will never die." With this belief in mind, the Muslims continued to spread the message of Allah and Islam, through a combination of teaching and military conquest. Within a hundred years of Mohammed's death, Islam had already spread over all of the Arabian peninsula (uniting the various tribes), most of the Middle East, North Africa, Spain, and Persia. However, during this same short period, Islam had already split into two main groups who disagreed on the question of who should lead Islam. The **Sunnis,** who are the larger group, believed that any just Muslim could serve as leader of Islam. Following the death of Mohammed, the Sunnis supported the appointment of the head of Mohammed's tribe as leader of Islam. The **Shi'ites,** the smaller of the two main sects, believed that the Islamic leader must be chosen by the previous leader. The Shi'ites believed that Mohammed's son-in-law, Ali, should have been the successor.

In spite of this disagreement over who should be the rightful successor, those who led the Muslims were a series of four **Caliphs** (leaders) who were elected by the people; since the Sunnis were more numerous, their will prevailed. However, the fourth of these Caliphs was Ali; the same person who the Shi'ites believed should have led the faith from the death of Mohammed. You might think that the appointment of Ali would heal the breach in Islam, but it did not. Rival factions continued to fight over the right to lead and, during the succession war, Ali was killed. The victor of the wars decided to move the administrative center of Islam to **Damascus,** from which he and his descendents ruled Islam for about a hundred years. They were called the **Umayyad Dynasty.** It was under the Umayyads that Islam grew throughout North Africa, Spain, and Persia. The Shi'ites were resentful of the Umayyads throughout their reign.

The end of the Umayyad dynasty occurred when another group, the **Abbasids,** headquartered in **Baghdad,** united the Shi'ites and gained support of the Sunnis against the corruption that had crept into the Umayyad reign. The Abbasids assumed control throughout all of Islam except Spain, where Umayyad-related leaders remained independent. This was the first break in the political unity of Islam, but would not be the last. After gaining control over most of Islamic territory, the focus of the Abbasids shifted from military conquest to the arts, sciences, and other cultural aspects of life. It was during the **Abbasid Dynasty** that Islam enjoyed its golden age. We will discuss the fruits of that wonderful time a little later in this chapter.

The golden age of Islam began to decay about 969 A.D. (358 A.H.), when local groups asserted their independence from the Abbasids, especially in North Africa and Persia. The emergence of these new leaders complicated the relationships between Muslims and Christians and, as we will see in a later chapter, led to the crusades in the twelfth to fourteenth centuries. The crusaders were defeated by **Saladin,** a Kurdish leader who successfully united Islam in North Africa and the Holy Land, but did not subdue the Abbasid capital of Baghdad. However, in 1258, the Abbasids were attacked by the **Mongols,** and Baghdad fell, ending the Abbasid reign.

No single group had sufficient power to unite all of Islam after the early Abbasids. In part, this was because the area of Islam had continued to expand under various local initiatives and was simply too diverse for any group to exert overall control. Occasionally, small groups would be united under a strong ruler who would establish a dynasty, but only two such dynasties were ever able to control vast territories. The first of these major dynasties arose in Central Asia after the Mongols under the leader **Tamarlane** and, later, his grandson, **Babar.** They were, in fact, descended from the Mongols, who had converted to Islam. They became known as the **Mughals,** a Persian rendering of the "Mongol." The Mughals conquered Persia and much of India, ruling both areas for many years. They brought great culture to Persia and India, leading to the blending of those two cultures and creating some of the most beautiful buildings in the world. More on this later.

The other major power in Islam after the Abbasids were the **Ottoman Turks.** The Turks, first the **Seljuks** and then the **Ottomans,** filled the vacuum left in the Middle East with the demise of the Abbasids. They expanded their power throughout that territory, eventually conquering the Byzantine Empire and also major areas in the Balkans. In the sixteenth century the Ottoman Turks threatened major areas in Europe, and were stopped in the conquest at the gates of Vienna. They also expanded westward from their Middle Eastern stronghold to, eventually, encompass control over the Arabian Peninsula and much of North Africa. The Ottoman Turks viewed themselves as the successors to the Abbasids, and acted as the rulers of all Islam. The Ottoman Turks continued to control vast territories in Africa, the Middle East, and southern Europe until the end of World War I.

Preserving and Adding to Creativity

Even with the divisions in Islam that we have discussed, Islam was still far more unified, both doctrinally and as a people, than the Christians or the scattered Jews. For this reason, and others, while the Jews were suffering through the Diaspora and the European Christians were languishing through the medieval era, the Islamic world was in its golden age of knowledge and culture. Trade and travel in the Islamic world were booming, streets were paved and lighted, and many workers became highly skilled artisans. The richness of Islamic culture can be seen in a few comparisons. The library in **Cordoba** had over 400,000 volumes, while the great **Benedictine monastery** in Switzerland had only 600 volumes at the same time. Furthermore, hundreds of schools were established for the study of religion, whereas most of Europe languished in illiteracy. Great Islamic scholars like **Averroes** (Ibn Rushd) and **Avicenna** (Ibn Sina) lived during this period, one working as a teacher and philosopher and writing his massive commentary of Aristotle, and the other advancing medical knowledge. Much later these scholars were discovered by Europeans, who then realized the greatness of the Islamic creativity and, moreover, gave these Muslims credit for preserving Greek knowledge while Europe was in the Dark Ages. In fact, the medical books of Avicenna, when finally discovered, were translated and used in Europe as textbooks for over 500 years.

The earliest great works of Islamic art are probably the great mosques built as Islam expanded during the Umayyad and early Abbasid Dynasties. One of the most beautiful of these mosques (now a shrine), the **Dome of the Rock,** was built in 685, in Jerusalem on the site where Mohammed ascended to heaven and beheld the glories of Allah's realm. Mohammed was transported to the site and, on his horse, lifted off a great rock on the top of a mount in Jerusalem. This site is at the same place as the ancient Jewish temple, and so is especially holy for Muslims and Jews (and Christians, too). The Jews refer to the place as "the Temple Mount" and the Muslims call it "the Noble Sanctuary." Therefore, today, there is conflict between the Jews and the Muslims over control of the location. In general, Jews worship at the bottom of the mount where the western wall of the temple, the only part of the temple still remaining, is exposed and accessible. Muslims go onto the mount itself and worship at the shrines and mosques that are there, including the Dome of the Rock and a large mosque called **Al Aqsa.** Other beautiful mosques are found throughout the Islamic world, including the Grand Mosque in Mecca (open only to Muslims) and the **Blue Mosque** in Istanbul, which served the Ottoman rulers.

Another great architectural wonder, the **Alhambra,** was built during the time the Muslims controlled Spain. The Alhambra is a castle complex overlooking the city of **Granada** that was built in the fourteenth century about a century before the end of the Islamic presence in Spain. Inside the many buildings and gardens that make up the Alhambra, the Islamic love of geometrical designs is seen in the beautiful carved stone ceilings, window grates, wall panels, and other decorative pieces (see Figure 16.3). In general, Islamic art avoids depicting humans and any other form that might be considered an idol. Hence, the use of geometric decorations is one of the most common motifs in Islamic architecture and art. A related form of decorative art employs calligraphy, that is, using beautiful writing as a decorative art. Mosques, especially, use calligraphy, and often feature the many ways of referring to Allah as the basis for the calligraphy.

Another beautiful palace is **Topkapi,** located at the end of the peninsula of Istanbul. This large complex was the headquarters of the

Figure 16.3 ■ View of the Court of the Lions in the Alhambra. *© 2010 by Rafael Ramirez Lee. Used under license of Shutterstock, Inc.*

Ottoman Empire, and today houses many wonderful artifacts such as possessions of the Prophet Mohammed, jewels of the Ottoman Sultans, extravagant royal thrones and symbols of power, and lovely furniture and other decorations of the Sultans' living quarters.

Perhaps the most famous Islamic building was from a later time in a different part of the world. This building, described by some as the most beautiful building in the world, is the **Taj Mahal,** shown in Figure 16.4. It was built in the sixteenth century in the city of **Agra,** India, by a Mughal leader as a tomb for his wife. The building is a perfectly symmetrical and balanced structure made from white marble extensively and beautifully inlaid with a flower motif consisting of semi-precious stones, gold, and silver. The lovely and restful park leading up to the entrance of the Taj Mahal represents paradise and invites a feeling of awe and peacefulness in those who visit.

The creativity of Islam was also demonstrated in their contributions to mathematics and science. The prevalence of Arabic words, many of which begin with "al," in several areas of math and science is an indication of their fundamental work. For instance, **algebra** was invented by the Muslims about 850. Other scientific terms from the Arabic include algorithm, alcohol, aldehyde, alkali, alum, almanac, and, of course, the ancient name of chemistry itself, alchemy. Other Arabic words include **zero** and **cipher,** both representing a concept in math that was probably discovered in India, but perfected in Arabia. The practical arts were also developed. The finest steel in the world, even long after the Middle Ages, was produced in Damascus, Syria, and Toledo, Spain. Metal working in both of those cities in gold and silver was also world famous, and continues until today. Contributions to astronomy can also be gauged by the many Arabic words we use today, such as azimuth, nadir, zenith, and many names of stars (such as Betelgeuse).

The Islamic proficiency in science was also seen in medicine, as has already been alluded to in mentioning Avicenna, whose textbooks became so important in Europe. Other medical advances include the discovery of the contagious spread of tuberculosis and other diseases, by an Islamic physician in central Asia about the year 1000. The description of wound cauterizing to prevent infection and a discussion of the crushing of bladder stones were given in a medical book written in the ninth century in Cordoba, Spain. A book listing 760 pharmaceutical drugs was published about the same time. Some Arab medical terms include syrup, elixir, soda and julep.

In addition to his contributions to medicine, Avicenna wrote major textbooks on physics. He generally followed the lead of Aristotle in describing several types of motion, although he disagreed with Aristotle on the nature of projectile motion. Avicenna asserted that a projectile kept moving due to a quality or power of movement impressed upon it, thus suggesting that if a projectile was thrown into a void, it would keep moving. He quantified this motion by saying that bodies would move with a velocity inversely proportional to their weight. This quantification leads directly to Newton's formulation for motion, expressed as $f = ma$.

Islamic scholars developed schools for learning this wealth of old and new knowledge. They

Figure 16.4 ■ *The Taj Mahal. Image © 2006 Jupiter Images Corporation.*

assembled scholars in specific places, like Baghdad, Cordoba and **Fez** (in Africa). These institutions were the precursors to modern universities.

Islamic literature is especially rich from the golden age when Baghdad was the capital. The tales of **Scheherazade,** as recorded in the *1001 Arabian Nights,* including such stories as "Ali Baba" and "Sinbad," are still enjoyed by both adults and, in derivative form, by children. The *Rubaiyat* of Omar Khayyam is a collection of poems that is both beautiful and evocative. One example is as follows:

Come, fill the Cup, and in the Fire of Spring
The Winter Garment of Repentance fling:
The Bird of Time has but a little way
To fly—and Lo! the Bird is on the Wing.[1]

Another well known verse from the *Rubaiyat* is as follows:

Here with a Loaf of Bread beneath the Bough,
A Flask of Wine, a Book of Verse—and Thou
Beside me singing in the Wilderness—
And Wilderness is Paradise enow.[2]

Unlike European Christian culture, Islamic creativity did not decline during the period we call the Middle Ages. On the contrary, that was the time of Islam's golden age. The vigor and teachings of Mohammed helped give Islam a desire for knowledge that led to a preservation of the knowledge of the past (such as that of the ancient Greeks) but also gave Islam a forward goal and great creativity. Moreover, the spread of Islam during this period, and the continued active trading and exploration, brought Islam into contact with many other cultures, which the Muslims investigated and, where appropriate, incorporated into their own culture.

Eventually, however, Islamic creativity and rule began to decline. The internal and external problems of the thirteenth and fourteenth centuries led to a reduction in Islamic territory and a beginning of isolationism that has persisted until today. There has been, moreover, a feeling among Muslims that because they are the true religion of Allah, they have a special right to receive creative promptings. Therefore, they will have more creativity and their developments will be better than those arising in non-Islamic cultures. That belief has not proven to be the case, at least over the last 400 years. Some Muslims will say that their creativity has been diminished by their nearly continuous domination by outside political entities. While that may be so, the evidence suggests that when Islam became isolated and chauvinistic (believing that they were the best and that anything foreign was inevitably inferior), their creativity declined. In many ways, they became like the ancient Egyptians of the New Kingdom and later, and the Chinese. They were not able to break free of their own rich heritage and explore new paths. Perhaps Islam's recent emergence into strong interactions with the rest of the world will help them regain the position of creative excellence that they once enjoyed.

Timeline—Important Dates

Date	Event
570 A.D.	*Birth of Mohammed*
610	*Founding of Islam*
622	*The Hegira*
632	*Death of Mohammed*
632–661	*Rule by the four good Caliphs*
661–750	*Umayyad Dynasty*
750–1258	*Abbasid Dynasty*
969–1171	*Fatimids control Egypt and the Levant*
1095–1291	*Christian crusades*
1169–1193	*Saladin rules over Egypt and the Levant*
1071–1260	*Seljuk Turks reign over Persia and Turkey*
1260–1517	*Mamluk Dynasty in Egypt*
1526–1858	*Mughal Dynasty in Persia and India*
1382–1919	*Ottoman Turk Empire*

Notes

1. Khayyam, Omar, *Rubaiyat,* Edward FitzGerald (trans.), First Edition, Number 7, ELF on-line version, http://www.arabiannights.org/rubaiyat/index2.html.
2. Khayyam, Omar, *Rubaiyat,* Edward FitzGerald (tr.), First Edition, Number 11, ELF on-line version, http://www.arabiannights.org/rubaiyat/index2.html.

Suggested Readings

Ahmed, Akbar S., *Living Islam,* Facts on File, 1994.

Burton, Richard (trans.), *Arabian Nights,* Adapted by Jack Zipes, Signet Classic, 1991.

Gilbran, Kahlil, *The Prophet,* Knopf, 1951.

Khyyam, Omar, *Rubaiyat,* Edward FitzGerald (trans.), St. Martin's Press, 1983.

Lewis, Bernard, *What Went Wrong?,* Oxford University Press, 2002.

Pickthall, Muhammad Marmaduke (text explanation and translation), *The Glorious Qur'an,* Muslim World League—Rabita, 1977.

Smullyan, Raymond, *The Riddle of Scheherazade,* Harcourt Brace, 1997.

Tahan, Malba, *The Man Who Counted,* Leslie Clark and Alastair Reid (trans.), Norton, 1993.

Early Medieval Europe

Creativity Dimmed

> Civilization requires a modicum of material prosperity—enough to provide a little leisure. But, far more, it requires confidence—confidence in the society in which one lives, belief in its philosophy, belief in its laws, and confidence in one's own mental powers . . . Vigor, energy, vitality: all the great civilizations—or civilizing epochs—have had a weight of energy behind them. People sometimes think that civilization consists in fine sensibilities and good conversation and all that. These can be among the agreeable results of civilization, but they are not what make a civilization, and a society can have these amenities and yet be dead and rigid.
>
> —*Kenneth Clark,* Civilisation *(BBC television series)*

After the Fall of the West

Medieval refers to the **Middle Ages**—that period between the fall of the Western Roman Empire in about 476 A.D. and the **Renaissance,** which began about 1400. For scholars living in the early Renaissance (and beyond), the Middle Ages were depreciated and ridiculed. They idealized the culture of ancient Greece and Rome and hoped to have a rebirth (*renaissance,* in French) of that ancient glory. Therefore, the time between the last, supposedly glorious days of European Rome and the rebirth that they were bringing about was an embarrassment that existed only as an interlude, an age in the middle.

Modern scholars have generally divided the Middle Ages into shorter segments that reflect some of the major differences that occurred. The first period, from 476 to about 1000, is the **Early Medieval Period.** The second period, from 1000 to about 1400 is known as the **High Middle Ages.** We will examine these two periods in the next several chapters; monitoring the dramatic changes in all aspects of life that occurred as people changed their views of creativity and of change itself.

The few hundred years following the collapse of the Western Roman Empire have been called the **Dark Ages.** That term is probably too harsh, as it implies that progress and creativity stopped completely. We prefer to think of creativity as being just dimmed during this period, thus allowing for some gradual progress and even for occasional bright lights when creativity flourished briefly. However it is termed, on the whole the Early Medieval Period experienced diminished creativity compared with other times that we have examined. A comparison between medieval Europe and Byzantium is especially interesting because Byzantium achieved glory and success while Europe saw its civilization disintegrate and creativity stagnate. Of course, conditions in Europe and Byzantium were not identical, but the two had much more in common than is usually recognized. Both faced internal strife and external enemies. Both were predominantly Christian. Both had general populations that were mostly Roman. Also, both were inheritors of the legacy and history of Rome, and of all the culture and institutions that came with that distinction. However, for a variety of reasons, creativity continued and civilization adapted and flourished in the Byzantine Empire (at least for a few hundred years), while it floundered (or at the least took a very different direction) in Europe, causing European society to struggle simply to survive. An examination of those reasons for creativity decline, and the results that followed, are the principal subjects of this chapter.

Immediately after the fall of Rome the nature of creativity and progress in Europe depended greatly on location. Italy was much different from the other parts of the Western Roman Empire because it, for a period, carried on many of the traditions of the Roman Empire. Spain, too, was unique because it was occupied by the Muslims. Over time, however, all these former Roman territories became much more homogeneous and more like the Germanic portions of Europe; Italy changing first and Spain changing much later. In this chapter we will first examine Italy and then England and then France, followed by a discussion of the homogeneity that occurred throughout all these countries and Germany. We will then look at the medieval church and its special position in European culture during the early Middle Ages. Spain was dominated by the Muslims during this early Medieval Period, as has already been discussed in the chapter on Islam, and will not be considered in this chapter.

Italy after the Fall

The first barbarian ruler in the west after the fall of the Roman Empire was Theodoric the Goth, who was likely a more capable ruler than any of his contemporaries ruling in Byzantium up to the reign of Justinian. Theodoric was an effective administrator, a shrewd general, a devoted Christian, and a patron of the arts. In truth, Theodoric made vast improvements to the area he conquered (which had greatly declined because of the general malaise of the late Roman Empire). Life under his reign was superior to what it had been during the last years of Roman rule in the west although his strange ways (for Romans) and absolute power must have put an edge on the existence of most Romans. If Theodoric was unloved (which in large part he was), it was due to his being a Goth rather than a Roman like the majority of his subjects, his ruthlessness, and his adherence to a branch of Christianity (Arianism) not well accepted by the largely orthodox Roman population.

Under Theodoric, a cultural and artistic revival took place in Ravenna, his capital. Theodoric built many chapels in the Roman style and decorated them with wonderful mosaics that depicted scenes from the scriptures and other religious themes. The art and architecture from this period in Ravenna rivals (and in some cases surpasses) the work being done in Constantinople, and is unique as it combines stylistic elements from Roman, Byzantine, and Gothic influences. Figure 17.1 shows the unique octagonal design of the cathedral built by Theodoric in Ravenna. (When Justinian came to power after the death of Theodoric and the conquest by Belisarius, the revival of Ravenna was continued, with many mosaics depicting Justinian and his wife, Theodora, as we discussed briefly in the chapter on Byzantium.)

Theodoric also encouraged learning, and was himself a sponsor of **Boethius,** the preeminent writer and intellectual of the day (early sixth century). Boethius devoted much of his writing to translating the Greek classics in Latin, including many writings of Aristotle, Euclid, Archimedes, and Ptolemy. Boethius also wrote a lengthy treatise on Greek music, which is important to modern scholars as it is our major source today on what Greek music was like. Boethius' greatest work was his *Consolation of Philosophy,* an attempt to reconcile his belief in Christianity with

Figure 17.1 ■ *Theodoric's church in Ravenna. Image © Angelo Hornak/Corbis.*

his lifelong quest to understand the pagan classics of Greece. The summation of this belief is best given in the last line of Boethius' treatise in defense of the Trinity, where he states: "As far as you are able, join faith to reason." Boethius was accused of involvement in a plot to overthrow Theodoric, and was executed; some now say without proper proof.

In spite of the stability and progress during the reign of Theodoric, several problems crept into Theodoric's kingdom even before he died. One of these problems was a lack of unity and commonality among the people. Theodoric's Italy remained a society divided between its Gothic rulers and its Roman masses. The Goths spoke a form of German; the Romans spoke Latin. The Goths practiced Arian Christianity, while the Romans were Catholics. The Goths viewed themselves as conquerors and rightful heirs to the legacy of Rome, while the Romans saw them as socially backward usurpers. Theodoric the Goth addressed this issue when he said, "An able Goth wants to be like a Roman; only a poor Roman would want to be like a Goth." The "us" versus "them" mentality proved difficult to overcome. Furthermore, the Goths fell prey to one of the same ills that continually plagued Rome—lack of a clear system of succession. Since Theodoric had no sons, there was great confusion after his death. That confusion, plus the division between the Roman populace and the Gothic leadership, invited an invasion by the Byzantines and, as we have already noted in a previous chapter, Justinian's army was able to conquer Italy. The time of Byzantine control was difficult for the Goths; they were removed from leadership positions and driven out of Italy.

Justinian's problems elsewhere in the empire led to the withdrawal of Byzantine troops, after only a few years of unification, and a vacuum of leadership was again created. That vacuum was filled by the **Lombards,** a Germanic tribe that was far less capable than Theodoric's Goths. The arrival of the Lombards caused a rapid decline in Italian society. Stable government broke down and, as we will discuss, brought a homogeneity of culture in Europe under a backward and oppressive German rule.

England

England, or **Britannia** as the Romans called it (and from which we get the English word Britain), was the furthest frontier of the Roman Empire and one of the last areas to be occupied by Rome. It proved to be a troublesome province. An initial Roman invasion under Julius Caesar was able to exact tribute from the **Britons (Celts),** but when Caesar returned to Rome, the Roman army left Britain and Celtic rule returned. The Romans again invaded in 55 A.D. and were able to subdue most of the Celtic tribes in the southern part of the island. However, trouble was always near the surface, as was evident from the fierce but short-lived revolt of **Queen Boadicea,** who destroyed several Roman-held cities and captured London, but when the Romans finally prevailed, she committed suicide rather than surrender. The Romans continued to slowly expand their holdings in Britain, but with great difficulty. Eventually, in 122 A.D., the emperor Hadrian decided to consolidate the boundaries of the territory that had been won to that time; he had a wall constructed across the northern frontier of the Roman-occupied lands in Britain. Hadrian's wall can still be seen today; it marks, roughly, the boundary between England and Scotland. Tribes north of the wall, such as the **Picts** and the **Caledonians,** were never subdued by the Romans.

The difficulties in controlling Britain led to the withdrawal of the Roman army in the early fifth century, when problems in other parts of the empire required a reallocation of the Roman army. Sensing a power vacuum and fleeing from flooding and other natural disasters in Germany, the **Angles** and the **Saxons,** two German tribes, invaded. They were resisted by the British Celtic tribes that, under Roman rule, had become Romanized in law, civil administration, and religion (becoming largely Christian) but were able to maintain much of their tribal identity and their language. One of the battles between the **Anglo-Saxons** and the Britons occurred at **Mount Baden** in about 500. The victorious leader of the Britons was **Ambrosius Aurelianus,** who many believe was the legendary **King Arthur.** A period of peace ensued, but after about 70 years the Anglo-Saxons succeeded in pushing the Celts into the far western parts of **Wales, Ireland, Scotland,** and the northern coast of France **(Brittany).** At this time the country became known as **Anglo-land (England).**

The legends of King Arthur are not without some historical backing. A Welsh poet reported some parts of the Arthurian legend in a book *(The Mabinogion)* written in 600. Reasonably good evidence confirms that a king named Arthur was born in **Tintagel,** a seacoast town in the west of England. **Cadbury,** an old castle in southwestern England, was identified as **Camelot** in writings as early as the tenth century. Another site, **Camlann,** in southwestern England, is reportedly the place where Arthur died in a battle in 542. The legend of the **Holy Grail** and traditions of the **Round Table** and knightly chivalry date from this time. The burial site for Arthur and **Guinevere** is **Glastonbury** Abbey, also in southwestern England. Legend also states that **Joseph of Arimathaea** built the first Christian church at Glastonbury. The site, called Glastonbury Tor (tower) which is now a hill in the Somerset marshes (see Figure 17.2), was previously an island called Avalon. It was the place where Joseph of Arimathaea landed when he took Mary, the mother of Christ, Mary Magdalene, and others away from Jerusalem following the resurrection of Christ. This church was the beginning of the **Celtic Christian Church** (that is, the Christian Church in England during the time of the Celtic rule), which resisted initial domination from the Catholic Church but, as a result of an English church council, was merged with the Catholic Church in the seventh century.

King Arthur gained more legendary status when **Geoffrey of Monmouth** represented him as a conqueror of Western Europe in his *History of the Kings of Britain* (1135). Arthur became widely popular when he was romanticized by **Chrétian de Troyes,** who published about a generation after Geoffrey and solidified many of the Arthurian legends. Then, when **Sir Thomas Malory** added additional stories and published *Le Morte d'Arthur* (1469), the stories of Arthur became immensely popular and widely known. Throughout history, other authors have contributed to Arthurian lore, either with a retelling of the legends or by adding new legends. Some of the most notable of these authors include Alfred Lord Tennyson, T. H. White, and Ernie Pyle. Writers in other countries have taken local myths and related them to characters found in the Arthurian tales. One of the most famous linkage legends is the story of **Siegfried and Brünhild** told in *Das Niebelungenlied* (written about 1200), which has been retold in some Wagnerian operas.

The legends of King Arthur relate his creative leadership style and other forward-thinking inno-

Figure 17.2 ■ Glastonbury Tor (tower). *© 2010 by Stephen Inglis. Used under license of Shutterstock, Inc.*

vations to create a wonderful society that has been the model for English rulers (and others) ever since his time. These innovations may have occurred, but they were short lived. The onslaught of the Angles and the Saxons from Germany proved to be too much for the Celts and soon almost all of England was under Anglo-Saxon control. Many Celts were pushed to the far west and north, in the mountains and valleys of Wales and Scotland. Those people still speak a **Celtic (Gaelic)** language, as the Latin of the Romans never was widely accepted in England. Those who remained in England were subjected to the same difficult and oppressive rule that others in Europe would experience under German rule, and which we will detail in the section on homogeneity of Europe. The land was broken into numerous minor kingdoms; wars of expansion and economic domination were nearly continuous. Most people in England adopted the Anglo-Saxon (Germanic) language, which became the basis of Old English.

Merovingian France

With the demise of the Roman state in 476, the area known as **Gaul** (present-day France) was susceptible to attack. The **Franks,** a tribe from the coastal region of current Holland and Belgium, were among the first to enter Gaul. The leader of the Franks was named **Clovis.** Through a combination of military power and political intrigues, Clovis was able to conquer the various local lords in the region and unite them under his rule. Thus, Clovis established the first European-style kingdom, the **Merovingian** Dynasty (which was named after Clovis' father, Merovech).

Having married a Catholic, Clovis converted to Christianity and was among the first of the Germanic Christians to accept Catholicism rather than Arianism. While there is no evidence that his conversion to Catholicism was insincere, it proved to be a politically astute move, for a couple of reasons. First, his Catholicism gave him an idealistic reason to expand his kingdom against the two Germanic tribes to his south, the **Visigoths** and the **Burgundians,** who were both Arian Christians and had a history of persecuting Catholic subjects. Clovis used this as justification to conquer them and bring their lands under his control. Second, by converting to Catholicism, he gained a degree of legitimacy among his Roman subjects, who were also Catholics.

His rule was given further legitimacy when Anastasius, the Byzantine emperor, asked Clovis to assist in driving the Visigoths from southern Gaul and then gave Clovis a gift of a scepter and robe to acknowledge his success in the rejection of Arian Christianity.[1] (Note that this interaction between the Byzantine Emperor and the German warrior-king illustrates the continuing claim of the Byzantine Emperors over Europe and the tacit agreement of the European ruler to overall rule of the emperor, at least at this time—the late fifth century.) Clovis also worked to unify his people by encouraging intermarriage between the Germanic Franks and the Roman Gauls. It is through this process that the language of the region moved from a variety of German to a rough and corrupted Latin, which was a precursor to French.

At his death in 511, Clovis divided his kingdom among his four sons, who then warred with one another for supremacy. The wars continued until only one of Clovis' sons remained alive, but he proved unequal to the task of uniting the divided kingdom, and it broke into several pieces. Wars and intrigues continued for the next 150 years as the rulers of the various Frankish kingdoms vied with each other for control of the entire kingdom of Clovis. Often the queens and mistresses of the Frankish kings were at the heart of these wars and intrigues. For example in 631, **Brunhilda,** queen of the east Frankish kingdom, declared war on the western kingdom after the western king murdered his wife, Galswintha, so that he could marry his mistress. (Brunhilda and Galswintha were sisters).

The later Merovingian kings were relatively weak, and generally allowed their advisors and ministers to govern. The largest Frankish kingdom was governed by the royal advisor, **Pepin of Herstal,** a generally capable administrator. The late Merovingian kings may have been uninterested in their kingdoms, but their advisors worked hard to improve and expand their holdings. Even though the Frankish kingdoms had been divided and their leaders weak since the time of Clovis, the Merovingians had been able to retain power because of the administration of men like Pepin, and the disorganization and weakness of the other peoples around them.

However, around 730, an invasion of Muslims from Spain (sometimes called the Moors who were actually a North African tribe that was converted to Islam and then recruited by the Arabs to assist them in conquering Spain) threatened the position of the Merovingians and, for that matter, all of Christian Europe. Fortunately for the Merovingians, Pepin's son **Charles** was an accomplished soldier, and proved to be an effective general. Leading the Frankish forces against the Muslims, he was able to defeat the Muslims in France between **Tours** and **Poitiers** (in 732) and prevent further Muslim military penetration into Europe. For this accomplishment Charles was given the surname **Martel,** meaning "hammer." At the death of his father, Charles Martel was chosen by the king to rule as his advisor. Like his father had done before him, Charles served the kingdom ably and, using his military prowess, was able to unite much of the Frankish kingdom.

With the majority of the kingdom of the Franks under unitary control, the Muslim threat repelled, and the able Charles Martel running the kingdom from his position as royal advisor, things were better than they had been in centuries for the Merovingian dynasty. When Charles died, his son, **Pepin the Short,** took his place as royal advisor and continued to lead the Frankish kingdom. Pepin, however, had designs on the throne. In 751 he succeeded in getting the backing of the pope, who supported him because of his obvious political strength, his dedication to the Catholic Church, and a donation to the Pope of land in central Italy. Pepin overthrew the last of the Merovingian kings and was named King of the Franks, thus starting what became known as the **Carolingian Dynasty.** We will discuss this very important dynasty later in this chapter, but first we need to examine how the Germanic tribal areas of Italy, England, and France grew to be a homogeneous Medieval Europe. We also need to understand the position of the Catholic Church, and its influence on the lives of the people, on culture, and on the governments that gradually emerged.

Homogenity in Medieval Europe

By the end of the sixth century, Germanic and Slavic tribes held power in Italy, England, and France and, of course, Germany and the rest of central Europe. These tribes were, before their interaction with the Roman Empire, nomadic barbarians. They knew little of agriculture and even less of trade. They lived from what they could find in the forests and fields, and when they left their native lands and entered Roman territory, they also lived from what they could steal from the Romans. Their society had been nomadic, so they did not build permanent structures or cities, and they were almost universally illiterate. Even a thousand years of interaction with Rome and Byzantium, first across strong boundaries and then from within the empires, did not significantly change their habits and customs. They had finally conquered Rome, driven the Byzantine army out of Italy, and converted to Christianity, yet they had not really learned to be civilized in the sense we have spoken about in the four river societies, or Greece and the Roman Empire, especially with respect to a recognition of the rule of law. So, when the final remnants of Roman infrastructure disintegrated and no government officials or law enforcers were able to keep the peace, the rule of tribal power became the rule of Europe.

Without any central authority, all manner of brigands and marauders rode the countryside, stealing from those who dared to travel (usually killing them as well) and raiding towns and villages when they needed food or wanted women. These roving bands had several fundamental effects on European society. First, warfare became a near constant condition, as competing tribes and smaller raiding groups fought for territorial control, plunder, and survival. Most of this warfare was small-scale local fighting, but that made little difference to the people and villages caught in the middle of it. Second, cities became nearly extinct and large towns rare, since large populations needed extensive agricultural trade and that trade became restricted as the highways became more dangerous. Most people began to live on family farms in or near small villages or hamlets, and these smaller dwelling places became essentially self-sufficient. Most people lived, married, and died within a few miles of where they were born. As already noted, Italy was under the control of the Lombards, led by constantly warring tribal chieftains, mimicking the life they had in the forests of Germany. England, too, was divided and war-ravaged. Even in France, where the Merovingians had some control, the influence of the Merovingian kings was only minimal at the local level; besides, the territory under Merovingian control was actually quite small. Hence, all of Europe experienced these same chaotic conditions.

Another major factor, not man-made, contributed to the demise of cities and greatly increased the difficulty of life for the common medieval European: a dramatic decrease in the average climatic temperature. Colder weather meant that crop yields generally declined and growing seasons had to be extended. Some land could not be used because it was too far north, too far up the mountain, or located in a cold valley. Most families could grow only enough for their own needs, and that took all of their efforts. People in the cities were forced to find small plots of land where they could grow their own food, and that required them to leave the cities and move to more isolated locales. Furthermore, except for trade with the few artisans who could survive in small villages, people could not buy finished goods. Therefore, people had to make their own farm implements (hoes, rakes, wagons, barrels, etc.), make their own clothes, make their own supplies (such as soap, grease for their wagons, candles, dishes, furniture, etc.), and even build their own homes. This all left little time for leisure, and that left little time for learning and the arts. The world was hard and life was short; theft, rape and murder were simply part of life. The only consolation and hope offered came from the Church, which offered the distant reward of a better life after death.

An interesting theory for the decrease in climatic temperature has recently been advanced.[2] Evidence of a major volcanic eruption occurring about the year 532 is quite good. Ice core samples from the polar regions show layers where a large amount of dirt fell with the snow over several years, thus suggesting that the atmosphere was filled with dusty debris, as would be expected following a large eruption. Also, contemporary records indicate that the sun was dimmed, even causing one writer to wonder if the sun would ever shine brightly again. Several historians recorded a period of total crop failures, perhaps for three years, as would be consistent with a volcanic eruption that scattered small dust particles in the air, migrating over their entire world. We have, in fact, evidence that societies in all continents suffered from crop failures and lower crop yields during this time. Other evidences are the reduced ring sizes found in trees that were growing during the mid-sixth century, and actual reports of hearing a major explosion in the southern Orient. In light of all this evidence, the assertion of a colder climate seems certain and the cause of the climate change, at least initially, could have been a volcanic eruption, probably in Indonesia.

Another terrible problem occurring in the mid-sixth century had a devastating effect on medieval life. This was an outbreak of the **Bubonic Plague** or **Black Death.** Historical records from Constantinople report the terrible plague that swept through the Byzantine Empire in the days of Justinian. It was, in fact, one of the reasons for the decrease of imperial power and withdrawal of Byzantine troops from Italy. Historical records also indicate that the plague was widespread in Europe during the same time, perhaps accentuated in its effect by the possible starvation that occurred because of the lower availability of food. Although less widely known than the plague outbreak that devastated Europe in the mid-fourteenth century, the sixth-century plague may have been worse in terms of the percentage of the population that died. Some estimate that in cities, where the effect of the plague was the worst, populations decreased by about 80 percent. Under the twin disasters of lower food output and devastation by the plague, with the additional problem of brigandage on the roads, it is no surprise that cities almost ceased to exist.

In an attempt to find some safety and stability amidst all of the turmoil, villagers began seeking creative ways to be protected, at least from the continuing thievery, rape, house burnings, and crop damage that they experienced on a fairly regular basis. Tired of the raids on their lands, and living in constant fear, villagers realized that most of the raids on their little village came from groups of German brigands who had become somewhat localized, living in the forests and countryside around the villages, since travel was also dangerous and difficult for them. In other words, both the people and the brigands had become localized. Some innovative villagers approached the brigands and suggested that a cooperative agreement might benefit all parties. The villagers offered to supply the brigands with food if the brigands would stop stealing. For the brigands, this meant that they would be given that which they had previously stolen. Even though the villagers were generally unprepared to defend themselves against their raids, the brigands realized that stealing was still more dangerous and required more effort than simply being given the food. The villagers also asked that the brigands protect them from raids by other brigand groups. The arrangement was accepted and soon became a standard for other villages. The brigands in one village then reached agreements with the **protector-brigands** of other villages that neither would raid in the other's territory. Some brigand groups grew to dominate a territory, and their leader would organize the smaller groups into units of loyalty to himself. He would be their **lord.** They would be his **vassals.** Because most of the brigands rode horses, they became known as "horsemen" or, in English, knights. The words for these knights in French, German, and many other languages also reflect the idea of horseman.

The scheme of collective promises eventually led to a system of taxes (in kind) where the villagers would pay taxes to the lord for the upkeep of his manor (usually a castle built in a central location to provide for defense) and the training and maintenance of the knights. Often these taxes were as much as half of all the goods produced by the farmer. When the peasants could not pay their taxes, they lost their land to the lord, who then allowed them to stay and work the land for him as tenant farmers. However, tenant farmers had no opportunity to repurchase their lands and no rights of inheritance, thus they became tied to the land as they had no property of their own and nowhere to go. They either chose to work the land for the lord or starve. They became **serfs.** Occasionally a family would leave in hopes of finding a better deal elsewhere, but conditions were still unsafe for traveling long distances and, with no money or property, the best they could hope for was being a tenant farmer for some other lord. That, combined with the fact that most people had no understanding of the world outside their village, meant that few peasants ever left their old family lands. Over time, as more and more families eventually had a poor crop and could not pay their taxes, more and more land came under the control of the local lords. Eventually nearly all land belonged to the lords, with the peasants being unable or unwilling to leave. Laws were eventually enacted to control and formalize these relationships, including the requirement of the serfs to stay on the land, generation after generation. It is out of this arrangement that the **feudal system** developed.

The cooler weather, the outbreak of plague, the general lack of legal infrastructure, the wandering bands of brigands who eventually became localized knights, and the localization of people into villages occurred throughout Europe. We can, therefore, talk about a rather homogeneous medieval society that characterized the bulk of Europeans. The people were tied to the land and worked every waking moment just to survive. This was the situation that led to the dimming of creativity and, to a large extent, the stagnation of culture. But, one other factor encompassed all of Europe and contributed to homogeneity. That factor was also vitally important in the lives of medieval Europeans, peasants and rulers—the Catholic Church.

The Role of the Medieval Church

Life in the early medieval ages was indeed a hard and miserable existence. However, even in the hardest of times (maybe especially in the hardest of times), people seek for hope and consolation. In a world filled with fear, isolation, ignorance, and the endless struggle just to survive, there seemed to be little hope of betterment in this life, so most people turned to the church and its promise of happiness in a life to come. The importance of the church can be seen in the importance of the Catholic bishop as suggested in the following quotation:

> *As Roman culture died out and was replaced by vibrant new barbarian growths, people forgot many things—how to read, how to think, how to build magnificently—but they remembered and they mourned the lost peace. Call them the people of the Dark Ages if you will, but do not underestimate the desire of these early medieval men and women for the rule of law. There was, moreover, one office that survived intact from the classical to the medieval polis (society); the office of Catholic bishop.*[3]

The Catholic Church was the ray of hope in the lives of the people of medieval Europe. Not yet officially split from the Orthodox variety of Christianity that dominated the Byzantine Empire and parts of Eastern Europe, the Latin church was by this time, in reality, a completely separate entity with different leadership and doctrines from its eastern cousin. The church offered hope, first of all through Catholic theology, namely the promise of happiness in the afterlife for followers who were faithful to the teachings of Christ and the tenets of the church. Another reason for hope was that the church was the last surviving institution left from the days of Roman glory, and as such served as a connection to a greater era. The Catholic Church, with its rules, ordinances, and hierarchy, provided the people of Europe with a sense of order, structure, and authority lacking in most people's lives. Life in medieval Europe was dreadfully mundane, filled with the repetitive daily chores and the constant grind of survival. The church was a chance to escape the drudgery and sameness of medieval life. Sundays provided an opportunity to escape routine and attend Mass, and to listen to the priest's sermon and receive his blessings and advice (the local priest probably being the most educated person a common peasant would know, although often they too were illiterate and ignorant). The church also provided a larger escape from life in the form of holidays and holy days, which were often accompanied by larger gatherings, feasting, and entertainment.

Another reason the church was so universally embraced is that it adapted itself to include much of the paganism that the Germanic tribes had believed in, prior to their conversion to Christianity. Many of Christianity's most holy days were held on old pagan festival days. Christmas was held on the **Saturnalia,** Easter was celebrated at the same time as the spring **fertility festival,** Pentecost was observed on **Floralia,** and All Soul's Day was placed on the same day as a pagan festival for the dead. (Interestingly, in modern times we have largely forgotten the Christian meaning of All Soul's Day and revived the pagan festival on the eve of that day—Halloween). This trend continued beyond just the observation of holy days. Many pagan sites of worship (forests, shrines, etc.) were converted to Christian holy places. Many saints took on the attributes of pagan gods. Incense was introduced into the Mass. Pagan animal sacrifices were changed to animal blessings, and these evolved into general blessings with holy water. Finally, pagan (Greek and Roman) philosophical concepts such as wisdom, justice, courage and temperance were added to Christian values such as faith, hope, and charity, and were incorporated into the doctrine of the church as values taught explicitly by Christian church fathers.

The church permeated all aspects of life. The local priest or monk performed infant blessings and baptism, officiated at marriages, conducted the mass of the church, took confessions and absolved sins, and offered last rites at death. No facet of medieval life was untouched by the church. The holidays celebrated were sanctioned by the church, some of the taxes paid went to the church, even the measurement of time was based on the monastic day. The monks were called to prayer seven times a day by ringing of bells, and these became the way villagers kept track of time. The prayers and times of day (called the **canonical hours**) were: matins/lauds—5 A.M., prime—6 A.M. (first hour of the day), terce—9 A.M. (third hour), sext—noon (sixth hour), none—3 P.M. (ninth hour), vespers—6 P.M. (evening prayers), and compline—7 P.M. (The many callings to prayer are reminiscent of the Islamic prayers, and we wonder if Mohammed might have patterned this Islamic pillar after the Christian monks of Arabia.) Simply put, the Catholic Church was the center of medieval life.

In the few larger towns scattered across Europe, the Catholic Church held even more power. The bishops in the towns had political power and influence because they had access to resources unavailable to most others, including the lords and nobles. Bishops had money, land (which was often donated by those seeking favors or willed to the church by people in hopes of getting into heaven), education, influence with major lords and with other bishops, and the ability to recruit and employ labor. Bishops vied with one another for larger and more influential bishoprics, and, later in the medieval period, would compete with one another in building taller, larger, and more elaborate churches in their towns.

The bishop of the city of Rome was recognized as the **pope,** a word meaning father and the equivalent of **"patriarch,"** which is the title given to the heads of the Eastern Orthodox Church. (The word "pope," as a designation for the leading bishop of the church was actually first used by the Armenian Orthodox Church.) However, in contrast to the pattern in the Eastern Church where the leading patriarch is the first among equals, the Roman pope was the solitary head of the Catholic Church. He based this claim on a direct lineage from Peter and an asserted granting to the Bishop of Rome the keys of presidency for the entire church. The pope also claimed bestowal of authority directly from Constantine, who actually controlled the church as the emperor. (This latter claim was, however, proven to be fictitious when the document detailing the imperial bestowal was proven to be a forgery in the later Middle Ages). Over time, in the western Christian church, the pope became the final authority, the infallible mouthpiece of God on Earth. However, while the other bishops recognized the pope's superiority in principle, he often held relatively little sway over the decisions these bishops made, especially during the early Middle Ages when communications and transportation were extremely difficult.

Throughout most of the Middle Ages there existed a civil state surrounding the city of Rome known as the **Papal States** and the pope served as its king. The Papal States were begun by the donation of land by Pepin the Short. Many of the popes were leaders of large armies, and used this political and military power to consolidate their power and expand the territory of the Papal States. The popes also employed an army of priests and monks as missionaries who were sent throughout Europe. Many of the unconverted barbarian tribes were brought into Christianity; those who practiced Arian Christianity, because of earlier conversions, were persuaded to switch to the doctrine and authority of Rome. Thus, while the early medieval popes generally had limited authority over the bishops in the far-flung branches of the Catholic Church, they were able to increase their political power and religious authority over the neighboring barbarians and heretics. The political involvement of the popes also brought political intrigue. Over more than 200 years in the medieval period, one-third of the popes died from strangulation, suffocation, mutilation, or some other violent act.

From time to time throughout the Middle Ages, church and secular leaders have felt that the church was in need of reform. Councils would be held and, sometimes, reform-minded popes would be chosen to correct the problems. Such a reform pope was **Gregory I,** who ruled from 590–604. In many ways, Gregory shaped the medieval Catholic Church.

Gregory was born at Rome in 540 to an aristocratic Roman family. While he seems to have always been a religious person, Gregory's early life was devoted to politics and public service; for a time he served as prefect of the city of Rome. The office had long since lost much of its grandeur and responsibility, but was still the highest political office in the city of Rome, and a position of some importance and respect. The reasons are lost to history, but sometime during the year 574 Gregory decided to resign his post as prefect and devote his life to God and become a monk. Gregory donated his personal estates to the church, and several monasteries were built on his former lands.

Gregory worked hard and served as a dedicated and faithful monk, rising through the church's monastic hierarchy quickly. After only five years, he was assigned to be ambassador for the Catholic Church in Constantinople. Having already given up his worldly life, Gregory found the grandeur and worldly atmosphere of the Byzantine court to be disturbing, and did his best to live as if he was still in the monastery. While in Constantinople Gregory studied and taught the scriptures, and worked to forward the views of the Latin church. A famous incident in Constantinople occurred when Gregory debated **Eutychius,** the Patriarch of Constantinople on the topic of the resurrection. Eutychius had published a treatise stating that the resurrected bodies of the righteous would be "impalpable, more light than air." Gregory objected to this view, stating that Christ's resurrected body had been palpable and not lighter than air, as evidenced in his appearance to the apostles on at least two occasions following his resurrection. A great debate ensued between the two and became so contested and bitter than eventually the Byzantine emperor brought them both before him and had them defend their views. In the end the emperor ruled that Gregory was correct, and ordered Eutychius' book burned. However, the debate had been so intense that both Gregory and Eutychius fell sick. Gregory slowly recovered but Eutychius only worsened, eventually recanting his error on his deathbed. In spite of Gregory's success in the debate, his overall mission to Constantinople was unproductive; after six years he was recalled to Rome. From his trip to Constantinople Gregory learned that reconciliation between the Roman and Byzantine churches was unrealistic. As pope, Gregory directed the Catholic Church on a path independent of any concern over reconciliation with the Orthodox Church of the east.

Upon his return to Rome, Gregory was appointed abbot at his former monastery, which he loved. His tenure there was to be short, however, as he soon was made the chief advisor, assistant, and personal secretary to **Pope Pelagius II.** It was while serving in this capacity that Gregory's political skills became useful and he was able to broker a peace agreement with the Lombards and thus avoid an attack by them on Rome.

The year 589 was a difficult year for the city of Rome. Flooding, disease, famine, and death scourged the once great city until all business stopped and the streets were deserted, save for the carts sent around to collect the dead. It was in the midst of this crisis, in February of 590, that Pope Pelagius II died. The modern system where the College of Cardinals elects the new pope was not yet in place, and the pope, while head of the church, was still the functioning Bishop of Rome in a more real and literal sense than he is today. For this reason, the popes in early medieval times were selected by the priests and people of the city of Rome, and the vote fell on the extremely popular Gregory. Gregory, who had always favored the cloistered life of the monastery, wrote a letter attempting to decline his election. The letter, however, fell into the hands of the prefect of Rome, who ensured that it was never delivered. Six months later Gregory was confirmed pope.

Gregory may not have aspired to the position, but once he became pope, he worked with vigor and vision. Pope Gregory was missionary oriented, and spent much of his time and energies working to convert barbarian Christians from Arian Christianity (deemed heretical by Catholicism) to the Nicene Creed as adopted by the Catholic Church. He also sent missionaries throughout Europe to convert the pagans, and advocated a church position of acceptance of many pagan practices, with gradual transformation of these practices into Christian-related rites. Pope Gregory, also a strong administrator, worked to standardize Catholic liturgy, which until this time often varied in its wording and practice from place to place. Gregory also allowed a simple form of music to be added to the mass. Today we refer to this style of singing as **Gregorian chant,** after its sponsor, Pope Gregory.

Pope Gregory was also a strong supporter of monasteries, promoting the monastic way of life as an honorable way to devote oneself to God. Many monasteries were built in isolated locations (reminiscent of those in the Eastern Church) but others were located in rich agricultural areas (see Figure 17.3) and became wealthy. He enforced the long-ignored rule, established in the fourth century, that stated that priests could not marry, although after his death, this rule was largely ignored. Gregory's fourteen-year tenure as pope helped shape the direction of the Catholic Church in the Middle Ages (and in the modern era). Despite his many and varied accomplishments, Gregory was sick for much of his time as pontiff, and died March 12, 604 A.D.[4]

Monasteries and convents were not uncommon before Gregory's election to the Papacy, but his support increased their number and influence. Indeed, the famous Benedictine order had been established more than a century prior to Gregory's ascension as pope. Yet, it is in large part because of Gregory's support that monastic life became a central part of Catholicism.

During the early medieval period, life in the monastery was at least as good as the lives of the common peasants of Europe. Monastic life was open to both men and women, and often a monastery was mixed, although separated. Women took care of the children left to the care of the monastery, while the men did the manual labor to provide for those who lived within. Of course, both sexes spent a fair amount of time in prayer, study, and meditation. Men also worked at translating and copying books, mostly the scriptures and other religious texts. Secular texts were often allowed to fall into ruin, ignored, or destroyed, as topics of study other than theology were generally frowned upon by the church. This practice helped contribute to Europe's loss of creativity, as much knowledge from the past was forgotten. Eventually books and the knowledge they contained had to be reintroduced to Europe through the Byzantine Empire, the Islamic world, and Ireland, which was far enough removed from barbarian invasions and the over-zealousness of some critics of non-catholic knowledge that many of their secular books in their possession were preserved.

Figure 17.3 ■ Saint Antimo Abbey in Tuscany (built in the 12th century).

The largest and most influential monastic order of the Middle Ages was the **Benedictine Order.** Benedict was a typical young Italian man of his day, the late fifth century. His family sent him to Rome to study rhetoric, the goal of which was to learn to argue convincingly. Uncomfortable with the basis of his study, and seeing his friends pursue immoral lives of pleasure, Benedict fled Rome in fear for his soul. Eventually he became a religious hermit living in the isolation of the mountains. Over time Benedict gained a reputation for holiness and devotion, and a group of nearby monks asked him to serve as their spiritual leader. Benedict told them he would be too strict for them, but they insisted and he relented. A short time later, Benedict's first followers decided he was indeed too strict and they attempted to poison him, but Benedict survived (and is now the patron saint against poisoning). Another more faithful group of devotees approached Benedict later and he agreed to become their leader, eventually establishing a series of monasteries, including the monastery at **Monte Cassino,** where he would write the **Benedictine Rule.**[5]

Monks and monasteries existed before Benedict (they were especially popular in the Orthodox Church in the Byzantine Empire) but they were just loose collections of men or women who wanted to devote their lives to God. Benedict changed monastic life forever at Monte Cassino by writing the Rules of the Master or Benedictine Rule and requiring those who lived in the monastery to be obedient to this rule. By introducing a common set of guidelines that had to be followed, Benedict created modern monasticism and transformed monasticism into a force that the church could use for educational and missionary purposes, and to test the faith and devotion of those who would devote their lives to the service of God. **Organized monasticism** was one of the few true creative breakthroughs of the early medieval period (along with the innovations of Pope Gregory I), and, as we shall see, will be the driving force behind much of the learning and creativity of the later medieval period.

Benedict's Rule would serve as the basis for all monastic orders, at least in the west, and was less self-abusive than **St. Basil's Rule,** which governed monastic life in the Orthodox Church in the east. The Benedictine Rule required vows of poverty, chastity, obedience, labor, and religious devotion. The rule also emphasized simple clothing, simple but sufficient food (only the sick ate meat, and wine was only permitted in small amounts), and enough sleep. The rule also provided for a well regimented day, with time divided between worship and manual labor. Indeed, the motto of the Order was "Work and pray." Each monastery was to be economically self-sufficient and was to provide for its own discipline, with abbots having the authority to flog or invoke other punishments. There was also an emphasis placed on learning. Originally the emphasis was simply placed on literacy, but was later shifted to the scholarly study of theology, with the focus not on new knowledge but on understanding the intricacies of God's creations. Thus, we find medieval religious study dwelt on questions such as how many angels could dance on the head of a pin, or if it was possible that God could make a boulder so large that he could not move it. Monastic life was not easy, and it was often lonely (monk comes from *mono*—alone); however, it could also be rewarding and could provide for opportunities not available to the common peasant.

Throughout the initial centuries of the early medieval period, all Europe was under the influence of the Catholic Church and, moreover, was amazingly homogeneous in both lifestyle and politics. However, as we have already noted, some strength and leadership had been demonstrated by the Merovingian dynasty in Frankish Gaul. That leadership was due largely to the innovative methods of the original Merovingian king, Clovis I, and then to the able administrators who helped the later kings of this dynasty. We introduced some of those able administrators and noted that, with Pepin the Short, the Merovingian Dynasty was overthrown and a new dynasty, the Carolingian, was born. It is to this new dynasty that we now turn our attention—the most creative and innovative force in the entire early medieval period.

The Carolingian Dynasty

A key feature of the **Carolingian Dynasty,** along with the promise to protect the church against invasion, was a strong and public acceptance of the Catholic Church and a corresponding support of the Carolingian kings by the papacy. Initially this reciprocal support led directly to the establishment of the Carolingians as rulers of France in place of the Merovingians. Later, the relationship with the papacy led to acceptance of the Carolingians as the rulers of Europe and the successors to the ancient Roman Caesars. In all this, the pope was able to further his claim as the leader of the western church and challenge the supremacy of the eastern church as the leader of Christendom.

Just to remind you of the situation in which we left the Carolingians earlier in this chapter, in 751 Pepin the Short had sought for and obtained support from the pope to be the ruler of the Franks, the largest and most powerful of the Germanic tribes. He gained that papal support because his family had shown excellent administrative and military capabilities for several generations as chief administrative officers for the Merovingian kings, who were the previous rulers of the Franks, and because Pepin was personally very devout, and a strong supporter of papal authority. He also gave the pope political control over the region in central Italy that became the Papal States.

The earliest years of Pepin the Short's reign were tenuous because King Pepin was, after all, a usurper. He fought against several other would-be kings and only over several years was he able to solidify his crown. When Pepin died, his sons jointly became kings, thus posing the potential of continued controversy and possible dissolution of the kingdom in warring factions. However, one of the brothers died shortly after Pepin's death and the remaining son, **Charlemagne** (Karl der Grosse, in German) took sole control of the kingdom. Charlemagne envisioned the kingdom of the Franks as a renewal of the Roman Empire, and himself as a Germanic emperor in the Roman style. Charlemagne patterned himself after Theodoric the Goth because Theodoric had been a powerful and (relatively) cultured Germanic king and, at least in the loosest sense, a Roman emperor. (He had been given the title Caesar by the Byzantine emperor as part of the mutual protection treaty between Theodoric's Italy and the Byzantine Empire). Charlemagne moved his capital to the village of **Aachen,** near the modern border of Germany, Belgium, and Holland, and set to work building a city modeled after the Ravenna of Theodoric's day. The highlight of Aachen was a cathedral, shown in Figure 17.4, built in the same octagonal style as the one Theodoric had built in Ravenna. That cathedral is decorated with marble and statues taken from the cathedral in Ravenna, which Charlemagne obtained on a trip to Italy; the cupola of the dome even has a mosaic done in the style of Ravenna. However, the church in Aachen is not an exact replica of the one in Ravenna. For example, the balcony of the church in Aachen has a throne for Charlemagne that is built to resemble King Solomon's throne as it is described in the Bible, thus further demonstrating the exalted vision of grandeur that was characteristic of Charlemagne's reign. This vision was, at least in part, re-

Figure 17.4 ■ *Charlemagne's church in Aachen.*
Image © Photoasia.com.

sponsible for the united drive we see both in Charlemagne and in those who surrounded him.

Charlemagne imitated Theodoric's military prowess as well as his artistic taste. Constantly at war with one enemy or another, Charlemagne led his troops in over 50 wars, and was able to unite most of Europe under his control. First, he was able to solidify his own territories, gaining firm control over all of France and most of western Germany. In an attempt to control eastern Germany, he spent over 30 years warring with the Saxons on his eastern border. At one point he became so frustrated with the Saxons' continuous rebellions that he ordered over 4,000 killed in one day. Eventually Charlemagne gained the upper hand and brought the eastern part of Germany under his control, at least nominally. Charlemagne also fought with the Lombards in the south, and eventually conquered all of northern Italy, including his beloved Ravenna, home of Theodoric. A map of the Carolingian Empire is given in Figure 17.5, which shows the division between his grandsons, discussed later. Charlemagne also fought with the Basques in northern Spain, but eventually had to withdraw when the Saxons revolted again in the east. The withdrawal from Spain was Charlemagne's only defeat, and he forbade others to talk about it.

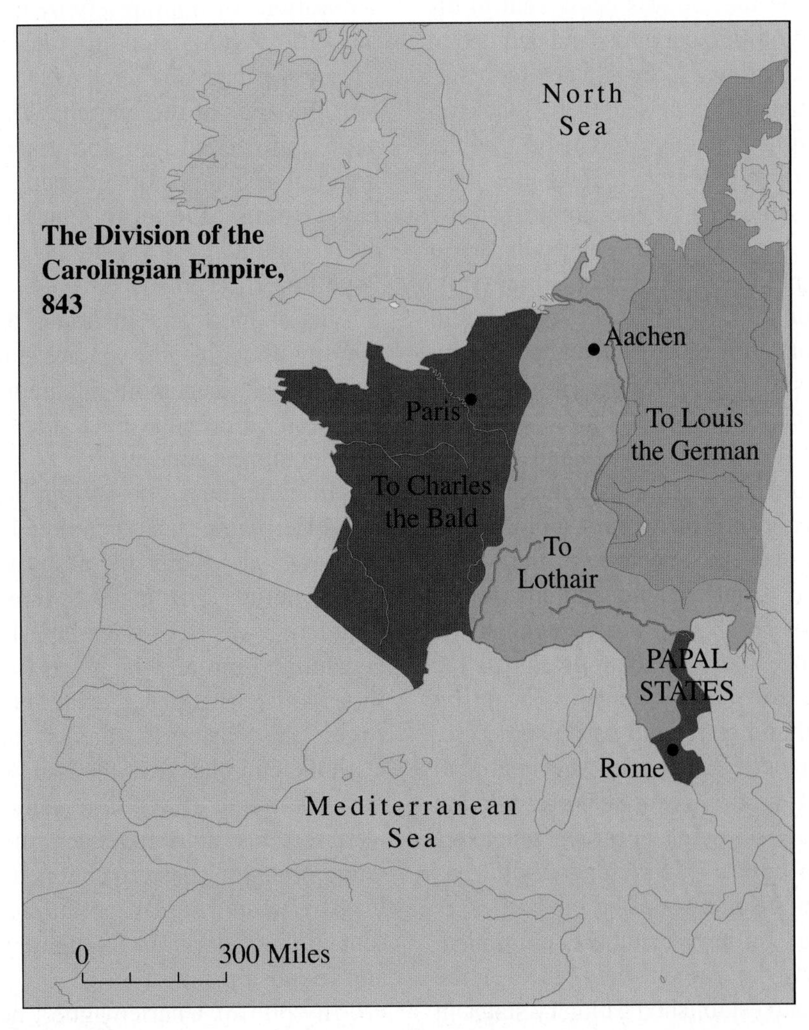

Figure 17.5 ■ *Charlemagne's empire, showing the divisions among his grandsons.*

The war with the Spaniards was also the inspiration for one of the few great pieces of literature to emerge from the early medieval period—the *Song of Roland.* Although it was not written until roughly 1100, it is based on an earlier oral rendering dating from the time of the battle, around the year 800. In Charlemagne's campaign with the Spaniards, his general was his nephew **Roland.** Roland led the troops into battle against the Spaniards and forced them to sue for peace, with the condition that they would become Christians and the Franks would leave Spain. The Franks, who were tired of war, agreed to this plan, began their march back to France, and sent an ambassador with the Spaniards to communicate their acceptance of the plan to their leaders. However, the ambassador felt that he was being sent to his death at the hands of the Spaniards, and decided to betray the Franks. Following the advice of the ambassador, the Spaniards renewed their attack on the Franks. Sensing that there might be trouble, the brave Roland volunteered to take the rear-guard position as the rest of the Frankish army left for France. A great battle ensued between Roland's troops and the Spaniards at **Roncesvals,** a pass in the mountains. Roland believed he could win the battle, and refused to endanger Charlemagne's troops with a cry for help. However, the Spaniards proved to be too great a force. About to perish just before the final defeat, Roland sounded an ivory war horn to warn Charlemagne and, while blowing the horn, Roland burst a blood vessel in his temple and died. Because of the heroic action of Roland, Charlemagne and his forces were prepared for the battle, turned against the Spanish, and drove them to their deaths in the River Ebro. The poem is written in a beautiful rhymed and rhythmic style, and while some creative license has been taken with the historical events, overall it is a fairly accurate representation of what occurred. The poem became immensely popular after the time of Charlemagne, and has often been used to inspire troops before battle.

Charlemagne's military conquests continued. Further in the east he gained victories over the Poles and Slavs, and established tributary states in those regions. His empire became the largest political entity in Europe since the days of the Romans. Charlemagne also solved the difficulty of raising an army in the feudal system. Instead of relying on his lords and other vassals to provide soldiers for his army, he simply confiscated the lands and properties of any lords who rebelled against him and used the funds he gained as a means to support a standing army. This standing army was probably the first to be seen in Europe since the collapse of the Roman Empire.

When Charlemagne first came to the throne, he had envisioned himself as an emperor and his kingdom as a new Rome. On Christmas day, in the year 800, that dream became a reality. Charlemagne was in Rome to show support for the new pope, **Leo III,** who had been the subject of false accusations of impropriety by his enemies within the city. While attending the pope's Mass on Christmas day, Charlemagne knelt in prayer before the altar of the church. While so doing, the pope approached him and placed upon him the imperial crown, anointed him, and named him **Holy Roman Emperor.** Charlemagne may have been genuinely surprised at the action, which Pope Leo III seems to have done out of gratitude for his support and in honor of Charlemagne's power, although some sources claim Charlemagne must have known about the intended action, since Leo would never have acted without first having Charlemagne's consent.

In either case, the Byzantines were outraged that a Germanic "usurper" would take the title that they felt was theirs by descent. However, it is worth noting that by this time Charlemagne's kingdom was considerably larger than the Byzantine Empire, which was slowly losing territory to the Muslims. Furthermore, the split between the eastern Orthodox and the western Catholic churches over the issue of icons and statues was raging at this time, and the pope desired to assert his independence from the Byzantine emperor and the eastern church. Charlemagne, for his part, treated the Byzantine emperors as equals, sent ambassadors, and sought out their support and friendship.

In spite of Charlemagne's new titles, life in Carolingian Europe was certainly not the equal of life during the glory days of Rome; however, Charlemagne faced many of the same problems as the Roman emperors. He had to devise methods to govern a large empire of diverse peoples and cultures. To do so, Charlemagne borrowed several ideas from ancient Rome, but then adapted them to his own circumstances. Realizing the importance of uniform laws, Charlemagne established a new legal code for his empire, asserting the supremacy of law, even stipulating that the king was subject to the law. However, the writings of Saint Augustine said that while a king was indeed subject to the law, he also had a special mandate from God, or a "divine right" to rule. Thus, God had chosen the ruler and placed him in his position, and in so doing sanctioned the actions of the king. Therefore, criticisms of the king could be considered as both treasonous and heretical, since the king was chosen by God. With divine right Charlemagne had devised a system that made the law a supreme and unifying force, while at the same time allowing himself relative freedom to act as he chose. The principle of **divine right of kings** was eventually adopted by most of the monarchs of Europe, and was the standard for the next 800 years; not seriously questioned or challenged until the English Civil War and the American and French revolutions.

To effectively administer this new legal system and solve legal disputes, Charlemagne also introduced a new office, the *missi dominici* or **agents of the lord king**—a legal court, tax collection agency, and local government office all rolled into one. Generally consisting of a member of the nobility and an abbot, it was the job of the *missi dominici* to supervise local sections of the empire, visit the districts and hold courts, investigate financial matters, and solve problems in general. A fairly effective way to administer a large empire, it helped keep the various localities more closely tied to the crown, and not to local lords whom Charlemagne generally did not trust and who he felt were a drain on his power.

Charlemagne's unification of much of Europe, his powerful army, and his new legal code and system of enforcement stabilized medieval society. War among the various Germanic tribes largely ceased, as Charlemagne had defeated most tribes. Banditry had been brought under reasonable control. Due to these improvements, life became better. Travel and trade were still dangerous and the people, now heavily taxed, were still desperately poor and struggled to survive, but much of the fear of daily life and constant threat of violence had been removed. With this burden removed, a brief period of light and learning began. While small in comparison to what had previously existed in the Roman Empire or what would occur later during the Renaissance, Charlemagne's Europe experienced a brief period of learning and creativity, now known as the **Carolingian Renaissance.**

Charlemagne had an interest in learning and the arts, and made efforts to introduce them into his kingdom. He summoned scholars from all parts of Europe and asked them to assist him. One scholar who had an exceptionally powerful influence was a monk, **Alcuin of York,** who was acquainted with the fine preservation work and historical writings of the monks from the area of Northumbria, in England; for example, **The Venerable Bede** was a Northumbrian monk who wrote the *Ecclesiastical History of the English Nation,* perhaps the best history written in the medieval period. At about this same time, another Northumbrian monk wrote *Beowulf,* an epic poem about **King Beowulf** of Sweden, who went on a quest and defeated fierce monsters (**Grendel** and his mother). *Beowulf* is probably the first sectarian writing in the English (Anglo-Saxon) language. Alcuin became a favorite of Charlemagne and was eventually made his chief advisor. The concepts of chivalry, so well developed in the court of Arthur and a tradition in England, may have been introduced to Charlemagne by Alcuin. These rules were adopted by Charlemagne as a method of controlling the knights and raising their devotion to God.

The Carolingian Renaissance was not limited to Northumbrian visitors in Charlemagne's court. Other scholars and monks throughout the kingdom copied books and built up libraries. This practice contributed to a revival in learning, at first only among the clergy in the monasteries, but eventually spreading to other schools. To facilitate copying of the manuscripts and learning from them, Charlemagne developed a new script and new rules for writing. The **Carolingian script** introduced small letters (equivalent to today's lower case), whereas previously only capitals had been used. The use of the small letters increased the amount of text that could be written on a single page, and also introduced the concept of capitalization of proper nouns, thus improving understanding. The Charlemagne writing system also introduced the concept of putting a space at the end of every word, a practice that, surprisingly, had not been followed previously. The spaces in the text allowed punctuation to be added, further improving understanding.

Learning was not limited to the scholars and clergy. Charlemagne had schools built in cathedrals throughout the empire, to be used by any who wanted to attend. The curriculum, written by Alcuin, featured both logic and science (which is still the basis for the "classical" curriculum today) and was based on the ideas of Boethius, again showing the admiration Charlemagne had for Theodoric the Goth. Logic was divided into grammar, rhetoric and dialectic; science was divided into arithmetic, geometry, astronomy, and music. Of course, many among the peasantry could not attend school, as they still had to work very long and hard just to survive, but just the opportunity for learning was remarkable, considering the state of Europe even a century before Charlemagne.

Unfortunately, Charlemagne could not sit on the throne forever, and in 814 he died. Dying with him was his unified kingdom. His son **Louis the Pious** succeeded to the throne but was a weak leader and administrator. After only a few years, Louis' three sons divided the kingdom among themselves and finalized the divided arrangement with the **Treaty of Verdun** in 843. Figure 17.5 shows this division. These kingdoms evolved into the present-day kingdoms of France, Germany, and Italy (and others), but they were never able to develop the military and cultural heights reached by Charlemagne. So it was that only 29 years after the death of Charlemagne, the Carolingian Dynasty, the brightest light of the medieval period, was dimmed and extinguished.

Post-Carolingian Invasions

Shortly after the division of the Carolingian Empire, a series of invasions disrupted the stability and the improved life gained under Charlemagne. The first of the invaders were the **Vikings** or, equivalently, **Norsemen,** who came from northern Europe. The Vikings or Norsemen were inhabitants of the Scandinavian countries. Initially they were dominated by the Dane tribe (living in modern-day Denmark) and later by the Norse tribe (living in modern-day Norway). They attacked all over the European continent, primarily for plunder, as they had very little initial interest in settling. Excellent seafarers, Viking ships were very fast and extremely seaworthy, allowing quick surprise attacks from great distances. These narrow and shallow-draft ships, like the one shown in Figure 17.6 could penetrate great distances up the many rivers of Europe, thus bringing Viking influence to the European interior as well as to the coastal zones.

The Vikings were particularly troublesome to the peoples living in the British Isles; they raided

Figure 17.6 ■ *Viking ship.*

and then eventually invaded and occupied most of the eastern part of England, much of Scotland, and much of Ireland. For many years, the eastern part of England was called "Dane Law" because it was administered by the **Danes.** The Norsemen also carried out extensive invasions into the area that is modern Russia, and even founded cities such as Kjiv. They also explored and settled regions unknown to the rest of Europe, including permanent settlements in Iceland and Greenland, and a settlement that was later abandoned in North America, in the modern Canadian province of Newfoundland.[6] Vikings settled along the northern coast of France in what is today called **Normandy** ("Northmen land"). The Vikings even conquered and settled some areas along the Mediterranean coast in France and Italy. Various Viking invasion routes are shown in Figure 17.7.

Another invasion of Europe came from the Magyars of eastern Europe and western Asia. They were a tribe that appeared in Europe in the early tenth century. Feeling pressure themselves from other peoples further east on the Asian steppes, the Magyars began to migrate west in search of land and plunder. When the Magyars swept into Europe on horseback and began their devastating attacks, they were mistakenly thought to be the return of the Huns, the fearsome horsemen who had plagued Europe centuries before at the start of the medieval period. The Magyar invasion was stopped before conquering Western Europe and then the Magyars retreated east of the Danube River where they settled. Interestingly, this is the same area that was settled by the Huns many centuries before when the Huns' invasion was also stopped. The confusion in Western European minds about the identity of the Magyars resulted in this land being called the land of the Huns (Hungary) even though in that country the locals refer to their country as the land of the Magyars. The language of the Magyars, called Hungarian by Western Europeans, is related to only one other European language—Finnish—suggesting that the Finns might also have originated in the Central Asian steppes.

A third invasion came from the Muslims in northern Africa. Islam had swept across the Arabian peninsula, northern Africa, southwestern Asia, and Spain in a matter of a few centuries, and

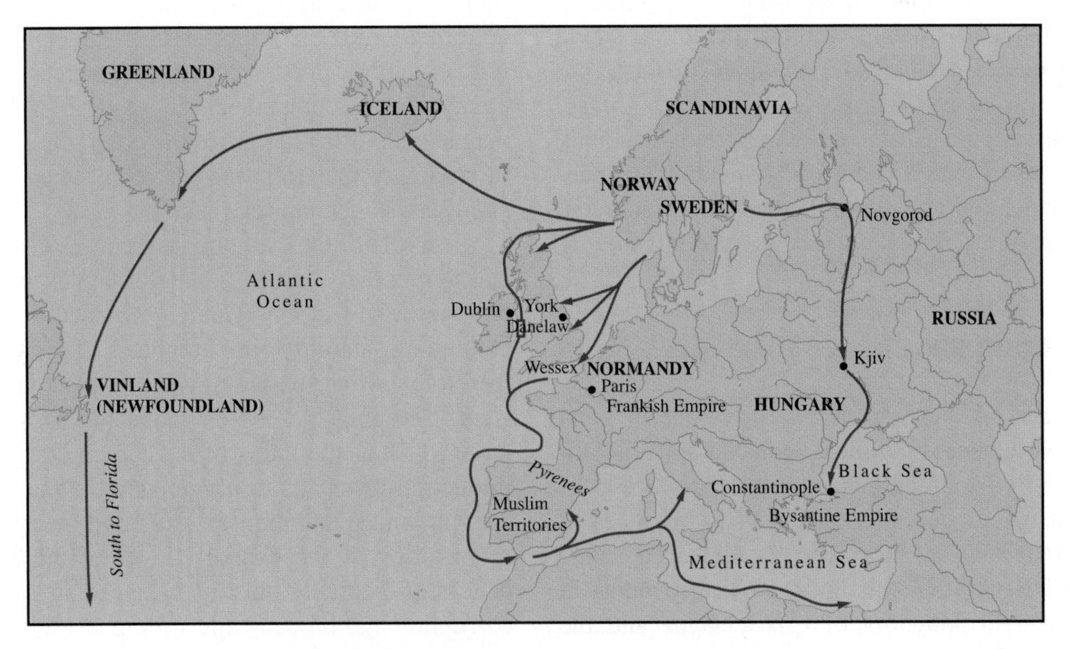

Figure 17.7 ■ *Invasions of the Vikings.*

was seen as a legitimate military and spiritual threat to Christian Europe. The Muslims themselves were less interested in converting Christians than in securing their interests in the Italian trade routes. First invading Sicily, then pouring up through Italy, the Muslim armies sacked Rome in 878. Unable to hold Rome, the Muslims fell back but retained a strong presence in Sicily, southern Italy, and the Mediterranean, until they were displaced by the Vikings in the tenth century.

The effect of the various invasions throughout Europe was to return the continent to a state of insecurity similar to that of the early medieval period. The invasions also further weakened the power of the Carolingian kings and the Anglo-Saxon kings, as they lacked the ability to protect their people. Needing protection and unable to get it from their kings, the peasantry looked to their local lords to once again fill this role, thus giving a boost to the feudal system, an institution that had been diminished during the reign of Charlemagne. In continental Europe, the Carolingian kings lost almost all of their authority; the political system reverted to being a loose collection of minor lords and nobles with control over relatively small geographic areas. Because the people needed protection, the various invasions also worked to strengthen the hold that the local nobility had on their peasants. Within Europe there was still a great deal of arable land available to farm, but there was a lack of people to work it. Consequently, people became more important than land; hence, there was a need for "ownership" of people, which led to a strengthening of serfdom and the loss of the rights of peasants to own land.

Summary

The early medieval period was not one of great creative advances. Political and economic circumstances left the continent in chaos and the people in ignorance and isolation. The instances of creativity and advancement that did occur came from the two stable institutions of early medieval Europe—the kingdom of Charlemagne and the Catholic Church. The creativity of the church occurred only with a few popes, such as Gregory I, and was largely squashed by the corruption and political intrigues of most popes and their supporting clergy. The creativity of Charlemagne was a short-lived respite from the normal drudgery and toil of the feudal system and, even worse, the chaos that reigned during most of the early medieval period when local lords were in control and warfare was rampant. Creativity and culture remained stagnated through much of the early medieval period. We wonder what creativity might have resulted if Charlemagne, Alcuin, and Pope Gregory had lived elsewhere or in another time.

Creativity in the Darkened Ages

Some factors that dramatically affected the creativity of this period should have become apparent through the course of this chapter. First, the fall of the Roman Empire really did diminish creativity, because the infrastructure that gave stability to society collapsed. Perhaps even more importantly, strong civil leadership disappeared. The importance of these two factors is contrasted in the continued strength of the Byzantine Empire, where both the infrastructure and strong leadership continued, versus Europe, where they did not. Further confirmation of the importance of leadership and infrastructure can be seen with the increased creativity that accompanied the reign of Charlemagne and, to further prove the point, the decline of creativity that followed his reign when chaos and weak leadership returned.

The role of the Catholic Church was also critical to creativity, but in a rather complex way. In one view, the Catholic Church provided the only continuing stability in European society and therefore gave the basis for whatever creativity existed. Certainly the church sponsored some creativity such as the fixing of the church liturgy, introduction of chants to accompany the mass, the copying and illustration of texts, and the writing of histories of the church. However, these evidences of creativity must be balanced against the corruption and bureaucratic stifling of the church hierarchy. Some areas of Europe outside the control of the Catholic Church, like Spain and the areas near Byzantium, did not experience the same decrease in creativity during this time period, thus suggesting a direct link, at least in part, between decreased creativity and the church. Therefore, the Catholic Church might be considered the air that is feeding the small light of creativity or the wind that is threatening to extinguish completely that small light. Both are true.

Perhaps the change in the weather was equally responsible for the decline of creativity. Worldwide evidence suggests that the weather got colder in the mid-sixth century, leading to a decrease in food production and forcing the people to work harder for their living. Plagues and general chaos further made the times nearly impossible for creative acts, which, in general, require some leisure time.

Whatever the reasons for the decline in creativity, the effects were felt across western Europe (with the exception of Spain) and recovery would not occur until nearly 500 years after the fall of the Roman Empire. When bright spots occurred, they were quickly extinguished or, at least, minimized. This did not happen by choice but, rather, as a result of the conditions. When some of the conditions changed, creativity again began to flourish. That is the subject of the next chapter.

Timeline—Important Dates

Date	Event
55–54 B.C.	*Julius Caesar invaded Britain and then abandoned it*
55 A.D.	*Conquest of Britain by the Romans*
122	*Revolt by Queen Boadicea*
About 409	*Romans abandon Britain*
About 409 to 570	*Anglo-Saxon conquest of Britain*
500	*Battle of Mount Baden, possibly won by King Arthur*
476	*Fall of the Western Roman Empire*
476–524	*Rule of Theodoric the Goth*
480–525	*Life of Boethius, who established 7-subject curriculum*
480–547	*Life of St. Benedict, who revised monastic rules*
481–511	*Reign of Clovis I, founder of the Merovingian Dynasty*
590–604	*Rule of Pope Gregory I*
732	*Battle of Tours stopped the Muslim advance in Europe*
751	*Pepin the Short established the Carolingian Dynasty*
768–814	*Reign of Charlemagne*
800	*Charlemagne named Holy Roman Emperor*
843	*Charlemagne's kingdom divided by his grandsons*
900–1000	*Invasions of the Norsemen, Magyars, and Muslims*

Notes

1. Norman, A. V. B., *The Medieval Soldier, 8–9,* Barnes & Noble, Inc., 1993. Online version: http://www.txdirect.net/users/rrichard/chlodo1.htm, June 27, 2001.
2. Keys, David, *Catastrophe,* Ballantine Books, 1999.
3. Cahill, Thomas, *How The Irish Saved Civilization,* Anchor Books, 1995, 69.
4. Hudleston, G. Roger, "Pope St. Gregory I (The Great)" *Catholic Encyclopedia,* Encyclopedia Press, Inc., 1913, Online version: http://www.ewtn.com/library/MARY/CEGREGRY.HTM, June 27, 2001.

5. Matz, Terry, "Saint Benedict," http://www.catholic.org/saints/saints/benedict.html, June 27, 2001.
6. Ritchie, Donald A. and Albert S. Broussard, *American History: The Early Years to 1877,* Glencoe/McGraw Hill 1997, 63.

Suggested Readings

Baigent, Michael, *Holy Blood, Holy Grail,* Dell, 1982.

Cahill, Thomas, *How The Irish Saved Civilization,* Anchor, 1995.

Gardner, Laurence, *Bloodlines of the Holy Grail,* Element, 1996.

Goodrich, Norma Lorre, *The Holy Grail,* Harper Perennial, 1992.

Hatto, A. T. (trans.), *The Nibelungenlied,* Penguin, 1969.

Keys, David, *Catastrophe,* Ballantine, 1999.

Mallory, Sir Thomas, *Le Morte d'Arthur,* Random House, 1993.

Matarasso, P. M. (trans.), *The Quest for the Holy Grail,* Penguin, 1969.

Ritchie, Donald A. and Albert S. Broussard, *American History: The Early Years to 1877,* Glencoe/McGraw-Hill 1997.

Wadell, Helen (trans.), *The Wandering Scholars,* Constable, 1934.

Article 29

Malory: Le Morte d'Arthur

Introduction

King Arthur was the legendary great king of England who instituted the code of chivalry in the land and created a bright moment of civilization in the midst of the Dark Ages. Troubadours and bards told tales involving King Arthur and his Knights of the Round Table throughout the Middle Ages. It is believed that these tales were based on an actual monarch who ruled sometime between the 5th and 8th centuries.

The stories of King Arthur have been perpetually popular enough to inspire the creation of several collections or adaptations of the stories over the last thousand years. One of the earliest and most popular of these collections is Sir Thomas Malory's *Le Morte D'Arthur.* The moral themes that lie at the foundation of the tales contained therein showcase the code of chivalry and the life of its adherents and their challenges.

Just as other great epics gave value and prestige to various nations, like the *Iliad* and the *Odyssey* did for the Greeks and the *Aeneid* for the Romans, the tales of Arthur create a great heritage for the English people. Other western Europeans have linked their heroic stories to the tales of Arthur (such as Lancelot for the French and Siegfried for the Germans) and have, therefore, enjoyed the same prestige and glory of their origins. Just as with the other great epics, the ethics and values of a society are developed. Therefore, these Arthurian tales should be compared to the *Iliad,* the *Odyssey,* and the *Aeneid.*

The stories contained in the selections below are still familiar to most of the western world. The first passage contains the forever-loved tale of the sword in the stone. The next two passages show references to the Holy Grail. The last passage gives the emotional tale of Arthur's death.

Chapter VI

How King Arthur Pulled Out the Sword Divers Times

Now assay, said Sir Ector unto Sir Kay. And anon he pulled at the sword with all his might, but it would not be. Now shall ye essay, said Sir Ector to Arthur. I will well, said Arthur, and pulled it out easily. And therewithal Sir Ector knelt to earth, and Sir Kay. Alas, said Arthur, my own dear father and brother, why kneel ye to me? Nay, nay, my lord Arthur, it is not so, I was never your father nor of your blood, but I wot well ye are of an higher blood than I weened ye were. And then Sir Ector told him all, how he was bitaken him for to nourish him, and by whose commandment, and by Merlin's deliverance. Then Arthur made great doole when he understood that Sir Ector was not his father. Sir, said Ector unto Arthur, will ye be my good and gracious lord when ye are king? Else

Malory, Sir Thomas, *Le Morte d'Arthur,* Random House, 1993.

were I to blame, said Arthur, for ye are the man in the world that I am most beholden to, and my good lady and mother your wife, that as well as her own hath fostered me and kept. And if ever it be God's will that I be king as ye say, ye shall desire of me what I may do, and I shall not fail you, God forbid I should fail you.

Chapter XVI

How Balin was Delivered by Merlin, and Saved a Knight That Would Have Slain Himself for Love

THEN Merlin came thither and took up Balin, and gat him a good horse, for his was dead, and bad him ride out of that country. I would have my damosel, said Balin. Lo, said Merlin, where she lieth dead. And King Pellam lay so, many years sore wounded, and might never be whole till Galahad the haughty prince healed him in the quest of the Sangreal, for in that place was part of the blood of our Lord Jesus Christ, that Joseph of Arimathea brought into this land, and there himself lay in that rich bed. And that was the same spear that Longius smote our Lord to the heart; and King Pellam was nigh of Joseph's kin, and that was the most worshipful man that lived in those days, and great pity it was of his hurt, for through that stroke, turned to great dole, tray and tene. Then departed Balin from Merlin, and said, in this world we meet never no more.

Then within a little while after, the king commanded that all people should avoid that none should be in that way there as the king would come. And so when this was done, these four men and these ladies laid hand on Sir Launcelot, and so they bare him into a tower, and so into a chamber where was the holy vessel of the Sangreal, and by force Sir Launcelot was laid by that holy vessel; and there came an holy man and unhylled that vessel, and so by miracle and by virtue of that holy vessel Sir Launcelot was healed and recovered. And when that he was awaked he groaned and sighed, and complained greatly that he was passing sore.

Chapter V

How King Arthur Commanded to Cast His Sword Excalibur into the Water, and How He Was Delivered to Ladies in a Barge

BUT I may not stand, mine head works so. Ah Sir Launcelot, said King Arthur, this day have I sore missed thee: alas, that ever I was against thee, for now have I my death, whereof Sir Gawaine me warned in my dream. Then Sir Lucan took up the king the one part, and Sir Bedivere the other part, and in the lifting the king swooned; and Sir Lucan fell in a swoon with the lift, that the part of his guts fell out of his body, and therewith the noble knight's heart brast. And when the king awoke, he beheld Sir Lucan, how he lay foaming at the mouth, and part of his guts lay at his feet. Alas, said the king, this is to me a full heavy sight, to see this noble duke so die for my sake, for he would have holpen me, that had more need of help than I. Alas, he would not complain him, his heart was so set to help me: now Jesu have mercy upon his soul! Then Sir Bedivere wept for the death of his brother. Leave this mourning and weeping, said the king, for all this will not avail me, for wit thou well an I might live myself, the death of Sir Lucan would grieve me evermore; but my time hieth fast, said the king. Therefore, said Arthur unto Sir Bedivere, take thou Excalibur, my good sword, and go with it to yonder water side, and when thou comest there I charge thee throw my sword in that water, and come again and tell me what thou there seest. My lord, said Bedivere, your commandment shall be done, and lightly bring you word again. So Sir Bedivere departed, and by the way he beheld that noble sword, that the pommel and the haft was all of precious stones; and then he said to himself: If I throw this rich sword in the water, thereof shall never come good, but harm and loss. And then Sir Bedivere hid Excalibur under a tree. And so, as soon as he might, he came again unto the king, and said he had been at the water, and had thrown the sword in the water. What saw thou there? said the king. Sir, he said, I saw nothing but waves and winds. That is untruly said of thee, said the king, therefore go thou lightly again, and do my commandment; as thou art to me lief and dear, spare not, but throw it in. Then Sir Bedivere returned again, and took the sword in his hand; and then him thought sin and shame to throw away that noble sword, and so efte he hid the sword, and returned again, and told to the king that he had been at the water, and done his commandment. What saw thou there? said the king. Sir, he said, I saw nothing but the waters wappe and waves wanne. Ah, traitor untrue, said King Arthur, now hast thou betrayed me twice. Who would have weened that, thou that hast been to me so lief and dear? and thou art named a noble knight, and would betray me for the richness of the sword. But now go again lightly, for thy long tarrying putteth me in great jeopardy of my life, for I have taken cold. And but if thou do now as I bid thee, if ever I may see thee, I shall slay thee with mine own hands; for thou wouldst for my rich sword see me dead. Then Sir Bedivere departed, and went to the sword, and lightly took it up, and went to the water side; and there he bound the girdle about the hilts, and then he threw the sword as far into the water, as he might; and there came an arm and an hand above the water and met it, and caught it, and so shook it thrice and brandished, and then vanished away the hand with the sword in the water. So Sir Bedivere came again to the king, and told him what he saw. Alas, said the king, help me hence, for I dread me I have tarried over long. Then Sir Bedivere took the king upon his back, and so went with him to that water side. And when they were at the water side, even fast by the bank hoved a little barge with many fair ladies in it, and among them all was a queen, and all they had black hoods, and all they wept and shrieked when they saw King Arthur. Now put me into the barge, said the king. And so he did softly; and there received him three queens with great mourning; and so they set them down, and in one of their laps King Arthur laid his head. And then that queen said: Ah, dear brother, why have ye tarried so long from me? alas, this wound on your head hath caught over-much cold. And so then they rowed from the land, and Sir Bedivere beheld all those ladies go from him. Then Sir Bedivere cried: Ah my lord Arthur, what shall become of me, now ye go from me and leave me here alone among mine enemies? Comfort thyself, said the king, and do as well as thou mayest, for in me is no trust for to trust in; for I will into the vale of Avilion to heal me of my grievous wound: and if thou hear never more of me, pray for my soul. But ever the queens and ladies wept and shrieked, that it was pity to hear. And as soon as Sir Bedivere had lost the sight of the barge, he wept and wailed, and so took the forest; and so he went all that night, and in the morning he was ware betwixt two holts hoar, of a chapel and an hermitage.

Article 30
Rudel: To His Love Afar

Introduction

The ideals of chivalry evolved over hundreds of years in the Middle Ages. Some parts of the Roman Catholic world were a long way from Rome and further ethical laws were needed to compensate for the differences in culture. A King's need to hold his powerful knights in check became the basis for the code of chivalry to which they were sworn. Many elaborate rituals and rules grew up to become the Chivalric code. Part of the code dealt with defending the honor of the court's lady. This behavior coincided with the increasing popularity of the Virgin Mary, and set women on a pedestal as subjects of admiration and love.

Plato's concepts of intangible perfect Forms had become the basis of much of Catholic dogma. Through the code of chivalry, Plato's philosophy became the basis of the popularized way of love. Hence, "Platonic love" and "courtly love" were coined to describe this love from afar and the committing of one's deeds to the honor of a lady, possibly without ever having even met her!

While we know almost nothing of the author of this poem, Jaufre Rudel, we are able to see the essence of chivalry in the words which he penned. The following poem comes from the age of chivalry (High Middle Ages) and describes the ideal of courtly love.

To His Love Afar

When the days lengthen in the month of May,
Well pleased am I to hear the birds
Sing far away.

And when from that place I am gone,
I hang my head and make dull moan,
Since she my heart is set upon
Is far away.

So far, that song of birds, flower o'the thorn,
Please me no more than winter morn,
With ice and sleet.
Ah, would I were a pilgrim over sea,
With staff and scrip and cloak to cover me,
That some day I might kneel me on one knee
Before her feet.

Most sad, most joyous shall I go away,
Let me have seen her for a single day,
My love afar.
I shall not see her, for her land and mine
Are sundered, and the ways are hard to find,
So many ways, and I shall lose my way,
So wills it God.

"To His Love Afar" by Rudel from *The Wandering Scholars,* translated by Helen Waddel. Constable, London, 1936. Reprinted by permission of Constable & Robinson Ltd.

[1]Paynimrie = paganism

Yet shall I know no other love but hers,
And if not hers, no other love at all.
She hath surpassed all.
So fair she is, so noble, I would be
A captive with the hosts of paynimrie[1]
In a far land, if so be upon me
Her eyes might fall.

God, who hath made all things in earth
that are,
That made my love, and set her thus afar,
Grant me this grace,
That I may some day come within a room,
Or in some garden gloom
Look on her face.

It will not be, for at my birth they said
That one had set this doom upon my
head,
—God curse him among men!—
That I should love, and not till I be dead,
Be loved again.

Nations, Crusades, and Mongols
Creativity Rekindled

> The difference [between human and animal evolution] is that human beings evolve externally to their bodies as well as internally through the process of natural selection. . . . [W]e are extending ourselves outward from our bodies into our environment, at the same time changing the environment within which we are operating in order to suit our own purposes. If it is too hot, we create refrigeration. It if is too cold, we learn to control fire, to build the hearth and chimney. Each extension increases our ability to adapt to change and to react to alterations in the environment that we may encounter. . . . Humankind does evolve. We do adapt to changing environments and changing conditions. But it is accomplished through the creation of artifacts, by a manipulation of the environment and an understanding of natural law that enables us to improve and re-create the environment in the form we find most advantageous.
>
> —*Paul A. Alcorn,* Social Issues in Technology, 3rd Ed.

Creativity and the Environment

Around the year 1000 A.D., the climate got warmer and creativity improved. This is the reverse of what happened in the sixth century when a downturn in climatic temperature, coupled with several natural disasters and adverse political changes, seemed to crush creativity. We should not be surprised that creativity is closely linked to the weather. From the beginning of civilization, we noted the need for water (rivers) but also saw that the earliest civilizations were located in warm-weather places. Because civilization and creativity require leisure time, places where nature is gentle are preferred, at least initially. As populations grew and humans learned to grow crops that would thrive in cooler climates and with less water, civilizations moved northward. The expansion of population to almost all parts of the world today is only possible because humans have solved the issues of food distribution and environmental control, thus allowing people in even inhospitable areas to enjoy leisure and creativity.

The inexorable expansion of civilization to fill the earth through human efforts to subdue nature have been integral to society since the days of Adam and Even when God said, "... Be fruitful, and multiply, and replenish the earth, and subdue it. . . ." (Genesis 1:28). The quotation at the beginning of this chapter expresses the same concept in a secular sense—humans have tried to subdue the environment since the beginning of human life on earth. Animals generally are reactive to nature, that is, accepting of what comes to them. Increasingly, as technology has continued to expand, humans have manipulated nature, even from the beginning of civilization. For example, early Mesopotamians developed canals to irrigate the land and to wash the salts out of the soil. But, even though the desire of humans might be to dominate nature, the means of doing that, technology, did not come all at once. Technology is cumulative. Thus, early humans were still largely reactive to nature, just a little higher than the animals in this regard. Steady technological progress was made through the early river societies, the Greeks, the Romans, and the Muslims, but humans remained largely reactive to their environment, as was clearly seen by the dimming of creativity in the early Middle Ages, largely because of colder weather, natural disasters, and political chaos. But, as we shall see, when the weather warmed and the political situation stabilized, beginning around the year 1000, creativity surged and life became better.

One aspect of civilization that saw major changes and improvements was the field of agriculture, where a series of inventions and insights allowed more and better food to be produced over a wider geographical area. This fortunate occurrence allowed European farmers to have a longer and more productive growing season. It also made more land usable for farming, especially in the north where long winters and poor soils had previously made agriculture nearly impossible.

One such helpful innovation was the **heavy plow.** Initially, in the days of the river civilizations and even into the early Greek period, wooden stick plows had dominated agriculture. Later, metal replaced the wooden plows but the design was essentially the same. These straight metal plows merely extended the life of a plow and allowed deeper tillage. These plows improved agriculture in the sandy soils of southern Europe, but did little in the heavy clay soils of northern Europe, where more than deeper tillage was needed to open the soil. The problem in the north was solved with the invention of the heavy plowshare. The heavy plowshare design was very different. It had a sharp point of iron to cut the soil, a plowshare blade mounted behind the sharp metal point that widened the cut, and a moldboard behind the share to lift up and turn the soil. It is illustrated in Figure 18.1. The new plow allowed the soil to be aerated, thus increasing its quality and growing capacity. It also created furrows and beds, and provided natural drainage to the fields, particularly useful because it allowed for the growth of wheat, a better staple crop than the grains that had previously dominated in northern Europe. Previous to this time wheat was rarely grown in Europe, as it was a middle-eastern plant that did poorly in the wetter European climate. The new metal plow also made tilling the heavy European soils easier, allowing for even more land to be used for agriculture. Because of the difficulty of acquiring the needed iron (it was difficult to work and expensive to buy), the use of the metal plow spread slowly, but its advantages were obvious. Combined with the warmer weather, Europe seemed to be ready for a substantial improvement in food supply.

The food situation seemed especially favorable in light of the development of the horse collar, an innovation that had gradually occurred over the early medieval period but became widespread about 1000. In Roman times, horses were harnessed using a strap around the horse's neck, with the load point located at the top of the strap. This

Figure 18.1 ■ *Medieval heavy plow.*

arrangement caused great stress on the horse because, with heavy loads, the strap pressed against the horse's windpipe. The strap arrangement gradually evolved, over several hundred years, into the **horse collar**—a device that puts the load on the horse's shoulders and allows the horse to pull heavy loads, such as the heavy metal plow. When further coupled with the use of horseshoes to give better traction and improved hoof wear, agricultural technology was in place for much higher food production. Horses also became more practical than oxen, the previous major beast of burden, for other uses besides pulling plows, including general transportation, and thus were better investments for farmers.

The **three-crop rotation system** was introduced and that, too, increased food production. Previously farmers had grown grain on half their field one season and then allowed that field to lie fallow the next or, when possible, grow a second crop, like beans, that did not deplete the nitrogen from the soil. Around the year 1000 the practice of dividing the field into three sections that could be rotated on a three-year cycle became widespread. Two sections were dedicated to grain and only one-third to the alternate crop. The placement of the alternate crop rotated through the three sections. Therefore, compared with the old two-year system, the amount of acreage devoted to grain production increased from 50 percent to 67 percent of the total. Coupled with more total acreage under cultivation and the better yields from warm weather, the food supply skyrocketed.

Other inventions that helped agriculture and food production included the expanded use and, sometimes, the invention of simple machinery. The use of water wheels, known in Roman times but not widely used, was greatly expanded. **Windmills** were invented (about 1185) to provide the needed power to turn mills and make grinding grains easier. Windmills were especially valuable where the land was relatively flat and water wheels were not effective (such as in the Netherlands). The water wheels and windmills provided power for a variety of other manufacturing needs, thus saving a great deal of manual and animal labor, and allowing more people to farm the newly viable land or pursue more specialized work. Hence, manufacturing became important for making textiles, barrels, wagons, and metal products.

As people ate enough food and had a wider variety of it, they became healthier, and as they became healthier, populations began to increase. England saw its population rise from one million to four million people in less than two hundred years; this increase was indicative of what was occurring all across Europe. This immense growth in population, combined with the improvements to agriculture, meant that people no longer had to grow their own food to survive, nor were all the peasants needed to work the land for the lords and nobles. Furthermore, as we will see, the rise of nations provided better internal stability and security, which greatly reduced the threat of brigand attacks on larger populations. The combination of these factors led to a rebirth of the town, which meant a greater interaction among people and a more rapid spread of ideas and technology.

Guilds were formed at this time, initially so that merchants could band together for safety when traveling to markets, and then later so that artisans could regulate quality and prices for their goods. Guilds became especially important as a means to help and control the many new people who were moving into the towns. The guilds insured an orderly transition of these people from farming to artisan goods production. They mandated quality standards in a particular product, controlled the apprentice system, stipulated pricing within a region, and even regulated acceptable manufacturing practices. While much good came from the guilds, eventually their restrictive practices imposed barriers to continuous product improvement and thus dampened creativity. The guild system eventually collapsed (after hundreds of years) when artisans became individually recognized for their work and creativity and the needs of a dynamic marketplace forced innovation on the manufacturing community.

During this time (from about the twelfth century) groups of cities joined together to control trade in their region. The most successful of these was the **Hanseatic League** in Northern Europe, which controlled not only land trade but most of the shipping in the Baltic Sea. The leagues were occasionally able to develop control over a particular commodity, thus increasing the price by controlling the supply. For example, during the days of Hanseatic League power, almost all the amber traded in the world flowed through the hands of the merchants of the league. This system is similar to the present-day control of the diamond market by the international diamond cartel.

The rise of the town was not an isolated occurrence confined to a few regions, but generally occurred all across the European continent. With the exception of Paris (which had grown very large as a trading town and center of government), most towns were still too small to be considered full-fledged cities; however, the existence of even mid-sized towns was a marked change from the nearly 500 years of isolated farm and village life that had dominated early medieval Europe. When people began to live together in communities once again, there was greater interaction, and that sparked creativity and change. The increased artisan work also led to greater creativity, since the artisans were more likely to produce creative works and to travel for trade purposes, which further increased mixing of cultures and gave people new ideas. Town life also helped create an environment where people had more leisure time, a condition needed for the development of the arts. Only when people can live without spending every waking moment struggling to survive can they produce fine art or find time and energy to go and appreciate what others have produced. Thus, town life helped the arts by providing the conditions needed for the development of both the artists and the audience.

Most of the towns that grew up at this time were still medieval in design and feel. Nearly all of the new towns were protected by a castle and city walls. The usual pattern was a castle atop a rise or hill overlooking the town in the valley below, generally with a defensive wall surrounding both. Often, other fortifications sat atop other hills nearby to increase the ability to defend the town. Usually a river or stream flowed through the valley to provide water and transportation. The town and castle formed a symbiotic relationship: The castle and its lord and knights provided protection to the town; in return, the town's economy, through taxes and direct supply of goods, provided the money for the upkeep of the local lord's estate, as well as sustenance for the knights and other soldiers who helped defend the town. It was a similar arrangement to the feudal system that existed in the countryside, with the exception that in towns the people were generally not tied to the land, and town taxes were often lower because there was a larger tax base. Some of the most noteworthy towns that can still be visited to see this medieval pattern are Oxford, Cambridge, and London in England; Heidelberg and Rothenberg, both in Germany; Prague, in the modern Czech Republic; Krakow, in Poland; Budapest, in Hungary; Orleans, in France; Rome, in modern Italy, which was the capital of the Catholic Church and was slowly being rebuilt; and several of the Italian city-states, such as Venice, Genoa, Florence, and Ravenna.

The diversity and increased mercantilism of the towns and cities led to other creative developments. One such development was the general quantification of European life. Until this time, most weight and distance measurements were imprecisely measured. For instance, the length unit, foot, was literally the length of the foot of the current king. When the king died or when traveling to a place with a different king, the measurement changed. Another example was the furlong, a distance originally associated with the obviously variable length of a furrow (the trench made by a plow). People began to standardize these and other measurements, such as temperature, hardness, and speed. Triangulation was introduced so that surveys could be made, thus improving the precision of area measurements for the laying out of the towns and the deeding of property. One important standardization was in the money used in England. The king established the **Trial of the Pyx** (which derives from the name for the boxes in which the coins were kept), during which money from the mint was compared to various standard coins to guarantee correct weight, size, and alloy content. Inevitably some deviations were encountered, but the crown set acceptable variation limits, thus establishing some important principles of the application of statistics to manufacturing.

Perhaps the most important change in quantification during this period was a revision of the **number system.** This revision began when a young Italian student, **Leonardo Pisano,** now known as **Fibonacci,** traveled to Algeria and was instructed by an Arab mathematician in the Hindu-Arabic number system (which we use today). Fibonacci saw the advantages of this system compared to the ponderous Roman numeral system in use at that time throughout Europe. After extensively studying the system, Fibonacci summarized his learning in the book *Liber Acaci (Book of the Abacus),* which he published in 1202. The book gave both theory and practical problems, including such topics as algebra, cubic equations, commercial bookkeeping, conversions of money, calculation of interest rates, and even the reproduction rate of rabbits, which, interestingly, follows the same mathematical form as the Greek Golden Ratio. After some demonstrations of the new number system, the book was enthusiastically received by the Holy Roman Emperor, and it quickly became the standard number system in Europe.[1]

Life in Europe was slowly improving. The darkest days were passed. The culture and creativity of Europe was beginning to wake from its 500-year slumber. The rise of nations that would begin during this period would help to centralize and stabilize government and offer the masses better protection. Also offering more protection, and thus helping to increase travel and trade, were the various orders of **knights** that sprung up to protect pilgrims journeying to holy sites. Interaction with other peoples and cultures also continued with the knights' crusades to the Holy Land. Further diversification was thrust upon Europe as they experienced the Mongol invasions. The creativity involved in establishing nations, fighting crusades, and leading raiding parties across much of the world might not be readily apparent. However, if we consider the organizational and motivational ability of those strong leaders who conquered the various nations, who then established the often original methods of governance, and who struggled with the problems of succession, we can see creativity demonstrated. We will now look at each of these factors of civilization development.

The French Nation

By the mid 900s, the Carolingian kings had lost virtually all their power and control over the land of the Franks. Power had reverted to the dukes, barons, and counts who had previously served as vassals to the kings. Throughout the Middle Ages and beyond, the nobility was divided into two major groups—the king or monarch, who was over the entire region and the dukes, barons, and counts who were local leaders (sometimes called the minor nobility). These two groups were bound together by oaths of loyalty and mutual protection but were often antagonistic to each other as power shifted with the strength and capabilities of the kings. Additional rulers in the territory were external invaders, such as the Vikings, who had conquered and then settled the north coast of France, today called Normandy. Another invasion, from Germany, gave the Burgundians control over the part of France bordering the Rhine valley. Many of these invaders blended with the local culture, even accepting the French language as their own.

In 987, several of the nobles in France met together and decided to cede some of their power to a king, thereby hoping to increase the military strength and political power of the Frankish region. The nobility elected **Hugh Capet** to serve as their king, and with this act unknowingly created the core of modern France. Initially the **Capetian kings** (descended from Hugh Capet) only controlled a small area around the cities of Paris and Orleans, called *Ile de France.* As time went on, the Capetian dynasty was able to expand its territorial holdings, strengthen the kingship, and solidify power. The original plan of the nobles who had elected Hugh Capet had been to keep the monarchy reliant upon the support of the nobility, so that the nobles would maintain power in the overall governance of the land. Unfortunately for the plans of the nobility, each king for the next

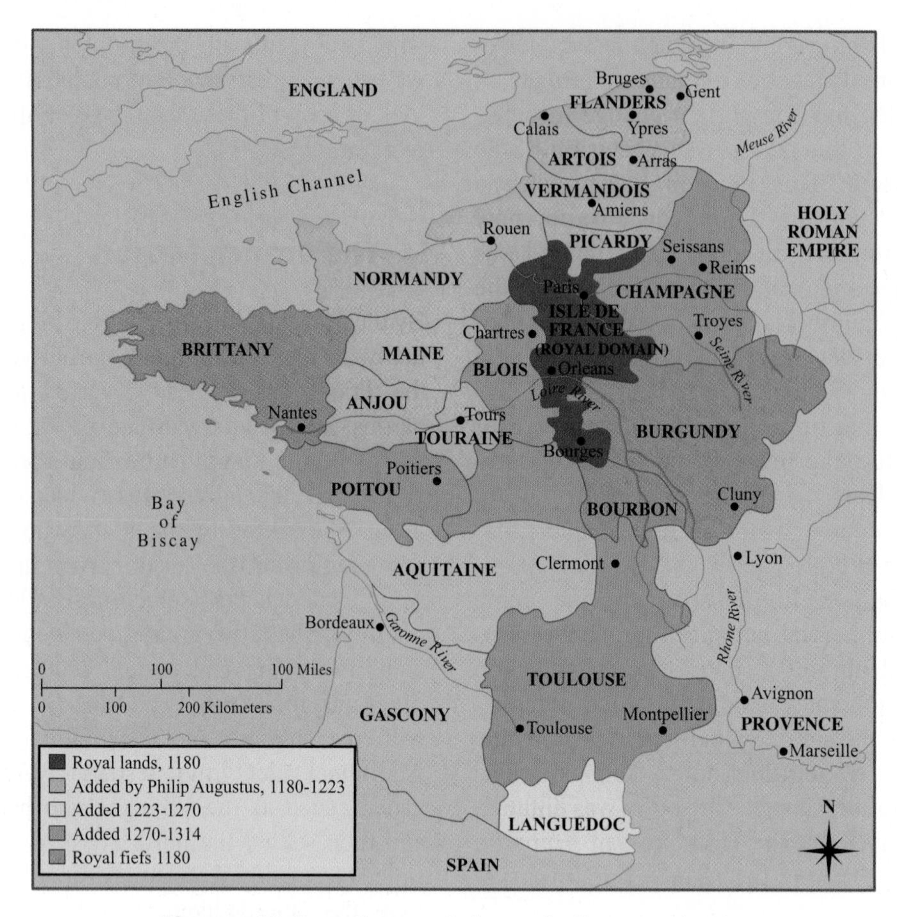

Figure 18.2 ■ *Extent of the early Capetian lands.*

300 years of the Capetian dynasty had a son who survived the king, thus avoiding succession crises. Without the problems of succession, the Capetian dynasty was able to expand its power and achieve dominance over the nobility. The extent of Capetian growth is shown in Figure 18.2.

The most aggressive campaign of territorial expansion during the Capetian dynasty occurred under the reign of **King Philip II** (called Augustus) between 1180 and 1223. In a difficult struggle, Philip was able to defeat **King John of England** and acquire the territory north of *Ile de France* up to and including Normandy. As Philip's kingdom grew, he needed more infrastructure and local government to oversee it, but did not want to empower his nobility any further for fear of limiting his own power. Philip found his solution by appointing local authorities, such as sheriffs, to serve as his direct agents. To ensure that these agents of the crown did not gain too much power themselves, Philip did not allow them to serve in their native area or allow them to own land in the region they presided over. Philip's decision to govern through appointed agents rather than his nobility was the first step in a continual effort by French kings to deny their nobility any control over the monarchy. The actions taken by the Capetian kings ensured that France would become the strongest and most unified of the early nations. When the Capetian Dynasty finally collapsed in the fourteenth century, the French and English kings would clash over sovereignty, but that is a subject we will discuss in a later chapter dealing with the end of the Middle Ages.

The German Nation

The eastern part of the old Carolingian Empire, the land that would eventually be known as Germany, was politically divided among local barons and lords who had complete control over their tiny fiefdoms. Eventually, like the Frankish lords, a loose union was desired, and the German princes agreed to a king. In keeping with the German tradition, the king was elected by the princes rather than assuming the throne through strict hereditary rights. (Elections were preferred because, it was believed, the princes could choose a king who was not too strong and therefore they could continue dominance over their local fiefdoms.)

In the mid-tenth century **Otto I,** called **the Great,** was elected to power. He believed in a strong central government, and fought against the local princes, eventually deposing the rebellious princes and replacing them with his relatives. He then broke up the princes' hereditary fiefdoms and awarded the parts to various bishops and other officials who were appointed by himself. He thus created a local bureaucracy that was loyal and, individually, not very powerful. Otto defeated the Magyars and others in Eastern Europe and then, at the invitation of the pope, he invaded Italy and defeated the king of the Lombards, who ruled northern Italy. In 962 the pope crowned Otto as Holy Roman Emperor, the title a previous pope had given Charlemagne. In the document accompanying the crowning of Otto, all future emperors were required to guarantee the pope's right to govern the Papal States, and all future papal candidates had to swear fealty to the emperors; therefore, as Holy Roman Emperor, Otto the Great was able to influence the choice of pope, govern much of Germany, and even expand beyond the normal German borders. His successors continued these privileges and forced the gradual expansion of the empire, although they were often challenged by princes who would take upon themselves the title of king of the Germans.

In 1056 a young prince was elected as Holy Roman Emperor **Henry IV (called Heinrich IV Römisher Kaiser, in German).** The Holy Roman Empire became another name for the collection of mostly German-speaking states which we commonly call Germany today. They comprised the eastern portion of Charlemagne's old empire. Sensing the weakness of the situation inherent in a very youthful emperor, the lords and barons of Germany appropriated royal lands and established independent treaties among themselves, thus weakening the power of the emperor. Several outside groups also invaded Germany and carved off peripheral territories. The church broke free of the influence of the emperor by reorganizing the method of choosing the pope—establishing the rule that the pope must be elected by the cardinals of the church. When Henry IV came to adulthood, he sought to regain the lost territory and the lost power. As we will see, he was successful in part, but created much enmity among the defeated rebellious princes and caused a strain with the church. Ultimately, the interaction between Henry IV and the Catholic Church established a weakness in the Holy Roman Empire that would never be fully repaired.

When the strongly reform-minded pope **Gregory VII** attempted to gain papal control over the local church in Germany, to the detriment of the young Henry IV, a serious conflict between the pope and the emperor ensued. Pope Gregory began to insist upon "freedom of the church" and the right of the church to handle its own affairs. As his first battle, Gregory chose the appointment of bishops. Up to this time, the king or local lord selected bishops for the region, a practice that had been insisted upon by several Roman and Byzantine Emperors as a way to ensure they had some control over the church. This practice was called **lay investiture.** Pope Gregory VII insisted that the power to appoint bishops lay solely within the church, and that the church would no longer sanction the appointment of bishops by secular authorities. To give his decree some bite, Gregory denied the right to say mass to any bishop appointed by any authority other than his own. Furthermore, Gregory threatened to excommunicate any secular ruler who ignored the edict. Holy Roman Emperor Henry IV, King Philip I of France, and the English king, William the Conqueror, all objected, but, initially, none dared act.

As time passed, Holy Roman Emperor Henry IV grew bolder, encouraged by the German bishops who were angry with Pope Gregory VII because of his harsh reforms. Eventually Henry IV ignored the papal edict and began to appoint bishops once again. When Henry refused to stop appointing bishops, Gregory excommunicated him and dissolved all oaths of fealty to Henry. The excommunication meant that Henry would not be saved in heaven and was ostracized from the general community. The cancellation of fealty oaths meant that Henry could not rely on the armies of the lords nor on their financial support, in essence, leaving his nobility to do as they pleased and throwing Germany into chaos. (This led to one of the great ironies of history, as the German clergy supported Henry against the pope, while the German nobility, in an attempt to gain more power, backed the pope against Henry).

Finding himself in a dire situation and his kingdom in disarray, Henry crossed the Alps and went to visit Pope Gregory at his mountain home. Upon arrival, Henry reportedly knelt in the snow (perhaps for several hours) and begged the pope to reinstate him, agreeing to accede to the pope's wishes. Henry was reinstated and then returned to Germany, restored order, raised an army, and marched on Rome. The war between Henry's armies and the pope's lasted for several years, but eventually Henry defeated Gregory and had the pope deposed and sent into exile. Henry then appointed a new pope, called by the Catholic Church an **anti-pope** because many, including the powerful Italian nobles, did not accept him.

Henry's victory was to be short-lived. Shortly after the appointment of the new pope, the Italian nobility rallied Pope Gregory's army and attacked Henry. This time Henry lost and was forced to abdicate his throne and title to his son, who then settled the conflict on terms favorable to the Italian nobility and papacy. Furthermore, Henry's conflict with the pope had lasting consequences that kept Germany from uniting into a nation. First, there arose out of these troubles reluctance among the German nobility to upset the pope or interfere in Italian affairs, although Holy Roman Emperors would, from time to time, attempt to exert their influence in Italy. Also, the German nobility decided to return the position of Holy Roman Emperor to an elected post, rather than an inherited monarchy, so that the emperor would be unable to act without the support of the various princes. This decision also had the unforeseen side effect of causing Germany to lose its central authority, as the center of power in Germany could be relocated with every new Holy Roman Emperor. Thus, the Holy Roman Emperor was a figurehead ruler of Germany, but in reality Germany reverted to a loose confederation of small German kingdoms. Voltaire, a famous writer of the seventeenth-century Enlightenment commented on the irony of the Holy Roman Empire by stating that it was "neither Holy, nor Roman, nor an Empire."

Various Holy Roman Emperors would attempt to unite Germany under a strong central leader, the most successful of whom was **Frederick Barbarossa** (r. 1152–1190), who conquered much of the old territory and subdued many of the princes, but died leading a crusade before he could establish a lasting dynasty. Germany would remain in this general state of weakened emperors and multiple principalities until the nineteenth century. Figure 18.3 is a map of medieval Germany showing the dozens of small states that resulted from the weak German monarch (Holy Roman Emperor).

The English Nation

From the time of their conquest over the Britons (Celts) in the seventh and eighth centuries, the history of England has been a constant struggle between the Anglo-Saxons and various powerful invaders who wanted control of the island. The Norsemen plagued much of Europe during the ninth and tenth centuries but the British Isles were the closest target by water and were hardest hit. The most important Anglo-Saxon king during this period, **Alfred the Great,** spent his entire reign fighting the Viking hordes. Much of the war went poorly for Alfred and his men. At their lowest point, King Alfred and the remaining Anglo-Saxons had been completely driven from the mainland to a tiny island off of the southern coast of England. Badly beaten and in virtual exile from his homeland, Alfred sat around a campfire and contemplated whether there was any hope or

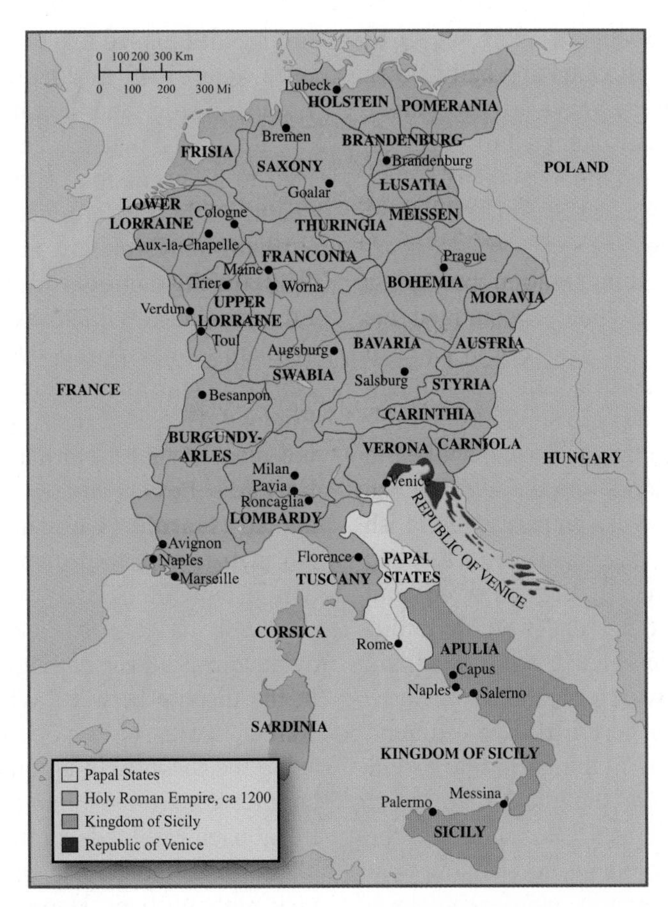

Figure 18.3 ■ The Holy Roman Empire showing the fractured nature of medieval Germany.

purpose in continuing the struggle against the Vikings. King Alfred eventually decided that he would continue the fight for his kingdom, and crossed back to mainland England, where he was able to raise a small army to add to his few remaining forces. This time Alfred and the Anglo-Saxons were more successful than before, and by the time of Alfred's death they had reclaimed the western half of England. Eastern England was called **Danelaw,** reflecting its Danish (Norse) kingship. The survival of even something of an Anglo-Saxon kingdom proved to be an even larger event than it appears to be, at least for those of English heritage. That's because if King Alfred would have been defeated, it would likely have resulted in the end of the English language.

Alfred set up an effective government over his part of England. He gave a set of laws that lasted for many years, fostered scholarship, and promoted and participated in the translation of many Latin works into English, thus giving England much of the cultural advancement that Charlemagne had given to France. For this, Alfred was called "the Great," the only English king so named. Perhaps more than other Europeans, the Anglo-Saxons assimilated the culture and language of foreign groups with whom they came in contact, either by trade or by war, leading to an enrichment of English culture that would later benefit the English by making their language and lifestyle excellent tools for creative purposes.

Alfred's son and grandson were able to drive the Danes from Danelaw and establish a unified Anglo-Saxon kingdom. The kings ruled with the assistance of a council of wise men who helped make laws and select the kings. Creatively, the kingdom was divided into about 40 **shires,** each of which was supervised by an **earl** and had its own court and **sheriff** (that is, **reeve of the shire**). Many smaller units were also created for local administration such as taxing and local court duties. This governing system was, at the time, the most effective in all of Europe.

The Anglo-Saxon administration brought a tenuous peace to England and encouraged the blending of the eastern and the western parts of England. In the blending process, the English language became richer and more subtle by assimilating parts of the Norse language, still spoken in the eastern part of England, into the Old English spoken in the west. The vocabulary of English was expanded by adding many new words that had similar meanings to existing English words but eventually took on meanings that were quite different. For example, the English word *shirt* and the Norse *skirt* originally described the same article of clothing, but later described two different, although related, items of clothing. Similar examples are the English *rear* and the Norse *raise; want* and *wish; skill* and *craft; skin* and *hide;* the list goes on. Later developments and language assimilations would further this word acquisition process and make English an extremely diverse and colorful language that could be creatively shaped and used by authors, poets, playwrights, and politicians.

Just before the year 1000, a new round of Viking invasions began. The Vikings, now warriors of a joint Danish and Norwegian kingdom, successfully drove out the English king and placed a Viking king, **Canute II,** on the throne of England. At the death of King Canute's sons, **Edward,** the Anglo-Saxon king who had been living in exile in Normandy (northern France), successfully invaded, drove out the Vikings, and made himself king over all of England. The arrival of Edward seemed to herald a new dawn of Anglo-Saxon greatness and glory in England. However, Edward had strong religious convictions (thus, the title "the Confessor") and had taken a vow of celibacy before taking the throne. Although King Edward did marry, he refused to break his vow, and it soon became obvious that no heir would be produced. This led to a chain of events that would once again have serious consequences for both English history and the English language.

Realizing that the absence of an heir could lead to a succession crisis and turmoil upon his death, King Edward declared that his cousin, William of Normandy, later known to history as **William the Conqueror,** was to be his successor. Edward chose William as a sign of gratitude to William's father, who had sheltered Edward in Normandy during the reign of the Danish kings in England. However, the Anglo-Saxon masses were not pleased that a Norman was to be their king. Edward's brother-in-law, an Anglo-Saxon duke named **Harold Godwinson,** used this anti-Norman feeling to declare himself Edward's true heir, even while King Edward was still alive.

As King Edward aged, disaster looked unavoidable as all across England people chose sides in the dispute between William and Harold. Edward sent Harold to Normandy in an effort to resolve the dispute. In an unusual twist of fate, the conflict between William and Harold looked as if it had been resolved in a most unusual way. While sailing off of the coast of France on his way to visit with William, Harold's vessel became shipwrecked. The French quickly rescued Harold, but when they discovered he was a wealthy noble and possible heir to the English throne, they held him for ransom. The ransom was paid by William of Normandy, who then held Harold prisoner himself, until Harold pledged to give up his claim to the English throne in favor of William. Taking Harold's vow seriously (it was sworn on the relic bones of a saint), William released Harold and allowed him to return to England, where he became Edward's chief counselor.

When King Edward died, Harold quickly assumed the throne for himself, thus breaking his oath, and while it is not completely clear, Edward may have actually changed his mind on his deathbed and declared for Harold. Whatever the case, both the English nobility and the commoners largely supported Harold's assumption of the throne. In Normandy, an angry William prepared to cross the English Channel and invade. He promised land in England to any knight who would join his cause. Before long William had assembled an army and built a navy to transport him and his army. Furthermore, the pope, citing Harold's broken promise to not seek the throne and King Edward's earlier declaration that William was to be his heir, publicly backed William as heir to the English crown.

Poor weather conditions delayed William's invasion of England, but it turned out to be a blessing in disguise, as the delay allowed William to strike a deal with the Vikings (who were, by this time, dominated by the Norwegians). The Norwegians agreed to attack England from the North. Harold had sent his armies south to meet William's invasion, but was forced to hurriedly send them north when the Norwegians invaded. Once Harold's forces were bogged down with the Norwegians in the north, William ordered his men across the English Channel, with the hope of sweeping up through the empty southern countryside and gaining easy victory. However, Harold was able to quickly dispatch the Norwegians and then march his troops south again to meet William. The two armies clashed at the **Battle of Hastings** near England's southern coast in 1066.

Harold's army was tired from two fast, forced marches and the battle with the Norwegians. However, William's forces were used to fighting defensive castle-warfare, not the open field style of fighting that took place in Hastings. Both sides were disadvantaged and the battle was even until William made a bold move. He instructed his troops to act as if they were defeated and retreat toward the coast. Thinking that victory was imminent, Harold's troops broke ranks and pursued the Normans in a mad rush. When William's men had gained a small rise, they reorganized with their archers on the sides of the hills while the main force slowly ascended the heights, waiting for Harold's disorganized troops to enter the valley below. Once Harold's troops were in the valley, William ordered his archers to fire and his main force to turn and attack. Harold and his forces continued to resist for a time but eventually Harold's personal guards were overcome; Harold was struck in the eye with an arrow, and killed. Soon after, Harold's forces surrendered and William was able to quickly conquer the rest of England.

The story of the conflict between William and Harold is told in a remarkable historical artifact, the **Bayeux Tapestry.** This historical masterpiece was created under the command of William. It tells the story from his point of view and was originally hung in a church in southern England to remind the Anglo-Saxons of why William's claim to the throne and his subsequent victory were favored by God. Today the tapestry hangs in a museum in Bayeux, a city in Normandy. It is unusually well preserved and the museum presentation is well done. All who travel in the area would benefit from visiting it.

Because William the Conqueror was not well loved throughout the English countryside, he appropriately took steps to solidify his power. He ordered a series of castles to be built to allow him to more easily control the English peasants. A typical Norman castle was made of stone whereas the Anglo-Saxons built timbered forts. Such a Norman castle is shown in Figure 18.4. William also took personal possession of all conquered lands, but wisely did not immediately remove all the Anglo-Saxon lords from their lands. Instead, William allowed Anglo-Saxon lords who would support him to keep their lands and titles, and gave the lands of those who would not to the knights who had fought for him. William also did not change the local infrastructure. He kept the office of sheriff as the local authority and link between the king and the local area, but did slowly replace the sheriffs with his loyal Norman supporters. William also secured his authority over the church, by giving the church gifts of land and only appointing Norman bishops. Thus, William quickly placed Normans in control of most aspects of English life without changing the structure of English daily life. Then, William ordered a complete census of his new holdings so that he would have an accurate idea of what exactly he ruled over. William's extensive census came to be known as the **Doomsday Book** (or Domeday Book) from the Anglo-Saxon word for judgment—doom. It was a population census and tax list that also recorded all of the possessions in the country, including animals and machinery. The Doomsday Book has been an invaluable historical reference giving insights into life in the medieval period.

Figure 18.4 ■ A typical Norman castle built to dominate the area near Bamburgh, England. *© 2010 by Kevin Eaves. Used under license of Shutterstock, Inc.*

After William's death there was a period of turmoil as his three sons fought among themselves for control of William's two kingdoms (Normandy and England). William had given Normandy to his oldest son and England to his second son, but left nothing to his youngest son, Henry. Due to a "terrible accident" when Henry and his brother were hunting together, the older brother was killed and Henry assumed the English throne as **Henry I of England.** Henry then conquered his other brother in Normandy and claimed both kingdoms for himself. Henry never had a son, so he chose his daughter, **Matilda,** as his heir. Upon his death Matilda tried to claim the English and Norman thrones but was opposed by a group of other claimants (especially her cousin **Stephan,** who became king for a short time) and the council of the lords. Eventually the crisis was resolved when Matilda agreed to give up her claim to the thrones in favor of her son, **Henry II of England** who succeeded Stephen.

Matilda was married to **Geoffrey of Anjou,** the ruler of a large area in France, thus Henry II became ruler over all of England, Normandy, and Anjou when the agreement was struck between Matilda and the English nobility to allow Henry II to take the throne. Henry had even larger designs, and planned to create influence for his family throughout Europe. First, he married **Eleanor of Aquitaine,** who was heiress to Aquitaine, another large French province. Eleanor had been married to the French king but the marriage was annulled when Eleanor reputedly had an affair while she and her first husband had been on a crusade. With his marriage to Eleanor, Henry controlled all of England and much (roughly half) of France. Henry also made politically astute marriages for his daughters, marrying them to the heirs of **Brittany** (another region of France), **Castile** (a territory in Spain), and **Sicily** (an Italian province) in an attempt to gain those thrones for his descendants.

Henry II also made changes to the English judicial system by creating **English common law,** which based the law on precedent rather than a code like the Code of Justinian that was still used by most European countries. Henry also introduced the concept of **trial by jury,** which he found to be more fair than **trial by ordeal,** the previous standard, which was still used across much of Europe. For example, under trial by ordeal, the accused might be dunked in water (considered to be a pure substance) and if they were guilty, the pure water would reject them, causing them to float; if the accused were innocent, they would be taken into the pure water and would sink (but maybe not live). The use of this system highlights the degree to which medieval Europe placed a greater emphasis on the afterlife than on earthly life, as it was excusable for the innocent to die because they were being freed from the hardship and toil of this life. The ending of the practice of trial by ordeal was a signal that medieval thinking was beginning to give way.

Henry's changes to the secular judicial system were generally accepted. However, Henry's attempts to make changes to the church met with greater opposition. Upset that clerics who committed crimes could not be tried in a secular court (under his jurisdiction), Henry demanded that the church change its policy, which stated that the clergy could only be tried in a church court. When the church refused to give in to Henry's demand, Henry appointed his good friend and political ally, **Thomas à Becket,** as the new **Bishop of Canterbury,** the highest religious position in England, so that he would have a supporter within the church. Once appointed, however, Becket took his new position seriously and, fearing to offend God, did everything in his power to defend the rights of the church, refusing to support Henry in his argument with the pope. Infuriated, Henry felt betrayed by his old friend. In a fit of frustration one day, Henry cried out, "Who will rid me of this pestilent cleric?" Unfortunately, four knights, eager to impress Henry with their loyalty, took him at his word and killed Thomas à Becket not far from the altar at Canterbury Cathedral. This act turned Becket into a martyr for the church (he was sainted) and a hero to the peasantry. Soon **Canterbury Cathedral** was one of the most popular pilgrimage destinations. The death of Becket made King Henry look like an ungodly monster; in the end he lost his battle with the church and submitted to a church-sanctioned punishment in order to save face and keep from being overly vilified by his own people.

Despite an attempt by his wife Eleanor to have Henry's kingdom divided among their sons upon his death, Henry's eldest son, **Richard I, the Lionhearted,** inherited the kingdom. Richard, however, was a pious man, and spent most of his life away from England, fighting in the crusades to reclaim the Holy Land from the Muslims (or languishing in prison waiting to be ransomed). While he was away, his younger brother **Prince John** (of the **Robin Hood** stories) ruled, although their mother Eleanor was the real power behind the throne. When Richard later died in yet another foreign battle, Eleanor made sure John inherited the throne.

After Eleanor's death, John's ineptitude led to disputes with both the church and his nobles. John disliked the church's nominee to be the new Archbishop of Canterbury and refused to appoint him, upsetting the church, which had great latitude in these matters since Becket's martyrdom and King Henry's submission. When John continued his defiance of the church, the pope decided to force the situation, and forbade any church services in England, thus, in the eyes of the faithful, denying the saving ordinances to all people. Under this intense pressure King John capitulated, but the relationship between church and state in England had been further damaged.

King John, probably sensing his own weakness and wanting to secure his power, refused to recognize many of the rights and privileges that the barons and other nobility had long enjoyed. The nobility also resented King John because he established high taxes in order to pay for his continuous wars with France, in which England had lost Normandy to the aggressive French king. The unrest of the nobility became so severe that the nobles drew up a document, **Magna Carta,** limiting the powers of the king, which the lords forced John to sign in the year 1215.

Magna Carta was a **bill of rights,** guaranteeing certain rights for the English nobility and limiting the power of John and all future English monarchs. It also guaranteed rights to the church. Magna Carta was a creative masterstroke in the field of political science. The signing of Magna Carta empowered and emboldened the English nobility, who then worked to gain further control over the English kings. King John's son, **Henry III of England,** tried to ignore the restrictions placed upon him by the Magna Carta. However, like his father, Henry was a weak king, and his nobility created administrative devices to ensure that the rights promised them in the Magna Carta were granted. One of the provisions of Magna Carta was that a council of nobles, or **parliament,** was to help the king govern. When King Henry III rejected this idea, the nobles refused to grant the king any money. (The nobles were the chief means of collecting taxes and thus controlled the ability of the Crown to get money.) This established the principle that parliament controls the king's purse strings. Five years later parliament tried to further limit the king, but this time the nobles' revolt was crushed. However, the principle of parliament as a limiting factor of the king continued to grow. Although Magna Carta was often ignored or circumvented by later monarchs, over time it was strengthened, and became the basis of English government. Thus, with Magna Carta, the English created the basis of limited-power government.

The Italian Nation

Rather than coalescing into a single political entity, Italy saw the rise of powerful city-states. The largest and most important of these, at least in the early to mid-medieval period, was the city of **Venice,** a key center for trade among Europe, the Byzantine Empire, and the Far East. The growth of the Italian trade cities was an important development for Europe, as the cultural and intellectual interaction that began to take place between Europe, Byzantium, and the Far East helped to force open and revive European society and creativity. The city of Venice dates from the late Roman Empire but was organized into a republic in 697 when the first Duke *(Doge)* was elected. This was during the time of Byzantine dominance of Italy and so the Duke was directly responsible to Ravenna, the Byzantine capital in Italy, and ultimately responsible to the Byzantine emperor. When Ravenna and most of Italy fell to the barbarian Lombards, Venice was not conquered, and remained affiliated with the Byzantine Empire. However, the distance between Venice and Byzantium, and the chaotic condition of Lombard Italy, kept Venice isolated and led to a semi-autonomous status. In the tenth century, Venice signed treaties with the Muslims, thus acting in opposition to the official position of the Byzantines. The gradual decline of the Byzantine Empire led to greater Venetian independence until, in the thirteenth century, Venice had become the most important trading center of Europe, politically independent of Byzantium.

Venice grew in importance because of its location as a crossroad between trade in the east and west. It was, throughout the period, the favored port for Byzantium trade with Europe, and also became the favored port for Muslim entry to Europe. During the period of the crusades and the European presence in the Holy Land, Venice was one of the major ports for shipping goods from Europe to the Holy Land. With the continuing military pressure on Constantinople from the Muslims and other groups such as the **Bulgars,** Venice developed its own trade system with the Orient.

Foremost among the Venetian oriental traders was **Marco Polo.** The Polo's were already a wealthy trading family when Marco Polo, along with his father and uncle, left on a trip to China. While in China, Marco Polo found favor with the Khan and became an advisor and eventually an ambassador for the Khan's government. Marco Polo was also a keen observer of the Chinese people and lifestyle, and kept notes of what he saw. Eventually, after 20 years, Marco Polo decided to return to Venice. At the time of his arrival, Venice was at war with the rival trading city of Genoa. On the way home he was captured by the Genoans and imprisoned. It was while in prison in Genoa that Marco Polo consolidated his notes and wrote his famous book *Travels.*

Throughout its history, Venice took several creative steps to glorify the city, gain prestige in the eyes of the world, and protect trade, which was the key to the city's success. The Venetians perfected the technology of driving massive pilings into the soft ground and then building atop the pilings so that their buildings would have solid foundations. This technique allowed them to continue to occupy the muddy islands that were such an excellent trading location, but were so difficult to build on. Wishing to gain prestige by having a famous patron saint, they stole the body of **St. Mark** from Alexandria in Egypt, where Mark had gone for missionary work and died. At the time, Alexandria was under the control of the Muslims and so, to ensure that they would not be stopped in their thievery, they packed the bones in barrels of pickled pork which, of course, is forbidden for Muslims to eat or even touch. Thus they were able to take the bones to Venice, where they constructed a great cathedral, based on the elaborate Byzantine style, to house Mark's body. The cathedral was next to the *doge's* palace, which was surrounded by a lovely plaza they named **Piazza San Marco** in honor of their new patron saint. Venice built the most powerful navy in the Mediterranean to protect their trading interests. Perhaps because of their success, Venetian government was remarkably stable. The *doge* was elected by a small city council of wealthy and powerful families. This group ruled the city in what has become the model example of an **oligarchy** (rule by a small elite).

The intense rivalry among the various Italian trading cities kept Italy from beginning to unify into a nation. The Italian situation was further complicated by the existence of the church-controlled Papal States in the middle of the peninsula and a separately ruled kingdom, Sicily and Naples, at the southern end. All of the city-states looked to Rome for religious direction, but they all feared Roman domination as well, and guarded their independence fiercely.

The earliest trading rival to Venice was **Genoa.** Its location at the northern end of the Ligurian Sea is similar to the location of Venice, except on the western side of the Italian peninsula, whereas Venice is on the eastern side. Genoese merchants traded in the eastern part of the Mediterranean and gained important trade concessions in Constantinople in the twelfth century, but the focus of Genoa was western Europe and North Africa.

Florence, located in the central section of northern Italy, is landlocked, although the area of dominance of Florence extended to the coast at Pisa, south of Genoa. Florence was focused on agricultural trade, especially wool, for its main industry. The Florentines developed strong trading relationships throughout Europe, and especially with the fabric-making centers of Flanders (in the low countries). The Florentines used their profits to establish important banks, which financed much of the growth in Europe that occurred after the year 1000. The growth of power, money, and influence in Florence in the late Middle Ages set the stage for the emergence of Florence as the leading cultural center of Italy and the birthplace of the Renaissance, but that is a story told in another place.

Central Italy was dominated by the Papal States, an area traditionally ruled by the pope, who claimed territorial authority from the times of the Roman emperors.

> *The foundation of the Pope's political claims was the* Donation of Constantine—*a document by which the Emperor Constantine the Great had allegedly divided the Roman Empire in two, transferred imperial authority over the Western Provinces to Bishop Sylvester of Rome and his successors, and reserved for himself only the eastern empire, governed from his newly-founded capital of "Constantinople." By the 1430s, the authenticity of this document had been accepted without question for more than five hundred years: in mediaeval political thought it had occupied a place like that of the Declaration of Independence in the American constitution today. Scholars now believe that the* Donation *was counterfeited during the eighth-century—possibly at a time when Pope Paul I was anxious to cut his ties with the iconoclastic authorities of the Byzantine Empire.*[2]

The popes fought several wars to defend their position as ruler of the Papal States. The size of the territory governed by the pope grew and declined with the various invasions of Germanic tribes, Byzantines, Holy Roman Emperors, and others, but the nominal existence of a papal state continued throughout the Middle Ages.

Southern Italy was ruled by several different groups during the Middle Ages. Known as the **Kingdom of Naples and Sicily** (sometimes united and sometimes separate from each other), it came under the domination of the Muslims, the Normans, the Germans, the Spanish, the Austrians, and the French.

Italy's location as a crossroad for trade and travel forced Italians to interact with other cultures, and spurred the creativity of the region. Furthermore, the rise of city-states sparked creativity in each region, as the city-states vied for power and prestige against one another and with other parts of Europe. A vibrant and creative Italy, through its focus on trade and survival, was forced to leave behind medieval thinking sooner than the other parts of Europe. But some events within Europe forced a new awareness, brought about by the movement of people across Europe into the Holy Land, their interactions with the various societies of the Mediterranean basin, and the awakening they gave to the rest of Europe upon their return. We speak, of course, of the crusades.

The Crusades

The origins of the crusades grew out of the battles between the Byzantines and the **Seljuk Turks** in the late eleventh century. The Seljuks, who were Muslims, had conquered Baghdad and much of the territory we call the Holy Land, including the city of Jerusalem. The fierceness of the Seljuks and their seeming disregard for Christians led the Byzantine emperor to issue a call for all Christians to unite in driving the Seljuks from the Holy Land. The Byzantine emperor also wanted to regain the territory that he had lost to the Seljuks.

At just this time, the eleventh century, Europeans were reawakening from the darkness of the early medieval period and therefore had more money and a desire for luxury goods that could be obtained from Byzantium and the Orient. Europeans saw the Seljuks as barriers to that trade. Furthermore, the nations of Europe had become stronger, and their kings desired to increase their prestige further by being the heroes who might secure the Holy Land for Christianity. A further factor that led to the crusades was the growing influence of the popes, who had exerted their influence in several confrontations with various European kings, as we have previously discussed in this chapter.

Muslims had controlled Jerusalem and the surrounding regions since the eighth century, but the Seljuk Turks were more militant than the previous rulers. The Byzantine emperor convinced the pope that action must be taken to maintain Christian access to the Holy Land. It was in this environment that **Pope Urban II** decided to call for a holy crusade to free the Holy Land from Muslim control. Pope Urban urged all knights to stop fighting each other and to band together in a common cause to free the Holy Land, which included Jerusalem and all the area surrounding it, even as far north as Syria (which is the area the Byzantine emperor wanted returned to him). To encourage Christians to volunteer, the pope offered **indulgences** (forgiveness of sins—past and future) to those who would go and fight. Enthusiasm for the crusades swept across Europe and thousands of knights, nobles, and peasants volunteered. And while the crusades would help open up Europe and bring an end to medieval thinking, the crusades were still a truly medieval institution. The crusades demonstrated medieval Europe's complete focus on the Catholic Church and the will of God, as warring nations and starving peasants alike stopped what they were doing to go and fight a holy war in a faraway land. (Can you imagine how different the reaction would be to such a call by the pope today?)

Knights and other crusaders marched across Europe in 1096 (the **First Crusade**), gathering strength as they went. By the time the crusaders reached the Holy Land they were a massive military force infused with tremendous religious zeal, and by 1099 most of the Holy Land, including Syria on the north and all of present-day Lebanon and Israel, plus much of Jordan and some of Egypt, had fallen to the Christian crusaders. The crusaders then established a European-style kingdom in Jerusalem and dependent kingdoms in other parts of the Holy Land. They crowned a king and selected lords and barons to serve as his vassals. The Europeans did not, however, give control of any of the newly conquered territories to the

Byzantine emperor. The emperor felt betrayed, and grew ever more resentful toward the crusaders. Eventually, the emperor even entered an alliance with the Muslims against the crusaders; as a result, Constantinople was sacked by the crusaders in one of the later crusades.

In light of their humiliating defeat, the Muslim community began a series of political maneuvers among the various factions and, eventually, a military leader (who was a Kurd) emerged as the Islamic leader. His name was **Saladin.** Taking advantage of the difficulties that the crusaders were having in supplying their crusader states in the Holy Land, and of the ineptness of some of the crusader military leaders who remained (after the conquerors returned to Europe), Saladin was able to reconquer Jerusalem and much of the land lost to the First Crusade.

Several more crusades received papal approval between 1100 and 1270, but all failed to reclaim the Holy Land, and most were disastrous embarrassments for the Europeans. The routes of the crusades are shown in Figure 18.5. During the **Third Crusade** the three most powerful kings of Europe—Richard the Lion-Hearted of England, Phillip Augustus of France, and Frederick Barbarosa of Germany—and others, volunteered to fight, but they arrived at different times and refused to coordinate their activities. Hence, Saladin was able to withstand their attacks. Richard was on the verge of reconquering Jerusalem when he was forced to seek a settlement with Saladin because Richard received word that his brother John, who was ruling in Richard's place, was attempting to make his kingship permanent. Then, to his horror, Richard was captured on the way home and held for ransom by a previous ally, the king of Austria, who was offended by Richard's arrogance during the crusade battles. The ransom was paid and Richard returned to England and set John aside. However, as we have already discussed, Richard was killed in a battle in Europe and John inherited the throne.

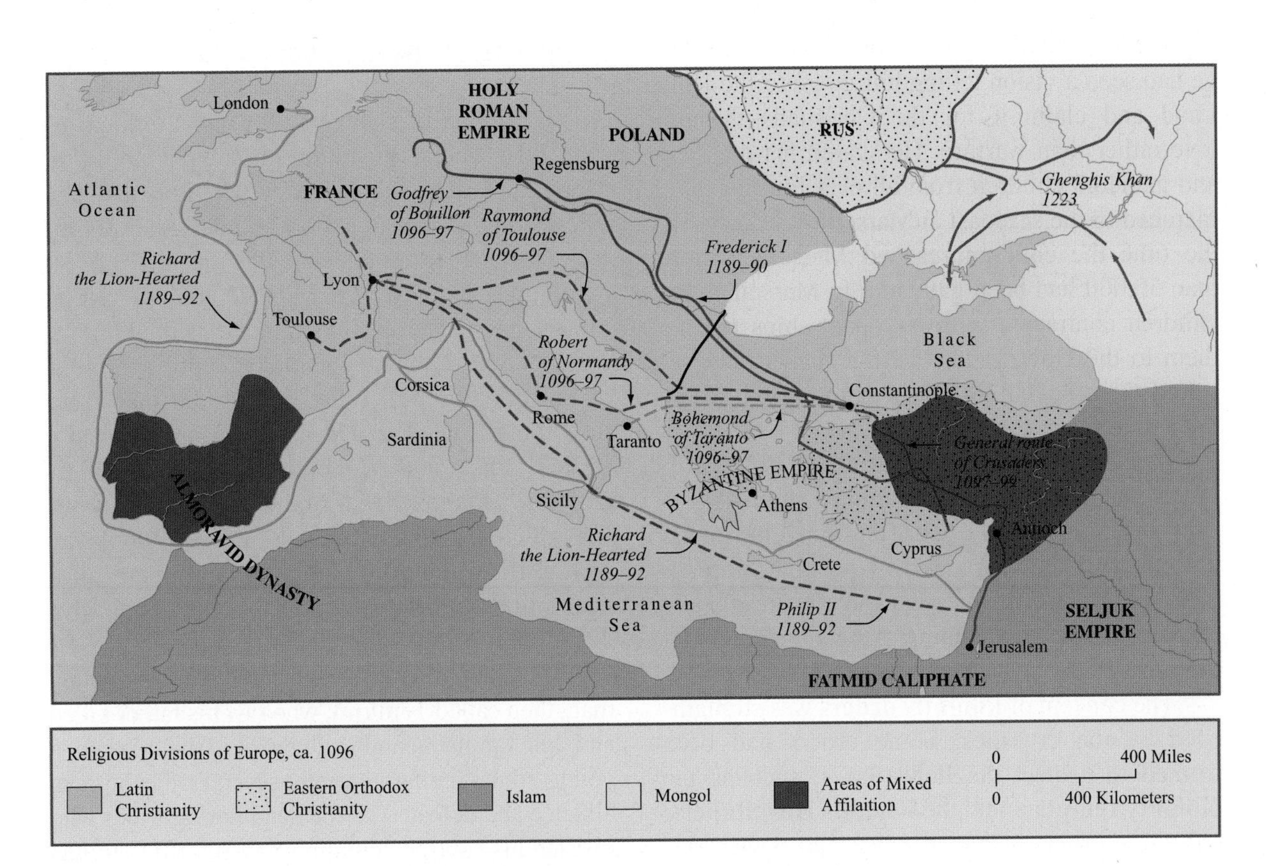

Figure 18.5 ■ *Routes of the crusades.*

The crusaders in the **Fourth Crusade** were so poor that they could not afford transport from Venice to Jerusalem. A deal was struck with the Venetian shipmasters that the crusaders could gain free passage if they would attack the city of **Zara** and give it to the Venetians, who wanted Zara for its lumber to build ships. Zara, however, was a Christian city, thus ending the goals of the crusades to only attack Muslims. In the end, the city of Zara was conquered and given to the control of Venice; the crusaders were never taken to Jerusalem, but instead were dropped off at Constantinople, where they sacked the city and then returned home to Europe when the Byzantine emperor, after several years, was able to mount an army and drive the crusaders from the city.

Later crusades were even more pointless and disastrous. One later crusade called for by the pope was against a small heretical group in southern France, and had nothing to do with reclaiming the Holy Land from Muslim control. Probably the most tragic of the crusades was the **Children's Crusade,** begun by a young boy who claimed that he had seen a vision telling him to go to the Holy Land and claim it for the Christians through love rather than warfare. He shared his message and gathered children from all over Europe as he marched to the seacoast at Marseilles, France. By the time the children reached Marseilles more than 30,000 had been gathered. In Marseilles the children contracted with merchant ships to take them to the Holy Land. The merchants then betrayed them by sailing to northern Africa, where the children were sold into slavery.

In spite of the eventual expulsion of the crusaders from the Holy Land and the many lost lives in trying to establish a Christian kingdom there, the effect of the crusades was positive, because they brought new knowledge back to Europe and accelerated the reawakening that had begun about the year 1000.

The concept of **knightly orders** was strengthened by the crusades. Some orders had been formed to protect the holy places, such as the **Knights Templars** and the **Knights Hospitaliers,** and these orders gained prestige and power as a result of the crusades. The knights in these orders took vows of loyalty and righteous living, much like monks, except that the intent was not to spread the word of God through preaching but to fight for God in foreign lands. Gradually these orders became so powerful that they were a threat to the kings of Europe, and the kings expelled the orders from their territories. Some knights fled to Cyprus, Malta, and northern Germany, where they continued their strong influence for many years.

Other knights, not members of orders, were also strengthened by the crusades. To control these knights proved somewhat easier than the orders, since these knights were sworn to fealty to lords and to the kings. They were required to live according to strict rules of behavior that had existed in tradition for generations and were codified in 1275 in a book entitled *Book of the Order of Chivalry.* For the next 200 years, the chivalrous knights set the standard for proper behavior of the ruling-warring class in Europe.

Mongol Invasions

Another influx of change swept into Europe, this time from across the Eurasian steppes and Ural Mountains, in the form of the Mongol invaders. The **Mongols** were a vicious and devastating military force that established the world's largest, contiguous land empire, but had limited lasting impact on the European continent, as they left almost as quickly as they came (except for regions in Eastern Europe). What Europe did take from the Mongols were new ideas in warfare and battle strategy, and a general wonderment at how differently the Mongols lived. And while the Europeans did not choose to adopt much of the Mongol way of life, the Mongol invasion did help open European minds to the possibility that they could live differently from the old medieval way.

The **Mongol Empire** began with a poor young man, then called **Temujin,** who saw his father killed and his family abandoned by his tribe. When a young adult, Temujin brought several tribes into an alliance and defeated all the neighboring tribes who resisted his control. Temujin was renamed **Genghis Khan** ("great leader") and began a process of plunder over an ever-increasing area. His troops conquered all of central Asia and then successfully invaded China, beginning the Yuan Dynasty. The Mongol armies, under Genghis Khan's successors, his sons, divided into two groups. The southern group attacked the Muslims and eventually sacked Baghdad; the northern group attacked Europe, conquered Kiev and Poland, and reached the gates of Vienna, where they were finally stopped.

The Mongols were superb horsemen who fought fiercely from horseback. It is reported that the Mongols could travel faster than any other cavalry force in history. In the desert, when other groups would have to stop and find water, the Mongols reportedly would nick the necks of their horses and drink the horses' blood to survive. One wonders at the endurance of the horses under this treatment. The terror of facing a Mongol horde was increased because they so effectively and creatively used intimidation as a weapon as well. The Mongols were so effective that the Europeans called them **Tartars,** meaning "those from Hell." The Mongols sent spies ahead of their main force, to spread rumors of the terrible atrocities inflicted on those who resisted the Mongol armies. When in battle, they used fierce war cries to scare their enemy, and often purposely killed their enemies' children so that they could not later seek revenge.

The Mongol soldiers were superbly trained for both infantry and cavalry warfare, and promoted according to skill rather than family connections (unlike in Europe). The cavalry and infantry were drilled to work together to defeat an enemy (again in Europe this was not the case; the cavalry, which was the nobility, would fight the other side's cavalry, while the peasant infantry fought the other peasant infantry). Furthermore, the Mongols developed a system of mounted messengers and signal flags to keep communication flowing during battles. They were deadly and efficient warriors, and the Europeans eventually adopted many of their tactics. The Mongols eventually established the largest contiguous land kingdom in history as shown in Figure 18.6.

The transition of ideas between Europe and the Mongols flowed both ways. However, the

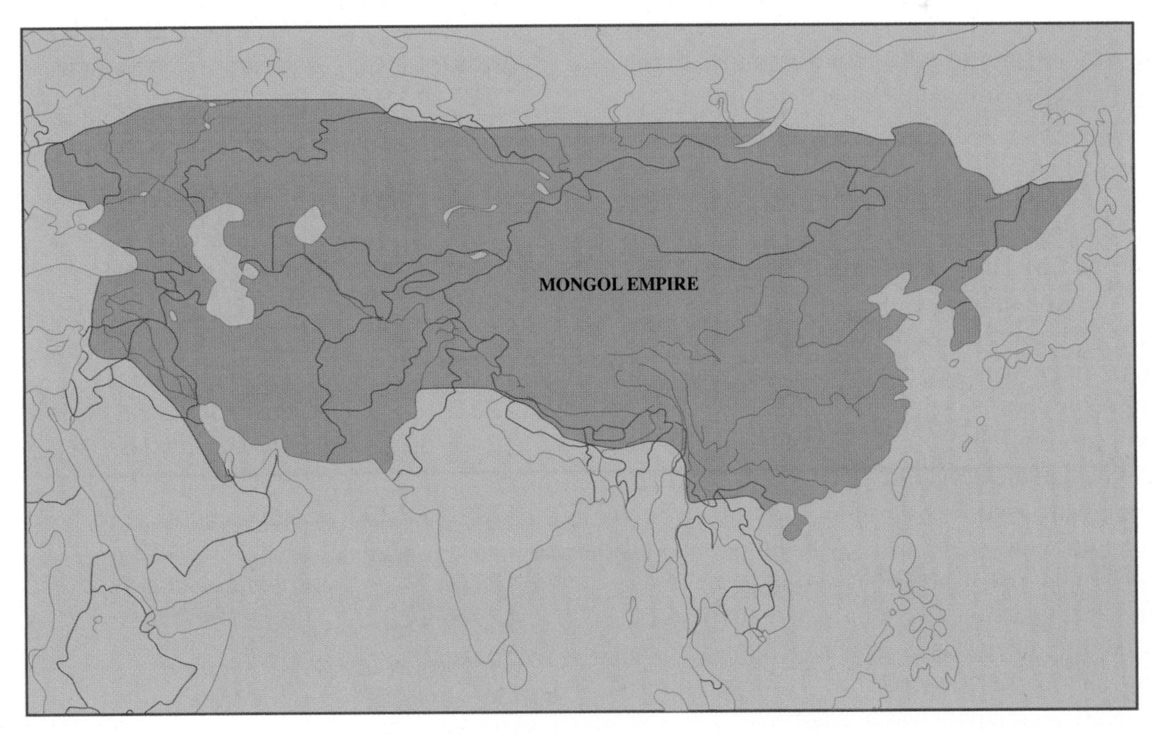

Figure 18.6 ■ The Mongol Empire

Khans were unable to keep what they conquered in Europe, because they had never learned to settle down, establish bureaucracy, and govern.

A Mongol leader in China, **Kublai Khan,** decided to spend less energy fighting and more energy governing. Kublai Khan established an elaborate bureaucratic system to help govern the large territory the Mongols had conquered, and to collect the profits from their control of the trade routes. Kublai Khan's acceptance of Marco Polo was in part an attempt to better understand European culture and government so that he could more effectively govern his empire. The Mongols in China were never well accepted by the Chinese people, especially the ruling bureaucrats, who had tremendous power in the Chinese government.

Toward the Future

Make no mistake—the later medieval period was still medieval. Daily life was still mostly mundane, occasionally dangerous, and always difficult. Education and intellectual thought still revolved around the Catholic Church. Opportunity for change and advancement was nearly nonexistent. Yet, in spite of what was the same, Europe slowly became different. Out of the political chaos of the early medieval period came the rise of nations. While still primarily based on feudalism, governments of the nations provided better security, an identification with a king (which instilled pride and a sense of belonging), a set of laws (which gave stability), and greater trade (which led to improvement in daily life). Via trade, crusades, and expansion, increased travel and better communication slowly began to be a part of European life. This progress, combined with improvements in agriculture, led to a rebirth of towns, which led to even more travel, trade, and communication. European civilization was definitely on the rise. It was able to wage wars in distant lands (wars that were only partially successful) and to defend itself against foreign invaders (also only partially successful). However, clearly the trend of creativity was upward.

Timeline—Important Dates

Date	Event
871–901 A.D.	*Reign of Alfred the Great of England*
962	*Otto I crowned Holy Roman Emperor in Germany*
987	*Hugh Capet begins reign as French king*
About 1000	*Warmer weather and other factors lead to increase in towns*
1066	*William I of Normandy successfully invades England*
1088	*Pope Gregory VII elected, conflict with Henry IV*
1096–1099	*First Crusade, ends in capture of Jerusalem*
1133–1189	*Henry II rules England*
1145–1149	*Second Crusade, led by Louis VII of France*
1152–1190	*Frederick I (Barbarossa) rules in Germany*
1162–1294	*Mongols raid in Asia, Middle East, and Europe*
About 1185	*Invention of the windmill*
1187–1192	*Third Crusade, led by Richard I, Frederick I, Phillip II*
1198–1204	*Fourth Crusade, sacks Constantinople*
1199–1216	*John rules England*
1202	Liber Abaci *establishes Arabic/Indian numerals*
1212	*Children's Crusade*
1215	*Signing of* Magna Carta
1217–1221	*Fifth Crusade, against Egypt*
1228–1229	*Sixth Crusade*
1248–1254	*Seventh Crusade*
1270	*Eighth Crusade*
1275–1292	*Marco Polo travels to China*

Notes

1. Bernstein, Peter L., *Against the Gods,* New York: Wiley, 1996, XXIV–XXVII (extracted).
2. Toulmin, Stephen and June Goodfield, *The Discovery of Time,* University of Chicago Press, 1965, 104–105.

Suggested Readings

Bernstein, Peter L., *Against the Gods,* Wiley, 1996.

Breay, Claire, *Magna Carta: Myths and Manuscripts,* British Library, 2002.

Chambers, James, *The Devil's Horsemen,* Atheneum, 1979.

Crosby, Alfred W., *The Measure of Reality,* Cambridge University Press, 1997.

Toulmin, Stephen and June Goodfield, *The Discovery of Time,* University of Chicago Press, 1965.

Tuchman, Barbara, *Bible and Sword,* New York University Press, 1956.

Article 31
Magna Carta

Introduction

Magna Carta was intended originally as a temporary solution to a standoff between a king and his barons, and not as the famed basis for present-day English Law. The nobility of England was fed up with over-taxation, losing wars with France, disputes between the king and the church, and poor legal representation. At the root of it all, though, was the power of the monarchy itself. The monarch believed that his power was based on divine right. The barons believed that the power should be limited. The church claimed that its power should be exercised independent of the king. When King John (ruled 1199–1216) was forced to sign *Magna Carta* by his barons, however, he assumed that he would be able to reprieve it shortly after and put the business behind him. The balance of power between the monarchs and barons would tilt either way for many years, but some of the principle rights in *Magna Carta* would survive through the centuries and remain in English Law.

Perhaps the three most significant changes in *Magna Carta* are presented below. They are:

1. The church's independence from secular law (article 1)
2. Right to a fair trial for the accused before any punishment (article 39)
3. The election of Parliament to ensure these rights for all (article 61)

Magna Carta should be read in light of other legal codes (such as the Code of Hammurabi and the Justinian Code) as well as modern legal codes.

Magna Carta

John, by the grace of God King of England, Lord of Ireland, Duke of Normandy and Aquitaine, and Count of Anjou, to his archbishops, bishops, abbots, earls, barons, justices, foresters, sheriffs, stewards, servants and to all his officials and loyal subjects, Greeting.

Know that before God, for the health of our soul and those of our ancestors and heirs, to the honour of God, the exaltation of the holy Church and the better ordering of our kingdom, at the advice of our reverend fathers Stephen, archbishop of Canterbury, primate of all England, and cardinal of the holy Roman Church. Henry archbishop of Dublin, William bishop of London, Peter bishop of Winchester, Jocelin bishop of Bath and Glastonbury. Hugh bishop of Lincoln. Walter bishop of Worcester. William bishop of Coventry. Benedict bishop of Rochester. Master Pandulf subdeacon and member of the papal household, Brother Aymeric master of the knighthood of the Temple in England. William Marshal earl of Pembroke, William earl of Salisbury, William earl of Warren, William earl of Arundel, Alan de

Galloway constable of Scotland, Warin Fitz Gerald, Peter Fitz Herbert, Hubert de Burgh seneschal of Poitou, Hugh de Neville, Matthew Fitz Herbert, Thomas Basset, Alan Basset, Philip Daubeny. Robert de Roppeley, John Marshal, John Fitz Hugh, and other loyal subjects:

1. First that we have granted to God, and by this present charter have confirmed for us and our heirs in perpetuity, that the English Church shall be free, and shall have its rights undiminished, and its liberties unimpaired. That we wish this so to be observed, appears from the fact that of our own free will, before the outbreak of the present dispute between us and our barons, we granted and confirmed by charter the freedom of the Church's elections—a right reckoned to be of the greatest necessity and importance to it—and caused this to be confirmed by Pope Innocent III. This freedom we shall observe ourselves, and desire to be observed in good faith by our heirs in perpetuity.
To all free men of our kingdom we have also granted, for us and our heirs for ever, all the liberties written out below, to have and to keep for them and their heirs, of us and our heirs:

39. No free man shall be seized or imprisoned, or stripped of his rights or possessions, or outlawed or exiled, or deprived of his standing in any other way, nor will we proceed with force against him, or send others to do so, except by the lawful judgement of his equals or by the law of the land.

61. Since we have granted all these things for God, for the better ordering of our kingdom, and to allay the discord that has arisen between us and our barons, and since we desire that they shall be enjoyed in their entirety, with lasting strength, for ever, we give and grant to the barons the following security:

The barons shall elect twenty-five of their number to keep, and cause to be observed with all their might, the peace and liberties granted and confirmed to them by this charter.

The twenty-five barons shall swear to obey all the above articles faithfully, and shall cause them to be obeyed by others to the best of their power.

We will not seek to procure from anyone, either by our own efforts or those of a third party, anything by which any part of these concessions or liberties might be revoked or diminished. Should such a thing be procured, it shall be null and void and we will at no time make use of it, either ourselves or through a third party.

63. It is accordingly our wish and command that the English Church shall be free, and that men in our kingdom shall have and keep all these liberties, rights, and concessions, well and peaceably in their fulness and entirety for them and their heirs, of us and our heirs, in all things and all places for ever.

Both we and the barons have sworn that all this shall be observed in good faith and without deceit. Witness the abovementioned people and many others.

Given by our hand in the meadow that is called Runnymede, between Windsor and Staines, on the fifteenth day of June in the seventeenth year of our reign *(i.e. 1215: the new regnal year began on 28 May).*

Church and University
Creative Thinking

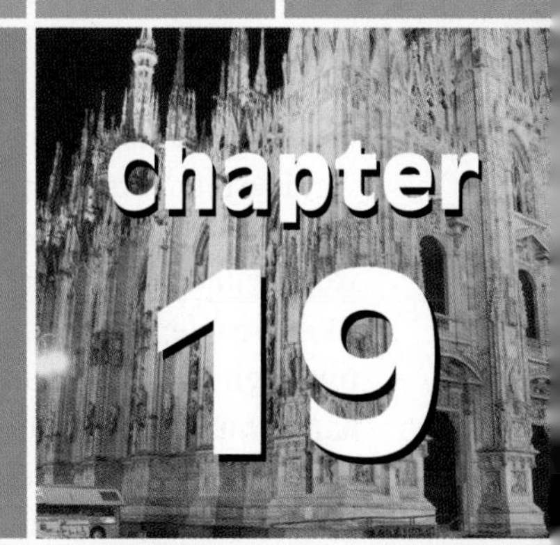

> Demonstration [of the existence of God] can be made in two ways: One is through the cause, and is called "a priory," and this is to argue from what is prior absolutely. The other is through the effect, and is called a demonstration "a posteriori"; this is to argue from what is prior relatively only to us. When an effect is better known to us than its cause, from the effect we proceed to the knowledge of the cause. And from every effect the existence of its proper cause can be demonstrated, so long as its effects are better known to us; because since every effect depends upon its cause, if the effect exists, the cause must pre-exist. Hence the existence of God, in so far as it is not self-evident to us, can be demonstrated from those of His effects which are known to us.
>
> —*Thomas Aquinas, Summa Theologica*

Religious Life at the New Millennium

As the end of the first millennium following the birth of Christ approached, the medieval mindset and its complete fixation on religion as an escape from life's difficulties and drudgery completely engulfed Europe. Many people believed that the year 1000 A.D. would be the end of the world, and that Christ would return and establish his kingdom on Earth. Others thought that the millennium marked the time when Satan would be let loose on the world (as if life in medieval times was not bad enough) based on the following passage from the Book of Revelation, "And I saw an angel come down from heaven having the key of the bottomless pit and a great chain in his hand. And he laid hold on the dragon, that old serpent, which is the Devil, and Satan, and bound him a thousand years . . . and after that he must be loosed a little season." (Revelation 20:1–3)

Anxiety swept across Europe, and regardless of whether one believed 1000 A.D. marked the second coming of Christ or the season of release of the Devil, many believed that the end of the earth as then known was imminent. During the last part of the tenth century, the devout took to the streets, crying repentance and making demonstrations of remorse for sin and hope for salvation. As the century drew to a close, much business and industry simply stopped, as people saw no point in undertaking any enterprises except the most temporary.

Despite their darkest predictions or greatest hopes, the start of the new millennium came and went without any major occurrence in the lives of most people. Europe as a whole breathed a collective sigh of relief. However, the entire millennial experience caused many Christians to reassess their personal lives, goals, and values. This reassessment caused an outburst of energy and creativity. In the last chapter we saw how warmer weather and new technologies led to an increase in city life and to the foundation of nations, both of which helped move Europe out of the dark ages and toward a better era. In this chapter we will examine the changes in the Catholic Church that began about the year 1000, and how those changes affected the religious life of the people and led to a dramatic change in the way scholars thought about religion and, ultimately, the world in general.

Personal Reform and Pilgrimages

Although Christians viewed the sacraments of the Catholic Church as necessary for salvation, many people felt that they needed a more direct contact with God to purge themselves of their sins. As we have already noted, one path to this purgation was the crusades, especially in light of the indulgence (forgiveness of sins) promised by the pope for all those who would join and fight. For others who did not want to fight, the **pilgrimage** was the ultimate reforming act. Some went on pilgrimage because their priest had mandated it as an act of penance for sin; some clergy went because they felt it was a fulfillment of their vows; others went on their own initiative, just to be more holy; and still others, perhaps, went for the adventure.

With the rise of nations and the accompanying strengthening of central authority, the roads were safer, so travel was not such a frightening experience. To be sure, there were still robbers and bandits, not to mention deceptive innkeepers and other rogues along the way, but overall the journey was reasonably safe. There were, moreover, orders of knights who had returned from their crusade and still were under vows to do the work of the Lord. Many of these knights saw the protection of pilgrims as a way to be both righteous and warlike, thus giving the pilgrims even greater security.

These pilgrimages often lasted for months, and pilgrims traveled to faraway destinations. Churches and monasteries along the main routes would provide food and lodging for the pilgrims. The pilgrims would dress distinctly so they could be readily identified and protected. The standard pilgrim attire was a simple long cloak, a large hat, a walking stick with a gourd attached for carrying water, and a necklace of scallop shells, which were the identifying icon of the pilgrim, especially those who went to **Santiago de Compostela** (burial site of St. James), the most popular pilgrimage site, which is located near the northwestern tip of Spain. A map showing the routes of pilgrims to Santiago is given in Figure 19.1. Other major pilgrimage sites were Jerusalem and the Holy Land, **Canterbury** in England (Thomas à Becket's burial place), Rome (center of the church), and later, **Lourdes, France** (site of miracles), and **Czestochowa,** Poland (famous for visions). These sites all remain popular as pilgrimage destinations today.

Cities that were major pilgrimage destinations, and even those along the major routes, generally thrived economically and culturally, as streams of pilgrims would journey to the city, spend their money, and share their way of life. As time passed, towns and cities began to recognize the economic, cultural, and political advantages to being a pilgrimage destination. Some towns took steps to make themselves more attractive to pilgrims. Inns were built, churches expanded, and soldiers assigned to protect the travelers. Other cities desiring to enjoy the benefits of the pilgrimage trade purchased relics (ancient religious artifacts such as the bones of saints, pieces of the true cross of Jesus, cloaks and other items of cloth associated with Jesus or the saints, and statues and paintings of Jesus, Mary, or the saints), so that people might come to visit their city. There was

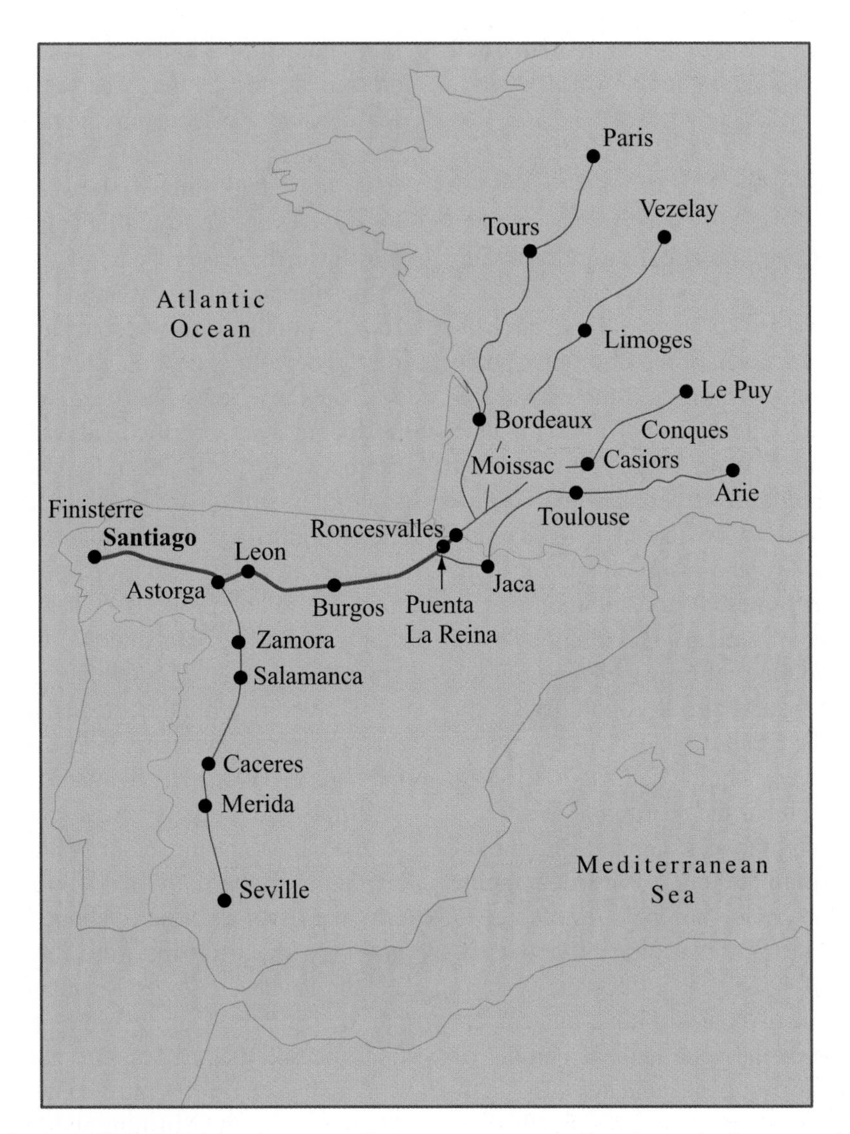

Figure 19.1 ■ *Map showing pilgrimage routes to Santiago de Compostela.*

also great prestige in owning a sacred relic. In some cases, the relics were instrumental in a miraculous cure or other sacred events and these also enhanced the appeal of a city for pilgrims.

At the same time, Europe was still a medieval-thinking society. The pilgrimages themselves were the product of a medieval-minded people. Their lives were still completely centered on the church, as is indicated by the fact that pilgrims went on these journeys at all. The trips were arduous, long, expensive, and in spite of knights and royal armies, still relatively dangerous. Nevertheless, people did travel more, but not much or often. Common European peasants in the later medieval period might go on one pilgrimage in their lifetime (if any at all). Otherwise they rarely went far from their home. Yes, communication was improved and ideas spread more quickly, but that was due in large part to the traveling knights, nobles, pilgrims, and crusaders who might pass through a village or, more likely, the largest town close to your village, where you might journey once a year to sell goods, purchase rare items, and find out what was happening in the world.

Church Reform

Just as many lay Christians sought to reform their lives during these times of change, many people—lay and clergy—wanted to change the Church itself. The dominant position of the Catholic Church during the late Roman period and the early Middle Ages had led to widespread corruption among church officials, and to many church practices that alienated the faithful and perpetuated the corruption. Church officials were forced to reexamine themselves, personally and institutionally, in light of the increased awareness of the common people and the emergence of nations. The kings of these nations were becoming effective checks on the power of the church, and also becoming rivals for the allegiance of the people.

As a result, several church councils were convened to try and combat the corruption and to reform various church practices. The most important of these councils were the four **Lateran Councils,** held in the Lateran palace in Rome from 1123 to 1215. The general thrust of the councils was to separate the church from secular influences, such as elimination of the involvement of kings and emperors in the election of the pope and the naming of bishops. The edicts from the councils also reaffirmed the celibacy of the clergy, specifically prohibiting clerics from marrying, having concubines, or even living in the same house with a woman. The church proclaimed its support for pilgrims and crusaders by giving rules for the safeguarding of their possessions and families, and by condemning those who molested or harmed pilgrims. Lateran Councils also repaired the church hierarchy after periods of turmoil following times when two men claimed to be pope. The rules of papal election, limiting the election to only the members of the College of Cardinals, and similar reforms, were also announced. The councils also addressed doctrinal and liturgical issues by, for example, defining the nature of the Eucharist and outlining the duties of members with respect to Easter celebration.

One religious and social issue that was not addressed by the church was the prejudice against Jews, which was becoming increasingly strident during this period. During the Early Medieval Period, Jews had rarely interacted with Christian Europe. Even in Roman times, Jews had lived mostly in the eastern part of the Roman Empire (which became the Byzantine Empire), so large Jewish populations were unknown in the Latin west. The sole exception was Spain where, under the Muslims, Jews had been welcomed and had prospered. A synergistic relationship seemed to occur between the Spanish Jews and the Muslims, such that some of the greatest Jewish scholars of the Middle Ages, **Maimonides** for example, emerged from this society. Muslims, too, benefited from the relationship, as evidenced in the respect they granted the Jews and the interactions of both groups in mutually promoting learning and science.

However, with the gradual re-conquering of Spain by the Christians, whose stages are shown in Figure 19.2, the relationship among Jews, Muslims, and Christians was dramatically altered. As the Christians inexorably gained more territory, beginning in the north and working toward southern Spain over a period of about 500 years (ending in 1492), the Muslims were forced further south and the Jews were forced to interact with the Christian conquerors. During some periods, the Christians insisted that all Muslims and Jews remaining in Christian territories must convert to Christianity. At other times the Muslims and Jews were allowed to quietly practice their religions, but at all times, there was a social pressure on them that restricted their religious practices. Hence, many Jews left Spain. Some went to other areas in Europe where small Jewish communities were established. These emigrant Jews were sometimes tolerated and sometimes persecuted. During some periods, the Jews would be literally expelled from entire countries. As a result, the Jews wandered from country to country looking for safe havens. Germany, Poland, and Russia were some of the most accommodating areas during the Middle Ages, and so many of the Jews moved there.

In spite of the occasional problems experienced in other western European countries, not all

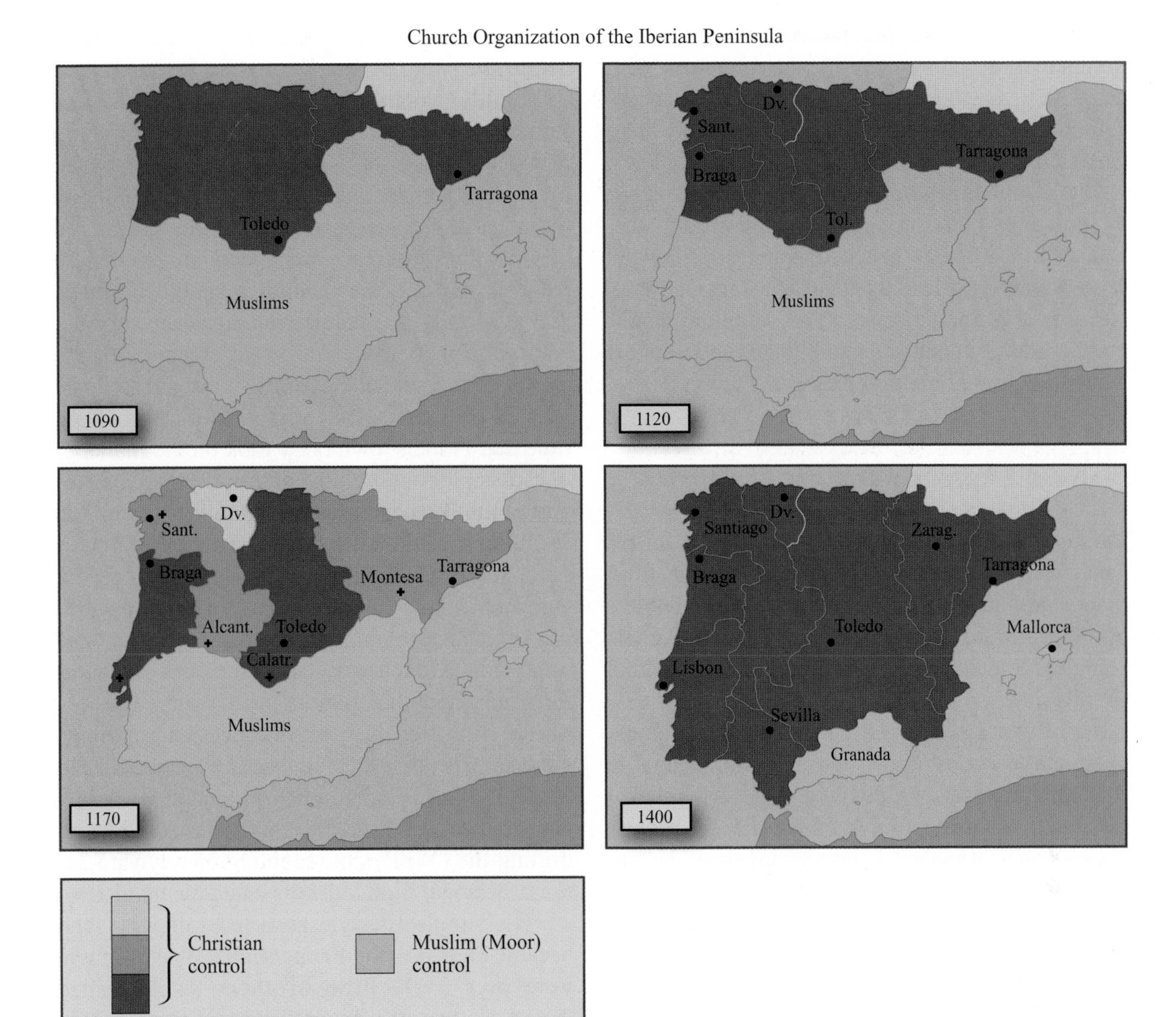

Figure 19.2 ■ *Stages of the Christian re-conquest of Spain.*

Jews moved away. Those who stayed were often able to prosper because, at the time, Christians were reluctant to lend (sometimes prohibited from lending) money at interest, and thus few Christians were bankers. Jews, therefore, accepted this role in society. Many became wealthy, but often also gained the ire of their customers and the community at large. For example, crusaders frequently needed to borrow money to finance the purchase of supplies, equipment, and transportation for the crusade. They resented paying interest for what, in their minds, was a religious duty. Of course, the Jews saw it otherwise. As a result, crusaders raided Jewish communities on their way to the Holy Land, blaming all Jews for the supposed evil of the Jewish bankers back home. When the crusaders returned home, their anger was rekindled as they were asked to repay the loans, and the Jews often suffered. (Shakespeare's *Merchant of Venice* illustrates the feelings of resentment toward Jewish bankers that were typical of Europe during this time, and later.)

Jews were also persecuted because, with the increased feeling of religiosity generally felt near 1000 A.D., any non-believers were suspect. Christians and the church wanted a society that was unified by religion and actions. The Jews were an impediment to that unity and so, directly or indirectly, both the people in general and the church in particular resented and restricted the Jews, sometimes leading to official persecution. Nevertheless, the Jews survived, albeit in small numbers and often in isolated villages and ghettos where they were ordered to live.

New Monastic Orders

Throughout the early Middle Ages, monasticism had been a major factor in European religious life. Many Christians had sought the serenity and order of monastic life. As a result, monasteries had become common; monks and nuns were viewed as among the best people in Christian society, because of their general piety. The rural isolation of the monasteries, especially those that followed the Benedictine rules of work and prayer, further contributed to the perception of these orders as pious, because they were not generally involved in the politics and scandals of the church in general. Hence, many wealthy landholders who hoped to improve their standing in the next life bequeathed large estates to these monasteries, giving land for new monasteries and also providing substantial wealth, as some of the land was merely continued as income property after the monasteries gained ownership. Estimates have suggested that the amount of church-owned land could have approached 30 percent of the total in some countries.

With this wealth, **abbots** (the heads of the monasteries) began to focus more on material things than on the spiritual needs of the monks. These leaders appeared to the common people as nothing but overlords. Monastery life began to be viewed less as a life of service to God in poverty and more of a way to live in luxury. As a result, two devoutly religious men took surprisingly similar paths to reform monastic life and, simultaneously, refocus the purposes of monastic living. These men were St. Francis and St. Dominic.

Saint Francis of Assisi, the son of wealthy Italian parents, joined a crusade and was captured and held for ransom. This traumatic experience must have changed his view of life because, upon his release, Francis gave away all his goods and began a life of poverty, study, and contemplation. He believed that the scriptures should be interpreted literally, and that led him to a deep personal commitment to Jesus and to all creatures of the world. Some said that Francis contemplated the passion of Jesus so intently and for such a long time that Francis' own body took on the marks of the cross (a process called **stigmata**). It is also reported that Francis' love of animals gave him the ability to speak to birds. (He glorified the animals in the hymn he composed—"All Creatures of Our God and King.") Toward human creatures, his love impelled him to find ways to serve those who might not be touched by God's servants. He therefore preached that people who would be holy should seek out those who needed help and give them aid. He also believed that holy people should maintain high personal integrity and strict obedience to the laws of God. He believed that by controlling the "Will" and repenting of wayward actions, personal righteousness could be attained.

His simple lifestyle attracted followers who became known as the **Franciscans.** By 1218 there were over 3,000 **little brothers** (as he called them). He saw the general movement of people from farms to towns, and believed that these new town dwellers needed God's care. He therefore encouraged his followers to enter the towns and find ways to serve those who lived there. To avoid the corruption that had beset the Benedictines, the Franciscans did not own land and therefore were not sustained by farming. Rather, they begged for their sustenance among the merchants of the town and others, like the nobility, who might agree with their actions. Therefore, the Franciscans were called a **mendicant** ("begging") order.

Saint Dominic, a Spaniard, likewise saw the problems associated with Benedictine wealth. In 1215 he organized a group of like-minded men who took vows of obedience, poverty, and chastity.

Like the Franciscans, the followers of Dominic owned no land and begged for their sustenance. They also lived in the towns and cities.

Dominic's order, which is formally called the **Order of Friars Preachers,** but is often called the **Dominicans,** believed that the "Intellect" needed to be filled, and that the true path could be attained through a correct understanding of the doctrines of God. Consequently, the Dominicans strongly emphasized education; many monks became scholars and teachers. Their intellectual rigor must have impressed other members of the church hierarchy, as several Dominicans became popes. Some Dominicans became famous as painters, especially **Fra Angelico** and **Fra Bartolomeo.** ("Fra" means "brother"). The Dominicans' emphasis on doctrinal purity led them to have powerful positions within the church at a time when the church was attempting to force a unity of the faith, not only in places where the church encountered non-Christians, like Spain, but also in the rest of Europe, where Christians who criticized the church or otherwise exhibited "questionable" behavior came under review. The church entity responsible for that doctrinal purity was the Inquisition.

Inquisition

After the crusades and the interactions with Byzantines, Muslims, Jews and others, there was a desire to unite all Christendom into a more homogeneous society in which all were strongly dedicated to the church. To this end, the church established a court, called the **Inquisition,** that was charged with the responsibility of rooting out heresy (incorrect beliefs) and dissent. The Inquisition may have also been organized to ensure church authority over doctrines in light of the increasingly strong attempts of kings and emperors to influence all aspects of church procedures and practices.

For whatever reason, the church appointed special judges, often taken from the Dominicans but also occasionally from the Franciscans and from the ranks of ordinary bishops, to investigate charges of heresy and dissent. The importance of these investigations is attested by the fact that the church judges had power of life and death. In medieval Europe where the church was the dominant institution (still more important than any nation, emperor, or king), such authority was not surprising.

Typically, the Inquisition judge would journey to a region where heresy was reported to be a serious problem. The judge would declare a month's period of grace, during which inhabitants could come forward, confess their sins, and receive an appropriate penance (such as a pilgrimage). During this period of confession, statements were often made by the penitents that led to accusations of others who might be involved in heretical activities. If those others did not confess during the grace period, they were investigated. Witnesses would be called and, upon two agreeing testimonies, a person could be convicted. The accused had great difficulty countering the witnesses, since friendly witnesses who would support the accused would rarely appear, for fear that they would be accused of assisting a heretic and, therefore, likewise be found guilty. Sometimes further investigation was sought to reinforce the testimony of the witnesses or, if two accusing witnesses were not forthcoming, to otherwise enlighten the situation. This additional investigation consisted of four methods of extracting open acknowledgement of forbidden acts or attitudes. These were the following: (1) threat of death by burning; (2) close confinement, often with curtailment of food; (3) visits from others who would attempt to convince a person of their errors; and (4) torture (known as "violent testimony"). Torture, which could not endanger life or limb, was sanctioned only after virtual certainty had been concluded, and was a method of solidifying the position of the court. Civil courts of the day also employed torture in similar situations. Some of the judges realized that torture did not favor the discovery of truth (one stating that "torture is deceptive and ineffectual"), but many others made torture a regular practice.

The final judgment was usually pronounced at a formal ceremony called the *auto-da-fé* (**act of faith**). The accused was allowed to confess at this time, and might be spared the ultimate punishments—death or perpetual imprisonment. Most of the judges were pious men who seemed to work within reasonable restraints (at least, in the given situation). Some, however, were excessive, such as the judge who, on one occasion, executed en masse about 180 people, whose trials all began and ended within a week. Later, when Rome found out about this person's excessive zeal, he was removed and eventually incarcerated for life.

The Inquisition was not used in all parts of Europe. The most active areas were in Italy, southern France, Germany, and Spain. The infamous **Spanish Inquisition** was active later than the period we are currently discussing (the last decades of the fifteenth century), and was an effort to expose and eliminate those who were Muslims who feigned conversion to Christianity but, in reality, harbored Muslim beliefs. The organizer of the Spanish Inquisition, **Fray Tómas Torquemada,** was a Dominican who relentlessly and cruelly pursued the Muslims turned pseudo-Christians, and the Jews. At one point he even defied the Spanish rulers who were about to accept a bribe from former Muslims who wanted to be exempt from the Inquisition. Torquemada eventually was responsible for the expulsion of all Jews from Spain in 1492.

Universities

Beginning in the twelfth century, Europe began to see the establishment of universities in several cities. Universities were started in the eighth century in several Muslim cities, most notably **Fez** in Morocco, which is the oldest continuous operating university in the world, and **Salamanca** in Spain, which was established as a Muslim center for the study of law but eventually moved to Christian control when the Muslims were driven from Salamanca. By the twelfth century the general European desire for personal reform and improvement, coupled with the Dominicans' emphasis on learning, had spurred the establishment of these universities. Another key factor was the rise of cities, which helped to produce a merchant middle class that had free time and money to spend. Some of the earliest European universities were located at Bologna (where the law school began in the 12th century), Paris (12th century), Oxford (12th century) and Cambridge (13th century), followed by many others in rapid succession, as can be seen from the map shown in Figure 19.3.

The undergraduate curriculum for these early European universities was a combination of religious study and the arts-and-science curriculum from Charlemagne's day. It included studies of rhetoric, logic, and grammar (called the *Trivium*)—subjects about the *structure* and *expression* of knowledge. Graduates from the *Trivium* curriculum were awarded a Bachelor of Arts degree. Those who wished could continue their studies by following a curriculum of arithmetic, geometry (which included geography and natural history), astronomy, and music (called the *Quadrivium*)—subjects about the *content* of knowledge. Graduates from this curriculum were awarded a Master of Arts degree. The *Trivium* and *Quadrivium* together are known as the **seven liberal arts** because they liberate the mind. The course of study usually took about four years, beginning at age 14. Graduates would then generally take jobs as clergy, professors, or bureaucrats, or go on for additional postgraduate studies. Three courses of postgraduate study were available—theology, medicine, and law—although not all universities had all three. Some universities became especially well known for a particular emphasis, such as the excellent reputation of the **University of Paris** for its school of theology. Those who completed postgraduate studies (taking as long as eight years for theology) were given the Doctor's degree.

Universities were generally of two different basic types. In one type the university was under the direction of some central authority such as the church, a city, or a group of professors. These were similar in structure to most modern universities. An example of this type was the University of Paris. The other type of university was owned by the students, who hired professors to come and teach them, much like a group tutoring arrangement. An example of this type was the **University of Bologna.** Both types of universities were valu-

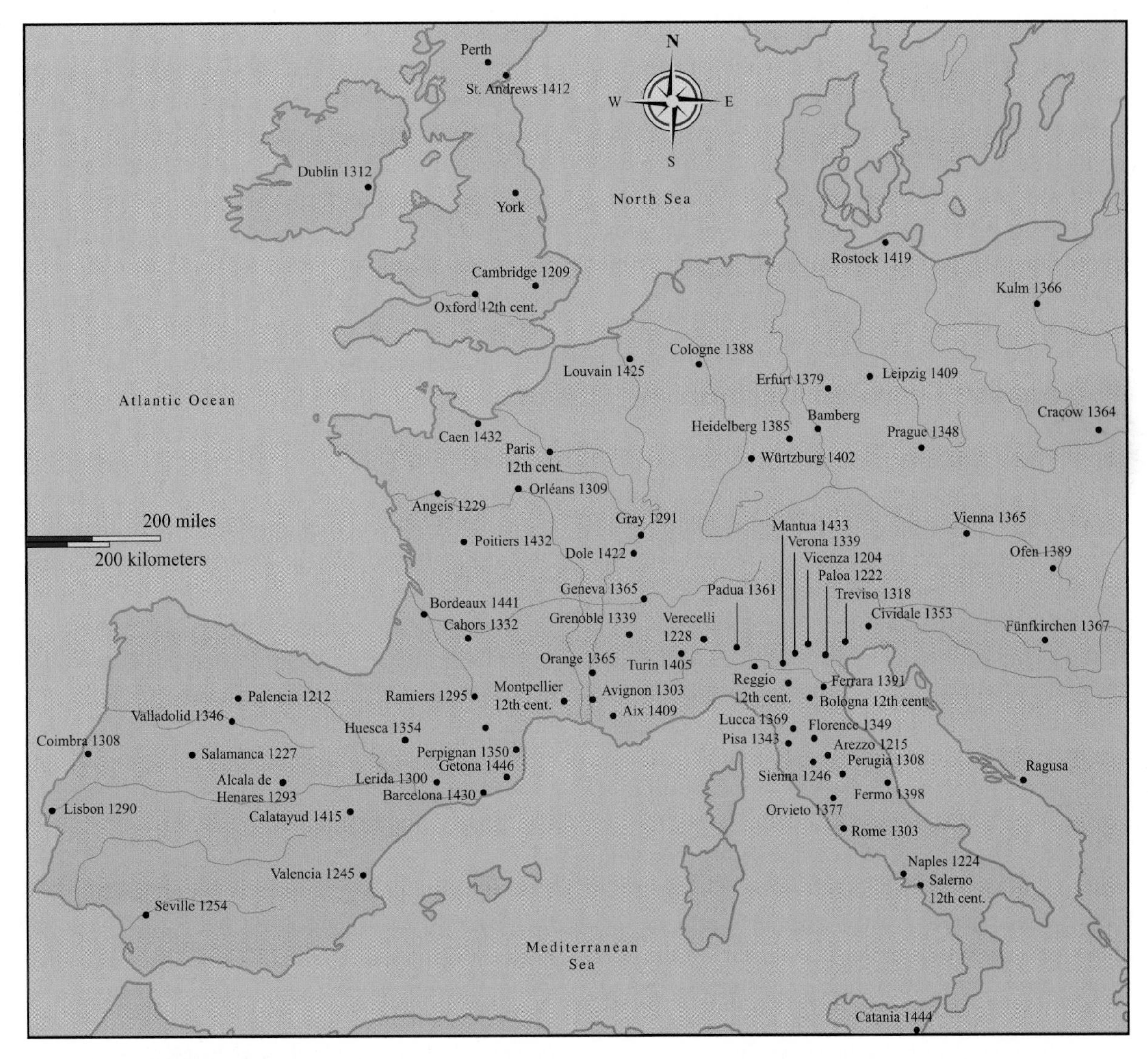

Figure 19.3 ■ *Medieval universities—locations and approximate starting dates.*

able for all the parties involved. Students liked them because the students could get better quality teaching when a large number of students were gathered in one place. Faculty liked universities because they had reasonable assurances of being paid and they could join with other faculty to discuss and improve. The church liked them because universities allowed the church to more easily control the type of teaching, thus ensuring that it was non-heretical. The cities liked them because they brought in money.

In spite of these advantages, universities sometimes (often) had crises. One crisis occurred when the arts and sciences (that is, the undergraduate school) of the University of Paris lost most of its funding. The University of Paris was sponsored by the church and, evidently, the church only wanted to continue its support of the theology faculty. The arts faculty moved away from the theology faculty and took up residence on the left bank of the Seine River, where it was forced to rely on wealthy patrons for survival. Foremost among the donors was

Robert de Sorbon, from whom we have derived the name **Sorbonne** for the arts campus in Paris today. The university section of Paris is called the **Latin Quarter** because the students who lived and studied there were taught in Latin. Some things about medieval and modern universities are surprisingly similar. Notes from medieval students complained of poor housing, high rent, terrible food, and lack of jobs upon graduation.

Monastic Learning Method

The earliest teaching method in the universities was derived from the methods used to teach monks throughout the Middle Ages, which was then adopted by the many church schools begun by Charlemagne and continued to be operated by the bishops. It is, therefore, not surprising that this method emphasized silence, obedience, and submission of will to the instructor. Typically, one monk would be assigned to be the instructor and would simply read from the scriptures and the writings of the church fathers. There was no dialogue between instructor and students.

One variation on the traditional monastic learning method was called **glossing.** The instructor, who in this case was likely the head of the abbey or a highly experienced teacher, would expound on a word or phrase encountered in the reading. Glossings might continue for a long time, as we can now determine because some glossings were written down. Perhaps the most famous set of glossings is from the famous monk **Bernard of Clairvaux** (1090–1153), an abbot near Paris. Saint Bernard gave sermons each morning to the monks in his abbey. We have records of 86 sermons dealing only with material taken from just the first two chapters of the Song of Solomon. Clearly he was not overly anxious to get through all the material. He strongly supported the monastic style of learning, and distrusted knowledge outside the purview of the church. He declared that unless the pursuit of knowledge was sanctified by a holy mission, it was a pagan act and therefore vile.

Bernard is also famous as one of the most pious men of his day. Over 90 monasteries were started that used his monastery as their model. Bernard strongly influenced the choice of a pope, and was a powerful force within the French court. He was deeply upset by the loss of the Holy Land following the initial victories of Saladin, and was instrumental in the formation of the Second Crusade and the establishment of the Knights Templar to protect the holy sites. Bernard was also the composer of the hymn, "Jesus, the Very Thought of You."

Saint Bernard is sometimes criticized for his opposition to a new method of teaching that began during his lifetime at the University of Paris. Whether you agree with Bernard or with those who sought to change teaching methods, the sincerity of Bernard has rarely been questioned. He believed, simply, that the proper pursuit of learning was to find God and improve our lives within the framework God has dictated. His criticism of the new university teaching method, later called scholasticism, was that the professors left the students in doubt concerning the doctrines of God.

Scholasticism

The fundamental premise of **scholasticism** was that there is basic agreement between philosophy (especially classical Greek philosophy) as understood through logic, and Christian theology, as given through revelation. The advocates of scholasticism therefore used logic and discussion, in a very organized and almost ritualistic way, to explore both classical philosophy and its ultimate links to and agreement with theology.

A typical classroom experience under scholasticism would begin with the professor's formulating a general question such as "Can a man see God?" The students could gather the next morning for reading from the scriptures and other books (such as those of the church fathers or from philosophers such as Aristotle) to develop a list of arguments (assertions) on each side of the question. The afternoon would be spent with professor and students discussing the arguments. This would be done using the **dialectic** (Socratic) method; that is, the professor would ask the student a question based on one of the arguments, and then the student would respond based on the readings or on his own logic. Because the students would have already studied the *Trivium,* they would be prepared for this type of logical discussion. The professor would then ask a counter-question, to which the student would again respond. This back-and-forth method would continue until all of the arguments had been thoroughly explored. Careful notes would be taken of these many exchanges by the students. They would hand in their notes at the end of the afternoon session. The next morning, after the professor had read the notes, he would meet with the students, summarize the arguments on both sides, and draw a final conclusion. The conclusion would show that logic and scriptures and doctrines of the church all coincide.

Professors who taught using the scholastic method also wrote books or treatises that explored various questions. In a scholastic treatise, two arguments or apparent contradictions were compared and contrasted, using logic to examine each side of the argument. The treatise typically stated the problem to be explored and then listed the arguments on both sides. Each of the arguments was explained in turn and then counter-arguments given. These counter-arguments would then be responded to from the initial point of view. When the arguments had been exhausted, the writer summarized the arguments and drew the conclusion. Any two opposing viewpoints could be examined, but the main purpose of most scholastic treatises was to reconcile discrepancies between philosophy and scriptural revelation or the doctrines of the Catholic Church. Occasionally theology and philosophy could not be reconciled, and in these cases theology took precedence over philosophy. It is through the writings and study of the scholastics that much of the doctrine of the early church fathers, such as Augustine, was solidified and fully accepted into Catholic doctrine.

The originator and strongest proponent of early scholasticism was **Peter Abelard** (1079–1142), the son of a knight in Brittany. Peter gave up his inheritance to become a student in theology and then a teacher at the University of Paris. He formally presented the idea of scholasticism in his book *Sic et Non* (Yes and No). In *Sic et Non* Abelard outlined the scholastic method and described how it is usually possible for man, through the use of logic and reason, to arrive at truth, even God's truths. Abelard did so by using the scholastic method to examine a series of debates. The topics or points of view of the arguments were merely demonstrative, since the focus was on the method and not the results. Abelard pointed out that his scholastic method could be applied to debates between two Catholic theologians just as easily as a theologian and a classicist. Scholasticism could even examine differences between the Bible and the church, and discover the reasoning behind those differences through the use of logic. Scholasticism also explored the idea that more than one truth could exist on an issue; an idea that was considered to be heretical to many within the Catholic Church.

Peter Abelard continued to trouble many within the church with his second book, *Scito te Ipsum* (Know Thyself). The premise of this book was that sin did not consist of deeds, which are not good or evil of themselves, but in intentions. Sin, Abelard argued, is not the thing done, but the consent of the person to something that they know is wrong. Abelard's views in *Scito te Ipsum* led to debate within the church over the nature of sin. Soon a great theological debate was raging over the topic. Abelard defended his view that knowingly consenting to a wrongful act constituted the sin, and Bernard de Clairvaux, the famous and influential monastic teacher, defended the view that sin was committing the wrongful act.

Bernard eventually gained the upper hand in the debate, not by proving Abelard wrong, but by attacking the scholastic method itself and undercutting the very means by which Abelard came to his decision. In essence, Bernard was arguing not that Abelard's conclusions were wrong, but that by reasoning out his conclusion he was sinning, since truth came through revelation. According to Bernard, if Abelard's conclusion were true, he must have received that knowledge through revelation, and since Abelard admitted that he came to his conclusion through logic and reason, not revelation, it could not be true, for no mind can comprehend the will of God.

In the end, at the insistence of Bernard de Clairvaux, Abelard was chastised. Despite the papal chastisement, Peter Abelard had convinced many that his views were correct, and he became one of the most popular teachers at the university. It was not Peter Abelard's controversial professional opinions, but his troublesome personal life that eventually got him into real trouble with the church and ended his teaching career. While teaching at the university in Paris, Abelard became romantically involved with one of his students, **Heloise,** the niece of a high church official. After a time Heloise became pregnant with Peter's child and they were later secretly married. However, Peter, a minor cleric, was forbidden to marry. Peter's difficult predicament caused him to vacillate and, in the midst of this personal turmoil, Heloise's uncle sent a gang of thugs after Peter and castrated him. Peter was forced to resign from the university and then had to make a choice about his relationship with Heloise. Peter suggested that they both enter monasteries rather than continue as a married couple. Heloise reluctantly agreed; she became a nun and, eventually, a leading force within the church. In spite of these hardships, Peter and Heloise stayed friends, and later in life published a book containing some of their love letters to one another.

Thomas Aquinas

Neither Peter Abelard's papal chastisement nor his subsequent fall from grace caused scholasticism to fall out of favor within the university community. Teaching was continued by others, including Albertus Magnus (the Great) who taught this method to the man who would become the greatest scholar since Augustine and the new champion of scholasticism, **Thomas Aquinas** (1225–1274). Thomas, the son of a wealthy family in southern Italy, showed an aptitude for learning and was schooled at the headquarters of the Benedictine order, **Monte Cassino.** Thomas' family hoped that he would become a prosperous Benedictine abbot like his uncle. When Monte Cassino was overrun by the troops of the Holy Roman Emperor, Thomas was sent to the University of Naples to study. While in Naples Thomas Aquinas became a Dominican monk.

When Thomas' father heard that Thomas had joined the Dominicans, he was very angry and sent men to capture him and bring him home. Thomas' family knew that the riches that could be obtained in the Benedictine order were impossible in the Dominican order and were, therefore, disappointed in Thomas' choice. Thomas was then imprisoned by his father in his family's castle, in the hope that it would cause Thomas to change his mind about joining the Dominicans. Thomas' father even went so far as to send a prostitute into Thomas' cell in the hope that she could induce Thomas to break his vow of chastity and then reconsider his life as a Dominican. Thomas drove her out of the room with a red hot poker from the fire and then branded the door with a cross to demonstrate his determination to remain loyal to his vows. After a year of imprisonment, Thomas' father realized his son was not going to abandon the Dominicans, and released him. Thomas had not wasted that year in prison, however; he had used the time to memorize the Bible.

After his release from home prison, Aquinas completed his studies in Naples and then went to the University of Paris to study theology. Life in Paris was difficult for Thomas, who had always been an outsider; and while he was respected for his intelligence, he was also teased by his peers, because Thomas was quite large and clumsy. One day while studying with a group of his classmates, a fellow student called to Thomas and pointed out the window, exclaiming that he saw a flying cow. Thomas slowly arose and went to the window to see for himself. Of course, there was no flying cow, and the other students ridiculed Thomas mercilessly. When Aquinas was asked how he could be so stupid as to believe there had been a flying cow, Thomas replied, "I would rather believe that there was a flying cow than that my friends would lie to me."

Aquinas became a pupil of the great Dominican monk and teacher **Albertus Magnus.** Albertus was the first medieval thinker to make a distinction between knowledge derived from science and knowledge derived from God. He also was the first in Europe to offer a comprehensive interpretation of Aristotle. Furthermore, Albertus reconciled the teachings of Aristotle (whom the church had banned) with the doctrine of the Catholic Church by rationalizing Aristotle's belief in natural cause and effect by arguing that God uses natural methods, and by downplaying Aristotle's views about the creation of the world by saying that Aristotle, as a philosopher, was unqualified to discuss the matter. It was under the guidance of Albertus Magnus that Thomas Aquinas became familiar with Aristotle and the methods of scholasticism.

After graduating from the University of Paris, Aquinas taught there for a time. He then returned to Italy, where he taught at three different universities. Aquinas was an expert in several languages, literature, astronomy, and mathematics, as well as theology. During his life Thomas Aquinas wrote over 40 books on theology, philosophy, and Biblical studies, his masterpiece being *Summa Theologica,* a three-part, 21-volume religio-philosophical treatise in which Aquinas combined Aristotelian teachings with Christian doctrine, thus completing the Catholic Church's reconciliation to, and adoption of, Aristotelian principles, as begun by Albertus Magnus. Aquinas was posthumously named a Doctor of the Church, the highest intellectual recognition possible in the Catholic Church.

Summa Theologica worked within the scholastic tradition and attempted to harmonize those things that are part of human learning (reason) with those supernatural truths revealed by God in the Bible and through the teachings of the church. To reach his conclusions, Aquinas generally took a middle path between philosophy and church doctrine. For Aquinas, truth was declared when the mind had seen a sufficient number of evidences to declare that something is so **(rule of evidence).** Aquinas was convinced that there was enough evidence in the world to conclude the existence of God, thus, there is a relationship between reason and revelation. This thinking is illustrated in the quotation at the beginning of this chapter, which gives part of Aquinas' famous proof of the existence of God. However, Aquinas also conceded that some theological truths, such as the Trinity of persons in God, and that God became a man, were unprovable by human logic.

Besides theology and philosophy, Thomas Aquinas also studied and wrote about secular topics discussed initially by Aristotle, such as government and science. Aquinas believed that no conditions allowed governments to violate the basic rights of mankind, which he viewed as education, religion, and reproduction. He also argued that rulers should implement laws and rules that were in harmony with the laws of God and beneficial for the people, and that if civil and divine law conflicted, people should support divine law. Aquinas' scientific writings were also ahead of their time and helped to improve the image of science by knocking away the general feeling that it was mystical and superstitious.

Creative Thinking

As we approached the year 1000 in our examination of history, we saw that warmer weather and improved technology allowed a large increase in population and a dispersion of people throughout Europe, even beginning to farm some areas not previously possible, thus greatly increasing the food supply. Some people moved into towns and began to specialize in their occupations. Overall, there was greater leisure time and greater creativity.

We also saw the emergence of strong and creative leaders who formed ruling dynasties that created and then strengthened nations. France, Germany, England, and Italy all emerged at this time. (Spain was in the midst of a battle to reconquer the land from the Muslims.) The rise of nations led to the crusades, which forced the interaction between Europe and the Byzantine and Muslim worlds, causing an awakening in Europe that further accelerated creativity.

During all this time the Catholic Church continued to rule the hearts and minds of Europeans. Strong kings were emerging, but the church and religion were still the dominant forces in a person's life. Many people sought to reform their lives, perhaps because of fear of the end of the world, but also because they believed that it was the right thing to do. Many went on pilgrimages to faraway places, and that also caused an awareness of the greater world, which led to increased creativity. Some of that awareness also led to demands to reform the corruption of the clerics and of the church itself. The church responded with a series of councils, which seemed to hold off the critics, at least for a while. New holy orders, the Franciscans and Dominicans, were also organized to oppose the corruption of the Benedictine order, which had dominated monastic life up to that time. These orders broke many of the old concepts of monastic living. We might ask, however, whether we believe they helped with creativity. To the extent that they furthered inquiry, they helped creativity. Remember that most of the great university teachers were Dominicans. However, to the extent that they enforced the dictates of the church through the Inquisition, creativity was harmed. The very people who thought *originally* were the ones most likely to be punished. This undoubtedly had a chilling effect on creativity.

The new greater awareness of people also led to the creation of universities. Scholars and students gathered together to learn, and inevitably, new learning methods were developed. The most important of these was scholasticism. In this method, questions and answers were given to address a topic of concern, usually a religious topic. The method allowed use of personal logic and also the logic and arguments of the classical Greek philosophers, especially Aristotle. However, the final conclusion would be that traditional Catholic doctrine was upheld.

We might pause to ask whether the system of scholasticism was beneficial to creativity in general. Critical thinking was obviously improved with scholasticism. It helped people see many sides of an issue and, even when the end conclusion was always orthodox, the ability to see other sides was of value. Again, creative thinking implies that different ideas can be tolerated, at least until proven to be in error. However, over time the scholastic method became as rigid as the old monastic teaching method with which it competed. The method of argumentation became the focus, and not the concepts being discussed. Therefore, in the long run, scholasticism was both beneficial and detrimental. It was beneficial because it broke one mold (rote learning), but detrimental because it became another mold (forced conclusions and rigid method). The mold of scholasticism would not be broken until the Scientific Awakening and the Enlightenment in the seventeenth and eighteenth centuries.

Timeline—Important Dates

Date	Event
1079–1142 A.D.	*Peter Abelard*
1090–1153	*Bernard of Clairvaux*
1123–1215	*Lateran Councils*
About 1150	*University of Paris formally established*
1209	*Franciscan Order established*
1215	*Dominican Order established*
1225–1274	*Thomas Aquinas*
1231	*Inquisition established*

Suggested Readings

Aquinas, Thomas, *Summa Theologica,* Great Books of the Western World, Encyclopedia Brittanica, 1952.

Bainton, Roland, H. (ed.), *The Medieval Church,* Krieger, 1962.

Article 32

Peter Abelard: Sic et Non

Introduction

The great philosopher and theologian Peter Abelard (1079–1142) was intended as a youth for a military career. But as he says, he abandoned Mars for Minerva, the profession of arms for that of learning. He left home as a wandering scholar seeking the most renowned teachers of the day and became the greatest thinker of his generation. His favorite area of study became Christian theology. He became a teacher of theology at the University of Paris. While there he gave private lessons to the niece of a nobleman, Heloise, and, when she became pregnant, they married. However, through an apparent misunderstanding regarding his desire to support her, Heloise's uncle had Abelard castrated. Abelard then joined a monastery and suggested that Heloise join a convent, which she did.

Abelard was perhaps most famous for his method of applying critical thought to issues in theology. Called the didactic, or dialectical method, it consists of showing both sides to every argument through a series of statements and counterarguments. Abelard would pose the questions and then occasionally let the students decide which side they supported. In this way, he tried to sharpen the minds of his students and teach them to make their own decisions, and base them on rational analysis of the arguments. The occasional suspension of conclusions gave many church officials great distress since they felt that the duty of a professor was to teach sound principles and not to allow the students to possibly be confused. One of Abelard's chief critics was Bernard of Clairvaux, a very powerful cleric.

The dialectical method is best exemplified by Abelard's classic theological work, *Sic et Non* ("Yes and No"). The following passage is an example of the didactic method from *Sic et Non.*

Sic et Non

Inasmuch as among the multitudinous words of the saints there are some which . . . not only [differ] but actually [contradict one another], we are not to judge lightly of these saints who themselves will judge the world. . . . If there are divine mysteries which we cannot understand in the spirit in which they were written, better to reserve judgment than to define rashly. We are not to rely on apocryphal writings and we must be sure that we have the correct text on the canonical. For example, Matthew and John say that Jesus was crucified at the sixth hour, but Mark at the third. This is an error of transcription in Mark. We are to observe because he carelessly incorporated the work of someone else, as Augustine confessed he had done with reference to Origen. We must bear in mind the diversity of situation in which particular sayings were uttered. In case of controversy between the saints, which cannot be resolved by reason, we should hold to that opinion which has the most ancient and powerful authority. And if sometimes the fathers were

---

Bainton, Roland, H., ed., *The Medieval Church.*

in error we should attribute this not to duplicity but ignorance, and if sometimes they were absurd, we are to assume that the text is faulty, the interpreter in error or simply that we do not understand.

Therefore it has seemed to us fitting to collect from the holy fathers apparently contradictory passages that tender readers may be incited to make inquiry after the truth. . . . By doubting we come to inquire, and by inquiry we arrive at the truth. . . . We are including nothing from the Apocrypha and nothing from the writings of Augustine which he later retracted.

Example XXXII. That God May Do all Things and that He May Not.

Chrysostom said that God is called almighty because it is impossible to find anything that is impossible for Him. Nevertheless He cannot lie, or be deceived, He cannot be ignorant. He cannot have a beginning or an end.

He cannot forget the past, be involved in the present or be ignorant of the future. Finally, He cannot deny Himself. Augustine said there are some things God can do as to His power, but not as to His justice. Being himself justice He cannot commit injustice. He is omnipotent in the sense that He can do what He wants. But He cannot die, He cannot change and He cannot be deceived.

Example XI. That the Divine Persons Differ from Each Other and That They Do Not.

Athanasius said there is one person of the Father, one of the Son and one of the Holy Spirit. The Father is not made, created or begotten. The son comes solely from the Father. He is not made or created but He is begotten. The spirit proceeds from the Father and the Son. He is not begotten or created but proceeding. But Pope Leo I said, "In the divine Trinity nothing is dissimilar, nothing unequal."

Article 33

Thomas Aquinas: Summa Theologica

Introduction

Thomas Aquinas (1225?–1274) may have been the most influential theologian of the Middle Ages. He was strongly influenced by St. Augustine but took a different approach and, as a result, changed some of the ways people thought about God, the Church, and the methods of arriving at truth.

Aquinas was born in Italy and, following the example of his famous uncle, became a monk of the Benedictine Order. Not too long after becoming a Benedictine monk, Aquinas was introduced to a new order of monks, the Dominicans. Aquinas loved the emphasis of the Dominicans on education and attempted to enroll in that order. However, when his parents heard of this move, they intervened and kept Thomas locked in his room for a year in an attempt to dissuade him. But, Thomas held firm and his parents eventually allowed Thomas to join the Dominicans. He then moved to Paris where he became a member of the faculty of the University of Paris.

At the University of Paris Aquinas was taught by Albert, sometimes called Albertus Magnus (Albert the Great), for his superb teaching and reasoning capability. Albert expanded the concepts and teaching method of Peter Abelard, called Dialectics, into a more comprehensive reasoning method which came to be known as Scholasticism. Albert taught this system to Aquinas who mastered the system and became its greatest exemplar. Aquinas succeeded Albert as a professor of theology at the University of Paris reinforcing the position of the University of Paris as the leading theological school in the world.

Aquinas' masterpiece is *Summa Theologica,* a massive work that uses the careful reasoning of the Scholastic method to explore ways to harmonize human reasoning and learning with the truths revealed by God. The method he employed was to ask a general question and then answer the question from one point of view. He then carefully reasoned this point of view, showing both the strengths and weaknesses. Then, he suggested alternate and opposing answers to the original question. These were then carefully analyzed showing both strengths and weaknesses. He then reintroduced the first point of view to answer the arguments of the second point of view. He responded from the second viewpoint. This process could be repeated several times until he finally came to a firm conclusion that was, often, between the opposing points of view.

The reasoning of man, often one of the viewpoints, was usually based on the teachings of Aristotle. Some have said that Aquinas made Aristotle into a Christian, and that comment has some merit since, in the end of the argument, Aquinas often shows how Aristotle's teachings could be reconciled with Christian theology. His work in justifying the teachings of Aristotle is similar to the way in which St. Augustine justified the teachings of Plato with Christian doctrine (although the methods of reasoning and writing of St. Augustine and St. Aquinas were very different). Nevertheless, these two Christian thinkers reconciled the teachings of

Plato and Aristotle with their understanding of Christian thought. Both Augustine and Aquinas became Doctors of the Church, a title indicating that their teachings were largely accepted and served as the basis of Catholic doctrine.

Summa Theologica

First Part: Treatise on the One God
Question 2: The Existence of God (Three Articles)

Second Article: Whether it can be demonstrated that God exists?

Objection 1: It seems that the existence of God cannot be demonstrated. For it is an article of faith that God exists. But what is of faith cannot be demonstrated, because a demonstration produces scientific knowledge; whereas faith is of the unseen (Heb. 11:1). Therefore it cannot be demonstrated that God exists.

Objection 2: Further, the essence is the middle term of demonstration. But we cannot know in what God's essence consists, but solely in what it does not consist; as Damascene says (De Fide Orth. i, 4). Therefore we cannot demonstrate that God exists.

Objection 3: Further, if the existence of God were demonstrated, this could only be from His effects. But His effects are not proportionate to Him, since He is infinite and His effects are finite; and between the finite and infinite there is no proportion. Therefore, since a cause cannot be demonstrated by an effect not proportionate to it, it seems that the existence of God cannot be demonstrated.

On the contrary, The Apostle says: "The invisible things of Him are clearly seen, being understood by the things that are made" (Rm. 1:20). But this would not be unless the existence of God could be demonstrated through the things that are made; for the first thing we must know of anything is whether it exists.

I answer that, Demonstration can be made in two ways: One is through the cause, and is called "a priori," and this is to argue from what is prior absolutely. The other is through the effect, and is called a demonstration "a posteriori"; this is to argue from what is prior relatively only to us. When an effect is better known to us than its cause, from the effect we proceed to the knowledge of the cause. And from every effect the existence of its proper cause can be demonstrated, so long as its effects are better known to us; because since every effect depends upon its cause, if the effect exists, the cause must pre-exist. Hence the existence of God, in so far as it is not self-evident to us, can be demonstrated from those of His effects which are known to us.

Reply to Objection 1: The existence of God and other like truths about God, which can be known by natural reason, are not articles of faith, but are preambles to the articles; for faith presupposes natural knowledge, even as grace presupposes nature, and perfection supposes something that can be perfected. Nevertheless, there is nothing to prevent a man, who cannot grasp a proof, accepting, as a matter of faith, something which in itself is capable of being scientifically known and demonstrated.

Reply to Objection 2: When the existence of a cause is demonstrated from an effect, this effect takes the place of the definition of the cause in proof of the cause's existence. This is especially the case in regard to God, because, in order to prove the existence of anything, it is necessary to accept as a middle term the meaning of the word, and not its essence, for the question of its essence follows on the question of its existence. Now the names given to God are derived from His effects; consequently, in demonstrating the existence of God from His effects, we may take for the middle term the meaning of the word "God".

Reply to Objection 3: From effects not proportionate to the cause no perfect knowledge of that cause can be obtained. Yet from every effect the existence of the cause can be clearly demonstrated, and so we can demonstrate the existence of God from His effects; though from them we cannot perfectly know God as He is in His essence.

Third Article: Whether God exists?

Objection 1: It seems that God does not exist; because if one of two contraries be infinite, the other would be altogether destroyed. But the word "God" means that He is infinite goodness. If, therefore, God existed, there would be no evil discoverable; but there is evil in the world. Therefore God does not exist.

Objection 2: Further, it is superfluous to suppose that what can be accounted for by a few principles has been produced by many. But it seems that everything we see in the world can be accounted for by other principles, supposing God did not exist. For all natural things can be reduced to one principle which is nature; and all voluntary things can be reduced to one principle which is human reason, or will. Therefore there is no need to suppose God's existence.

On the contrary, It is said in the person of God: "I am Who am." (Ex. 3:14)

I answer that, The existence of God can be proved in five ways.

The first and more manifest way is the argument from motion. It is certain, and evident to our senses, that in the world some things are in motion. . . . [Now], whatever is in motion must be put in motion by another. If that by which it is put in motion be itself put in motion, then this also must needs be put in motion by another, and that by another again. But this cannot go on to infinity, because then there would be no first mover, and, consequently, no other mover; seeing that subsequent movers move only inasmuch as they are put in motion by the first mover; as the staff moves only because it is put in motion by the hand. Therefore it is necessary to arrive at a first mover, put in motion by no other; and this everyone understands to be God.

The second way is from the nature of the efficient cause. In the world of sense we find there is an order of efficient causes. There is no case known (neither is it, indeed, possible) in which a thing is found to be the efficient cause of itself; for so it would be prior to itself, which is impossible. Now in efficient causes it is not possible to go on to infinity, because in all efficient causes following in order, the first is the cause of the intermediate cause, and the intermediate is the cause of the ultimate cause, whether the intermediate cause be several, or only one. Now to take away the cause is to take away the effect. Therefore, if there be no first cause among efficient causes, there will be no ultimate, nor any intermediate cause. . . . Therefore it is necessary to admit a first efficient cause, to which everyone gives the name of God.

The third way is taken from possibility and necessity, and runs thus. We find in nature things that are possible to be and not to be, since they are found to be generated, and to corrupt, and consequently, they are possible to be and not to be. But it is impossible for these always to exist, for that which is possible not to be at some time is not. Therefore, if everything is possible not to be, then at one time there could have been nothing in existence. Now if this were true, even now there would be nothing in existence, because that which does not exist only begins to exist by something already existing. Therefore, if at one time nothing was in existence, it would have been impossible for anything to have begun to exist; and thus even now nothing would be in existence—which is absurd. Therefore, not all beings are merely possible, but there must exist something the existence of which is necessary. But every necessary thing either has its necessity caused by another, or not. Now it is impossible to go on to infinity in necessary things which have their necessity caused by another, as has been already proved in regard to efficient causes. Therefore we cannot but postulate the existence of some being having of itself its own necessity, and not receiving it from another, but rather causing in others their necessity. This all men speak of as God.

The fourth way is taken from the gradation to be found in things. Among beings there are some more and some less good, true, noble and the like. But "more" and "less" are predicated of different things, according as they resemble in their different ways something which is the maximum, as a thing is said to be hotter according as it more nearly resembles that which is hottest; so that there is something which is truest, something best, something noblest and, consequently, something which is uttermost being; for those things that are greatest in truth are greatest in being. . . . Therefore there must also be something which is to all beings the cause of their being, goodness, and every other perfection; and this we call God.

The fifth way is taken from the governance of the world. We see that things which lack intelligence, such as natural bodies, act for an end, and this is evident from their acting always, or nearly always, in the same way, so as to obtain the best result. Hence it is plain that not fortuitously, but designedly, do they achieve their end. Now whatever lacks intelligence cannot move towards an end, unless it be directed by some being endowed with knowledge and intelligence; as the arrow is shot to its mark by the archer. Therefore some intelligent being exists by whom all natural things are directed to their end; and this being we call God.

Reply to Objection 1: As Augustine says (Enchiridion xi): "Since God is the highest good, He would not allow any evil to exist in His works, unless His omnipotence and goodness were such as to bring good even out of evil." This is part of the infinite goodness of God, that He should allow evil to exist, and out of it produce good.

Reply to Objection 2: Since nature works for a determinate end under the direction of a higher agent, whatever is done by nature must needs be traced back to God, as to its first cause. . . . For all things that are changeable and capable of defect must be traced back to an immovable and self-necessary first principle, as was shown in the body of this Article.

Middle Ages Architecture
High Creativity

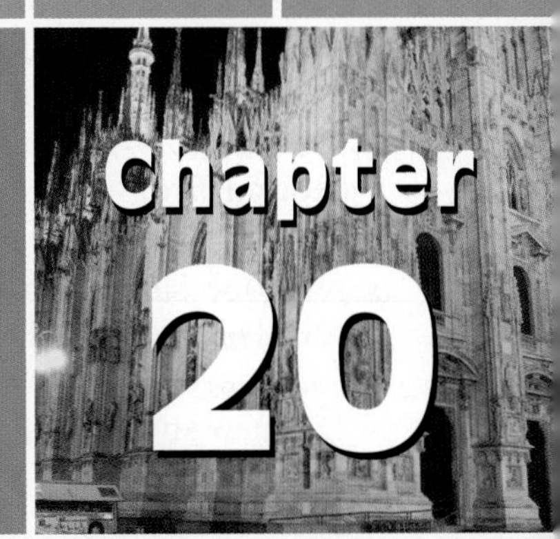

> The defining technology of the high Middle Ages was . . . the Gothic cathedral. It is hard to say too much about Gothic cathedrals. They combine immensity with a delicacy of balance and detail that must be seen to be believed. . . . The people who created this art appear to have been without formal educations . . . they probably knew nothing of formal geometry, and it is unlikely they made any calculations. Most astonishing of all, they built without working drawings. The medieval cathedral builder learned his empirical art . . . through apprenticeship.
>
> —*John Lienhard,* The Engines of Our Ingenuity, p. 29.

The Roman Legacy in Architecture

The Romans were wonderful builders. As we discussed in the chapter on Roman science, technology, and art, they took the best architectural components from throughout the world and improved them. They built roads, aqueducts, triumphal arches, temples, coliseums, hippodromes, and entire cities with many conveniences (such as running water and sewers) not seen again for a thousand years. Most of these architectural accomplishments were made from materials such as stones alone, stones with mortar, and, when they finally understood how to use it, concrete. They understood the engineering principles of support and force distribution so they used, as appropriate, posts and lintels, arches, arcades, barrel vaults, round vaults, and domes. We can still marvel at some of these magnificent constructions.

But, we might ask, did the Romans pass this architectural knowledge on to succeeding societies? In the case of the Byzantine Empire, the true successor (continuation) of the Roman Empire, the answer is yes! The Byzantines, at least for a while, used the best of the Roman architecture and then went even further. However, in the case of Western Europe, the answer is less sure. The political chaos of Western Europe seemed to inhibit most construction of major buildings. When the political situation solidified, as when Charlemagne came to power, buildings were constructed after the Roman style, that is, with arches and generally thick and substantial walls. The thick walls may have also reflected the needs of these buildings beyond just style, as some were fortresses. But even the churches had thick walls. This style is appropriately called Romanesque (Roman-like).

After the awakening of progress around the year 1000 and even after the further advances in knowledge brought about by the First Crusade and pilgrimages, a new architectural style was created. This new style was, finally, Western Europe's first major architectural improvement over the Roman style. The people of the time thought of this new style in terms of height and light. The creation of this style might have even given the basis of the term **"High" Middle Ages,** which is used to describe the period from about 1200 A.D. to the beginning of the Renaissance. We call this new style the Gothic, but we could just as easily call it the "expression of height and light"—truly an expression of "high creativity." The Gothic style did not spring from nothing, however. It was influenced by the Byzantine and also by the Romanesque. We should take a close look at those styles before considering the Gothic.

Byzantine Architecture

In the chapter on the Byzantine Empire we briefly mentioned the building of *Hagia Sophia.* Built originally by Constantine and then rebuilt by Justinian after a fire, this beautiful building was the largest and most important church in Christendom throughout the Middle Ages. It also was the only major innovation to the Roman style in the Christian world until Gothic architecture was developed.

The most innovative architectural concept of *Hagia Sophia* was the use of a dome set on top of a basilica, rather than just on top of a simple drum, as was the case with the Pantheon in Rome. This is seen in Figure 15.2, the external view of the church, in Figure 20.1 (interior view) and in Figure 20.2 which shows the ground plan of *Hagia Sophia.* The larger area of the basilica and its rectangular shape required transition to the round shape of the dome. The transition was creatively made by transferring the load of the dome onto pillars, thus allowing the walls of the dome to be reduced in thickness from what they might otherwise have been. This reduction allowed windows to be put into the dome, which gave the appearance of a ring of light, suggesting the presence of the Holy Spirit and reinforcing the overall theme of *Hagia Sophia* (Holy Wisdom). **Procopius,** a Byzantine historian, said at the time, "The dome [of *Hagia Sophia*] is a work admirable and terrifying . . . seeming not to rest on the masonry below it, but to be suspended by a chain of gold from the height of the sky." The transitions

Figure 20.1 ■ Hagia Sophia (interior). *© 2010 by Faraways. Used under license of Shutterstock, Inc.*

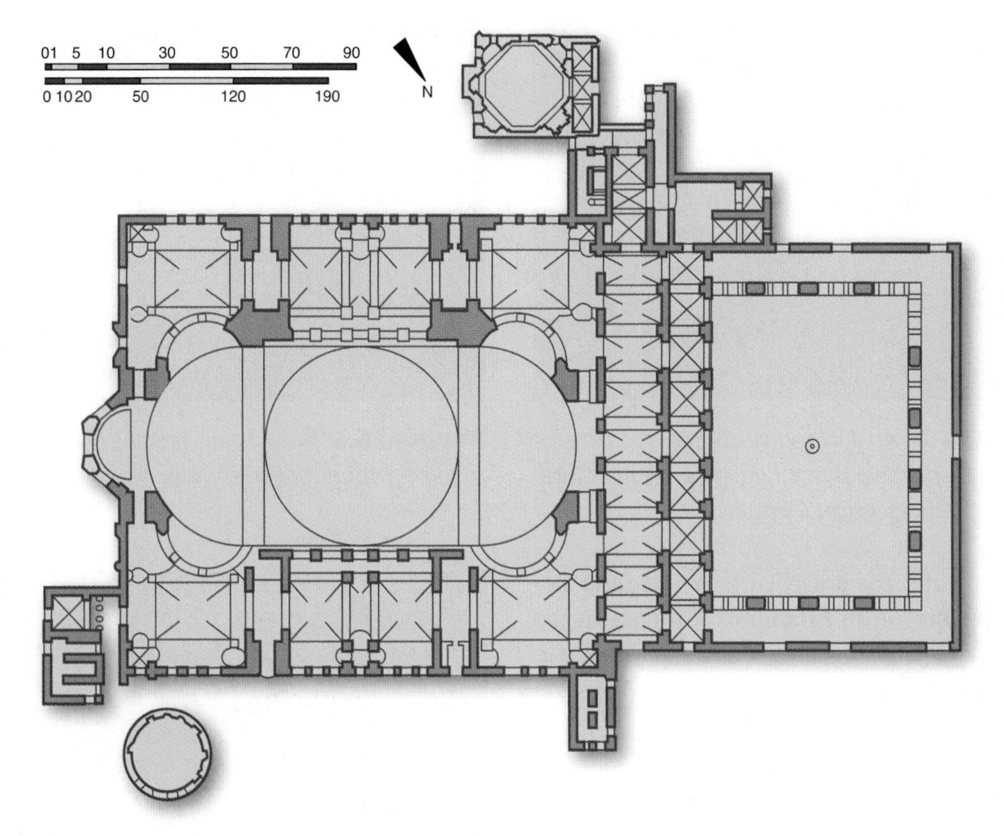

Figure 20.2 ■ *Ground plan of* Hagia Sophia.

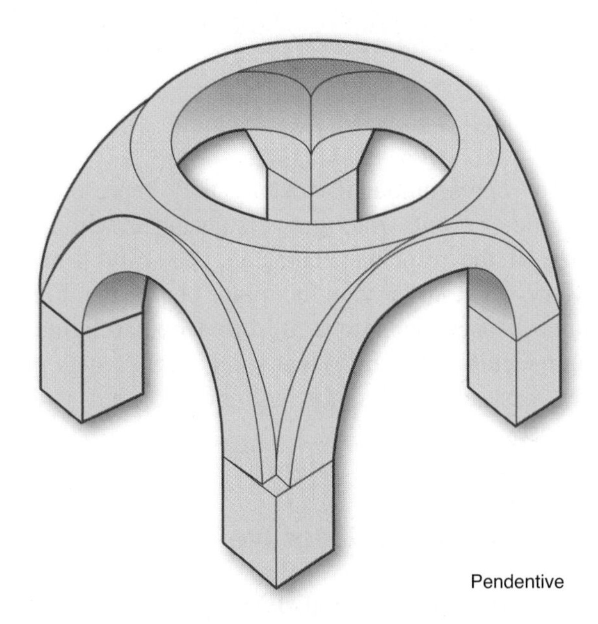

Figure 20.3 ■ *Diagram of a pendentive.*

that allowed this architecture were called **pendentives,** and a diagram is given in Figure 20.3. The pendentives are structural elements between the tops of the arches that bend inward and around to form a circular opening on which the dome can rest. The style of *Hagia Sophia,* that is, a dome over a large rectangular space with pendentives, was later copied in many Muslim mosques.

Not just coincidentally, when the Byzantine Empire entered a period of political stagnation following Justinian (especially from the 7th to the 8th centuries), the architecture of the empire also stagnated. The only significant architectural innovation was the incorporation of **onion domes** in the churches of the Orthodox Church. These domes, which are a blend of Byzantine, Persian, and Slavic influences, are beautiful reminders of the once great Byzantine Empire and its lasting

Figure 20.4 ■ *An Orthodox church (St. Basil's in Moscow), showing Byzantine style architecture.* *Image © 2006 Jupiter Images Corporation.*

Figure 20.5 ■ *Norman castle, showing the Roman arch and massive walls.* *Image from Corel.*

influence on the eastern Mediterranean and beyond. A picture of an **Orthodox Church** in the Byzantine style (with onion domes) is given in Figure 20.4.

Romanesque Architecture

The architecture of Western Europe continued the basic elements of the Roman style, that is, arches and thick, massive walls. This style, called **Romanesque,** was used for fortress castles throughout Europe, but especially by the Normans when they conquered England. A typical Norman castle is shown in Figure 20.5.

Romanesque churches were also built with arches and massive walls, even though, presumably, they were not fortresses. (See Figure 20.6.) Note that Roman-like, semicircular arches are used for the doorways and the windows, typical of the Romanesque style. The height of the walls of the churches required these thick and massive walls. These churches, therefore, had rather dark interiors, since the walls were so thick that windows were necessarily small and infrequent. That darkness limited the ability to meaningfully decorate the interior of the churches, so many Romanesque churches were elaborately decorated on their exterior, especially over the main entrance where everyone might see it. In keeping with the general nature of medieval art, the decorations were representational; that is, they represented people or events of religious importance, with the size of the principal characters, like Christ and Mary, often larger than the minor characters. Figures in such depictions are often both religious and secular, indicating that some of the kings of the past and the saints will be glorified with Christ.

Figure 20.6 ■ *A Romanesque church.* *Image © Archivo Iconografico, S. A./Corbis.*

Gothic Architecture

The **Gothic** architectural style began with the reconstruction of the abbey church of **St-Denis,** just outside of Paris. (The name "Gothic" arose because some writers in the seventeenth century thought that the style was invented by the Goths or, alternately, as a pejorative meaning "barbarous" or rude, because the style did not follow classic designs.) **Abbot Suger,** head of the church at St-Denis and an advisor to the crown, wanted to show his support for the French king, Louis VI, by making St-Denis the most important religious site in Europe. The church at St-Denis already had several things in its favor. It possessed several relics supposedly brought back from the Holy Land by Charlemagne; there were reports of several miracles and visions having taken place there; and it was near a famous trade fair, which already brought people into the area. Furthermore, the St-Denis abbey had a historical significance, especially to the French, as Charlemagne had first been crowned there; it was the burial location for many French monarchs, and it was named after **Saint Denis,** a martyr for French Christianity and the patron saint of France.

Suger hoped to capitalize on these advantages by rebuilding parts of the old abbey into a great and elaborate church where pilgrims would come to worship. Abbot Suger redesigned his church with elements that had largely already been used in various places, but never altogether in one building. The reconstructed abbey was to employ an arch concept, the **pointed arch,** that would allow much higher and thinner walls than had previously been possible. This was possible because the pointed arch directs the weight force above the arch more downward than does a Roman-style semicircular arch, where much of the thrust is outward. Figure 20.7 shows the forces in both a rounded and pointed arch. The types of vaults that are created when rounded and pointed arches intersect are also depicted. Coupled with flying buttresses, also shown in Figure 20.7, which support the walls from a distance rather than using massive pillars, the walls could be filled with windows that could allow light to enter the church and also provide locations for further decorations using stained glass. The external decorations of the Romanesque style were retained and elaborated. Using these engineering improvements, Gothic churches were larger, taller, more light-filled, and more decorated than any other church or cathedral in Europe.

When the St-Denis abbey was refurbished, it more than fulfilled Abbot Suger's vision. St-Denis abbey became one of the most popular pilgrimage destinations in Europe, bringing money to the city, glory to France, and greater importance to Suger and his successors. Other cities saw the success of the St-Denis abbey and began to build even larger and more spectacular churches and cathedrals, in hopes of gaining prestige and making themselves successful pilgrimage destinations. Some of the most successful were the cathedral in **Reims** (which was the location where French kings were crowned); the cathedral in **Chartres, France,** which is, perhaps, the best example of the complete Gothic style; and **Notre Dame in Paris,** perhaps the most famous Gothic cathedral, shown in Figure 20.8. Note in particular the pointed window frames, which are typical of the interior arches as well. Flying buttresses can be seen extending from the back and sides of the church.

A floor plan of a typical Gothic cathedral, drawn in Figure 20.9, is helpful in seeing the massiveness of the engineering problems, such as the enormous spans, and the overall religious nature of the edifice; it is in the form of a Latin cross. The floor plan also helps our understanding of the terminology used in describing these cathedrals. Cathedrals were laid out facing east, with the main entrance usually on the west end where the **narthex** (entry chamber) is noted. This layout is to remind the attendees of the resurrection, which is traditionally toward the east, as attested to by most Christian burials, which also face east. The main, large center portion of the church is the **nave.** It is here that the magnificence of the Gothic style is most evident, because of the very high ceiling and the wide spans. The roof is supported by large columns along the sides of the nave. These columns, along with the outside walls, carry the downward force from the roof. The nave leads directly to the intersection of the arms with the main part of the cross. The arms, called the **transepts,** are identified as **north** and **south.** The **pulpit** and **lectern** are often

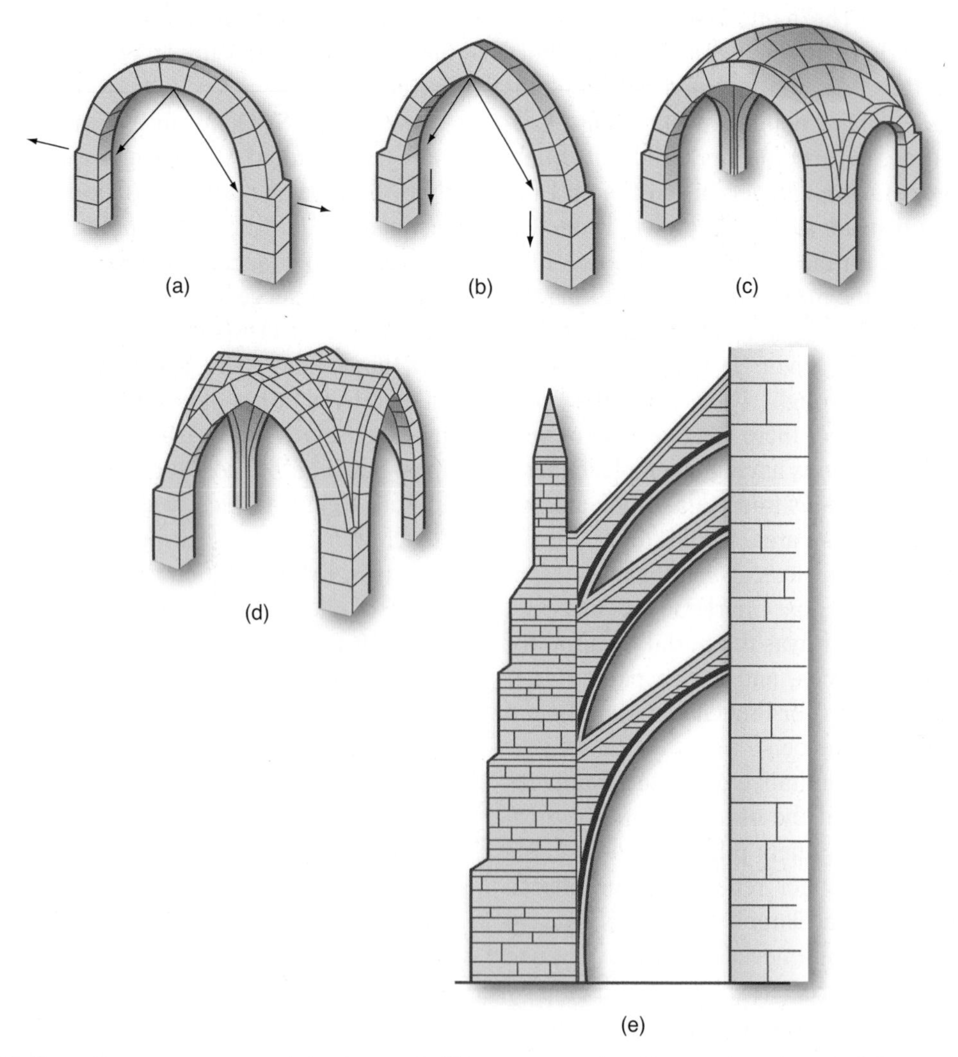

Figure 20.7 ■ *Forces on a semicircular arch* **(A)** *compared with a pointed arch* **(B);** *and the dome vault* **(C)** *created when semicircular arches intersect, compared with the ribbed vault* **(D)** *when pointed arches intersect. Flying buttresses are depicted in* **(E).**

in this area. Beyond the intersection of the cross is the **chancel.** The choir often sits on benches arrayed along the sides of the chancel, so the area is also called the **choir.** Beyond the chancel is the **sanctuary,** in which the **altar** is located. The altar in some churches is located at the entrance to the chancel, just beyond the intersection of the cross. The end of the building is the **apse.** Outside the columns that define the outer edge of the nave is the **ambulatory,** a place where people can walk (which is the origin of the name). Outside the ambulatory are **chapels.** These small rooms may have small altars for prayer or might have baptism fonts, or confessionals, or might be places of burial for families. The chapels are sometimes decorated with paintings and other religious artifacts.

The construction of larger, taller, and more spectacular churches and cathedrals became a matter of civic pride and technological virtuosity for the various towns, while it provided the local bishops or abbots with increased prestige and power within the church. Thus, before long, cities were

Figure 20.8 ■ Gothic Cathedral, Notre Dame de Paris. *© 2010 by Nadinelle. Used under license of Shutterstock, Inc.*

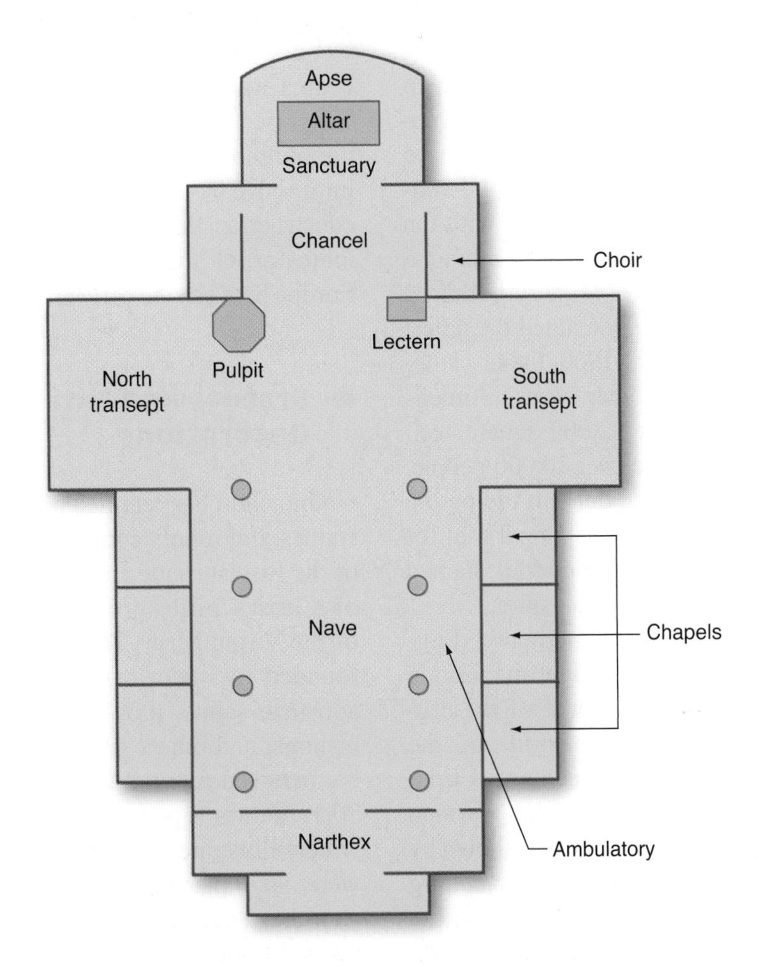

Figure 20.9 ■ *Floor plan of a typical Gothic cathedral.*

Figure 20.10 ■ Milan cathedral. *© 2010 by Tomas Sereda. Used under license of Shutterstock, Inc.*

Figure 20.11 ■ *Exterior decorations typical of both Romanesque and Gothic styles. Image © 2006 Jupiter Images Corporation.*

competing to build the biggest and best churches. Begun in 1194, the spire of Chartres Cathedral reached 122 feet. **Amiens Cathedral,** begun in 1220, reached 140 feet to replace Chartres cathedral as the tallest building in Europe. In 1247 **Beauvais Cathedral** was begun; upon completion its spire reached 157 feet, but it collapsed shortly after the completion of the cathedral. Eventually the trend spread outside of France, with the spire of the cathedral of Strasbourg reaching a height of 466 feet, as high as a 47-story building! **Strasbourg Cathedral's** spire remained the tallest stone structure in Europe until 1960. Other cathedrals tried to impress in other ways. Amiens Cathedral was colossal, over 82,900 square feet, large enough to accommodate over 10,000 people. Chartres Cathedral had a maze done in tile on the floor for decoration and to serve as a final trial for pilgrims, to go along with its wonderful stained glass windows, many statues, and tall spire.

Other countries, especially Germany, England, and Italy, slowly began to adopt the Gothic style. The travel and religious fervor of the crusades helped to spread the popularity of the Gothic style, and helped it to be seen as a Christian style rather than a French style. German Gothic cathedrals accentuated height, as shown by the massive height of the spire of Strasbourg Cathedral and the huge towers that adorned the cathedral in **Cologne.** The English Gothic style focused on a perpendicular feeling to the architecture and is especially well done in the church at King's College, Cambridge. Italian Gothic saw an interesting variation on the Gothic theme. It used wooden ceilings and, therefore, the roof and beams were lighter and the large exterior flying buttresses were not needed to support the walls of the building. The cathedral in **Milan** is especially impressive (see Figure 20.10). The wave of Gothic construction that swept across Europe is a great indicator of the changes that had occurred in Europe between the early and late medieval periods.

Statues and External Decorations

Gothic churches retained and elaborated upon the statues and reliefs common in the most elaborate of the Romanesque churches. Typical scenes were of Christ's birth, crucifixion, and judgment, or of the Virgin Mary. These scenes were often surrounded by statues, in partial or full relief, of apostles, saints, prophets, kings, queens, popes, bishops, and others who the craftsmen or designers believed merited inclusion and honor. Figure 20.11 shows a portal on the Chartres Cathedral, which illustrates this type of art. Some statues were also placed on top of the spires of the churches, giving both decoration and weight, needed to help immobilize the pillars so that they would give proper support.

Figure 20.12 ■ *Stained glass windows in Chartres Cathedral. Image from Corel.*

Figure 20.13 ■ *Interior of Sainte-Chapelle in Paris. Image from Corel.*

Gargoyles were often added to the exterior of cathedrals to frighten evil spirits away from the church. In some cases, such as with Notre Dame in Paris, the gargoyles are partially hollow so that they can also serve as rain spouts.

Stained Glass Windows

Cathedrals also competed on the basis of decorations. Stained glass windows are, of course, the most famous of these decorations. These windows are a special art form that became identified with the Gothic style because of the ability to use so much glass in Gothic cathedrals, and the technical capability in materials and artisanship that was present during the High Middle Ages. Some of the most impressive of the stained glass windows from the Gothic period are shown in Figure 20.12. Rich benefactors often donated the costs for the windows. These benefactors are remembered by name, or occasionally by portrait, in the window. In some churches the windows were donated by guilds that wanted to both decorate the church and illustrate their craft. One of the best examples is in Chartres where, among others, the winemakers, tanners, and silversmiths all have windows.

An especially impressive church, because of its stained glass, is **Sainte-Chapelle in Paris.** This small church was built as part of the royal palace, and so it was exquisite in its execution. The windows cover nearly the entire surface of the walls, and depict the stories of the Old and New Testament. The interior of the Sainte-Chapelle is shown in Figure 20.13. In this church we see a deeper intent of stained glass windows beyond just decoration. They were to teach the people the stories of the Bible. Since many people were illiterate, these pictorial representations communicated the stories that would build faith.

Creativity and Politics

We began this chapter by pointing out that the development of architecture after the fall of the Western Roman Empire was linked to the political stability of the area in which the buildings were built. Where political stability existed, the architecture was innovative. Sometimes the political leaders used the magnificence of the buildings to convey their own magnificence. This has been the case since the days of ancient Egypt, Pericles in ancient Athens, and the Roman emperors. When political chaos was the rule, no strong leader could fund the construction of great buildings nor was architectural progress made, at least that could be seen. Such was the condition throughout most of the Early Middle Ages.

When strong kings arose and nations developed, great buildings soon followed. These were both fortresses and monuments to the king, like the Norman castles, but major innovations in architecture were not seen. Some other buildings, like Romanesque churches, were monuments to religion, and did not seem to be linked to a particular monarch, although certainly the stability derived from a strong monarch was a catalyst for their construction. (These great cathedrals, both in the Romanesque time and later in the Gothic, were built over decades, sometimes even centuries, and so their construction often spanned the reigns of several monarchs, thus giving the cathedrals an independence from any particular monarch.)

The creativity of Europe at the beginning of the High Middle Ages resulted in one of the great innovations in architecture—the Gothic cathedral. It showed a good understanding of engineering principles, and also captured the grandeur of the times, with a glorious church and nation. The economic benefits of such an edifice, in terms of pride and pilgrims, were not lost on the builders. Just the task of erecting such a building must have been an economic boon to an area, provided, of course, funding was adequate.

These great edifices were more than just churches. They became symbols of the pride of the people in an area, and of their devotion to their religion. They were works of art, from the high vaulted roofs, constructed with skill and bravery, to the stained glass windows that still give us awe, to the exterior statues and gargoyles that impress us with their sheer number and complexity. We can think of the Gothic cathedral as the symbol of the High Middle Ages. Religion is clearly the central focus, but political stability is also there. Present, too, are the artistic and engineering skills of the people that have developed since the time of the Romans. We see the materials and the themes as depicting an awareness of the greater world beyond just their local village or town, especially a desire for pilgrimage and for personal reform and devotion. In the architectural and visual arts, creativity was moving to new heights.

Timeline—Important Dates

Date	Event
532 A.D.	Hagia Sophia *rebuilt by Emperor Justinian*
500–1100	*Period of Romanesque architecture*
1150	*Abbot Suger remodeled St.-Denis in Gothic style*
1163–1285	*Notre Dame de Paris built*
1194–1260	*Chartres Cathedral built*
1248	*Sainte-Chapelle built*

Suggested Readings

Adams, James L., *Flying Buttresses, Entropy, and O-Rings,* Harvard University Press, 1991.

Follett, Ken, *Pillars of the Earth,* Signet, 1990.

Leinhard, John, *The Engines of Our Ingenuity,* Oxford University Press, 2000.

Stokstad, Marilyn, *Art History,* Prentice Hall and Abrams, 1995.

The Builders, National Geographic Society, 1992.

Middle Ages Arts and Literature

To "Hell" with Creativity

I AM THE WAY INTO THE CITY OF WOE.
I AM THE WAY TO A FORSAKEN PEOPLE.
I AM THE WAY INTO ETERNAL SORROW.

SACRED JUSTICE MOVED MY ARCHITECT.
I WAS RAISED HERE BY DIVINE OMNIPOTENCE,
PRIMORDIAL LOVE AND ULTIMATE INTELLECT.

ONLY THOSE ELEMENTS TIME CANNOT WEAR
WERE MADE BEFORE ME, AND BEYOND TIME I STAND.
ABANDON ALL HOPE YE WHO ENTER HERE.

These mysteries I read cut into stone
Above a gate. And turning I said: "Master,
What is the meaning of this harsh inscription?"

And he then as initiate to novice:
"Here must you put all division of spirit
And gather your soul against all cowardice.

This is the place I told you to expect.
Here you shall pass among the fallen people,
Souls who have lost the good of intellect."

—*Dante Aligheri,* Divine Comedy

The Arts in the Middle Ages

All art forms were religious in the early Middle Ages. The themes were religious, the objectives or purposes of the art were religious, and the styles were religious. Then, with the dramatic social changes that began to occur around the year 1000, some secular influences slowly crept into the arts. Some people welcomed these few non-religious innovations as ways to expand the views of people and thereby improve society. Others saw the changes as devilish and pagan, and felt that they were leading society to hell.

We will trace these changes in each of the major art forms of the Middle Ages—music, visual arts, and literature. The trend of increased secularization of the arts continued inexorably through the Middle Ages, ultimately culminating in the Renaissance. Sometimes the changes were in themes, which were the easiest secular influences to identify, but changes in objectives and styles were also made and, in the end, may have had a more lasting influence on the arts.

From the standpoint of creativity, the opposing forces give us pause to think. Not all people in all situations are in favor of the changes that accompany creativity. Sometimes change might not be good, especially if people are worse off for the change being made. In the case of Middle Ages arts, the changes seemed progressive, but we should not blithely assume that creativity is always accepted and enjoyed by all people.

Medieval Music

The earliest medieval music was an extension of monastic prayer chanting. We can imagine how the monks added tonal changes to their chants to help them remember the words, deepen meaning, and add interest. This music was **monophonic,** that is, one melody line sung in unison. Monophony preserved the clarity of the words and encouraged contemplation, as would have been consistent with the purposes of monastic life. There was no beat or regular rhythm to disrupt the reverent sound or stir the passions. Further, these simple chants, properly known as **plainchant** or **songchant,** were sung without accompaniment and thus needed melodic simplicity. The melodies were highly **conjunct;** that is, the intervals between one note and the next were small, which added to the spirit of reverence and facilitated singing by untrained voices without written music. The melody matched closely to the words so that, in general, one note linked with one syllable. At the time of **Pope Gregory I,** in the sixth century, plainchants were adapted to the singing of segments of the mass and formally accepted as part of the church liturgy. From that time onward, the chants were known as **Gregorian chants** in honor of Pope Gregory.

To appreciate the way music was used in the mass, it is useful to understand the structure of the mass. The accepted mass was divided in two parts—the **Proper** and the **Ordinary.** The Proper consisted of those segments that changed from day to day depending on the liturgical calendar. For example, the segments in the Proper would be different on Easter, Christmas, Advent, and every other day, depending on what particular saint is celebrated on that day. The Ordinary consisted of those segments of the mass that were always the same, regardless of what day the mass was said. The Ordinary and Proper portions were interspersed through the mass with one segment of the Proper, the **Introit,** said first, followed by segments of the Ordinary—the **Kyrie** and the **Gloria**—and then further segments of the Proper, and then of the Ordinary, and so on to the end of the mass. A table showing the relationship between the Proper and Ordinary segments and the order of their presentation is shown in Figure 21.1. The music for the mass usually focused on the Ordinary because it did not change and therefore a single composition could be performed on any day, rather than just once a year, as would be the case if the music were for the Proper.

One of the first changes to plainchant music, occurring perhaps in the eighth century, was the introduction of a lead or solo voice. The **lead voice** would sing part of the chant and then, either in response or accompanying, the **group voices** would join in. During the portions of the chant sung by the lead voice, additional complexities in

The Mass—Presentation Order

Proper (change daily)	Ordinary (fixed)
■ Introit	
	■ Kyrie
	■ Gloria
■ Collect	
■ Epistle	
■ Gradual	
■ Alleluia (or Tract)	
■ Evangelium	
	■ Credo
■ Offertory	
■ Secret	
■ Preface	
	■ Sanctus
■ Canon	
	■ Angus Dei
■ Communion	
■ Post-Communion	

Figure 21.1 ■ *Ordinary and proper parts of the mass, showing the presentation order of the segments.*

the music were possible. One of the earliest was the introduction of **melisma**—putting more than one note to a syllable—which was easiest to do during the solo portion. Furthermore, the melismas allowed the soloist to show some virtuosity. However, these changes were all subject to the papal restriction that music could not obscure the text of the mass, regardless of how it was performed.

As with many other aspects of European culture, music was changed even more around the year 1000. A highly creative innovation of this period was the development of **formal music notation.**

Figure 21.2 ■ Medieval music notation for a Gregorian chant. *© 2010 by KariDesign. Used under license of Shutterstock, Inc.*

Previously the sequence of notes was merely indicated by a rising or lowering of marks on a page. **Guido d'Arezzo,** a Benedictine monk, used a four-line staff as a reference for the pitches. He soon realized that voices would cover a wider range than could be easily indicated with just a single staff, and so he also invented the use of treble and bass clefs and assigned a name to each of the notes, from *a* to *g*. He also began the practice of naming the sounds of a scale (do, re, mi, etc.) and gave six of the scale notes the names *ut, re, mi, fa, sol, la* which he derived from the first syllables of a hymn to St. John the Baptist, in which the lines are "***Ut*** queant laxis." "**Re**sonare fibris," "**Mi**ra gestorum," "**Fa**muli tuorum," "**Sol**ve polluti," and "***La***bil reaturm." Each line of the hymn begins one note higher than the preceding line. The major terms of music such as crescendo, forte, and so on, were largely developed by d'Arezzo, and he established the pattern, using Italian, for music notation that has continued, with many more terms being added, until the present day. An example of a slightly later medieval music script is shown in Figure 21.2.

A major challenge to the simplicity of plainchant occurred around 1000 with the introduction of a new kind of music—the **organum,** which consists of a plainchant melody to which a second melody has been added. The melodies are sung simultaneously and are of equal importance. This type of music is called, in general, **polyphony,** which means "many melodies" and would be contrasted to monophony, the one-melody system of original plainchant. The presence of two melodies required that they be coordinated in some manner. One way was to use the plainchant as a fundamental, called a ***cantus firmus,*** to which the other melody was synchronized. Usually the syllables and notes of the *cantus firmus* were greatly extended, so that the second melody could be creatively elaborative with melismas. Hence, the voice singing the *cantus firmus* needed to be capable of sustaining notes for a long time and was, therefore, called the **tenor,** from the Italian word *tenere,* which means "to hold." The two voices could move in parallel (one voice shadowing the other) or in contrast or counterpoint (the second voice moving around the first).

When a third melody was eventually introduced, the need for a more defined method of synchronizing the melodies became evident. This was done by adding rhythm or beat to the music. Sometimes an instrumental accompaniment, perhaps playing the *cantus firmus* part, was also added to assist in coordination of the melodies, perhaps assisting in staying on pitch, and to add interest and variation. The multi-voiced ***organum*** flourished in Paris, chiefly at the Cathedral of Notre Dame and became typical of this new musical creation. Some believe that the beautiful heights of the gothic cathedral were inspiration to the composers who allowed the second and third voices to range highly in the upper registers of the human voice. One of the composers associated with Notre Dame Cathedral, **Perotin,** was especially innovative in creating music for four simultaneous voices. Some of this creativity may have been spurred along by a practice that began about this time—the composer signing the music and thus taking personal credit for his work. The earliest known signed piece was by **Léonin.** The composers of the **Notre Dame School** wanted their works to be distinctive and used musical innovation as a way to differentiate themselves. This innovation was much easier with the complexity of polyphonic textures than with traditional plainchant.

As indicated at the beginning of this chapter, secularization gradually entered Middle Ages music. The opening for non-church music came with another innovation in music—the addition of independent words to some of the music lines in the *organum.* This new music was called ***motet*** from the French word *mot* ("word"). Although the original additional word lines were religious, with time French love poems were used for texts and it was then clear that the purposes of the songs had changed from religious devotions to devotions of another sort. This innovation led directly to troubadour and other secular music of the court and countryside. But, before we discuss that, we need to examine one more innovation in the field of religious music.

Toward the end of the Middle Ages, a group of composers began to talk of their work as ***ars nova*** ("new art" or "new technique"). They developed new musical intricacies by combining multivoiced *motets* with radically different rhythms, sometimes in each of the melodies, so that all voices seemed independent. The result was, to some, a cacophony of sounds that had little resemblance to music and certainly made the mass confusing. Others enjoyed the radical uniqueness of *ars nova* produced by composers such as the Frenchman **Guillaume de Mauchat,** and his young English admirer, **Geoffrey Chaucer.** Such divisions of musical taste would not be seen again until the late nineteenth and twentieth centuries. The new music was highly disagreeable to many church leaders because, in their view, the complex rhythms and polyphonic textures obscured the words. They believed that the words were critically important, since they conveyed the meaning of the mass. The music should not interfere with the clarity of understanding. These church leaders may have also objected to the music on other terms. In the end, the pope agreed with the objecting leaders and he issued a ban on all polyphonic music to accompany the mass. This ban remained in place (although not always enforced) until highly creative composers in the Renaissance showed that music could be both polyphonic and textually clear at the same time. We will speak of these composers in the second volume of this work.

Truly secular music found its first home in the royal courts of the emerging nations of medieval Europe. As the kings and barons gained strength and independence from the church, they also began to enjoy music suited to their secular lifestyle rather than just the religious nature of church music. The performers, who were often also the composers, were called **troubadours** after a southern French (Provençal) word *trobar* meaning "to sing poetry." In other places these traveling musicians were called *trouvères* (northern France), *Minnesingers* (Germany) from the word *Minne,* which means ideal or chivalric love and, more generally, **minstrels.**

The troubadour tradition was originally derived from the Arabic singers of Spain. The songs were performed in the native language and were often accompanied by a stringed instrument such as the lyre or lute. The subjects of the musical pieces were usually about love. They could be dedications to the beloved of the performer, but could also be poems about famous lovers (such as Lancelot and Guinevere) or just generalized love ballads.

These minstrel songs did much to promote the development and unity of native languages. They also increased the popularity and sales of secular books, such as the Arthurian legends we discussed in a previous chapter. The troubadours provided entertainment in a period when life was still very difficult. Hence, they quickly became fixtures at the trade fairs that sprang up around the Gothic cathedrals and other important cities during the latter part of the Middle Ages. The frequent performances of secular music gave it legitimacy and wide acceptance.

Painting and Visual Arts

Painting throughout the Middle Ages was mostly representational. That is, it depicted scenes, usually religious, where the characters represented someone in particular, such as Christ, Mary, or a saint, and the positions and sizes of the figures in the painting were depicted according to their importance and not by their actual appearance. These early paintings gave flat, two-dimensional representations of the scenes and people. That was especially important with icons, which we discussed in the earlier chapter on Byzantium, since icons were considered doorways through which a person, while in prayer, could enter the presence of God. Other medieval art, like the mosaics of Ravenna, were likewise two-dimensional. In mosaics, the key feature was to show the presence of certain people, like Emperor Justinian and Empress Theodora, and not to convey any particular scene. When a scene was depicted, such as Christ being baptized, the two-dimensional style was still employed, with a continuing emphasis on representation effects.

Another example of medieval art was the decoration that was done to manuscripts. Some of the texts were beautifully illustrated with scenes from the stories of the text on that page, but more general decorations were also common. To further enhance their beauty, some of the illustrations were enhanced with gold or silver. These are called **illuminated manuscripts** because they reflected light. A picture of a medieval manuscript is shown in Figure 21.3. These beautiful manuscripts were an important type of art in the early medieval period.

Figure 21.3 ■ A medieval illustrated manuscript.

A few medieval churches, especially in the latter part of the thirteenth century in Italy, began to be decorated with paintings and frescoes, perhaps because the new architectural styles (such as the Gothic) allowed sufficient light to enter that the decorations could be seen. This wall art recaptured themes of some ancient frescoes and mosaics that depicted life in the homes of wealthy Minoans and, later, Athenians and Romans. The Roman city of Pompeii, which was covered by ashes from the eruption of Mount Vesuvius in 79 A.D., is a place where such ancient wall decorations can still be seen. These were also two-dimensional, both ancient and medieval (a fresco is a painting done on wet plaster and is therefore very durable after drying.)

Around the latter part of the fourteenth century, a young Italian artist, Giotto di Bondone (called **Giotto** today), was given some church wall art commissions, in which he took a dramatic and important step in the development of painting. He began to depict the figures realistically. In particular, he presented the figures as freely moving solid (three-dimensional) figures in a convincing spatial arrangement. An example of his art is shown in Figure 21.4, entitled ***Lamentation,*** part of a series of frescoes decorating the **Arena Chapel** in Padua, Italy. Even though some representational features remain, such as the angels in the heavens, the departure from a strict two-dimensional painting is striking. Note how Giotto shaded the clothing of the people to convey both solidity of the figures and direction of the light. The cloth is also finely treated to convey, in some cases, its diaphanous nature and, in other cases, the elaborate borders. Of particular creativity was Giotto's ability to convey reality in the expressions of the people and their gestures. He showed further creativity in the positions of the people and in the background, where he attempted to display, in a reasonable but not yet correct way, perspective. In *Lamentation,* all these elements were meant to convey the sadness of the moment. Note also the dramatic descent of the rocky ledge with its barren tree (symbols of death in the Middle Ages), which directs our attention toward Mary, who is holding the deceased Christ in her arms. Instead of mere representations, Giotto conveyed real sorrow throughout the painting. Giotto set the stage for the period that was on the distant horizon, the Italian Renaissance. He was the finest and most advanced of the Middle Ages painters.

Figure 21.4 ■ *Giotto's* Lamentation, *from the Arena Chapel in Padua, Italy.* *Image © Photoasia.com.*

The use of realistic techniques suggested, to some painters, that real life could be painted in current time rather than the religious focus, which always forced a depiction of past events. We see, therefore, the beginnings of **portrait painting** and **landscapes.** But, critics said that the portraits raised the issue of pride, and that landscapes were inherently inferior because they did not involve people, who were the highest of God's creations. These attitudes persisted for many years, thus leading to a generally slower development of landscape art.

The painting of non-religious themes led to a much greater problem for some of the church leaders. That problem was the introduction of themes from Greek and Roman mythology. These themes were obviously pagan; the church leaders felt that Christian society was threatened by the pagan depictions. The nudity in many of the pagan themes was also highly objectionable. This attitude was later seen clearly during the Renaissance when pagan themes had become prominent. These pagan works were opposed by **Savonarola,** a monk in the city of Florence, at the heart of the Renaissance, who gained control of the government of the city and then acted to destroy as much of the pagan art as he could. He sponsored a bonfire in the center of the city, into which many artworks were cast and destroyed. However, Savonarola was eventually discredited and the church acted to remove him. Pagan themes returned, but many of the artists were deeply affected and they did not personally return to pagan themes. We will discuss the rise of pagan themes in the Renaissance in the second volume of this work.

Literature

The year 1000 A.D. was also a time for changes in literature. Arthurian legends, of which we have already spoken, became popular through the works of Chrétien de Troyes and then, later, Sir Thomas Malory. These stories blended well with other popular books of the time about **courtly love** and the behavior of lords, ladies, knights and dragons. The books on courtly love not only provided entertainment for those who could read (or be read to), but they also gave instructions to the knights and ladies on the proper way to behave. These rules became the basis of noble society and remained strongly in force until the fifteenth century. Some of the rules are both interesting and entertaining to us now:[1]

- Marriage is no real excuse for not loving.
- No one should be deprived of love without the very best of reasons.
- A true lover does not desire to embrace in love anyone except his beloved.
- When made public, love rarely endures.
- The easy attainment of love makes it of little value; difficulty of attainment makes it prized.
- Every lover regularly turns pale in the presence of his beloved.
- When a lover suddenly catches sight of his beloved, his heart palpitates.
- Good character alone makes any man worthy of love.
- Real jealousy always increases the feeling of love.
- He, who the thought of love vexes, eats and sleeps very little.
- Love can deny nothing to love.
- A man who is vexed by too much passion usually does not love.

Some concepts of courtly love have remained in our society even to the present, especially in the genre of the romantic novel. We leave it to you to decide which of the concepts are really expressions of true love.

Dante

The greatest writer of the Middle Ages was **Dante Alighieri** (1265–1321), a scholar and politician born in Florence, who became entangled in local politics and was exiled from his native city. While in exile, Dante became an itinerant scholar and writer. The book ***Divine Comedy*** is his great masterpiece. Many consider it the greatest work written in Italian and one of the greatest literary works of all time. Some have said that more words of analysis have been written about this book than any other, save perhaps the Bible. Whether that is true we can't say, but of this we are certain: *Divine Comedy* was very important in the time it was written, largely solidifying the Italian language, and has remained an important text ever since, for its insight into Dante's view of Catholic doctrine about the afterlife, its beautiful language, and the view of the Middle Ages that he incorporated into the characters and themes of this great work.

This great work of Dante contains much about the politics of Florence (and all of northern Italy and much of southern Germany) as well as comments about past history and the church. The politics of Dante's time focused on the continuing conflicts between the popes and the Holy Roman Emperors. We saw the roots of this conflict when we discussed the confrontation between Holy Roman Emperor Henry IV and Pope Gregory VII over the issue of lay investiture, in a previous chapter. The conflicts between popes and emperors continued for hundreds of years. Political parties were formed that supported both sides. Those who favored the papal position were called the

Guelphs and those supporting the emperor were the **Ghibellines.** Cities and principalities throughout Italy and Germany became strongholds for one side or the other; sometimes neighboring areas taking opposite views. For example, Florence was traditionally Guelph but nearby Siena was Ghibelline. Guelph and Ghibelline cities fought with each other and were, additionally, influenced by outside forces such as the kings of France, as well as the popes and emperors. The time of Dante, and the generation just before and after his birth, were especially turbulent times in Florence. In the midst of the turmoil, with control of Florence changing from Guelph to Ghibelline and back again, the Guelph party split into two factions—the whites and the blacks—who represented, respectively, the moderates and the purists. The politics of this time were, to say the least, complex.

Dante, a white Guelph, was appointed to the city council of Florence. When a feud broke out between the blacks and the whites, he was a member of the contingent that was sent to Rome to seek the pope's help in subduing the feud. (The feud began as a quarrel between two families, much like the feud described by Shakespeare in *Romeo and Juliet.*) While Dante was in Rome, the French king invaded Florence and asserted his support of the black faction. The city government changed from white to black and those who were in the previous government were exiled on trumped-up charges. Dante was one of those exiles. He was never to return to Florence. His wife and children stayed in Florence and so Dante lived the remaining 20 years of his life without the association of his wife, although he was close to at least one of his daughters. Dante was bitter about his exile, trying many times, especially at the beginning of his exile, to return to Florence. Dante died in Ravenna and is buried there in a beautiful tomb just outside a Franciscan church. After Dante's success, the city of Florence also built a tomb for Dante in the cathedral church **Santa Croce** where other Florentine greats are buried, such as Michelangelo. However, the Florentine tomb, though beautiful and clearly labeled for Dante, stands empty. This probably reflects Dante's feelings about Florence at the end of his life.

The reasons behind the refusal of Dante's wife to join him in exile are not clear. One reason may be Dante's feelings about another woman, **Beatrice,** who played an important role in Dante's life even though his actual association with her was fleeting and quite distant. In that age of courtly love, Dante fell in love (courtly) with Beatrice when he was nine and she was seven. They didn't speak until the next time they met, nine years later, when she called him by name. Dante believed, perhaps correctly, that Beatrice had been equally smitten with love at their first encounter and had harbored these feelings throughout the intervening nine years, just as he had. Perhaps they even expressed these feelings of mutual love. However, by the time of their second encounter, both Dante and Beatrice had been promised to others by their respective families. (Arranged marriages were common, and the commitments were often made early in the children's teens.) Both Dante and Beatrice married their intended spouses and then Beatrice died when she was only 20 years old.

This love affair was to affect Dante throughout his entire life. He wrote a book of prose and poems about his life in Florence *(Vita Nuova)* and dedicated it to Beatrice; it contained some love poems about her. As we will see, Beatrice also played an important role in the *Divine Comedy.* Dante's wife was not mentioned. When the daughter to whom Dante was close became a nun, she took Sister Beatrice as her religious name.

Divine Comedy is about Dante's journey through the afterlife. It is a comedy, not because it has jokes, but because it begins with sadness and ends with happiness. The "divine" part of the title was added by others because it talks about religious themes and ends in the presence of God, and because it was deemed to be a book of great perfection. The book is an epic poem (the same genre as the *Iliad* and the *Aeneid*), combining spirituality, politics, life experiences, and character growth, all told in a beautiful poetic style. The work is divided into a **Prologue, Inferno, Purgatory,** and **Paradise.** Within each section are major groupings called **cantos.** The prologue is one canto, and then there are thirty-three cantos in each of the three other parts, for a total of one hundred. Each canto is divided into three-line verses **(tercets)** that rhyme the first and third line. The second line in each tercet is rhymed with the first and third lines of the following tercet. This primary organization is both simple and beautiful. There is also an underlying organization in the book that demonstrates numerology, symbolism, and a symmetry that is revealed to the careful reader. Even though Dante spoke several languages (including Latin, the language of education of the day), he chose to write *The Divine Comedy* in a dialect of Italian that became the standard, thus solidifying the Italian language, much as Shakespeare later solidified modern English.

The story begins when Dante finds that he is lost in a forest. This beginning is interesting because we see Dante as both the principal character of the story and also as the author, even though the book is not strictly autobiographical. He is lost in the forest because of a spiritual confusion, and seems to reflect the confusion in the life of Dante (the author), which is reflected in the life of Dante (the pilgrim). This intermingling of author and pilgrim continues throughout the book. Therefore, problems of the pilgrim are probably problems of the author, although the pilgrim is also meant to represent all humankind. Clearly, however, the author's special association with the pilgrim is evident in, for example, the role of Beatrice in the book as the pilgrim's helper and companion in Paradise. With this duality in mind, the book holds great pathos.

The pilgrim's confusion occurs in the midpoint of his life, at age 35, when he has gone half way through the Biblical age of 70 years. The date of the story is set in the year 1300, when the author also was 35, as can be determined from the inclusion of events up to that year but not afterwards, even though the book was actually written many years after 1300. In the woods, the pilgrim is about to be attacked by three beasts, but is saved by **Virgil,** the great Roman epic poet, who will be the guide and counselor to Dante through the first part of the book. The journey through the afterlife is intended to help Dante see his life clearly and to resolve the confusion and turmoil that he feels. In other words, by understanding the purpose of life, Dante will gain solace and dedication to a spiritual goal.

Virgil leads Dante to the gates of hell as the beginning of the journey. The quotation at the beginning of this chapter reflects the despair ("Abandon all hope") that all must feel upon entering hell, or, as it is called in the book, Inferno. Dante's journey proceeds downward through a series of nine circles or levels until the bottom of hell is reached. A diagram of the pathway through inferno is shown in Figure 21.5. Details of the circles are given in Figure 21.6. As the travelers go deeper into hell, the sins increase in severity, at least in Dante's view. The depths of hell are for murderers and traitors such as Cain, Brutus, and Judas Iscariot. Satan himself is at the bottom.

The levels of hell represent places where sinners suffer punishments that are appropriate for their type of sin. One example is those who commit suicide. They are changed into trees because they did not value a body enough to keep theirs. Another is the lustful, who are blown about by strong winds, forever in the presence of the person with whom they committed their lustful sin, but unable to touch, since all the people are ghost-like and pass through each other. The winds are symbolic of the fleeting nature of lustful emotions and the diaphanous bodies signify the unsubstantial nature of emotions and lust. At each of the levels, Dante typically sees people whom he knows or knows about. In some cases Dante speaks to the people to investigate their circumstances and the nature of their sin. In the circle of lust Dante meets a woman and her lover. She tells Dante that she and her husband's brother were at home alone one day and began to read a tale of Lancelot and Guinevere. As the characters in the book became more intimately involved, so too did the woman and her brother-in-law, until they finally committed adultery. Dante creatively reflects the thinking errors of the woman who first blames love itself for her sin; that is, love made her do it. Then she blamed the book she was reading, because it led her to the sin. She could not seem to accept blame herself. That, of course, is part of her continuing sin and, evidently, her punishment. The woman and her

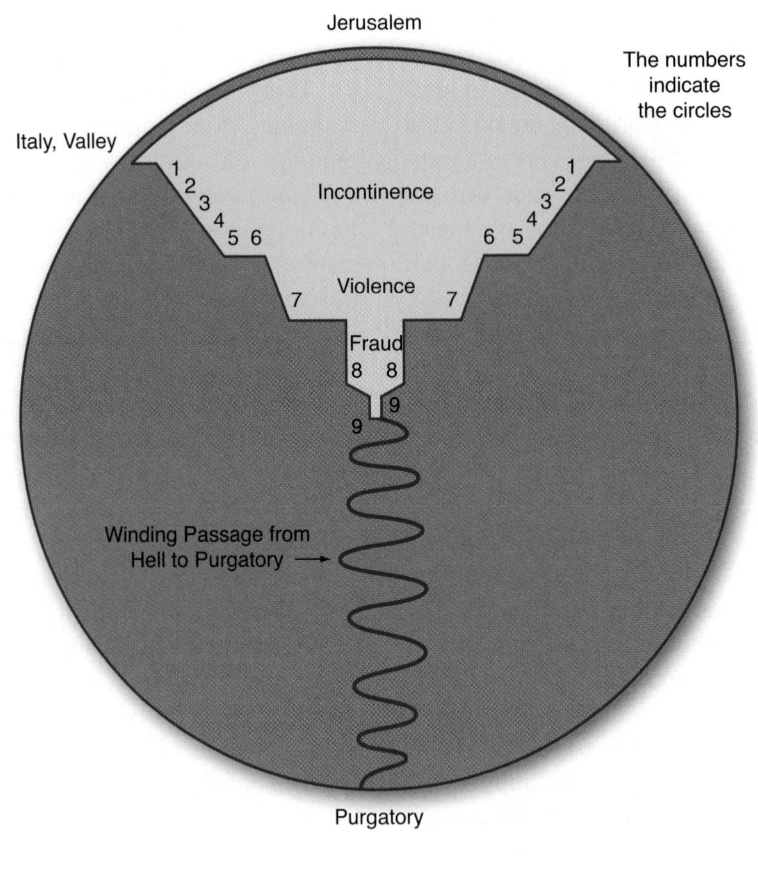

Figure 21.5 ■ *Representation of the pathway through Inferno, and the location of Purgatory, from Divine Comedy.*

lover were real people whose story became widely known in Italy at the time of Dante. Other people Dante encounters are historical figures, popes who Dante felt had committed serious sins, kings who were tyrants, and others whom Dante knew in real life. The politics of Italy and the Catholic Church are certainly evident throughout Dante's travels, providing a wonderful window for us to view life in the fourteenth century.

When Dante and Virgil finally reach the bottom of hell, they climb on Satan and enter a tunnel that takes them through the earth to the opposite side, where they finally emerge into the night and see the stars. One example of the symmetry of Dante's work is reflected in his use of the word *stelle* ("stars") as the last word in each of the three parts of the book.

Dante and Virgil find themselves at the foot of the mountain of Purgatory. They begin their assent and soon find that those who are capable of repentance can have their sins remitted by working on them as they climb. Each of the seven deadly sins (pride, envy, wrath, sloth, avarice/greed, gluttony, and lust/lasciviousness)

Selected Outline of The Inferno

Upper Hell (Incontinence)		
Region	**Sinners**	**Punishments**
Vestibule	Neutrals	Run after banners
Circle I	Limbo	Virtuous pagans—melancholy
Circle II	Lustful	Blown forever by storm winds
Circle III	Gluttons	Discomfort, all senses punished
Circle IV	Hoarders and wasters	Push great rocks against each other
Circle V	Wrathful/sullen	Immersed in slime
Lower Hell, Malice (Violence and Fraud)		
Circle VI	Heretics	In burning tombs
Circle VII	Violent	Lake of boiling blood or turned into trees (suicides)
Circle VIII	Fraud (10 levels)	Tormented by demons, in excrement, heads backwards, etc.
Circle IX	Treason	Buried in lake of ice

Figure 21.6 ■ *Details of the levels of Inferno.*

must be overcome. The pilgrims are marked on their foreheads with a "p" (*peccato,* Italian for "sin") for each of the sins that they must strive with. As the sin is conquered, the "p" disappears. When Dante nears the top of Purgatory, Virgil leaves and Dante is taken across the River of Forgetfulness. On the other side he is met by Beatrice, who then becomes his guide. He is given several riddles but cannot solve them. Beatrice reminds him that he cannot understand everything and that he needs understanding beyond his native intelligence. Dante faints with remorse, but when he awakens, he has forgotten all his sins. Dante is then taken to another river, where drinking the water restores his memory of good deeds.

The pilgrim and his guide then enter Paradise (heaven), which lies in seven spheres above the earth. Heaven's levels are divided by virtues rather than sins. Each level is arranged for Dante's benefit. Dante is greeted by Peter, James, and John, who question him on the issues of faith, hope, and love. Dante says his understanding of love is based on both reason and revelation, at which the hosts of heaven shout for joy. In the circle of the sun Dante meets two great intellects of history—St. Aquinas, a Dominican who praises the Franciscans, and St. Bonaventure, a Franciscan who praises the Dominicans. Dante is then met by his final guide—Bernard of Clairvaux. Beatrice leaves, as she was a good guide for illustrating the general virtues, but Dante now needs a more specific model and Bernard, a poet, teacher, crusader, reformer, and devout churchman, is the perfect example for Dante. After some contemplation, Dante realizes that he must become a crusader for truth and write a book about what he has seen and learned, as he believes Bernard would do if he were in Dante's place. Dante sees that he can overcome even his admitted weaknesses (lust and pride) by modeling his life after Bernard's. Dante then rises to meet God, who is situated at the

Figure 21.7 ■ *A painting of the Empyrean, by Gustave Doré. Image © Bettmann/Corbis.*

center of a rose-like arrangement with all of the hosts of heaven around Him like petals. This is the Empyrean. An etching of this scene, done by 19th-century illustrator, Gustave Doré, is shown in Figure 21.7.

The story of Dante's travels and the people whom he meets are only part of the art of the *Divine Comedy.* Numerical symbolism abounds, as well as other subtle intricacies in organization and underlying structure. Numerology was widely practiced during the Middle Ages in both Christian and Jewish literature. It was a method of communicating religious subtleties. For example, in Christian writings, the number 3 was seen as symbolic of the trinity; 4 was a symbol of the world since there were four elements in the Aristotelian world; 7 meant completeness, 10 was perfection, and 100 was super-perfection. Many other numbers also had special significance. The overall organization of *Divine Comedy* was certainly based on this type of numerology. There is 1 introductory canto, 33 cantos in Inferno, 33 cantos in Purgatory, and 33 cantos in Paradise for a total of 100–super-perfection. (Note that 33 is also the age of Christ when he died, thus adding further to the importance of this number.) In the Inferno there are 9 circles and 1 vestibule, for 10 locations. In purgatory there are 7 terraces plus an ante-purgatory plus a shore of purgatory plus an after-purgatory, for 10 locations. In paradise there are 10 heavens.

Even at a micro level, the symbolism and numerology are impressive. Each tercet has 3 lines of verse and 33 syllables, with 11 syllables per line. The rhyming pattern throughout—ABA/BCB/CDC—links the tercets together to give a unity to the entire work. The unity of the work is also expressed in features such as the ending word "stars" of each section—Inferno, Purgatory, and Paradise—as has already been mentioned. Also, the first verses of all three sections talk about water. The sixth verses of each section talk about politics (of Florence, Italy and the world, respectively). Some analysts have noted that the central verse of the entire work discusses "Roma," which is an anagram for "amor," Italian for "love," and have noted that Roma (the church and state) as well as love are the central themes of the book. Some may dismiss the numerology either as being fortuitous or as inventions of later analysts, but clearly some of the symmetry and organization were intended by Dante.

Standing back from the organization and symbolism in the work, we might ask, "What is the objective of this massive work?" It is an epic and, like other epics we have considered, it has a purpose. The *Odyssey* was about adventure, loyalty, and home; the *Aeneid* gave Romans a magnificent history and a set of values; and the *Divine Comedy* is about spiritual fulfillment and introspection. Dante wanted people to look at their lives in view of the consequences of their decisions and actions. For Dante, making choices was critical, and (he seemed to assert) there is no such thing as not making a choice. He also asserts that each person is responsible for his or her actions (or inactions), and these determine their place in the afterlife. There is no pre-destination, nor are there any gray areas. The criteria for making a choice are based on Christian principles—What would Jesus do in this situation? Is this action based on love of others? If continued to eternity, will this action result in happiness or pain? In Dante's book, hell is having what you, a sinful mortal, choose forever; but heaven is having what God chooses forever. Dante realizes that even the book itself is to be written, not for glory or gain, but to communicate the message of God. When he reaches that realization, he is ready to enter God's presence.

Petrarch

About a generation after Dante, Italian literature began an important transition, from religious writings such as *Divine Comedy* to secular writings that valued the wisdom and culture of ancient Greece and Rome, even to the point of ridiculing the culture of the Middle Ages. In fact, the term "Middle Ages" was invented during this time as a way of isolating and depreciating the period between the fall of the western Roman Empire and the rise of the new-found appreciation for the ancient classics. This new movement, which continued and grew until it flowered fully in the Renaissance, was called **Humanism.** The early leader of the movement was **Francesco Petrarch.**

Petrarch (1304–1374) was an ardent follower of Dante, and was seen as the successor to Dante. Just as Dante had written love poems about Beatrice, Petrarch wrote love poems about his **Laura,** whom he met in a church when he was 22, but he never had any association with her. In this, he followed the example of Dante. Petrarch's disciple, another Italian humanist, **Boccaccio,** also followed the pattern of courtly love for a woman who never became directly involved in his life. Boccaccio's love was called *Fiammetta,* "little flame."

Petrarch and the other humanists of his day believed that studying the ancient past could reveal truths that, in a Christian setting, would lead people to live better Christian lives. They saw valuable ethical teachings in the ancient writings, and also beauty and culture that had been lost and needed to be restored. They therefore advocated studies of these writings so that a person could be "liberated" from the narrow view of the medieval age. This concept today is the basis of a "liberal education." Petrarch was a strong advocate of liberating education and creative thinking, as can be seen in his statement, "The mind is not a vessel to be filled but a fire to be kindled."

We can, therefore, see Petrarch as a bridge between the strictly religious views of the medieval times and the more secular and even pagan views of the Renaissance. For some people, the paganism of these ancients was so offensive that they could not accept what had been written by them. For others, the paganism was incidental to the truths communicated; more often than not, the truths could be reconciled with Christian values, somewhat like Aquinas had done for Aristotelian thinking and Augustine had done for Plato's works. At this early stage, Petrarch was widely acclaimed for his writings. He was summoned to Rome, where he was crowned with a laurel wreath as the poet laureate in Rome. (He was also offered the position in France.) To show that he could be both a humanist and a Christian, he placed the laurel wreath on the tomb of St. Peter. Certainly this acceptance encouraged others, especially in Italy, to accept the writings of ancient Greece and Rome. This acceptance laid the foundations of the Renaissance and may be a chief reason why the Renaissance first took root in Italy.

Chaucer

Near the same time that Petrarch was writing humanistic poems in Italy, a new kind of writing was emerging in England. This new writing was also a combination of religion and secularism, but in England something else was involved. That additional factor was the language itself. England was moving from Old English to Middle English and the most famous of the writers using this new language was **Geoffrey Chaucer.** Before we examine his works, however, we should examine what was happening to the English language.

The basis of English is German as it was spoken, originally, by the Anglo-Saxons; that ancient language is known today as **Old English.** As we have already seen in a previous chapter, Old English was modified by the inclusion of Norse words, but these, too, were Germanic in origin, so the effect on the basic structure of the language was small. Further small changes to the language occurred when subjects such as Christianity were discussed and written, as in early Old English versions of the Bible. Again, the changes were largely within the existing structure of Old English. An interesting example is the method of creating a new word when Old English did not have an appropriate term. The practice, called **kenning,** was to combine two existing Old English words to match the meaning of the new term as closely as possible. For example, when translating the Bible, there was no Old English term for "disciple," so a new term was needed. The invented term was "learning-knight," which gives a delightful new dimension to disciple. Another example was the translation of John the Baptist. After kenning, his name was rendered as John the "Fully-wetter."

The invasion of the Normans in 1066 caused a much greater and longer-lasting change in English. The Normans spoke French and, although they continued to be socially separated from the Anglo-Saxon peasants, with time English began to change. It is interesting that those who spoke English seemed to have made a fundamental decision about how they viewed their language—a view that was decidedly different from those who spoke French. The English speakers saw English as an acquisitive language, that is, willing to acquire words from other languages rather than make up the words from already existing words. Kenning seemed to be a dead concept in the new Anglo and Norman world; simple word adoption had taken its place. This view likely occurred because the English speakers were the lower class and they would benefit, economically and culturally, from accepting the words spoken by the Norman nobility. We see this trend in the types of words that were adopted. Many words came from French court life, such as prince, game, poor, rich, master, court, prison, and prove. Castle, a French word, described the new rock-walled fortresses better than the Old English word for fortress, timberhall. English adopted the word "chivalry" and many of the other knightly terms from the French word for horseman and French words that described the actions of the English/Norman nobility.

Sometimes the new word was adopted even though Old English had a near cognate. When this happened, both words might be retained but could have different meanings because of the varying contexts in which they were used. Using modern French and German to illustrate the differences between the Norman and Anglo-Saxon languages, we can see how the new French words would enter the English language. Imagine a Norman nobleman who was hungry for some meat. He might ask his servant to go and buy a butchered cow (*boeuf,* in French) to get the food. The servant would go to an Anglo-Saxon peasant and, pointing to the cow, ask that the peasant kill the *kuh* (German for cow) so that it could be served to the nobleman. When the *kuh* of the peasant was served to the nobleman, it would be called *boeuf.* Both *kuh* and *boeuf* are really the same, since in their original languages they describe both the animal and the meat. In English, however, the animal is the cow (Germanic-derived) and the meat is beef (French-derived). Similar examples are calf *(kalb)* and veal *(veau);* swine *(schwein)* and pork *(porc),* and stool *(stuhl)* and chair *(chaise).* The concept can also be seen in house *(haus),* where an Anglo-Saxon lived, and mansion *(maison),* where a nobleman lived, which has, of course, given English the concept of mansion for a big house where the nobility would live.

Sometimes the Latin of the church was also adopted into English. The marriage ceremony, which needed to be understood by all people, included the words for love from Anglo-Saxon, French, and Latin and all are still preserved in the marriage phrase: love (Anglo-Saxon), honor (French), and cherish (Latin). All really meant "love" in medieval times. Many other examples in both church and legal affairs (such as stop, cease, and desist) illustrate this same seemingly redundant use of words.

As England began to interact with Europe through trade or wars, English was further enriched. Sometimes words from Arabic were taken into the language (alcohol, algebra, alchemy, zero, etc.) or, perhaps, from Spanish or Italian. Some interesting enrichments came from differences between the Norman French dialect and the Parisian dialect. For example, the Norman "c" was the equivalent of the Parisian "ch" and those differences have been retained in the following English words: cattle (Norman) versus chattel (Parisian), castle versus chateau, and cap versus chapeau. Likewise, the Norman "w" is equivalent to the Parisian "gu" to give us the English following words: warden (Norman) versus guardian (Parisian), wiley versus guile, and war versus guerre.

The interactions of the languages caused English to be a chaos of words and, inevitably, varying rules of grammar. Around the thirteenth and fourteenth centuries, the English speakers began to change the grammar rules to get consistency. Probably because English was the language of the peasants and because the basic concept of English had already been to acquire rather than preserve, the grammar rules became decidedly simpler than those in any of the other languages. Some of the changes were to eliminate the purely grammatical distinction between genders of words. Gone were the *der, die,* and *das* of German and also the *le* and *la* of French. In English, it is "the car" and "the auto," whereas in German it is *"der Wagen"* and *"das Auto,"* even though, in both languages, the words all have the same meaning. Similarly "the house" and "the castle" use the same article, whereas in French it is *"la maison"* and *"le château."* Gone too was the declension of nouns and adjectives. We can see this in the following sentences: "The father *(der Vater)* is old" (nominative case) versus "He gives the father *(dem Vater)* a book" (dative case). The German article is different depending on the case. It can get even more complex when both the adjective and the noun change, as in the following: "The child *(das Kind)* is small" (nominative case) versus "Give the child *(dem Kinde)* a book" (dative case). English also became a language of word order (syntax) rather than a language of endings (inflections). This meant that an English speaker could change meaning by saying "The man is short" versus "Is the man short?" When word endings were critically important, as they were in Old English, rhyming by making the ends of the words sound alike was difficult. Therefore, Old English obtained a poetic feel by using alliteration (words with similar beginnings), rather than through rhyming the end of the words, which became the normal rhyming method after the medieval period.

After all these changes, a new language emerged. It was called **Middle English.** It combined parts of both French and Old English, and simplified both. It was acceptable to both the Anglo-Saxon peasantry and the Norman nobility. The English court finally agreed to speak the same language as the commoners when Middle English was made the official language of the court (for all official documents as well as common speech) in the fifteenth century. Even with these dramatic changes, English retained its Anglo-Saxon (German) origins, especially in common speech. Two quotations from *The Story of English* reveal how English could benefit from its foreign imports and also how it could remain largely Anglo-Saxon.

> *The English language has three characteristics that can be counted as assets in its world state. First of all, unlike all other European languages, the gender of every noun in modern English is determined by meaning, and does not require a masculine, feminine or neuter article. . . . The second practical quality of English is that it has a grammar of great simplicity and flexibility. Nouns and adjectives have highly simplified word-endings. Nouns can become verbs and verbs nouns in a way that is impossible in other languages. . . . Above all, the great quality of English is its teeming vocabulary, 80 percent of which is foreign-born.*[2]

And,

> *Computer analysis of the language has shown that the 100 most common words in English are all of Anglo-Saxon origin. These roots are important. Anyone who speaks or*

> *writes English in the late twentieth century is using accents, words, and grammar which, with several dramatic modifications, go all the way back to the Old English of the Anglo-Saxons. There is an unbroken continuity from here to there. When, in 1940, Winston Churchill wished to appeal to the hearts and minds of the English-speaking people it is probably no accident that he did so with the plain bareness for which Old English is noted: 'We shall fight on the beaches; we shall fight on the landing grounds, we shall fight in the fields and in the streets, we shall fight in the hills; we shall never surrender.' In this celebrated passage, only surrender is foreign—Norman-French.*[3]

Despite its emergence as a strong and viable language, Middle English still needed to be solidified in literature. The person who did that was the foremost writer in this new language—Geoffrey Chaucer (1340–1400). He seemed to be just the right person at just the right time. He was born of a wealthy merchant father who gave him the best education possible, including several trips to Europe, where young Chaucer learned several languages. He was keenly interested in music, astronomy, physics, and medicine, and wrote papers on them in Latin. As a young man, he fought in the Hundred Years War and was captured and held for ransom, some of which was paid by the king of England. When released, he was involved in court life and therefore understood both the arts and politics. His writings reveal this varied background in the many classical allusions he made and the wide vocabulary he employed.

Chaucer's greatest work, ***Canterbury Tales,*** is great literature and it also gives wonderful insights into the historical setting of the fourteenth century. In this it is similar to the *Divine Comedy.* Both books also helped solidify their respective languages and became standards against which other works have been compared. Both selected a dialect that they felt would be most appropriate as the standard. Chaucer, interestingly, included several other dialects but clearly used them as dialects for individuals in the story and not as the standard language. Their books also tell much about their respective authors' lives. In both cases the authors are pilgrims who are characters in their book. Both books are rhymed and metered (Chaucer's is pentameter). Both authors also composed poems apart from their masterpieces. Chaucer's were light poems for amusement. He also translated various writings from French to English.

The language of *Canterbury Tales* can be sensed from the beginning lines of the introduction in the prologue. These are given in Figure 21.8 as Chaucer wrote them in Middle English. The language may be somewhat difficult to understand, at least until you get accustomed to it, so a Modern English version of the same selection is given in Figure 21.9. The French influence can be seen immediately in the following words, all taken from French: licour, vertu, engendred, Zephirus, corages, pilgrimages, and

Here bygynneth the Book of the Tales of Caunterbury

Whan that Aprill, with his shoures soote
The droghte of March hath perced to the roote
And bathed every veyne in swich licour,
Of which vertu engendred is the flour;

Whan Zephirus eek with his sweete breeth
Inspired hath in every holt and heeth
The tendre croppes, and the yonge sonne
Hath in the Ram his halfe cours yronne,
And smale foweles maken melodye,

That slepen al the nyght with open eye—
(So priketh hem Nature in hir corages);
Than longen folk to goon on pilgrimages
And palmeres for to seken straunge strondes
Top ferne halwes, kowthe in sondry londes;

And specially from every shires ende
Of Engelond, to Caunterbury they wende,
The hooly blisful martir for the seke
That hem hath holpen, whan that they were seeke.

Figure 21.8 ■ *Opening lines of the prologue of* Canterbury Tales, *in the Middle English.*

Here begins the Book of the Tales of Canterbury

When April with his showers sweet with fruit
The drought of March has pierced unto the root
And bathed each vein with liquor that has power
To generate therein and sire the flower;

When Zephyr also has, with his sweet breath,
Quickened again, in every holt and heath,
The tender shoots and buds, and the young sun
Into the Ram one half his course has run,
And many little birds make melody

That sleep through all the night with open eye
(So Nature pricks them on to ramp and rage)—
Then do folk long to go on pilgrimage,
And palmers to go seeking out strange strands,
To distant shrines will known in sundry lands.

And specially from every shire's end
Of England they to Canterbury wend,
The holy blessed martyr there to seek
Who helped them when they lay so ill and weak.

Figure 21.9 ■ *Opening lines of the prologue of* Canterbury Tales, *in modern English.*

palmers. Some features of Old English were also retained, such as the alliteration "shoures soote," "holt and heath," and "hem hath holpen." The mixture of words from Old English and French allowed Chaucer to control the meter and rhyme, plus give interest and beauty in the images created through the word selection. The classical allusions common throughout are also seen in this introduction with the reference to "Zephirus" (west winds) and "Hath in the Ram" (Aries of the Zodiac). The literary beauty is noted in the way the introduction begins with a wide view of nature and the skies, then moves in to see specific plants and birds, then to people; but the first view of people is worldly, then from all over England, then finally to those who are in the group going to Canterbury. The changes in view are dramatic, almost cinematic, as might be seen at the beginning of a movie.

The prologue of *Canterbury Tales* goes on to explain the setting and the organization of the book. A group of pilgrims is at an inn near London and about to travel to Canterbury on pilgrimage. The innkeeper suggests that they tell stories along the way to pass the time. He says that after the pilgrimage is over, he will give a free dinner to whomever tells the best story. The prologue then continues with a vibrant and lyrical description of each pilgrim. The descriptions often give subtle insights into the people. For example, the prioress is concerned about appearances and always crooks her finger when she drinks and always wipes her mouth after each bite. She is said to speak French whenever possible, but her French is of the English type, that is, spoken with a rather crude accent. In another prologue, the knight proudly outlines his many military engagements—so many in fact that we wonder if it is possible that one man could have been in so many places in his life. Perhaps the knight was too righteous and loyal to be real. In stories such as these, we get a delightful and sometimes satirical picture of each pilgrim. We also glimpse life in the medieval period.

After the prologue, we read the stories of several pilgrims. Each story reveals the personality and the interests of the storyteller. For example, the knight's tale is about chivalrous romance, using the concepts of courtly love; the miller's tale is a bawdy tale of a wife's sexual cheating on her husband; the wife of Bath tells about husbands who unsuccessfully try to squelch their wives; the tale of the reeve (administrative agent) is written in the dialect of the north, and some people are made to sound like simpletons. Sadly, the stories end before the group gets to Canterbury, so all the tales are not known, nor do we know the winner or the conclusion of the journey. However, the descriptions of each pilgrim and the stories we have are superb literature and insightful history.

Summary

Some people in the Middle Ages applauded the changes in the arts and literature, while others condemned them. The church seemed to accept the changes except when objectives of the church, such as hearing the words of the mass or the blatant introduction of paganism, were compromised; then there were clearly some limitations imposed by the church. But we might ask whether those limitations actually restricted creativity. It could be argued, especially by moderns, that creativity is always restricted when limitations are imposed. Dante would probably not agree. He wrote what was in his heart and seemed to use his book as a personal catharsis, without any noticeable inhibition by the church. Chaucer, likewise, seemed to write without any dampening of his creativity. Petrarch was aware of the need to respect the position of the church, but he did not seem restricted and, in fact, felt free to criticize as inferior the time of history in which the church was dominant. Sometimes creativity is actually enhanced because of the need to stay within limitations of one sort or another. Look at the way the limitations of meter and rhyme enhanced the creativity of both Dante and Chaucer. True, the limitations made the task more difficult, but maybe those limitations also made the accomplishment more enjoyable, both for the creator and for us.

Timeline—Important Dates

Date	Event
About 600 A.D.	*Gregorian chants authorized by Pope Gregory I*
990–1050	*Guido D'Arezzo develops musical notation*
About 1000	Organum *developed*
About 1000	*Arthurian legends appear in popular literature*
1163–1190	*Léonin is first composer recognized by name*
About 1150	*Troubadour music begins*
About 1200	Motet *developed*
About 1300	Ars Nova *developed*
1265–1321	*Dante Alighieri*
1319–1321	*Publication of the* Divine Comedy
1267–1337	*Giotto di Bondone*
1304–1374	*Francesco Petrarch*
1340–1400	*Geoffrey Chaucer*
1387–1400	*Writing and publication of* Canterbury Tales

Notes

1. Cabellanus, *The Art of Courtly Love,* Columbia University Press, 1960, extracted.
2. Robert McCrum, et. al., *The Story of English* (New York: Penguin Books, 1992), 30.
3. McCrum, 45.

Suggested Readings

Capellanus, Andreas, *The Art of Courtly Love,* John Jay Parry (trans.), Columbia University Press, 1960.

Chaucer, Geoffery, *Canterbury Tales,* J. U. Nicolson (trans.), Covici, Friede, 1934.

Dante, *The Divine Comedy,* John Ciardi (trans.), New American Library, 1970.

Kacirk, Jeffrey, *Forgotten English,* Morrow, 1997.

McCrum, Robert, William Cran, and Robert MacNeil, *The Story of English,* Penguin, 1992.

Pearl, Matthew, *The Dante Club,* Random House, 2004.

Article 34
Dante: Divine Comedy

Introduction

Dante Alighieri (1265–1321) was born in Florence and quickly became one of the great intellectuals of his period. His extensive published work proves his great love for literature, philosophy, theology, and science. Caught in the middle of a power struggle, he was falsely accused of a crime and exiled from his hometown. Dante lived the rest of his life in this exile, spending the years wandering through northern Italy and working on his masterpiece, the *Divine Comedy.*

The *Divine Comedy* is widely recognized as the greatest piece of literature from the Middle Ages. It relates a journey through hell, purgatory, and heaven (paradise). He wrote this massive work in exquisite Italian, using the preferred parts of many dialects, thus solidifying the Italian language that is used today. The work is not only filled with Dante's understanding of Christian doctrine, it is full of numerical and natural symbolism as well. Dante imbues personality in the book by using the love of his life (Beatrice), mentors, and heroes as his guides and as occupants of wonderful realms in the afterlife. He also includes enemies and others for whom he had contempt in various places of suffering. He includes references to events of his period, thus giving an insight into late Middle Ages life. Dante poured his soul into this work, treating his feelings on such topics as the consequences of sin, the relationship between love and divinity, truth, knowledge, and choices.

The following selections from *Divine Comedy* are shared here to provide a taste of that symbolism and personal feeling. The readings begin with Dante lost in a woods, symbolic of a mid-life crisis. He encounters a guide, Virgil, who takes him on a tour through the afterlife. He travels first to Inferno where he sees people suffering. Their punishment is fitted to their sins. You should read carefully to determine the meanings of this relationship and who are the sinners being punished. In your readings about Purgatory, note the differences in tone and feeling. There is progress here and hope for a better place. Finally in Paradise, the worthy of the world are blessed by their location. Dante will be given the chance to be here also, but he will move on to the glory of God. Note the importance of love in the final stages of his journey. The work is called divine because it is about the plan of God. It is a comedy because it ends happily with Dante learning the importance of giving love to others and then being taken into God's presence.

The Inferno

Canto I

The Dark Wood of Error

Midway in his allotted threescore years and ten, Dante comes to himself with a start and realizes that he has strayed from the True Way into the

Dark Wood of Error (Worldliness). As soon as he has realized his loss, Dante lifts his eyes and sees the first light of the sunrise (the Sun is the Symbol of Divine Illumination) lighting the shoulders of a little hill (The Mount of Joy). It is the Easter Season, the time of resurrection, and the sun is in its equinoctial rebirth. This juxtaposition of joyous symbols fills Dante with hope and he sets out at once to climb directly up the Mount of Joy, but almost immediately his way is blocked by the Three Beasts of Worldliness: THE LEOPARD OF MALICE AND FRAUD, THE LION OF VIOLENCE AND AMBITION, and THE SHE-WOLF OF INCONTINENCE. These beasts, and especially the She-Wolf, drive him back despairing into the darkness of error. But just as all seems lost, a figure appears to him. It is the shade of VIRGIL, Dante's symbol of HUMAN REASON.

Virgil explains that he has been sent to lead Dante from error. There can, however, be no direct ascent past the beasts: the man who would escape them must go a longer and harder way. First he must descend through Hell (The Recognition of Sin), then he must ascend through Purgatory (The Renunciation of Sin), and only then may he reach the pinnacle of joy and come to the Light of God. Virgil offers to guide Dante, but only as far as Human Reason can go. Another guide (BEATRICE, symbol of DIVINE LOVE) must take over for the final ascent, for Human Reason is self-limited. Dante submits himself joyously to Virgil's guidance and they move off.

Midway in our life's journey, I went astray
from the straight road and woke to find myself
alone in a dark wood. How shall I say

what wood that was! I never saw so drear,
so rank, so arduous a wilderness! 5
Its very memory gives a shape to fear.

Death could scarce be more bitter than that place!
But since it came to good, will recount
all that I found revealed there by God's grace.

How I came to it I cannot rightly say, 10
so drugged and loose with sleep had I become
when I first wandered there from the True Way.

But at the far end of that valley of evil
whose maze had sapped my very heart with fear!
I found myself before a little hill 15

and lifted up my eyes. Its shoulders glowed
already with the sweet rays of that planet
whose virtue leads men straight on every road,

and the shining strengthened me against the fright
whose agony had wracked the lake of my heart 20
through all the terrors of that piteous night.

Just as a swimmer, who with his last breath
flounders ashore from perilous seas, might turn
to memorize the wide water of his death—

so did I turn, my soul still fugitive 25
from death's surviving image, to stare down
that pass that none had ever left alive.

And there I lay to rest from my heart's race
till calm and breath returned to me. Then rose
and pushed up that dead slope at such a pace 30

each footfall rose above the last. And lo!
almost at the beginning of the rise
I faced a spotted Leopard, all tremor and flow

and gaudy pelt. And it would not pass, but stood
so blocking my every turn that time and again 35
I was on the verge of turning back to the wood.

This fell at the first widening of the dawn
as the sun was climbing Aries with
those stars
that rode with him to light the new creation.

Thus the holy hour and the sweet season 40
of commemoration did much to arm my fear
of that bright murderous beast with their
good omen.

Yet not so much but what I shook with dread
at sight of a great Lion that broke upon me
raging with hunger, its enormous head 45

held high as if to strike a mortal terror
into the very air. And down his track,
a She-Wolf drove upon me, a starved horror

ravening and wasted beyond all belief.
She seemed a rack for avarice, gaunt
and craving. 50
Oh many the souls she has brought to
endless grief!

She brought such heaviness upon my spirit
at sight of her savagery and desperation,
I died from every hope of that high summit.

And like a miser—eager in acquisition 55
but desperate in self-reproach when
Fortune's wheel
turns to the hour of his loss—all tears
and attrition

I wavered back; and still the beast pursued,
forcing herself against me bit by bit
till I slid back into the sunless wood. 60

And as I fell to my soul's ruin, a presence
gathered before me on the discolored air,
the figure of one who seemed hoarse from
long silence.

At sight of him in that friendless waste I cried:
"Have pity on me, whatever thing you are, 65
whether shade or living man."
And it replied:

"Not man, though man I once was, and
my blood
was Lombard, both my parents Mantuan.
I was born, though late, *sub Julio,* and bred

in Rome under Augustus in the noon 70
of the false and lying gods. I was a poet
and sang of old Anchises' noble son

who came to Rome after the burning of Troy.
But you—why do *you* return to
these distresses
instead of climbing that shining Mount
of Joy 75

which is the seat and first cause of man's bliss?"
"And are you then that Virgil and
that fountain
of purest speech?" My voice grew
tremulous:

"Glory and light of poets! now may that zeal
and love's apprenticeship that I poured out 80
on your heroic verses serve me well!

For you are my true master and first author,
the sole maker from whom I drew
the breath
of that sweet style whose measures have
brought me honor.

See there, immortal sage, the beast I flee. 85
For my soul's salvation, I beg you, guard
me from her,
for she has struck a mortal tremor
through me."

And he replied, seeing my soul in tears:
"He must go by another way who
would escape
this wilderness, for that mad beast
that fleers 90

before you there, suffers no man to pass.
She tracks down all, kills all, and knows
no glut,

but, feeding, she grows hungrier than
she was.

She mates with any beast, and will mate
with more
before the Greyhound comes to hunt
her down. 95
He will not feed on lands nor loot,
but honor

and love and wisdom will make straight his way.
He will rise between Feltro and Feltro,
and in him
shall be the resurrection and new day

of that sad Italy for which Nisus died, 100
and Turnus, and Euryalus, and the
maid Camilla.
He shall hunt her through every nation of
sick pride

till she is driven back forever to Hell
whence Envy first released her on
the world.
Therefore, for your own good, I think
it well 105

you follow me and I will be your guide
and lead you forth through an eternal place.
There you shall see the ancient spirits tried

in endless pain, and hear their lamentation
as each bemoans the second death of souls. 110
Next you shall see upon a burning mountain

souls in fire and yet content in fire,
knowing that whensoever it may be
they yet will mount into the blessed choir.

To which, if it is still your wish to climb, 115
a worthier spirit shall be sent to guide you.
With her shall I leave you, for the King
of Time,

who reigns on high, forbids me to come there
since, living, I rebelled against his law.
He rules the waters and the land and air 120

and there holds court, his city and his throne.
Oh blessed are they he chooses!" And I
to him:
"Poet, by that God to you unknown,

lead me this way. Beyond this present ill
and worse to dread, lead me to Peter's gate 125
and be my guide through the sad halls
of Hell."

And he then: "Follow." And he moved ahead
in silence, and I followed where he led.

Notes

1. *Midway in our life's journey:* The Biblical life span is threescore years and ten. The action opens in Dante's thirty-fifth year, i.e., A.D. 1300.

17. *that planet:* The Sun. Ptolemaic astronomers considered it a planet. It is also symbolic of God as He who lights man's way.

31. *each footfall rose above the last:* The literal rendering would be: "So that the fixed foot was ever the lower." "Fixed" has often been translated "right" and an ingenious reasoning can support that reading, but a simpler explanation offers itself and seems more competent: Dante is saying that he climbed with such zeal and haste that every footfall carried him above the last despite the steepness of the climb. At a slow pace, on the other hand, the rear foot might be brought up only as far as the forward foot. This device of selecting a minute but exactly centered detail to convey the whole of a larger action is one of the central characteristics of Dante's style.

THE THREE BEASTS. These three beasts undoubtedly are taken from *Jeremiah,* v, 6. Many additional and incidental interpretations have been advanced for them, but the central interpretation must remain as noted. They foreshadow the three divisions of Hell (incontinence, violence, and fraud) which Virgil explains at length in Canto XI, 16–111. I am not at all sure but what the She-Wolf is better interpreted as Fraud and the Leopard as Incontinence. Good arguments can be offered either way.

38–39. *Aries . . . that rode with him to light the new creation:* The medieval tradition had it that the sun was in Aries at the time of the Creation. The significance of the astronomical and religious conjunction is an important part of Dante's intended allegory. It is just before dawn of Good Friday A.D. 1300 when he awakens in the Dark Wood. Thus his new life begins under Aries, the sign of creation, at dawn (rebirth) and in the Easter season (resurrection). Moreover the moon is full and the sun is in the equinox, conditions that did not fall together on any Friday of 1300. Dante is obviously constructing poetically the perfect Easter as a symbol of his new awakening.

69. *sub Julio:* In the reign of Julius Caesar.

95. *The Greyhound . . . Feltro and Feltro:* Almost certainly refers to Can Grande della Scala (1290–1329), great Italian leader born in Verona, which lies between the towns of Feltre and Montefeltro.

100–101. *Nisus, Turnus, Euryalus, Camilla:* All were killed in the war between the Trojans and the Latians when, according to legend, Aeneas led the survivors of Troy into Italy. Nisus and Euryalus (*Aeneid,* IX) were Trojan comrades-in-arms who died together. Camilla (*Aeneid,* XI) was the daughter of the Latian king and one of the warrior women. She was killed in a horse charge against the Trojans after displaying great galantry. Turnus (*Aeneid,* XII) was killed by Aeneas in a duel.

110. *the second death:* Damnation. "This is the second death, even the lake of fire." (*Revelation,* xx, 14)

118. *forbids me to come there since, living, etc.:* Salvation is only through Christ in Dante's theology. Virgil lived and died before the establishment of Christ's teachings in Rome, and cannot therefore enter Heaven.

125. *Peter's gate:* The gate of Purgatory. (See *Purgatorio,* IX, 76 ff.) The gate is guarded by an angel with a gleaming sword. The angel is Peter's vicar (Peter, the first Pope, symbolized all Popes; *i.e.,* Christ's vicar on earth) and is entrusted with the two great keys.

Some commentators argue that this is the gate of Paradise, but Dante mentions no gate beyond this one in his ascent to Heaven. It should be remembered, too, that those who pass the gate of Purgatory have effectively entered Heaven.

The three great gates that figure in the entire journey are: the gate of Hell (Canto III, 1–11), the gate of Dis (Canto VIII, 79–113, and Canto IX, 86–87), and the gate of Purgatory, as above.

Canto III

The Vestibule of Hell
The Opportunists

The Poets pass the Gate of Hell and are immediately assailed by cries of anguish. Dante sees the first of the souls in torment. They are THE OPPORTUNISTS, those souls who in life were neither for good nor evil but only for themselves. Mixed with them are those outcasts who took no sides in the Rebellion of the Angels. They are neither in Hell nor out of it. Eternally unclassified, they race round and round pursuing a wavering banner that runs forever before them through the dirty air; and as they run they are pursued by swarms of wasps and hornets, who sting them and produce a constant flow of blood and putrid matter which trickles down the bodies of the sinners and is feasted upon by loathsome worms and maggots who coat the ground.

The law of Dante's Hell is the law of symbolic retribution. As they sinned so are they punished. They took no sides, therefore they are given no place. As they pursued the ever-shifting illusion of their own advantage, changing their courses with every changing wind, so they pursue eternally an elusive, ever-shifting banner. As their sin was a darkness, so they move in darkness. As their own guilty conscience pursued them, so they are pursued by swarms of wasps and hornets. And as their actions were a moral filth, so they run eternally through the filth of worms and maggots which they themselves feed.

Dante recognizes several, among them POPE CELESTINE V, but without delaying to speak to any of these souls, the Poets move on to ACHERON, the first of the rivers of Hell. Here the newly-arrived souls of the damned gather and wait for monstrous CHARON to ferry them over to punishment. Charon recognizes Dante as a living man and angrily refuses him passage. Virgil forces Charon to serve them, but Dante swoons with terror, and does not reawaken until he is on the other side.

I AM THE WAY INTO THE CITY OF WOE.
I AM THE WAY TO A FORSAKEN PEOPLE.
I AM THE WAY INTO ETERNAL SORROW.

SACRED JUSTICE MOVED MY ARCHITECT.
I WAS RAISED HERE BY DIVINE OMNIPOTENCE, 5
PRIMORDIAL LOVE AND ULTIMATE INTELLECT.

ONLY THOSE ELEMENTS TIME CANNOT WEAR
WERE MADE BEFORE ME, AND BEYOND TIME I STAND.
ABANDON ALL HOPE YE WHO ENTER HERE.

These mysteries I read cut into stone 10
above a gate. And turning I said: "Master,
what is the meaning of this harsh inscription?"

And he then as initiate to novice:
"Here must you put by all division of spirit
and gather your soul against all cowardice. 15

This is the place I told you to expect.
Here you shall pass among the fallen people,
souls who have lost the good of intellect."

So saying, he put forth his hand to me,
and with a gentle and encouraging smile 20
he led me through the gate of mystery.

Here sighs and cries and wails coiled and recoiled
on the starless air, spilling my soul to tears.
A confusion of tongues and monstrous accents toiled

in pain and anger. Voices hoarse and shrill 25
and sounds of blows, all intermingled, raised
tumult and pandemonium that still

whirls on the air forever dirty with it
as if a whirlwind sucked at sand. And I,
holding my head in horror, cried: "Sweet Spirit, 30

what souls are these who run through this black haze?"
And he to me: "These are the nearly soulless
whose lives concluded neither blame nor praise.

They are mixed here with that despicable corps
of angels who were neither for God nor Satan, 35
but only for themselves. The High Creator

scourged them from Heaven for its perfect beauty,
and Hell will not receive them since the wicked
might feel some glory over them." And I:

"Master, what gnaws at them so hideously 40
their lamentation stuns the very air?"
"They have no hope of death," he answered me,

"and in their blind and unattaining state
their miserable lives have sunk so low
that they must envy every other fate. 45

No word of them survives their living season.
Mercy and Justice deny them even a name.
Let us not speak of them: look, and pass on."

I saw a banner there upon the mist.
Circling and circling, it seemed to scorn
all pause. 50
So it ran on, and still behind it pressed

a never-ending rout of souls in pain.
I had not thought death had undone so many
as passed before me in that mournful train.

And some I knew among them; last of all 55
I recognized the shadow of that soul
who, in his cowardice, made the
Great Denial.

At once I understood for certain: these
were of that retrograde and faithless crew"
hateful to God and to His enemies. 60

These wretches never born and never dead
ran naked in a swarm of wasps and hornets
that goaded them the more the more
they fled,

and made their faces stream with bloody gouts 65
of pus and tears that dribbled to their feet
to be swallowed there by loathsome
worms and maggots.

Then looking onward I made out a throng
assembled on the beach of a wide river,
whereupon I turned to him: "Master, I long

to know what souls these are, and what
strange usage 70
makes them as eager to cross as they
seem to be
in this infected light." At which the Sage:

"All this shall be made known to you when we
stand
on the joyless beach of Acheron." And I
cast down my eyes, sensing a reprimand 75

in what he said, and so walked at his side
in silence and ashamed until we came
through the dead cavern to that
sunless tide.

There, steering toward us in an ancient ferry
came an old man with a white bush of hair, 80
bellowing: "Woe to you depraved
souls! Bury

here and forever all hope of Paradise:
I come to lead you to the other shore,
into eternal dark, into fire and ice.

And you who are living yet, I say begone 85
from these who are dead." But when he
saw me stand
against his violence he began again:

"By other windings and by other steerage
shall you cross to that other shore.
Not here! Not here!
A lighter craft than mine must give
you passage." 90

And my Guide to him: "Charon, bite back
your spleen:
this has been willed where what is
willed must be,
and is not yours to ask what it may mean."

The steersman of that marsh of ruined souls,
who wore a wheel of flame around
each eye, 95
stifled the rage that shook his woolly jowls.

But those unmanned and naked spirits there
turned pale with fear and their teeth began
to chatter
at sound of his crude bellow. In despair

they blasphemed God, their parents, their time
on earth, 100
the race of Adam, and the day and the hour
and the place and the seed and the womb
that gave them birth.

But all together they drew to that grim shore
where all must come who lose the fear
of God.
Weeping and cursing they come for
evermore, 105

and demon Charon with eyes like burning coals
herds them in, and with a whistling oar
flails on the stragglers to his wake of souls.

As leaves in autumn loosen and stream down
until the branch stands bare above its tatters 110
spread on the rustling ground, so one by one

the evil seed of Adam in its Fall
cast themselves, at his signal, from
the shore
and streamed away like birds who hear
their call.

So they are gone over that shadowy water, 115
and always before they reach the
other shore
a new noise stirs on this, and new
throngs gather.

"My son," the courteous Master said to me,
"all who die in the shadow of God's wrath
converge to this from every clime
and country. 120

And all pass over eagerly, for here
Divine Justice transforms and spurs them so
their dread turns wish: they yearn for what
they fear.

No soul in Grace comes ever to this crossing;
therefore if Charon rages at your presence 125
you will understand the reason for
his cursing."

When he had spoken, all the twilight country
shook so violently, the terror of it
bathes me with sweat even in memory:

the tear-soaked ground gave out a sigh of wind 130
that spewed itself in flame on a red sky,
and all my shattered senses left me. Blind,

like one whom sleep comes over in a swoon,
I stumbled into darkness and went down.

Notes

7–8. *Only those elements time cannot wear:* The Angels, the Empyrean, and the First Matter are the elements time cannot wear, for they will last to all time. Man, however, in his mortal state, is not eternal. The Gate of Hell, therefore, was created before man. The theological point is worth attention. The doctrine of Original Sin is, of course, one familiar to many creeds. Here, however, it would seem that the preparation for damnation predates Original Sin. True, in one interpretation, Hell was created for the punishment of the Rebellious Angels and not for man. Had man not sinned, he would never have known Hell. But on the other hand, Dante's God was one who knew all, and knew therefore that man would indeed sin. The theological problem is an extremely delicate one.

It is significant, however, that having sinned, man lives out his days on the rind of Hell, and that damnation is forever below his feet. This central concept of man's sinfulness, and, opposed to it, the doctrine of Christ's ever-abounding mercy, are central to all of Dante's theology. Only as man surrenders himself to Divine Love may he hope for salvation, and salvation is open to all who will surrender themselves.

8. *and beyond time I stand:* So odious is sin to God that there can be no end to its just punishment.

9. *Abandon all hope ye who enter here:* The admonition, of course, is to the damned and not to those who come on Heaven-sent errands. The Harrowing of Hell (see Canto IV, note to l. 53) provided the only exemption from this decree, and that only through the direct intercession of Christ.

57. *who, in his cowardice, made the Great Denial:* This is almost certainly intended to be Celestine V, who became Pope in 1294. He was a man of saintly life, but allowed himself to be convinced by a priest named Benedetto that his soul was in danger since

no man could live in the world without being damned. In fear for his soul he withdrew from all worldly affairs and renounced the Papacy. Benedetto promptly assumed the mantle himself and became Boniface VIII, a Pope who became for Dante a symbol of all the worst corruptions of the Church. Dante also blamed Boniface and his intrigues for many of the evils that befell Florence. We shall learn in Canto XIX that the fires of Hell are waiting for Boniface in the pit of the Simoniacs, and we shall be given further evidence of his corruption in Canto XXVII. Celestine's great guilt is that his cowardice (in selfish terror for his own welfare) served as the door through which so much evil entered the Church.

80. *an old man:* Charon. He is the ferryman of dead souls across the Acheron in all classical mythology.

88–90. *By other windings:* Charon recognizes Dante not only as a living man but as a soul in grace, and knows, therefore, that the Infernal Ferry was not intended for him. He is probably referring to the fact that souls destined for Purgatory and Heaven assemble not at his ferry point, but on the banks of the Tiber, from which they are transported by an Angel.

100. *they blasphemed God:* The souls of the damned are not permitted to repent, for repentance is a divine grace.

123. *they yearn for what they fear:* Hell (allegorically Sin) is what the souls of the damned really wish for. Hell is their actual and deliberate choice, for divine grace is denied to none who wish for it in their hearts. The damned must, in fact, deliberately harden their hearts to God in order to become damned. Christ's grace is sufficient to save all who wish for it.

133–134. DANTE'S SWOON. This device (repeated at the end of Canto V) serves a double purpose. The first is technical: Dante uses it to cover a transition. We are never told how he crossed Acheron, for that would involve certain narrative matters he can better deal with when he crosses Styx in Canto VII. The second is to provide a point of departure for a theme that is carried through the entire descent: the theme of Dante's emotional reaction to Hell. These two swoons early in the descent show him most susceptible to the grief about him. As he descends, pity leaves him, and he even goes so far as to add to the torments of one sinner. The allegory is clear: we must harden ourselves against every sympathy for sin.

Canto V

Circle Two
The Carnal

The Poets leave Limbo and enter the SECOND CIRCLE. Here begin the torments of Hell proper, and here, blocking the way, sits MINOS, the dread and semi-bestial judge of the damned who assigns to each soul its eternal torment. He orders the Poets back; but Virgil silences him as he earlier silenced Charon, and the Poets move on.

They find themselves on a dark ledge swept by a great whirlwind, which spins within it the souls of the CARNAL, those who betrayed reason to their appetites. Their sin was to abandon themselves to the tempest of their passions: so they are swept forever in the tempest of Hell, forever denied the light of reason and of God. Virgil identifies many among them. SEMIRAMIS is there, and DIDO, CLEOPATRA, HELEN, ACHILLES, PARIS, and TRISTAN. Dante sees PAOLO and FRANCESCA swept together, and in the name of love he calls to them to tell their sad story. They pause from their eternal flight to come to him, and Francesca tells their history while Paolo weeps at her side. Dante is so stricken by compassion at their tragic tale that he swoons once again.

So we went down to the second ledge alone;
a smaller circle of so much greater pain
the voice of the damned rose in a
bestial moan.

There Minos sits, grinning, grotesque, and hale.
He examines each lost soul as it arrives 5
and delivers his verdict with his coiling tail.

That is to say, when the ill-fated soul
appears before him it confesses all,
and that grim sorter of the dark and foul

decides which place in Hell shall be its end, 10
then wraps his twitching tail about himself
one coil for each degree it must descend.

The soul descends and others take its place:
each crowds in its turn to judgment,
each confesses,
each hears its doom and falls away
through space. 15

"O you who come into this camp of woe,"
cried Minos when he saw me turn away
without awaiting his judgment, "watch
where you go

once you have entered here, and to whom
you turn!
Do not be misled by that wide and
easy passage!" 20
And my Guide to him: "That is not
your concern;

it is his fate to enter every door.
This has been willed where what is willed
must be,
and is not yours to question. Say no more."

Now the choir of anguish, like a wound, 25
strikes through the tortured air. Now
I have come
to Hell's full lamentation, sound
beyond sound.

I came to a place stripped bare of every light
and roaring on the naked dark like seas
wracked by a war of winds. Their
hellish flight 30

of storm and counterstorm through time
foregone,
sweeps the souls of the damned before
its charge.
Whirling and battering it drives them on,

and when they pass the ruined gap of Hell
through which we had come, their
shrieks begin anew. 35
There they blaspheme the power of
God eternal.

And this, I learned, was the never-ending flight
of those who sinned in the flesh,
the carnal and lusty
who betrayed reason to their appetite.

As the wings of wintering starlings bear
them on 40
in their great wheeling flights, just so
the blast
wherries these evil souls through
time foregone.

Here, there, up, down, they whirl and,
whirling, strain
with never a hope of hope to comfort them,
not of release, but even of less pain. 45

As cranes go over sounding their harsh cry,
leaving the long streak of their flight in air,
so come these spirits, wailing as they fly.

And watching their shadows lashed by wind,
I cried:
"Master, what souls are these the very air 50
lashes with its black whips from side
to side?"

"The first of these whose history you would
know,"
he answered me, "was Empress of
many tongues.
Mad sensuality corrupted her so

that to hide the guilt of her debauchery 55
she licensed all depravity alike,
and lust and law were one in her decree.

She is Semiramis of whom the tale is told
how she married Ninus and succeeded him
to the throne of that wide land the
Sultans hold. 60

The other is Dido; faithless to the ashes
of Sichaeus, she killed herself for love.
The next whom the eternal tempest lashes

is sense-drugged Cleopatra. See Helen there,
from whom such ill arose. And
great Achilles, 65
who fought at last with love in the
house of prayer.

And Paris. And Tristan." As they whirled above
he pointed out more than a thousand shades
of those torn from the mortal life by love.

I stood there while my Teacher one by one 70
named the great knights and ladies of
dim time;
and I was swept by pity and confusion.

At last I spoke: "Poet, I should be glad
to speak a word with those two
swept together
so lightly on the wind and still so sad." 75

And he to me: "Watch them. When next
they pass,
call to them in the name of love that drives
and damns them here. In that name they
will pause."

Thus, as soon as the wind in its wild course
brought them around, I called: "O
wearied souls! 80
if none forbid it, pause and speak to us."

As mating doves that love calls to their nest
glide through the air with motionless
raised wings,
borne by the sweet desire that fills
each breast—

Just so those spirits turned on the torn sky 85
from the band where Dido whirls
across the air;
such was the power of pity in my cry.

"O living creature, gracious, kind, and good,
going this pilgrimage through the sick night,
visiting us who stained the earth with blood, 90

were the King of Time our friend, we would
pray His peace
on you who have pitied us. As long as
the wind
will let us pause, ask of us what you please.

The town where I was born lies by the shore
where the Po descends into its ocean rest 95
with its attendant streams in one
long murmur.

Love, which in gentlest hearts will
soonest bloom
seized my lover with passion for that
sweet body
from which I was torn unshriven to
my doom.

Love, which permits no loved one not to love, 100
took me so strongly with delight in him
that we are one in Hell, as we were above.

Love led us to one death. In the depths of Hell
Caïna waits for him who took our lives."
This was the piteous tale they stopped
to tell. 105

And when I had heard those world-offended
lovers
I bowed my head. At last the Poet spoke:
"What painful thoughts are these your
lowered brow covers?"

When at length I answered, I began: "Alas!
What sweetest thoughts, what green and

young desire 110
led these two lovers to this sorry pass."

Then turning to those spirits once again,
I said: "Francesca, what you suffer here
melts me to tears of pity and of pain.

But tell me: in the time of your sweet sighs 115
by what appearances found love the way
to lure you to his perilous paradise?"

And she: "The double grief of a lost bliss
is to recall its happy hour in pain.
Your Guide and Teacher knows the truth
of this. 120

But if there is indeed a soul in Hell
to ask of the beginning of our love
out of his pity, I will weep and tell:

On a day for dalliance we read the rhyme
of Lancelot, how love had mastered him. 125
We were alone with innocence and
dim time.

Pause after pause that high old story drew
our eyes together while we blushed
and paled;
but it was one soft passage overthrew

our caution and our hearts. For when we read 130
how her fond smile was kissed by such
a lover,
he who is one with me alive and dead

breathed on my lips the tremor of his kiss.
That book, and he who wrote it, was
a pander.
That day we read no further." As she
said this, 135

the other spirit, who stood by her, wept
so piteously, I felt my senses reel
and faint away with anguish. I was swept

by such a swoon as death is, and I fell,
as a corpse might fall, to the dead floor of Hell. 140

Notes

2. *a smaller circle:* The pit of Hell tapers like a funnel. The circles of ledges accordingly grow smaller as they descend.
4. *Minos:* Like all the monsters Dante assigns to the various offices of Hell, Minos is drawn from classical mythology. He was the son of Europa and of Zeus who descended to her in the form of a bull. Minos became a mythological king of Crete, so famous for his wisdom and justice that after death his soul was made judge of the dead. Virgil presents him fulfilling the same office at Aeneas' descent to the underworld. Dante, however, transforms him into an irate and hideous monster with a tail. The transformation may have been suggested by the form Zeus assumed for the rape of Europa—the monster is certainly bullish enough here—but the obvious purpose of the brutalization is to present a figure symbolic of the guilty conscience of the wretches who come before it to make their confessions. Dante freely reshapes his materials to his own purposes.
8. *it confesses all:* Just as the souls appeared eager to cross Acheron, so they are eager to confess even while they dread. Dante is once again making the point that sinners elect their Hell by an act of their own will.
27. *Hell's full lamentation:* It is with the second circle that the real tortures of Hell begin.
34. *the ruined gap of Hell:* See note to Canto IV, 53. At the time of the Harrowing of Hell a great earthquake shook the underworld shattering rocks and cliffs. Ruins resulting from the same shock are noted in Canto XII, 34, and Canto XXI, 112 ff. At the beginning of Canto XXIV, the Poets leave the *bolgia* of the Hypocrites by climbing the ruined slabs of a bridge that was shattered by this earthquake.

THE SINNERS OF THE SECOND CIRCLE (THE CARNAL): Here begin the punishments for the various sins of Incontinence (The sins of the She-Wolf). In the second circle are punished those who sinned by excess of sexual passion. Since this is the most natural sin and the sin most nearly associated with love, its punishment is the lightest of all to be found in Hell proper. The Carnal are whitled and buffeted endlessly through the murky air (symbolic of the beclouding of their reason by passion) by a great gale (symbolic of their lust).

53. *Empress of many tongues:* Semiramis, a legendary queen of Assyria who assumed full power at the death of her husband, Ninus.

61. *Dido:* Queen and founder of Carthage. She had vowed to remain faithful to her husband, Sichaeus, but she fell in love with Aeneas. When Aeneas abandoned her she stabbed herself on a funeral pyre she had had prepared.

According to Dante's own system of punishment, she should be in the Seventh Circle (Canto XIII) with the suicides. The only clue Dante gives to the tempering of her punishment is his statement that "she killed herself for love." Dante always seems readiest to forgive in that name.

65. *Achilles:* He is placed among this company because of his passion for Polyxena, the daughter of Priam. For love of her, he agreed to desert the Greeks and to join the Trojans, but when he went to the temple for the wedding (according to the legend, Dante has followed) he was killed by Paris.

74. *those two swept together:* Paolo and Francesca (PAH-oe-loe; Frahn-CHAY-ska).

Dante's treatment of these two lovers is certainly the tenderest and most sympathetic accorded any of the sinners in Hell, and legends immediately began to grow about this pair.

The facts are these. In 1275 Giovanni Malatesta (Djoe-VAH-nee Mahl-ah-TEH-stah) of Rimini, called Giovanni the Lame, a somewhat deformed but brave and powerful warrior, made a political marriage with Francesca, daughter of Guido da Polenta of Ravenna. Francesca came to Rimini and there an amour grew between her and Giovanni's younger brother Paolo. Despite the fact that Paolo had married in 1269 and had become the father of two daughters by 1275, his affair with Francesca continued for many years. It was sometime between 1283 and 1286 that Giovanni surprised them in Francesca's bedroom and killed both of them.

Around these facts the legend has grown that Paolo was sent by Giovanni as his proxy to the marriage, that Francesca thought he was her real bridegroom and accordingly gave him her heart irrevocably at first sight. The legend obviously increases the pathos, but nothing in Dante gives it support.

102. *that we are one in Hell, as we were above:* At many points of the *Inferno* Dante makes clear the principle that the souls of the damned are locked so blindly into their own guilt that none can feel sympathy for another, or find any pleasure in the presence of another. The temptation of many readers is to interpret this line romantically: *i.e.,* that the love of Paolo and Francesca survives Hell itself. The more Dantean interpretation, however, is that they add to one another's anguish (a) as mutual reminders of their sin, and (b) as insubstantial shades of the bodies for which they once felt such great passion.

104. *Caïna waits for him:* Giovanni Malatesta was still alive at the writing. His fate is already decided, however, and upon his death, his soul will fall to Caïna, the first ring of the last circle (Canto XXXII), where lie those who performed acts of treachery against their kin.

124–125. *the rhyme of Lancelot:* The story exists in many forms. The details Dante makes use of are from an Old French version.

126. *dim time:* The original simply reads "We were alone, suspecting nothing." "Dim time" is rhyme-forced, but not wholly outside the legitimate implications of the original, I hope. The old courtly romance may

well be thought of as happening in the dim ancient days. The apology, of course, comes after the fact: one does the possible then argues for justification, and there probably is none.

134. *that book, and he who wrote it, was a pander:* "Galeotto," the Italian word for "pander," is also the Italian rendering of the name of Gallehault, who, in the French Romance Dante refers to here, urged Lancelot and Guinevere on to love.

Canto XXXIV

Ninth circle: Cocytus	*Compound Fraud*
Round Four: Judecca	*The Treacherous*
The Center	*to Their Masters Satan*

"On march the banners of the King," Virgil begins as the Poets face the last depth. He is quoting a medieval hymn, and to it he adds the distortion and perversion of all that lies about him. "On march the banners of the King—of Hell." And there before them, in an infernal parody of Godhead, they see Satan in the distance, his great wings beating like a windmill. It is their beating that is the source of the icy wind of Cocytus, the exhalation of all evil.

All about him in the ice are strewn the sinners of the last round, JUDECCA, named for Judas Iscariot. These are the TREACHEROUS TO THEIR MASTERS. They lie completely sealed in the ice, twisted and distorted into every conceivable posture. It is impossible to speak to them, and the Poets move on to observe Satan.

He is fixed into the ice at the center to which flow all the rivers of guilt, and as he beats his great wings as if to escape, their icy wind only freezes him more surely into the polluted ice. In a grotesque parody of the Trinity, he has three faces, each a different color, and in each mouth he clamps a sinner whom he rips eternally with his teeth. JUDAS ISCARIOT is in the central mouth, BRUTUS and CASSIUS in the mouths on either side.

Having seen all, the Poets now climb through the center, grappling hand over hand down the hairy flank of Satan himself—a last supremely symbolic action—and at last, when they have passed the center of all gravity, they emerge from Hell. A long climb from the earth's center to the Mount of Purgatory awaits them, and they push on without rest ascending along the sides of the river Lethe, till they emerge once more to see the stars of Heaven, just before dawn on Easter Sunday.

"On march the banners of the King of Hell,"
my Master said. "Toward us. Look straight ahead:
can you make him out at the core of the frozen shell?"

Like a whirling windmill seen afar at twilight,
or when a mist has risen from the ground— 5
just such an engine rose upon my sight

stirring up such a wild and bitter wind
I cowered for shelter at my Master's back,
there being no other windbreak I could find.

I stood now where the souls of the last class 10
(with fear my verses tell it) were covered wholly;
they shone below the ice like straws in glass.

Some lie stretched out; others are fixed in place
upright, some on their heads, some on their soles; 15
another, like a bow, bends foot to face.

When we had gone so far across the ice
that it pleased my Guide to show me the foul creature
which once had worn the grace of Paradise,

he made me stop, and, stepping aside, he said:
"Now see the face of Dis! This is the place 20
where you must arm your soul against all dread."

Do not ask, Reader, how my blood ran cold
and my voice chocked up with fear. I cannot write it:
this is a terror that cannot be told.

I did not die, and yet I lost life's breath: 25
imagine for yourself what I became,
deprived at once of both my life
and death.

The Emperor of the Universe of Pain
jutted his upper chest above the ice;
and I am closer in size to the
great mountain 30

the Titans make around the central pit,
than they to his arms. Now, starting from
this part,
imagine the whole that corresponds to it!

If he was once as beautiful as now
he is hideous, and still turned on his Maker, 35
well may he be the source of every woe!

With what a sense of awe I saw his head
towering above me! for it had three faces:
one was in front, and it was fiery red;

the other two, as weirdly wonderful, 40
merged with it from the middle of
each shoulder
to the point where all converged at the top
of the skull;

the right was something between white and bile;
the left was about the color that one finds
on those who live along the banks of
the Nile. 45

Under each head two wings rose terribly,
their span proportioned to so gross a bird:
I never saw such sails upon the sea.

They were not feathers—their texture and
their form
were like a bat's wings—and he beat
them so 50
that three winds blew from him in one
great storm:

it is these winds that freeze all Cocytus.
He wept from his six eyes, and down
three chins
the tears ran mixed with bloody froth
and pus.

In every mouth he worked a broken sinner 55
between his rake-like teeth. Thus he
kept three
in eternal pain at his eternal dinner.

For the one in front the biting seemed to play
no part at all compared to the ripping:
at times
the whole skin of his back was
flayed away. 60

"That soul that suffers most," explained
my Guide,
"is Judas Iscariot, he who kicks his legs
on the fiery chin and has his head inside.

Of the other two, who have their heads thrust
forward,
the one who dangles down from the
black face 65
is Brutus: note how he writhes without
a word.

And there, with the huge and sinewy arms, is
the soul
of Cassius.—But the night is coming on
and we must go, for we have seen
the whole."

Then, as he bade, I clasped his neck, and he, 70
watching for a moment when the wings
were opened wide, reached over dexterously

and seized the shaggy coat of the king demon;
then grappling matted hair and frozen crusts
from one tuft to another, clambered down. 75

When we had reached the joint where the
great thigh
merges into the swelling of the haunch,
my Guide and Master, straining terribly,

turned his head to where his feet had been
and began to grip the hair as if he were
climbing; 80
so that I thought we moved toward
Hell again.

"Hold fast!" my Guide said, and his breath
came shrill
with labor and exhaustion. "There is
no way
but by such stairs to rise above such evil."

At last he climbed out through an opening 85
in the central rock, and he seated me
on the rim;
then joined me with a nimble
backward spring.

I looked up, thinking to see Lucifer
as I had left him, and I saw instead
his legs projecting high into the air. 90

Now let all those whose dull minds are
still vexed
by failure to understand what point it was
I had passed through, judge if I was
perplexed.

"Get up. Up on your feet," my Master said.
"The sun already mounts to middle tierce, 95
and a long road and hard climbing
lie ahead."

It was no hall of state we had found there,
but a natural animal pit hollowed from rock
with a broken floor and a close and
sunless air.

"Before I tear myself from the Abyss," 100
I said when I had risen, "O my Master,
explain to me my error in all this:

where is the ice? and Lucifer—how has he
been turned from top to bottom: and how
can the sun
have gone from night to day so suddenly?" 105

And he to me: "You imagine you are still
on the other side of the center where
I grasped
the shaggy flank of the Great
Worm of Evil

which bores through the world—you *were*
while I climbed down, 110
but when I turned myself about,
you passed
the point to which all gravities are drawn.

You are under the other hemisphere where
you stand;
the sky above us is the half opposed
to that which canopies the great dry land.

Under the mid-point of that other sky 115
the Man who was born sinless and
who lived
beyond all blemish, came to suffer and die.

You have your feet upon a little sphere
which forms the other face of the Judecca.
There it is evening when it is morning here. 120

And this gross Fiend and Image of all Evil
who made a stairway for us with his hide
is pinched and prisoned in the ice-pack still.

On this side he plunged down from heaven's
height,
and the land that spread here once hid
in the sea 125
and fled North to our hemisphere for fright;

and it may be that moved by that same fear,
the one peak that still rises on this side
fled upward leaving this great cavern here.

Down there, beginning at the further bound 130
of Beelzebub's dim tomb, there is a space
not known by sight, but only by the sound

of a little stream descending through the
hollow

it has eroded from the massive stone
in its endlessly entwining lazy flow." 135

My Guide and I crossed over and began
to mount that little known and
lightless road
to ascend into the shining world again.

He first, I second, without thought of rest
we climbed the dark until we reached
the point 140
where a round opening brought in
sight the blest

and beauteous shining of the Heavenly cars.
And we walked out once more beneath
the Stars.

Notes

1. *On march the banners of the King:* The hymn (*Vexilla regis prodeunt*) was written in the sixth century by Venantius Fortunatus, Bishop of Poitiers. The original celebrates the Holy Cross, and is part of the service for Good Friday to be sung at the moment of uncovering the cross.
17. *the foul creature:* Satan.
38. *three faces:* Numerous interpretations of these three faces exist. What is essential to all explanation is that they be seen as perversions of the qualities of the Trinity.
54. *bloody froth and pus:* The gore of the sinners he chews which is mixed with his slaver.
62. *Judas:* Note how closely his punishment is patterned on that of the Simoniacs (Canto XIX).
67. *huge and sinewy arms:* The Cassius who betrayed Caesar was more generally described in terms of Shakespeare's "lean and hungry look." Another Cassius is described by Cicero (*Catiline,* III) as huge and sinewy. Dante probably confused the two.
68. *the night is coming on:* It is now Saturday evening.
82. *his breath came shrill: Cf.* Canto XXIII, 85, where the fact that Dante breathes indicates to the Hypocrites that he is alive. Virgil's breathing is certainly a contradiction.
95. *middle tierce:* In the canonical day tierce is the period from about six to nine A.M. Middle tierce, therefore, is seven-thirty. In going through the center point, they have gone from night to day. They have moved ahead twelve hours.
128. *the one peak:* The Mount of Purgatory.
129. *this great cavern:* The natural animal pit of line 98. It is also "Beelzebub's dim tomb," line 131.
133. *a little stream:* Lethe. In classical mythology, the river of forgetfulness, from which souls drank before being born. In Dante's symbolism it flows down from Purgatory, where it has washed away the memory of sin from the souls who are undergoing purification. That memory it delivers to Hell, which draws all sin to itself.
143. *Stars:* As part of his total symbolism Dante ends each of the three divisions of the *Commedia* with this word. Every conclusion of the upward soul is toward the stars, God's shining symbols of hope and virtue. It is just before dawn of Easter Sunday that the Poets emerge—a further symbolism.

The Purgatorio

Canto XII

THE FIRST CORNICE *The Proud*

The Rein of Pride
The Angel of Humility

VIRGIL instructs Dante to arise from where he has been walking bent beside Oderisi and to move on. Dante follows obediently, and soon Virgil points out to him THE REIN OF PRIDE carved in thirteen scenes into the stone beneath their feet. The scenes portray dreadful examples of the destruction that follows upon great pride.

The Poets pass on and find THE ANGEL OF HUMILITY approaching to welcome them. The Angel strikes Dante's forehead with his wings and, though Dante does not discover it till later,

THE FIRST P instantly disappears without a trace, symbolizing the purification from the sin of Pride. The Poets pass on, up a narrow ASCENT TO THE SECOND CORNICE, but though the way is narrow, Dante finds it much easier than the first, since steps have been cut into it, and since he is lighter by the weight of the first P. As they climb they hear the first beatitude, Beati pauperes spiritu, *ring out behind them, sung by the Angel of Humility.*

Toward us, dressed in white, and with a face
serenely tremulous as the Morning Star,
the glorious being came, radiant
with Grace. 90

First his arms and then his wings spread wide.
"Come," he said, "the stars are near,
and now
the way is easy up the mountainside.

Few, all too few, come answering to this call.
O sons of man, born to ascend on high, 95
how can so slight a wind-puff make
you fall?"

Straight to where the rock was cut he led.
There he struck my forehead with
his wings,
then promised us safe journeying ahead.

When a man has climbed the first slope
toward the crown 100
on which is built the church that overhangs
at the Rubaconte, the well-managed town,

the abrupt ascent is softened on his right
by steps cut in the rock in other days,
before the stave and ledger had
grown light— 105

just so the bank here, plunging like a slide
from the Round above, has been
made easier,
though towering cliffs squeeze us from
either side.

We set out on the climb, and on the way
Beati pauperes spiritu rang out, 110
more sweetly sung than any words
could say.

Ah, what a difference between these trails
and those of Hell: here every entrance fills
with joyous song, and there with
savage wails!

We were going up the holy steps, and though 115
the climb was steep, I seemed to feel
much lighter
than I had felt on level ground below.

"Master," I said, "tell me what heaviness
has been removed from me that I can climb
yet seem to feel almost no weariness." 120

He answered: "When the *P*'s that still remain,
though fading, on your brow, are
wiped away
as the first was, without a trace of stain—

then will your feet be filled with good desire:
not only will they feel no more fatigue 125
but all their joy will be in mounting higher."

A man with some strange thing lodged
on his hat
will stroll, not knowing, till the stares
of others
set him to wonder what they're staring at:

whereat his hand seeks out and verifies 130
what he suspected, thus performing for him
the office he could not serve with his eyes—

just so, I put my right hand to my brow,
fingers outspread, and found six
letters only
of those that had been carved there
down below

by the Angel with the keys to every grace;
at which a smile shone on my Master's face.

Notes

89. *the Morning Star:* Venus. Note that the Angel Boatman of Canto II was first seen as a ruddy glow and compared to Mars.
90. *the glorious being:* The Angel of Humility.
92. *now:* Now that the soul has been purged of the heaviness of Pride. The Angel is about to remove the first *P.*
96. *so slight a wind-puff:* The Angel of Humility is specifically concerned with Pride. In that context, the feeble wind seems best interpreted as the vanity of earthly ambition as compared to the eternal good of the soul.

100–105. The church is San Miniato, built on a rise across the Arno from Florence. The Rubaconte (now Ponte alle Grazie) is the bridge that leads most directly to San Miniato. An old account explains: "Issuing from the gate [in the city walls] to go to San Miniato, one finds at first, only one road by which to climb. Then the road forks. And the one on the climber's right hand has the stairs."

"Well managed" is, of course, ironic when applied to Florentine affairs. The "stave" was formerly an official measure, primarily for salt, which was taxed. One of the Chiaramontesi family, as head of the Salt Tax Department, had given rise to a famous scandal by auditing the salt in with a full stave and auditing it out with a lightened one thus shaving a certain quantity from each transaction. The "ledger" had grown light when two officials ripped out a page to remove evidence of graft. The exact date of these events are disputed, but both took place in Dante's time and both were widely known. The matter of the lightened stave even became the subject for a mocking popular ditty.

110. *Beati pauperes spiritu:* "Blessed are the poor in spirit: for theirs is the kingdom of Heaven." (*Matthew,* v, 3.) Each time Dante leaves one of the Cornices, he hears sung one of the beatitudes from the Sermon on the Mount. Dante does not specify in this instance that it is the Angel who sings. At each subsequent ascent, however, the beatitude is sung by the Angel who has allowed the Poets to pass. It should be clear that Dante is not likely to break so firm a part of his pattern without special reason. One must conclude, therefore, that it is the Angel who sings.

Canto XXX

THE EARTHLY PARADISE — *Beatrice*

Virgil Vanishes

The procession halts and the Prophets turn to the chariot and sing "Come, my bride, from Lebanon." They are summoning BEATRICE, who appears on the left side of the chariot, half-hidden from view by showers of blossoms poured from above by A HUNDRED ANGELS. Dante, stirred by the sight, turns to Virgil to express his overflowing emotions, and discovers that VIRGIL HAS VANISHED.

Because he bursts into tears at losing Virgil DANTE IS REPRIMANDED BY BEATRICE. The Angel Choir overhead immediately breaks into a Psalm of Compassion, but Beatrice, still severe, answers by detailing Dante's offenses in not making proper use of his great gifts. It would violate the ordering of the Divine Decree, she argues, to let Dante drink the waters of Lethe, thereby washing all memory of sin from his soul, before he had shed the tears of a real repentance.

When the Septentrion of the First Heaven,
which does not rise nor set, and which
has never
been veiled from sight by any mist but sin,

and which made every soul in that high court
know its true course (just as the lower Seven 5
direct the helmsman to his earthly port),

had stopped; the holy prophets, who till then
had walked between the Griffon and

those lights,
turned to the car like souls who cry
"Amen."

And one among them who seemed sent from
Heaven 10
clarioned: *"Veni, sponsa, de Libano,"*
three times, with all the others joining in.

As, at the last trump every saint shall rise
out of the grave, ready with voice
new-fleshed
to carol *Alleluliah* to the skies; 15

just so, above the chariot, at the voice
of such an elder, rose a hundred Powers
and Principals of the Eternal Joys,

all saying together: *"Benedictus qui venis";*
then, scattering flowers about on every side: 20
"Manibus o date lilia plenis."

Time and again at daybreak I have seen
the eastern sky glow with a wash of rose
while all the rest hung limpid and serene,

and the Sun's face rise tempered from its rest 25
so veiled by vapors that the naked eye
could look at it for minutes undistressed.

Exactly so, within a cloud of flowers
that rose like fountains from the
angels' hands 30
and fell about the chariot in showers,

a lady came in view: an olive crown
wreathed her immaculate veil, her
cloak was green,
the colors of live flame played on her gown.

My soul—such years had passed since
last it saw
that lady and stood trembling in
her presence, 35
stupefied by the power of holy awe—

now, by some power that shone from her above
the reach and witness of my mortal eyes,
felt the full mastery of enduring love.

The instant I was smitten by the force,
which had already once transfixed my soul 40
before my boyhood years had run
their course,

I turned left with the same assured belief
that makes a child run to its mother's arms
when it is frightened or has come to grief, 45

to say to Virgil: "There is not within me
one drop of blood unstirred. I recognize
the tokens of the ancient flame." But he,

he had taken his light from us. He had gone.
Virgil had gone. Virgil, the gentle Father 50
to whom I gave my soul for its salvation!

Not all that sight of Eden lost to view
by our First Mother could hold back
the tears
that stained my cheeks so lately washed
with dew.

"Dante, do not weep yet, though Virgil goes. 55
Do not weep yet, for soon another wound
shall make you weep far hotter tears
than those!"

As an admiral takes his place at stern or bow
to observe the handling of his other ships
and spur all hands to do their best—
so now, 60

on the chariot's left side, I saw appear
when I turned at the sound of my own name
(which, necessarily, is recorded here),

that lady who had been half-veiled from view
by the flowers of the angel-revels.
Now her eyes 65
fixed me across the stream, piercing
me through.

And though the veil she still wore, held in place
by the wreathed flowers of wise
Minerva's leaves,
let me see only glimpses of her face,

her stern and regal bearing made me dread 70
her next words, for she spoke as one
who saves
the heaviest charge till all the rest are read.

"Look at me well. I am she. I am Beatrice.
How dared you make your way to this
high mountain?
Did you not know that here man lives
in bliss?" 75

I lowered my head and looked down at the
stream.
But when I saw myself reflected there,
I fixed my eyes upon the grass for shame.

I shrank as a wayward child in his distress
shrinks from his mother's sternness,
for the taste 80
of love grown wrathful is a bitterness.

Notes

1. *the Septentrion of the First Heaven:* The Septentrion is the seven stars of the Big Dipper. Here Dante means the seven candelabra. They are the Septentrion of the First Heaven (the Empyrean) as distinct from the seven stars of the dipper which occur lower down in the Sphere of the Fixed Stars.
2. *which does not rise nor set:* The North Star does not rise or set north of the equator, but the Septentrion, revolving around the North Star, does go below the horizon in the lower latitudes. This Septentrion of the First Heaven, however, partaking of the perfection and constancy of Heaven, neither rises nor sets but is a constant light to mankind. So these unchanging lights guide the souls of man on high, as the "lower Seven" (line 5), in their less perfect way, guide the earthly helmsmen to their earthly ports.
7. *the holy prophets:* The twenty-four elders who represent the books of the Old Testament. (See XXIX, 64, note.)
10. *one among them: The Song of Solomon.*
11. *Veni, sponsa, de Libano:* "Come [with me] from Lebanon, my spouse." *Song of Solomon,* iv, 8. This cry, re-echoed by choirs of angels, summons Beatrice, who may be taken here as revelation, faith, divine love, hence as the bride of the spirit, to Dante (man's redeemed soul).
17–18. *a hundred Powers and Principals:* Angels.
19. *Benedictus qui venis:* "Blessed is he who cometh." (*Matthew,* xxi, 9.)
21. *Manibus o date lilia plenis:* "Oh, give lilies with full hands." These are the words of Anchises in honor of Marcellus. (*Aeneid,* VI, 883.) Thus they are not only apt to the occasion but their choice is a sweetly conceived last literary compliment to Virgil before he vanishes.
31. *a lady:* Beatrice. She is dressed in the colors of Faith (white), Hope (green), and Caritas (red).
34. *since last it saw:* Beatrice died in 1290. Thus Dante has passed ten years without sight of her.
36. *stupefied:* Dante describes the stupor of his soul at the sight of the living Beatrice in *La Vita Nuova,* XIV, and XXIV. Then, however, it was mortal love; here it is eternal, and the effect accordingly greater.
54. *washed with dew:* By Virgil. I, 124.
55. *Dante:* This is the only point in the *Commedia* at which Dante mentions his own name. Its usage here suggests many allegorical possibilities. Central to all of them, however, must be the fact that Dante, in ending one life (of the mind) and beginning a new one (of faith), hears his name. The suggestion of a second baptism is inevitable. And just as a child being baptized is struck by the priest, so Beatrice is about to strike him with her tongue before he may proceed to the holy water.

64. *that lady:* There are thirty-four Cantos in the *Inferno* and this is the thirtieth of the *Purgatorio,* hence the sixty-fourth Canto of the *Commedia.* This is the sixty-fourth line of the sixty-fourth Canto. In Dante's numerology such correspondences are always meaningful. Six plus four equals ten and ten equals the sum of the square of trinity and unity. Obviously there can be no conclusive way of establishing intent in such a structure of mystic numbering, but it certainly is worth noting that the line begins with "that lady." The Italian text, in fact, begins with *vidi la donna, i.e.,* I saw the lady [who represents the sum of the square of trinity plus unity?]. The lady, of course, is Beatrice.
68. *wise Minerva's leaves:* The olive crown.
80. *his mother's sternness:* Beatrice appears in the pageant as the figure of the Church Triumphant. The Church is the mother of the devout and though she is stern, as law decrees, her sternness is that of a loving mother.

The Paradiso

Canto XXXIII

THE EMPYREAN

St. Bernard
Prayer to the Virgin
The Vision of God

ST. BERNARD offers a lofty PRAYER TO THE VIRGIN, asking her to intercede in Dante's behalf, and in answer Dante feels his soul swell with new power and grow calm in rapture as his eyes are permitted the DIRECT VISION OF GOD.

There can be no measure of how long the vision endures. It passes, and Dante is once more mortal and fallible. Raised by God's presence, he had looked into the Mystery and had begun to understand its power and majesty. Returned to himself, there is no power in him capable of speaking the truth of what he saw. Yet the impress of the truth is stamped upon his soul, which he now knows will return to be one with God's Love.

Virgin Mother, daughter of thy son;
humble beyond all creatures and
more exalted;
predestined turning point of
God's intention;

thy merit so ennobled human nature
that its divine Creator did not scorn 5
to make Himself the creature of
His creature.

The Love that was rekindled in Thy womb
sends forth the warmth of the eternal peace
within whose ray this flower has come
to bloom.

Here, to us, thou art the noon and scope 10
of Love revealed; and among mortal men,
the living fountain of eternal hope.

Lady, thou art so near God's reckonings
that who seeks grace and does not
first seek thee
would have his wish fly upward
without wings. 15

Not only does thy sweet benignity
flow out to all who beg, but oftentimes
thy charity arrives before the plea.

In thee is pity, in thee munificence,
in thee the tenderest heart, in thee unites 20
all that creation knows of excellence!

Now comes this man who from the final pit
of the universe up to this height has seen,
one by one, the three lives of the spirit.

He prays to thee in fervent supplication 25
for grace and strength, that he may raise
his eyes
to the all-healing final revelation.

And I, who never more desired to see
the vision myself than I do that he
may see It,

add my own prayer, and pray that
it may be 30

enough to move you to dispel the trace
of every mortal shadow by thy prayers
and let him see revealed the Sum of Grace.

I pray thee further, all-persuading Queen,
keep whole the natural bent of his affections 35
and of his powers after his eyes have seen.

Protect him from the stirrings of man's clay;
see how Beatrice and the blessed host
clasp reverent hands to join me as I pray."

The eyes that God reveres and loves the best 40
glowed on the speaker, making clear the joy
with which true prayer is heard by the
most blest.

Those eyes turned then to the Eternal Ray,
through which, we must indeed believe,
the eyes
of others do not find such ready way. 45

And I, who neared the goal of all my nature,
felt my soul, at the climax of its yearning,
suddenly, as it ought, grow calm
with rapture.

Bernard then, smiling sweetly, gestured to me
to look up, but I had already become 50
within myself all he would have me be.

Little by little as my vision grew
it penetrated further through the aura
of the high lamp which in Itself is true.

What then I saw is more than tongue can say. 55
Our human speech is dark before the vision.
The ravished memory swoons and
falls away.

As one who sees in dreams and wakes to find
the emotional impression of his vision
still powerful while its parts fade from
his mind— 60

just such am I, having lost nearly all
the vision itself, while in my heart I feel
the sweetness of it yet distill and fall.

So, in the sun, the footprints fade from snow.
On the wild wind that bore the
tumbling leaves 65
the Sybil's oracles were scattered so.

O Light Supreme who doth Thyself withdraw
so far above man's mortal understanding,
lend me again some glimpse of what I saw;

make Thou my tongue so eloquent it may 70
of all Thy glory speak a single clue
to those who follow me in the world's day;

for by returning to my memory
somewhat, and somewhat sounding in
these verses,
Thou shalt show man more of Thy victory. 75

So dazzling was the splendor of that Ray,
that I must certainly have lost my senses
had I, but for an instant, turned away.

And so it was, as I recall, I could
the better bear to look, until at last 80
my vision made one with the Eternal Good.

Oh grace abounding that had made me fit
to fix my eyes on the eternal light
until my vision was consumed in it!

I saw within Its depth how It conceives 85
all things in a single volume bound by Love,
of which the universe is the scattered leaves;

substance, accident, and their relation
so fused that all I say could do no more
than yield a glimpse of that
bright revelation. 90

I think I saw the universal form
that binds these things, for as I speak
these words
I feel my joy swell and my spirits warm.

Twenty-five centuries since Neptune saw
the *Argo's* keel have not moved
all mankind, 95
recalling that adventure, to such awe

as I felt in an instant. My tranced being
stared fixed and motionless upon
that vision,
ever more fervent to see in the act of seeing.

Experiencing that Radiance, the spirit 100
is so indrawn it is impossible
even to think of ever turning from It.

For the good which is the will's ultimate object
is all subsumed in It; and, being removed,
all is defective which in It is perfect. 105

Now in my recollection of the rest
I have less power to speak than any infant
wetting its tongue yet at its mother's breast;

and not because that Living Radiance bore
more than one semblance, for It
is unchanging 110
and is forever as it was before;

rather, as I grew worthier to see,
the more I looked, the more
unchanging semblance
appeared to change with every change
in me.

Within the depthless deep and clear existence 115
of that abyss of light three circles shone—
three in color, one in circumference:

the second from the first, rainbow
from rainbow;
the third, an exhalation of pure fire
equally breathed forth by the other two. 120

But oh how much my words miss my
conception,
which is itself so far from what I saw
that to call it feeble would be
rank deception!

O Light Eternal fixed in Itself alone,
by Itself alone understood, which from Itself 125
loves and glows, self-knowing
and self-known;

that second aureole which shone forth in Thee,
conceived as a reflection of the first—
or which appeared so to my scrutiny—

seemed in Itself of Its own coloration 130
to be painted with man's image. I
fixed my eyes
on that alone in rapturous contemplation.

Like a geometer wholly dedicated
to squaring the circle, but who cannot find,
think as he may, the principle indicated— 135

so did I study the supernal face.
I yearned to know just how our
image merges
into that circle, and how it there
finds place;

but mine were not the wings for such a flight.
Yet, as I wished, the truth I wished
for came 140
cleaving my mind in a great flash
of light.

Here my powers rest from their high fantasy,
but already I could feel my being turned—
instinct and intellect balanced equally

as in a wheel whose motion nothing jars— 145
by the Love that moves the Sun and the
other stars.

Notes

1–39. ST. BERNARD'S PRAYER TO THE VIRGIN MARY. No reader who has come this far will need a lengthy gloss of Bernard's prayer. It can certainly be taken as a summarizing statement of the special place of Mary in Catholic faith. For the rest only a few turns of phrase need underlining. 3. *predestined turning point of God's intention:* All-foreseeing God built his whole scheme for mankind with Mary as its pivot, for through her He would become man. 7. *The Love that was rekindled in thy womb:* God. In a sense he withdrew from man when Adam and Eve sinned. In Mary He returned and Himself became man. 35. *keep whole the natural bent of his affections:* Bernard is asking Mary to protect Dante lest the intensity of the vision overpower his faculties. 37. *Protect him from the stirrings of man's clay:* Protect him from the stirrings of base human impulse, especially from pride, for Dante is about to receive a grace never before granted to any man and the thought of such glory might well move a mere mortal to an hubris that would turn glory to sinfulness.

40. *the eyes:* Of Mary.

50. *but I had already become: I.e.,* "But I had already fixed my entire attention upon the vision of God." But if so, how could Dante have seen Bernard's smile, and gesture? Eager students like to believe they catch Dante in a contradiction here. Let them bear in mind that Dante is looking directly at God, as do the souls of Heaven, who thereby acquire—insofar as they are able to contain it—God's own knowledge. As a first stirring of that heavenly power, therefore, Dante is sharing God's knowledge of St. Bernard.

54. *which in Itself is true:* The light of God is the one light whose source is Itself. All others are a reflection of this.

65–66. *tumbling leaves . . . oracles:* The Cumean Sybil (Virgil describes her in *Aeneid,* III, 441 ff.) wrote her oracles on leaves, one letter to a leaf, then sent her message scattering on the wind. Presumably, the truth was all contained in that strew, could one only gather all the leaves and put the letters in the right order.

76–81. How can a light be so dazzling that the beholder would swoon if he looked away for an instant? Would it not be, rather, in looking at, not away from, the overpowering vision that the viewer's senses would he overcome? So it would be on earth. But now Dante, with the help of all heaven's prayers, is in the presence of God and strengthened by all he sees. It is by being so strengthened that he can see yet more. So the passage becomes a parable of grace. Stylistically it once more illustrates Dante's genius: even at this height of concept, the poet can still summon and invent new perceptions, subtlety exfoliating from subtlety.

The simultaneous metaphoric statement, of course, is that no man can lose his good in the vision of God, but only in looking away from it.

85–87. The idea here is Platonic: the essence of all things (form) exists in the mind of God. All other things exist as exempla.

88. *substance:* Matter, all that exists in itself. *accident:* All that exists as a phase of matter.

92. *these things:* Substance and accident.

109–114. In the presence of God the soul grows ever more capable of perceiving God. Thus, the worthy soul's experience of God is a constant expansion of awareness. God appears to change as He is better seen. Being perfect, He is changeless within Himself, for any change would be away from perfection.

130–144. The central metaphor of the entire *Comedy* is the image of God and the final triumphant in-Godding of the elected soul returning to its Maker. On the mystery of that image, the metaphoric symphony of the *Comedy* comes to rest.

In the second aspect of Trinal-unity, in the circle reflected from the first, Dante thinks he sees the image of mankind woven into the very substance and coloration of God. He turns the entire attention of his soul to that mystery, as a geometer might seek to shut out every other thought and dedicate himself to squaring the circle. In *Il Convivio,* II, 14, Dante asserted that the circle could not be squared, but that impossibility had not yet been firmly demonstrated in Dante's time and mathematicians still worked at the problem. Note, however, that Dante assumes the impossibility of squaring the circle as a weak mortal example of mortal impossibility. How much more impossible, he implies, to resolve the mystery of God, study as man will.

The mystery remains beyond Dante's mortal power. Yet, there in Heaven, in a moment of grace, God revealed the truth to him in a flash of light—revealed it, that is, to the God-enlarged power of Dante's emparadised soul. On Dante's return to the mortal life, the details of that revelation vanished from his mind but the force of the revelation survives in its power on Dante's feelings.

So ends the vision of the *Comedy,* and yet the vision endures, for ever since that revelation, Dante tells us, he feels his soul turning ever as one with the perfect motion of God's love.

Article 35

Chaucer: Canterbury Tales

Introduction

Geoffrey Chaucer (1340–1400) was the son of a London merchant who received a good education and traveled widely. He became an expert in physics, medicine and astronomy and wrote papers on them in Latin. Being from the upper middle class, his writings legitimized a class of people (the middle class) that still hadn't gained the power they would in the Renaissance and beyond.

Chaucer is most famous for his collection of stories, *Canterbury Tales.* It is the tales told to pass the time away by 30 pilgrims on their way to Canterbury. Each of the 30 pilgrims comes from a different profession and has a unique personality given through Chaucer's prologue to the tales and within the construction of each tale. With so many different characters, the book is a valuable insight into the way of life during the Middle Ages. Most importantly, however, it was the standardization and legitimization of Middle English. Latin and French were the languages of the nobility and upper class in Medieval England. Chaucer took a risk by publishing in a "vulgar" tongue, but was successful due to his usage of the best parts of each English dialect. Thus, the language of trade today—English—owes much to this pioneer of the tongue.

Presented here are selections from the prologue, about several pilgrims plus the Knight's Tale and the Canon's Tale. The prologue contains a lively introduction to each of the pilgrims. The Knight's Tale is an example of the bliss and agony of courtly love. The Canon Yeoman's Tale illustrates the Middle Ages fascination with alchemy and proves that scams have always been part of civilization.

The Prologue

Here Begins the Book of the Tales of Canterbury

When April with his showers sweet with fruit
The drought of March has pierced unto the root
And bathed each vein with liquor that has power
To generate therein and sire the flower;
When Zephyr also has, with his sweet breath,
Quickened again, in every holt and heath,
The tender shoots and buds, and the young sun
Into the Ram one half his course has run,
And many little birds make melody
That sleep through all the night with open eye
(So Nature pricks them on to ramp and rage)—
Then do folk long to go on pilgrimage,
And palmers to go seeking out strange strands,
To distant shrines well known in sundry lands.
And specially from every shire's end
Of England they to Canterbury wend,
The holy blessed martyr there to seek
Who helped them when they lay so ill and weak.
Befell that, in that season, on a day
In Southwark, at the Tabard, as I lay
Ready to start upon my pilgrimage
To Canterbury, full of devout homage,
There came at nightfall to that hostelry
Some nine and twenty in a company
Of sundry persons who had chanced to fall
In fellowship, and pilgrims were they all
That toward Canterbury town would ride.
The rooms and stables spacious were and wide,
And well we there were eased, and of the best.
And briefly, when the sun had gone to rest,
So had I spoken with them, every one,
That I was of their fellowship anon,

And made agreement that we'd early rise
To take the road, as you I will apprise.
But none the less, whilst I have time and space,
Before yet farther in this tale I pace,
It seems to me accordant with reason
To inform you of the state of every one
Of all of these, as it appeared to me,
And who they were, and what was their degree,
And even how arrayed there at the inn;
And with a knight thus will I first begin.

The Knight

A knight there was, and he a worthy man,
Who, from the moment that he first began
To ride about the world, loved chivalry,
Truth, honour, freedom and all courtesy.
Full worthy was he in his liege-lord's war,
And therein had he ridden (none more far)
As well in Christendom as heathenesse,
And honoured everywhere for worthiness.
At Alexandria, he, when it was won;
Full oft the table's roster he'd begun
Above all nations' knights in Prussia.
In Latvia raided he, and Russia,
No christened man so oft of his degree.
In far Granada at the siege was he
Of Algeciras, and in Belmarie.[1]
At Ayas was he and at Satalye[2]
When they were won; and on the Middle Sea
At many a noble meeting chanced to be.
Of mortal battles he had fought fifteen,
And he'd fought for our faith at Tramissene[3]
Three times in lists, and each time slain his foe.
This self-same worthy knight had been also
At one time with the lord of Palatye[4]
Against another heathen in Turkey:
And always won he sovereign fame for prize.
Though so illustrious, he was very wise
And bore himself as meekly as a maid.

[1]Benimarim (the name of a tribe), in Morocco.

[2]Modern Adalia, in Asia Minor.

[3]Modern Tlemçen, in Algeria.

[4]Modern Balat.

He never yet had any vileness said,
In all his life, to whatsoever wight.(man)
He was a truly perfect, gentle knight.
But now, to tell you all of his array,
His steeds were good, but yet he was not gay.
Of simple fustian wore he a jupon
Sadly discoloured by his habergeon;
For he had lately come from his voyage
And now was going on this pilgrimage.

The Squire

With him there was his son a youthful squire,
A lover and a lusty bachelor,
With locks well curled, as if they'd laid in press.
Some twenty years of age he was, I guess.
In stature he was of an average length,
Wondrously active, aye, and great of strength.
He'd ridden sometime with the cavalry
In Flanders, in Artois, and Picardy,
And borne him well within that little space
In hope to win thereby his lady's grace.
Prinked out he was, as if he were a mead,
All full of fresh-cut flowers white and red.
Singing he was, or fluting, all the day;
He was as fresh as is the month of May.
Short was his gown, with sleeves both long and
wide.
Well could he sit on horse, and fairly ride.
He could make songs and words thereto indite,
Joust, and dance too, as well as sketch and write.
So hot he loved that, while night told her tale,
He slept no more than does a nightingale.
Courteous he, and humble, willing and able,
And carved before his father at the table.

The Yeoman

A yeoman had he,[5] nor more servants, no,
At that time, for he chose to travel so;
And he was clad in coat and hood of green.

[5]That is, the Knight.

A sheaf of peacock arrows bright and keen
Under his belt he bore right carefully
(Well could he keep his tackle yeomanly:
His arrows had no draggled feathers low),
And in his hand he bore a mighty bow.
A cropped head had he and a sun-browned face.
Of woodcraft knew he all the useful ways.
Upon his arm he bore a bracer gay,
And at one side a sword and buckler, yea,
And at the other side a dagger bright,
Well sheathed and sharp as spear point in the light;
On breast a Christopher[6] of silver sheen.
He bore a horn in baldric all of green;
A forester he truly was, I guess.

The Prioress

There was also a nun, a prioress,
Who, in her smiling, modest was and coy;
Her greatest oath was but "By Saint Eloy!"
And she was known as Madam Eglantine.
Full well she sang the services divine,
Intoning through her nose, becomingly;
And fair she spoke her French, and fluently,
After the school of Stratford-at-the-Bow,
For French of Paris was not hers to know.
At table she had been well taught withal,
And never from her lips let morsels fall,
Nor dipped her fingers deep in sauce, but ate
With so much care the food upon her plate
That never driblet fell upon her breast.
In courtesy she had delight and zest.
Her upper lip was always wiped so clean
That in her cup was no iota seen
Of grease, when she had drunk her draught of
wine.
Becomingly she reached for meat to dine.
And certainly delighting in good sport,
She was right pleasant, amiable—in short.
She was at pains to counterfeit the look
Of courtliness, and stately manners took,
And would be held worthy of reverence.
But, to say something of her moral sense,
She was so charitable and piteous
That she would weep if she but saw a mouse
Caught in a trap, though it were dead or bled.
She had some little dogs, too, that she fed
On roasted flesh, or milk and fine white bread.
But sore she'd weep if one of them were dead,
Or if men smote it with a rod to smart:
For pity ruled her, and her tender heart.
Right decorous her pleated wimple was;
Her nose was fine; her eyes were blue as glass;
Her mouth was small and therewith soft and red;
But certainly she had a fair forehead;
It was almost a full span broad, I own,
For, truth to tell, she was not undergrown.
Neat was her cloak, as I was well aware.
Of coral small about her arm she'd bear
A string of beads and gauded[7] all with green;
And therefrom hung a brooch of golden sheen
Whereon there was first written a crowned "A,"
And under, *Amor vincit omnia.*

The Physician

With us there was a doctor of physic;
In all this world was none like him to pick
For talk of medicine and surgery;
For he was grounded in astronomy.
He often kept a patient from the pall
By horoscopes and magic natural.
Well could he tell the fortune ascendent
Within the houses for his sick patient.
He knew the cause of every malady,
Were it of hot or cold, of moist or dry,
And where engendered, and of what humour;
He was a very good practitioner.
The cause being known, down to the deepest root,
Anon he gave to the sick man his boot.
Ready he was, with his apothecaries,
To send him drugs and all electuaries;
By mutual aid much gold they'd always won—
Their friendship was a thing not new begun.
Well read was he in Esculapius,
And Deiscorides, and in Rufus,

---

[6]That is, an image of Saint Christopher.

[7]In a rosary the beads marking divisions are called gauds.

Hippocrates, and Hali, and Galen,
Serapion, Rhazes, and Avicen,
Averrhoës, Gilbert, and Constantine,
Bernard, and Gatisden, and John Damascene.
In diet he was measured as could be,
Including naught of superfluity,
But nourishing and easy. It's no libel
To say he read but little in the Bible.
In blue and scarlet he went clad, withal,
Lined with a taffeta and with sendal;
And yet he was right chary of expense;
He kept the gold he gained from pestilence.
For gold in physic is a fine cordial,
And therefore loved he gold exceeding all.

The Knight's Tale

In searching through the heap of enemy dead,
Stripping them of their gear from heel to head,
The busy pillagers could pick and choose,
After the battle, what they best could use;
And so befell that in a heap they found,
Pierced through with many a grievous, bloody wound,
Two young knights lying together, side by side,
Bearing one crest, wrought richly, of their pride,
And of those two Arcita was the one,
The other knight was known as Palamon.
Not fully quick, nor fully dead they were,
But by their coats of arms and by their gear
The heralds readily could tell, withal,
That they were of the Theban blood royal,
And that they had been of two sisters born.
Out of the heap the spoilers had them torn
And carried gently over to the tent
Of Theseüs; who shortly had them sent
To Athens, there in prison cell to lie
For ever, without ransom, till they die.
Thus passed by year by year and day by day,
Till it fell out, upon a morn in May,
That Emily, far fairer to be seen
Than is the lily on its stalk of green,
And fresher than is May with flowers new
And in the garden, as the sun up-rose,
She sauntered back and forth and through each close,
Gathering many a flower, white and red,
To weave a delicate garland for her head;
And like a heavenly angel's was her song.
The tower tall, which was so thick and strong,
And of the castle was the great donjon,
(Wherein the two knights languished in prison,
Of whom I told and shall yet tell, withal),
Was joined, at base, unto the garden wall
Whereunder Emily went dallying.
Bright was the sun and clear that morn in spring,
And Palamon, the woeful prisoner,
As was his wont, by leave of his gaoler,
Was up and pacing round that chamber high,
From which the noble city filled his eye,
And, too, the garden full of branches green,
Wherein bright Emily, fair and serene,
Went walking and went roving up and down.
This sorrowing prisoner, this Palamon,
Being in the chamber, pacing to and fro,
And to himself complaining of his woe,
Cursing his birth, he often cried "Alas!"
And so it was, by chance or other pass,
That through a window, closed by many a bar
Of iron, strong and square as any spar,
He cast his eyes upon Emilia,
And thereupon he blenched and cried out "Ah!"
As if he had been smitten to the heart.
And at that cry Arcita did up-start,
Asking: "My cousin, why what ails you now
That you've so deathly pallor on your brow?
This Palamon replied and said again:
It's not our prison that caused me to cry.
But I was wounded lately through the eye
Down to my heart, and that my bane will be.
The beauty of the lady that I see
There in that garden, pacing to and fro,
Is cause of all my crying and my woe.
I know not if she's woman or goddess;
But Venus she is verily, I guess."
And on that word Arcita looked to see
This lady who went roving to and fro.
And in that look her beauty struck him so
That, if poor Palamon is wounded sore,
Arcita is as deeply hurt, and more.
And with a sigh he said then, piteously:
"The virgin beauty slays me suddenly
Of her that wanders yonder in that place;

And save I have her pity and her grace,
That I at least may see her day by day,
I am but dead; there is no more to say."
Palamon knit his brows and stood at bay.
"It will not prove," he said, "to your honour
After so long a time to turn traitor
To me, who am your cousin and your brother,
Sworn as we are, and each unto the other,
That never, though for death in any pain,
Never, indeed, till death shall part us twain,
Either of us in love shall hinder other,
No, nor in any thing, O my dear brother;
But that, instead, you shall so further me
As I shall you. All this we did agree.
Such was your oath and such was mine also.
You dare not now deny it, well I know.
Thus you are of my party, beyond doubt.
And now you would all falsely go about
To love my lady, whom I love and serve,
And shall while life my heart's blood may preserve.
Nay, false Arcita, it shall not be so.
I loved her first, and told you all my woe,
As to a brother and to one that swore
To further me, as I have said before.
For which you are in duty bound, as knight,
To help me, if the thing lie in your might,
Or else you're false, I say, and downfallen."
Then this Arcita proudly spoke again:
"You shall," he said, "be rather false than I;
And that you're so, I tell you utterly;
For *par amour* I loved her first, you know.
What can you say? You know not, even now,
Whether she is a woman or goddess!
Yours is a worship as of holiness,
While mine is love, as of a mortal maid;
Wherefore I told you of it, unafraid,
As to my cousin and my brother sworn.
Let us assume you loved her first, this morn;
Know you not well the ancient writer's saw
Of 'Who shall give a lover any law?'
Love is a greater law, aye by my pan,[1]
Than man has ever given to earthly man.
And therefore statute law and such decrees
Are broken daily and in all degrees.
A man must needs have love, maugre his head.
He cannot flee it though he should be dead,
And be she maid, or widow, or a wife.
And yet it is not likely that, in life,
You'll stand within her graces; nor shall I;
For you are well aware, aye verily,
That you and I are doomed to prison drear
Perpetually; we gain no ransom here.
Love if you like; for I love and aye shall;
And certainly, dear brother, that is all.
Here in this prison cell must we remain
And each endure whatever fate ordain."
Great was the strife, and long, betwixt the two,
If I had but the time to tell it you,
Save in effect. It happened on a day
(To tell the tale as briefly as I may),
A worthy duke men called Pirithous,
Who had been friend unto Duke Theseüs,
Since each had been a little child, a chit,
Was come to visit Athens and visit
His play-fellow, as he was wont to do,
Pirithous loved Arcita, too, that knight,
Having known him in Thebes full many a year;
And finally, at his request and prayer,
And that without a coin of ransom paid,
Duke Theseüs released him out of shade,
Freely to go where'er he wished, and to
His own devices, as I'll now tell you.
The compact was, to set it plainly down,
As made between those two of great renown:
That if Arcita, any time, were found,
Ever in life, by day or night, on ground
Of any country of this Theseüs,
And he were caught, it was concerted thus,
That by the sword he straight should lose his head.
He had no choice, so taking leave he sped
Homeward to Thebes, lest by the sword's sharp
edge
He forfeit life. His neck was under pledge.
How great a sorrow is Arcita's now!
How through his heart he feels death's heavy blow;
He weeps, he wails, he cries out piteously;
He thinks to slay himself all privily.
Said he: "Alas, the day that I was born!
I'm in worse prison, now, and more forlorn;
Now am I doomed eternally to dwell
No more in Purgatory, but in Hell.

[1]Pan: the brain-pan; the skull.

Alas, that I have known Pirithous!
For else had I remained with Theseüs,
Fettered within that cell; but even so
Then had I been in bliss and not in woe.
Only the sight of her that I would serve,
Though I might never her dear grace deserve,
Would have sufficed, oh well enough for me!
O my dear cousin Palamon," said he,
"Yours is the victory, and that is sure,
For there, full happily, you may endure.
In prison? Never, but in Paradise!
Oh, well has Fortune turned for you the dice,
Who have the sight of her, I the absence.
For possible it is, in her presence,
You being a knight, a worthy and able,
That by some chance, since Fortune's changeable,
You may to your desire sometime attain.
But I, that am in exile and in pain,
Stripped of all hope and in so deep despair
That there's no earth nor water, fire nor air,
Nor any creature made of them there is
To help or give me comfort, now, in this—
Surely I'll die of sorrow and distress;
Farewell, my life, my love, my joyousness!
And on the other hand, this Palamon,
When that he found Arcita truly gone,
Such lamentation made he, that the tower
Resounded of his crying, hour by hour.
The very fetters on his legs were yet
Again with all his bitter salt tears wet.
"Alas!" said he, "Arcita, cousin mine,
With all our strife, God knows, you've won the wine.
You're walking, now, in Theban streets, at large,
And all my woe you may from mind discharge.
You may, too, since you've wisdom and manhood,
Assemble all the people of our blood
And wage a war so sharp on this city
That by some fortune, or by some treaty,
You shall yet have that lady to your wife
For whom I now must needs lay down my life.
For surely 'tis in possibility,
Since you are now at large, from prison free,
And are a lord, great is your advantage
Above my own, who die here in a cage.
For I must weep and wail, the while I live,
In all the grief that prison cell may give,
And now with pain that love gives me, also,
Which doubles all my torment and my woe."
Now when Arcita unto Thebes was come,
He lay and languished all day in his home,
Since he his lady nevermore should see,
But telling of his sorrow brief I'll be.
Had never any man so much torture,
No, nor shall have while this world may endure.
Bereft he was of sleep and meat and drink,
That lean he grew and dry as shaft, I think.
His eyes were hollow and ghastly to behold,
His face was sallow, all pale and ashen-cold,
Upon a night, while sleeping in his bed,
He dreamed of how the winged God Mercury
Before him stood and bade him happier be.
And thus he spoke: "To Athens shall you wend;
For all your woe is destined there to end."
And on that word Arcita woke and started.
And with that word he caught a great mirror,
And saw how changed was all his old colour,
And saw his visage altered from its kind.
And right away it ran into his mind
That since his face was now disfigured so,
By suffering endured (as well we know),
He might, if he should bear him low in town,
Live there in Athens evermore, unknown,
Seeing his lady well-nigh every day.
And right anon he altered his array,
Like a poor labourer in mean attire,
And all alone, save only for a squire,
Who knew his secret heart and all his case,
And who was dressed as poorly as he was,
To Athens was he gone the nearest way.
And to the court he went upon a day,
And at the gate he proffered services
To drudge and drag, as any one devises.
And to be brief herein, and to be plain,
He found employment with a chamberlain
Was serving in the house of Emily;
He said "Philostrates" would name him right.
But half so well beloved a man as he
Was never in that court, of his degree;
His gentle nature was so clearly shown,
That throughout all the court spread his renown.
They said it were but kindly courtesy
If Theseüs should heighten his degree
And put him in more honourable service

Wherein he might his virtue exercise.
And thus, anon, his name was so up-sprung,
Both for his deeds and sayings of his tongue,
That Thesëus had brought him nigh and nigher
And of the chamber he had made him squire,
There was no man that Thesëus loved more.
And in such bliss I leave Arcita now,
And upon Palamon some words bestow.
  In darksome, horrible, and strong prison
These seven years has now sat Palamon,
Wasted by woe and by his long distress.
  It fell out in the seventh year, in May,
That, shortly after midnight, Palamon,
By helping of a friend, broke from prison,
And fled the city, fast as he might go;
And to a grove that grew hard by, with stride
Of furtive foot, went fearful Palamon.
In brief, he'd formed his plan, as he went on,
That in the grove he would lie fast all day,
And when night came, then would he take his way
Toward Thebes, and there find friends, and of
    them pray
Their help on Thesëus in war's array;
And briefly either he would lose his life,
Or else win Emily to be his wife;
This is the gist of his intention plain.
  Now I'll return to Arcita again,
On a path he wandered up and down,
Near which, and as it chanced, this Palamon
Lay in the thicket, where no man might see,
For sore afraid of finding death was he.
He knew not that Arcita was so near:
  Arcita, having sung, began to speak,
And sat him down, sighing like one forlorn.
"Alas," said he, "the day that I was born!
How long, O Juno, of thy cruelty,
Wilt thou wage bitter war on Thebes city?
Alas! Confounded beyond all reason
The blood of Cadmus and of Amphion;
Of royal Cadmus, who was the first man
To build at Thebes, and first the town began,
And first of all the city to be king;
Of his lineage am I, and his offspring,
By true descent, and of the stock royal:
And now I'm such a wretched serving thrall,
That he who is my mortal enemy,
I serve him as his squire, and all humbly.
And even more does Juno give me shame,
For I dare not acknowledge my own name;
But whereas I was Arcita by right,
Now I'm Philostrates, not worth a mite.
Alas, thou cruel Mars! Alas, Juno!
Thus have your angers all our kin brought low,
Save only me, and wretched Palamon,
Whom Theseus martyrs yonder in prison.
And above all, to slay me utterly,
Love has his fiery dart so burningly
Struck through my faithful and care-laden heart,
My death was patterned ere my swaddling-shirt.
You slay me with your two eyes, Emily;
You are the cause for which I now must die.
For on the whole of all my other care
I would not set the value of a tare,
So I could do one thing to your pleasance!"
And with that word he fell down in a trance
That lasted long; and then he did up-start.
  This Palamon, who thought that through his
    heart
He felt a cold and sudden sword blade glide,
For rage he shook, no longer would he hide.
But after he had heard Arcita's tale,
As he were mad, with face gone deathly pale,
He started up and sprang out of the thicket,
Crying: "Arcita, oh you traitor wicked,
Now are you caught, that crave my lady so,
For whom I suffer all this pain and woe,
And are my blood, and know my secrets' store,
As I have often told you heretofore,
And have befooled the great Duke Thesëus,
And falsely changed your name and station thus:
Either I shall be dead or you shall die.
You shall not love my lady Emily,
But I will love her, and none other, no;
For I am Palamon, your mortal foe.
And though I have no weapon in this place,
Being but out of prison by God's grace,
I say again, that either you shall die
Or else forgo your love for Emily.
Choose which you will, for you shall not depart."
  This Arcita, with scornful, angry heart,
When he knew him and all the tale had heard,
Fierce as a lion, out he pulled a sword,
And answered thus: "By God that sits above!
Were it not you are sick and mad for love,

And that you have no weapon in this place,
Out of this grove you'd never move a pace,
But meet your death right now, and at my hand.
For I renounce the bond and its demand
Which you assert that I have made with you.
What, arrant fool, love's free to choose and do,
And I will have her, spite of all your might!
But in as much as you're a worthy knight
And willing to defend your love, in mail,
Hear now this word: tomorrow I'll not fail
(Without the cognizance of any wight)
To come here armed and harnessed as a knight,
And to bring arms for you, too, as you'll see;
And choose the better and leave the worse for me.
And meat and drink this very night I'll bring,
Enough for you, and clothes for your bedding.
And if it be that you my lady win
And slay me in this wood that now I'm in,
Then may you have your lady, for all of me."
  This Palamon replied: "I do agree."
And thus they parted till the morrow morn,
When each had pledged his honour to return.
  Arcita rode into the town anon,
And on the morrow, ere the dawn, he bore,
Secretly, arms and armour out of store,
Enough for each, and proper to maintain
A battle in the field between the twain.
So on his horse, alone as he was born,
He carried out that harness as he'd sworn;
And in the grove, at time and place they'd set,
Arcita and this Palamon were met.
There was no "good-day" given, no saluting,
But without word, rehearsal, or such thing,
Each of them helping, so they armed each other
As dutifully as he were his own brother;
And afterward, with their sharp spears and strong,
They thrust each at the other wondrous long.
You might have fancied that this Palamon,
In battle, was a furious, mad lion,
And that Arcita was a tiger quite:
Like very boars the two began to smite,
Like boars that froth for anger in the wood.
Up to the ankles fought they in their blood.
And leaving them thus fighting fast and fell,
Forthwith of Theseüs I now will tell.
  Clear was the day, as I have told ere this,
When Theseüs, compact of joy and bliss,
With his Hippolyta, the lovely queen,
And fair Emilia, clothed all in green,
A-hunting they went riding royally.
And to the grove of trees that grew hard by,
In which there was a hart, as men had told,
Duke Theseüs the shortest way did hold.
  And when this duke was come upon that land,
Under the slanting sun he looked, anon,
And there saw Arcita and Palamon,
Who furiously fought, as two boars do;
The bright swords went in circles to and fro
So terribly, that even their least stroke
Seemed powerful enough to fell an oak;
But who the two were, nothing did he note.
This duke his courser with the sharp spurs smote,
And in one bound he was between the two,
And lugged his great sword out, and cried out:
    "Ho!
No more, I say, on pain of losing head!
By mighty Mars, that one shall soon be dead
Who smites another stroke that I may see!
But tell me now what manner of men ye be
That are so hardy as to fight out here
Without a judge or other officer,
As if you rode in lists right royally?"
  This Palamon replied, then, hastily,
Saying: "O Sire, what need for more ado?
We have deserved our death at hands of you.
Two woeful wretches are we, two captives
That are encumbered by our own sad lives;
And as you are a righteous lord and judge,
Give us not either mercy or refuge,
But slay me first, for sacred charity;
But slay my fellow here, as well, with me.
Or slay him first; for though you learn it late,
This is your mortal foe, Arcita—wait!—
That from the land was banished, on his head.
And for the which he merits to be dead.
For this is he who came unto your gate,
Calling himself Philostrates—nay, wait!—
Thus has he fooled you well this many a year,
And you have made him your chief squire, I hear;
And this is he that loves fair Emily.
For since the day is come when I must die,
I make confession plainly and say on,
That I am that same woeful Palamon
Who has your prison broken, viciously.

I am your mortal foe, and it is I
Who love so hotly Emily the bright
That I'll die gladly here within her sight.
Therefore do I ask death as penalty;
But slay my fellow with the same mercy,
For both of us deserve but to be slain."
This worthy duke presently spoke again,
Saying: "This judgment needs but a short session:
Your own mouth, aye, and by your own confession,
Has doomed and damned you, as I shall record.
There is no need for torture, on my word.
But you shall die, by mighty Mars the red!"
But then the queen, whose heart for pity bled,
Began to weep, and so did Emily
And all the ladies in the company.
Great pity must it be, so thought they all,
That ever such misfortune should befall:
For these were gentlemen, of great estate,
And for no thing, save love, was their debate.
They saw their bloody wounds, so sore and wide,
And all cried out—greater and less, they cried:
"Have mercy, lord, upon us women all!"
And down upon their bare knees did they fall,
And shortly, when his ire was thus grown pale,
He looked up to the sky, with eyes alight,
And spoke these words, as he would promise plight:
Lo, here, Arcita and this Palamon,
That were delivered out of my prison,
And might have lived in Thebes right royally,
Knowing me for their mortal enemy,
And also that their lives lay in my hand;
And yet their love has wiled them to this land,
Against all sense, and brought them here to die!
Look you now, is not that a folly high?
Who can be called a fool, except he love?
I will forgive your trespass, and forget,
At instance of my sweet queen, kneeling here,
Aye, and of Emily, my sister dear.
And you shall presently consent to swear
That nevermore will you my power dare,
Nor wage war on me, either night or day,
But will be friends to me in all you may;
I do forgive this trespass, full and fair."
And then they swore what he demanded there,
And, of his might, they of his mercy prayed,
And he extended grace, and thus he said:
"To speak for royalty's inheritress,
Although she be a queen or a princess,
Each of you both is worthy, I confess,
When comes the time to wed: but nonetheless,
I speak now of my sister Emily,
The cause of all this strife and jealousy—
You know yourselves she may not marry two,
At once, although you fight or what you do:
One of you, then, and be he loath or lief,
Must pipe his sorrows in an ivy leaf.
That is to say, she cannot have you both,
However jealous one may be, or wroth.
Therefore I put you both in this decree,
That each of you shall follow his own quest,
Free of all ransom or of fear from me;
And this day, fifty weeks hence, both shall be
Here once again, each with a hundred knights,
Armed for the lists, who stoutly for your rights
Will ready be to battle, to maintain
Your claim to love. I promise you, again,
Upon my word, and as I am a knight,
That whichsoever of you wins the fight,
That is to say, whichever of you two
May with his hundred, whom I spoke of, do
His foe to death, or out of boundary drive,
Then he shall have Emilia to wive
Who looks up lightly now but Palamon?
Who leaps for you but Arcita the knight?
And who could tell, or who could ever write
The jubilation made within that place
Where Theseüs has shown so fair a grace?
But down on knee went each one for delight
And thanked him there with all his heart and might,
And specially those Thebans did their part.
And thus, with high hopes, being blithe of heart,
They took their leave; and homeward did they ride
To Thebes that sits within her old walls wide.
The day of their return is forthcoming,
When each of them a hundred knights must bring
The combat to support, as I have told;
And into Athens, covenant to uphold,
Has each one ridden with his hundred knights,
Well armed for war, at all points, in their mights.
And certainly, 'twas thought by many a man
That never, since the day this world began,
Speaking of good knights hardy of their hands,

Wherever God created seas and lands,
Was, of so few, so noble company.
For every man that loved all chivalry,
And eager was to win surpassing fame,
Had prayed to play a part in that great game;
And all was well with him who chosen was.
For if there came tomorrow such a case,
You know right well that every lusty knight
Who loves the ladies fair and keeps his might,
Be it in England, aye or otherwhere,
Would wish of all things to be present there
To fight for some fair lady. *Ben'cite!*
'Twould be a pleasant goodly sight to see!
There might you see, riding with Palamon,
Lycurgus' self, the mighty king of Thrace;
Black was his beard and manly was his face.
With Arcita, in tales men call to mind,
The great Emetrëus, a king of Ind,
Upon a bay steed harnessed all in steel,
Covered with cloth of gold, all diapered well,
That Sunday night, ere day began to spring,
When Palamon the earliest lark heard sing,
Although it lacked two hours of being day,
Yet the lark sang, and Palamon sang a lay.
With pious heart and with a high courage
He rose, to go upon a pilgrimage
Unto the blessed Cytherea's shrine
(I mean Queen Venus, worthy and benign).
And at her hour he then walked forth apace
Out to the lists wherein her temple was,
And down he knelt in manner to revere,
And from a full heart spoke as you shall hear.
"Fairest of fair, O lady mine, Venus,
Daughter of Jove and spouse to Vulcanus,
Thou gladdener of the Mount of Citheron,
By that great love thou borest to Adon,
Have pity on my bitter tears that smart
And hear my humble prayer within thy heart.
Alas! I have no words in which to tell
The effect of all the torments of my hell;
My heavy heart its evils can't bewray;
I'm so confused I can find naught to say.
But mercy, lady bright, that knowest well
My heart, and seëst all the ills I feel,
Consider and have ruth upon my sore
As truly as I shall, for evermore,
Well as I may, thy one true servant be,
And wage a war henceforth on chastity.
If thou wilt help, thus do I make my vow,
To boast of knightly skill I care not now,
Nor do I ask tomorrow's victory,
Nor any such renown, nor vain glory
Of prize of arms, blown before lord and churl,
But I would have possession of one girl,
Of Emily, and die in thy service;
Find thou the manner how, and in what wise.
And if thou wilt not so, O lady, cede,
I pray thee, that tomorrow, with a spear,
Arcita bear me through the heart, just here.
For I'll care naught, when I have lost my life,
That Arcita may win her for his wife.
This the effect and end of all my prayer,
Give me my love, thou blissful lady fair."
Now when he'd finished all the orison,
His sacrifice he made, this Palamon,
Right piously, with all the circumstance,
Albeit I tell not now his observance.
But at the last the form of Venus shook
And gave a sign, and thereupon he took
This as acceptance of his prayer that day.
For though the augury showed some delay,
Yet he knew well that granted was his boon;
And with glad heart he got him home right soon.
Three hours unequal[2] after Palamon
To Venus' temple at the lists had gone,
Up rose the sun and up rose Emily,
And to Diana's temple did she hie.
When kindled was the fire, with sober face
Unto Diana spoke she in that place.
"O thou chaste goddess of the wildwood green,
By whom all heaven and earth and sea are seen,
Queen of the realm of Pluto, dark and low,
Goddess of maidens, that my heart dost know
For all my years, and knowest what I desire,
Oh, save me from thy vengeance and thine ire
That on Actaeon fell so cruelly.
Chaste goddess, well indeed thou knowest that I
Desire to be a virgin all my life,
Nor ever wish to be man's love or wife.

[2]Hours unequal: hours formed by dividing the daylight by twelve. Hence, in May, hours of longer duration than sixty minutes.

I am, thou know'st, yet of thy company,
A maid, who loves the hunt and venery,
And to go rambling in the greenwood wild,
And not to be a wife and be with child.
I do not crave the company of man.
Now help me, lady, since thou may'st and can,
By the three beings who are one in thee.
For Palamon, who bears such love to me,
And for Arcita, loving me so sore,
This grace I pray thee, without one thing more,
To send down love and peace between those two,
And turn their hearts away from me: so do
That all their furious love and their desire,
And all their ceaseless torment and their fire
Be quenched or turned into another place;
And if it be thou wilt not show this grace,
Or if my destiny be moulded so
That I must needs have one of these same two,
Then send me him that most desires me.
Behold, O goddess of utter chastity,
The bitter tears that down my two cheeks fall.
Since thou art maid and keeper of us all,
My maidenhead keep thou, and still preserve,
And while I live a maid, thee will I serve."

The fires blazed high upon the altar there,
While Emily was saying thus her prayer,
And wept, till it was pitiful to hear.
But thereupon Diana did appear,
With bow in hand, like any right huntress,
And said: "My daughter, leave this heaviness.
Among the high gods it has been affirmed,
And by eternal written word confirmed,
That you shall be the wife of one of those
Who bear for you so many cares and woes;
But unto which of them I may not tell.
I can no longer tarry, so farewell.
The fires that on my altar burn incense
Should tell you everything, ere you go hence,
Of what must come of love in this your case."

At the next hour of Mars, and following this,
Arcita to the temple walked, that is
Devoted to fierce Mars, to sacrifice
With all the ceremonies, pagan-wise.
With sobered heart and high devotion, on
This wise, right thus he said his orison.

"O mighty god that in the regions cold
Of Thrace art honoured, where thy lordships hold,
And hast in every realm and every land
The reins of battle in thy guiding hand,
And givest fortune as thou dost devise,
Accept of me my pious sacrifice.
If so it be that my youth may deserve,
And that my strength be worthy found to serve
Thy godhead, and be numbered one of thine,
Then pray I thee for ruth on pain that's mine.
I'm young, and little skilled, as knowest thou,
With love more hurt and much more broken now
Than ever living creature was, I'm sure;
For she who makes me all this woe endure,
Whether I float or sink cares not at all,
And ere she'll hear with mercy when I call,
I must by prowess win her in this place;
And well I know, too, without help and grace
Of thee, my human strength shall not avail.
Then help me, lord, tomorrow not to fail,
For sake of that same fire that once burned thee,
The which consuming fire so now burns me;
And grant, tomorrow, I have victory.
Mine be the toil, and thine the whole glory!
Now, lord, have pity on my sorrows sore;
Give me the victory. I ask no more."

With ended prayer of Arcita the young,
The rings that on the temple door were hung,
And even the doors themselves, rattled so fast
That this Arcita found himself aghast.
The armour of God Mars began to ring,
And with that sound there came a murmuring,
Low and uncertain, saying: "Victory!"
For which he gave Mars honour and glory.
And thus in joy and hope, which all might dare,
Arcita to his lodging then did fare,
Fain of the fight as fowl is of the sun.

But thereupon such quarrelling was begun,
From this same granting, in the heaven above,
'Twixt lovely Venus, goddess of all love,
And Mars, the iron god armipotent,
That Jove toiled hard to make a settlement;
Until the sallow Saturn, calm and cold,
Who had so many happenings known of old,
Found from his full experience the art
To satisfy each party and each part.

"Now my dear daughter Venus," quoth Saturn,
Now weep no more. I'll see, with diligence,
That Palamon, who is your own true knight,

Shall have his lady, as you hold is right.
Though Mars may help his man, yet none the less
Between you two there must come sometime
peace,
And though you be not of one temperament,
Causing each day such violent dissent,
I am your grandsire and obey your will;
Weep then no more, your pleasure I'll fulfill."

The mighty Theseüs, from sleep awakened
By songs and all the noise that never slackened,
Kept yet the chamber of this rich palace,
Till the two Theban knights, with equal grace
And honour, were ushered in with flourish fitting.
Duke Theseüs was at a window sitting,
Arrayed as he were god upon a throne.
Then pressed the people thitherward full soon,
To see him and to do him reverence,
Aye, and to hear commands of sapience.

A herald on a scaffold cried out "Ho!"
Till all the people's noise was stilled; and so,
When he observed that all were fallen still,
He then proclaimed the mighty ruler's will.

"The duke our lord, full wise and full discreet,
Holds that it were but wanton waste to meet
And fight, these gentle folk, all in the guise
Of mortal battle in this enterprise.
Wherefore, in order that no man may die,
He does his earlier purpose modify.
No man, therefore, on pain of loss of life,
Shall any arrow, pole-axe, or short knife
Send into lists in any wise, or bring;
Nor any shortened sword, for point-thrusting,
Shall a man draw, or bear it by his side.
Nor shall a knight against opponent ride,
Save one full course, with any sharp-ground
spear;
Unhorsed, a man may thrust with any gear.
And he that's overcome, should this occur,
Shall not be slain, but brought to barrier,
Whereof there shall be one on either side;
Let him be forced to go there and abide.
And if by chance the leader there must go,
Of either side, or slay his equal foe,
No longer, then, shall tourneying endure.
God speed you; go forth now, and lay on sure.
With long sword and with maces fight your fill.
Go now your ways; this is the lord duke's will."

Then were the gates closed, and the cry rang loud:
"Now do your devoir, all you young knights
proud!"

The heralds cease their spurring up and down;
Now ring the trumpets as the charge is blown;
And there's no more to say, for east and west
Two hundred spears are firmly laid in rest;
And the sharp spurs are thrust, now, into side.
Now see men who can joust and who can ride!
Now shivered are the shafts on bucklers thick;
One feels through very breast-bone the spear's
prick;
Lances are flung full twenty feet in height;
Out flash the swords like silver burnished bright.
Helmets are hewed, the lacings ripped and shred;
Out bursts the blood, gushing in stern streams red.
With mighty maces bones are crushed in joust.
One through the thickest throng begins to thrust.
There strong steeds stumble now, and down goes
all.
One rolls beneath their feet as rolls a ball.
One flails about with club, being overthrown,
Another, on a mailed horse, rides him down.
One through the body's hurt, and haled, for aid,
Spite of his struggles, to the barricade,
As compact was, and there he must abide;
Another's captured by the other side.
At times Duke Theseüs orders them to rest,
To eat a bite and drink what each likes best.
And many times that day those Thebans two
Met in the fight and wrought each other woe;
Out leaps the blood and makes their two sides red.

But sometime comes the end of every deed;
And ere the sun had sunk to rest in gold,
The mighty King Emetreüs did hold
This Palamon, as he fought with Arcite,
And made his sword deep in the flesh to bite;
And by the force of twenty men he's made,
Unyielded, to withdraw to barricade.
And, trying hard to rescue Palamon,
The mighty King Lycurgus is borne down;
And King Emetreüs, for all his strength,
Is hurled out of the saddle a sword's length,
So hits out Palamon once more, or ere
(But all for naught) he's brought to barrier.
His hardy heart may now avail him naught;
He must abide there now, being fairly caught

By force of arms, as by provision known.
Who sorrows now but woeful Palamon,
Who may no more advance into the fight?
And when Duke Theseüs had seen this sight,
Unto the warriors fighting, every one,
He cried out: "Hold! No more! For it is done!
Now will I prove true judge, of no party.
Theban Arcita shall have Emily,
Who, by his fortune, has her fairly won."
This fierce Arcita doffs his helmet soon,
And mounted on a horse, to show his face,
He spurs from end to end of that great place,
Looking aloft to gaze on Emily;
And she cast down on him a friendly eye
(For women, generally speaking, go
Wherever Fortune may her favor show);
And she was fair to see, and held his heart.
But from the ground infernal furies start,
From Pluto sent, at instance of Saturn,
Whereat his horse, for fear, began to turn
And leap aside, all suddenly falling there;
And Arcita before he could beware
Was pitched upon the ground, upon his head,
And lay there, moving not, as he were dead,
His chest crushed in upon the saddle-bow.
And black he lay as ever coal, or crow,
So ran the surging blood into his face.
Anon they carried him from out that place,
With heavy hearts, to Theseüs' palace.
There was his harness cut away, each lace,
And swiftly was he laid upon a bed,
For he was yet alive and some words said,
Crying and calling after Emily.
The sum of all is, Arcita must die,
And so he sends a word to Emily,
And Palamon, who was his cousin dear;
And then he said to them as you shall hear.
"Naught may the woeful spirit in my heart
Declare one point of how my sorrows smart
To you, my lady, whom I-love the most;
But I bequeath the service of my ghost
To you above all others, this being sure
Now that my life may here no more endure.
Alas, the woe! Alas, the pain so strong
That I for you have suffered, and so long!
Alas for death! Alas, my Emily!
Alas, the parting of our company!
Alas, my heart's own queen! Alas, my wife!
My soul's dear lady, ender of my life!
What is this world? What asks a man to have?
Now with his love, now in the cold dark grave
Alone, with never any company.
Farewell, my sweet foe! O my Emily!
Oh, take me in your gentle arms, I pray,
For love of God, and hear what I will say.
"I have here, with my cousin Palamon,
Had strife and rancour many a day that's gone,
For love of you and for my jealousy.
May Jove so surely guide my soul for me,
To speak about a lover properly,
With all the circumstances, faithfully—
That is to say, truth, honour, and knighthood,
Wisdom, humility and kinship good,
And generous soul and all the lover's art—
So now may Jove have in my soul his part
As in this world, right now, I know of none
So worthy to be loved as Palamon,
Who serves you and will do so all his life.
And if you ever should become a wife,
Forget not Palamon, the noble man."
And with that word his speech to fail began,
For from his feet up to his breast had come
The cold of death, making his body numb.
And furthermore, from his two arms the strength
Was gone out, now, and he was lost, at length.
Only the intellect, and nothing more,
Which dwelt within his heart so sick and sore,
Began to fail now, when the heart felt death,
And his eyes darkened, and he failed of breath.
But on his lady turned he still his eye,
And his last word was, "Mercy, Emily!"
With passing in their length of certain years,
All put by was the mourning and the tears
Of Greeks, as by one general assent;
And then it seems there was a parliament
At Athens, upon certain points in case;
Among the which points spoken of there was
The ratifying of alliances
That should hold Thebes from all defiances.
Whereat this noble Theseüs, anon,
Invited there the gentle Palamon,
Not telling him what was the cause and why;
But in his mourning clothes, and sorrowfully,
He came upon that bidding, so say I.

And then Duke Theseüs sent for Emily.
When they were seated and was hushed the place,
And Theseüs had mused a little space,
Ere any word came from his full wise breast,
His two eyes fixed on whoso pleased him best,
Then with a sad face sighed he deep and still,
And after that began to speak his will.
"The Primal Mover and the Cause above,
When first He forged the goodly chain of love,
Great the effect, and high was His intent;
Well knew He why, and what thereof He meant;
For with that goodly chain of love He bound
The fire, the air, the water, and dry ground
In certain bounds, the which they might not flee;
All men perish, the king as well as page;
Some in their bed, and some in the deep sea,
And some in the wide field—as it may be;
There's naught will help; all go the same way. Aye,
Then may I say that everything must die.
Who causes this but Jupiter the King?
He is the Prince and Cause of everything,
Converting all back to that primal well
From which it was derived, 'tis sooth to tell.
And against this, for every thing alive,
Of any state, avails it not to strive.
"Then is it wisdom, as it seems to me,
To make a virtue of necessity,
And calmly take what we may not eschew,
And specially that which to all is due.
Whoso would balk at aught, he does folly,
And thus rebels against His potency.
And certainly a man has most honour
In dying in his excellence and flower,
When he is certain of his high good name;
For then he gives to friend, and self, no shame.
And gladder ought a friend be of his death
When, in much honour, he yields up his breath,
Than when his name's grown feeble with old age;
For all forgotten, then, is his courage.
Hence it is best for all of noble name
To die when at the summit of their fame.
The contrary of this is wilfulness.
Why do we grumble? Why have heaviness
That good Arcita, chivalry's fair flower,
Is gone, with honour, in his best-lived hour.
Out of the filthy prison of this life?
Why grumble here his cousin and his wife
About his welfare, who loved them so well?
Can he thank them? Nay, God knows, not! Nor tell
How they his soul and their own selves offend,
Though yet they may not their desires amend.
"What may I prove by this long argument
Save that we all turn to merriment,
After our grief, and give Jove thanks for grace.
And so, before we go from out this place,
I counsel that we make, of sorrows two,
One perfect joy, lasting for aye, for you;
And look you now, where most woe is herein,
There will we first amend it and begin.
"Sister," quoth he, "you have my full consent,
With the advice of this my Parliament,
That gentle Palamon, your own true knight,
Who serves you well with will and heart and might,
And so has ever, since you knew him first—
That you shall, of your grace, allay his thirst
By taking him for husband and for lord:
Lend me your hand, for this is our accord.
Let now your woman's pity make him glad
For he is a king's brother's son, by gad;
And though he were a poor knight bachelor,
Since he has served you for so many a year,
And borne for you so great adversity,
This ought to weigh with you, it seems to me,
For mercy ought to dominate mere right."
Then said he thus to Palamon the knight:
"I think there needs but little sermoning
To make you give consent, now, to this thing.
Come near, and take your lady by the hand."
Between them, then, was tied that nuptial band,
Which is called matrimony or marriage,
By all the council and the baronage.
And thus, in all bliss and with melody,
Has Palamon now wedded Emily.
And God, Who all this universe has wrought,
Send him His love, who has it dearly bought.
For now has Palamon, in all things, wealth,
Living in bliss, in riches, and in health;
And Emily loved him so tenderly,
And he served her so well and faithfully,
That never word once marred their happiness,
No jealousy, nor other such distress.
Thus ends now Palamon and Emily;
And may God save all this fair company! Amen.

The Canon Yeoman's Tale

There is a canon of religion known
Among us, who'd contaminate a town,
Though 'twere as great as Nineveh the free,
Rome, Alexandria, Troy, and others three.
His tricks and all his infinite treacherousness
No man could write down fully, as I guess,
Though he should live unto his thousandth year.
In all this world for falsehood he's no peer;
For in his terms he will so twist and wind
And speak in words so slippery of kind,
When he communicates with any wight,
That he soon makes a fool of him outright,
Unless it be a devil, as he is.
In London was a priest, an annualeer[1]
Who had therein dwelt many a quiet year,
A man so pleasant and so serviceable
To the goodwife who shared with him her table,
That she would never suffer him to pay
For board or clothing, went he ever so gay;
Of spending-silver, too, he had enow.
No matter; I'll proceed as I said, now,
And tell about the canon all my tale,
Who gave this priest good cause to weep and wail.
This canon false, he came, upon a day
Into the chaplain's chamber, where he lay,
Beseeching him to lend him a certain
Amount in gold, the which he'd pay again.
"Lend me a mark," said he, "for three days, say,
And when that time's done, I will it repay.
And if you find me false, I shall not reck
If, on a day, you hang me by the neck!"
This priest brought him a mark, and quickly, too,
Whereat this canon thanked him, said adieu,
And took his leave and went forth on his way,
And brought the money back on the third day,
And to the priest he gave his gold again,
Whereof this priest was wondrous glad, 'tis plain.
"Truly," he said, "it no wise bothers me
To lend a man a noble, or two, or three,
Or any modest thing that is my own,
To him who has the disposition shown
That in no wise will he forgo to pay;
To such a man I never can say nay."
"What!" cried this canon, "Should I be untrue?"
Nay, that for me would be a thing quite new.
Truth is a thing that I will ever keep
Unto that day, at last, when I shall creep
Into my grave, or elsewise God forbid!
Trust this as surely as you trust your creed.
I thank God, and in good time be it said,
That there was never yet man ill repaid
For gold or silver that to me he lent,
Nor ever falsehood in my heart I've meant.
And, sir," said he, "out of my privity,
Since you have been so very good to me,
And showed to me so great a nobleness,
Somewhat to quit you for your kindliness,
I'll show to you, and if you'd learn it here,
I'll teach you plainly all the methods dear
I use in working at philosophy.
Give it good heed, for you'll see with your eye
I'll do a masterpiece before I go."
"Yes?" asked the priest, "Yes, sir, and will you so?
Mary! Thereof I pray you heartily."
"Right at your service, sir, and truthfully,"
Replied the canon, "else, may God forbid!"
And then this canon took a crucible
Out of his bosom, showing it to the priest.
"This instrument," said he, "you see—at least
Take in your hand, and put yourself therein
An ounce of quicksilver, and here begin,
And in God's name, to be philosopher!
There are but few to whom I would proffer
To make my science clear and evident.
For you shall learn here, by experiment,
That this quicksilver will I mortify
Right in your sight anon, without a lie,
And make it as good silver and as fine
As any that's in your purse or in mine,
Or elsewhere, aye, and make it malleable;
Otherwise hold me false, unfit as well
Among good folk for ever to appear.
I have a powder here that cost me dear,
Shall do all this, for it's the root of all
My craft; you'll see what shall therewith befall.
Dismiss your man and let him stay without,
And shut the door fast while we are about

[1]A priest employed in singing anniversary masses.

Our secret work, that no man may espy
The way we work in this philosophy."
All was then done as canon had decreed;
This servant took himself straight out, indeed,
Whereat his master barred the door anon,
And to their labour quickly they were gone.
The priest, at this damned canon's ordering,
Upon the fire anon did set this thing,
And blew the fire and busied him full fast;
Within the crucible the canon cast
A powder (I know not whereof it was
Compounded, whether of chalk, or maybe glass,
Or something else—it was not worth a fly)
To blind the priest with; and he bade him high
The coals to pile the crucible above.
"In token of how much I bear you love,"
This canon said, "your own two hands, and none
Other, shall do this thing that shall be done."
"Thank you," the priest replied, and was right glad,
And heaped the coals up as the canon bade.
And while he laboured thus, this fiendish wretch,
This canon false—may him the foul Fiend fetch!—
Out of his bosom took a beechen coal,
Wherein right cunningly he'd bored a hole
In which, before, he'd put of silver limail
An ounce, and which he'd stopped up, without fail,
With blackened wax, to keep the filings in.
And understand you well that this false gin
Was not made there, but it was made before;
He took this coal whereof I spoke above,
And in his hand he bore it privily.
And while the priest did pile up busily
The burning coals, as I told you ere this,
This canon said: "My friend, you do amiss;
This is not piled up as it ought to be;
But soon I shall amend all that," said he.
"Now let me thereof have a hand the whiles,
For I've great pity on you, by Saint Giles!
You are right hot, I see well how you sweat,
Take here a cloth and wipe away the wet."
And while the simple priest did wipe his face,
This canon took his coal, and with grave grace,
Laid it above and well to middleward
Upon the crucible, and blew it hard
Until the flames did blaze up hot again.
"Now give us drink, sir," said the canon then,
"For soon all shall be well, I undertake;
Let us sit down, and let us merry make."
And when this treacherous canon's beechen coal
Was burnt, then all the filings from the hole
Into the crucible fell down anon;
As so, in reason, it must needs have done,
Since so well centred over it it was;
But thereof nothing knew the priest, alas!
He deemed that all the coals alike were good,
For of the trick he nothing understood.
And when this alchemist was ready, he
Said to the priest: "Rise up and stand by me;
And since I know that metal mould you've none,
Go sally forth and bring here a chalk-stone;
For I will make one of the very shape
That ingot moulds have, if I can them ape.
And, too, bring in with you a bowl or pan
Full of clear water, and you'll see, dear man,
How well our business here shall thrive, in brief.
And yet, that you may have no unbelief,
Or think that somehow I'm not doing right,
I'll never be a moment out of sight,
But go with you and come with you again."
He took the chalk and shaped it in such wise
As moulds are made, as further I'll apprise.
I say, he took, then, out of his own sleeve
A tain[2] of silver (Hell the man receive!)
Which was an ounce, no more or less, in weight;
Now here's the trick, the way of which I'll state!
He shaped his mould in length and breadth to be
Like to the tain of silver, as you see,
So slyly that the priest this never spied;
And in his sleeve did then the model hide;
And from the fire he took his crucible
And poured it in the mould, for all went well,
And in the bowl of water then did cast
The mould and all, and bade the priest, at last:
"Seek what there is, put in your hand and grope,
And you shall find there silver, as I hope;
What—devils out of Hell!—should it else be?
Filing of silver silver is!" cried he.
He put his hand in and a tain took out
Of silver fine, and glad, you cannot doubt,
Was this priest when he saw that it was so.

[2]Tain: a thin slice.

And to the canon thus he spoke and said:
"For love of God, Who for us all was dead,
And as I may requite it unto you,
What shall this recipe cost? Come, tell me now?"
"By 'r Lady," said this canon, "it is dear,
I warn you well; for now in England here
One friar and I are all who can it make."
"No matter," said he, "now, sir, for God's sake,
What shall I pay? Oh, tell me this, I pray!"
"Truly," said he, "it is right dear, I say;
Sir, in one word, if this thing you will have,
You shall pay forty pounds, so God me save!
And were it not for friendship shown ere this
To me, you should pay more than that, ywis."
This priest the sum of forty pounds anon
In nobles fetched, and gave them, every one,
To this said canon for this said receipt;
His business was all fraud and all deceit.
"Sir priest," he said, "I do not care to lose
My secret craft, and I would 'twere kept close;
So, as you love me, keep it privily;
For if men knew all of my subtlety,
By God above, they'd have so great envy
Of me, because of my philosophy,
I should be slain, there'd be no other way."
"Nay, God forbid!" replied the priest. "What say?
Far rather would I spend all coin, by gad,
That I possess (and else may I grow mad!)
Than that you fall in any such distress."
"For your good will, I wish you all success,"
Replied the canon, "farewell, many thanks."
He went, and ne'er the priest this mountebank's
Face saw thereafter; and when this priest would
Make his own test, at such time as he could,
Of this receipt, farewell! it would not be!
Lo, thus bejaped and thus beguiled was he!
And thus he had his introduction in
The way men fall to ruin and to sin.

End of the Middle Ages

Survival and Creative Change

> Printing with movable type was both inspiration and perspiration, an idea and an invention. The birth of the idea sounds as if it ought to have been a sudden revelation, a Eureka! moment like the one that inspired Archimedes to leap from his bath with his famous yell. But ideas seldom jump into the mind from nowhere. If they do, like Leonardo da Vinci's sketch for a helicopter, they remain science fictions until technological advance makes them seem prescient. Ideas are seeded in frameworks of previous growths and need those same frameworks—in this case, punch-making, casting, metallurgical skills, wine- and oil-pressing, paper-making—to flourish.
>
> —*John Man,* Gutenberg, *John Wiley and Sons, 2002, p. 122*

The Worst Century

Some periods of time seem to be just terrible. Such a time was the century from roughly 1350 to 1450, which might qualify as the worst century in history. It was a time of devastating plague, continuous state of war, religious corruption, and intolerant government. Not that these were unique to this hundred years, but during this period all seemed to grow in intensity, as if by some evil combination, until a climax was reached that profoundly changed all aspects of civilization. The foundation on which European civilization was built cracked and partially crumbled, resulting in, perhaps, the most profound change in a society that had ever occurred.

It would have been impossible to live in these times and not experience the change. Even if you were a peasant in a faraway village, you would sense the change when you went to church; you would know a difference when the sheriff came to collect your taxes; you would, perhaps, be drafted into an army to fight for a king you had little allegiance to; and you might quake in fear when your neighbors or family members died from the hideous plague. Even your calendar might be different. After the century was over, you would think differently about the church, the government, and your own life. You might begin to think about changing your personal circumstances and even learning how to read, so that you could become more informed. Who knows what might happen then?

In the broad view, the worst century was culminated by a period of technological innovations that had then, and continues to have now, the deepest cultural ramifications. The man responsible for the most astounding of these technological changes has been recognized by the media and by popular opinion as the most important man of the millennium between 1000 and 2000. The change was the invention of printing using movable type, and the man was Gutenberg. Yet, as seen in the quotation at the beginning of this chapter, his contribution was as much hard work as genius. That combination is, of course, the essence of creativity. But, before we talk about him, we must survive the worst century in history.

The Basic Structure of Society

From the beginning of the Middle Ages, and perhaps even before, a person's place in society was determined at birth. All humans, at least those in European society, were linked together in what was called the **Great Chain of Being.** It was a model in which every individual was linked to every other individual in a social network. The top of the great chain was God. He was linked to earth in two lines. The first was to His representatives on earth—the pope, the bishops, and the other clergy down to the priest in the local church and the monk in the monastery outside of the village. Another line from God went to the king, who was linked to his (the king's) dukes, barons, earls, and other vassals even down to the knight and the local king's representative. That kingly line continues to all the commoners in the cities, villages, and countryside who toil on the farms and in the shops of the realm.

Not only did all the people feel linked together, but they also all understood their duties. If society was to function properly, all persons had to accomplish the tasks assigned to them. Few people could change their basic responsibilities, although some farmers could move to the city and become artisans—but only because their duty of growing food was being adequately done by others. A person who wanted to enter a religious community would probably not be the child who was to inherit the land, as that might cause disruption in the Great Chain. Most people were born to a position and they died in that position. The oppressively static nature of society was a problem for some people, but there was little that they could do about it.

This basic societal structure could also be viewed in a slightly different model. It could be seen as three groups of people, each with different duties and privileges. We call the three groups the **Three Estates** and they are designated as follows:

- The First Estate is the church and clergy, and their responsibility is to pray.
- The Second Estate is the nobility, and their responsibility is to fight and rule.
- The Third Estate is the commoners, and their responsibility is to work.

Aside from the people who move from the common class into the clergy (and their number was small since the clergy was largely composed of minor nobility), few could change from one estate to another. The clergy and the nobility ferociously defended their positions and allowed little mixing of duties or privileges.

The governmental system that accompanied the Great Chain of Being and the Three Estates was **feudalism.** Lords controlled vast amounts of land and allowed peasants to work the land and share in the proceeds. The lords gave allegiance to kings and promised to fight for the king, should the king require them to do so. In turn, the lords were the beneficiaries of loyalties from knights, who received their maintenance from the lords and fought at their command.

The feudal system had served the purposes of European society for nearly a millennium, but some major problems were causing it to break down. For example, what would happen if a lord died and was succeeded by a young child or a daughter who could not fulfill the duty to fight for the king? The rules of feudalism allowed the child or daughter to pay the king a fee in lieu of military service. The king used the money to hire knights (or others) to fight in place of those who might have served otherwise. This practice introduced the concept of fighting by the commoners—a concept that mixed the responsibilities of the estates and, therefore, brought changes in the basics of society.

When a king or great lord died, the fealty oaths that bound together the kings, lords, and knights had to be re-established. Normally this was not a problem, but what would happen if a king were to die and then two kings claimed to be the rightful successor? To whom should the lords and knights swear allegiance? Furthermore, what were the status and feudal responsibility of people who lived in towns and cities? They were not part of any lord's domain. Were they, then, under the direct control of the king, or might they not be part of the feudal system at all?

These problems, and many others, brought into doubt the value of the Great Chain of Being and of the three estates. Society was clearly struggling with old models and new situations. Then, on top of all this potential for change, society experienced the confluence of devastations mentioned at the beginning of this chapter. As a result, society changed. Let's now examine the changes that shook all parts of society; they can best be understood by looking at each of the divisions of society—the Three Estates—in turn.

Changes in the First Estate

The First Estate was the Catholic Church and its clergy. Its influence permeated virtually every aspect of life in the Middle Ages. The calendar was liturgical (beginning with Easter and then marked by major holy days throughout the year, which were reinforced by weekly reminders of the days as the people went to mass each Sunday). Church attendance was frequent and included in addition to weekly mass, baptisms, confirmation, confession, marriage, blessings, and last rites. The church was the center of the community. Some of the churches were large cathedrals that gave great pride to the city and brought in much economic benefit.

The popes in the fourteenth century were often corrupt and increasingly non-religious, despite attempts by the church to reform the papacy. Popes readily accepted money to forgive any sin or to grant any special dispensation. While popes were no longer appointed by emperors and kings, some of the emperors and kings did not agree with those rules, and attempted, often successfully, to exert their authority over the popes. As we will shortly see, this church-state conflict caused a major division in the church, from which it did not survive intact.

Bishops became increasingly distant from their congregations. Many bishops, who were the only officers to perform confirmations, did so perfunctorily, such as riding into a town to perform them and never leaving horseback or carriage; those wishing to be confirmed lined up in the street and approached him as he sat majestically aloof. Bishops actively sought **benefices** (areas under a bishop's control from which he collected taxes) in many parts of the country and could not, therefore, service them properly.

Priests were also increasingly distant from the people. They often lectured on philosophical concepts that were above the people's capabilities to understand. Benedictines were isolated in their monasteries. Friars, especially Dominicans, became increasingly caught up in university education. Some monks began to enforce doctrinal purity through the Inquisition, which caused a rift in the towns where people were tried and punished. People were forced to pay for many of the sacraments (baptism, penance, confirmation, marriage, and extreme unction). Priests widely ignored celibacy. It has been reported that 23 percent of the sexual crimes were committed by clerics, who represented only 2 percent of the population. Some nunneries allowed male visitors and gave sexual services.

The withdrawal or estrangement from the clergy of the church forced people to adopt other methods to connect to God. One method was to adopt personal signs of religious behavior that were independent of the church. For example, people would make the sign of the cross at many different times, such as marking a loaf of bread with a cross before cutting it, or if something unusual happened, especially if it frightened them or appeared to be a bad omen. Relics were adopted widely, especially if some miracle was associated with the relic. The worship of the Virgin Mary became a substitute for association with the clergy. Mary became a substitute for the church.

Throughout all this corruption, the church resisted change, as can be seen in the following quotation from a fourteenth-century cardinal:

> *The church is the work of God and, like all of God's works, it is perfect . . . The church is independent of any earthly power, not merely in regard to her lawful end and purpose, but also in regard to whatever means she may deem suitable and necessary to attain them.*

The church seemed ripe for a major crisis. The trigger was a dispute between **Phillip IV of France** and **Pope Boniface VIII.** Pope Boniface had been elected pope in 1294 under some rather curious circumstances. The previous pope was a hermit who had been elected as a compromise because the cardinals couldn't agree. After a short time in office, the hermit pope resigned, perhaps under pressure from Boniface, who was elected as the new pope but was not well accepted. At just this time, Phillip IV issued a tax on non-church land in France held by the clergy (which had previously been exempt from taxes), which Boniface commanded them not to pay, asserting the independence of church officials and their holdings from secular authority. Various political moves by both king and pope, including **papal bulls** (declarations of truth) and a threatened excommunication, led King Phillip to seize Pope Boniface and hold him in prison. Although Boniface was soon released, he died shortly thereafter. Following the 8-month papacy of Benedict XI who may have died of poisoning (1303), Phillip was able to secure the election of **Clement V,** who annulled Boniface's bulls and supported Phillip's persecution of the Knights Templars, who were exiled from France and whose wealth the king appropriated. Clement V further supported Phillip by moving the headquarters of the church out of Rome and to the city of **Avignon,** now in southern France (Figure 22.1). This move began what has been called the **Babylonian Captivity of the Catholic Church.** (The historical reference of this name is to when the Jews were taken as captives to Babylon by King Nebuchadnezzar of Babylonia in the 6th century B.C. thereby denying them rights to access the temple in Jerusalem and, in other ways, changing their religion.)

The Avignon papacy lasted from 1309 to 1376 and covered the reign of seven popes, all generally loyal to the king of France. The focus of the Avignon popes was generally on financial and bureaucratic matters as they tried to re-establish the papacy in the new city. The popes built a beautiful palace in Avignon (which can be toured today) and attempted to restore some of the grandeur that existed in Rome. As a result, the Avignon popes were constantly looking for money. Some of the services for fees, all of which were against church rules, included the following: simony (selling church positions), overlooking age limitations (which meant that bishoprics could be purchased and filled by youths), forgiving sins, legitimizing children (many the children of clerics), permitting nuns to keep maids, allowing marriage within the prohibited degrees of sanguinity, trading with infidels (Muslims) for a share of the proceeds, receipt of stolen goods by merchants, exclusion of minimum requirements for clergy (such as literacy), misuse of the office of pardoner (to sell indulgences), and allowance of clergy to extort payments by threatening excommunication.

Another example showing just how widespread the clerical corruption had become comes from an instruction book given to young priests—*Handling Synne, 1303.* The author of the book, Robert Manning of Brunne, felt it necessary to specifically proscribe selling their vestments to itinerant actors to use as costumes.

Rome fell into near ruin during the Avignon papacy. Without the presence of church headquarters and the many residents and visitors who followed, Rome had little economic support. The population dropped to less than half. Buildings were abandoned, including several churches; some of these were even used to stable animals.

The plight of Rome was critical. Some in the church became alarmed and determined to do

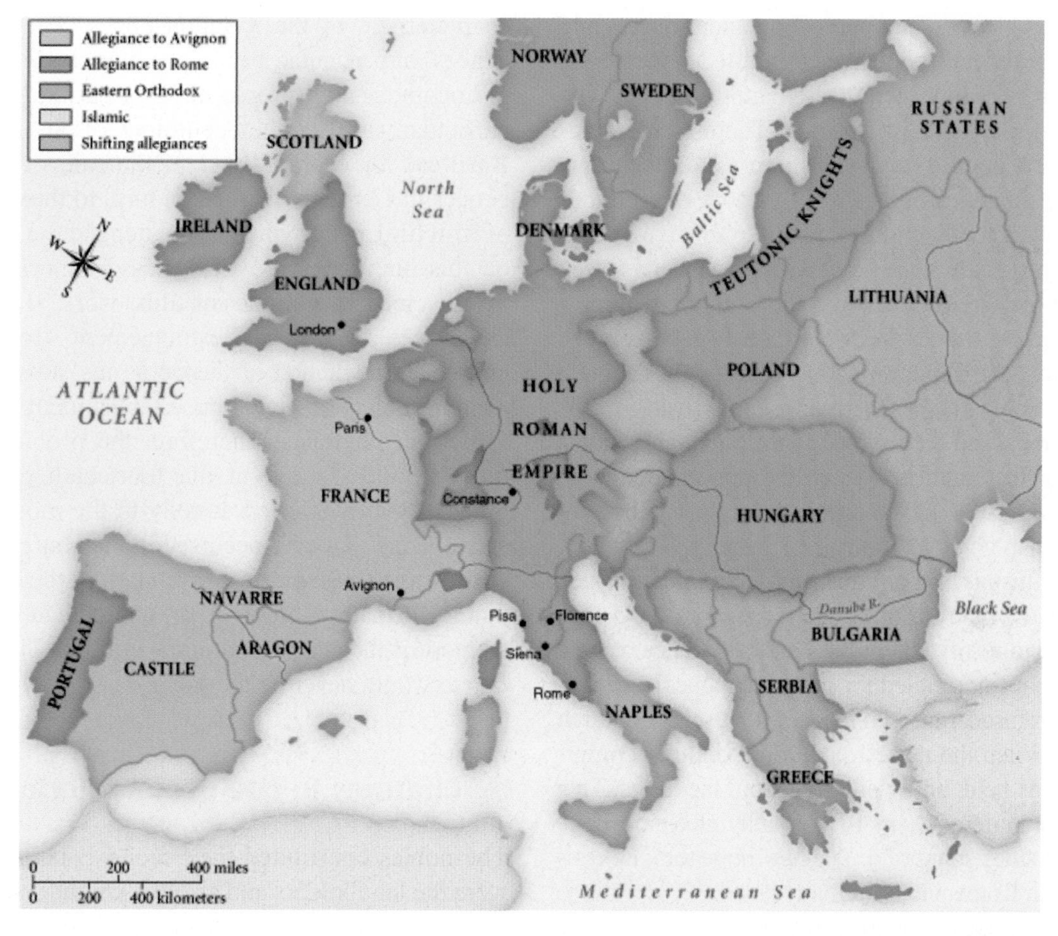

Figure 22.1 ■ *Map of France, showing the location of Avignon and the division of Europe over the election of two popes.*

something about it. One such person was **Catherine of Siena,** who was widely recognized (but not yet officially designated) as a saint. She had received the marks of Christ's death on her hand, feet, and sides (stigmata) thus certifying her saintliness (although the marks were only visible to her). She had practiced asceticism from the age of nine, and ate almost nothing. She had urged a crusade and believed that her will and that of God were identical. She began a campaign to restore the papacy to Rome and convinced Pope Gregory XI that if he did not return to Rome to die, he would not go to paradise and Rome would fall to the Holy Roman Emperor, thus eliminating the Papal States. Pope Gregory returned to Rome over the objections of the king of France, most of the cardinals, his advisors, and even his own father. He died after only one year in Rome. The rest of the papal courts remained in Avignon.

The rules of the church required that the new pope be elected in the city where the previous pope had died. Therefore, the cardinals (most of them French) convened in Rome but, when there, were threatened with violence (from the Roman citizens) if they did not elect an Italian as pope. Acceding to the demands of the crowds, they selected a new pope from Naples, but the cardinals forced him to accept Avignon as the papal home and headquarters of the church as a condition of his being elected. The cardinals returned to Avignon but the new pope, breaking his promise, stayed in Rome. The cardinals, claiming that the previous election had been done under duress and also that the new pope had committed several serious errors (sins), then elected another pope, who took up residence in Avignon. There were, therefore, two popes—both of whom were elected by the legitimate cardinals. The two popes excommunicated each other and set about to form their own college of cardinals. This caused what has been called the **Great Schism** of the Catholic Church.

Europe was divided over which pope was the authentic one. France obviously backed the Avignon pope. England and Germany, long rivals of the French, backed the Roman pontiff. Scotland, long a rival of the English, backed the pope in Avignon. The position of the countries of Europe can be seen in the map given in Figure 22.1. After several years, the confusion and animosities of the situation led the kings of the various countries to convene a conference to resolve the issue. The conference elected a new pope and called for both rival popes to resign. They refused, thus creating a three-pope church mess. When the newest pope died, another conference was held, under pressure from the kings. That second conference, in 1417, finally elected a pope that all sides supported. The new pope took up residence in Rome and Avignon receded.

The popes following the reunification of the church were, again, beset with financial and administrative difficulties. Rome needed to be rebuilt and the Papal States had diminished in power and land. Papal corruption continued and seemed to fall to a new low with the election of the **Borgia** pope, **Alexander VI.** He had many mistresses and reportedly even bore children from his own illegitimate daughter—**Lucrezia Borgia,** who later also may have poisoned her husband. **Caesare Borgia,** a brother, poisoned his older brother to gain power. Caesare Borgia, was the model for **Machiavelli's** novel, *The Prince,* which details the concepts of exploitation and suppression as a way for princes to remain in power. Alexander VI was the pope who resolved the dispute between Spain and Portugal over newly discovered territories in the New World, a topic we will discuss in the next chapter.

The financial woes of the new Roman pontiffs led to continuation of many fund-raising activities characteristic of the Avignon popes. The indulgences, in particular, became an important source of income, and were sometimes earmarked for particular causes. The rebuilding of **St. Peter's Basilica,** for example, led to the sale of indulgences in Germany that led, in turn, to the actions of **Martin Luther** when he challenged the church on this point. As we will discuss in more detail in the second volume of this work, Luther's challenges led to his estrangement from the church, his defiance of the pope, his subsequent excommunication, and the establishment of the Protestant churches. Therefore, the problems of the Catholic Church in the fourteenth century, great as they were, led directly to the most massive change that ever occurred in the church—the **Protestant Reformation.** Even before the Protestant Reformation, however, the church had lost the support of the people and of the nobility. The First Estate would never be the same.

Changes in the Second Estate

The nobles constituted the Second Estate. These were the landholders and also the knight-warriors. They claimed their position in the Second Estate by birth; where a person wished to exercise some privilege of the class, such as participation in a knightly tournament, a proof of genealogy was required. The nobility paid no taxes (at least in some countries like France) and were generally above the common law, so that they could do almost whatever they liked to a person of the lower class.

In peacetime the life of a nobleman was filled with military practice followed by long sessions of leisure and dining. Dinners were ultra-lavish and extensive. Records of a dinner for 800 nobles reported that four courses of ten dishes each were served. The dishes consisted of two items that complemented each other, such as roast capons and partridges, meat and fish aspics, lark pasties (pies) and rissoles (pressings) of beef marrow, black puddings and sausages, and lampreys and savory rice. Some meals were built around delicacies that were almost unbelievable such as, in one case, a course featuring hummingbird tongues.

One wonders how the chefs were able to get enough to make just one plate, let alone to serve many people at a banquet. The place settings were of gold and velvet. After dinner the 800 guests moved to a large room where the taking of Jerusalem by the First Crusade was re-enacted, complete with bodies of water, Christ rising from the tomb, hell opening its mouth, Noah's flood, and the decapitation of John the Baptist (using ox blood and a fake head).

The Second Estate was governed by the rules of chivalry rather than the rules of the land (which governed the commoners) and the rules of the church (in which they had lost confidence). The commoners resented this apparent lack of legal consequences, but there was little that could be done. It seemed, correctly as it turned out, that initial changes to the Second Estate would have to come from within.

Those changes began with the **Hundred Years War** (1337–1453) between England and France, over the ownership of lands (which England claimed in France) and the right to the French throne. The major territorial claims and battle locations of the Hundred Years War are shown in the map given in Figure 22.2. When the last Capetian king died, there was no direct heir and the succession came into question. A Valois duke assumed the French throne but was disputed by the English monarch, who was closely related through marriage and descent, as well as being the holder of vast territories in France. To enforce their claim, the English sent an army to France and, in the several battles, for example at **Crécy** and **Poitiers,** the English were victors—surprising in view of the vast numerical superiority of the French army.

The English victories were largely due to two related and recent English innovations in warfare. The first innovation was a natural consequence of some difficulties in the feudal system that we discussed previously in this chapter. That was the presence of a large contingent of commoners in the English army; various lords had purchased exemption from their martial duties and, consequently, the king had hired commoners as soldiers. Previous armies had used commoners, but never to the extent of this English army. These lightly dressed commoners (at least compared to the heavily-armed French knights) were able to move quickly and effectively in the soft and muddy ground of the battles, whereas the knights sunk into the mud. The second innovation was the weaponry employed by these commoners—the **long bow.** Originally developed by the Welsh, the advantages of this eight-foot bow were quickly seen by the English, and their army was outfitted with these weapons. Those major advantages were the range and the lethality against an armored knight. These bows were large and powerful—some requiring tremendous strength just to string. They could engage an enemy at a far greater distance than any other weapon. Also, they were powerful enough to launch an arrow that could, apparently, penetrate the heavy armor of the day. However, the long bow could not be effectively fired from horseback so they were not appropriate weapons for the knights (who were always mounted). The English king equipped his paid infantry men with this lethal weapon.

What a difference the long bow made in the battles of the Hundred Years War! The English would launch their first salvo from a great range, thus causing confusion in the French ranks and forcing a premature charge by the French knights. During the charge, the English reloaded and, when the French knights came into close proximity, but before hand-to-hand combat could begin, the English bowmen fired again, penetrating the French armor and killing most of the knights. The remaining French knights were frustrated, not only because the English infantry would then withdraw, but also because the knights wanted to fight English knights in glorious hand-to-hand combat, but rarely were given the opportunity. The results of these battles were consistent English victories. In one battle, the French king was captured and taken to England as a prisoner. There he agreed to cede much more French land to the English and pay a large ransom. The French king was then returned to France and set free. The English were not, however, able to enforce the agreement, largely because of internal battles in England.

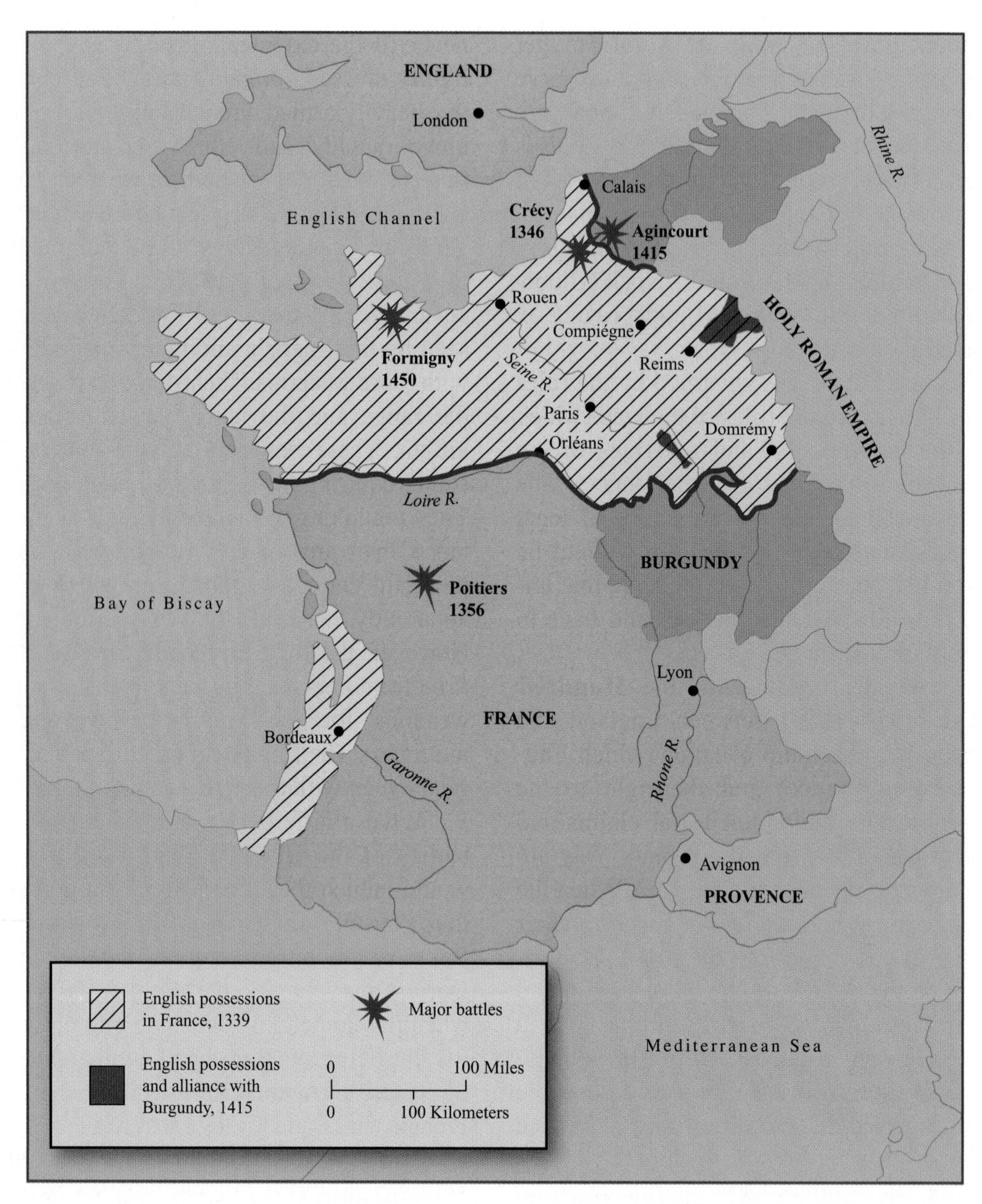

Figure 22.2 ■ *Major battle locations and territorial claims during the Hundred Years War.*

From time to time, as English kings gained control over their own country, they would again mount armies and invade France. One such example was under **Henry V.** He met the French troops at **Agincourt,** in northern France. On the night before the battle Henry saw great apprehension in the faces of his troops as he walked among them. The apprehension was undoubtedly because of the vastly superior numbers and supplies of the French army. To fire up his troops, Henry gave a passionate speech, at least according to Shakespeare, that excited and rededicated his soldiers, so that they won a startling victory the next day. (This speech is called the **"St. Crispin's Day speech,"** named in honor of the saint's day on which it was given; it is reproduced in part in Figure 22.3.) Henry took, as

Henry:
If we are mark'd to die, we are enow
To do our country loss; and if to live,
The fewer men, the greater share of honour.
God's will! I pray thee, wish not one man more.
By Jove, I am not covetous for gold,
Nor care I who doth feed upon my cost;
It yearns me not if men my garments wear;
Such outward things dwell not in my desires.
But if it be a sin to covet honour,
I am the most offending soul alive.
No, faith, my coz, wish not a man from England.
God's peace! I would not lose so great an honour
As one man more methinks would share from me
For the best hope I have. O, do not wish one
more!
Rather proclaim it, Westmoreland, through my
host,
That he which hath no stomach to this fight,
Let him depart; his passport shall be made,
And crowns for convoy put into his purse;
We would not die in that man's company
That fears his fellowship to die with us.
This day is call'd the feast of Crispian.
He that outlives this day, and comes safe home,
Will stand a tip-toe when this day is nam'd,
And rouse him at the name of Crispian.
He that shall live this day, and see old age,
Will yearly on the vigil feast his neighbours,
And say 'To-morrow is Saint Crispian.'
Then will he strip his sleeve and show his scars,
And say 'These wounds I had on Crispian's day.'
Old men forget; yet all shall be forgot,
But he'll remember, with advantages,
What feats he did that day. Then shall our names,
Familiar in his mouth as household words—
Harry the King, Bedford and Exeter,
Warwick and Talbot, Salisbury and
Gloucester—
Be in their flowing cups freshly rememb'red.
This story shall the good man teach his son;
And Crispin Crispian shall ne'er go by,
From this day to the ending of the world,
But we in it shall be remembered—
We few, we happy few, we band of brothers;
For he to-day that sheds his blood with me
Shall be my brother; be he ne'er so vile,
This day shall gentle his condition;
And gentlemen in England now-a-bed
Shall think themselves accurs'd they were not
here,
And hold their manhoods cheap whiles any
speaks
That fought with us upon Saint Crispin's day.

Figure 22.3 ■ *St. Crispin's Day speech by Shakespeare, from* King Henry V *(IV, iii).*

a prize, the princess of France to be his wife and a commitment that he would succeed to the French throne upon the death of the king. Again, troubles at home prevented the English from enforcing this agreement.

After a few years, the English were able to again press their demands. They controlled much of France north of the Loire Valley and attempted to expand their holdings by attacking Orleans. They put the city under siege, but then a turning point of the war occurred. This was brought about by the presence of a young girl, **Joan of Arc** *(Jean d'Arc),* as the nominal head of the French army that was sent to relieve the siege. Among the nobles she was an uncertain and, by some, vilified young maid. However, to the commoners she was a fulfillment of a folk prophecy that stated a young woman would come to save France. Upon her appearance, the French army was energized, and the **Siege of Orleans** was lifted. She then pressed for the **dauphin** (next in line to the throne) to accept the throne and be crowned in the cathedral at Reims. The dauphin was eventually crowned as **Charles VII,** but Joan of Arc was captured (by the French Burgundians who were allies of the English), turned over to the English, tried as a witch, and then burned at the stake. Nevertheless, Charles was able to win a group of victories that drove the English from almost all of their French territory and effectively ended the Hundred Years War.

The consequences of the war for the Second Estate were profound. The warrior class (knights) was shown to be vulnerable and, therefore, not adequately able to perform the duty for which their class existed. Moreover, this vulnerability was against common soldiers, an insult that the knights could not ignore. Consequently, the knights lost the respect of the people. When the lords dismissed them because they were expensive to maintain and no longer effective in fighting, the knights pillaged the countryside, and thus further angered the people. The kings oppressed the knight orders by removing their tax-exempt status and then, as we have already seen, expelling them and confiscating their lands. The knights shortly disappeared as a class. Their demise was largely because they were not creative enough to find another way to fight in light of the long bow development.

The changes in the fourteenth century strengthened the kings, the only nobles with sufficient funds to employ large commoner armies, which became the most effective force in war. The kings also realized that navies were important, as trade competition increased and exploration began (which is discussed in the next chapter), and only they had funds to build these navies. In short, the nobles (secondary lords) lost their warrior status and became only landholders, and politicians. As cities continued to grow and money moved into the hands of the commoners, even these traditional roles began to be challenged, but those challenges were done within the system already in place, at least until the revolutions in England, America, and France many years later.

Changes in the Third Estate

The population trends that began about the year 1000 continued and intensified into the fourteenth century so that several major cities had been created (Paris being the largest) and numerous towns of reasonable size dotted the map of Europe. With the rise of cities and towns, the power of some commoners—the **Third Estate**—grew. These were the merchants who were able to profit from trade and investments that arose as people became more sophisticated in their desires, and as the population continued to grow. In Italy, the nobility used their money to enter mercantilism and thus defined a new role for themselves. (The **Medici family** of Florence was one of these families that gained great wealth and prestige from trade and manufacturing.) In contrast, English nobility continued to focus on income from their land and to largely ignore the merchant trade of the cities. Consequently, a strong merchant class formed among the commoners. These later became the backbone of English trade and, ultimately, the power of the country.

In rural settings, little had changed, at least at first. People still worked the land, largely as serfs or peasant farmers, but they realized that changes were occurring and they became aware of the advances of the city people. After several years, the rural peasants revolted in an attempt to gain more privileges. These revolts were not fully armed rebellions, because the peasants didn't have the resources to attack the king. Instead, they were raids by a few, and crimes by single individuals. However, the riots became epidemic and soon gave the villagers a reputation for lawlessness. (The word "villain" comes from "villager.")

In 1347 the world of the village and of the city dweller changed radically, at least for those who survived. This was the year of the beginning of the **Great Plague** or **Black Death.** It started, we believe, when a ship that had been trading in the Black Sea arrived in Genoa with most of the sailors dead. The disease quickly spread out from the Italian port into the countryside and then on to other countries. A map showing the spread of the plague is given in Figure 22.4. Two forms of the plague presented. The first was characterized by the development of large swellings **(buboes)** about the size of an egg under the armpit and in the groin. The buboes oozed blood and pus. The spread of boils and black blotches over the entire body (from internal bleeding) then occurred. Death came in a few days. This type of plague, called the **Bubonic Plague** after the buboes, was spread by fleas that lived on the rats that were

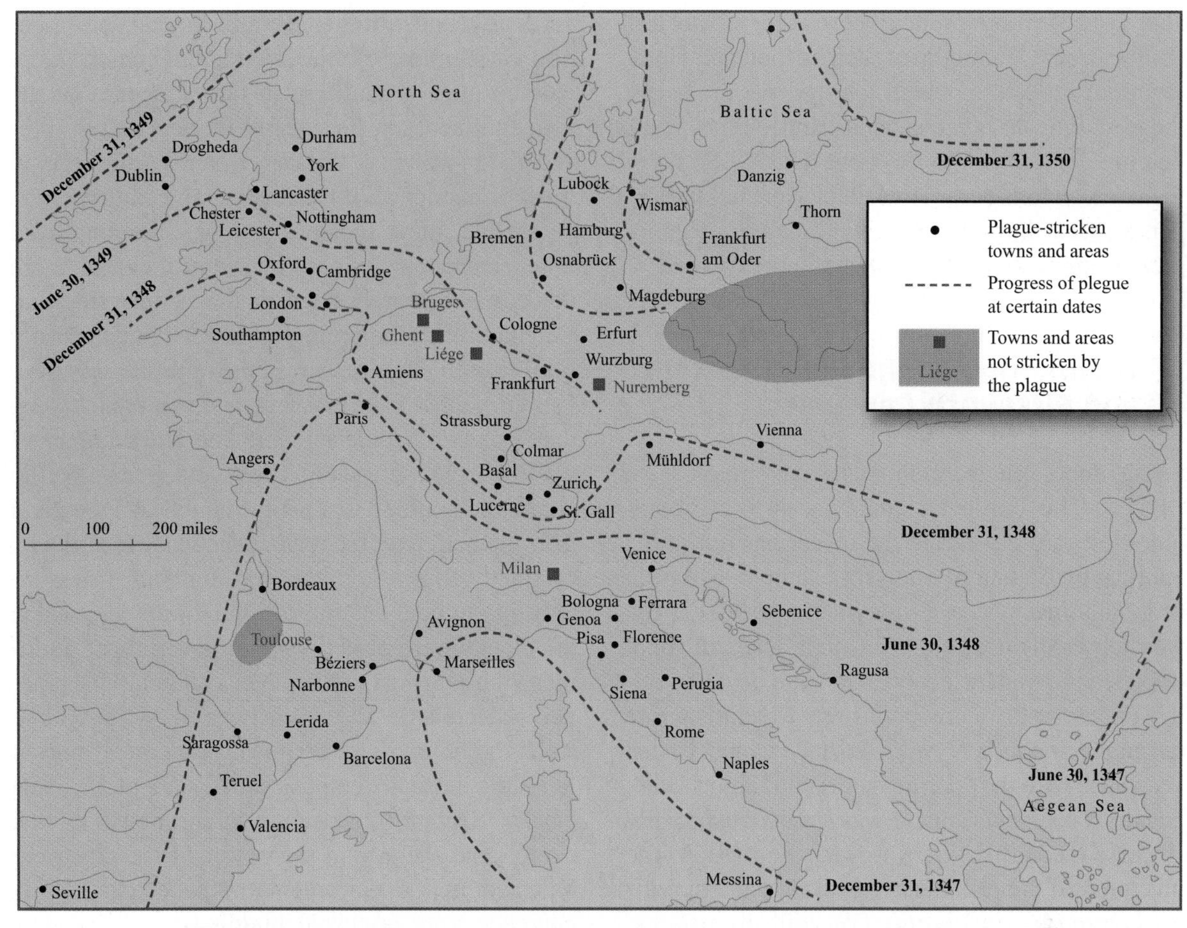

Figure 22.4 ■ *Map of the spread of the Bubonic Plague, 14th century.*

everywhere during the Middle Ages, and then by direct contact with infected tissues. The second type of plague, called the **Pneumonic Plague,** was characterized by a continuous fever and the spitting of blood, from the involvement of the respiratory system. There was extensive coughing, which spread the disease through the air. Death was within hours. In both cases the blood, breath, sweat, issues from the buboes, urine, coughed blood, and excrement all smelled incredibly foul. Most of Europe was infected; it is estimated that one third of the population of Europe died in a five-year period. Some believe that the plague was especially severe because both types were present at the same time. Others say that the concentration of people in the cities made the epidemic worse. Still others say that this plague, while certainly bad, was not much more severe than others that had occurred from time to time, but records were better. (An especially bad plague occurred during the time of Justinian in about 530 A.D.) This last view gains credibility because outbreaks of plague continued throughout the next 200 years.

The results of the plague were especially felt among the Third Estate. Most families lost one or more members; commoners in the cities may have lost even more. This meant that the labor force was drastically reduced at exactly the time when trade was expanding and the skills of labor were needed. The power of the commoners therefore increased. They were able to demand and receive better terms for their labor on the land. Those in the cities were able to make more money because there was less competition. Commodities such as food and clothing were in excess, which lowered the prices for those willing to wear second-hand clothes, thus helping commoners to be more healthy. Some of the excess cloth became available for making paper, a recent import from China. Other technologies became important, as we will now consider.

Technology in the Fourteenth and Fifteenth Centuries

Some important technologies were imported to Europe. The European creativity in these technologies was seen not in the inventions but in the application of them. **Paper,** for example, had been originally invented in China in about 100 A.D. but was not widely used outside China. Then, in about 800, Islamic traders discovered it and began to utilize paper for the many books that Muslims wrote during their Golden Age. Europe, which traded very little with the Islamic world until about 1000, began to use paper, but it was limited, especially since few could read. However, about 1450, the invention of the printing press made paper a critical commodity in Europe. (We will discuss that invention later in this chapter.) **Eyeglasses,** also invented in the East, were used by some but demand was low until the printing press was invented. The **compass** was also invented in China and imported to Europe after 1000. Its use was limited, however, until the kings began to build their navies and increase trade among the far-flung parts of Europe. More will be said about this in the next chapter when we discuss the creative way that sailors were taught to use the compass.

A major invention that did originate in Europe was the **mechanical clock,** which dated from about 1400. The first major advancement in timekeeping since the water clock of ancient times, these new mechanical clocks utilized gravity to pull weights, which activated the catch-and-release mechanisms that were the technological innovation that allowed clocks to be invented. When springs became part of clocks in the sixteenth century, the clocks could be oriented non-vertically, and **watches** were invented. The scientific principles of the pendulum clock were worked out (by **Galileo**) in the latter part of the sixteenth century, but clearly the technology preceded the science, as was the case throughout most of history until the nineteenth century.

While rural societies enjoyed the improved timekeeping capability of mechanical clocks, these devices were rarely seen in the countryside and were not really important for the regulation of daily rural life. In cities, however, the opposite was true. People wanted to be efficient, and that meant using the clock to schedule appointments and set hours of work. Clocks were set in towers and given a bell to chime the hours so that people could easily see and hear them all over the town. (The word for "clock" originally comes from the word for "bell.") It is interesting to note that most of the towers into which the clocks were placed were in government buildings, like a city hall, rather than a church. This practice reflects several key changes in society. First, since the church was still using canonical time, it felt little need to enthusiastically adopt the new clocks. Second, the decline in the power of the church and the rise in the power of the city were reflected in the placement of the clocks. Third, churches were often old buildings, and few new ones were being built, at least in comparison to the many new governmental buildings. Finally, the funding of the clocks was often provided by the merchants, and they felt more control over the municipal governments than over the church.

Some inventions of this period were important to general manufacturing, such as the **lathe** and the **brace and bit.** The lathe allowed hard materials, like metal and wood, to be shaped on a machine, thus improving the quality and the speed of the shaping over manual techniques. The brace and bit allowed holes to be easily made in hard substances, thus improving manufacturing efficiencies. Another major manufacturing advance was the invention of the **spinning wheel,** which improved upon the hand-held **distaff** (a rod or staff that collected the yarn as it was being spun, using a spinning bob). The foot-powered spinning wheel, in which the wheel and spindle were connected by a belt, vastly improved production rates.

This was the first use of **distributed power** in manufacturing equipment.

Johannes Gutenberg, a craftsman in the city of **Mainz, Germany,** was responsible for the greatest invention of the age. He showed the brilliant insight and the hard work that are the key to creativity. The series of inventions necessary to bring about successful printing using movable type was finally culminated with the establishment of a commercial and successful printing operation in 1455. To understand the extent of Gutenberg's accomplishment, we should first examine the history of printing and of paper.

Some of the elements of **printing**—paper and printing using wooden blocks—existed in China years previously. The Chinese system was not practical for mass-producing books because the wooden printing blocks wore out quickly and the carving of non-alphabetic figures, such as Chinese characters, was a major task that just couldn't be done practically for the quantities that would be required for mass-produced books. The Chinese needed an alphabet and metal type to really take advantage of movable block printing. Both alphabet and metal type were available in nearby Korea, but the Chinese were loath to accept the innovations of the Koreans and so the Chinese continued to only print complex characters on paper using wooden blocks.

Gutenberg's first realization was that letters needed to be the basis of the printing system and that metal type was required so that the type would last for several hundred printings. The current method of making metal pieces, both in the Orient and in the West, was to carve each individually by hand, using a block of metal and sharp metal-working tools. However, the task of carving the hundreds and perhaps thousands of metal type-pieces required for just one book was so daunting that it could not be practically done. (The many pieces of type were needed because not only would one page need to be set, requiring dozens of types of each letter in the alphabet, but other pages would also have to be simultaneously set so that the entire job could be printed in a reasonable period of time.) Gutenberg conceived of the system that is diagrammed in Figure 22.5, derived from John Man's important biography, *Gutenberg* (2002). The first step in the process was to carve a single punch into the shape of the letter desired, using traditional metal-working techniques. This part was called the **punch** or **patrix.** The patrix was then used to punch the type pattern into a softer piece of metal, called the **matrix.** The matrix was then enclosed by a clever little hand-assembled **mold** that was formed by two pieces of metal that fit over the matrix, with a cavity into which the molten type metal could be poured. When the molten metal cooled, a **type-piece** was completed, and it could be used to do the actual printing. Note that in this system, the types were cast (as opposed to carved) and so many hundreds could be produced quickly and inexpensively. Eventually the matrix would wear out because of its repeated use in casting the types, but that was not a problem because a new matrix could be easily made by punching a new piece of soft metal with the patrix.

Gutenberg had to solve several metallurgical problems as he made this invention. He had to choose the metals for the patrix, matrix, and type-pieces. All would typically be different from each other. The metal for the type-pieces was an especially difficult problem to solve, because it needed to be easily meltable but still be hard enough to withstand the pressures of printing. Gutenberg also had to solve the related problems of the ink and paper. The Chinese paper was too soft to be used for printing letters. It did not give good letter definition; it also wicked the ink outward, thus forcing the letters to be set far apart so that they would be clearly distinguishable. Gutenberg developed a harder paper that seemed to be correct for printing close-set letters, but then needed to formulate inks that would seep into the paper without wicking extensively. The inks also needed to dry in a reasonable time, and to be inexpensive. He was able to accomplish these difficult tasks. After all of these problems were solved, he still had the challenge of forcing the types into the paper. He realized that a winepress, with some reasonable modifications, would work for this purpose.

When all was completed, he sought a printing project that was large enough to make some

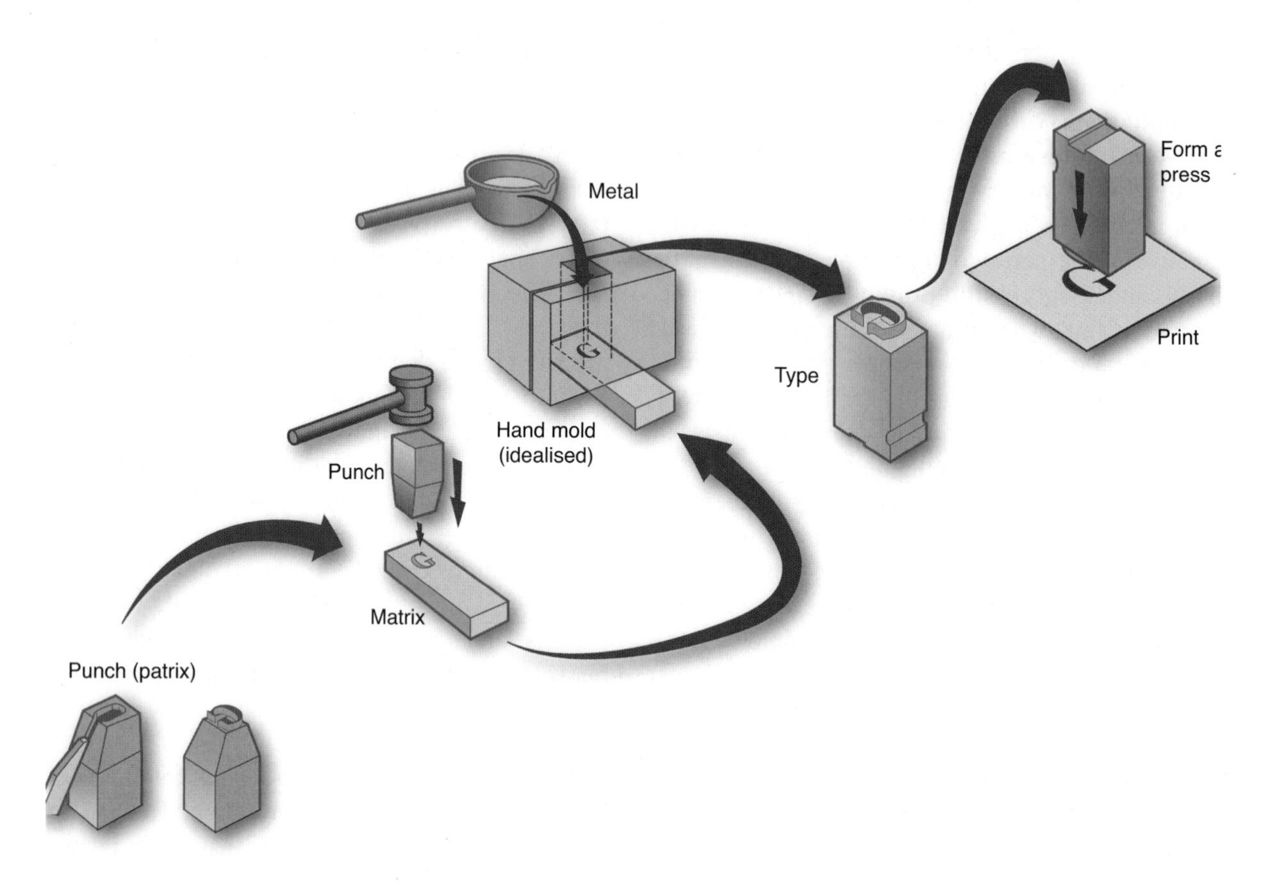

Figure 22.5 ■ *Gutenberg's invention.*

money for himself and his investor partners, but not so large that thousands of type-pieces would be required. He found a job with the local bishop who wanted to sell indulgences. The purchase of the indulgence was receipted with one-sheet printed **certificates of payment** and corresponding **forgiveness explanation.** This single sheet only required a few dozen types of each letter, but the sheet was printed in high volume so that Gutenberg could make a nice profit. After this success, Gutenberg decided to print Bibles. These were much more extensive, and required vast numbers of types, but he knew that the Bibles would be distributed among churches and monasteries throughout Europe and would likely bring in more printing business.

The effects of Gutenberg's invention were immediate and widespread. The public was growing more wealthy and literate because of the increase in trade. Moreover, the taste for books among the public was growing rapidly, fueled to some extent by the introduction into Europe of many ancient Greek texts because of the fall of Constantinople in 1453 (essentially the same time as Gutenberg's invention). People also had more time for leisure, especially those who lived in cities. Only a few years following Gutenberg's invention, **pamphlets,** which could be purchased inexpensively, were developed and became widely circulated throughout Europe. Two generations after Gutenberg, when Martin Luther began his campaign to win the hearts of the German people, he used pamphlets extensively. Because of the printing press, the people of Europe had become predominately literate, thus affording Luther a vast audience for his ideas.

The End of the Middle Ages

The gradual changes that began about 1000 culminated in a set of sweeping changes that fundamentally changed the social structure of Europe. These changes caused each of the three estates—the church, the nobility, and the commoners—to alter their lifestyles and to accommodate the new realities of an increasing urban population and a growing middle class. Money and power were becoming more widely distributed, forcing acceptance of the changes. The process was, however, slow. The church and the nobility were inherently conservative. They did not seek, nor did they readily accept, change. They were largely non-creative. But the merchants and craftsmen of the urban middle class were just the opposite. They wanted change, and realized that creative innovations in politics, social structure, and technology could bring them about. That process began in earnest and continued unabated to the present time, accelerating with each passing century. The best example of the new technology was, of course, Gutenberg and his movable-type printing system.

Timeline—Important Dates

Date	Event
1304 A.D.	*Conflict between King Phillip IV Pope Boniface VIII*
1309–1378	*Avignon Papacy*
1337–1453	*Hundred Years War*
1347	*Beginning of the Great Plague*
1378–1415	*The Great Schism*
About 1400	*Mechanical clocks invented*
1412–1431	*Joan of Arc*
1455	*Gutenberg invents movable type and printing press*

Suggested Readings

Burke, James, *The Day the Universe Changed,* Back Bay, 1985.

Man, John, *Gutenberg,* Wiley, 2002.

Manchester, William, *A World Lit Only by Fire,* Little, Brown, 1993.

Tey, Josephine, *The Daughter of Time,* Simon & Schuster, 1951.

Tuchman, Barbara W., *A Distant Mirror,* Ballantine, 1978.

Age of Exploration
Discovering Creativity

> The story you have heard about Christopher Columbus was backwards. Columbus was the guy that had it wrong. There was a good reason that everyone laughed at him. Christopher Columbus wanted to sail west to Asia. It was an incredibly stupid idea. The leading navigators and scientists knew that the earth was round. But they also knew that Asia was much too far away to be reached by sailing west. Fifteenth century boats were incapable of making the journey. If it hadn't been for the totally unexpected intervention of the Americas, Columbus and his crews would have died at sea somewhere southeast of Hawaii. Columbus had the facts all wrong. But Columbus's idea, wrong as it was, did get him out of a centuries-old rut. When he was finally given the resources to test his idea, he made a brilliant discovery. It was not the discovery he wanted to make, or thought he had made, but it was still important. All bad ideas are potential "Chris Concepts." They may not be the solution you are looking for, but they could still carry you forward to a solution that no one has even imagined. . . . Bad ideas, or Chris Concepts, are essential to developing good solutions. Innovation is rarely a direct line from problem to solution. The path to a great solution twists, turns, and doubles back. Along the way there are many failures that are essential to developing the final solution.
>
> —*Scott Thorpe,* How to Think Like Einstein, *Barnes & Noble Books, Inc., 2000, p. 47–49*

Is Discovery a Creative Act?

As the above quotation suggests, Columbus was more lucky than smart. Yet, he was a determined advocate who eventually was able to obtain the resources he needed to embark on his great adventure. The work he did to get the resources was clever and creative. The various methods he used to settle the dissent among his crew were creative. He might be called creative in the way he maintained his reputation as the foremost explorer of the age. He was even creative in obtaining regal dispensations and additional funding after he had demonstrated ineptness for political leadership. But, was the discovery of the Americas a creative act?

The answer can best be given after we have examined the history of the Age of Exploration which began, in earnest, with the fall of Constantinople in

1453. The first national group to embark on an organized quest for discovery of the world were not the Spanish; they were still too occupied with driving the Muslims (Moors) out of their country. The honor of being the first to really explore belongs to the Portuguese. We will, therefore, examine first why exploration became so important, and then why Portugal was the place where it was first organized. We will then see why Spain became so dominant in exploration. The explorations of other countries in this same period will be examined and then, after all, we will revisit the question of discovery and creativity.

Why the Age of Exploration Occurred

Trade before the **fall of Constantinople** to the Turks in 1453 had been centered in the Mediterranean basin. That trade had been important from nearly the beginning of civilization. It led the Phoenicians to establish colonies in North Africa and southern Europe, it gave the Greeks interactions with other cultures that led to prosperity and creativity, it was a principal factor in the rise and continued strength of the Roman Empire, it sustained the Byzantine Empire, it helped the Muslims extend their empire, it provided means for the crusaders to establish crusader states in the Holy Land, and it led to the rise of Italian city-states as the most prosperous centers of Europe in the late Middle Ages.

In spite of the dangers and difficulties placed on trade during Europe's medieval period, a dribble of trade goods continued to flow into Europe from Asia. This trade was dominated by the Byzantine Empire in Constantinople and the Italian city-state of Venice, which was initially under Byzantine control and later became a republic. Working together, Venice and Byzantium were able to import items such as silk, spices, and chinaware into Europe and, in the process, make great profits. The newly arising nations of Europe, hungry for cash and prestige, had dreams of trade with the East as well, and hoped to make money through selling their own trade goods, and by cutting out the Byzantine and Italian middle men. However, the Venetians and Byzantines jealously guarded their trade routes and the profits they brought. European attempts to control the established trade routes proved to be futile. Because of the traditional ties between Venice and the Byzantines, Venetian overland trade was permitted through Byzantine territory, as in the case of Marco Polo. Attempts by European nations to develop their own overland routes to the East proved too dangerous and costly to be profitable, thus leaving the Venetians and Byzantines to control a virtual monopoly over trade with the Far East. Genoa was able to gain a strong position in the western Mediterranean and, toward the end of the Byzantine Empire, had become a rival to Venice in the eastern Mediterranean.

With the fall of Constantinople, the situation changed. The natural relationships between Christian Europe and the Christian Byzantine Empire were ruptured. The new owners of Constantinople, the Turks, distrusted the Christians and, moreover, wanted to dominate trade in the Mediterranean themselves and especially control any connection between Europe and Asia. Their lands were located at the junction of the two continents and, therefore, they had the means to enforce their desires. They allowed only two cities trade concessions—Venice and Genoa—and both of these were highly restricted and became more restricted with time.

Although many other groups, especially Arabs, traded with India and the spice islands of present-day Indonesia and Malaysia, if those goods were to be transported to Europe, the pathway was through Turkish-controlled territory, especially Constantinople. Even overland trade routes, like the Silk Road, were controlled by the Turks. As they expanded their territorial power to include North Africa, their ability to dominate the trade between Europe and Asia became nearly absolute. They didn't stop trade—they just ensured that all of it flowed through their hands, so that they could profit from it. Goods were literally off-loaded from ships traveling from the Orient and then reloaded onto ships traveling to Europe, with the Turks charging for the service. It is no wonder that commodities from Asia were so costly when they finally reached Europe. All this occurred at a time when European desires for these

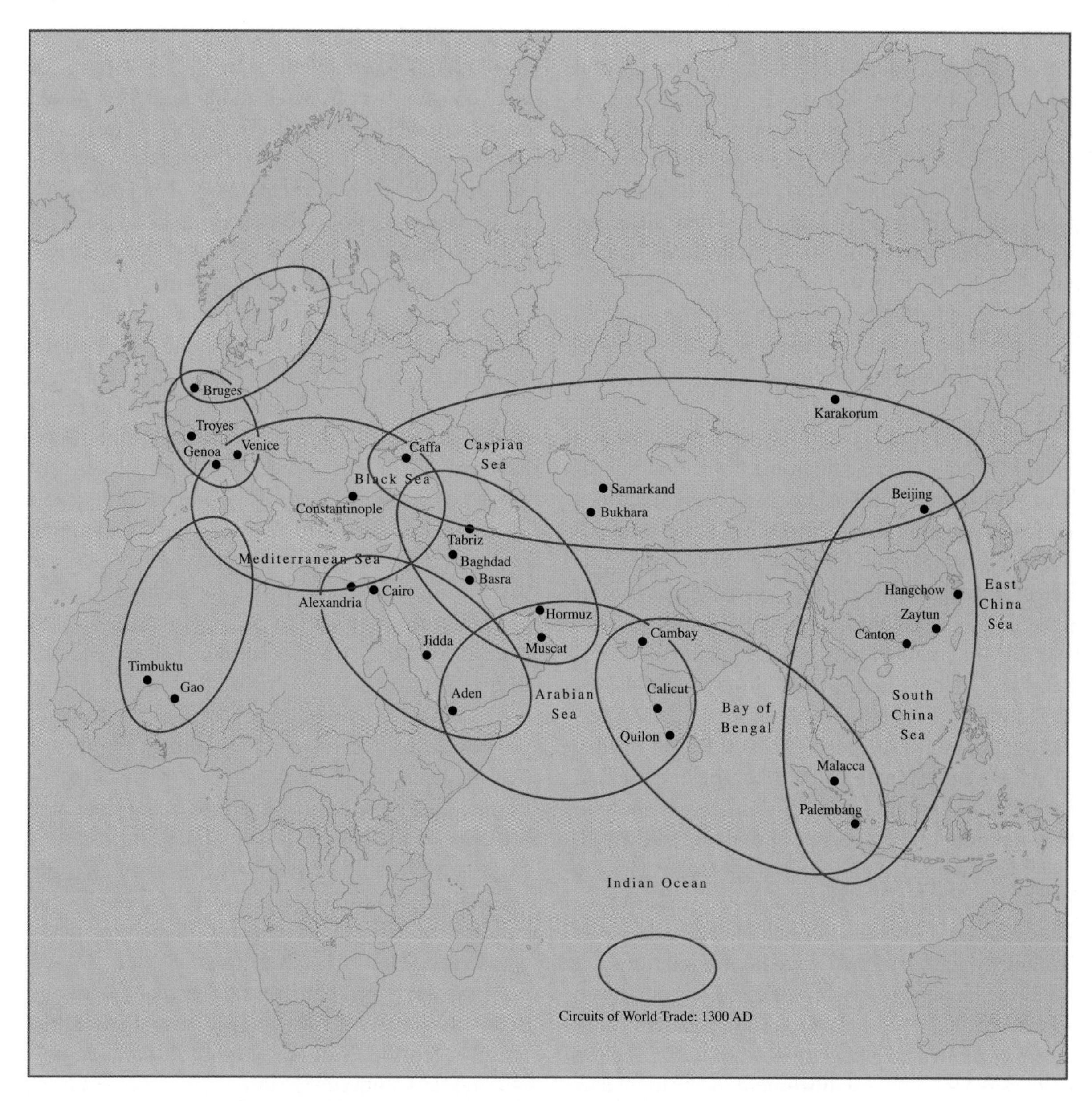

Figure 23.1 ■ *Major trading zones in the late Middle Ages.*

goods was high and growing higher. The major trading zones in the Middle Ages are pictured in Figure 23.1 and the position of Constantinople at the center of Europe/Asian trade is clear.

The years directly following the fall of Constantinople were important for European history and creativity. Should Europe learn to work with and rely on the Muslim world for trade with the Far East, or attempt to break the Muslim monopoly at the risk of losing the trade wars and permanently being cut off from Asian goods? Some states believed that co-operation was the key. The trading concessions to Venice and Genoa allowed these cities to maintain facilities in Istanbul (Constantinople), thus making them the exclusive transporters of the Asian goods into the ports of Europe. The normal trade pathway was from Asia to Constantinople, or some other Turkish-controlled port on the Black Sea, with goods then transferred to Italian ships that entered Europe through Venice and Genoa, and then by land into northern Europe. The goods being produced in Europe, such as woolen cloth, were made in manufacturing facilities in northern Europe (Flanders being the largest) and then transported by land to Italy, where they were loaded onto ships in Venice and Genoa. This system greatly enriched the Italians and, thereby, led directly to the creation of the prosperous merchant-banking families that sponsored the growth of art and culture we call the Renaissance. We will discuss that in great detail in Volume Two of this series.

For other states, the possible profits and wealth from a successful trade route to the Far East proved too lucrative to resist; several nations began to develop fleets of trading ships to challenge the Muslim-Italian trade monopoly. This decision launched Europe's **Age of Exploration** and fueled an economic, technological, political, and cultural rebirth across Europe, further contributing to the forces that brought about the Renaissance. Furthermore, as Europe reached out, Europeans began to shape the destiny and history of other peoples, nations, and continents, making the Age of Exploration a pivotal time in the history not only of Europe, but of much of the world.

The Spanish and the Portuguese, relatively poor countries on the far southwestern corner of Europe, were almost completely left out of the trading system. But their growing populations desired the luxury goods of Asia and, especially in the case of the Portuguese; their leaders were strongly motivated and creative. This combination of factors led to the establishment of Portugal as a major trading country, perhaps unexpectedly to some, but the logic could be seen after the fact. They were the first of the nations to attempt to break the monopoly of the Muslims (and their Italian partners).

The Portuguese Explorations

After the Muslims were driven from Portugal in 1140, the Portuguese were resentful and economically weak. Surrounded by the larger, wealthier, more unified, and more powerful Spain, and the vast and unknown Atlantic Ocean, the Portuguese were constantly concerned about being dominated by the Spanish and cut off from contact with the rest of the world. (In this, they were much like the Scots in their resentment of England.) The Portuguese had good reason to be concerned, as Portugal had very little in its favor. Portugal was one of Europe's poorest nations. Most Portuguese lived with large, extended families crammed together in small houses. The economy of Portugal was almost completely based on the trade of dried fruits and dried fish, items not particularly lucrative or necessarily in high demand. Furthermore, Portugal was a loose society, with no strong religious ties, social contract, or powerful ruling family to bind the nation and people. The combination of Portugal's weakness and Spain's strength meant that Portugal only retained its autonomy and independence through astute political alliances. The most important of these political alliances came from **King John I of Portugal,** founder of the **Aviz dynasty.** King John married an English princess whose family had a claim to the throne of Castile in Spain, thus gaining the backing of England for Portugal and a degree of legitimacy in the eyes of the Spanish. King John and the Aviz dynasty were able to finally bring some strength and stability to the Portuguese crown. One of the children of King John and his English princess was **Prince Henry the Navigator.**

Prince Henry had his first contact with the riches of Muslim Africa in 1415 when he and his brothers led the Portuguese army in the conquest of **Cuerta** (Ceuta), a Muslim stronghold and trading center in Morocco. They hoped to use Cuerta as a way to improve their trade with Islamic Africa. However, Cuerta proved to be much less than the great prize Henry and the Portuguese had originally envisioned, as the Muslims simply quit using Cuerta as a trading center; leaving the city with little value to the Portuguese. However, Henry was not to be deterred in his attempts to bring the riches of Africa and the East to Portugal. He looked farther afield.

Because of Portugal's location on the southwest corner of Europe, the logical direction for exploration and increased trade was toward Africa. Prince Henry, who would become known to history as Henry the Navigator, strongly promoted the exploration of the western coast of Africa and the adjacent islands, and ordered his merchant captains to explore specific areas as part of their assigned duties. Henry was also given a papal bull bestowing on Portugal the exclusive right to explore, colonize, baptize, and exploit the west coast of Africa and the islands off the African coast. He realized, however, that the Portuguese would need to become much better sailors than they currently were, because the Atlantic seas were much rougher than the Mediterranean. Also, the exploration of new lands would mean that navigational skills would be imperative to master. Henry felt that a school, dedicated to maritime pursuits, would be the answer to these problems. He believed that this school should be located near the proposed port for African exploration and away from the turmoil and politics of the court in Lisbon. He therefore established a school and technological center for maritime pursuits in **Sagres,** a city on Portugal's southern coast.

Prince Henry's maritime center in Sagres proved to be an educational and creative center that was unparalleled in European history in its advancement of navigation. Henry brought together the brightest minds of his day in navigation and seafaring skills. Europe's greatest cartographers and instrument-makers came to draw up the newest, most accurate maps and charts, and to design better navigational tools. The best sailors were brought in to instruct others in sailing. Innovations from all over the world, such as the compass, were brought to Sagres. The techniques of making these instruments and the methods of employing them were expanded and improved.

The crowning moment of Prince Henry's maritime center was the designing and building of a new ocean-going ship, the **caravel.** The ships of the Mediterranean were relatively flat-bottomed and therefore could not maneuver well in the rougher waters of the Atlantic Ocean. Compared to these previous ships, the caravel was faster and more maneuverable, and had a deep cargo area for the movement of large quantities of trade goods.

Figure 23.2 ■ *Depiction of a caravel.*

The caravel could also be easily equipped with side cannons, which became increasingly important as gunpowder and cannons were developed in the waning years of the Middle Ages. A caravel is depicted in Figure 23.2.

Nearly every year, Henry's captains explored a little further south along the West African coast; by Henry's death in 1460, the Portuguese had reached the **Gold Coast** in sub-Saharan Africa and had established several trading posts on the African coasts and islands. Great wealth was available from the precious metals, ivory, and jewels—and after some time, slaves—that were found in Africa. The slaves were used in the Portuguese sugar plantations along the coast and, eventually, were transported to the Caribbean after the time of Columbus. This was the first instance of the enslavement of people based on race.

Prince Henry's vision of Portuguese trade expansion was in large part realized during his life, as Portugal developed the best navy in Europe and was able to establish trade with much of West Africa independent of the Muslims (although the Muslims still controlled the lucrative trade with the Far East). Possibly an even more important accomplishment achieved under Henry the Navigator's direction was the breaking of the fear barrier. At Henry's command, Portuguese sailors sailed further south and further from the coast than was believed safe or possible. Once these limits were broken and the dangers largely proven to be imaginary, the Portuguese grew even bolder, and began to sail longer distances and further from shore, allowing for many of the great discoveries that would soon occur.

After Henry the Navigator's death, other Portuguese leaders saw the opportunities that trade with Africa could bring the small nation. They continued Henry's policies of maritime power and exploration. **King John II** continued to send Portuguese sailors to explore the western African coast and even made attempts to permanently colonize some areas. One Portuguese captain, **Bartholomew Diaz,** was able to round the **Cape of Good Hope** on the southern tip of Africa. He recognized that he had entered a new ocean, but returned to Portugal without exploring further. This was a tremendous achievement, as it opened the possibility of sailing to Asia.

Perhaps the successes of the African trade and the potential for direct trade with Asia led King John to reject the plan of an Italian captain, Christopher Columbus, who had been trained in the Portuguese school and had made several voyages on behalf of Portugal. Perhaps, also, King John realized the error in Columbus' calculations and realized that sailing west to Asia was not practical because it was too far for the ships of the day. King John recognized his mistake and the potential problem for Portugal after Columbus returned triumphantly from his voyage to the "Indies" on behalf of Spain. King John II died in 1495, leaving his successor, **King Manuel the Fortunate,** to deal with the aftermath of Columbus' trip and the potential danger it presented to the Portuguese. King Manuel and the Portuguese were terrified that they would not be able to capitalize on their African possessions and knowledge of sailing around the Cape of Good Hope if the Spanish arrived in India first by sailing west. Fearing that they were losing their advantage, King Manuel quickly commissioned **Vasco da Gama** to round the Cape and sail to India.

Vasco da Gama knew from previous accounts that sailing directly down the African coast was slow and dangerous, due to shallow waters and unfavorable winds. Because speed was vital in recouping the Portuguese position in trade with India, Vasco da Gama elected to use the westward trade wind, sailing far out into the Atlantic Ocean on a southwestern course and then use other trade winds, which blew eastward, to sail quickly back toward the tip of Africa, and then swing around the Cape. This method worked reasonably well, although it did make much of his crew nervous as they sailed out of sight of land for over four months. Once around the Cape of Good Hope, the Portuguese made several stops on the East African coast to trade and restock their ships. After a last stop in Kenya, Vasco da Gama and his ships sailed across the Indian Ocean and landed in India, south of Bombay. To his dismay Vasco da Gama found that the Arabs already controlled the harbor. He had to sneak into port and load up with spices before the Arabs saw and stopped him. With the ships full of spices and other goods, the Portuguese quickly slipped away and returned home; arriving back in Lisbon to a hero's welcome after two full years. This was the longest duration of any voyage to that date. A map of his trip is shown in Figure 23.3.

King Manuel saw the potential of the new route to India and also understood that to overcome the entrenched position of the Arabs in India and eastern Africa, he would have to use force. He quickly sent Vasco de Gama back with more trade vessels, and several warships. The Portuguese were able to destroy much of the Arab trading fleet and soon controlled the entire spice-producing region from Africa to India to the Malay Peninsula to China, largely because the Portuguese caravels had guns, whereas the Arab ships did not. The Portuguese then established several large and well defended trading ports such as **Goa** in India and **Macao** in China, as well as many smaller posts at various other locations in the **Spice Islands.** Once the Portuguese presence was firmly entrenched in the Far East, Portugal made efforts to dominate the region. This established a pattern of European dominance and colonization that would spread throughout the world and would continue until World War I ended the colonial era over four centuries later. And while India itself never officially became a Portuguese colony (with the exception of the trading port of Goa), it certainly fell under

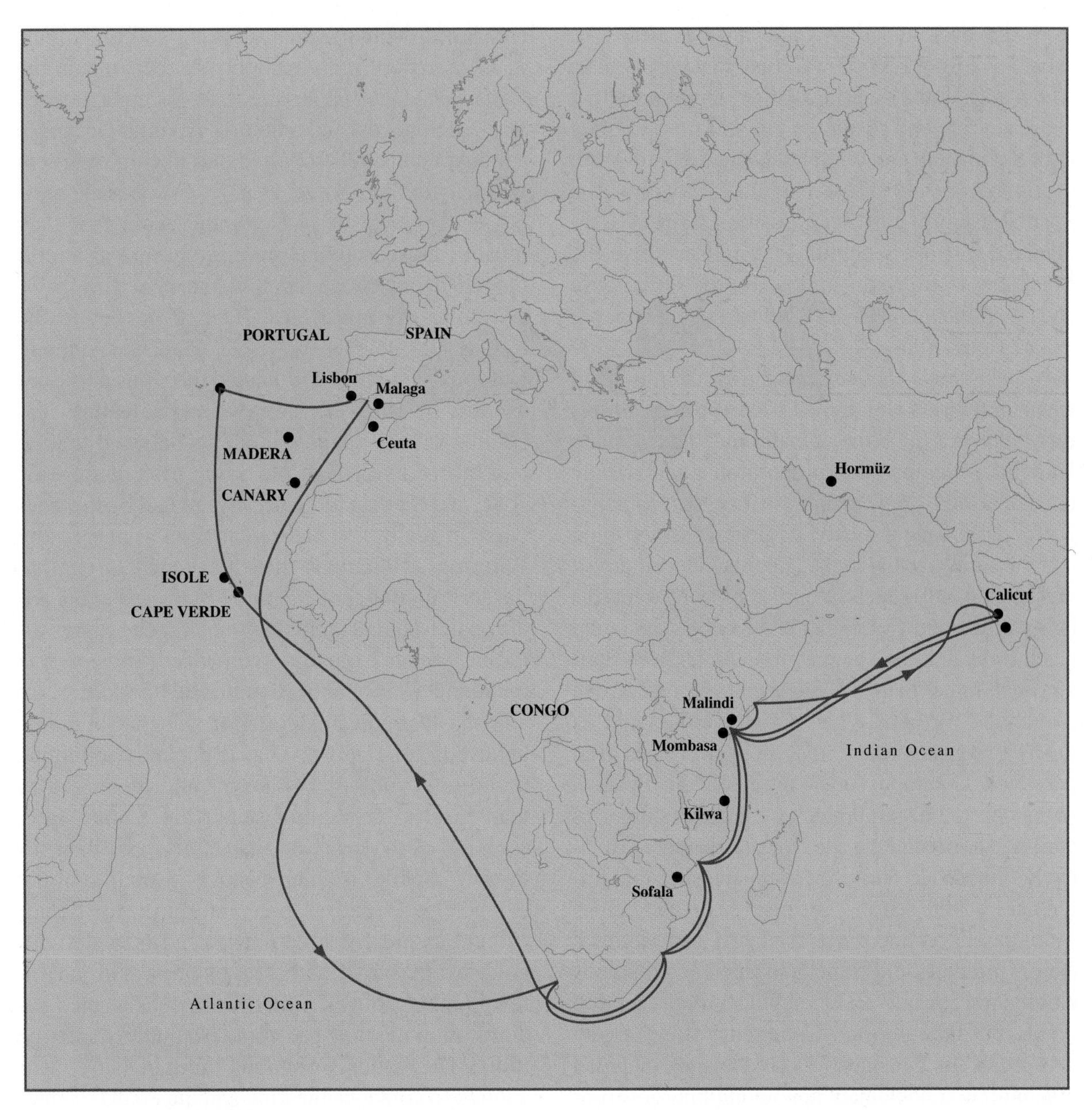

Figure 23.3 ■ *Map showing the route of Vasco da Gama from Portugal to India.*

Portugal's sphere of influence. Thus, the creative vision begun by Henry the Navigator was accomplished through Portuguese technological and navigational creativity, which resulted in achievements such as the caravel and sailing away from the African coast to use the trade winds to travel more quickly. The effects of the Portuguese trading dominance in Asia on the Asians will be discussed more fully in the next chapter.

The Spanish Explorations

Spain was aware of Portuguese probing down the African coast, making contacts, and establishing trade with the Africans, and feared that the Portuguese would eventually discover a sea route to the lucrative trade with India and the Far East. Spain was concerned that if Portugal succeeded, they might have to pay the Portuguese for goods from the East, and that would not be cheap. An even worse possibility was that the Portuguese, who always looked to their larger neighbor with a degree of fear and suspicion, might refuse to trade with Spain at all and completely cut them off from the luxury items of the Far East. However, the Spanish were in a difficult position, as they were involved in (just concluding) a fight to drive the Muslims out of Spain; moreover, the Portuguese had a significant head start, better ships, and more experienced sailors.

These were the circumstances facing Spain when an Italian sailor named **Christopher Columbus** approached **King Ferdinand** and **Queen Isabella** of Spain with a proposal that had already been rejected by the Portuguese. Contrary to popular modern legend, most Europeans did not think that the earth was flat in the late fifteenth century (it was mostly only superstitious sailors who kept this belief alive) and Columbus believed that he could reach India and the Far East more quickly by sailing west, rather than seeking a route around Africa (which the Portuguese had not yet verified and, as far as Europeans knew, may not have even been possible). Columbus' idea intrigued the Spanish monarchs and his arguments were convincing. According to Columbus, the voyage would be relatively short. (He had underestimated the circumference of the earth, because his calculations were based on incorrect medieval astronomical data.) Ferdinand and Isabella listened to Columbus closely and considered funding his proposed expedition, but they rejected Columbus' offer, largely because of his demands. Those demands included making him a nobleman, appointing him governor of any lands claimed for Spain, and providing a commission of 10 percent on all transactions that took place in the newly acquired territory. Columbus left the Spanish court disappointed, but determined to find success elsewhere, and began making plans to go to France and England to make his proposal. However, before Columbus could leave for France, some of his friends convinced Ferdinand and Isabella to fund his expedition; he was recalled to court and told to prepare for his voyage.

Columbus gathered his crew and made preparations aboard his three ships—the **Nina, Pinta,** and **Santa Maria**—finally setting sail on August 3, 1492. After briefly resupplying the ships in the Canary Islands, Columbus and his men headed west into the vast and unknown Atlantic Ocean. In spite of being well supplied and having excellent weather for the voyage, by early October the crew began to get restless. Columbus, sure that they must be close to India, promised to turn around if they had not found land in the next few days. Columbus' promise never had to be put to the test, as on October 12, 1492, land was sighted. Columbus and his crew landed the ships and went ashore, naming the island **San Salvador** and claiming it for Spain. Columbus believed that he had reached an island off of the eastern coast of Asia, and that his idea and voyage had been a success. In reality he had reached an island in the **Bahamas.** Columbus then proceeded to explore the surrounding territory and discovered many additional islands, including the larger islands of **Cuba,** which Columbus convinced himself was mainland China, and **Hispaniola** (modern Haiti and the Dominican Republic), which Columbus believed to be Japan. On Hispaniola Columbus found gold and other valuables and proceeded to load his two remaining ships (the Santa Maria sank off of the coast of Hispaniola) and then return to Spain, leaving behind a small colony named **Natividad.** Upon returning to Spain, Columbus presented Ferdinand and Isabella with gold, exotic birds, herbs, and spices, and even a few human captives, which Columbus termed Indians, thinking they had come from the vicinity of India. The goods Columbus brought back were enough to convince the king and queen that he had succeeded in his quest for the Far East, and they immediately granted him funds for a second voyage and the promise that he would be governor of the new colony.

Columbus returned to the Americas and found Natividad destroyed and its inhabitants killed by the islands' natives. Columbus then built a new colony with stronger fortifications which he named **La Isabela,** and he then took control as governor. One of Columbus' first acts as governor was to begin to kill and enslave the native peoples in retaliation for their killing of the Spaniards at

Natividad. Columbus remained at La Isabela for over two years before deciding to return to Spain in early 1496, leaving his two brothers in charge of the colony. Arriving in Spain, Columbus learned that Spain was at war with France and that the gold and other riches being extracted from "the Indies" was sorely needed to fund continued hostilities. Therefore, Columbus was almost immediately sent back to the New World on a third voyage. Upon arriving in Hispaniola, Christopher Columbus found the colony in disarray and tensions running high between his brothers and the mayor of La Isabela. The chiefs of the local tribes, as well as many of the Spaniards, led by the mayor, were upset at changes made by Columbus' brothers in the gold production process that favored some Spaniards over others and exploited the native work force. Christopher Columbus stepped in, resuming his position as governor, and took drastic steps to get the colony back in order, including imprisoning and hanging several Spaniards. The mayor and his supporters then wrote so many letters of complaint back to Spain, attacking Columbus, his harsh methods, and his brothers' interference in the gold process, that Ferdinand and Isabella sent a magistrate to arrest the three Columbus brothers, and they were shipped back to Spain in chains.

Columbus was brought before the king and queen, where he related his version of the events. The Spanish monarchs had him released from bonds and declared him a superior mariner, but questioned his ability to govern. The decision was made to strip Columbus of his governorship and appoint another governor on Hispaniola; but then, as a vote of confidence in Columbus, Ferdinand and Isabella pledged funds for a fourth voyage to the New World in hopes of finding a passage that led to India. (It was still believed that Columbus had found China and Japan and that India lay somewhere further west.) Obviously, Columbus was unable to find a passage to India, and returned home to Spain in 1505. Christopher Columbus lived his last year in Spain in comfort, if not wealth, but was emotionally distressed that the Spanish crown had never made good on its promise of property and gold. He went to court to seek redress for this supposed wrong, only to be rejected by Ferdinand. (Columbus' biggest supporter, Queen Isabella, had died the previous year). Columbus himself died shortly thereafter, on May 20, 1506, never realizing that he had not gone to Asia.

Immediately following his first voyage, Columbus realized the importance of ensuring that Spain could dominate all the new territories that he had discovered. He believed that the pope could give Spain that preferred position, and therefore he approached **Pope Alexander VI,** a Spaniard who was related to the Borgia family of Italy, to gain the territorial concession. The pope was open to such an idea because he saw an opportunity to resolve the conflicts that might arise between Spain and Portugal, but he wanted to guarantee the rights of the Portuguese and other Christian monarchs as well. He issued a papal decree stating that the Spanish would have possession of any unclaimed lands to the west of a line running down the mid-Atlantic 100 leagues (300 miles) west of the Cape Verde Islands. Portugal was given possession rights to any unclaimed lands to the east of the line. The Portuguese became unhappy with the position of the line when they realized how large the New World was and renegotiated a new line that was 370 leagues west of the Cape Verde Islands. This new treaty, signed in the Spanish town of Tordesillas in 1494 by the Portuguese, the Spanish and the pope, is called the **Treaty of Tordesillas.** The first agreement missed all of South America but the tip of Brazil, but the second agreement gave Portugal a major holding in Brazil, which they defended vigorously. Brazil was the lone Portuguese colony in the Americas. These lines are shown in Figure 23.4.

Eventually it became apparent to the Spanish that Columbus had not reached the Far East. Not yet realizing the value of the Americas, they continued their quest to find a sea route to the Orient. The new Spanish king, **Charles I** (also called Charles V of the Holy Roman Empire), was bitterly disappointed that the New World stood between them and the Indies, and felt very worried that the Portuguese would beat them to the riches to be found there. In an attempt to somehow establish a Spanish presence

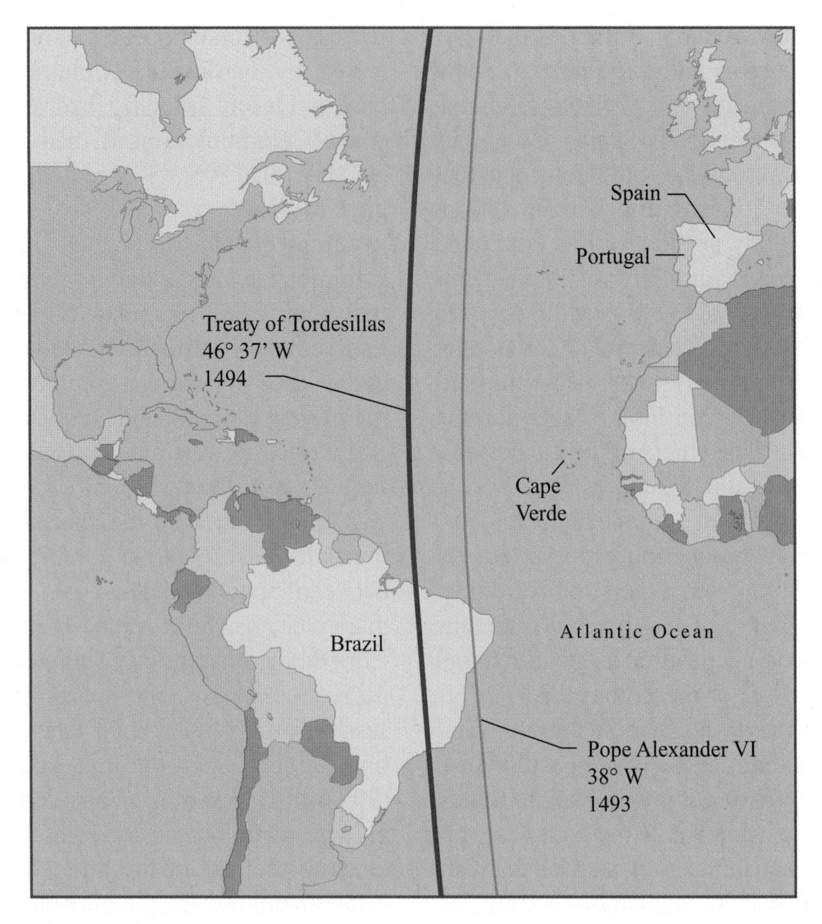

Figure 23.4 ■ *Map showing the original line of demarcation and the subsequent adjustment—the Treaty of Tordesillas.*

in the Indies, Charles commissioned **Ferdinand Magellan** to seek a route around the Americas and to the Far East. His voyage proved how long and perilous such a trip would be. Having gained the support of both the Spanish crown and the church, Magellan and his crew embarked on their voyage in five ships with two years' supplies. From the beginning, there were troubles, as the Spanish captains of the four other ships resented Magellan's captaincy over them and plotted to kill him. (Magellan was Portuguese, but had disavowed his home country when the Portuguese refused to support his ideas.) The murder plot was discovered and the ringleader, **Captain Cartegena,** was imprisoned.

Eventually Magellan crossed the Atlantic and he and his crew anchored off of the coast of Brazil so that they could restock the ships with food and fresh water. Magellan was careful to avoid trouble with the Portuguese who controlled Brazil, and stayed far from the Portuguese colonies. After the brief pause, the ships headed south along the coast of South America looking for a way around South America. Magellan investigated several large rivers in hopes that they might cut across the landmass. These investigations were fruitless, and took considerable time so that, as they sailed further south, the weather got so cold and forbidding that Magellan decided it would be suicidal to continue. He ordered that they put ashore and set up a winter quarters (in modern day Patagonia). This decision renewed the old hostilities, and **Captain Mendoza,** one of the Spanish captains, released Captain

Cartegena from prison. Cartegena then led another mutiny against Magellan. This time Magellan put it down ruthlessly by having Captains Mendoza and Quesada, another of the Spanish captains, executed, Captain Cartegena marooned alone on an island off the coast of Patagonia (Argentina), and several others imprisoned.

Magellan's troubles continued. In spite of his decision to stop for the winter, he sent out the ship *Santiago* to look for a way around the continent. While exploring for the passage, the *Santiago* hit rough seas and sank, leaving Magellan with only four ships. In August, with the weather warming, Magellan announced it was time to set sail again; by October they had found the strait around the southern tip of South America that would later be named the **Strait of Magellan.**

The strait was a tricky passage and it took the ships 38 days to successfully navigate through. The time lost getting through the strait was a big concern, but an even larger concern to befall Magellan and his crew was that, while attempting to pass the strait, the captain of the *San Antonio* decided to turn around and return to Spain. This was a crushing blow to Magellan and his crew, as the *San Antonio* was carrying the majority of the supplies for the voyage. The sailors on the three remaining vessels now had to forage for fresh food and water. It was early November when Magellan's expedition entered the Pacific Ocean. However, upon seeing the ocean, Magellan rejoiced, mistakenly thinking that the Spice Islands and the Far East were now only two or three sailing days away. Magellan did not comprehend the massiveness of the Pacific Ocean. It would take four months to cross, and conditions were terrible. The water on the ships went putrid and yellow in color, but the men were forced to drink it, as they had no other. Food ran out as well and the sailors survived by eating sawdust, leather, and rats. Scurvy ran rampant as the sailors lacked fresh fruit or any other source of vitamin C. Many sailors died of disease and starvation. The crews would have likely all died if they had not accidentally discovered the island of **Guam** in early March.

Finally, on March 28, 1521, Magellan and his men arrived in the Philippines, making Ferdinand Magellan the first person to completely sail around the world, as he had sailed to the Philippines by going east from Europe as part of the crew on a Portuguese ship in his youth. They stopped in the Philippines for rest and resupply and went ashore, where Magellan befriended a local chief. In an attempt to help his new friend, Magellan foolishly got involved in a local power struggle and was killed. Lacking the crew to maintain three ships, the expedition's new leader, **Sebastian del Cano,** ordered one ship burned. The two remaining ships went on to the Spice Islands, where they loaded spices and other luxury items to take back to Spain. Insistent that at least some of the hard-earned treasure make it back to Spain, Captain Cano took his ship west around Africa, and ordered the other ship to sail east back across the Pacific Ocean toward Spain. The eastbound ship never made it back. Cano and his ship were the only ship of the original five to return to Spain, thus becoming the first vessel and crew to circumnavigate the globe in one trip.

The Spanish claimed the Philippines as their territory and asserted that the Philippines were their side of the line of demarcation, extended around the world, and would, therefore, belong to Spain. Because the navigators of the day had no reliable way to determine longitude, the Portuguese were forced to allow the Spanish to control the Philippines even though the Philippines are actually within the Portuguese region, as can be seen from the map in Figure 23.5.

Spain slowly realized that its possessions in the **New World** were far vaster and possibly far more lucrative that they had originally thought. The Spanish began to focus more of their energies and attention on their holdings in the Americas. However, the New World still was a highly uncertain venture that included high costs, great risks, and no guarantee of profits at the end of the voyage. The high-risk threshold discouraged the Spanish crown from investing large sums of money. Thus, a new breed of Spanish sailor/explorers came to preeminence. These men were the **conquistadores,** essentially private adventurers who were encouraged but not financially supported by the Spanish crown. The men were often

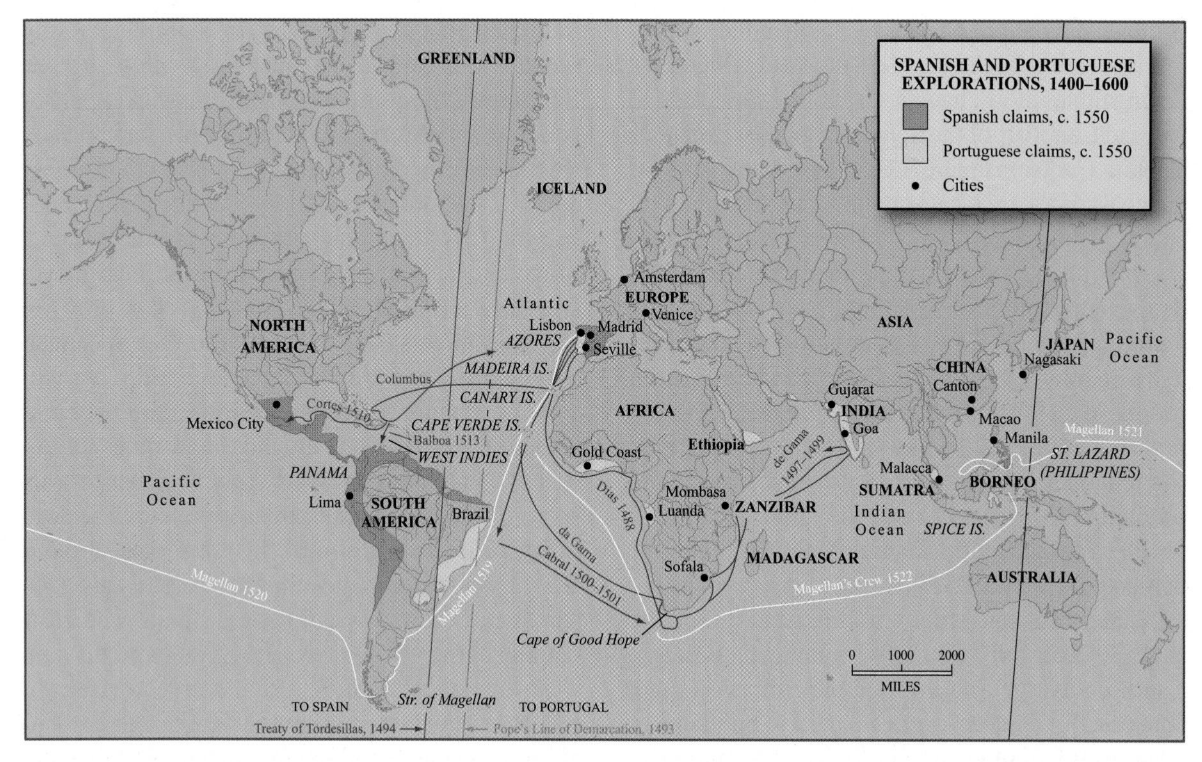

Figure 23.5 ■ *Subsequent discoveries by Portugal and Spain, and the line of demarcation showing the Asian extension.*

from impoverished families and were looking to make money and gain a reputation. The financing came from the wealthy bankers of Barcelona, who were willing to take greater risks than the crown in order to get a percentage of any profits.

The greatest of the Spanish conquistadores was **Hernan Cortes (Cortez),** conqueror of **Mexico** and the native **Aztecs** who lived there. Cortes was nearly the stereotypical conquistador. He was born in the province of Extremadura, a region along the Portuguese border and one of the poorest regions of Spain, to hard-working but poor parents. Cortes decided, after a failed attempt at the University of Salamanca, that he would make his reputation and gain a fortune going to the New World. So, at age 19, Cortes sailed for the Indies, where he settled in Cuba and became well known as an able soldier while fighting in skirmishes with the local native peoples.

The native peoples, who had regular contact with the Spanish, eventually realized that they could not defeat the Spanish in battle. The natives may have had a great numerical advantage, but they simply could not compete with the technology of the Spanish, who had guns, armor, artillery, and mastery of the horse. Rather than fight with the Spanish, the native peoples in the immediate vicinity began to leave peace offerings for the Spanish. Originally the offerings were of gold and other precious items, but eventually grew to include slaves captured from other tribes. This proved to be a stroke of great fortune for Cortes, as one of the captured slave girls happened to speak Aztec. Her name was **Malinsi,** but Cortes called her **"Mi lengua"** ("my tongue") and she became his lover and interpreter. From Malinsi, Cortes learned of the great Aztec Empire inland on the mainland, rich in gold and other precious items. She also told him it was well defended by a large army, but that many of the smaller vassal kings hated the Aztec king, **Montezuma,** and would support anyone that would seek his removal from power.

A small expedition of roughly 500 Spanish soldiers led by Cortes left Cuba and arrived on the Mexican mainland in the spring of 1519 (Cortes was 34), where they established a camp at what is now the city of **Veracruz.** However, the lack of supplies and the constant skirmishes took their toll on Cortes' men; many were openly calling for the abandonment of Veracruz and a return to Cuba. When his men complained that too many had been killed with fevers or in Indian attacks, Cortes responded, "Then let us bury our dead at night so that our enemies will think that we are immortal." Cortes was unwilling to leave without going further inland to seek out the Aztecs. When mutiny seemed nearly unavoidable, Cortes had the ships burned in the harbor so that the men could not leave. Soon after, the Spanish began the 250-mile march to the northwest to the main city of the Aztecs, present-day **Mexico City.** As Malinsi had said, many Indian tribes along the way were anxious to depose Montezuma, and joined with the Spanish. When the army reached the city, they were both amazed and terrified. It was everything they had hoped for—splendid and opulent grandeur—yet at the same time it was immediately apparent that they were vastly outnumbered and completely at the mercy of the Aztecs.

However, fate or luck was on the side of Cortes and the Spanish, as they had arrived on the Mexican coast the very day that the Aztec holy men had foreseen that the Plumed Serpent, the Great White God **Quetzalcoatl,** would return. Messengers of Montezuma had seen their arrival and had sped back to Mexico City with word that the gods had come back with lances that spit fire, and with warriors with two heads and six legs, and that they lived in houses that floated. Thus, rather than being wiped out, Cortes and his men were hailed as gods and invited into the city. Once in the city, they took Montezuma hostage and began to loot the city's treasures, setting up Christian shrines and ravaging the people. Eventually the Aztecs realized that these were not the long-awaited gods, and drove the Spanish out, but it was too late. Cortes returned with more men and armaments and conquered the Aztec Empire.

The Aztecs fought with courage and numbers, but they were at a severe strategic and technological disadvantage. Furthermore, the Aztecs lived in a world deeply governed by religion, and while they fought with bravery, they may have lacked heart, as their own religious tradition contemplated their subjugation to a white god (Quetzalcoatl).

Cortes was not the only great Spanish conquistador. Several others helped to claim territory and fortune for Spain. **Francisco Pizarro,** who conquered the **Incas** and claimed the area of Peru for Spain, **Orellana,** who explored the entire Amazon River basin looking for cinnamon and gold, **Cabeza de Vaca,** who lived among the natives in Texas and Northern Mexico, and **Francisco Coronado,** who explored the plains of North America in search of **El Dorado** (the legendary city of gold)—men like these and others helped to bring most of what is now North and South America under the dominion of the Spanish. The Spanish continued to harvest great riches of gold, silver, and other precious goods from the Americas for over 200 years. A list of major explorers is given in Figure 23.6.

The Northern European Countries

Spain and Portugal were the early naval and colonial powers in the Atlantic. Explorers and sailors from these countries claimed vast new continents, and economic and strategic islands, for their king and their god. In the process the explorers made a name for themselves and sometimes a fortune. Europe's other two major Atlantic-facing nations, England and France, got a later start in the colonial game and therefore were left to fight over the areas that the Spanish and Portuguese had ignored—chiefly North America. The English hoped to find a northwest passage to Asia by going around the New World to the north. The French were more content to extract the limited valuable resources that the northern part of the continent offered, namely animal furs and timber. While the trapping of beaver and other animals, and the cutting of timber, were not as lucrative as

Year	Explorer	Sponsor	Area Explored
1418–1460	Various	Portugal	Madeira, Azores, West African coast to Cape Verde
1487–1488	Diaz	Portugal	African coast to Cape of Good Hope
1492	Columbus	Spain	Bahamas, Santo Domingo
1493	Columbus	Spain	West Indian Islands
1497–1498	Cabot	England	Newfoundland, Nova Scotia
1497–1499	da Gama	Portugal	Cape of Good Hope, Indian Ocean
1498	Columbus	Spain	Trinidad, Venezuela
1499	Vespucci	Spain	Northeastern coast of S. America
1500	Cabral	Portugal	Brazil, Indian Ocean to W. India
1502–1504	Columbus	Spain	Central American Coast
1519–1522	Magellan	Spain	Circumnavigation, Cape Horn, Pacific Ocean
1524	Verrazano	France	American coast from Virginia to Newfoundland
1533, 1534	Cartier	France	Quebec, St. Lawrence River
1577–1580	Drake	England	Circumnavigation, west coast of N. and S. America

Figure 23.6 ■ *List of major explorers, 1400–1600.*

the extraction of gold and other precious items was for Spain and Portugal, it did have an added and unexpected side benefit of encouraging colonization and an economy based on trade rather than extraction. These factors proved to be a model that allowed England and France to dominate later colonial wars and become economic powers long after Spain and Portugal had extracted all the easy wealth from their colonies.

Largely because England was excluded from the most lucrative colonies by Spain and Portugal, and to a lesser extent by France, England had to find other ways to profit from the New World. One creative way England achieved this was through the use of **privateers.** Privateers were essentially pirates but with some limited (secret) backing by the English monarch. The privateers agreed to not attack English sailing vessels and to share a portion of the profits that they took from foreign ships with the English crown. In return, **Queen Elizabeth I** (reigned 1558–1603), the monarch who promoted the scheme, allowed them to keep large amounts of the confiscated goods (far more than they could make as honest shipping merchants) and did not attempt to arrest them for their pirating activities. English ports the world over became safe havens for privateers when fleeing from foreign adversaries.

The greatest and most renowned of all the privateers was **Francis Drake,** a master sailor and an excellent pirate, who particularly delighted in robbing and tormenting the Spanish. On one trip Drake raided several Spanish ports in South America, stealing over 25,000 pesos in gold from one ship in the port of Valparaiso alone. Then, in order to avoid capture by the enraged Spanish, Drake and his crew became the first Englishmen to circumnavigate the Earth. While on this voyage Drake claimed parts of California and Indonesia for England. Drake had captured over 26 tons of gold and silver on this one voyage alone, and when he returned to England, the Queen's portion alone was 47,000 gold crowns—enough to pay off all of England's foreign debt as well as operate the country for several years. Drake continued to be a thorn in Spain's side by later commanding the English victory against the **Spanish Armada** despite overwhelming odds in Spain's favor. For his services to the English crown (and as a wound to Spanish pride) Francis Drake, the privateer, was knighted by Queen Elizabeth I.

Sir Francis Drake and the other privateers not only brought in large sums of money to England's treasury, but also explored most of the world and gained a vast knowledge of accurate geography and sailing expertise for England. Both of these factors became vital in helping shape England's navy into the greatest in the world. Their navy allowed England to eventually dominate the oceans and go from being an afterthought in the grab for colonies to having an empire so vast that it could truly be said that, "The sun never sets on the British Empire." Ironically, when the British had finally conquered the Spanish and French so that they had vast holdings in the Caribbean (which occurred a hundred years after Drake), the pirates who remained were a constant source of irritation and loss of profits to the English.

Discovery and Creativity

The **Age of Discovery** is a prime example of people and nations using their creativity to better themselves and to bring them wealth and glory. It is a time when many people were thinking in new and exciting ways. Portugal's Prince Henry the Navigator, who recognized that the way out of Spanish dominance and Portuguese poverty was by turning to the sea, was a prime example of this creativity. He understood that training and technology were keys to success. The caravel is a reminder of his foresight.

The Italian sailor Christopher Columbus should be respected for his determined and creative efforts to find the financing for his dream. He continued to creatively exploit his discoveries by establishing political and religious concessions. His error in calculation of the earth's diameter turned out to be unimportant, except to give him the confidence to creatively manage his sailors and to promote the supposed value of his discovery. In truth, the riches were even greater than if he had been correct in his geographical assessments.

The Spanish conquistadores were creative in their willingness to use information brought to them by the natives of the New World and their ability to take advantage of the customs and religious traditions of the indigenous peoples. Their ruthless fighting methods were also creative in dominating the natives.

The French and English were creative for making the best of a bad situation. Finding themselves late to the colonial game and occupying lands not rich in gold, they made do with what they had. The French purposely worked to make fur hats and coats a popular fashion in Europe so as to increase the value of their prime export. England created the privateers, and improved their navy to the point that they were eventually able to dominate the oceans of the world and be the earth's primary economic and military power.

The importance of the **Age of Exploration** on later history is difficult to over-emphasize. The shift of trade moved out of the Mediterranean and into the Atlantic. The Mediterranean became just a lake. The riches of the world moved first to the Iberian Peninsula and then to northern Europe, and with those riches came political and military power. It would take nearly a hundred years for these changes to be fully realized, but when they were, the center of creativity would move northward as well.

Discovery can be creative for many reasons. It can be a creative idea and it can be a creative implementation. We might tend to dismiss the discovery of the world because it is obvious to us that what was done would have been inevitable and, besides, the discoverers were sometimes wrong in their ideas. However, "discovery" is present in many other fields besides exploration of the world, and most people would have no problem calling those efforts creative. For example, science is really just discovery of nature and scientists are often initially wrong in their assessments. Even art is a discovery of ways to manipulate principles of symmetry, color, tone, and form; combined, of course, with talent, which comes from or is at least enhanced by hard work and practice. Creative hard work and practice would certainly be traits of those creative individuals who discovered the world during the Age of Exploration.

Timeline—Important Dates

Date	Event
1394–1460 A.D.	*Henry the Navigator*
1453	*Constantinople falls to the Ottoman Turks*
1487–1488	*Diaz discovers Cape of Good Hope*
1492	*Columbus discovers Americas*
1493–1494	*Treaty of Tordesillas*
1497–1499	*Da Gama sails to India*
1497	*Cabot sails to America for England*
1519–1522	*Magellan's voyage around the world*
1519–1521	*Cortes in Mexico*
1533	*Cartier exploration of America for France*
1577–1580	*Drake circumnavigates the world*

Suggested Readings

Milton, Giles, *Nathaniel's Nutmeg,* Penguin, 1999.

Prescott, William H., *History of the Conquest of Peru,* Dent, 1968.

The Discovered World

Unknown Creativity

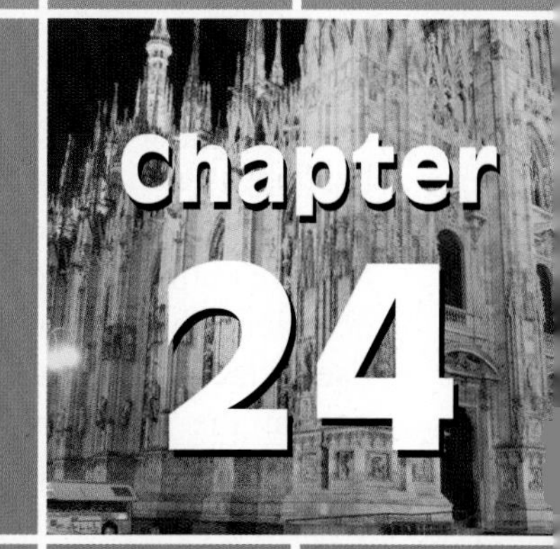

At the beginning of the age of exploration, the greatest seafaring nation in the world was China. China had a huge navy. Their massive ships were centuries ahead of European technology. Chinese merchants plied trade routes all over the South Pacific and Indian Oceans. The Chinese Admiral Cheng Ho led many expeditions that visited and charted ports as far as the East Coast of Africa. China was well on its way to becoming the preeminent nation in the world. Unfortunately, Chinese leaders learned the wrong things from Cheng Ho's expeditions. They concluded that they had nothing to learn from the outside world because outside technology, products, and societies were so obviously inferior to their own. China banned foreign travel and let its navy and merchant marines rot in port. Much smaller and less advanced nations like Portugal, Spain, England, and even the tiny Netherlands, vigorously pursued seaborne trade and exploration. It took centuries for them to catch up to where China had been, but they did. And they came to dominate the world, including controlling much of China.

—*Scott Thorpe,* How to Think Like Einstein, *Barnes & Noble, 2000, p. 51.*

The World Outside Europe throughout the European Middle Ages

We examined the early civilizations of India and China at the beginning of this book and traced their development from the dawn of civilization to about the second century A.D. We left those societies to look at the Greek societies and then the successor society—Rome. After the fall of the Roman Empire in the west, we looked at, in turn, the Byzantine Empire, the Islamic Empire, and the European Middle Ages. In all three we continued our examination to about the same year—1500 A.D. This was the time when European discoverers again encountered the greater world. It is, therefore, appropriate for us now to pick up the story of India and China, and to tell the story of the history of Japan, Africa, and pre-Columbian America, which we have not heretofore considered. We will trace all their histories up to about 1500 A.D.

The creative output of each of these areas varied greatly over the millennium prior to 1500. Each of the regions made important creative advances that have affected the entire world's civilization, as well as advances that have been important locally. Each region also had times when creative output was low. However, in spite of their occasional high creativity, these regions did not rise to the level of world dominance. The quotation at the beginning of this chapter suggests that the Chinese became complacent with their own society and underestimated the potential for progress in other regions. Cultural differences might also have caused the non-Europeans eventually to fall behind. Environmental and geographical issues might also have played a part. Therefore, as we examine these non-European cultures, we should strive to see what caused them to progress creatively, and also what might have limited their progress.

India

Indian society around the first and second centuries A.D. consisted of many relatively small kingdoms that were blends of the ancient Aryan and Dravidian cultures. One of these kingdoms emerged in the fourth century to dominate most of northern India and form the **Gupta Empire** (320–535). We see an interesting dichotomy in the Guptas. The first three leaders of their empire were all very powerful military leaders; the great Indian military/religious epic, *Mahabharata,* was written during this time, further demonstrating the military side of Gupta society. However, the Guptas delighted in continuing their empire through political manipulations and strategic marriages, rather than through force. This combination proved beneficial to India, as the Guptas were able to create a period of peace and prosperity that gave India a golden age.

Much of the lasting Hindu culture developed during the Gupta period, perhaps because of the *Mahabharata* and another key epic, the *Ramayana.* The first is a collection of stories, some of which date from ancient times of India, recorded as a unified book at the time of the Guptas. In this regard, it is like other epics we have considered—the *Iliad,* the *Odyssey,* and the *Aeneid.* The language of this great Indian epic is **Sanskrit.** The other great Indian epic created during this time is somewhat different. The *Ramayana* is the story of the incarnation of the god **Vishnu** as the warrior Rama. However, the *Ramayana* is not a fixed text but, rather, a core story that gains much of its life through the retelling, often in the unique words of the storyteller. In this regard, it preserves the oral tradition of India. Just as with the *Mahabharata,* the *Ramayana* is religious and moral in its tone. These two join the *Bhagavad-Gita,* written in the fifth century B.C., as the most important Hindu books.

Many other cultural achievements of India were made during the Gupta period, for example, the development of the numeral system, which is the basis of the system we use today (transmitted to us through the Arabs), and the decimal system. Indian medicine focused on pharmacopoeia and diseases readily understood from external examinations of the body, since religious injunctions against contact with dead bodies prevented studies of physiology and anatomy. Nevertheless, Indian medicine was quite advanced in this period.

An invasion by the Huns from central Asia brought an end to the Gupta golden age but, after a few generations, Hindu rulers were able to reorganize significant parts of their empire, because the Huns were little interested in occupying and ruling the lands they plundered. This was a period of darkness for India, which, interestingly, corresponded to the dark period in Europe that followed the fall of the Western Roman Empire, also brought on, in part, by an invasion of the Huns. The reorganized Hindu kingdoms that drove out the Huns were less religiously tolerant than the Guptas. Religious persecutions of the Buddhists became so severe that most Buddhists moved out of India. Even today, few Buddhists live in the land that gave birth to their religion.

The wave of Islamic conquests that began in Arabia reached India in the eighth century A.D., driving out the Hindu rulers in most of India. From this time forward, there were no significant

Hindu rulers in India until modern times; rather, India was ruled by outside monarchs. Initially the **Muslim Umayyads** conquered much of India but they were replaced in the eleventh century by **Abbasid Muslims,** who made Delhi their Indian capital. This period is called the **Delhi Sultanate.** Despite the influx of many Muslims from surrounding territories, and the conversion of many native Indians to Islam, the majority of Indians continued as Hindus. Muslim leaders allowed the building of large, beautifully ornate Hindu temples, very high, ethereal structures that invoked the same religious devotions among Hindus that Gothic cathedrals did for Christians in Europe at about the same time. Some temple sites were the size of a city, and included walls for defense and elaborately decorated entrance gates. One temple had more than 800 statues, and another had more than 6,000 priests. A complex built around a lake had more than 7,000 separate temple buildings. A Hindu temple of this period is shown in Figure 24.1. Indian influence spread throughout Southeast Asia and strongly influenced the architecture of temples in other places, such as Angkor Wat in Cambodia.

In 1398 the Delhi Sultanate fell to a ferocious descendent of Genghis Khan, **Tamarlane,** an Islamic leader who swept down from Samarkind, in central Asia. Tamarlane proclaimed his family the new rulers of India and ruled as a powerful central authority from **Samarkind.** But, as is so often the case in history, the son is not the father, and Tamarlane's son was driven out of his capital by Afghan tribes. He fled to Persia, where he lived comfortably but without any empire. This left India without any central leader or government, so local kings filled the power vacuum. The Portuguese arrived in India during this time. Thus, much of Portugal's early success in dominating India, particularly the coastal regions, was due to the fact that there was simply no strong government to oppose them once they had defeated the Arab traders. The Portuguese, however, did not have enough manpower to completely fill the national power vacuum, and were content to control the coast and the spice-producing regions.

Figure 24.1 ■ *The Konark Sun Temple (Hindu), built in the thirteenth century A.D. Image from Corel.*

In 1526 Tamarlane's grandson, **Babur the Tiger,** invaded and eventually conquered the whole of India with the exception of Goa and the other areas directly under Portuguese control. Babur established the **Mughal Dynasty,** which would rule India until the British occupation two centuries later. Babur was able to unite the country, where many of his predecessors had not, because of his willingness to grant important government positions to both Hindus and Muslims, reducing much of the religious tension that existed within India. Babur and his Mughal descendants also allowed the Portuguese (and eventually other Europeans) to serve as bureaucrats in the government, which kept the Europeans happy and trade markets open and favorable.

The Mughals became rich from trade with the Europeans and lavished their money on beautiful palaces and other symbols of royalty. The **peacock throne,** encrusted with gold, emeralds, diamonds, pearls, and rubies was built by these rulers. One Mughal ruler, **Shah Jehan,** built a tomb for his wife that is widely considered the most beautiful building in the world. This is the **Taj Mahal,** located in the city of Agra. A photo of the Taj Mahal is given in Figure 16.4 (which was described previously in the chapter on Islam). The walls of the building are of white marble decorated with a floral pattern made of inlaid precious and semi-precious stones and gold. It is wonderfully symmetrical, and reflects a pleasing architectural style that shows Persian (with perhaps some Byzantine), Indian, and Muslim influences.

The Mughals were weakened by internal disputes that allowed local rulers **(maharajas)** to exert strong control over their small kingdoms. These local leaders were often supported and influenced by the European trading countries. Persia conquered large portions of India in 1739, taking the peacock throne, but did not continue to rule the country. The British sensed the power vacuum in India after the withdrawal of the Persians, and began to establish political control over the country in order to protect their commercial interests. This led to India becoming a part of the **British Empire** in 1784.

China

The **Qin Dynasty** (221–207 B.C.), from which China got its name, and the **Han Dynasty** (206 B.C.–220 A.D.), which is the name of the largest ethnic group in China, were discussed in the chapter on the River Societies, which began civilization. These two dynasties set the pattern for much of Chinese culture by building the Great Wall, establishing the Silk Road, beginning the practice of elaborate tombs (such as the Terra Cotta warriors in Xi'an), inventing porcelain, and developing sophisticated bronze vessels and works of art. However, these periods of high creativity were not to last. A period of disunity and chaos overtook China from the third to the sixth centuries A.D. There were no national leaders during this time. This dark period coincided with the dark periods in Europe and India.

During part of this time, three separate kingdoms dominated Chinese government. The **Three Kingdoms Period** (200–250 A.D.) is a time when several legends were born that have strongly affected Chinese culture, much like the legends of King Arthur have contributed to Western culture. One legend tells about a confrontation between a northern army and an army from the south who met on opposite sides of a great river. Both armies readied for what they all knew would be the deciding battle of the war. The northern army was tired, a long way from home, and short on many supplies, including arrows, but they developed a creative plan. They commandeered boats along their side of the river and fashioned straw mannequins, which they dressed in uniforms and set in the boats. Keeping the boats tied together and to the shore, they pushed the boats into the early-morning, mist-covered river. The southern army guards saw the boats and sounded the alarm. The southerners shot many arrows into the mannequins. The northern army pulled the boats back to shore, retrieved the arrows, and then crossed the river and successfully defeated the southern army using the captured arrows to replenish their depleted supply.

Another legend tells of a great general who was surveying the fortifications of a city during a time of war. The general took a small detachment of troops with him because the rest of his army was occupied in a battle elsewhere. When the enemy troops happened upon the city, their forward scouts saw the general inside the walls of the city with what appeared to be only a few troops. The scouts hurried back to tell their commander the good news. The great general's spies were in the area around the city and returned to tell him that he was vastly outnumbered by the enemy and should quickly flee. However, instead of running away, the great general asked his second-in-command to join him for a game of chess, which they played in a small flat area above the main gate of the city wall where they could be easily seen. The general also told his troops to practice drilling in front of the city walls in clear view. When the enemy general got to the city, he saw the obvious nonchalance of the great general and, instead of attacking as he was urged to do by his advisors, the enemy general said that the great general would never leave himself in such an exposed situation, and so it must be a trap. The enemy therefore withdrew.

The **Tang Dynasty** (618–960 A.D.) brought creativity back to life in China. Their capital, **Xi'an** (formerly called Chang'an), may have been the largest city in the world at this time, with a population of perhaps one million. Buddhism, which had been introduced during the period of disunity, flourished under the Tangs, with many monasteries established and temples built. This was a period of great technological progress, including the invention of woodblock printing and gunpowder. The conquest of Persia by the Muslims caused the Persian crown prince to take refuge in China, and many Persian styles were introduced.

During the Tang Dynasty the Chinese people were willing to accept art and technology from outside China, as can be seen from the Persian influence and the adoption of Buddhism. Clearly this acceptance also helped the Chinese become the most advanced society in the world during the Tang period. The Chinese were even able to accept rule by **Wu Zeitan,** the only female head of state in China's history. She was born in 623 A.D. to the royal family and given a wide education in the arts. At 14, she became a concubine of the emperor and soon became one of his favorites because of her artistic capabilities and sharp mind. She was assigned to work in the imperial study, where she became acquainted with official documents and affairs of state. When she was 26 the emperor died and, following custom, all the former emperor's concubines were sent from the court to nunneries. The new emperor became aware of Wu Zeitan and visited her in the nunnery several times, becoming enchanted with her wit and beauty. He soon summoned her to court, where she became his concubine. Through a series of palace intrigues, she rose from the status of concubine to become the favorite of the emperor and then was made wife and empress. She was esteemed by her husband and recommended new ideas in agriculture (such as new irrigation systems), tax reduction (which were scaled so that as a person created more goods, the taxes decreased as a percentage), social reform (increasing the role of women and ridiculing the Confucian belief that women were inferior, thus promoting Buddhism over Confucianism). She was personally brilliant and also served as a conduit for new ideas from a large intellectual elite. Throughout this time she carefully cultivated friendships with the powerful advisors to the emperor. Those who opposed her were exiled. After five years of marriage to the emperor, he suffered a crippling stroke and she assumed control of the state. She created a secret police to monitor the activities of any who would oppose her and, as her confidence and power grew, she ruthlessly eliminated all opposition (including her own daughter), and ruled as an absolute monarch. When the emperor finally died, he was replaced by a son (not one of Wu's children) who proved to be very independent. Wu had him removed and then installed one of her own sons to sit as a puppet emperor while she continued to rule. As she grew older, her son gained power and at the age of 82 she was deposed. She died within the same year and was buried next to her husband in the outskirts of Xi'an. She insisted on a simple tomb that seems to invite history to judge whether this woman who ruled China on her own power will be remembered for good or bad.

Several centuries of pressure from central Asian tribes, combined with domestic instability, led to the collapse of the Tang Dynasty and the establishment of the **Song Dynasty** (960–1259 A.D.). The Song emperors were wary of the power of the many lords who dominated local regions (much like the feudal system in Europe) and moved to reduce the power of these local leaders. The Song emperors installed a system of bureaucrats (sometimes called the **literati** because they were highly educated and conducted the schooling in the empire and ran the government bureaucracy). These bureaucrats were promoted on the basis of merit and not patronage. They reported directly to imperial headquarters so that the emperor could control the workings of the government throughout all regions. While it is true that the bureaucrats did not control the armies in all the territories, simply administering the local governments gave them tremendous power and successfully balanced the power of the local lords.

Just as in Europe at about the same time, the warmer world climate allowed **rice** to replace **millet** as the staple crop, increasing food availability so that the increasing population could move into cities. The cities in China began to grow as centers of trade, industry, and maritime commerce. The landed elite lived in the provincial centers alongside the shopkeepers, artisans, and merchants. A mercantile class arose as printing and education spread, private trade grew, and a market economy began to link the coastal provinces with the interior. Landholding and government employment were no longer the only means of gaining wealth and prestige. Culturally, the Song refined many of the developments of the previous centuries, such as historical writings, painting, calligraphy, and hard-glazed porcelain. Technology continued to rapidly move forward, as evidenced by the invention of the **compass** and the establishment of a coin and paper money system to replace barter.

About the year 1100, the Song moved their capital from northern China to the south, occasioned by pressure from the warlike nomadic invaders that the Song leaders were unable to control. Eventually the northern part of China was brought under the control of people who were not native Chinese, creating a split in the Song Dynasty and leading to a strong feeling of Chinese nationalism in the south, where the intellectuals sought to preserve what they viewed as the ancient Chinese culture. Song intellectuals believed that answers to all philosophical and political questions could be found in the Confucian classics and Taoism. This renewed interest in the ancient sages coincided with the decline of Buddhism, which the Song regarded as foreign and failing to give practical guidelines for real life.

The approach of the southern Song intellectuals was intended to teach the rulers how to govern their realm, but was also applied to every individual in China, with the individual's realm considered to be their area of influence. In the aggregate, all these areas of influence would contribute to the entire realm and so every person felt a part in contributing to the welfare of China and, ultimately, to the betterment of the world. According to the intellectuals, a person's "realm" could only be controlled when their "family" was under control. The "family" can only be put under control when the "person" is under control. The "person" is put under control when the "consciousness" or "reality" is under control and that is done after getting "thinking" under control. "Thinking" is mastered by "investigating the nature of things," which leads to an understanding of nature and the actions of people. When "investigation of things" is done correctly, "thinking" is extended and the mind is clarified. This clarification of the mind leads to correct actions, because actions are controlled by the thoughts. With proper actions by a "person," the "family" can then be ordered and so on to the "realm." There is, therefore, a hierarchy of activities that begins with an "investigation of things" and proceeds to control over the "realm" and then world peace and harmony. However, all of these activities should be carried out simultaneously, so that a person would always be working on all facets of inner thoughts and outer control. Confucius even stated that these activities should be done even when a person is alone, thereby suggesting that personal integrity is a critical facet of human behavior and that personal and public lives should be the same.

The "investigation of things" is an attempt to discover the patterns of the world, which is called the ***Li*** and is strongly Taoist in concept. The perception of the *Li* depends on the ability of people to orient their inner force (called the ***Chi***) to gain the clarity necessary to really see the patterns of *Li*. Hence, a person investigates intellectually and emotionally by learning and by practicing mind and body control to gain power over the *Chi*.

The Song Dynasty emphasized their linkage with the culture of the past. Like the ancient Egyptians, they resisted new concepts and tried to always justify their ideas as being simply restatements of ancient concepts. There was a distrust of the new and a reverence for the old. Therefore, even though the ideas might be creative and new, they were always couched as being merely reiterations of the old. This attitude limited creativity in Chinese society.

The Song Dynasty continued for another hundred years until they were finally overrun by nomadic invaders from the north—the Mongols. The leader of the Mongols who invaded China was Genghis Khan, whom we discussed in a previous chapter. His partial conquest of China was completed by his son and grandsons, one of whom was **Kublai Khan,** who took the title of Emperor of China and ruled from Beijing, establishing the **Yuan Dynasty** (1260–1368).

The Mongol rulers were never able to fit into Chinese society. They spoke a different language, dressed differently, and had vastly different customs. They were shunned by the Chinese elite and bureaucrats, thus forcing Kublai Khan and his successors to supplement their own expertise with foreign advisors and diplomats (one of whom was Marco Polo). This distanced the Yuan rulers from the Chinese people and a feeling of distrust ensued. The Chinese elite, excluded from government, focused on cultural pursuits. Theater, literature, and opera flourished. Private schools were founded because the government schools were forced to teach concepts foreign to the Chinese. The Chinese were not allowed freedom to travel or promote trade with foreigners but foreigners were allowed to capitalize on trade inside China. These policies led to a reduction of trade and to severe economic difficulties. These difficulties were worsened by the disastrous attempt of the Yuan leaders to invade Japan. Most of the Chinese fleet sank during the fierce storm that arose during the invasion attempt. In the end, the Yuan emperors were never able to win the support of the Chinese people; uprisings against the emperors throughout China coalesced under a commoner who rose to become emperor and founded the **Ming Dynasty** (1368–1644).

The first of the Ming emperors was constantly worried about being deposed, and so he moved the capital to Nanjing and increased police control over the people. He and his Ming successors were also obsessed with the thought that China might be invaded, and increased military spending accordingly. The third Ming emperor believed that Nanjing was not as safe as the old capital, and so he returned the capital to the well-fortified Beijing. In that city the Ming rulers completed the **Forbidden City**—a large and beautiful palace complex that can be visited and enjoyed today. The Great Wall was expanded and improved. The Ming emperors encouraged the growth of merchant trade to increase the money in the empire, and returned the intellectual basis of Chinese society to the old values of Confucius and Tao. Chinese society sought to return to the glorious days of the past, just as Europe was in its Renaissance and seeking to do the same. And, just as the European Renaissance gave the world great art objects, so too did the Ming Dynasty. Porcelain works were especially good; one excellent example is pictured in Figure 24.2. Unfortunately, the increased trade did little to stimulate Chinese creativity. As the quotation at the beginning of the chapter states, the Chinese were so advanced that they saw little of value in other countries. This attitude led them to draw inward, which led to a diminishing of the rate of creative growth such that other countries, especially those in Europe, gained precedence over them. Internal struggles eventually led to the demise of the Ming Dynasty and rise of the **Qing Dynasty,** which lasted until 1911 and will be discussed in the next volume of this work.

■ Japan

Early Japanese culture was nomadic and largely not recorded. Settlement was probably from Korea. The introduction of rice in about the first century B.C. led to the development of agriculture

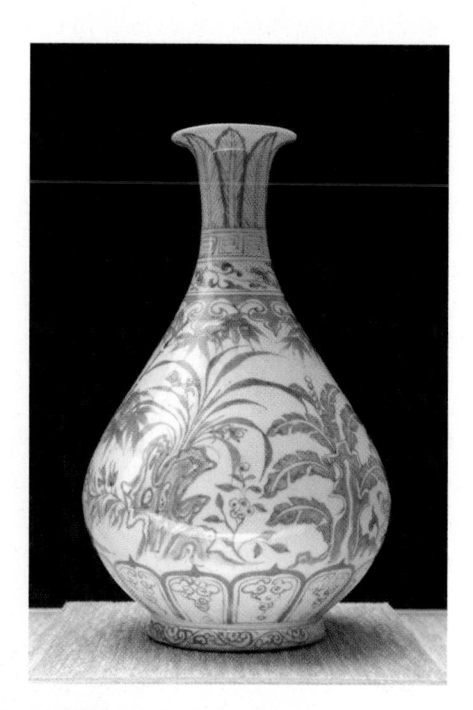

Figure 24.2 ■ *Ming vase. Image © Karen/Corbis Sygma.*

and city-based societies with the accompaniment of division of labor and social classes.

The **Yamato** (later called **Nara**) Period (538–794 A.D.), marked the unification of major parts of Japan under a single ruler who was located in what is now Nara prefecture. Many Chinese influences were absorbed by the Japanese, perhaps via Korea, including Chinese writing and Buddhism, but these were changed to reflect the Japanese culture. For example, Buddhism was blended with **Shinto,** the ancient belief in gods of nature and ancestral worship that dominates Japanese culture until today. The Japanese embracing of Buddhism can be seen in the many Buddhist monasteries and shrines throughout the country. Some of these are enormous; among the largest wooden structures in the world. One shrine is pictured in Figure 24.3. The rise of power among various Buddhist sects threatened imperial power and, as a result, the seat of government was moved from Nara to several other cities as religious and political influences dictated.

The establishment of the capital in Heian **(Kyoto)** ushered in a golden age (794–1185 A.D.). Japanese culture became fixed on "good taste" and established many rituals to assist in following the accepted rules of society. Chinese culture, which had often influenced governmental policies and culture, was even more strongly modified. A unique Japanese writing style was developed. The emperor came to be dominated by the **Fujiwara clan,** who established themselves as regents over several emperors during the **Heian Period** through political intrigues and intermarriage, eventually establishing a hereditary claim to the regency. As in Europe at about the same time, local warrior lords began to proliferate throughout the Japanese countryside. These lords hired soldiers to assist them in the many small wars that were fought in efforts to increase their territories and prestige. The country became feudal.

The **Kamakura Period** (1185–1333) arose because of the power of the local lords. A succession crisis in the imperial family set off a short period of uncertainty that was resolved by the two most powerful warrior clans. This marked a change in Japanese government as the warriors became increasingly powerful, even to the point of

Figure 24.3 ■ *Buddhist Temple.* Image from Corel.

appointing a military leader, a *shogun,* to be the head of state, who exercised his power from the town of Kamakura. This move established a government in parallel to the official imperial court in Kyoto. It was during this time that the Yuan Dynasty emperors in China attempted to invade Japan. The Kamakura leaders were forced to spend enormous amounts of money to prepare for what appeared to be a long and difficult war. However, the Japanese were saved by what they called *kamikaze* (the "divine wind"), which destroyed the Chinese invasion fleet. The great war expenditures were the undoing of the Kamakuras, and power shifted once again to Kyoto. The emperors in Kyoto were weak, so new *shoguns* arose, starting the **Muromachi-Momoyama Period** (1333–1603), named for a district in Kyoto where the government buildings were located. After a few generations, the warrior lords of the countryside (now called *daimyo*) again rose in power and a series of civil wars dominated Japan. It was during this time that the Portuguese landed in Japan and introduced both Christianity and firearms. Many *daimyo* supported the Portuguese presence, as it brought increased trade and money to those ports that welcomed the Europeans.

In 1568 a very powerful *daimyo* succeeded in capturing Kyoto and controlling the government. He began to eliminate his enemies, including the leaders of several Buddhist sects. However, the *daimyo* was assassinated, thus precipitating a civil war. The victor then eliminated his enemies and gained total military control. He destroyed many of the castles that had been built over the period of the civil wars, and succeeded in uniting Japan under his solitary control, as had not happened for hundreds of years. He expelled the Christian missionaries and executed some of the converts. He then set out to achieve his dream of conquering China. He invaded Korea and captured Seoul, but his army was met by the Chinese army; he was forced to retreat and eventually evacuate Korea. He died the following year.

A new *daimyo* was appointed *shogun* by the emperor; he moved his capital to Edo **(Tokyo),** thus beginning the **Edo Period** (1603–1868). This is the period when the warriors *(samurai)* undertook their vows of behavior *(bushido)* and became the most powerful class in Japan. Many of Japanese cultural characteristics, like the tea ceremony, began during the Edo period. We will discuss this period in the next volume of this work, as it is the government in power when Japan was forced to open its ports to western trade in the nineteenth century.

Throughout its history, Japan was influenced by Chinese culture. At the beginning, the Japanese adopted Chinese ways with only minor modifications, and these existed parallel to the ancient Japanese religion and practices. Then, with increasing Japanese self-confidence, the culture adopted from China was modified to blend with ancient Japanese culture and create something new. The rise of war lords who were against foreign influences led to a Japanese isolation that brought about a unique culture that we can still see in the Japanese people.

Africa

Africa is an immense continent with almost impenetrable forests and other navigational difficulties. These factors have led to many disparate cultures and have prevented the development of a unified African civilization. We must, therefore, speak of African regions rather than single governing entities. We must also be aware that the original African cultures were strongly influenced by invading forces—first by the Muslims and then by the Europeans.

The history of northern Africa has already been discussed, at least in part, in previous chapters on Egypt, the Hellenistic Empire, the Roman Empire, the Byzantine Empire, and the Islamic Empire. The culture of northern Africa reflected the strong influences of these various empires and added some unique local flavor. However, it is fair to say that the principal cultural features were those that were brought into the area, realizing that Egypt was obviously indigenous to Africa but, to a large degree, has always been apart from the rest of Africa.

The geographical isolation of southern, **sub-Saharan Africa** delayed the introduction of many technologies and other cultural aspects of the rest of the world. For example, iron was not introduced into southern Africa until 200 B.C., about a millennium after its use in Mesopotamia. To be sure, some trade occurred before 1000 B.C., but it was limited to a few port cities. The kingdom of **Sheba,** which some have located in present-day **Ethiopia,** was a powerful trading partner to Israel in the time of King Solomon, about 970 B.C. When later traders arrived, they encountered some isolated but quite powerful civilizations, such as the **Kush,** who lived along the southern Nile and dominated the area from 750 B.C. to 350 A.D. They claimed descent from Solomon and the Queen of Sheba. The **Bantu**-speaking people seemed to dominate much of the rest of pre-Muslim Africa, but gave little more than their basic language and did not establish effective rule over any large or integrated area.

The Muslims strongly influenced East African culture, as can be seen from the language of the dominant **Swahili tribes,** which is a combination of Bantu with many Arabic words. Trade in the area was predominantly toward the north and east, as would be expected in a time when Arabs dominated trade in the Indian Ocean. After Vasco da Gama, the Portuguese displaced the Arabs as the trading partners. The traders depended upon the coastal-living Swahili to transport the goods to and from the African interior. Some of the peoples there were tribal hunter-gatherers with little interest in or contact with the outer world. However, some sophisticated civilizations were developed, as can be seen from the ruins of the **Great Zimbabwe,** which began about 500 A.D. A building of this society is given in Figure 24.4. This seemingly large society collapsed about 1600 under the aggressive influence of neighboring groups. The Portuguese arrived about that time, seeking slaves and gold. This led to a further decay of the Zimbabwe society.

Figure 24.4 ■ *A building from Great Zimbabwe.*
Image © David Reed/Corbis.

West African society began around the **Senegalese River** and grew to be powerful through trade along caravan routes along the southern rim of the **Sahara.** Trade goods from the western region included gold, hides, ivory, pepper, and slaves, expanding into central Africa by rivers. The West Africans established trade routes between the major rivers, such as between the **Nile** and the **Niger,** by overland trails, which they supervised. When the Muslims arrived in West Africa, most of the people converted. The trade routes became even stronger, since they also served as transportation routes for pilgrims to Mecca.

Africa's unique cultures were largely suppressed by foreign domination and the lack of technological currency. This became even more obvious after the time of the European colonial expansion in the seventeenth, eighteenth, and nineteenth centuries. However, with independence, much of Africa has awakened to its indigenous past, and a revival of ancient culture is underway, paralleling the push for modernity. This dual track is potentially frustrating but, on the other hand, could be the source of creative inspiration.

Pre-Columbian America

The arrival of Columbus, and the Europeans who followed him, heralded a time of great change for the native inhabitants of America. Columbus' "In-

Figure 24.5 ■ *Stone head from the Olmec civilization. Image from Corel.*

dians" were noble and proud peoples, many of whom had impressive histories and accomplished much of lasting value. The **Olmecs** were the first great civilization of the Americas. Like their historical counterparts in Egypt, Mesopotamia, and the Yellow and Indus River valley civilizations, they seemed to have no precursor civilizations, and were based in fertile river valleys of southeastern Mexico, beginning about 2200 B.C. Little is known of the Olmec civilization except for the massive stone heads that they left. Olmec society seemed to have collapsed about 400 B.C. A picture of a head is shown in Figure 24.5.

The **Mayan civilization** developed about the time that the Olmecs were disappearing, but there does not seem to be any connection between them. Mayan civilization, which was spread over much of meso-America (Mexico and Central America), is characterized by many seemingly isolated cities, each with several temple pyramids and numerous houses for priests and other city dwellers. Perhaps this desire for city life is because of the jungle environment of these people and the dangers of living outside a city. A typical pyramid temple of the Mayan culture is pictured in Figure 24.6. The pyramid is strangely reminiscent of those in Egypt and, even more, the Mesopotamian ziggurats. Some Mayan temples in south-central Guatemala have been dated from 400 B.C. These early pyramids are the prototypes for the many others in northern Guatemala, Belize and Mexico, which are far more numerous. Most of these latter temples were built in the Mayan classical period (100–850 A.D.). Many of the cities were fortified with surrounding ditches and embankments. Mayan buildings did not have arches but used the post-and-lintel style like the early Egyptians and Mesopotamians. The many similarities between the Egyptians/Mesopotamians and the Mayans has led some to speculate that the societies may have been related. That idea led **Thor Heyerdahl** to build and sail a reed boat, the **Ra II,** from Egypt to America.

The Mayans were advanced in other ways. They had a complex pictograph language that is part idea-related and part phonic, somewhat like Egyptian hieroglyphs. They developed accurate calendars, astronomical observatories, math (including the concept of zero), and sophisticated agricultural techniques. Their society seems to have been strongly religious. Who knows what other knowledge about them has been lost when the Spanish burned the **Mayan bark books** in the 1540s?

Another Central American society was centered in **Teotihuacan,** an area near present-day Mexico City. These people were probably related to the Mayan, as their civilizations overlap in time and have many similarities. Teotihuacan, the largest city in the Americas, showed evidence of a strong merchant class with extensive trading areas. Irrigation was permanent, to support the large population in the dry climate of central Mexico. The residents of Teotihuacan were strongly militaristic and eventually conquered the Mayans. These people were worshippers of the sun, as well as other deities such as the plumed serpent, Queztecoatl.

The Teotihuacan society was conquered by the **Toltecs** (700–1200 A.D.), who were then conquered by the **Aztecs** (1200–1550). Both of these societies seem to have adopted many of the practices of the

Figure 24.6 ■ *Pyramid temple of the Mayan civilization (Palenque site). Image from Corel.*

residents of Teotihuacan. The Aztecs built their capital, **Tenochitlan,** on the present site of Mexico City where, according to their legend, an eagle ate a snake and thus designated the location as a holy place. They, too, were strongly religious and practiced human sacrifice, as can be borne out by the many skeletal remains in various pools in front of altars. They were also strongly militaristic and probably obtained many of the sacrificial victims from the people they conquered. The Aztecs are the people who ruled Mexico when Cortes invaded.

Other important civilizations existed in the Americas. The **Incas of Peru** were just as sophisticated and as ruthless as the Aztecs. They succeeded an earlier Peruvian society centered near **Nazca** that left incredibly interesting markings on the land (see Figure 24.7). These markings seem to depict religious or cultural events or symbols on a scale that is overwhelming. Other societies that created quite sophisticated buildings and left interesting signs were the **Anasazi** and **Hopi** of the southwestern United States. In other parts of South and North America the natives seemed to be mostly tribal and nomadic.

Despite significantly outnumbering the Europeans, at least for the first century or two following the discovery of America by Columbus, the natives in America lost their land and their lives to the ever-increasing numbers of Europeans who settled on their shores. While many of the native peoples fought European encroachment, in the end the Europeans took over quite easily. A variety of factors contributed to the downfall of the American natives and the triumph of the Europeans.

The largest factor was the susceptibility of the natives to **European diseases.** The vast numerical superiority that the natives enjoyed was generally useless, as contact with the Europeans almost always brought death to the nearby Indians. The Native Americans had not built up natural immunities to the many European diseases; sicknesses such as **small pox, chicken pox, measles,** and even certain strands of **flu** would wipe out entire native populations. It is estimated that 80 percent of the Native American population was killed by diseases brought by the Europeans. This exchange of foreign diseases worked the other way as well, as the native population introduced syphilis to the

Figure 24.7 ■ Markings at Nazca. *© 2010 by gary yim. Used under license of Shutterstock, Inc.*

population of Europe. However, European diseases proved to be much more deadly to Native Americans than vice versa.

The Europeans had a distinct technological edge. The huge ocean-going ships and navigational instruments allowed Europeans to dominate the seas and waterways, while the domestication of the horse, and tools such as saddles and bridles, allowed the Europeans to move swiftly over land. Europeans had a distinct technological advantage in the area of warfare as well. Guns, cannons, body armor, and fortified cities all gave a military edge to the Europeans.

Native American religious beliefs also played into European hands. Many Native American peoples mistook the arriving Europeans for the return of their gods, so instead of being cautious, they were welcoming and friendly. Often the Europeans gained positions of power and began exploiting the natives before the natives realized their mistake. The most famous example was when the Spanish conquistador Cortes was believed to be the Aztec god Queztecoatl because of his beard and white skin. Some Native American religions benefited the Europeans because of the natives' belief that their defeat by warfare or disease was caused by the stronger god of the Europeans. Many natives would then convert to the "stronger" deity, in this case Christianity. However, when Native Americans converted to Christianity, they left behind much of their culture and history, as well as their religion. Indian religions also helped the Europeans whenever a native king was captured, because the kings were considered divine. Thus, as was the case with **Montezuma** of the Aztecs and **Atahualpa** of the Incas, once the king was in the hands of the Europeans, they could influence the commands of the native ruler and the people would not question his commands, to their possible disadvantage.

Still another advantage for the Europeans was the lack of unity among the natives. Many of the native civilizations were long-time enemies who distrusted each other as much as, if not more than, they did the Europeans. Thus, the natives were unable to unite into a cohesive unit to defend themselves; and, as numbers were the Native Americans' major advantage, the refusal or inability to unite proved fatal to their cultures and civilizations. Sometimes this lack of cohesiveness even doomed individual groups, such as both the Aztecs and Incas, which were tyrannies hated by other tribes in the vicinity. All this created a vacuum of power, which the Europeans were quick to fill.

Native American societies were able to resist European advances for many years, but that was more a function of the vast territory than of the ability of the natives to resist the technological advantages of the European. However, some have continued to resist accepting European culture and attempted to maintain some degree of their own. This has been difficult.

Summary of Discovered Countries

Some of the societies discovered by the European explorers were as ancient and as advanced as any in the world. Still, each of these societies, for a variety of reasons, later came under the domination of the Europeans. Those reasons are worth reconsidering. When the Europeans arrived in the sixteenth century, India had been dominated by foreign powers (chiefly Muslims and Persians) for hundreds of years, so there was little sense of national identity. Local rulers (maharajahs) were anxious to benefit from European trade and so they allowed the Europeans to set up trading colonies. Over the ensuing years, the normal upheavals of a society, such as local warfare between the maharajahs, led the Europeans to protect their trade routes and investments by assuming ever greater control, until the entire Indian subcontinent was under European control.

China was quite different from India. Few foreign powers had controlled China. (The Mongolian Yuan Dynasty was the most important exception.) Moreover, Chinese culture was much more advanced than European during the entire European Middle Ages. Many creative inventions were made in China during this period, such as paper, gunpowder, and the compass. However, two factors seemed to slow future progress in China. The first was a feeling of superiority that led to isolationism and eventually to relative stagnation. The other factor was the inability of the Chinese to exploit their inventions. While they used paper for printed materials, Chinese writing did not lend itself to high-volume printing. Changing to a system of printing like that employed in Europe would have required a major cultural change, and the Chinese were unwilling to explore the advantages of the alphabet. Gunpowder, too, was a great invention but its application to military uses was made by the Europeans. Then, when the Europeans attempted to dominate China from the seventeenth century onward, European guns and artillery were turned against the Chinese.

Japan borrowed from China but eventually decided that isolation would lead to a better society. It may have, in some respects, but it also led to some problems, which were successfully exploited by the Europeans when interactions finally occurred. The Japanese were convinced that the old ways of the warriors were best, especially when those ways were tied to traditions and honor. Those old ways included a dependence on swords and an avoidance of any more modern weapons. In this, the Japanese were much like the French knights at the beginning of the Hundred Years War—convinced that their way of fighting was the only honorable way and, therefore, determined to continue with the methods that had been in effect for centuries. The Europeans did not have those values and so, when confrontations with the Japanese arose, the advanced weaponry of the Europeans was able to overwhelm the Japanese system. Culturally, the Japanese have attempted to conserve their past, and, to a great extent, that was successful until very modern times.

The Africans suffered from isolation, both from other societies and also from others within Africa itself. This isolation led to vulnerability, because of a lack of information about the latest technology, and stagnant creativity, because of the lack of interactions with other cultures. This all led, of course, to an inferior position in warfare and trade. Perhaps the isolation led to a lack of motivation for progress because there was little knowledge of the advantages in other societies. Hence, when the Europeans finally arrived at the shores of Africa, the European culture dominated in warfare and the Africans became colonies.

The Native Americans also lacked some of the motivations that drove the Europeans. The Native Americans did not know about the spices and other riches to be gained from other parts of the world, nor did they realize that the Europeans had ready-made markets for such goods. Some Native Americans may have traveled to the South Seas (Polynesia), but we have no evidence that they returned with spices and a trading contract. As was the case with Africa, isolation created technological disadvantages for the native Americans. The pre-Columbian civilizations of the Americas such as the Aztecs, Incas, Hopi, Mayans, and many others of the Caribbean and plains and forests, were often highly advanced, with, undoubtedly, much to offer world civilization. All of these peoples had cultures, traditions, histories, religions, and languages that would largely be lost with the arrival of the Europeans.

It is interesting that many cultural situations are similar between disparate societies at roughly the same time. For instance, Europe, China, India, and the Mayans all experienced major upheavals and a definite downturn in their culture in the sixth century A.D. Some have said that this may have been due to a great catastrophe such as a massive volcanic eruption that darkened the skies for several years and led to lower worldly temperatures. That might be true. It might also have been due to the invasion of the Huns, both in Europe and in India at about the same time. Perhaps some other catastrophe occurred in Central Asia, the homeland of the Huns, that caused their migrations both eastward and westward.

But other events were also similar. Feudalism became the dominant social system in Europe and China about 800 A.D.. People began to have more food, and that led to a movement of people into the cities about the year 1000 in both China and Europe. The middle class began to emerge as a force in all of these cultures as a result of the movement to cities and the emphasis on trade. Elevated architecture, temples, and cathedrals dominated both Europe and India in the period just after 1100. European, Japanese, and Chinese rulers moved to decrease the power of the local lords and increase their own power by establishing bureaucracies and permanent armies. The Mongol invasion was, of course, felt in Islamic society and in Europe, but China also suffered from the domination of these outside people. In both the European and Chinese cases, after the Mongols were driven out, the societies reached greater heights of culture and, in the not too distant future, they both tried to return to the glories of a past epoch.

Throughout the Middle Ages, Europeans were culturally behind many of the societies we have examined in this chapter. But then the Europeans went ahead, just as the Middle Ages were ending. This began the period of European dominance. The factors that led to that domination were undoubtedly complex. The study of those factors is one of the key elements in the creative history of the world from 1500 to the present. That is the subject of volume two in this work.

Timeline—Important Dates

Date	Event
About 2200 B.C.–400 B.C.	*Olmecs occupy Mexico*
970 B.C.	*Kingdom of Sheba (probably in Africa)*
750 B.C.–350 A.D.	*Kush kingdom dominates southern Nile area*
400 B.C.–850 A.D.	*Mayan Civilization in Mexico and Central America*
221–207 B.C.	*Qin Dynasty in China*
206 B.C.–220 A.D.	*Han Dynasty in China*
220–618 A.D.	*Period of chaos and intellectual darkness in China*
320–535	*Gupta Empire in India*
500–1600	*The Great Zimbabwe dominates southern Africa*
535	*Hun invasion of India, followed by minor Hindu rulers*

538–794	*Nara (Yamato) Period in Japan*
618–960	*Tang Dynasty in China*
690–705	*Wu Zeitan rules China as only female emperor*
700–1200	*Toltecs settle in Mexico*
About 750	*Muslims conquer India and establish the Delhi Sultanate*
794–1185	*Heian Age in Japan*
960–1259	*Song Dynasty in China*
1185–1333	*Kamakura Period in Japan*
1200–1550	*Aztec period in Mexico*
1259–1368	*Yuan (Mongol) Dynasty in China*
1333–1603	*Muromachi-Momoyama Period in Japan*
1368–1644	*Ming Dynasty in China*
1398	*Tamarlane conquers the Delhi Sultanate*
1526	*Babur establishes the Mughal Empire in India*
1603–1868	*Edo Period in Japan*
1644–1911	*Qing (Manchurian) Dynasty in China*

Suggested Readings

Clavell, James, *Shogun,* Dell, 1980.

Heyerdahl, Thor, *Kon-Tiki,* Washington Square Press, 1973.

Article 36

Prescott: Conquest of Peru

Introduction

The story of the conquest of the Americas by the Spanish Conquistadors is both an awe-inspiring tale of adventure and a sorrowful tale of destruction. Although the records surviving from the Conquistadors' hands were all doctored to rationalize their actions, their tales are virtually the only records we have of what the Pre-Columbian inhabitants of the Americas were like.

This passage, written for us by historian William Prescott, comes originally from Francisco de Xeres, the secretary to Francisco Pizarro, the commander of the Conquistadors who conquered the Incan Empire. This selection details the capture of the Inca King, his ransom, and his execution by the Spanish. Portrayed here is the most amazing theme of all the conquest of the Americas: how a small band of a few hundred soldiers was able to subdue a nation of millions. Accounts of the indigenous people's fear of artillery and charging cavalry (both new to them) are entertaining and sad. The portrayal of the life of a Conquistador is interesting, but their lust for gold is somewhat disturbing. Their true motivation of greed is masked as well as possible by the initiative of Christian missionary work.

Conquest of Peru

It was not long before sunset when the van of the royal procession entered the gates of the city. First came some hundreds of the menials, employed to clear the path from every obstacle, and singing songs of triumph as they came, "which, in our ears," says one of the Conquerors, "sounded like the songs of hell!" Then followed other bodies of different ranks, and dressed in different liveries. Some wore a showy stuff, checkered white and red, like the squares of a chess-board. Others were clad in pure white, bearing hammers or maces of silver or copper; and the guards, together with those in immediate attendance on the prince, were distinguished by a rich azure livery, and a profusion of gay ornaments, while the large pendants attached to the ears indicated the Peruvian noble.

Elevated high above his vassals came the Inca Atahuallpa, borne on a sedan or open litter, on which was a sort of throne made of massive gold of inestimable value. The palanquin was lined with the richly-coloured plumes of tropical birds, and studded with shining plates of gold and silver.

At this moment Fray Vicente de Valverde, a Dominican friar, Pizarro's chaplain, and afterwards Bishop of Cuzco, came forward with his breviary, or as other accounts say, a Bible, in one hand, and a crucifix in the other, and, approaching the Inca, told him that he came by order of his commander to expound to him the doctrines of the true faith, for which purpose the Spaniards had come from a great distance to his country. The friar then explained, as clearly as he could, the mysterious doctrine of the Trinity, and, ascending high in his account, began with the creation of man, thence passed to his fall, to his subsequent redemption by Jesus Christ, to the crucifixion, and

Prescott, William H., *History of the Conquest of Peru,* J. M. Dent & Sons, Inc., 1968.

the ascension, when the Saviour left the Apostle Peter as his Vicegerent upon earth. This power had been transmitted to the successors of the Apostle, good and wise men, who, under the title of Popes, held authority over all powers and potentates on earth. One of the last of these Popes had commissioned the Spanish emperor, the most mighty monarch in the world, to conquer and convert the natives in this western hemisphere; and his general, Francisco Pizarro, had now come to execute this important mission. The friar concluded with beseeching the Peruvian monarch to receive him kindly; to abjure the errors of his own faith, and embrace that of the Christians now proffered to him, the only one by which he could hope for salvation; and, furthermore, to acknowledge himself a tributary of the Emperor Charles the Fifth, who, in that event, would aid and protect him as his loyal vassal.

The eyes of the Indian monarch flashed fire, and his dark brow grew darker as he replied, "I will be no man's tributary! I am greater than any prince upon earth. Your emperor may be a great prince; I do not doubt it, when I see that he has sent his subjects so far across the waters; and I am willing to hold him as a brother. As for the Pope of whom you speak, he must be crazy to talk of giving away countries which do not belong to him. For my faith," he continued, "I will not change it. Your own God, as you say, was put to death by the very men whom he created. But mine," he concluded, pointing to his deity,—then alas! sinking in glory behind the mountains,—"my God still lives in the heavens, and looks down on his children."

He then demanded of Valverde by what authority he had said these things. The friar pointed to the book which he held as his authority. Atahuallpa, taking it, turned over the pages a moment, then, as the insult he had received probably flashed across his mind, he threw it down with vehemence, and exclaimed, "Tell your comrades that they shall give me an account of their doings in my land. I will not go from here till they have made me full satisfaction for all the wrongs they have committed."

The friar, greatly scandalised by the indignity offered to the sacred volume, staid only to pick it up, and, hastening to Pizarro, informed him of what had been done, exclaiming at the same time, "Do you not see, that, while we stand here wasting our breath in talking with this dog, full of pride as he is the fields are filling with Indians! Set on at once! I absolve you." Pizarro saw that the hour had come. He waved a white scarf in the air, the appointed signal. The fatal gun was fired from the fortress. Then springing into the square, the Spanish captain and his followers shouted the old war-cry of "St. Jago and at them!" It was answered by the battle-cry of every Spaniard in the city, as, rushing from the avenues of the great halls in which they were concealed, they poured into the *plaza,* horse and foot, each in his own dark column, and threw themselves into the midst of the Indian crowd. The latter, taken by surprise, stunned by the report of artillery and muskets, the echoes of which reverberated like thunder from the surrounding buildings, and blinded by the smoke which rolled in sulphurous volumes along the square, were seized with a panic. They knew not whither to fly for refuge from the coming ruin. Nobles and commoners—all were trampled down under the fierce charge of the cavalry, who dealt their blows right and left, without sparing; while their swords, flashing through the thick gloom, carried dismay into the hearts of the wretched natives, who now, for the first time, saw the horse and his rider in all their terrors. They made no resistance,—as, indeed, they had no weapons with which to make it.

Meanwhile the fight, or rather massacre, continued hot around the Inca, whose person was the great object of the assault. His faithful nobles, rallying about him, threw themselves in the way of the assailants, and strove, by tearing them from their saddles, or, at least, by offering their own bosoms as a mark for their vengeance, to shield their beloved master.

At length, weary with the work of destruction, the Spaniards, as the shades of evening grew deeper, felt afraid that the royal prize might, after all, elude them; and some of the cavaliers made a desperate attempt to end the affray at once by taking Atahuallpa's life. But Pizarro, who was nearest his person, called out with stentorian voice, "Let no one, who values his life, strike at the Inca;" and, stretching out his arm to shield him, received a wound on the hand from one of his own men,—the only wound received by a Spaniard in the action.

The struggle now became fiercer than ever round the royal litter. It reeled more and more, and at length several of the nobles who supported it having been slain, it was overturned, and the Indian prince would have come with violence to the ground, had not his fall been broken by the efforts of Pizarro and some other of the cavaliers, who caught him in their arms. The imperial *borla* was instantly snatched from his temples by a soldier named Estete, and the unhappy monarch, strongly secured, was removed to a neighbouring building, where he was carefully guarded.

All attempt at resistance now ceased. The fate of the Inca soon spread over town and country. The charm which might have held the Peruvians together was dissolved. Every man thought only of his own safety. Even the soldiery encamped on the adjacent fields took the alarm, and, learning the fatal tidings, were seen flying in every direction before their pursuers, who in the heat of triumph showed no touch of mercy.

Pizarro paid every attention to his royal captive, and endeavoured to lighten, if he could not dispel, the gloom which, in spite of his assumed equanimity, hung over the monarch's brow. He besought him not to be cast down by his reverses, for his lot had only been that of every prince who had resisted the white men. They had come into the country to proclaim the Gospel, the religion of Jesus Christ, and it was no wonder they had prevailed, when his shield was over them. Heaven had permitted that Atahuallpa's pride should be humbled, because of his hostile intentions towards the Spaniards, and the insults he had offered to the sacred volume. But he bade the Inca take courage and confide in him, for the Spaniards were a generous race, warring only against those who made war on them, and showing grace to all who submitted!—Atahuallpa may have thought the massacre of that day an indifferent commentary on this vaunted lenity.

It was not long before Atahuallpa discovered, amidst all the show of religious zeal in his conquerors, a lurking appetite more potent in most of their bosoms than either religion or ambition. This was the love of gold.

In the hope, therefore, to effect his purpose by appealing to the avarice of his keepers, he one day told Pizarro, that, if he would set him free, he would engage to cover the floor of the apartment on which they stood with gold. Those present listened with an incredulous smile; and, as the Inca received no answer, he said, with some emphasis, that "he would not merely cover the floor, but would fill the room with gold as high as he could reach;" and, standing on tiptoe, he stretched out his hand against the wall. All stared with amazement; while they regarded it as the insane boast of a man too eager to procure his liberty to weigh the meaning of his words.

The apartment was about seventeen feet broad, by twenty-two feet long, and the line round the walls was nine feet from the floor. This space was to be filled with gold; but it was understood that the gold was not to be melted down into ingots, but to retain the original form of the articles into which it was manufactured, that the Inca might have the benefit of the space which they occupied. He further agreed to fill an adjoining room of small dimensions twice full with silver, in like manner; and he demanded two months to accomplish all this.

Several weeks had now passed since Atahuallpa's emissaries had been despatched for the gold and silver that were to furnish his ransom to the Spaniards. But the distances were great, and the returns came in slowly: they consisted for the most part of massive pieces of plate, some of which weighed two or three *arrobas,*—a Spanish weight of twenty-five pounds. On some days articles of the value of thirty or forty thousand *pesos de oro* were brought in, and occasionally of the value of fifty or even sixty thousand *pesos.* The greedy eyes of the Conquerors gloated on the shining heaps of treasure, which were transported on the shoulders of the Indian porters; and, after being carefully registered, were placed in a safe deposit under a strong guard. They now began to believe that the magnificent promises of the Inca would be fulfilled; but as their avarice was sharpened by the ravishing display of wealth, such as they had hardly dared to imagine, they became more craving and impatient. They made no allowance for the distance and the difficulties of the way, and loudly inveighed against the tardiness with which the royal commands were executed. They even suspected Atahuallpa of devising this scheme only to gain a pretext for communicating with his subjects in distant places, and of proceeding as dilatorily as possible in order to secure time for the execution of his plans. Rumours of a rising among the Peruvians were circulated, and the Spaniards were in apprehension of some general and sudden assault on their quarters. Their new acquisitions gave them additional cause for solicitude: like a miser, they trembled in the midst of their treasures.

The Inca himself now loudly demanded his freedom. The proposed amount of the ransom had, indeed, not been fully paid. It may be doubted whether it ever would have been, considering the embarrassments thrown in the way by the guardians of the temples, who seemed disposed to secrete the treasures, rather than despoil these sacred depositories to satisfy the cupidity of the strangers. It was unlucky, too, for the Indian monarch, that much of the gold, and that of the best quality, consisted of flat plates or tiles, which, however valuable, lay in a compact form that did little towards swelling the heap. But an immense amount had been already realised, and it would have been a still greater one, the Inca might allege, but for the impatience of the Spaniards. At all events, it was a magnificent ransom, such as was never paid by prince or potentate before.

Meanwhile the old rumours of a meditated attack by the natives began to be current among the soldiers. They were repeated from one to another, gaining something by every repetition. An immense army, it was reported, was mustering at Quito, the land of Atahuallpa's birth, and thirty thousand Caribs were on their way to support it.

The rumours of a rising among the natives pointed to Atahuallpa as the author of it.

"What treason is this," said the general, "that you have meditated against me,—me, who have ever treated you with honour, confiding in your words, as in those of a brother?" "You jest," replied the Inca, who, perhaps, did not feel the weight of this confidence; "you are always jesting with me. How could I or my people think of conspiring against men so valiant as the Spaniards? Do not jest with me thus, I beseech you." "This," continues Pizarro's secretary, " he said in the most composed and natural manner, smiling all the while to dissemble his falsehood, so that we were all amazed to find such cunning in a barbarian."

"Am I not," said he to Pizarro, "a poor captive in your hands? How could I harbour the designs you impute to me, when I should be the first victim of the outbreak? And you little know my people, if you think that such a movement would be made without my orders; when the very birds in my dominions," said he, with somewhat of an hyperbole, "would scarcely venture to fly contrary to my will."

But these protestations of innocence had little effect on the troops, among whom the story of a general rising of the natives continued to gain credit every hour. A large force, it was said, was already gathered at Guamachucho, not a hundred miles from the camp, and their assault might be hourly expected. The treasure which the Spaniards had acquired afforded a tempting prize, and their own alarm was increased by the apprehension of losing it. The patroles were doubled. The horses were kept saddled and bridled. The soldiers slept on their arms; Pizarro went the rounds regularly to see that every sentinel was on his post. The little army, in short, was in a state of preparation for instant attack.

A court was organised, over which the two captains, Pizarro and Almagro, were to preside as judges.

He was found guilty,—whether of all the crimes alleged we are not informed,—and he was sentenced to be burnt alive in the great square of Caxamalca. The sentence was to be carried into execution that very night.

When Atahuallpa was bound to the stake, with the faggots that were to kindle his funeral pile lying around him, Valverde, holding up the cross, besought him to embrace it, and be baptised, promising that, by so doing, the painful death to which he had been sentenced, should be commuted for the milder form of the *garrote,*—a mode of punishment by strangulation, used for criminals in Spain.

The unhappy monarch asked if this were really so, and, on its being confirmed by Pizarro, he consented to abjure his own religion, and receive baptism. The ceremony was performed by Father Valverde, and the new convert received the name of Juan de Atahuallpa, the name of Juan being conferred in honour of John the Baptist, on whose day the event took place.

Atahuallpa expressed a desire that his remains might be transported to Quito, the place of his birth, to be preserved with those of his maternal ancestors. Then turning to Pizarro, as a last request, he implored him to take compassion on his young children, and receive them under his protection. Was there no one in that dark company who stood grimly around him, to whom he could look for the protection of his offspring? Perhaps he thought there was no other so competent to afford it, and that the wishes so solemnly expressed in that hour might meet with respect even from his conqueror. Then, recovering his stoical bearing, which for a moment had been shaken, he submitted himself calmly to his fate: while the Spaniards, gathering around, muttered their *credos* for the salvation of his soul! Thus, by the death of a vile male-factor perished the last of the Incas!

Retrospective
Creativity Revisited

> Creativity is the engine that drives cultural evolution.
>
> —*M. Csikszentmihalyi (World renowned expert in creativity)*
>
> and
>
> There are indeed certain instances in which social/cultural realities largely determine the possibility or lack of possibility for developing creativity in a given field.
>
> —*D. H. Feldman (World renowned expert in creativity)*

Creativity and Society

As a careful reading of the above quotations will reveal, one expert suggests that creativity is the cause of changes in society while the other suggests that social/cultural realities change creativity. Our guess is that they actually agree, and that the relationship between creativity and society is complex and mutually dependent. We have seen this interdependence throughout this book. For example, the environmental isolation of Egypt must have influenced the closed nature of their society and the eventual drying-up of their creativity. Likewise, the rocky, poor soil of Greece and its physical penetration into the sea meant that Greece would interact with other lands through trade, which then made Greece highly creative through synthesis of all these disparate ideas. In these examples we see the effect of the environment on creativity.

On the other hand, the creativity of Archimedes clearly affected the environment of Syracuse when they fought the Romans. Likewise, the creativity of Homer, Virgil, and Dante affected the intellectual and cultural environments subsequent to the writing of their books, and continues to influence our own time. We can, therefore, feel confident that both environment and creativity are involved whenever we examine the creativity of a civilization.

Mesopotamian Creativity

The creativity of the Mesopotamian civilization may have been the most profound in the ancient world. The very nature of history seems to have been changed when the Mesopotamians discovered how to domesticate grains so that agriculture could be practiced on a grand scale. This discovery allowed some people to form cities and to differentiate their occupations. With cities, social classes and rule by law inevitably followed.

Creativity in technology was seen early in Mesopotamian life. The artisans of Mesopotamia seem to have been responsible for the shift from using ceramics to metals—first copper, bronze, and brass and then, after several hundred years, to iron. These creative innovations meant that one culture could dominate another in warfare and the use of other tools. For example, the chariot was invented by one Mesopotamian group but then improved with iron wheels by a later, conquering empire. Similar situations happened repeatedly in Mesopotamia. There were many different empires that sequentially ruled the region over the nearly four millennia that Mesopotamia was a major influence on the world's politics. The periodic invasions brought new knowledge, but the old knowledge was not forgotten. We saw, for example, the retention of cuneiform writing through several empires, each with their own language. We also saw the accumulation of data about the motions of the sun, moon, planets, and stars across the earthly sky. These data were analyzed and the concepts of the Zodiac emerged after many years, along with number systems and measurement scales that we still employ today, such as the number of minutes in an hour, seconds in a minute, and degrees in a circle.

Religion in Mesopotamia was not especially creative, save for one group—the Hebrews. All others were idol-worshippers of many gods, but the Hebrews worshiped only one God and, moreover, had a book of writings from prophets and historians that informed the people of God's will. For the Hebrews, the religion and the book were not creative—they were the work of God, and that did not depend on the creativity of humans. However, the preservation of this monotheistic religion in the face of the many conquerors and various interactions with other (usually more powerful) societies certainly reflects a high degree of creativity.

What lessons about creativity can we learn from the Mesopotamians? First, the climate of warm, long growing seasons, good native grasses, and plentiful water provided the conditions for large-scale agriculture to begin, thus attesting to the importance of the environment on creativity. We also see that the mixing of societies through war can build creativity (although it can also destroy, as we will see in later societies). The Mesopotamians didn't really stop being creative at the end of their long period of historical dominance. They were simply subsumed by a more powerful culture, the Hellenistic Greeks, who mixed their culture with Mesopotamian culture and extended the resultant culture synergistically, just as other conquerors had done. In this last case, however, the new culture was so strongly Greek that it became identified with the new culture rather than the old.

Egyptian Creativity

Egyptians are the other side of the coin from the Mesopotamians. The Egyptians were largely isolated, because of the deserts and sea that surrounded them. Therefore, few conquerors were able to occupy Egypt and few cross-cultural interactions were experienced. So, were the Egyptians creative and, if so, what might have provided the seeds for their creativity?

The many innovations of the ancient Egyptians reflect a high creativity. Some of those include the architectural wonders of the pyramids and the temples, papyrus, hieroglyphs, a superb calendar system, very useful number system, and art that clearly influenced other societies. But we notice an interesting pattern in the timing of these creative advances: Most occurred in the earliest years of Egyptian civilization. During these productive years the Egyptians were struggling to define their civilization. They had just united the upper and lower kingdoms of the Nile and were solidifying their power against their neighbors (including from time to time against the Mesopotamians). But, even when the Egyptians successfully conquered a neighboring land, the Egyptians retreated to Egypt, looting but not occupying the conquered territory. This characteristic probably limited the amount of interaction and understanding that the Egyptians could gain from the conquered culture. Hence, the Egyptians benefited little from these conquests (except for the booty). Why did the Egyptians return to Egypt rather than occupy, as did the various Mesopotamian conquerors? The answer is simple—religion. The Egyptian religion was built around the concept of resurrection to an afterlife. But they believed that resurrection could only occur if the body was buried in Egyptian soil. So the pharaohs took their armies back to Egypt after each war. Moreover, they built huge burial places, like the pyramids, to give further evidence of their belief in the importance of the afterlife.

This dependence on religion meant that the priests were extremely important in Egyptian society. They administered the burial procedures and dictated the nature of the worship that would ensure proper adherence to the rules of the gods so that resurrection was certain. These priests strongly resisted change. The very nature of religion seems to require a steadiness and consistency. The preferred position of the priests in Egyptian society eventually gave them power over all in the land except the pharaoh himself, and toward the latter period, even over the pharaoh. Hence, barriers to change were erected, both physical and psychological. When this occurred, the creativity of the Egyptians waned. Isolation proved to be highly detrimental to progress.

Indian Creativity

Indian society was much like Mesopotamian. There were few natural defenses on the western border of the Indian subcontinent and so the land was overrun by several outside groups. Most of these stayed to occupy and therefore added their culture to the existing one. In one invasion, by the Aryans, some attempts were made to preserve the separateness of the two societies or, perhaps, to control the conquered people by separating them into castes. The caste system was creatively tied to religion to make it both acceptable and permanent. This creative innovation has persisted, at least to some degree, until the present time. It has, therefore, accomplished what was intended. Most modern citizens would see the caste system as a great evil because it restricted people to positions in society that stifled change and freedom. In that regard, the caste system certainly slowed creativity. We can see, therefore, that creative changes are not necessarily good (at least from our current perspective). On the other hand, the caste system was creative in its application and in the stability it gave to Indian society.

In spite of the possible dampening of creativity in some castes from the Aryan invasion, the Indians contributed many important innovations to world civilization. Several important religions came from India, including Hinduism, Jainism, Sikhism, and Buddhism. We also received our current numeral system, including the concept of zero, from the Indians. Some of the most beautiful and impressive buildings from India reflect the mixing of the Indian, Persian, Muslim, and other influences that built together to create the Indian culture.

Chinese Creativity

Just as the Indian culture has many similarities to the Mesopotamian, the Chinese culture has similarities to the Egyptian. Both China and Egypt were isolated. Therefore, much of their creativity was internally generated. It is interesting that one important contribution from both China and Egypt was writing, and the similarities between Egyptian and Chinese writing are astounding. For example, both developed highly complex pictograph writing methods and both invented highly important writing materials (papyrus and paper). We might ask whether the use of picture writing had a positive or negative effect on creativity. Because it was difficult to do, only the elite could master it, inevitably leading to a limitation on the number of people who became highly educated.

Their writing systems strengthened the hold of the priests and bureaucrats, who were the class that could read. On the other hand, pictographs may force the mind to think more broadly, although evidence of this is scant. On the whole, pictograph writing seems to have reduced overall creativity.

The Chinese did not have a religious belief in the afterlife as did the Egyptians, but a key development in Chinese culture that became almost like a religion had the same effect in stifling creativity. That development was the establishment of an incredibly powerful bureaucracy based upon the principles of Confucius. To many Chinese, both ancient and modern, the Confucian concepts were a religion. Those concepts controlled how people treated each other, and gave goals and aspirations to life. Combined with the teachings of Taoism, Confucianism became a way of life. And, like the priests of Egypt, the bureaucrats of China who taught and practiced Confucianism resisted change and stifled creativity.

Over the years, the Chinese made some other important creative contributions, like the compass and gunpowder, but these were poorly exploited, largely because of the feeling of superiority and isolation that permeated Chinese culture. In this attitude, the Chinese and Egyptians were similar. In the final analysis, the Chinese contributions were probably not as plentiful as might have occurred if Chinese thinking would have been more open.

Greek and Hellenistic Creativity

From the earliest Greek society, the Minoans of Crete, trade was essential for survival. Trade led to interactions with other societies, and that increased creativity. For example, the Greeks saw the meticulous recordkeeping of the Mesopotamians and then went further and asked not just what was happening in the heavens but why the heavenly bodies moved as they did. This type of questioning led to the development of natural philosophy, which is, today, science. It took the inquiring and questioning mind of the Greeks to believe that humans were capable of discovering everything about everything, and not just to assume that any unexplained event was caused by the gods (as was the case with the Mesopotamians). This same pattern of thinking led to the development of philosophy and the wonderful work of Socrates, Plato, and Aristotle. Some have said that no new concepts in philosophy have been proposed since the days of these Greeks.

The traders from Greece also noted the usefulness of writing. They understood cuneiform and hieroglyphics, but found the writing method of the Phoenicians to be much more valuable. The Greeks adopted and then adapted the Phoenician alphabet. As one expert, P. Hitti, has said in his book *The Near East in History,* "The alphabet was the most significant of the boons conferred upon mankind by Phoenicia. It is generally considered the greatest invention ever made by man." The adaptation by the Greeks made that significant contribution even more significant. The Greeks added vowels. This seemingly minor change made a tremendous difference. The new alphabet reflected the way words were actually spoken, thus not only making the recording of information and its later interpretation more precise, but also giving the power of writing to all who wanted to expend a relatively small amount of effort and become literate. Great oral stories like the *Iliad* and the *Odyssey* were written and widely circulated. Other writings were similarly made, on subjects such as the pantheon of the gods, history, and philosophy. Moreover, plays were written to entertain and analyze Greek society. The effect of the alphabet writing system was just the opposite of Chinese and Egyptian pictographs—the alphabet enhanced creativity.

The combination of trade and education (which was enhanced by the accessibility of the alphabet) increased the number of people who became involved in society. There was no single priest or bureaucratic class to control society's actions. Instead, the people became intimately involved in controlling their own affairs. This situation led to democratic rule and the accompanying insistence on the rule of law for all members of society. We are, of course, the beneficiaries of that creative change.

From the earliest days of Greek society, some time was devoted to leisure. The Minoans depicted their leisure activities on the walls of their homes. Later Mycenaean culture, although focused on war, likewise had time for leisure and pleasure, if we can judge from the extraordinary time for conducting the war at Troy and returning to home afterwards. During the days of Athens, leisure was used for thinking, socializing, attending dramas, and appreciation of art. Hence, a market was created for artistic works, and creativity flourished even more.

An interesting paradox should be noted about the time in Athens called the Golden Age of Greece. Leisure was surely important, but so was war. A fierce war between the Athenians and other Greek city-states, led by Sparta, persisted throughout the Golden Age. We would assume that war diminished leisure time and used up resources that might otherwise go toward the arts. Somehow the war and the Golden Age coexisted. There is little evidence of cultural benefit from the war, perhaps because the basic culture of all the participants was similar.

When Alexander conquered the Persian Empire, all of Mesopotamia and Egypt came under Greek influence. Generally, the people of these conquered areas liked Greek (now called Hellenistic) culture, and adopted it. The Greek language became dominant in the region and remained so for hundreds of years. This widespread acceptance of Greek values and methods influenced thinking for all the Mediterranean basin, especially for the new conquerors, the Romans.

Roman Creativity

The Romans took creative concepts from all that they encountered, sometimes changing them to fit Roman needs. Examples date from the earliest days of the Roman Republic when they took the concept of the arch from the Etruscans and used it extensively in Roman architecture thereafter. Then, when Greece came under Roman control, the culture of Greece was adopted unabashedly. The Romans sometimes copied the Greeks, as with many sculptures and dramas. However, the Romans sometimes changed the Greek form to fit Roman values. Whereas Greek sculpture was generic, Roman modifications became portraiture. Whereas Greek drama was intellectual and based on Greek history, Roman drama focused on the sensual and current.

Some aspects of Roman culture were uniquely Roman. For example, they established a government that was markedly different from any others. The Romans feared kingship and its power, so they developed a system of checks and balances that is the model from which the American government was derived. Even in the alphabet and number system, the Romans were unique; Roman letters and numbers were used throughout the Middle Ages in Europe (and still today in the case of the letters). Roman aqueducts and buildings, while using the Etruscan arch, were massive engineering accomplishments that went far beyond anything seen before. The road system was also wonderfully unique and useful.

The Romans borrowed but also created. Just the modifications were sufficient to qualify as creative works, but they often went far beyond mere modifications. The Romans managed the greatest empire in history for the longest period of time. That alone would suggest that they were highly creative.

Byzantine Creativity

The Byzantine Empire tried to continue the Roman legacy. It developed few new creative ideas. The isolation of Byzantium, which began with the rise of Islam and continued as the power of the Byzantine Empire diminished, must have dampened Byzantine creativity. However, a few innovations suggest that creativity was not entirely dead. For example, the beautiful mosaics found in Ravenna, the magnificence of the Hagia Sophia, and the lovely icons show that religious creativity flourished, at least until a Byzantine emperor tried to destroy them.

The Byzantines did make some interesting innovations in war and trade. They invented Greek

Fire, that devastating flammable liquid that made the Byzantine navy invincible. They also used the existing geography of Constantinople to erect impregnable defenses.

The Byzantines also established preferred ports, such as Venice, where trade could be done easily and profitably. Venice was certainly the beneficiary of Byzantine culture but added its own creative works to develop a unique state that grew in power and influence, roughly in direct relationship to the decline of the Byzantine state itself. Therefore, just as the Byzantine state was a continuation of the Roman, so too was the Venetian a continuation of the Byzantine. As the Byzantines understood the value of past glories, so too did the Venetians, as shown by their stealing of the bones of St. Mark to give their city a well-known patron saint. Hence, the benefits of European trade in the latter Middle Ages were indirectly attributable to Byzantium. So, too, was the rise of the Renaissance, which was fueled by that trade and by the learning that entered Europe when Constantinople fell in 1453.

Islamic Creativity

The relatively primitive tribes of Arabia that first took Islam to the world maintained their basic values and language but clearly added the cultures of the conquered territories to their own. By the time Islam had reached its own golden age, most of the creativity occurring in the world was in Islamic states. Beautiful architecture and literature attested to the high degree of culture, and also indicated their religious prohibition against images. Some of the most beautiful buildings in the world, such as the Taj Mahal and the Dome of the Rock, reflect the nature of Islamic art. We have discussed the effect of writing in other societies; Islamic writing has a unique and highly creative place. Because Arabic is the language of Islam's holy book, the use of Arabic script as an art form became widely adopted. Many buildings and other artifacts were decorated with this script, often illustrating the various forms of the titles of Allah.

As with the Jews and Christians, much of Islamic creativity was inspired by God. Some may question whether this constitutes creativity, because the changes are mandated by someone else. But the same argument can be said about any knowledge coming from others, even from the past. God gave instructions but then asked those to whom he talked to use their own creativity in implementing what God said.

Islamic science and learning were also highly developed. The Muslims retained the wisdom of the Greeks, which they inherited from the lands of the eastern Mediterranean they conquered, but also added Indian, Spanish, and native Arabic influences. The result was a highly developed knowledge of mathematics, number systems, medicine, and philosophy, and a unique and highly innovative literary tradition.

As Islam continued to spread, for example to India, these cultural influences followed, resulting in further mixing of cultures and, in our opinion, further refinement of the arts and architecture. In most cases, the native culture remained, but Islamic influences were added. This is true, for example, in India and Indonesia.

We might ask whether the crusades were good or bad for Islamic creativity. In one way, they were definitely good: They forced the emergence of a new leadership in Islam that proved to be extremely capable, and united Islam again, after many years of fractured rule. That unification led to the creation of the Ottoman Empire and the establishment of a second golden age for Islam. The crusades also gave interactions with the Europeans, but this was probably more beneficial to the Europeans than the Muslims. Europe was culturally far behind; but some lessons of warfare and commerce were learned and later employed throughout the Islamic Empire.

Medieval European Creativity

Great scholarly debates have arisen over the nature of creativity in Europe during the Middle Ages. Some have said that creativity all but stopped, and have called the early medieval period the Dark Ages. Others have said that the fall of the Western Roman Empire was not immediately significant and that society continued in much the same way as prior to the fall, at least for several decades and perhaps for a few hundred years. Based upon the absence of creative innovations, we tend to favor the view that the fall of the Western Roman Empire in 476 A.D. was very significant, and that society changed dramatically. However, other influences might have contributed about as much to the demise of creativity as did the change in politics. For example, the cooler weather and the probable major outbreak of disease, coupled with the admittedly worsening lawlessness, meant that city populations were devastated and the few people who survived the disasters were forced to flee to the countryside. These conditions also meant that people had to work extremely hard and for very long hours just to survive. They had little time for leisure and, therefore, little time for creativity. These years may not have been the Dark Ages, but they were surely dim.

About the year 1000 A.D., both the political climate and the temperature climate began to change. People were more secure and the warmer weather led to more food. People again began to move to the cities and specialize in occupations other than farming. This diversity led to great increases in creativity. The great Gothic cathedrals, literature, and art are but the most obvious developments.

The role of the Catholic Church in affecting creativity deserves special mention. In some ways the church was the only sponsor of creativity during the Early Medieval Period. What little art and learning were accomplished was done in, and at the request of, the church. The mass was created and with it the music of the church. Art was used to decorate the churches, both statues and, later, stained glass windows. Church monks preserved what little remained of the knowledge of the past. The church gave stability to society.

However, the church also stifled change and actively persecuted any who would be different enough to be called heretics. In this regard, the medieval church was like the ancient religion of Egypt. Change was anathema to church officials. For much of the Middle Ages, church education was restricted, generally, to those who studied church affairs. This restriction led to ever-increasing theological depth, but not to much new thinking. An exception was the rise of scholasticism, which restored some vigor to thinking and helped advance learning in universities. Those same universities adopted non-religious teaching, such as law and medicine, which further advanced creativity, although slowly.

Politics and war in the Middle Ages had both positive and negative effects on creativity. During the early period, when war was nearly constant, creativity was suppressed. Occasionally, as with Charlemagne, a strong military leader would subdue his enemies and that would give a respite from war and allow a period of creativity to develop, but only if the monarch was himself creative. Eventually nations developed, and with that, many strong kings. Even though these kings often warred against each other, the stability that resulted from nations was beneficial to creativity overall.

Language was developing in many ways during the Middle Ages. The Latin of the Romans was retained in some areas, mixed with the German of the new rulers, to create new languages such as French and Italian. In Spain, the mixture of languages also included Arabic. England never adopted Roman Latin and so the invasion of the Angles and the Saxons brought a new language that dominated the existing Celtic tongues. That new Anglo-Saxon language, with its German origins and later additions from Norse languages, became the basis of Old English. After the Norman Conquest, the French of the Normans was gradually blended with Old English in many creative ways, giving rise to Middle English, which had an enormous vocabulary because, in the tradition of English, words from both languages were adopted into the new tongue. The existence of this highly diverse language seemed to give a boost to creativity, as it allowed a natural mixing of thoughts as well as words.

Perhaps, however, the greatest influence on medieval creativity in Europe was the absence or presence of interactions among cultures. When there were few interactions, people lost lateral-thinking creativity. When interactions began again, probably with the crusades, many aspects of creativity began too. The Europeans were astounded by what they encountered in the Holy Land. Upon their return, the crusaders began to change European culture. Luxury goods were in demand. Learning increased. Cathedrals were built, as much for prestige of the local rulers and cities and to encourage trade as to glorify God. Sponsorship of creativity was clearly important in buildings, and in other aspects of culture as well. Kings established businesses to attempt to monopolize trade in certain goods. The learning of the Muslims and the exchange of knowledge from one part of Europe to another led to a dramatic increase in technological developments. The most important of these was Gutenberg's printing press. With the dramatic increase in book availability following Gutenberg, Europeans began to improve their personal knowledge and with that, returned to the situation that had existed in ancient Greece and Rome—a democratization of knowledge and power. The population became consumers of culture; many individuals had the time and the incentive to fill the needs of the new and vibrant society through creative developments.

Explorations began of necessity for Portugal and then became important economically for other countries as they followed Portugal's lead. We might ask if discovery is a creative act, since the thing discovered is already there. In the case of territorial discovery, that seems to be a legitimate question. However, what about discovery of the patterns of nature? We call that science, and few would question the creativeness of great scientific discoveries; yet, as with new lands, they were always there. Hence, discovery seems to qualify as a creativity activity, especially when the entire discovery process is evaluated, including the obtaining of a sponsor, convincing the crew to work together, and managing or securing the territories discovered.

Trends in Creativity

We have summarized the creativity of various societies and it is now appropriate to ask, What are the trends we see in creativity throughout history? We have identified a few.

War and Peace/Safety

War can be both beneficial and detrimental to creativity. Conquerors bring new ideas and, consequently, greater lateral thinking usually occurs. Often, the conquerors will accept much of the existing culture and overlay their own, to give a richer and more fertile seedbed for creativity. War can also be an incentive to creativity, as, for example, the wonderfully ingenious devices invented by Archimedes to stave off the Romans when they attacked Syracuse. Periods of war and threatened war can motivate creative developments that later move into non-war applications so that general civilization is improved.

If war is so disruptive that normal civilization cannot continue, creativity might be diminished. We have seen examples of both situations in our study of history. The Golden Age of Greece occurred during a period of war, but little negative effect was evident. On the other hand, the chaos that followed the fall of the Western Roman Empire was a major disruptive factor. Today we have seen technological advances like the computer and cell phones arise from war efforts.

It is not always predictable whether war, or any other catastrophic event, will negatively affect creativity. While it may be true that the nature of the catastrophe determines whether creativity will be negatively affected, it may be equally likely that personal environments, not general conditions, have the greater effect. Going even further in this analysis, personal environments may not even be the key but, rather, how people choose to react to their environments. In the days of the Greeks, many of the playwrights resented the war and openly spoke out against it, using their plays as their voice. Hence, they chose to fight against the war, and that choice spurred their creativity. On the other hand, the people of the Dark Ages were discouraged and isolated (and, perhaps, overworked) by war and its accompanying chaos, and they chose to not be creative.

The effect on creativity of choosing to react to a personal environment in various ways has been studied by a famous psychologist, **Mihaly Csikszentmihalyi,** who interviewed over a hundred highly creative people and reported on the conditions under which they were most creative. The study identified several pairs of conditions, shown in Figure 25.1, which represent opposite environments and personal traits.[1] Surprisingly, these creative people were often able to be creative under a variety of conditions. They adjusted their thinking to account for the immediate situation. This ability illustrates a trait of creativity that we addressed in the Prologue to this book—the ability of creative persons to control their thinking. Creativity requires use of both the left and right sides of the brain, and these highly creative people were able to choose which side of the brain to use, depending on their environment. For example, if they were surrounded by many people, they chose their right side to get ideas from diverse stimuli, but if they were alone, their left sides were more active, as they entered into an analytical mode. We think that choosing activities that encourage right-brain or left-brain activity depending on the nature of the personal environment at the moment is a key to being highly creative. Therefore, whether society is at war or relaxing in peace is less important, generally, than how the creative person chooses to respond. An exception is, of course, if war withdraws the very tools that must be used to be creative, as, for instance, when a person is taken from home to fight in the war. But, even situations like incarceration have proven to be useful for creative work as, for instance, when Marco Polo was imprisoned after his time in the Orient; that prison period gave him time to write the book describing his travels. Another similar circumstance was Thomas Aquinas' home imprisonment, wherein he had the time to memorize the Bible.

A person's control over the environment is only possible within certain limits. As we have seen, sometimes society is so chaotic or repressive that freedom is lost. While it is important to have some personal regimentation to force creative acts to be done, the loss of freedom of action may be devastating. Charles Thompson interviewed Dr. Yoshiro NakaMats, holder of more patents than any other person in history, and Dr. NakaMats commented as follows:

So you feel that creativity comes from a balance of regimentation and freedom? Yes, but freedom is most important of all. Genius lies in developing complete and perfect freedom within a human being. Only then can a person come up with the best ideas.[2]

Pairs of Attributes and Environments for Creativity

Pairs of Attributes and Environments for Creativity
■ Depth/breadth
■ Focused/relaxed
■ Smart/uncertain
■ Disciplined/playful
■ Realistic/imaginative
■ Introverted/extroverted
■ Humble/proud
■ Traditional/rebellious
■ Objective/passionate
■ Pain/pleasure

Figure 25.1 ■ *Ability to choose or balance attributes and the environment.*

Interactions with Other Societies

The Greeks were the most obvious example of the value of interactions with other societies, but most of the truly creative societies also exhibited this factor during the times when they were creative. The absence of interactions led to a reduction in creativity. These interactions increase the ability of a society to think laterally and that obviously increases creativity.

The importance of new knowledge on creativity was recently revealed in a study of scientists at a large organization.[3] Three different groups were identified. In the first group were those who contributed widely and frequently to the organization—the innovators/creators. The second group also contributed, but generally only in their narrow field—the implementers. The third group made almost no contributions—the slugs. An analysis of many factors that might affect the ability of these scientists to contribute led to the following findings: The major (only significant) difference among the groups was their reading habits. The innovators/creators read widely and avidly. The implementers read almost exclusively in their narrow field. The slugs read almost nothing. We believe that this study confirms that new knowledge, from reading or interactions with new people and societies, leads to creativity, because it fosters lateral thinking.

Arthur Koestler, a leading expert on creativity, has coined a phrase to describe the process of learning from one field and applying it to another. The term is **bisociative.** To put this concept into practice, one professor required that every time the students went to the library to do their specific research, they had to walk at random through the shelves of other disciplines and grab one book without perusal and read it, too, and somehow incorporate the "foreign" book into their research.

The ability to read and learn new information will be even more important in the future than in the past. **Alvin Toffler,** author of *Future Shock,* said, "The illiterate of the twenty-first century will not be those who cannot read and write, but those who cannot learn, unlearn, and relearn."[4]

Borrow and Improve

The Romans were the world's best borrowers and improvers. Their success was clearly evident in the many technological and cultural legacies that we enjoy even today, not to mention their reign as the longest and most important empire in history. We believe that improving on borrowed ideas is not only acceptable, but is actually essential. Few ideas (perhaps none) are created out of nothing. Sir Isaac Newton commented that if he had seen further, it was because he stood on the shoulders of giants, among whom he cited Archimedes. **Arthur Koestler** has suggested that creativity isn't making something out of nothing but, rather, recombining ideas that already separately exist.

The ability to see value in what others have done (and perhaps abandoned or underutilized) is a key to creativity. The Europeans saw the value of gunpowder in weapons, whereas the Chinese did not. The Greeks understood the value of adding vowels to an alphabet, whereas the Phoenicians did not (probably because the Phoenician language was Semitic, which was usually written without vowels, whereas the Greek language was Indo-European, which is vowel-intensive). Nevertheless, the Greeks added the vowels and the Phoenicians did not. The Indians saw the value of zero, whereas the Romans did not. **Albert Szent-Gyorgyi,** Nobel laureate in Physiology and Medicine, said, **"Discovery consists of looking at the same thing as everyone else and thinking something different."**

Leisure

We have already discussed the effect of societal and personal environments on creativity. As was mentioned, there are some circumstances that may be so disruptive that individuals cannot be creative. One such circumstance is when people's environments are so oppressive that they must spend every possible moment on just survival. Aristotle said that leisure is required for creativity and, of course, leisure requires time away from the press of working to survive. (That may actually be the definition of leisure.) We saw this situation most evident in the early Middle Ages when the cold weather and the breakdown of society forced people onto small, marginally productive farms with few interactions beyond their own village. Leisure time was rarely available and creativity suffered along with the people.

The relationship between people's needs and their motivation for various activities has been studied by **Abraham Maslow.** He ranked the needs of individuals and noted that motivation for action is tied closely to the level of the needs. That concept is depicted in Figure 25.2. Those lower needs, if not satisfied, have an overwhelming effect on a person's motivation. Simply put, we must fulfill them. If the political and economic situation is so bad that these needs are in question, then an individual loses sight of all other tasks. Hence, in

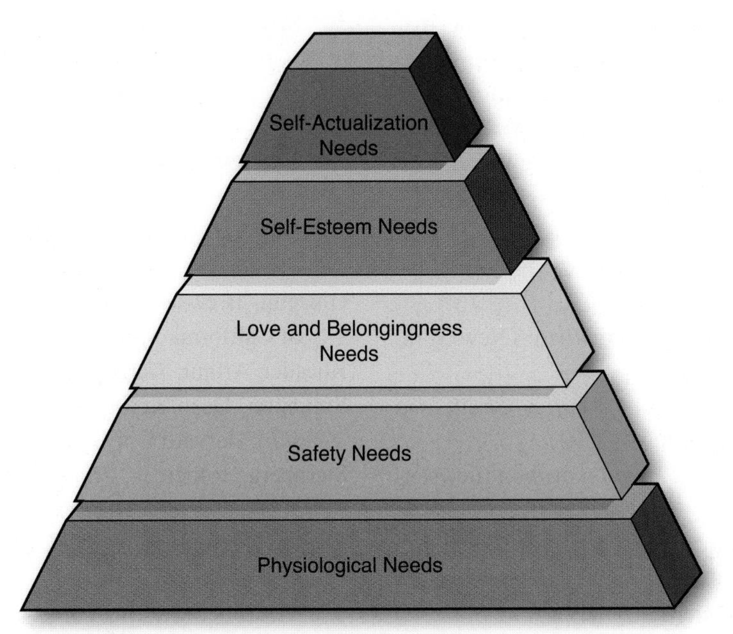

Figure 25.2 ■ *Maslow's hierarchy of human needs.*

the situation of the early Middle Ages, when survival and shelter were in question, there was little time for leisure and the pursuit of higher needs such as self-fulfillment, a key part of cultural creativity. However, if the lower needs are met, then the higher needs are worked on. These higher needs are the ones that relate most directly to creativity in the arts and sciences. This is another way of demonstrating the link between leisure and creativity.

Leisure time is especially important if we want to let our subconscious mind do some of the work for us, as we discussed in the Prologue. As **Scott Thorpe** has astutely observed:

> *Solving a problem is like looking for valuable antiques. You will find only junk unless you know what you are looking for. Great new ideas are too different from our current thinking, and too similar to nonsolutions to be casually recognized. But when we know what to look for, the probability of finding a great solution soars. The ancient genius Archimedes took baths all of his life, and each time he entered the bath, the water rose. But only when he was looking for a way to measure the volume of the king's crown did he recognize the rising water as a brilliant volume-measuring solution. He was so excited that he ran naked from the bath. To find a breakthrough that exciting, you must have a clear vision of the solution that you are seeking. Then you too can recognize your answer when you step into it.*[5]

Ending Comments

The story of Archimedes, one of our favorite creative people, brings us to the end of this volume.We have found a few trends in the history of creativity. Perhaps you will find others. The insights to be gathered from this approach to history are, in our opinion, just now becoming evident.

We invite all readers to creatively search the historical record for other interactions between creativity and history. Some additional trends will be discussed in the next volume of this work, which covers the period from 1500 A.D. to the present.

Notes

1. Mihaly Csikszentmihalyi, *Creativity* (New York: HarperPerennial, 1996).
2. Charles "Chic" Thompson, *What a Great Idea* (New York: HarperPerennial, 1992).
3. Roger Firestien, *Insights into Innovation* (newsletter, 2004).
4. Alvin Toffler (author of *Future Shock*), quoted in Scott Thorpe, *How to Think Like Einstein,* (New York: Barnes & Noble, 2000), 26.
5. Scott Thorpe, *How to Think Like Einstein* (New York: Barnes & Noble, 2000), 26.

Suggested Readings

De Bono, Edward, *Lateral Thinking,* Harper & Row, 1970.

Ghiselin, Brewster, *The Creative Process,* University of California Press, 1952.

Koestler, Arthur, *The Act of Creation,* Arkana, 1989.

Simonton, Dean Keith, *Genius, Creativity & Leadership,* Harvard University Press, 1984.

Sternberg, Robert J., *Handbook of Creativity,* Cambridge University Press, 1999.

Thorpe, Scott, *How to Think Like Einstein,* Barnes & Noble, 2000.

Weiner, Robert Paul, *Creativity & Beyond,* State University of New York Press, 2000.

Index

S

T

U